D0762531

Valued Gleim Aviation Customer,

When we inspected the final printed copies of the Gleim Sport, Privat ... ound Instructor FAA Knowledge Test books for the 2015 editions, we notec ... sectional chart excerpts were not printed to our quality standards. Certain charts were ... reproduced as clearly as they should have been, and some colors were depicted inaccurately. To compensate for these printing errors, we have reproduced all sectional chart excerpts for the affected products in this insert.

Each chart has the same figure number as it does in the corresponding book. To pair a chart in the book with its reproduction in this insert, simply match the figure numbers. For your convenience, they have been sorted by product and arranged numerically.

We at Gleim deeply regret this printing error and apologize for any confusion it may have caused. We always do our best to exceed your expectations and strive to provide the highest quality educational materials possible.

Good luck in your studies, and please fly safely.

Sincerely,

Gleim Publications, Inc.

TABLE OF CONTENTS

NOTE: The FAA prints the charts published in their Airman Knowledge Testing Supplements to the wrong scale. By printing the charts to the wrong scale, the FAA is testing to see if you checked your plotter to the scale printed on the chart to make sure the chart is accurate. Because our goal at Gleim is to prepare you for your Knowledge Test, our reproductions of the charts are also not to scale. For more information on how to correctly use these charts, refer to your FAA Knowledge Test book.

Copyright © 2014 Gleim Publications, Inc. All rights reserved. Duplication prohibited.
Reward for information exposing violators. Contact copyright@gleim.com.

Sport/Private: Figure 21

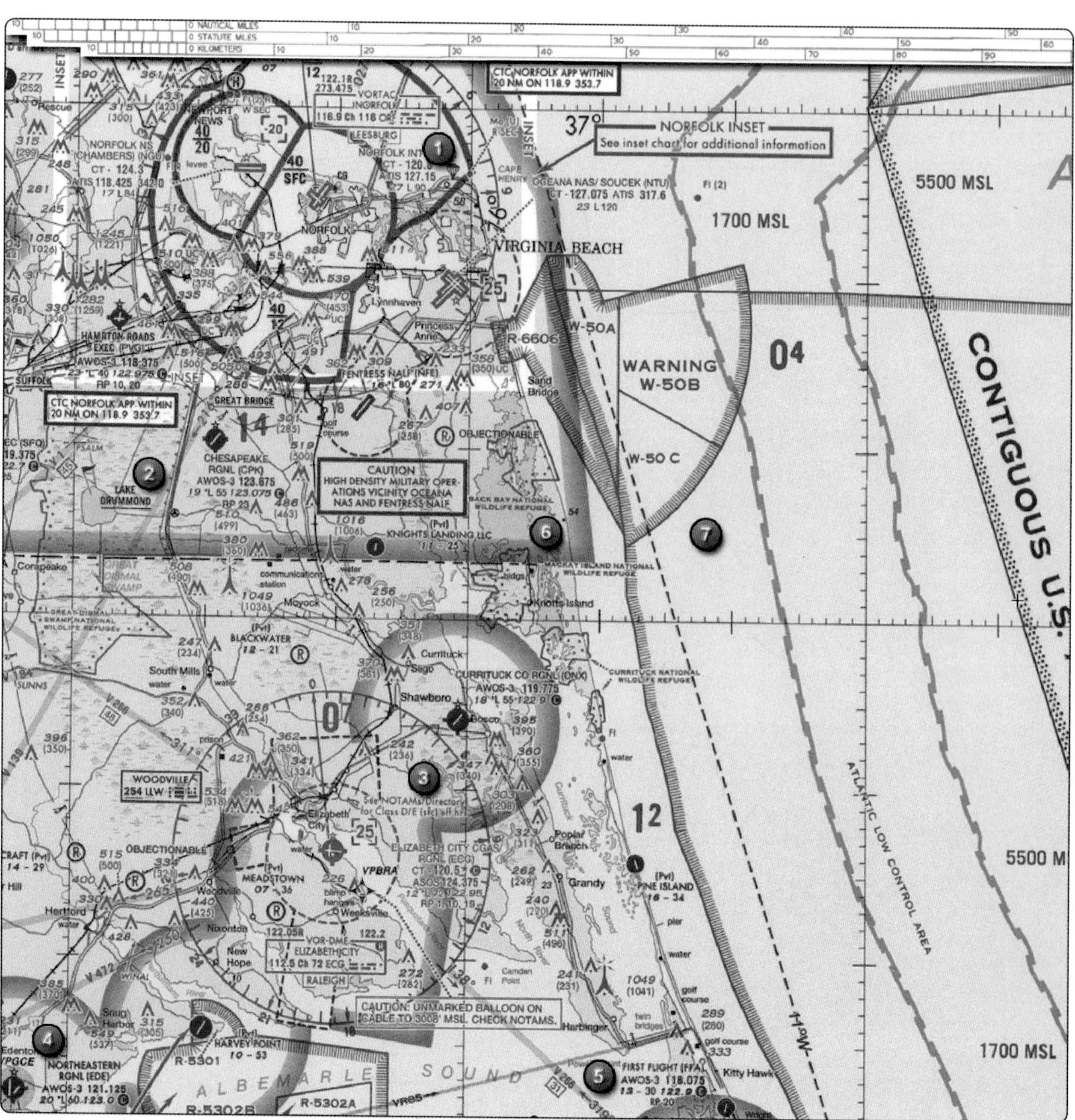

Figure 21. Sectional chart excerpt.

Sport/Private: Figure 22

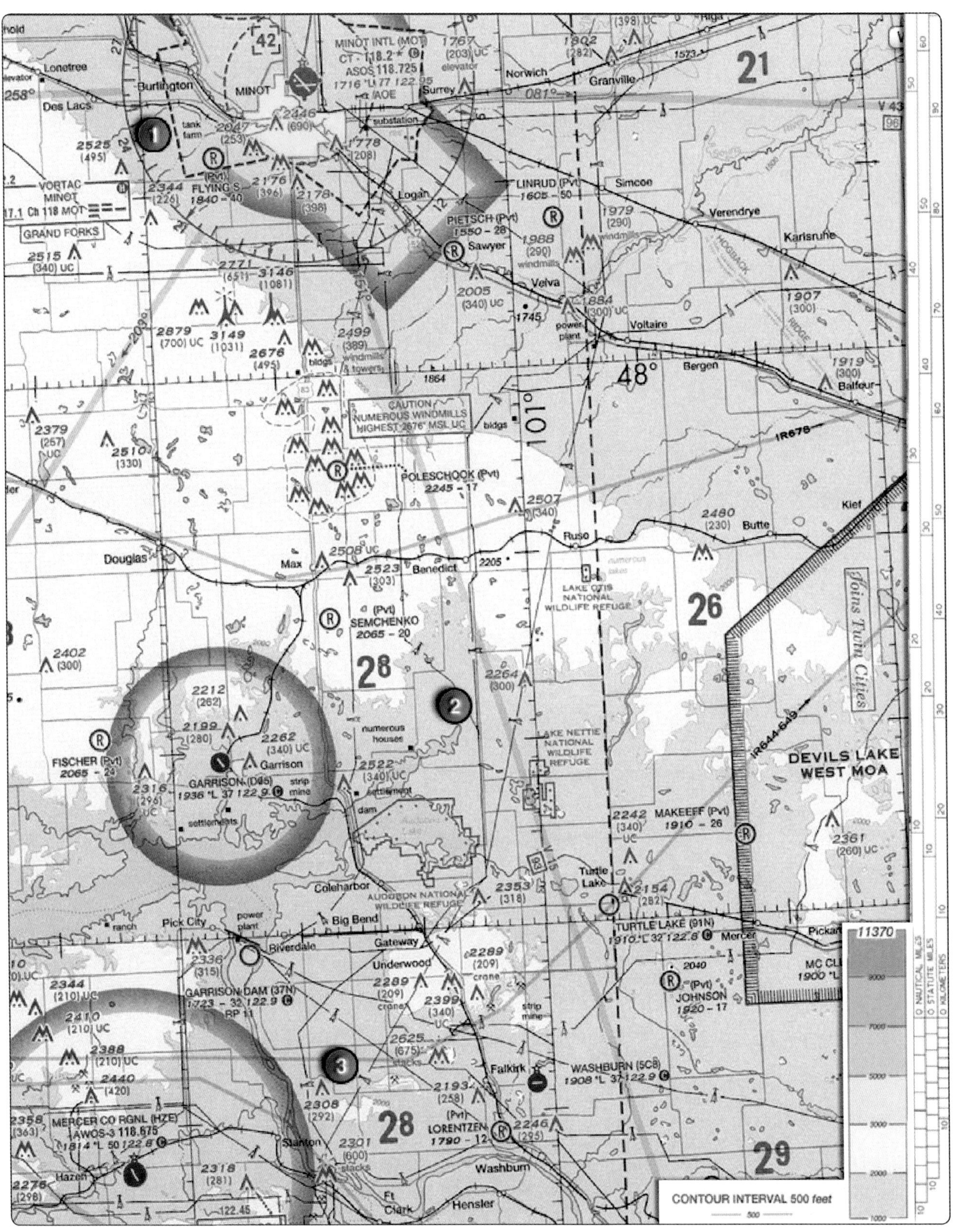

Figure 22. Sectional chart excerpt.

Sport/Private: Figure 23

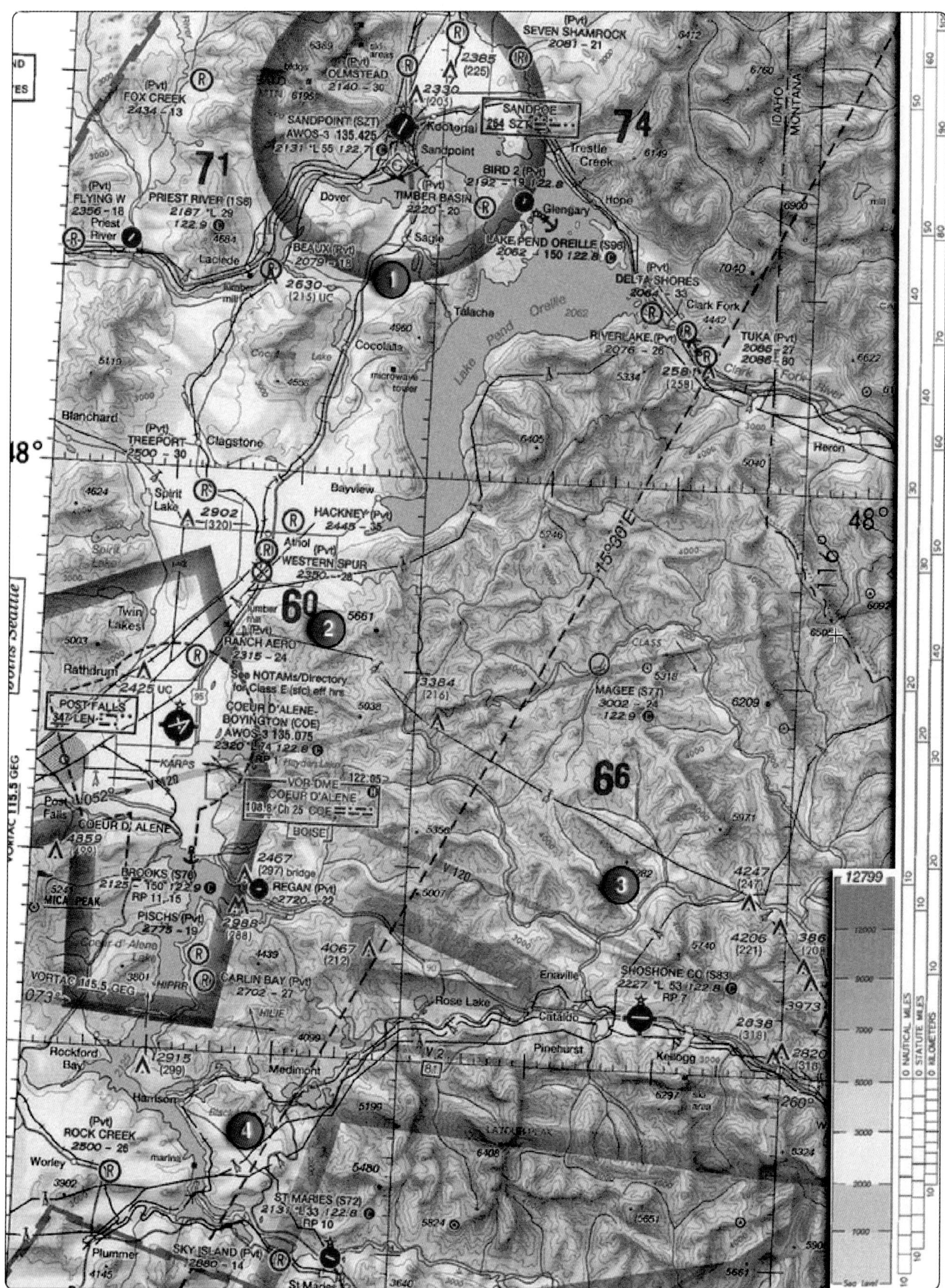

Figure 23. Sectional chart excerpt.

Sport/Private: Figure 24

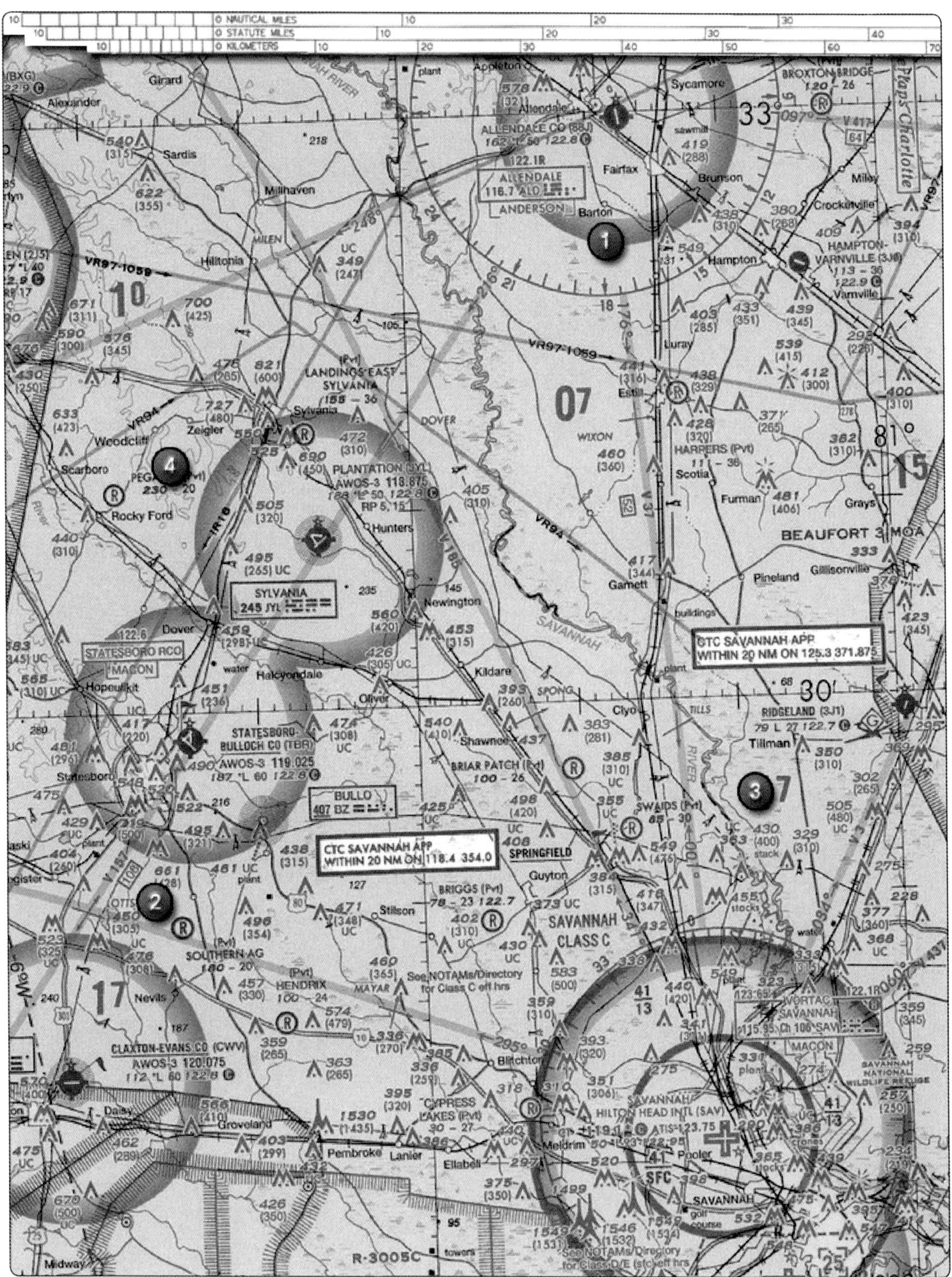

Figure 24. Sectional chart excerpt.

Sport/Private: Figure 25

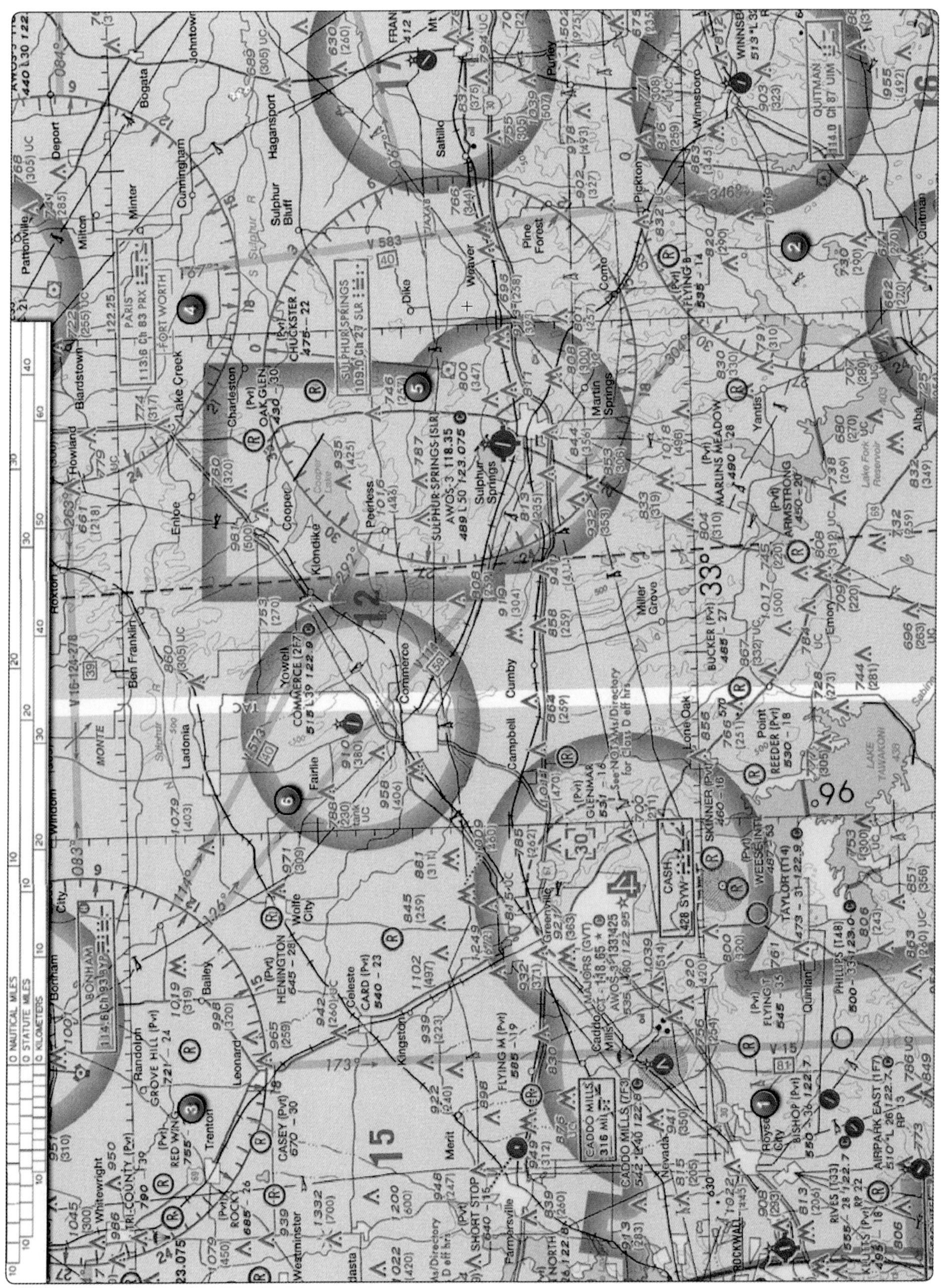

Figure 25. Sectional chart excerpt.

Sport/Private: Figure 26

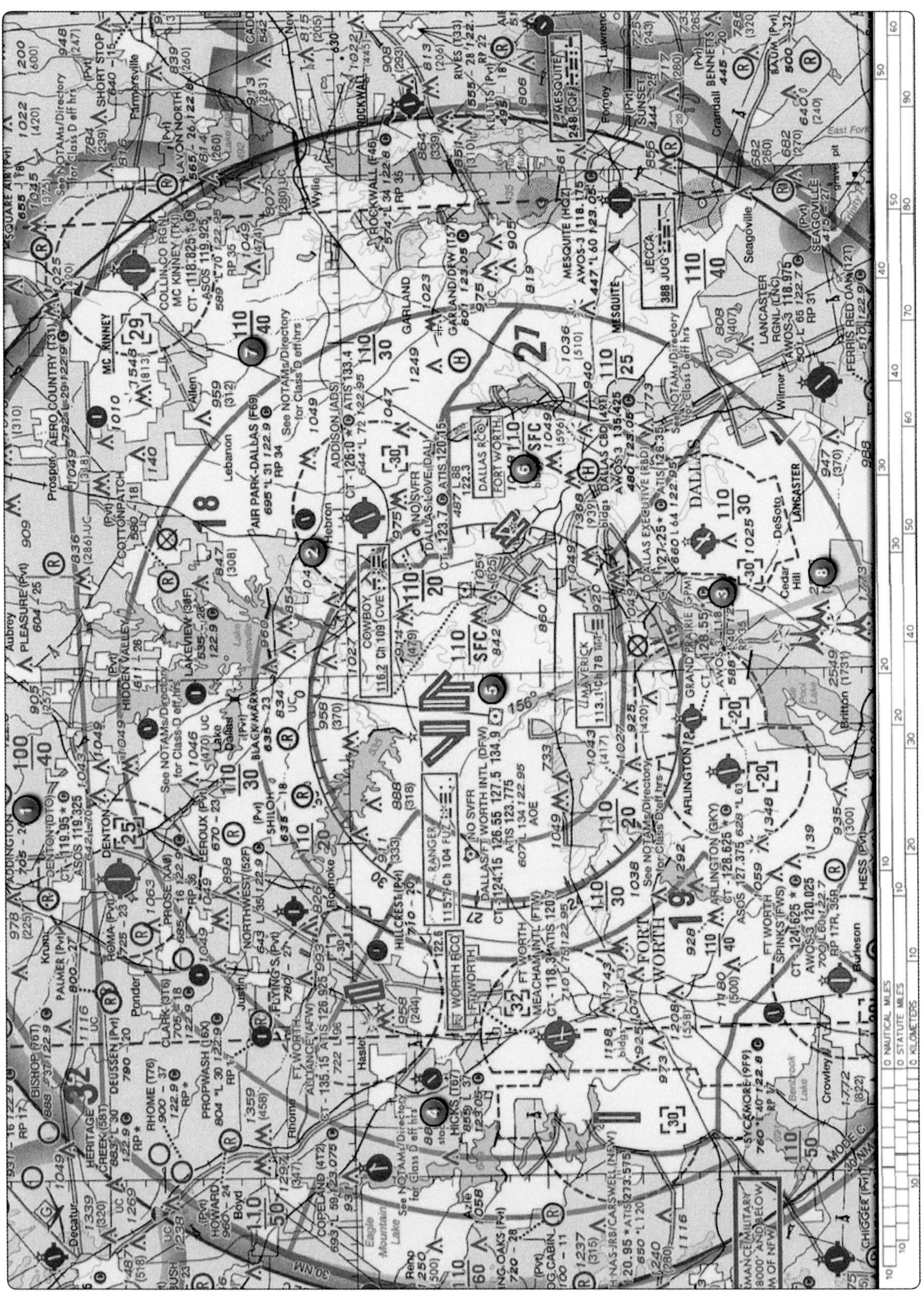

Figure 26. Sectional chart excerpt.

Sport/Private: Figure 27

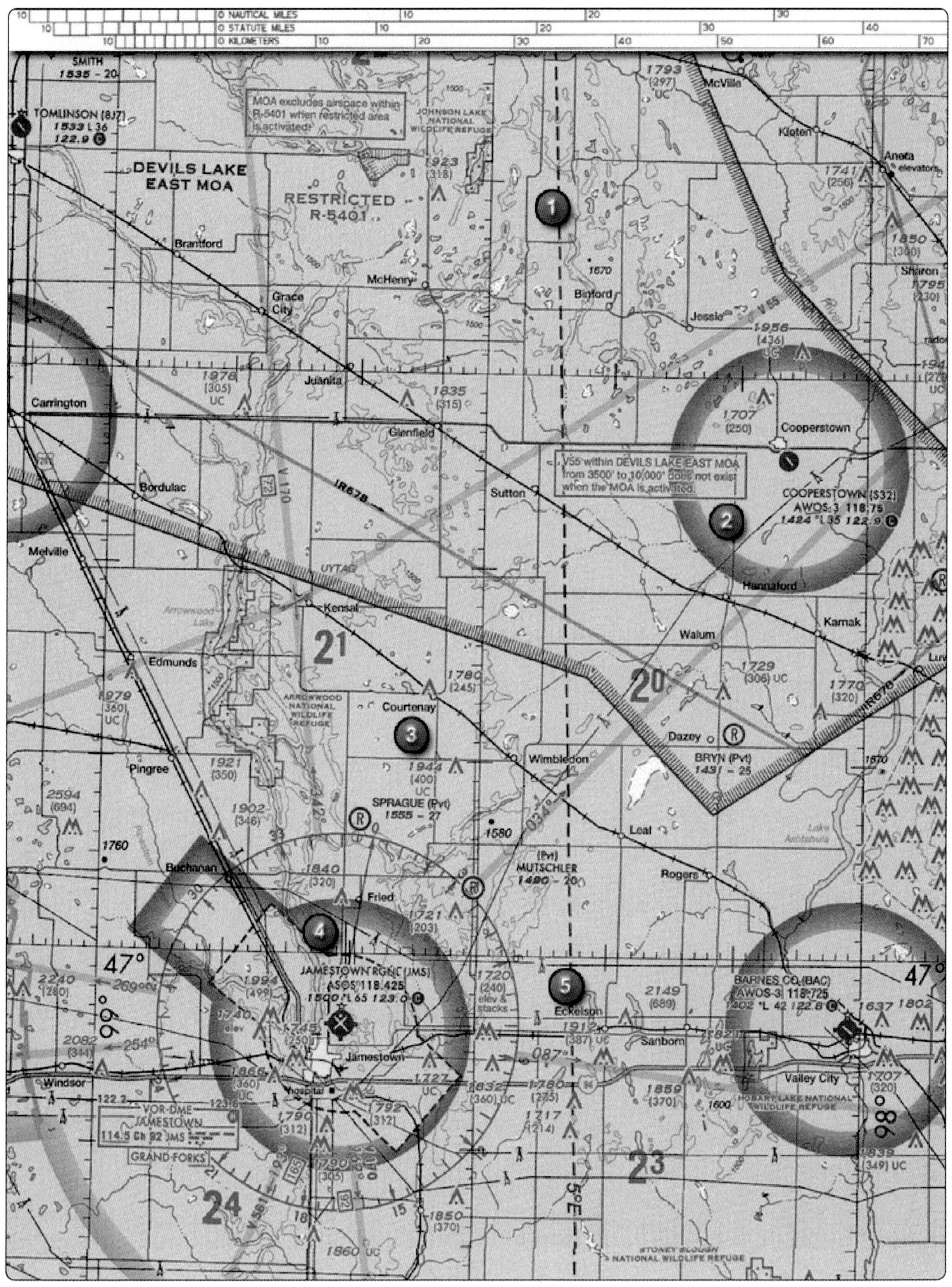

Figure 27. Sectional chart excerpt.

Sport/Private: Figure 60

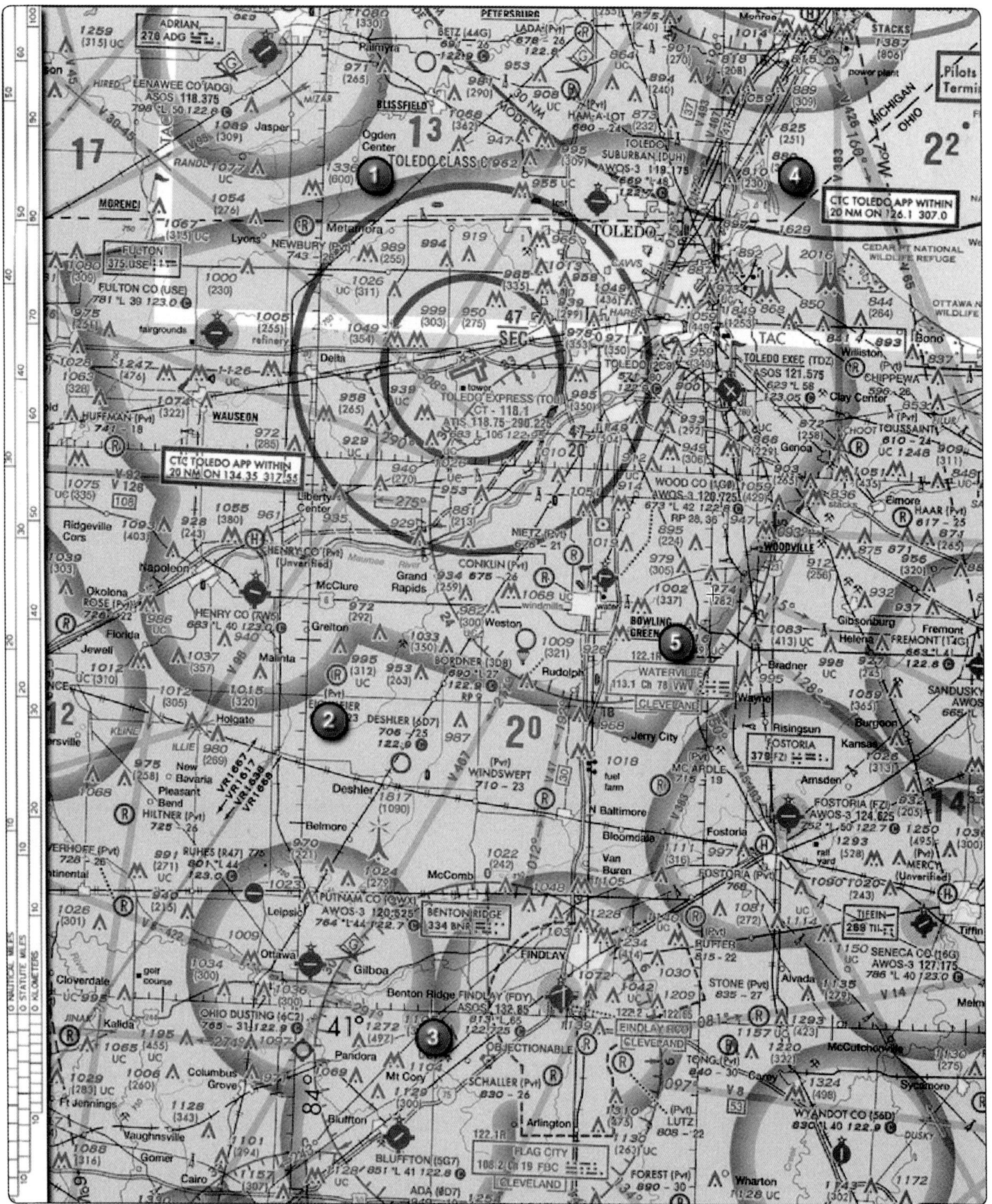

Figure 60. Sectional chart excerpt.

Sport/Private: Figure 70

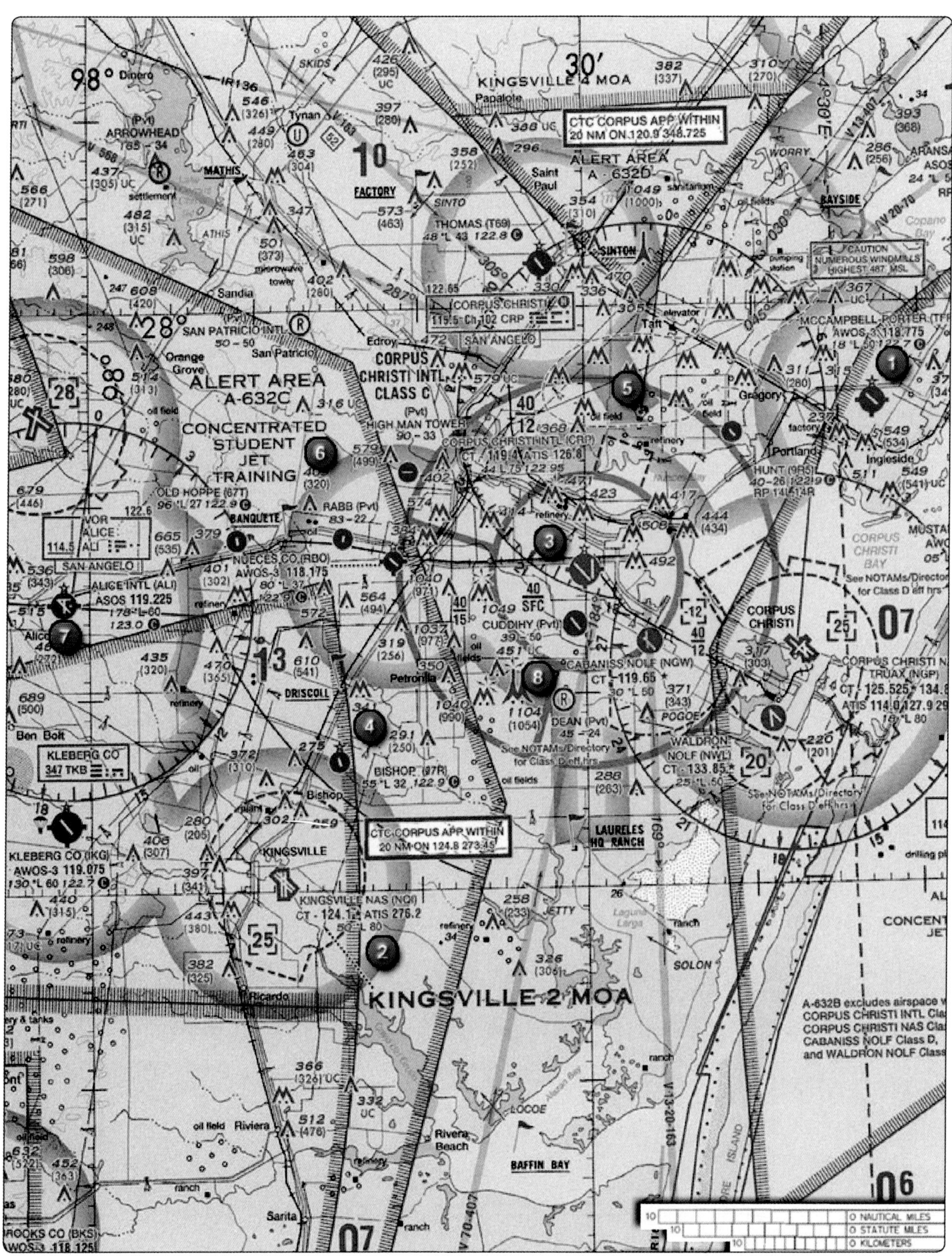

Figure 70. Sectional chart excerpt.

Sport/Private: Figure 71

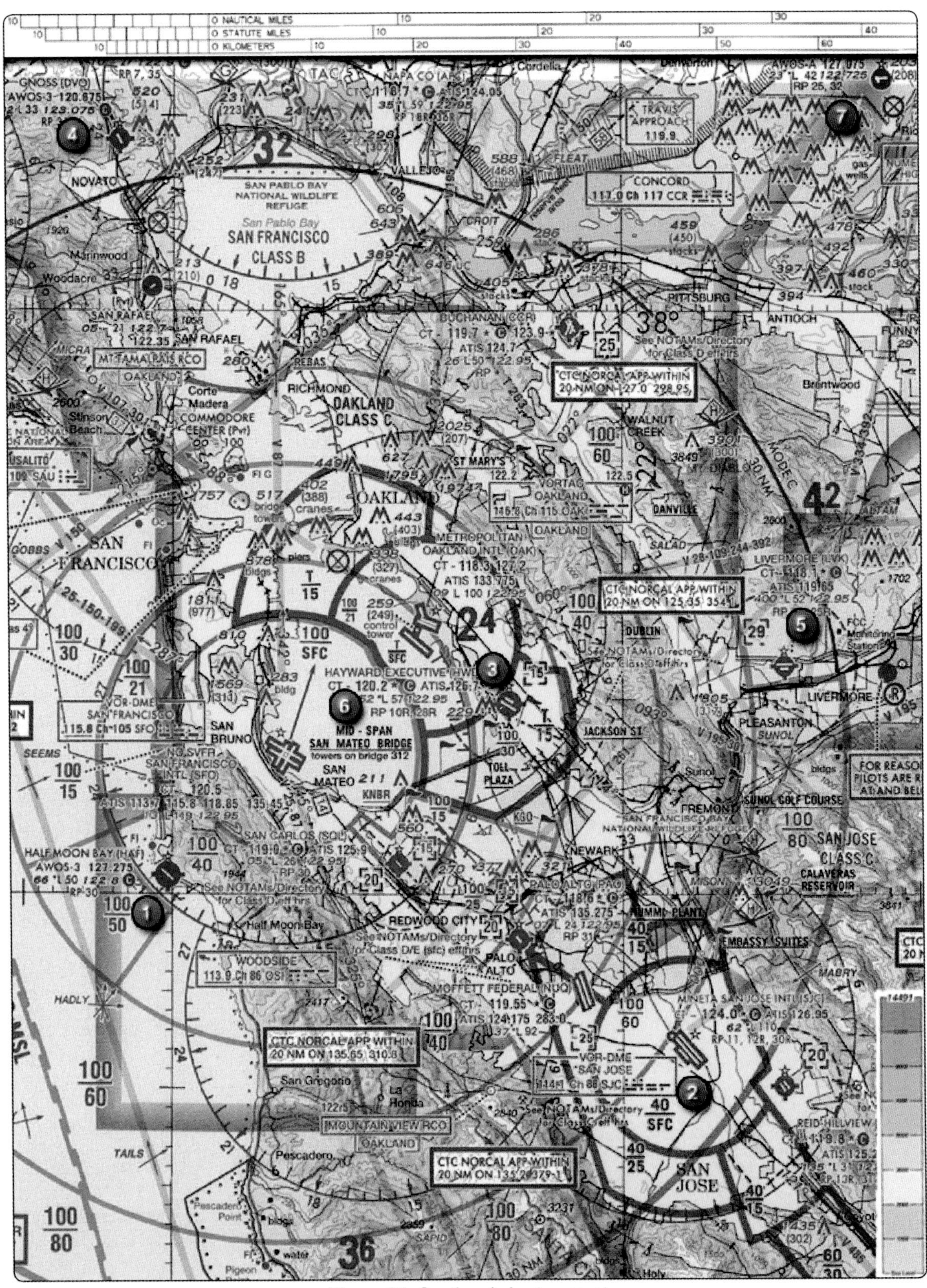

Figure 71. Sectional chart excerpt.

Sport/Private: Figure 72

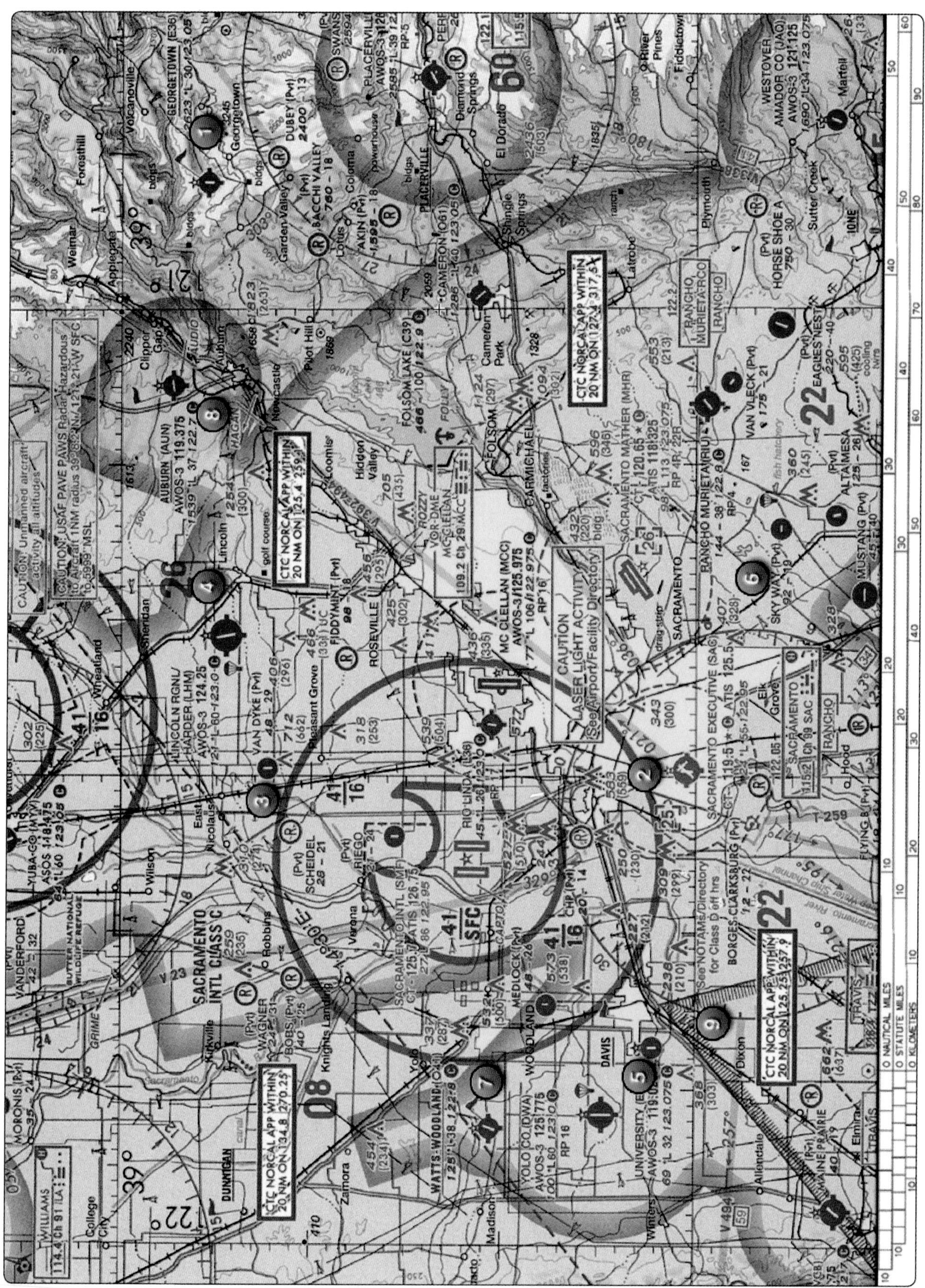

Figure 72. Sectional chart excerpt.

Sport/Private: Figure 75

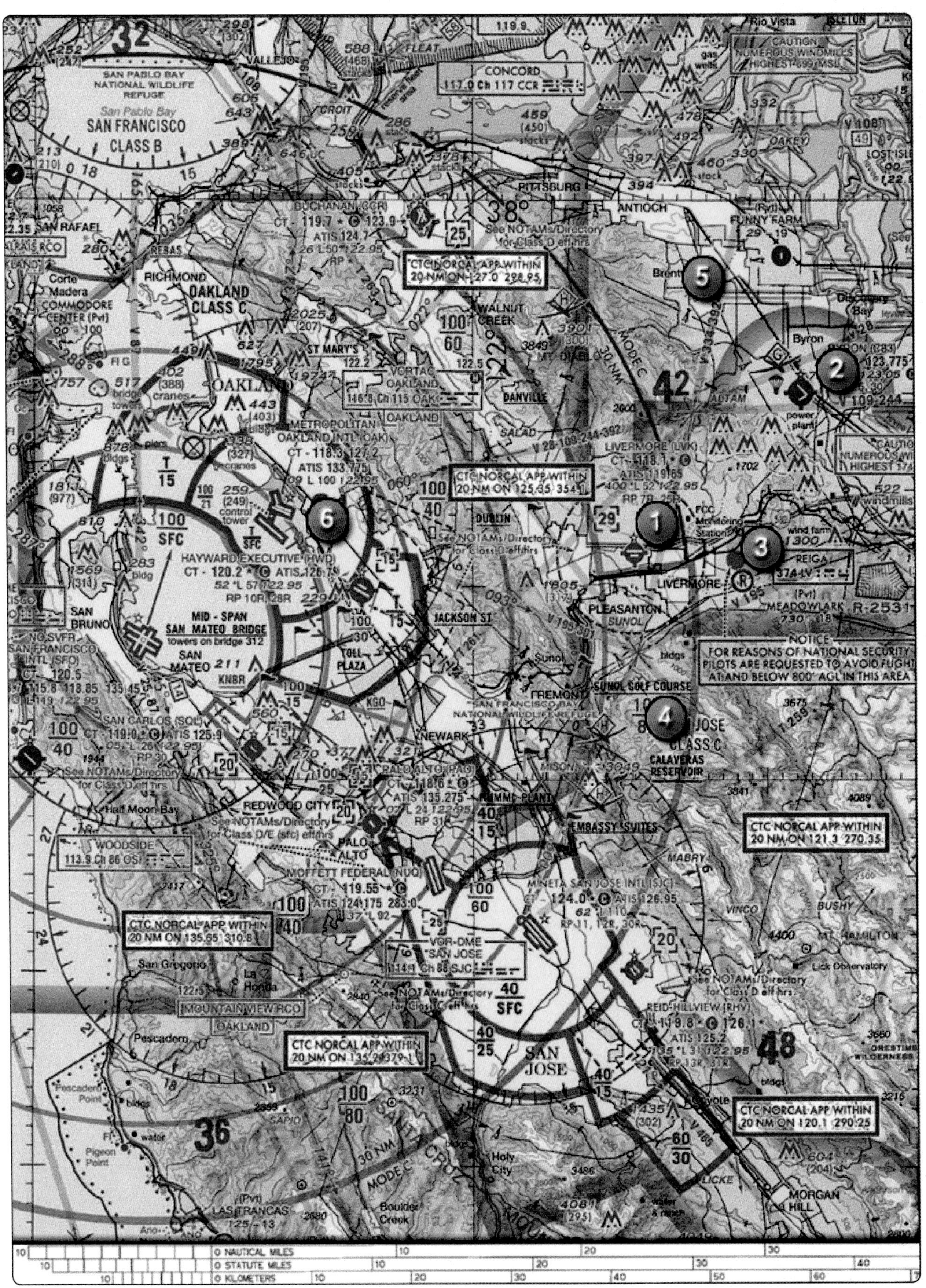

Figure 75. Sectional chart excerpt.

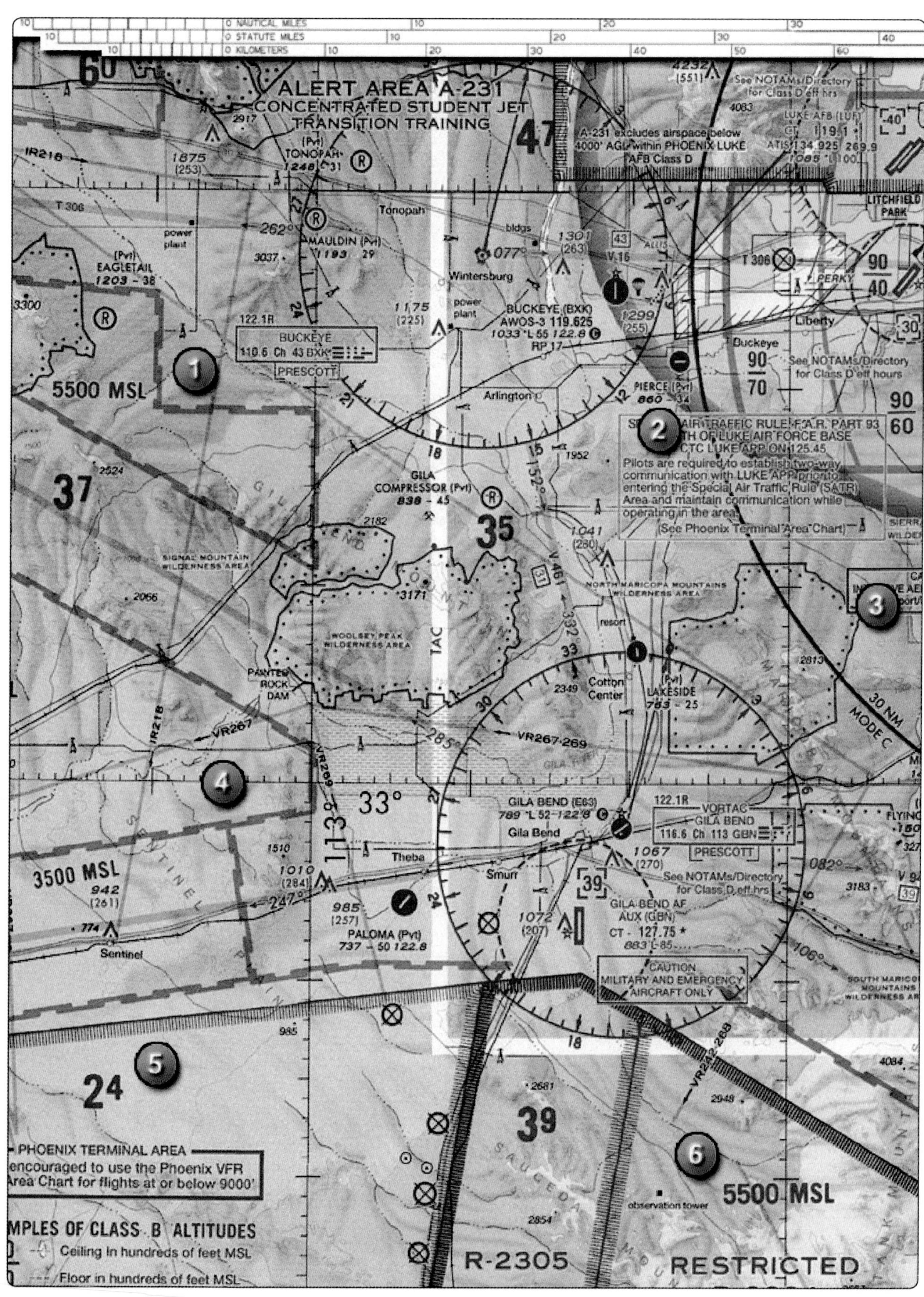

Figure 76. Sectional chart excerpt.

Sport/Private: Figure 77

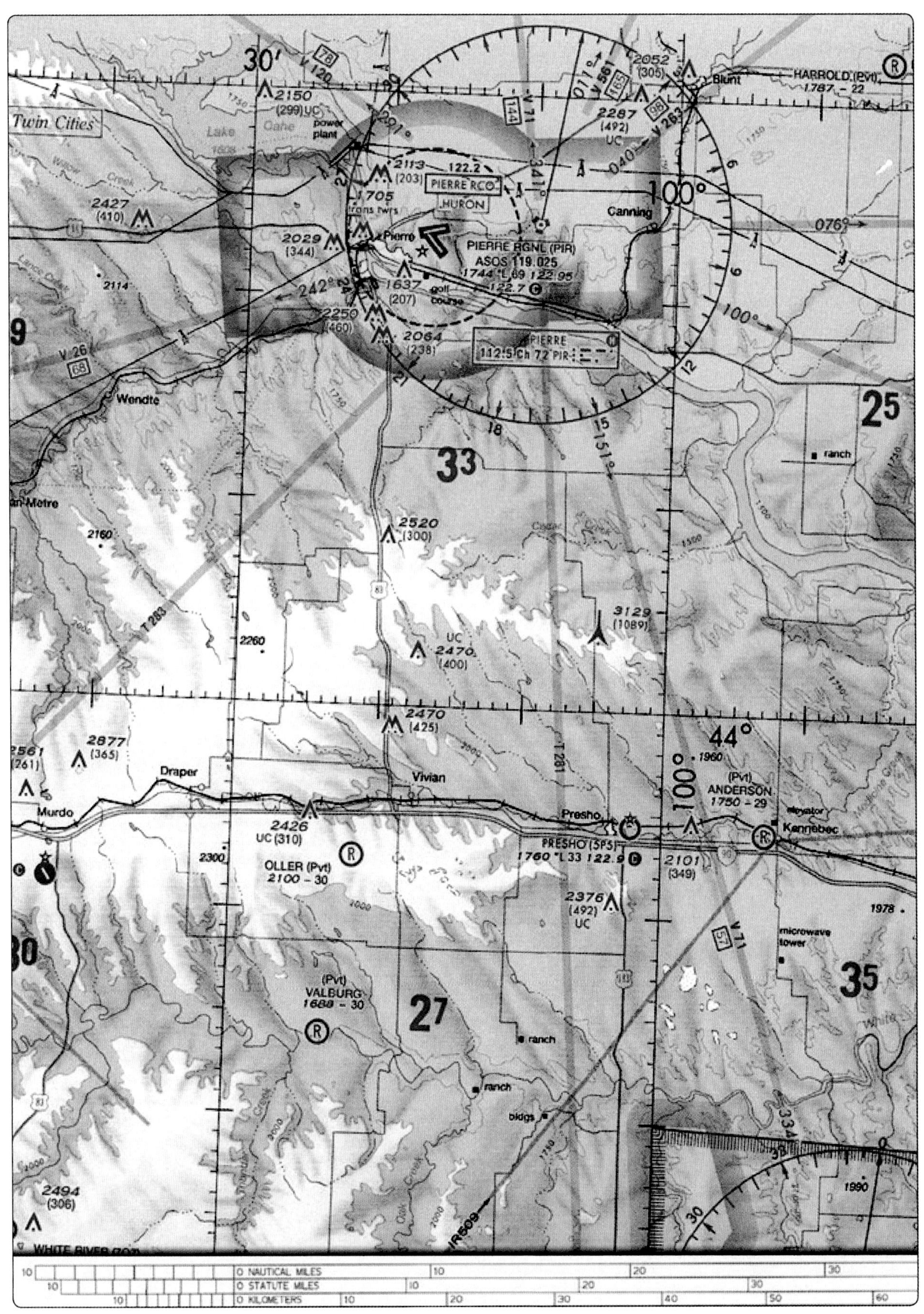

Figure 77. Sectional chart excerpt.

Sport/Private: Figure 79

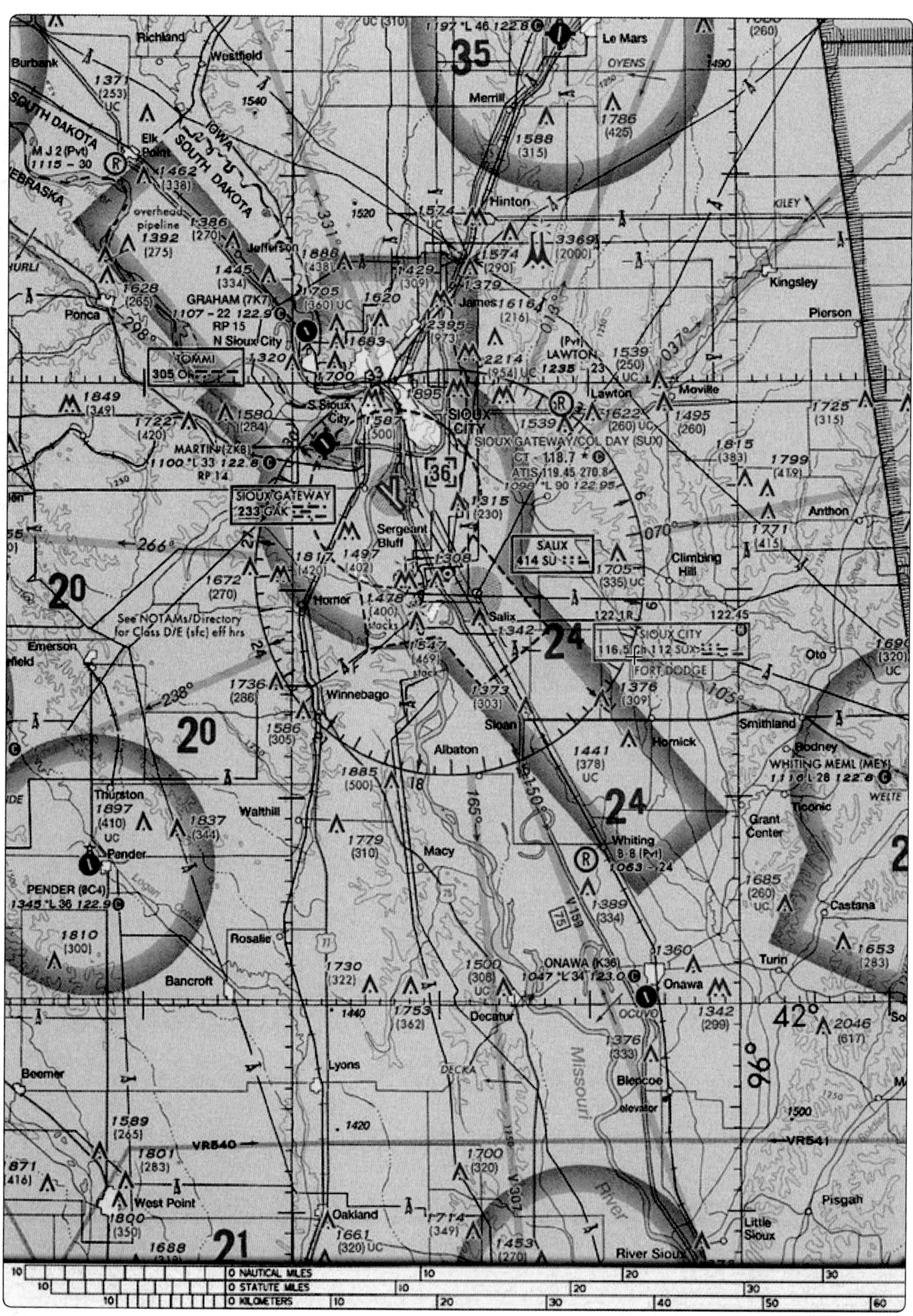

Figure 79. Sectional chart excerpt.

Sport/Private: Figure 81

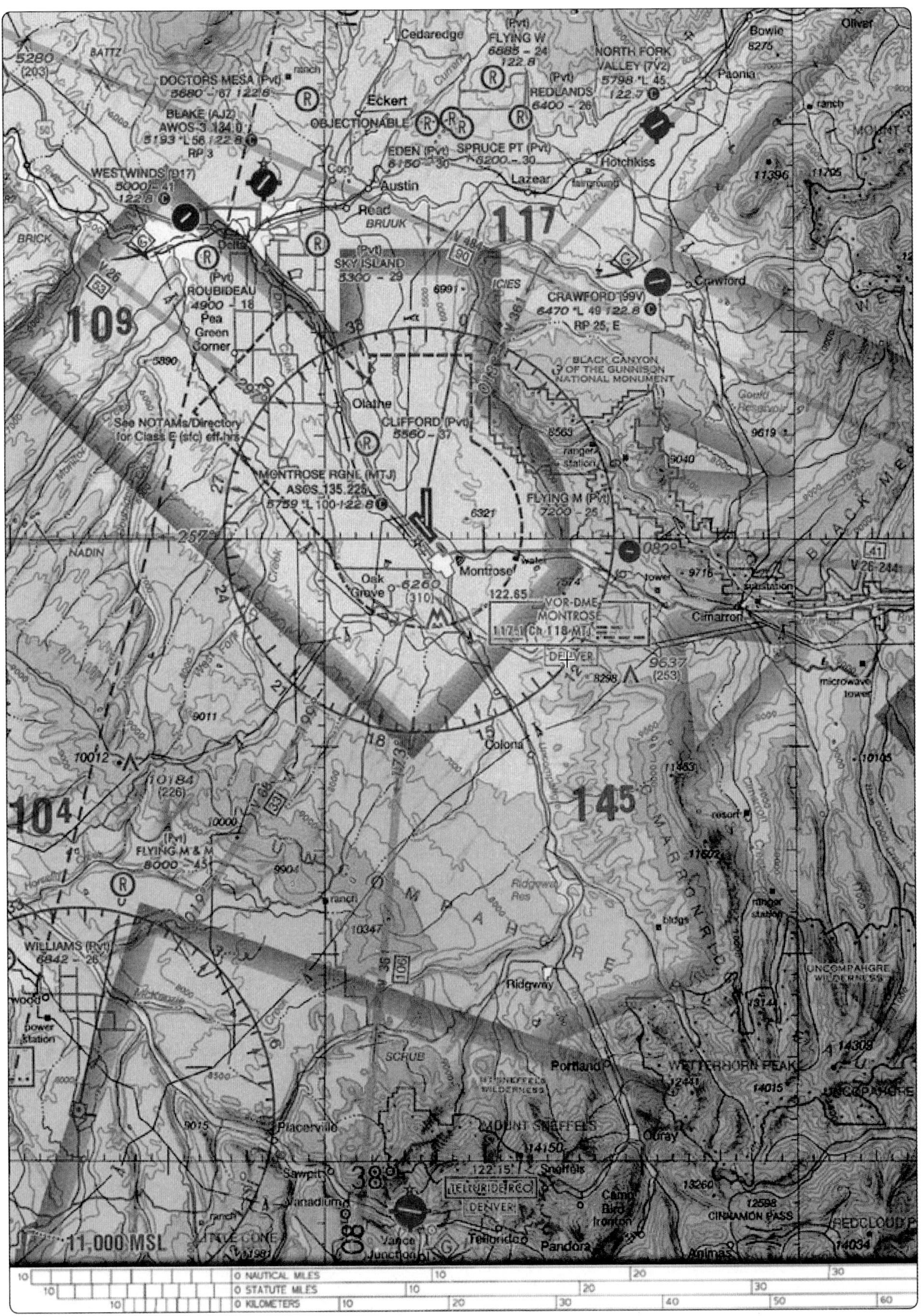

Figure 81. Sectional chart excerpt.

Commercial: Figure 52

Figure 52. – Sectional Chart Excerpt.

Commercial: Figure 53

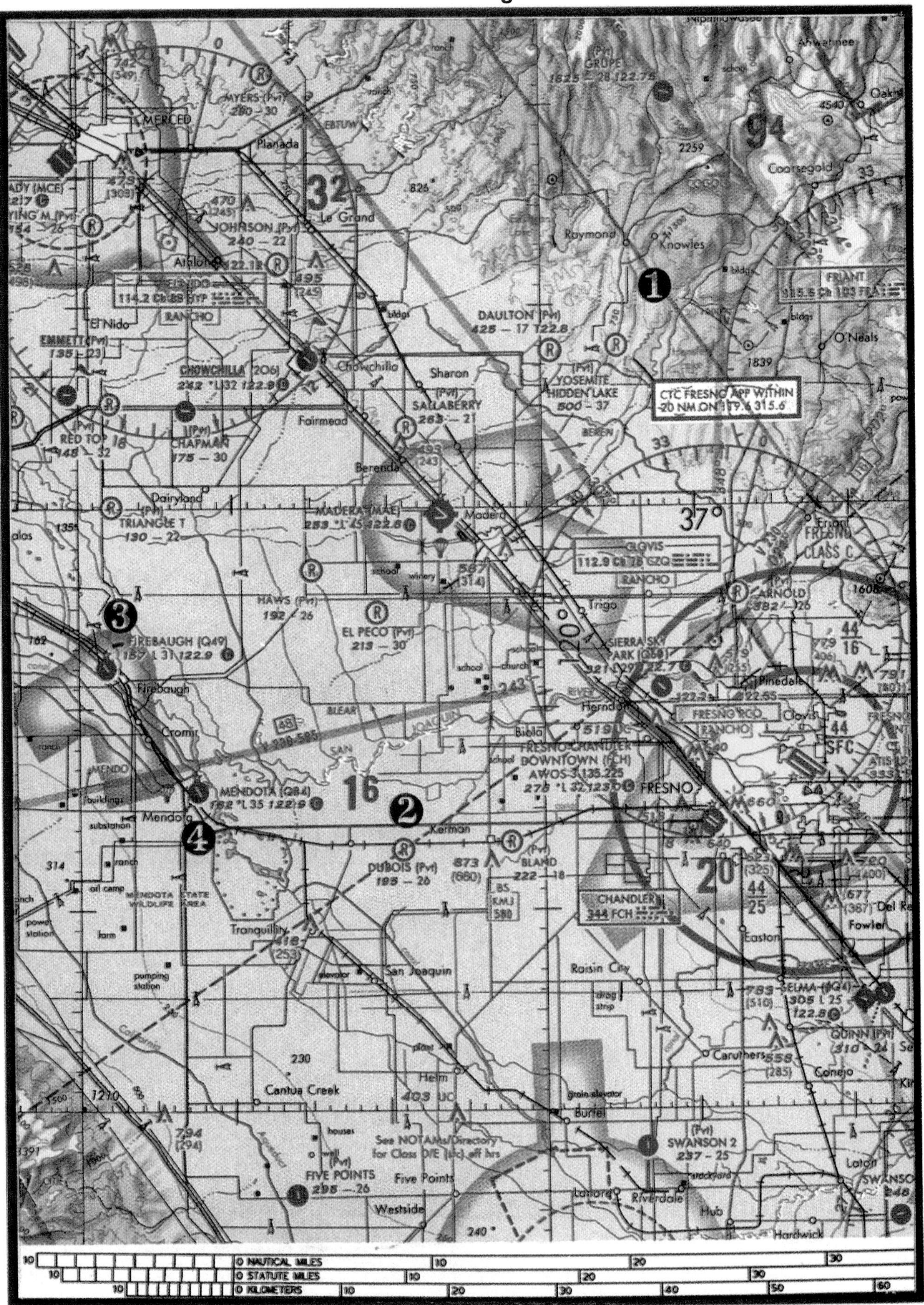

Figure 53. – Sectional Chart Excerpt.

Commercial: Figure 54

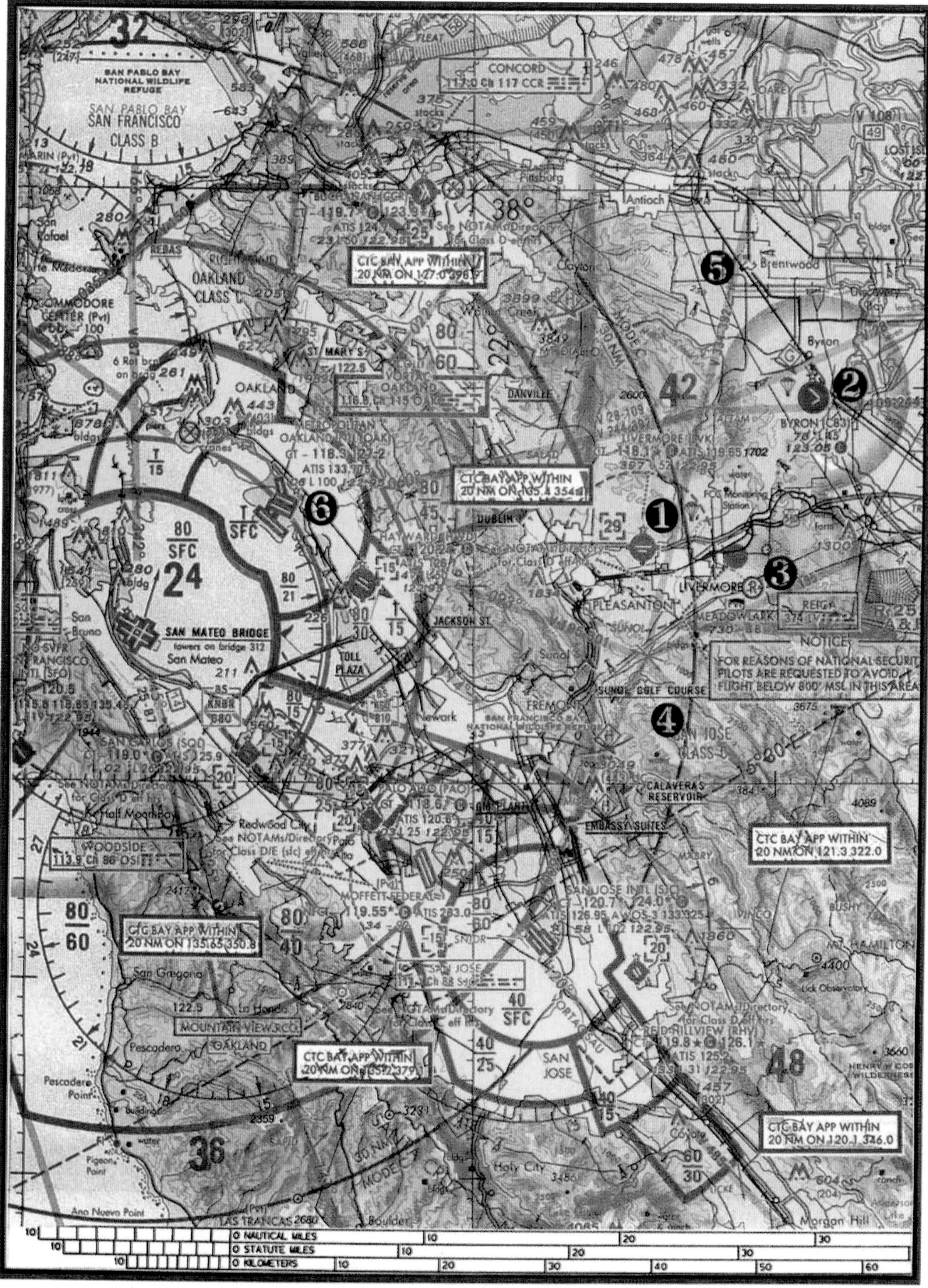

Figure 54. – Sectional Chart Excerpt.

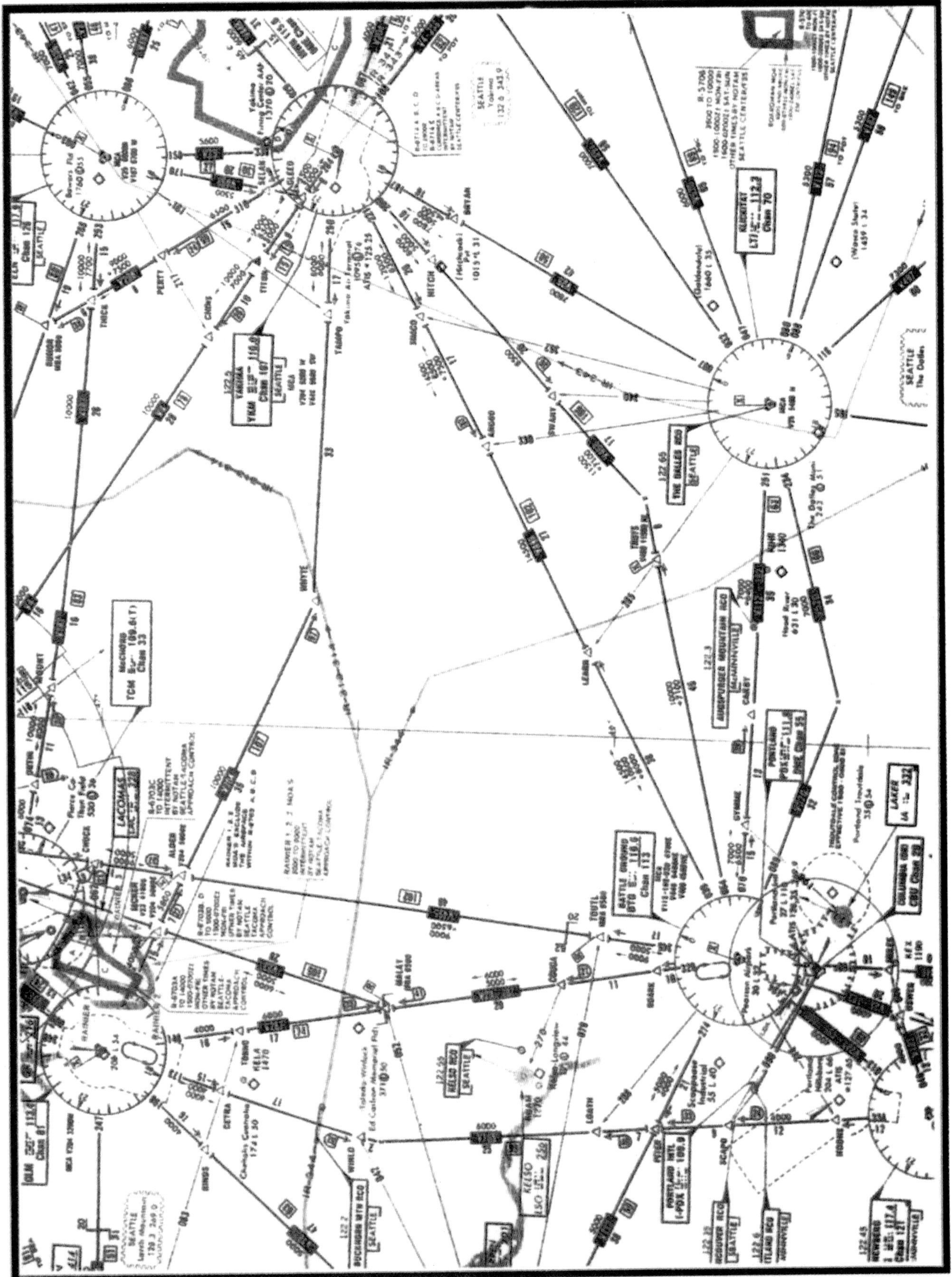

Figure 55. – En Route Low Altitude Chart Segment.

Flight/Ground Instructor: Figure 44

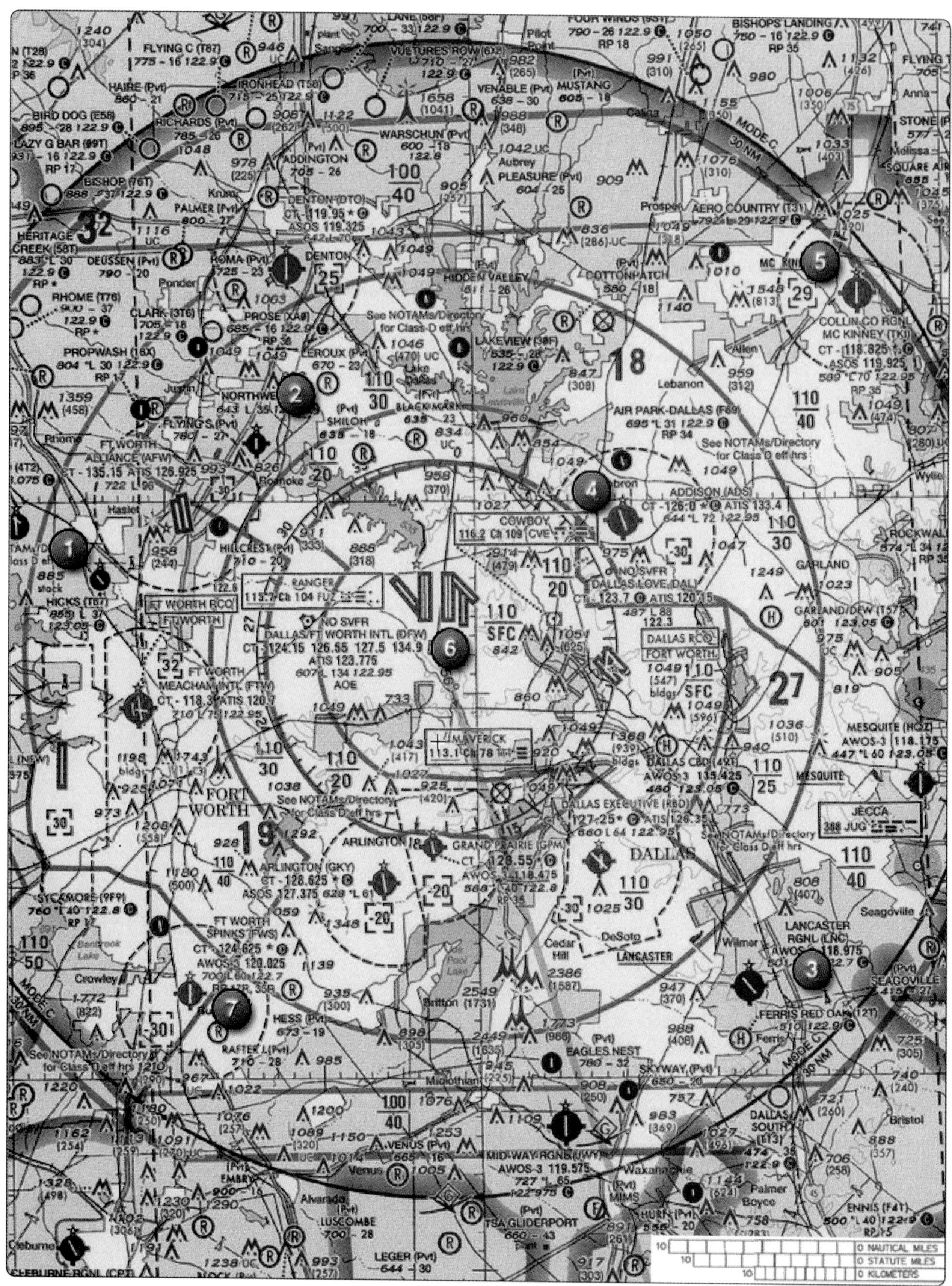

Figure 44. Sectional chart excerpt.

Flight/Ground Instructor: Figure 45

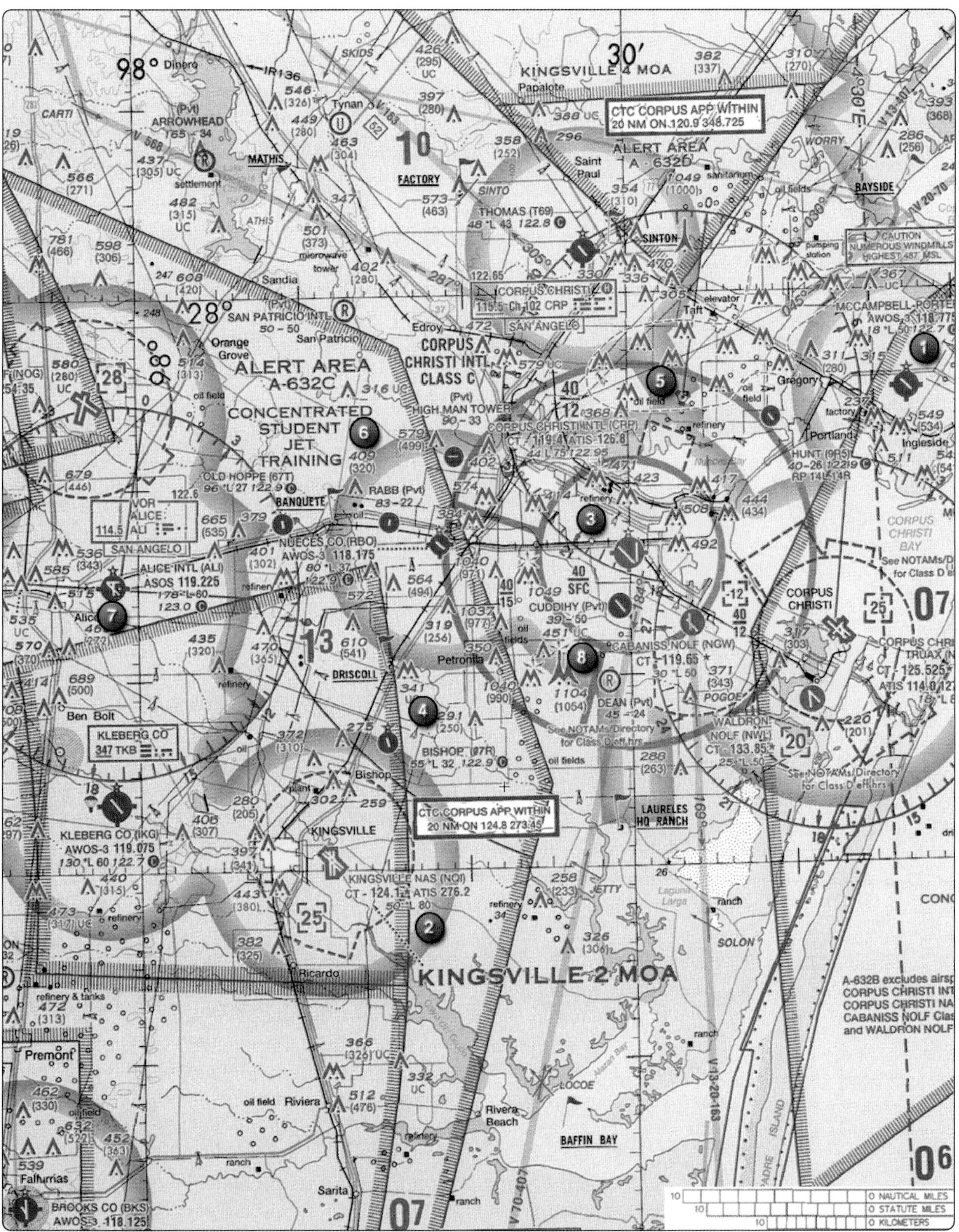

Figure 45. Sectional chart excerpt.

Flight/Ground Instructor: Figure 46

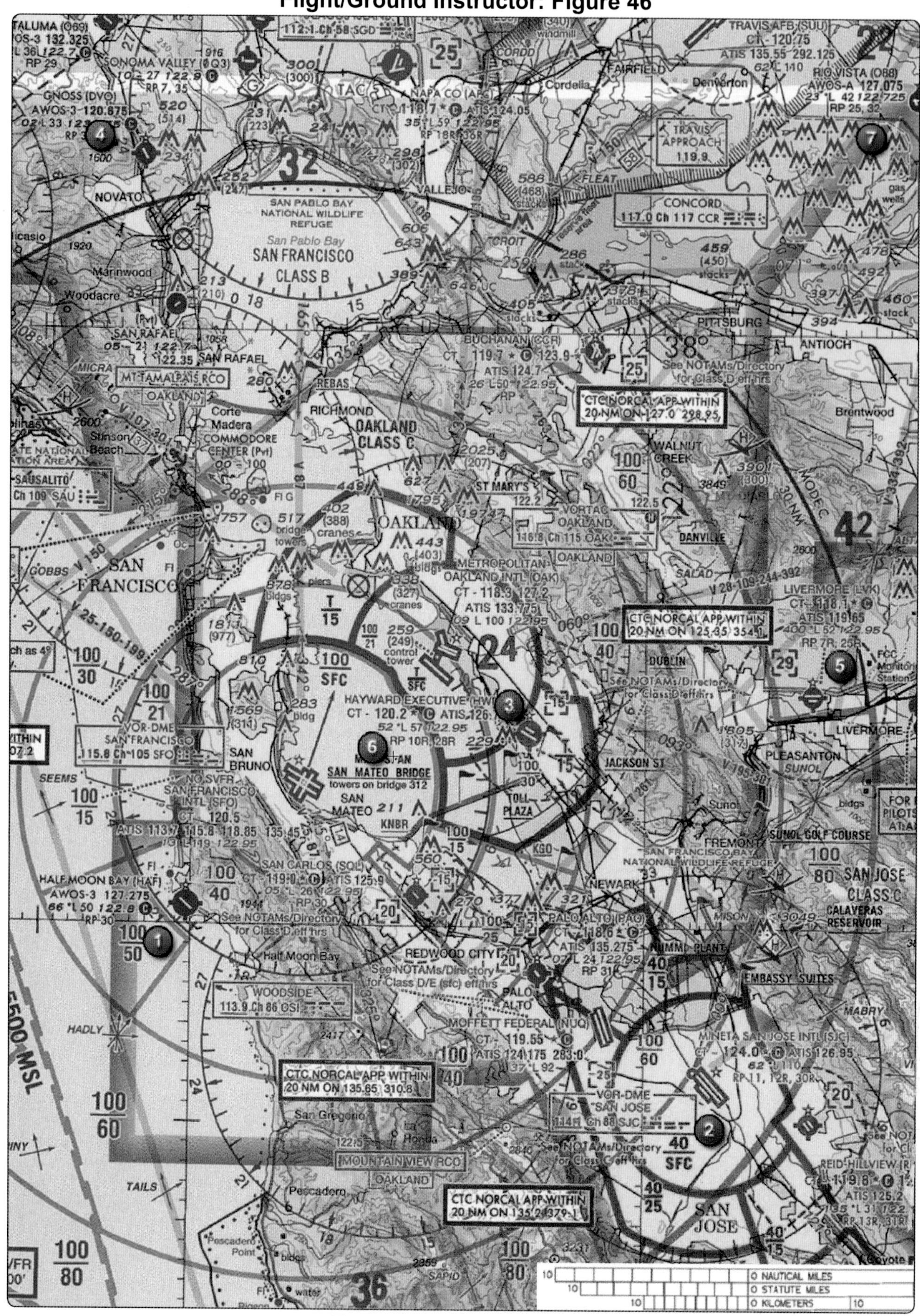

Figure 46. Sectional chart excerpt.

IF FOUND, please notify and arrange return to owner. This text is an important study guide for the owner's career and/or exam preparation.

Name: ______________________ Email: ______________________

Address: ______________________

City, State, ZIP: ______________________ Telephone: (____) ______________________

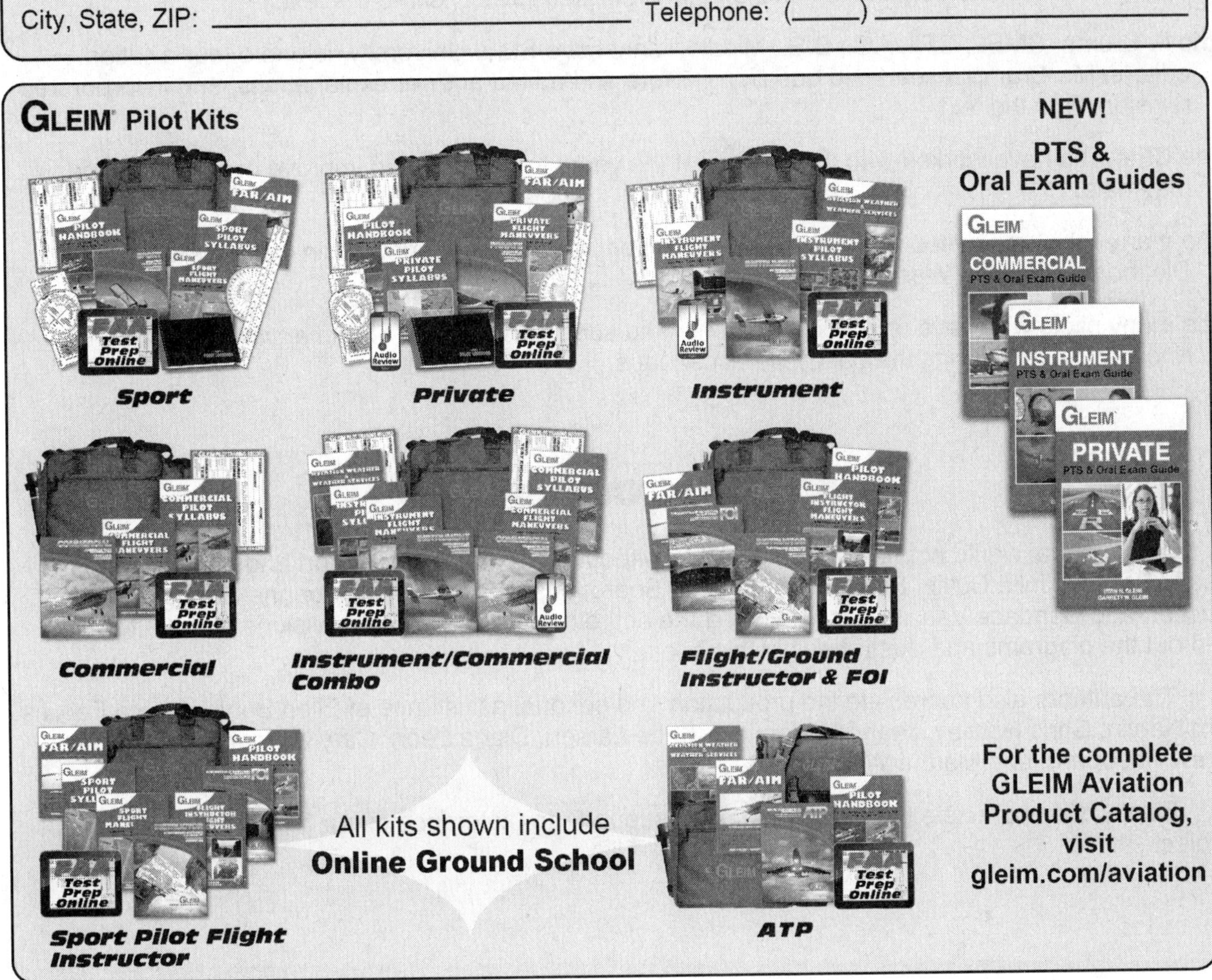

Additional copies of *Commercial Pilot Knowledge Test* are available from

Gleim Publications, Inc.
P.O. Box 12848 • University Station
Gainesville, Florida 32604

gleim.com
aviationteam@gleim.com

(352) 375-0772
(800) 87-GLEIM or (800) 874-5346
Fax: (352) 375-6940

The price is $19.95 (subject to change without notice). Orders must be prepaid. See the product listing at the back of the book and order online or call us. Shipping and handling charges apply to all orders. Add applicable sales tax to shipments within Florida.

Gleim Publications, Inc., guarantees the immediate refund of all resalable texts, unopened and un-downloaded Test Prep Software, and unopened and un-downloaded audios returned within 30 days of purchase. Aviation Test Prep Online may be canceled within 30 days of purchase if no more than the first study unit has been accessed. Other Aviation online courses may be canceled within 30 days of purchase if no more than two study units have been accessed. This policy applies only to products that are purchased directly from Gleim Publications, Inc. No refunds will be provided on opened or downloaded Test Prep Software or audios, partial returns of package sets, or shipping and handling charges. Any freight charges incurred for returned or refused packages will be the purchaser's responsibility. Returns of books purchased from bookstores and other resellers should be made to the respective bookstore or reseller. For more information regarding the Gleim Return Policy, please contact our offices at (800) 874-5346.

REVIEWERS AND CONTRIBUTORS

James Chaney, Gold Seal CFI, CFII, MEI, AGI, and IGI, is the Gleim 141 Chief Flight Instructor and one of our aviation editors. Mr. Chaney has 13 years of experience as a Flight Instructor, Stage Check Instructor, Assistant Chief Flight Instructor, Chief Flight Instructor, and Director of Flight Operations. He has taught Aviation English at various universities in China. Mr. Chaney researched changes, wrote and edited additions, and incorporated revisions into the text.

Eric L. Crump, CMEL, CFII, AGI, B.S., Middle Tennessee State University, is one of our aviation editors. Mr. Crump researched questions, wrote and edited answer explanations, and incorporated revisions into the text.

The CFIs who have worked with us throughout the years to develop and improve our pilot training materials.

The many FAA employees who helped, in person or by telephone, primarily in Gainesville, Orlando, Oklahoma City, and Washington, DC.

The many pilots who have provided comments and suggestions about *Commercial Pilot FAA Knowledge Test* during the past several decades.

A PERSONAL THANKS

This manual would not have been possible without the extraordinary effort and dedication of Jacob Brunny, Julie Cutlip, Eileen Nickl, Teresa Soard, Justin Stephenson, Joanne Strong, Elmer Tucker, and Candace Van Doren, who typed the entire manuscript and all revisions and drafted and laid out the diagrams and illustrations in this book.

The authors also appreciate the production and editorial assistance of Ellen Buhl, Jessica Felkins, Jim Harvin, Chris Hawley, Jeanette Kerstein, Katie Larson, Diana León, Cary Marcous, Shane Rapp, Drew Sheppard, and Martha Willis.

Finally, we appreciate the encouragement, support, and tolerance of our families throughout this project.

If you purchased this book without a cover, you should be aware that it is probably stolen property. Old editions of our books are reported to us as “unsold and destroyed,” and neither the author nor the publisher has received any payment for this “stripped book.” Please report the sale of books without covers by calling (800) 874-5346.

Environmental Statement -- This book is printed on recyclable, environmentally friendly groundwood paper, sourced from certified sustainable forests and produced either TCF (totally chlorine-free) or ECF (elementally chlorine-free).

2015 EDITION

COMMERCIAL PILOT

FAA KNOWLEDGE TEST

for the FAA Computer-Based Pilot Knowledge Test

Commercial Pilot - Airplane *Military Competency - Airplane*

by

Irvin N. Gleim, Ph.D., CFII

and

Garrett W. Gleim, CFII

ABOUT THE AUTHORS

Irvin N. Gleim earned his private pilot certificate in 1965 from the Institute of Aviation at the University of Illinois, where he subsequently received his Ph.D. He is a commercial pilot and flight instructor (instrument) with multi-engine and seaplane ratings and is a member of the Aircraft Owners and Pilots Association, American Bonanza Society, Civil Air Patrol, Experimental Aircraft Association, National Association of Flight Instructors, and Seaplane Pilots Association. He is the author of flight maneuvers and practical test prep books for the sport, private, instrument, commercial, and flight instructor certificates/ratings and the author of study guides for the sport, private/recreational, instrument, commercial, flight/ground instructor, fundamentals of instructing, airline transport pilot, and flight engineer FAA knowledge tests. Three additional pilot training books are *Pilot Handbook*, *Aviation Weather and Weather Services*, and *FAR/AIM*.

Dr. Gleim has also written articles for professional accounting and business law journals and is the author of widely used review manuals for the CIA (Certified Internal Auditor) exam, the CMA (Certified Management Accountant) exam, the CPA (Certified Public Accountant) exam, and the EA (IRS Enrolled Agent) exam. He is Professor Emeritus, Fisher School of Accounting, University of Florida, and is a CFM, CIA, CMA, and CPA.

Garrett W. Gleim earned his private pilot certificate in 1997 in a Piper Super Cub. He is a commercial pilot (single- and multi-engine), ground instructor (advanced and instrument), and flight instructor (instrument and multi-engine), and he is a member of the Aircraft Owners and Pilots Association and the National Association of Flight Instructors. He is the author of study guides for the sport, private/recreational, instrument, commercial, flight/ground instructor, fundamentals of instructing, and airline transport pilot FAA knowledge tests. He received a Bachelor of Science in Economics from The Wharton School, University of Pennsylvania. Mr. Gleim is also a CPA (not in public practice).

Gleim Publications, Inc.
P.O. Box 12848 · University Station
Gainesville, Florida 32604
(352) 375-0772
(800) 87-GLEIM or (800) 874-5346
Fax: (352) 375-6940
Internet: www.gleim.com
Email: admin@gleim.com

For updates to the first printing of the 2015 edition of
Commercial Pilot FAA Knowledge Test

Go To: www.gleim.com/updates

Or: Email update@gleim.com with **CPKT 2015-1** in the subject line. You will receive our current update as a reply.

Updates are available until the next edition is published.

ISSN 1553-6904
ISBN 978-1-58194-521-8

This edition is copyright © 2014 by Gleim Publications, Inc. Portions of this manuscript are taken from previous editions copyright © 1988-2013 by Gleim Publications, Inc.

First Printing: August 2014

ALL RIGHTS RESERVED. No part of this material may be reproduced in any form whatsoever without express written permission from Gleim Publications, Inc.

SOURCES USED IN *COMMERCIAL PILOT FAA KNOWLEDGE TEST*

The first lines of our answer explanations contain citations to authoritative sources of the answers. These publications can be obtained from the FAA (www.faa.gov) and aviation bookstores. These citations are abbreviated as provided below:

AC	Advisory Circular
ACL	Aeronautical Chart Legend
AFNA	Aerodynamics for Naval Aviators
AFH	*Airplane Flying Handbook*
AIM	*Aeronautical Information Manual*
A&PM PH	*Airframe and Powerplant Mechanics Powerplant Handbook*
AvW	*Aviation Weather*
AWBH	*Aircraft Weight and Balance Handbook*
AWS	*Aviation Weather Services*
FAR	Federal Aviation Regulations
FI Comp	Flight Computer
IFH	*Instrument Flying Handbook*
NTSB	National Transportation Safety Board Regulations
PHAK	*Pilot's Handbook of Aeronautical Knowledge*

HELP!!

This 2015 edition is designed specifically for pilots who aspire to the Commercial Certificate. Please send any corrections and suggestions for subsequent editions to the authors, c/o Gleim Publications, Inc. The last page in this book has been reserved for you to make comments and suggestions. It can be torn out and mailed to Gleim Publications, Inc. Alternatively, email aviation@gleim.com.

A companion volume, ***Commercial Pilot Flight Maneuvers and Practical Test Prep***, focuses on the FAA practical test, just as this book focuses on the FAA knowledge test. Save time, money, and frustration--order today! Refer to the product listing at the back of the book and then order online or call us. Please bring these books to the attention of flight instructors, fixed-base operators, and others with a potential interest in acquiring their pilot ratings and certificates. Wide distribution of these books and increased interest in flying depend on your assistance and good word. Thank you.

Our answers have been carefully researched and reviewed. Inevitably, there will be differences with competitors' books and even the FAA. If necessary, we will develop an UPDATE for ***Commercial Pilot FAA Knowledge Test***. Visit our website or email update@gleim.com as described above for the latest updates and information on all of our products. Updates for this 2015 edition will be available until the next edition is published. To continue providing our customers with first-rate service, we request that questions about our materials be sent to us via email to aviation@gleim.com. The appropriate staff member will give each question thorough consideration and a prompt response. Questions concerning orders, prices, shipments, or payments will be handled via telephone by our competent and courteous customer service staff.

TABLE OF CONTENTS

NOTE: The FAA no longer releases the complete database of test questions to the public. Instead, sample questions are released on the Airmen Testing page of the FAA website on a quarterly basis. These questions are similar to the actual test questions, but they are not exact matches.

Gleim utilizes customer feedback and FAA publications to create additional sample questions that closely represent the topical coverage of each FAA knowledge test. In order to do well on the knowledge test, you must study the Gleim outlines in this book, answer all the questions under exam conditions (i.e., without looking at the answers first), and develop an understanding of the topics addressed. You should not simply memorize questions and answers. This will not prepare you for your FAA knowledge test, and it will not help you develop the knowledge you need to safely operate an aircraft.

Always refer to the Gleim update service (www.gleim.com/updates) to ensure you have the latest information that is available. If you see topics covered on your FAA knowledge test that are not contained in this book, please contact us at aviation@gleim.com to report your experience and help us fine-tune our test preparation materials.

Thank you!

PREFACE

The primary purpose of this book is to provide you with the easiest, fastest, and least expensive means of passing the commercial pilot (airplane) knowledge test. The publicly released FAA knowledge test bank does **not** have questions grouped together by topic. We have organized them for you. We have

1. Reproduced all previously released knowledge test questions published by the FAA. We have also included additional similar test questions, which we believe may appear in some form on your knowledge test.
2. Reordered the questions into 86 logical topics.
3. Organized the 86 topics into 11 study units.
4. Explained the answer immediately to the right of each question.
5. Provided an easy-to-study outline of exactly what you need to know (and no more) at the beginning of each study unit.

Accordingly, you can thoroughly prepare for the FAA pilot knowledge test by

1. Studying the brief outlines at the beginning of each study unit.
2. Answering the question on the left side of each page while covering up the answer explanations on the right side of each page.
3. Reading the answer explanation for each question that you answer incorrectly or have difficulty answering.
4. Facilitating this Gleim process with our **FAA Test Prep Online**. Our software allows you to emulate the FAA test (CATS or PSI/LaserGrade). By practicing answering questions on a computer, you will become at ease with the computer testing process and have the confidence to PASS. See pages 16 and 17.
5. Using our **Online Ground School**, which provides you with our outlines, practice problems, and sample tests. This course is easily accessible through the Internet. Also, we give you a money-back guarantee with our **Online Ground School**. If you are unsuccessful, you get your money back!

The secondary purpose of this book is to introduce ***Commercial Pilot Flight Maneuvers and Practical Test Prep*** and ***Pilot Handbook***.

Commercial Pilot Flight Maneuvers and Practical Test Prep is designed to help prepare pilots for their flight training and the FAA commercial pilot practical test. Each task, objective, concept, and requirement is explained, analyzed, illustrated, and interpreted so pilots will be totally conversant with all aspects of the commercial pilot practical test.

Pilot Handbook is a textbook of aeronautical knowledge presented in easy-to-use outline format, with many charts, diagrams, figures, etc., included. While this book contains only the material needed to pass the FAA knowledge test, ***Pilot Handbook*** contains the textbook knowledge required to be a safe and proficient pilot.

Many books create additional work for the user. In contrast, this book and its companion, ***Commercial Pilot Flight Maneuvers and Practical Test Prep***, facilitate your effort. They are easy to use. The outline/illustration format, type styles, and spacing are designed to improve readability. Concepts are often presented as phrases rather than as complete sentences – similar to notes that you would take in a class lecture.

Also, recognize that this study manual is concerned with **airplane** flight training, not balloon, glider, or helicopter training. We are confident this book, **FAA Test Prep Online**, and/or **Online Ground School** will facilitate speedy completion of your knowledge test. We also wish you the very best as you complete your commercial pilot certificate, in subsequent flying, and in obtaining additional ratings and certificates.

Enjoy Flying Safely!

Irvin N. Gleim
Garrett W. Gleim

August 2014

INTRODUCTION: THE FAA PILOT KNOWLEDGE TEST

The beginning of this Introduction explains how to obtain a commercial pilot certificate, and it explains the content and procedures of the Federal Aviation Administration (FAA) knowledge test, including how to take the test at a computer testing center. The remainder of this Introduction discusses and illustrates the Gleim **Online Ground School** and **FAA Test Prep Online**. Achieving a commercial pilot certificate is fun. Begin today!

Commercial Pilot FAA Knowledge Test is one of three books contained in the Gleim **Commercial Pilot Kit**. The other two books are

1. ***Commercial Pilot Flight Maneuvers and Practical Test Prep***
2. ***Commercial Pilot Syllabus***

Commercial Pilot Flight Maneuvers and Practical Test Prep presents each flight maneuver you will perform in outline/illustration format so you will know what to expect and what to do before each flight lesson. This book will thoroughly prepare you to complete your FAA practical (flight) test confidently and successfully.

Commercial Pilot Syllabus is a step-by-step syllabus of ground and flight training lesson plans for your commercial pilot training.

While the following books are not included in the Commercial Pilot Kit, you may want to purchase them if you do not already have them:

Pilot Handbook is a complete pilot reference book that combines over 100 FAA books and documents, including *AIM*, FARs, ACs, and much more. Aerodynamics, airplane systems, airspace, and navigation are among the topics explained in ***Pilot Handbook***. This book, more than any other, will help make you a better and more proficient pilot.

FAR/AIM is an essential part of every pilot's library. The Gleim ***FAR/AIM*** is an easy-to-read reference book containing all of the Federal Aviation Regulations (FARs) applicable to general aviation flying, plus the full text of the FAA's *Aeronautical Information Manual (AIM)*.

The Gleim ***Aviation Weather and Weather Services*** combines all of the information from the FAA's *Aviation Weather* (AC 00-6), *Aviation Weather Services* (AC 00-45), and numerous FAA publications into one easy-to-understand book. It will help you study all aspects of aviation weather and provide you with a single reference book.

WHAT IS A COMMERCIAL PILOT CERTIFICATE?

A commercial pilot certificate is identical to your private pilot certificate except it allows you to fly an airplane and carry passengers and/or property for compensation or hire. The certificate is sent to you by the FAA upon satisfactory completion of your training program, the pilot knowledge test, and a practical test. A sample commercial pilot certificate is reproduced below.

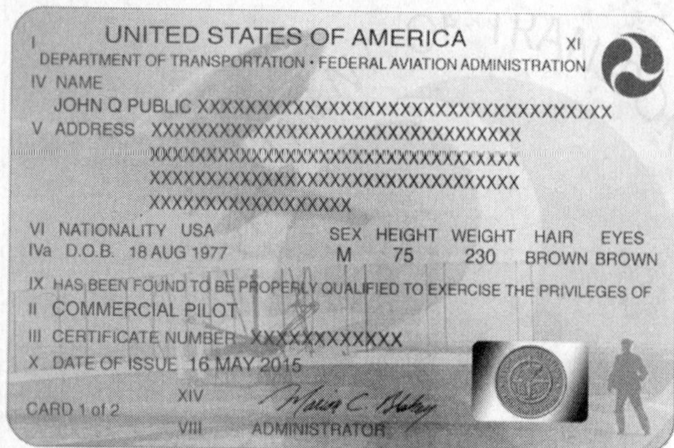

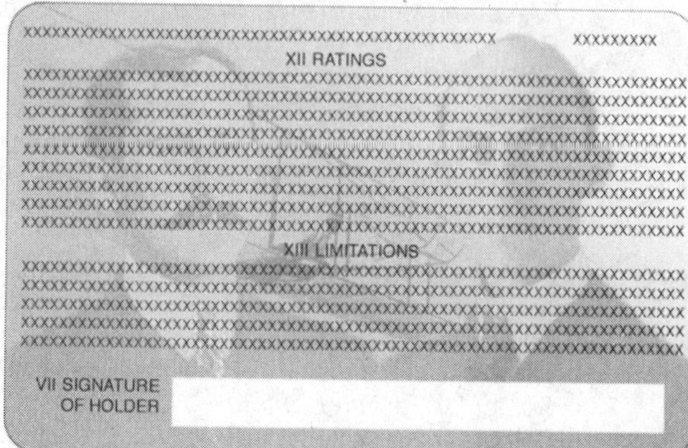

REQUIREMENTS TO OBTAIN A COMMERCIAL PILOT CERTIFICATE

1. Be at least 18 years of age and hold at least a private pilot certificate.
2. Be able to read, speak, write, and understand the English language. (Certificates with operating limitations may be available for medically related deficiencies.)
3. Hold at least a current third-class FAA medical certificate. Later, if your flying requires a commercial pilot certificate, you must hold a second-class medical certificate.
   a. You must undergo a routine medical examination, which may only be administered by FAA-designated doctors called aviation medical examiners (AMEs).
      1) For operations requiring a commercial pilot certificate, a second-class medical certificate expires at the end of the last day of the month, 1 year after the date of examination shown on the certificate.
      2) For operations requiring a private or recreational pilot certificate, any class of medical certificate expires at the end of the last day of the month either
         a) 5 years after the date of examination shown on the certificate, if you have not reached your 40th birthday on or before the date of examination, or
         b) 2 years after the date of examination shown on the certificate, if you have reached your 40th birthday on or before the date of examination.
   b. Even if you have a physical handicap, medical certificates can be issued in many cases. Operating limitations may be imposed depending upon the nature of the disability.
   c. Your certificated flight instructor (CFI) or fixed-base operator (FBO) will be able to recommend an AME.
      1) Also, the FAA publishes a directory that lists all authorized AMEs by name and address. Copies of this directory are kept at all FAA offices, ATC facilities, and Flight Service Stations (FSSs).

4. Receive and log ground training from an authorized instructor or complete a home-study course (such as studying this book, ***Commercial Pilot Flight Maneuvers and Practical Test Prep***, and ***Pilot Handbook*** or using the Gleim **Online Ground School**) to learn
   a. *Applicable Federal Aviation Regulations...that relate to commercial pilot privileges, limitations, and flight operations*
   b. *Accident reporting requirements of the National Transportation Safety Board*
   c. *Basic aerodynamics and the principles of flight*
   d. *Meteorology to include recognition of critical weather situations, windshear recognition and avoidance, and the use of aeronautical weather reports and forecasts*
   e. *Safe and efficient operation of aircraft*
   f. *Weight and balance computations*
   g. *Use of performance charts*
   h. *Significance and effects of exceeding aircraft performance limitations*
   i. *Use of aeronautical charts and a magnetic compass for pilotage and dead reckoning*
   j. *Use of air navigation facilities*
   k. *Aeronautical decision making and judgment*
   l. *Principles and functions of aircraft systems*
   m. *Maneuvers, procedures, and emergency operations appropriate to the aircraft*
   n. *Night and high-altitude operations*
   o. *Procedures for operating within the National Airspace System*
5. Pass a knowledge test with a score of 70% or better. All FAA tests are administered at FAA-designated computer testing centers. The commercial pilot test consists of 100 multiple-choice questions selected from the airplane-related questions in the FAA's commercial pilot test bank; the balance of questions are for balloons, helicopters, etc. The FAA's published airplane-related questions, along with our own similar questions, are reproduced in this book with complete explanations.
6. Accumulate flight experience (FAR 61.129). You must log at least 250 hr. of flight time as a pilot that consists of at least
   a. 100 hr. in powered aircraft, of which 50 hr. must be in airplanes
   b. 100 hr. as pilot in command flight time, which includes at least
      1) 50 hr. in airplanes
      2) 50 hr. in cross-country flight of which at least 10 hr. must be in airplanes
   c. 20 hr. of training in the areas of operation required for a single-engine or multi-engine rating that includes at least
      1) 10 hr. of instrument training of which at least 5 hr. must be in a single-engine or multi-engine airplane, as appropriate
      2) 10 hr. of training in an airplane that has a retractable landing gear, flaps, and controllable pitch propeller, or is turbine-powered
         a) For a multi-engine rating, the airplane must be a multi-engine airplane and meet the other requirements.
      3) One cross-country flight of at least 2 hr. in a single-engine or multi-engine airplane (as appropriate) in daytime conditions, consisting of a total straight-line distance of more than 100 NM from the original point of departure
      4) One cross-country flight of at least 2 hr. in a single-engine or multi-engine airplane (as appropriate) in nighttime conditions, consisting of a straight-line distance of more than 100 NM from the original point of departure
      5) 3 hr. in a single-engine or multi-engine airplane (as appropriate) with an authorized instructor in preparation for the practical test within the preceding 2 calendar months from the month of the test

d. 10 hr. of solo flight (sole occupant of the aircraft) or 10 hr. of flight time performing the duties of pilot in command in a single- or multi-engine airplane (as appropriate) with an authorized instructor, training in the areas of operations required for a single- or multi-engine rating (as appropriate), which includes at least
   1) One cross-country flight of not less than 300 NM total distance, with landings at a minimum of three points, one of which is a straight-line distance of at least 250 NM from the original departure point
      a) In Hawaii, the longest segment need have only a straight-line distance of at least 150 NM.
   2) 5 hr. in night-VFR conditions with 10 takeoffs and 10 landings (with each landing involving a flight in the traffic pattern) at an airport with an operating control tower

e. The 250 hr. of flight time as a pilot may include 50 hr. in an approved flight simulator or training device that is representative of a single-engine or multi-engine airplane (as appropriate) and provided the aeronautical experience was obtained from an authorized instructor in a flight simulator or flight training device that represents that class of airplane appropriate to the rating sought.

7. Hold an instrument rating. As a commercial pilot you are presumed to have an instrument rating. If not, your commercial certificate will be endorsed with a prohibition against carrying passengers for hire on flights beyond 50 NM, or at night.

8. Demonstrate flight proficiency (FAR 61.127). You must receive and log ground and flight training from an authorized instructor in the following areas of operations for an airplane category rating with a single-engine or multi-engine class rating.
   a. *Preflight preparation*
   b. *Preflight procedures*
   c. *Airport and seaplane base operations*
   d. *Takeoffs, landings, and go-arounds*
   e. *Performance maneuvers*
   f. *Ground reference maneuvers (single-engine only)*
      1) *Multi-engine operations (multi-engine only)*
   g. *Navigation*
   h. *Slow flight and stalls*
   i. *Emergency operations*
   j. *High-altitude operations*
   k. *Postflight procedures*

9. Alternatively, enroll in an FAA-certificated pilot school or training center that has an approved commercial pilot certification or test course (airplane).
   a. These are known as Part 141 schools or Part 142 training centers because they are authorized by Part 141 or Part 142 of the FARs.
      1) All other regulations concerning the certification of pilots are found in Part 61 of the FARs.

10. Successfully complete a practical (flight) test, which will be given as a final exam by an FAA inspector or designated pilot examiner. The flight test will be conducted as specified in the FAA's Commercial Pilot Practical Test Standards (FAA-S-8081-12).
   a. FAA inspectors are FAA employees and do not charge for their services.
   b. FAA-designated pilot examiners are proficient, experienced flight instructors and pilots who are authorized by the FAA to conduct practical tests. They do charge a fee.

The FAA's Commercial Pilot Practical Test Standards are outlined and reprinted in the Gleim ***Commercial Pilot Flight Maneuvers and Practical Test Prep*** book.

FAA PILOT KNOWLEDGE TEST AND TESTING SUPPLEMENT

1. This book is designed to help you prepare for and pass the following FAA knowledge tests:
   a. Commercial Pilot-Airplane (CAX), which consists of 100 questions and has a 3-hour time limit.
   b. Military Competency-Airplane (MCA), which consists of 50 questions covering FARs (see Study Unit 4) and airspace (see Study Unit 3).
      1) The MCA knowledge test time allowed is 2 hours.
2. The FAA figures are contained in a book titled *Computer Testing Supplement for Commercial Pilot*, which you will be given to use at the time of your test.
   a. For the purpose of test preparation, all of the FAA figures are reproduced in this book. We have included color images for some figures. These images are all located together in Study Unit 9 and are appropriately cross-referenced in the questions and outlines they relate to.
3. In an effort to develop better questions, the FAA frequently **pretests** questions on knowledge tests by adding up to five "pretest" questions. The pretest questions will not be graded.
   a. You will NOT know which questions are real and which are pretest, so you must attempt to answer all questions correctly.
   b. When you notice a question NOT covered by Gleim, it might be a pretest question.
      1) We want to know about each pretest question you see.
      2) Please email (aviation@gleim.com) or call (800-874-5346) with your recollection of any possible pretest questions so we may improve our efforts to prepare future commercial pilots.

FAA'S KNOWLEDGE TESTS: CHEATING OR UNAUTHORIZED CONDUCT POLICY

The following is taken verbatim from an FAA knowledge test. It is reproduced here to remind all test takers about the FAA's policy against cheating and unauthorized conduct, a policy that Gleim consistently supports and upholds. Test takers must click "Yes" to proceed from this page into the actual knowledge test.

14 CFR part 61, section 61.37 Knowledge tests: Cheating or other unauthorized conduct

(a) An applicant for a knowledge test may not:

(1) Copy or intentionally remove any knowledge test;

(2) Give to another applicant or receive from another applicant any part or copy of a knowledge test;

(3) Give assistance on, or receive assistance on, a knowledge test during the period that test is being given;

(4) Take any part of a knowledge test on behalf of another person;

(5) Be represented by, or represent, another person for a knowledge test;

(6) Use any material or aid during the period that the test is being given, unless specifically authorized to do so by the Administrator; and

(7) Intentionally cause, assist, or participate in any act prohibited by this paragraph.

(b) An applicant who the Administrator finds has committed an act prohibited by paragraph (a) of this section is prohibited, for 1 year after the date of committing that act, from:

(1) Applying for any certificate, rating, or authorization issued under this chapter; and

(2) Applying for and taking any test under this chapter.

(c) Any certificate or rating held by an applicant may be suspended or revoked if the Administrator finds that person has committed an act prohibited by paragraph (a) of this section.

FAA PILOT KNOWLEDGE TEST QUESTION BANK

In an effort to keep applicants from simply memorizing test questions, the FAA does not currently disclose all the questions you might see on your FAA knowledge test. We encourage you to take the time to fully learn and understand the concepts explained in the knowledge transfer outlines contained in this book. **Using this book or other Gleim test preparation material to merely memorize the questions and answers is unwise and unproductive, and it will not ensure your success on your FAA knowledge test.** Memorization also greatly reduces the amount of information you will actually learn during your study.

The questions and answers provided in this book include all previously released FAA questions in addition to questions developed from current FAA reference materials that closely approximate the types of questions you should see on your knowledge test. We are confident that by studying our knowledge transfer outlines, answering our questions under exam conditions, and not relying on rote memorization, you will be able to successfully pass your FAA knowledge test and begin learning to become a safer and more competent pilot.

FAA QUESTIONS WITH TYPOGRAPHICAL ERRORS

Occasionally, FAA test questions contain typographical errors such that there is no correct answer. The FAA test development process involves many steps and people and, as you would expect, glitches occur in the system that are beyond the control of any one person. We indicate "best" rather than correct answers for some questions. Use these best answers for the indicated questions.

Note that the FAA corrects (rewrites) defective questions as they are discovered; these changes are explained in our updates (see page iv). However, problems due to faulty or out-of-date figures printed in the FAA Computer Testing Supplements are expensive to correct. Thus, it is important to carefully study questions that are noted to have a best answer in this book. Even though the best answer may not be completely correct, you should select it when taking your test.

REORGANIZATION OF FAA QUESTIONS

1. In the public FAA knowledge test question bank releases, the questions are **not** grouped together by topic; i.e., they appear to be presented randomly.
   a. We have reorganized and renumbered the questions into study units and subunits.
2. Pages 309 through 315 contain a list of all the questions in FAA learning statement code order, with cross-references to the study units and question numbers in this book.
   a. For example, question 10-26 is assigned the code PLT001, which means it is found in Study Unit 10 as question 26 in this book and is covered under the FAA learning statement, "Calculate a course intercept."
   b. Questions relating to helicopters, gliders, balloons, etc., are excluded.

HOW TO PREPARE FOR THE FAA PILOT KNOWLEDGE TEST

1. Begin by carefully reading the rest of this Introduction. You need to have a complete understanding of the examination process prior to initiating your study. This knowledge will make your studying more efficient.
2. After you have spent an hour analyzing this Introduction, set up a study schedule, including a target date for taking your knowledge test.
   a. Do not let the study process drag on and become discouraging; i.e., the quicker, the better.
   b. Consider enrolling in an organized ground school course, like the Gleim **Online Ground School**, or one held at your local FBO, community college, etc.
   c. Determine where and when you are going to take your knowledge test.

3. Work through Study Units 1 through 11.

   a. All previously released questions in the FAA's commercial pilot knowledge test question bank that are applicable to airplanes have been grouped into the following 11 categories, which are the titles of Study Units 1 through 11:

Study Unit 1 -- Airplanes and Aerodynamics	Study Unit 6 -- Aeromedical Factors and Aeronautical Decision Making (ADM)
Study Unit 2 -- Airplane Instruments, Engines, and Systems	Study Unit 7 -- Aviation Weather
Study Unit 3 -- Airports, Air Traffic Control, and Airspace	Study Unit 8 -- Aviation Weather Services
Study Unit 4 -- Federal Aviation Regulations	Study Unit 9 -- Navigation: Charts, Publications, Flight Computers
Study Unit 5 -- Airplane Performance and Weight and Balance	Study Unit 10 -- Navigation Systems
	Study Unit 11 -- Flight Operations

   b. Within each of the study units listed, questions relating to the same subtopic (e.g., thunderstorms, airplane stability, sectional charts, etc.) are grouped together to facilitate your study program. Each subtopic is called a subunit.

   c. To the right of each question, we present

      1) The correct answer

      2) The appropriate source document for the answer explanation

AC	Advisory Circular	*AWS*	*Aviation Weather Services*
ACL	Aeronautical Chart Legend	FAR	Federal Aviation Regulations
AFNA	Aerodynamics for Naval Aviators	Fl Comp	Flight Computer
AFH	*Airplane Flying Handbook*	*IFH*	*Instrument Flying Handbook*
AIM	*Aeronautical Information Manual*	NTSB	National Transportation Safety Board Regulations
A&PM PH	*Airframe and Powerplant Mechanics Powerplant Handbook*	*PHAK*	*Pilot's Handbook of Aeronautical Knowledge*
AvW	*Aviation Weather*		
AWBH	*Aircraft Weight and Balance Handbook*		

         a) The codes may refer to an entire document, such as an advisory circular, or to a particular chapter or subsection of a larger document.

            i) See page 319 for a complete list of abbreviations and acronyms used in this book.

      3) A comprehensive answer explanation, including

         a) A discussion of the correct answer or concept

         b) An explanation of why the other two answer choices are incorrect

4. Each study unit begins with a list of its subunit titles. The number after each title is the number of questions that cover the information in that subunit. The two numbers following the number of questions are the page numbers on which the outline and the questions for that particular subunit begin, respectively.

5. Begin by studying the outlines slowly and carefully. The outlines in this part of the book are very brief and have only one purpose: to help you pass the FAA knowledge test.

   a. **CAUTION:** The **sole purpose** of this book is to expedite your passing the FAA knowledge test for the commercial pilot certificate. Accordingly, all extraneous material (i.e., not directly tested on the FAA knowledge test) is omitted, even though much more information and knowledge are necessary to be proficient and fly safely. This additional material is presented in four related Gleim books: ***Commercial Pilot Flight Maneuvers and Practical Test Prep***, ***FAR/AIM***, ***Aviation Weather and Weather Services***, and ***Pilot Handbook***.

6. Next, answer the questions under exam conditions. Cover the answer explanations on the right side of each page with a piece of paper while you answer the questions.

Remember, it is very important to the learning (and understanding) process that you honestly commit yourself to an answer. If you are wrong, your memory will be reinforced by having discovered your error. Therefore, it is crucial to cover up the answer and make an honest attempt to answer the question before reading the answer.

   a. Study the answer explanation for each question that you answer incorrectly, do not understand, or have difficulty with.
   b. Use our **Online Ground School** or **FAA Test Prep Online** to ensure that you do not refer to answers before committing to one AND to simulate actual computer testing center exam conditions.

7. Note that this test book contains questions grouped by topic. Thus, some questions may appear repetitive, while others may be duplicates or near-duplicates. Accordingly, do not work question after question (i.e., waste time and effort) if you are already conversant with a topic and the type of questions asked.
8. As you move through study units, you may need further explanation or clarification of certain topics. You may wish to obtain and use the following Gleim books described on page 1:
   a. ***Commercial Pilot Flight Maneuvers and Practical Test Prep***
   b. ***Pilot Handbook***
   c. ***FAR/AIM***
   d. ***Aviation Weather and Weather Services***
9. Keep track of your work. As you complete a subunit, grade yourself with an A, B, C, or ? (use a ? if you need help on the subject) next to the subunit title at the front of the respective study unit.
   a. The A, B, C, or ? is your self-evaluation of your comprehension of the material in that subunit and your ability to answer the questions.
      A means a good understanding.
      B means a fair understanding.
      C means a shaky understanding.
      ? means to ask your CFI or others about the material and/or questions, and read the pertinent sections in ***Commercial Pilot Flight Maneuvers and Practical Test Prep*** and/or ***Pilot Handbook***.
   b. This procedure will provide you with the ability to quickly see (by looking at the first page of each study unit) how much studying you have done (and how much remains) and how well you have done.
   c. This procedure will also facilitate review. You can spend more time on the subunits that were more difficult for you.
   d. **FAA Test Prep Online** provides you with your historical performance data.

Follow the suggestions given throughout this Introduction and you will have no trouble passing the FAA knowledge test the first time you take it.

With this overview of exam requirements, you are ready to begin the easy-to-study outlines and rearranged questions with answers to build your knowledge and confidence and PASS THE FAA's COMMERCIAL PILOT KNOWLEDGE TEST.

The feedback we receive from users indicates that our materials reduce anxiety, improve FAA test scores, and build knowledge. Studying for each test becomes a useful step toward advanced certificates and ratings.

MULTIPLE-CHOICE QUESTION-ANSWERING TECHNIQUE

Because the commercial pilot knowledge test has a set number of questions (100) and a set time limit (3 hours), you can plan your test-taking session to ensure that you leave yourself enough time to answer each question with relative certainty. The following steps will help you move through the knowledge test efficiently and produce better test results.

1. **Budget your time.** We make this point with emphasis. Just as you would fill up your gas tank prior to reaching empty, so too should you finish your exam before time expires.
   a. If you utilize the entire 3-hour time limit, that allows you 1.8 minutes per question.
   b. If you are adequately prepared for the test, you should finish it within 60-90 minutes.
      1) Use any extra time you have to review questions that you are not sure about, cross-country planning questions with multiple steps and calculations, and similar questions in your exam that may help you answer other questions.
   c. Time yourself when completing study sessions in this book and/or review your time investment reports from the Gleim **FAA Test Prep Online** to track your progress and adherence to the time limit and your own personal time allocation budget.
2. **Answer the questions in consecutive order.**
   a. Do **not** agonize over any one item. Stay within your time budget.
      1) We suggest that you skip cross-country planning questions and other similarly involved computational questions on your first pass through the exam. Come back to them after you have been through the entire test once.
   b. Mark any questions you are unsure of and return to them later as time allows.
      1) Once you initiate test grading, you will no longer be able to review/change any answers.
   c. Never leave a multiple-choice question unanswered. Make your best educated guess in the time allowed. Remember, your score is based on the number of correct responses. You will not be penalized for guessing incorrectly.
3. **For each multiple-choice question,**
   a. **Try to ignore the answer choices.** Do not allow the answer choices to affect your reading of the question.
      1) If three answer choices are presented, two of them are incorrect. These choices are called **distractors** for good reason. Often, distractors are written to appear correct at first glance until further analysis.
      2) In computational items, the distractors are carefully calculated such that they are the result of making common mistakes. Be careful, and double-check your computations if time permits.
   b. **Read the question carefully** to determine the precise requirement.
      1) Focusing on what is required enables you to ignore extraneous information, to focus on the relevant facts, and to proceed directly to determining the correct answer.
         a) Be especially careful to note when the requirement is an **exception**; e.g., "Which of the following is **not** a type of hypoxia?"
   c. **Determine the correct answer** before looking at the answer choices.
   d. **Read the answer choices carefully.**
      1) Even if the first answer appears to be the correct choice, do **not** skip the remaining answer choices. Questions often require the "best" answer of the choices provided. Thus, each choice requires your consideration.
      2) Treat each answer choice as a true/false question as you analyze it.

e. **Click on the best answer.**

1) You have a 33% chance of answering the question correctly by blindly guessing; improve your odds with educated guessing.
2) For many multiple-choice questions, at least one answer choice can be eliminated with minimal effort, thereby increasing your educated guess to a 50-50 proposition.

4. After you have been through all the questions in the test, consult the question status list to determine which questions are unanswered and which are marked for review.
   a. Go back to the marked questions and finalize your answer choices.
   b. Verify that all questions have been answered.

EDUCATED GUESSING

The FAA knowledge test sometimes includes questions that are poorly worded or confusing. Expect the unexpected and move forward. Do not let confusing questions affect your concentration or take up too much time; make your best guess and move on.

1. If you don't know the answer, make an educated guess as follows:
   a. Rule out answers that you think are incorrect.
   b. Speculate on what the FAA is looking for and/or the rationale behind the question.
   c. Select the best answer or guess between equally appealing answers. Your first guess is usually the most intuitive. If you cannot make an educated guess, re-read the stem and each answer choice and pick the most intuitive answer. It's just a guess!
2. Avoid lingering on any question for too long. Remember your time budget and the overall test time limit.

SIMULATED FAA PRACTICE TEST

Appendix A, "Commercial Pilot Practice Test," beginning on page 291, allows you to practice taking the FAA knowledge test without the answers next to the questions. This test has 100 questions randomly selected from the airplane-related questions in our commercial pilot knowledge test bank. Topical coverage in this practice test is similar to that of the FAA knowledge test.

It is very important that you answer all 100 questions in one sitting. You should not consult the answers, especially when being referred to figures (charts, tables, etc.) throughout this book where the questions are answered and explained. Analyze your performance based on the answer key that follows the practice test.

It is even better to practice with Test Sessions in the Gleim **FAA Test Prep Online**. These simulate actual computer testing conditions, including the screen layouts, instructions, etc., for CATS and PSI/LaserGrade.

For more information on the Gleim **FAA Test Prep Online**, see pages 16 and 17.

PART 141 SCHOOLS WITH FAA PILOT KNOWLEDGE TEST EXAMINING AUTHORITY

The FAA permits some FAR Part 141 schools to develop, administer, and grade their own knowledge tests as long as they use questions from the FAA test bank, similar to the questions in this book. The FAA does not provide the correct answers to the Part 141 schools, and the FAA only reviews the Part 141 school test question selection sheets. Thus, some of the answers used by Part 141 test examiners may not agree with the FAA or with those in this book. The latter is not a problem but may explain why you may miss a question on a Part 141 pilot knowledge test using an answer presented in this book.

AUTHORIZATION TO TAKE THE FAA PILOT KNOWLEDGE TEST

Before taking the commercial pilot knowledge test, you must receive an endorsement from an authorized instructor who conducted the ground training or reviewed your home-study in the areas listed in item 4. on page 3, certifying that you are prepared to pass the knowledge test.

For your convenience, a standard authorization form for the commercial pilot knowledge test is reproduced on page 317, which can be easily completed, signed by a flight or ground instructor, torn out, and taken to the test site.

Note that if you use the Gleim **FAA Test Prep Online** or **Online Ground School**, the program will generate an authorization signed in facsimile by Dr. Gleim that is accepted at all CATS and PSI/LaserGrade locations.

NOTE: An instructor endorsement is not required for the Military Competence Airplane (MCA) test.

WHEN TO TAKE THE FAA PILOT KNOWLEDGE TEST

1. You must be at least 16 years of age to take the commercial pilot knowledge test.
2. You must prepare for the test by successfully completing a ground instruction course or by using this book as your self-developed home study course.
   a. See "Authorization to Take the FAA Pilot Knowledge Test" above.
3. Take the FAA knowledge test within 30 days of beginning your study.
   a. Get the knowledge test behind you.
4. Your practical test must follow within 24 months.
   a. Otherwise, you will have to retake your knowledge test.

WHAT TO TAKE TO THE FAA PILOT KNOWLEDGE TEST

1. An approved flight computer (ideally the one that you use to solve the test questions in this book, i.e., one you are familiar with and have used before)
2. Navigational plotter
3. A pocket calculator you are familiar with and have used before (no instructional material for the calculator is allowed)
4. Authorization to take the knowledge test (see above and page 317)
5. Proper identification that contains your
   a. Photograph
   b. Signature
   c. Date of birth
   d. Actual residential address, if different from your mailing address

NOTE: Paper and pencils are supplied at the examination site.

COMPUTER TESTING CENTERS

The FAA has contracted with two computer testing services to administer FAA knowledge tests. Both of these computer testing services have testing centers throughout the country. To register for the knowledge test, call one of the computer testing services listed below. More information can be found at www.gleim.com/testing_centers.

CATS (800) 947-4228 PSI/LaserGrade (800) 211-2754

COMPUTER TESTING PROCEDURES

When you arrive at the testing center, you will be required to provide positive proof of identification and documentary evidence of your age. The identification must include your photograph, signature, and actual residential address if different from the mailing address. This information may be presented in more than one form of identification. Next, you will sign in on the testing center's daily log. Your signature on the logsheet certifies that, if this is a retest, you meet the applicable requirements (see "Failure on the FAA Pilot Knowledge Test" on page 14) and that you have not passed this test in the past 2 years. Finally, you will present your logbook endorsement or authorization form from your instructor, which authorizes you to take the test. A standard authorization form is provided on page 317 for your use. Both **FAA Test Prep Online** and **Online Ground School** generate an authorization signed in facsimile by Dr. Gleim that is accepted at all CATS and PSI/LaserGrade locations.

Next, you will be taken into the testing room and seated at a computer terminal. A person from the testing center will assist you in logging onto the system, and you will be asked to confirm your personal data (e.g., name, Social Security number, etc.). Then you will be given an online introduction to the computer testing system, and you will take a sample test. If you have used our **FAA Test Prep Online**, you will be conversant with the computer testing methodology and environment and will breeze through the sample test. You will be allowed 3 hours to complete the actual test, which equates to 1.8 minutes per question. When you have completed your test, an Airman Computer Test Report will be printed out, validated (usually with an embossed seal), and given to you by a person from the testing center. Before you leave, you will be required to sign out on the testing center's daily log.

Each testing service has certain idiosyncrasies in its paperwork, scheduling, and telephone procedures as well as in its software. It is for this reason that our **FAA Test Prep Online** emulates both of the FAA-approved computer testing companies.

YOUR FAA PILOT KNOWLEDGE TEST REPORT

1. You will receive your FAA Pilot Knowledge Test Report upon completion of the test. An example test report is reproduced below.
   a. Note that you will receive only one grade as illustrated.
   b. The expiration date is the date by which you must take your FAA practical test.
   c. The report lists the FAA learning statement codes of the questions you missed so you can review the topics you missed prior to your practical test.

Federal Aviation Administration
Airman Computer Test Report

EXAM TITLE: Commercial Pilot Airplane

NAME: Jones David John

ID NUMBER: 123456789 TAKE: 1

DATE: 07/14/14 SCORE: 82 GRADE: Pass

....

Knowledge area codes in which questions were answered incorrectly. See appropriate FAA knowledge test study guide. A code may represent more than one incorrect response.

PLT013 PLT041 PLT332 PLT442

EXPIRATION DATE: 07/31/16

DO NOT LOSE THIS REPORT

....

Authorized instructor's statement (if applicable).

I have given Mr./Ms. ______________________ additional instruction in each subject area shown to be deficient and consider the applicant competent to pass the test.

Last ______________________ Initial _____ Cert. No. ________ Type _____

Signature ________________________

2. Use the FAA Listing of Learning Statement Codes on pages 303 through 308 to determine which topics you had difficulty with.
   a. Look them over and review them with your CFI so (s)he can certify that (s)he reviewed the deficient areas and found you competent in them when you take your practical test. Have your CFI sign off your deficiencies on the FAA Pilot Knowledge Test Report.
3. Keep your FAA Pilot Knowledge Test Report in a safe place because you must submit it to the FAA inspector/examiner when you take your practical test.

FAILURE ON THE FAA PILOT KNOWLEDGE TEST

1. If you fail (score less than 70%) the knowledge test (which is virtually impossible if you follow the Gleim system), you may retake it after your instructor endorses the bottom of your FAA Pilot Knowledge Test Report certifying that you have received the necessary ground training to retake the test.
2. Upon retaking the test, you will find that the procedure is the same except that you must also submit your FAA Pilot Knowledge Test Report indicating the previous failure to the computer testing center.
3. Note that the pass rate on the commercial pilot knowledge test is about 96%; i.e., less than 1 out of 10 fail the test initially. Reasons for failure include
   a. Failure to study the material tested and mere memorization of correct answers. (Relevant study material is contained in the outlines at the beginning of Study Units 1 through 11 of this book.)
   b. Failure to practice working through the questions under test conditions. (All of the previously released FAA questions appear in Study Units 1 through 11 of this book.)
   c. Poor examination technique, such as misreading questions and not understanding the requirements.

This Gleim Knowledge Test book will prepare you to pass the FAA knowledge test on your first attempt! In addition, the Gleim ***Commercial Pilot Flight Maneuvers and Practical Test Prep*** book will save you time and frustration as you prepare for the FAA practical test.

Just as this book organizes and explains the knowledge needed to pass your FAA knowledge test, ***Commercial Pilot Flight Maneuvers and Practical Test Prep*** will assist you in developing the competence and confidence to pass your FAA practical test.

Also, flight maneuvers are quickly perfected when you understand exactly what to expect before you get into an airplane to practice the flight maneuvers. You must be ahead of (not behind) your CFI and your airplane. Our flight maneuvers books explain and illustrate all flight maneuvers so the maneuvers and their execution are intuitively appealing to you. Visit www.gleim.com/aviation or call (800) 874-5346 and order today!

GLEIM ONLINE GROUND SCHOOL

1. Gleim **Online Ground School (OGS)** course content is based on the Gleim Knowledge Test books, **FAA Test Prep Online**, FAA publications, and Gleim reference books. The delivery system is modeled on the Gleim FAA-approved online **Flight Instructor Refresher Course**.
   a. Online Ground School courses are available for
      1) Private Pilot
      2) Sport Pilot
      3) CFI/CGI
      4) FOI
      5) Instrument Pilot
      6) Commercial Pilot
      7) ATP
      8) Flight Engineer
      9) Canadian Certificate Conversion
   b. OGS courses are airplane-only and have lessons that correspond to the study units in the Gleim FAA Knowledge Test books.
   c. Each course contains study outlines that automatically reference current FAA publications, the appropriate knowledge test questions, FAA figures, and Gleim answer explanations.
   d. OGS is always up to date.
   e. Users achieve very high knowledge test scores and a near-100% pass rate.
   f. **Gleim Online Ground School is the most flexible course available!** Access your OGS personal classroom from any computer with Internet access 24 hours a day, 7 days a week. Your virtual classroom is never closed!
   g. **Save time and study only the material you need to know!** Gleim **Online Ground School** Certificate Selection will provide you with a customized study plan. You save time because unnecessary questions will be automatically eliminated.
   h. **We are truly interactive. We help you focus on any weaker areas.** Answer explanations for wrong choices help you learn from your mistakes.

Register for Gleim Online Ground School today:
www.gleim.com/OGS

or

Demo Study Unit One for FREE at
www.gleim.com/aviation/Demos

GLEIM FAA TEST PREP ONLINE

Computer testing is consistent with aviation's use of computers (e.g., DUATS, flight simulators, computerized cockpits, etc.). All FAA knowledge tests are administered by computer.

Computer testing is natural after computer study and computer-assisted instruction is a very efficient and effective method of study. The Gleim **FAA Test Prep Online** is designed to prepare you for computer testing because our software can simulate both CATS and PSI/LaserGrade. We make you comfortable with computer testing!

FAA Test Prep Online contains all of the questions in this book, context-sensitive outline material, and on-screen charts and figures. It allows you to choose either Study Mode or Test Mode.

In Study Mode, the software provides you with an explanation of each answer you choose (correct or incorrect). You design each Study Session:

Topic(s) and/or FAA learning statement codes you wish to cover
Number of questions
Order of questions -- FAA, Gleim, or random
Order of answers to each question -- Gleim or random
Questions marked and/or missed from last session -- test, study, or both
Questions marked and/or missed from all sessions -- test, study, or both
Questions never seen, answered, or answered correctly

In Test Mode, you decide the format: CATS or PSI/LaserGrade. When you finish your test, you can and should study the questions missed and access answer explanations. The software emulates the operation of FAA-approved computer testing companies. Thus, you have a complete understanding of how to take an FAA knowledge test and know exactly what to expect before you go to a computer testing center.

The Gleim **FAA Test Prep Online** is an all-in-one program designed to help anyone with a computer, Internet access, and an interest in flying pass the FAA knowledge tests.

Study Sessions and Test Sessions

Study Sessions give you immediate feedback on why your answer selection for a particular question is correct or incorrect and allow you to access the context-sensitive outline material that helps to explain concepts related to the question. Choose from several different question sources: all questions available for that library; questions from a certain topic (Gleim study units and subunits); questions that you missed or marked in the last sessions you created; questions that you have never seen, answered, or answered correctly; questions from certain FAA learning statement codes; etc. You can mix up the questions by selecting to randomize the question and/or answer order so that you do not memorize answer letters.

You may then grade your study sessions and track your study progress using the performance analysis charts and graphs. The Performance Analysis information helps you to focus on areas where you need the most improvement, saving you time in the overall study process. You may then want to go back and study questions that you missed in a previous session, or you may want to create a Study Session of questions that you marked in the previous session. All of these options are made easy with **FAA Test Prep Online**'s Study Sessions.

After studying the outlines and questions in a Study Session, you can further test your skills with a Test Session. These sessions allow you to answer questions under actual testing conditions using one of the simulations of the major testing services. In a Test Session, you will not know which questions you have answered correctly until the session is graded.

Recommended Study Program

1. Start with Study Unit 1 and proceed through study units in chronological order. Follow the three-step process below.
   a. First, carefully study the Gleim Outline.
   b. Second, create a Study Session of all questions in the study unit. Answer and study all questions in the Study Session.
   c. Third, create a Test Session of all questions in the study unit. Answer all questions in the Test Session.
2. After each Study Session and Test Session, create a new Study Session from questions answered incorrectly. This is of critical importance to allow you to learn from your mistakes.

Practice Test

Take an exam in the actual testing environment of either of the major testing centers: CATS or PSI/LaserGrade. **FAA Test Prep Online** simulates the testing formats of these testing centers, making it easy for you to study questions under actual exam conditions. After studying with **FAA Test Prep Online**, you will know exactly what to expect when you go in to take your pilot knowledge test.

On-Screen Charts and Figures

One of the most convenient features of **FAA Test Prep Online** is the easily accessible on-screen charts and figures. Several of the questions refer to drawings, maps, charts, and other pictures that provide information to help answer the question. In **FAA Test Prep Online**, you can pull up any of these figures with the click of a button. You can increase or decrease the size of the images, and you may also use our drawing feature to calculate the true course between two given points (required only on the private pilot knowledge test).

Instructor Sign-Off Sheets

FAA Test Prep Online is capable of generating an instructor sign-off for FAA knowledge tests that require one. This sign-off has been approved by the FAA and can be presented at the computer testing center as authorization to take your test--you do NOT need an additional endorsement from your instructor.

In order to obtain the instructor sign-off sheet for your test, you must first answer all relevant questions in **FAA Test Prep Online** correctly. Then, select “Sign-Off Sheets” under the “Additional Features” area on the Main page. If you have answered all of the required questions, the instructor sign-off sheet will appear for you to print. If you have not yet answered all required questions, a list of the unanswered questions, along with their location, will appear.

Order FAA Test Prep Online today
(800) 874-5346 • gleim.com

or

Demo Study Unit One for FREE at
www.gleim.com/aviation/Demos

Free Updates and Technical Support

Gleim offers FREE technical support to all users of the current versions. Call (800) 874-5346, send an email to support@gleim.com, or fill out the technical support request form online (www.gleim.com/support/form.php). Additionally, Gleim **FAA Test Prep Online** is always up to date. The program is automatically updated when any changes are made, so you can be confident that Gleim will prepare you for your knowledge test. For more information on our email update service for books, turn to page iv.

Update Service

Visit the GLEIM® website for free updates,

which are available until the next edition is published.

gleim.com/updates

STUDY UNIT ONE
AIRPLANES AND AERODYNAMICS

(7 pages of outline)

This study unit contains outlines of major concepts tested, sample test questions and answers regarding airplanes and aerodynamics, and an explanation of each answer. The table of contents above lists each subunit within this study unit, the number of questions pertaining to that particular subunit, and the pages on which the outlines and questions begin, respectively.

Recall that the **sole purpose** of this book is to expedite your passing of the FAA pilot knowledge test for the commercial pilot certificate. Accordingly, all extraneous material (i.e., topics or regulations not directly tested on the FAA pilot knowledge test) is omitted, even though much more knowledge is necessary to become a proficient commercial pilot. This additional material is presented in *Pilot Handbook* and *Commercial Pilot Flight Maneuvers and Practical Test Prep*, available from Gleim Publications, Inc. See the product listing at the back of the book and order online at www.gleim.com.

1.1 FLAPS

1. One of the main functions of flaps during the approach and landing is to increase angle of attack, which causes the wing to produce the same amount of lift at a slower airspeed.
2. The raising of flaps increases the stall speed.

1.2 AIRPLANE WINGS

1. Spoilers are fitted to many modern turbojets and other high performance aircraft.
    a. These aircraft are very clean aerodynamically and land at very high speeds.
        1) Spoilers fitted to the top of the wing can be deployed automatically or at the command of the PIC to disrupt airflow and destroy lift.
            a) When deployed just after landing, spoilers allow the brakes to be more effective.
2. Rectangular wings generally are designed so that the wing root stalls first, with the stall progression toward the wingtip.
3. A change in the angle of attack of the wing changes the lift, drag, and airspeed.
4. The angle of attack of a wing directly controls the distribution of positive and negative pressure acting on the wing.
5. Frost on the upper surface of airplane wings disrupts the smooth flow of air over the top of the wing (which increases drag) and causes the airplane to stall at higher airspeeds and lower angles of attack than normal.

1.3 STALLS

1. The angle of attack at which a wing stalls (critical angle of attack) remains constant regardless of
   a. Weight
   b. Dynamic pressure (a component of the Bernoulli equation, which explains lift in pressure differentials)
   c. Bank angle
   d. Pitch attitude
2. Stall speed is affected by the airplane's
   a. Weight
   b. Load factor
   c. Power setting
3. The stalling speed is most affected by variations in airplane loading, i.e., weight and CG.
   a. V_A is listed in the AFM/POH on all recently designed aircraft. V_A defines the maximum speed at which an airplane can be safely stalled.
4. Turbulence can increase stall speed due to increased load factors.
   a. Slowing to V_A protects the airplane from excessive load stresses while providing a safe margin above stall speed.
5. Stall recovery becomes progressively more difficult when the CG moves aft.
6. Stall speed tables for various configurations at different angles of bank are provided for some airplanes, such as illustrated in Figure 2 on page 29.
   a. Note that the table portrays situations for a given weight at four angles of bank in two configurations (gear and flaps up or down) and with power on or off.
   b. Note that, generally, stall speeds are lower with gear and flaps down.
   c. Also, stall speeds are higher as bank increases.
7. Over-the-top spin
   a. The aircraft can stall, then begin a spin. This begins as a cross-control stall.
      1) It usually occurs in the traffic pattern, when turning base to final.
         a) The pilot compensates for over-shooting the runway centerline with rudder alone.
         b) The proper action would be to increase the rate of turn while maintaining a coordinated turn.
      2) Improperly trained pilots are apt to hold the bank constant and try to increase the rate of turn by adding more rudder in an effort to get aligned with the runway centerline.
      3) While in this skidding turn, the aileron on the inside of the turn increases drag on the wing, slowing it down and decreasing its lift, which requires more aileron application.
      4) The airplane will then begin an uncommanded roll toward the inside wing. This roll may occur so quickly that it is possible the bank will be vertical or past vertical before it can be stopped.
      5) The airplane may continue to roll to an inverted position, which is usually the beginning of an over-the-top spin.

1.4 SPINS

1. Recovery from spins as well as stalls may become difficult when the CG is too far rearward.
   a. The rotation of a spin is always around the CG.

1.5 LIFT AND DRAG

1. An airplane wing produces lift resulting from relatively higher air pressure below the wing surface and lower air pressure above the wing surface.
   a. Lift is defined as the force acting perpendicular to the relative wind.
   b. An increase in the angle of attack will increase drag.
      1) Drag acts parallel to the flight path.
2. In all steady-state flight, including descent, the sum of all forward forces equals the sum of all rearward forces, and the sum of all upward forces equals the sum of all downward forces.
   a. During the transition from straight-and-level flight to a climb, the angle of attack must be increased and lift is momentarily increased.
3. Any given angle of attack has a corresponding airspeed to provide sufficient lift to maintain a given altitude.
   a. As airspeed decreases, the airfoils generate less lift. Accordingly, to maintain altitude, the angle of attack must be increased to compensate for the decrease in lift.
   b. To generate the same amount of lift as altitude increases, the airplane must be flown at a higher true airspeed for any given angle of attack.
4. As the angle of bank increases, the vertical component of lift decreases and the horizontal component of lift increases.
5. As airspeed increases, lift and parasite drag increase as the square of the increase in airspeed; e.g., doubling airspeed quadruples lift and parasite drag.
   a. Induced drag is a by-product of lift and is also greatly affected by changes in airspeed.
6. Graphs including curves of the component of lift, the component of drag, and the lift/drag (L/D) ratio are frequently prepared to demonstrate the effect of the angle of attack on drag, lift, and the lift/drag ratio. See Figure 3 on page 35.
   a. For any given angle of attack, the L/D ratio can be converted into altitude loss (in feet) per forward distance traveled.
   b. Of interest is that the L/D ratio can be the same for two different angles of attack.
      1) EXAMPLE: At 3° angle of attack and at slightly over 12° angle of attack, the L/D ratio is approximately 10.

7. In the diagram below, as airspeed increases above the maximum lift/drag (L/D_{MAX}) speed, total drag on the airplane increases due to the increased parasite drag. Note that Figure 1 on page 33 is basically the same graph.
   a. As airspeed decreases below the L/D_{MAX} speed, total drag increases due to increased induced drag.

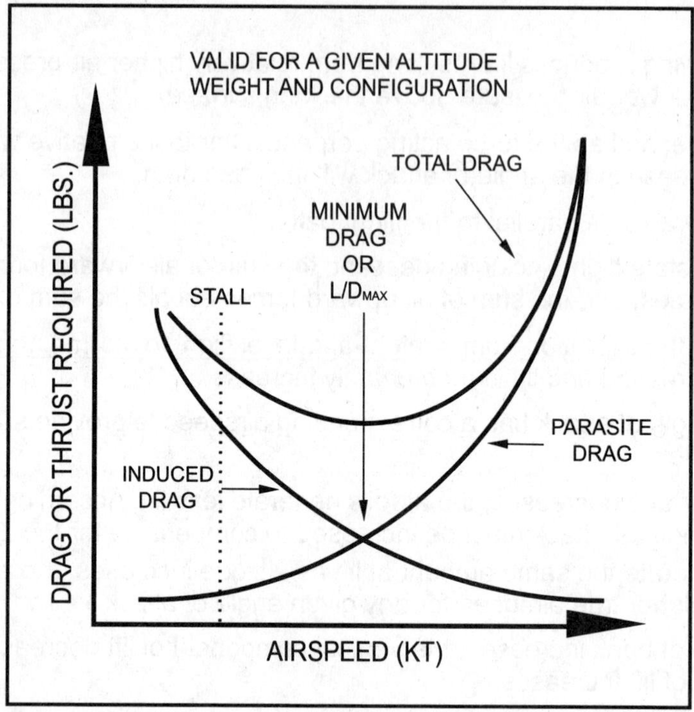

8. By definition, the L/D_{MAX} ratio is at the minimum (lowest) point of the total drag curve.
   a. The minimum point in the total drag curve is the point where the parasite drag and induced drag curves intersect.
9. In a propeller-driven airplane, the airspeed resulting in L/D_{MAX} will provide the maximum range and maximum glide distance.
10. When flaps are extended, lift and drag increase.

1.6 GROUND EFFECT

1. Ground effect is due to the interference of the ground (or water) surface with the airflow patterns about the airplane in flight.
   a. When an airplane is within a distance of its wingspan to the surface, a change occurs in the three-dimensional flow pattern around the airplane because the vertical component of the airflow around the wing is restricted by the Earth's surface.
      1) This change alters the wing's upwash, downwash, and wingtip vortices.
         a) The reduction of the wingtip vortices alters the spanwise lift distribution and reduces the induced angle of attack and induced drag.
2. An airplane leaving ground effect experiences an increase in induced drag and requires more thrust.
3. While in ground effect, an airplane needs a lower angle of attack to produce the same lift as when out of ground effect.
   a. If the same angle of attack is maintained in ground effect as when out of ground effect, lift will increase and induced drag will decrease.

1.7 AIRPLANE STABILITY

1. Stability is the inherent ability of an object (e.g., airplane), after its equilibrium is disturbed, to return to its original position. In other words, a stable airplane will tend to return to the original condition of flight if disturbed by a force such as turbulent air.
2. Static stability is the initial tendency that the airplane displays after its equilibrium is disturbed.
   a. Positive static stability can be illustrated by a ball inside a round bowl. If the ball is displaced from its normal resting place, it will eventually return to its original position at the bottom of the bowl.
   b. Neutral static stability can be illustrated by a ball on a flat plane. If the ball is displaced, it will come to rest at some new, neutral position and show no tendency to return to its original position.
   c. Negative static stability is actually instability. It can be illustrated by a ball on the top of an inverted round bowl. Even the slightest displacement of the ball will activate greater forces, which will cause the ball to continue to move in the direction of the applied force (e.g., gravity).
3. Dynamic stability is the overall tendency that the airplane displays after its equilibrium is disturbed.
   a. Positive dynamic stability is a property that dampens the oscillations set up by a statically stable airplane, enabling the oscillations to become smaller and smaller in magnitude until the airplane eventually settles down to its original condition of flight.
   b. Neutral dynamic stability means the oscillations remain unchanged.
   c. Negative dynamic stability is actually dynamic instability. It means the oscillations tend to increase.
4. An airplane is said to have
   a. Longitudinal stability about the lateral axis
   b. Lateral stability about the longitudinal axis
   c. Directional stability about the vertical axis
5. If an airplane is loaded to the rear of its CG range, it will tend to be unstable about its lateral axis.

1.8 TURNS

1. At a constant altitude in a coordinated turn, each airspeed has a specific, unvarying rate and radius of turn for each angle of bank.
   a. An increase in airspeed in a level, coordinated turn with a constant bank results in an increase in the radius and a decrease in the rate of turn.
   b. Steepening the bank and decreasing the airspeed results in an increase in the rate of turn and a decrease in the radius.
2. With a constant bank angle, the load factor will be constant regardless of
   a. The rate of turn
   b. Airspeed
   c. Weight
3. As bank is increased, additional vertical lift converts into horizontal lift, decreasing available vertical lift.
   a. Thus, an increased angle of attack (back elevator pressure) is required in order to maintain a constant altitude during the turn.
4. When airspeed is increased during a level turn, the angle of attack must be decreased or the angle of bank increased to maintain level altitude.
5. A standard rate turn is, by definition, 2 min. for 360°, or 3°/second.

1.9 LOAD FACTOR

1. Load factor is the ratio between the total airload imposed on the wing in flight and the gross weight of the airplane.
   a. The amount of excess load that can be imposed on an airplane's wings varies directly with the airplane's speed and the excess lift available.
      1) At low speeds, little excess lift is available, so little excess load can be imposed.
      2) At high speeds, the wings' lifting capacity is so great that the load factor can quickly exceed safety limits.
   b. An increased load factor will cause an airplane to stall at a higher airspeed.
   c. As bank angle increases, the load factor increases. The wings not only must carry the airplane's weight but also must bear the centrifugal force.
      1) The determinant of load factor in level, coordinated turns is the amount of bank.
      2) A change of airspeed does not affect load factor given a constant angle of bank, although it does directly affect the rate and radius of turn.
2. Load factor (or G units) is a multiple of the regular weight or, alternatively, a multiple of the force of gravity.
   a. Unaccelerated straight flight has a load factor of 1.0 (by definition).
   b. A 60° level bank has a load factor of 2.0. Thus, a 3,000-lb. airplane in a 60° bank would require the wings to provide lift for 6,000 pounds.
   c. The best indication of positive or negative Gs is the change in how heavy (positive) or light (negative) you feel in your seat.
3. Maximum safe load factors (limit load factors):
   a. Normal category airplanes are limited to 3.8 and –1.52 Gs.
   b. Utility aircraft are limited to 4.4 and –1.76 Gs.
   c. Aerobatic aircraft are limited to 6.0 and –3.0 Gs.
4. When baggage or other areas of the plane are placarded for weight, they are placarded for gross weight. The airplane is designed to accommodate the specified Gs (3.8, 4.4, 6.0) given the weight placarded.
5. A "stall speed/load factor" graph relates these variables to the degree of bank angle for a particular airplane, as illustrated in Figure 4 on page 40.
   a. Determine the load factor (or G units) for any bank angle by finding the bank angle on the horizontal axis, moving vertically up to the intersection with the load factor curve, and then proceeding horizontally to the left of the graph to find the number of G units on the vertical load factor scale.
   b. To determine the increase in stall speed for any load factor, begin with the load factor on the far left vertical scale and move horizontally to the graph on the right to intersect the load factor curve. From that point of intersection, move up vertically to the intersection with the stall speed curve. From that point, move horizontally to the left to the vertical axis to determine the percentage increase in stall speed.

1.10 TRANSONIC AND SUPERSONIC FLIGHT

1. Transonic and supersonic flight speeds are expressed in terms of true airspeed in knots to the speed of sound in knots. This ratio is called the **Mach number**.
   a. This ratio is not fixed because the speed of sound varies with altitude and temperature.
2. At low flight speeds, the study of aerodynamics is greatly simplified by the fact that air may experience relatively small changes in pressure with only negligible changes in density.
   a. This airflow is termed incompressible since the air may undergo changes in pressure without apparent changes in density.
   b. The study of airflow at high speeds must account for these changes in air density and must consider that the air is compressible and there will be compressibility effects.
   c. Local airflow velocities around an aerodynamic shape can be greater than flight speed.
      1) Thus, an aircraft can experience compressibility effects at flight speeds well below the speed of sound.
3. Since an aircraft can have both subsonic and supersonic airflows simultaneously, certain regimes have been defined.
   a. Subsonic: Mach numbers below 0.75.
   b. Transonic: Mach numbers from 0.75 to 1.20.
   c. Supersonic: Mach numbers from 1.20 to 5.00.
   d. Hypersonic: Mach numbers above 5.00.
4. The **critical mach number** is the highest flight speed possible without supersonic flow.
   a. Accelerating past critical Mach is associated with trim and stability changes, an increase in drag, and a decrease in control surface effectiveness.

QUESTIONS AND ANSWER EXPLANATIONS: All of the commercial pilot knowledge test questions chosen by the FAA for release as well as additional questions selected by Gleim relating to the material in the previous outlines are reproduced on the following pages. These questions have been organized into the same subunits as the outlines. To the immediate right of each question are the correct answer and answer explanation. You should cover these answers and answer explanations while responding to the questions. Refer to the general discussion in the Introduction on how to take the FAA knowledge test.

Remember that the questions from the FAA knowledge test bank have been reordered by topic and organized into a meaningful sequence. Also, the first line of the answer explanation gives the citation of the authoritative source for the answer.

QUESTIONS

1.1 Flaps

1. One of the main functions of flaps during the approach and landing is to

A. decrease the angle of descent without increasing the airspeed.

B. provide the same amount of lift at a slower airspeed.

C. decrease lift, thus enabling a steeper-than-normal approach to be made.

Answer (B) is correct. *(PHAK Chap 5)*

DISCUSSION: Extending the flaps increases the wing camber, the wing area (some types), and the angle of attack of the wing. This allows the wing to provide the same amount of lift at a slower airspeed.

Answer (A) is incorrect. Flaps increase, not decrease, the angle of descent without increasing the airspeed. Answer (C) is incorrect. Flaps increase, not decrease, lift. They also increase induced drag.

2. Which is true regarding the use of flaps during level turns?

A. The lowering of flaps increases the stall speed.

B. The raising of flaps increases the stall speed.

C. Raising flaps will require added forward pressure on the yoke or stick.

Answer (B) is correct. *(PHAK Chap 5)*

DISCUSSION: Raising the flaps decreases the wing camber and the angle of attack of the wing. This decreases wing lift and results in a higher stall speed.

Answer (A) is incorrect. Flaps decrease, not increase, the stall speed. Answer (C) is incorrect. Raising the flaps will decrease the lift provided by the wings. Thus, back, not forward, pressure on the yoke or stick is required to maintain altitude.

1.2 Airplane Wings

3. Some aircraft are fitted with wing spoilers to decrease

A. drag.

B. takeoff speed.

C. lift.

Answer (C) is correct. *(PHAK Chap 4)*

DISCUSSION: Some aircraft require the use of spoilers. Many modern high-speed aircraft are very clean aerodynamically. Upon landing, spoilers are deployed on the top of the wing to reduce lift and improve braking performance.

Answer (A) is incorrect. Spoilers increase drag while subsequently reducing lift. Answer (B) is incorrect. Spoilers are not used on takeoff. Spoilers reduce lift, the opposite of what is required for optimal takeoff performance.

4. An aircraft airfoil is designed to produce lift resulting from a difference in the

A. negative air pressure below and a vacuum above the airfoil's surface.

B. vacuum below the airfoil's surface and greater air pressure above the airfoil's surface.

C. higher air pressure below the airfoil's surface and lower air pressure above the airfoil's surface.

Answer (C) is correct. *(PHAK Chap 3)*

DISCUSSION: As air molecules flow over the top portion of the wing, which is cambered, they travel a greater distance than the molecules that flow over the relatively flat underside of the wing. The airflow over the top of the wing is forced to accelerate. It is this increase in velocity that causes a pressure differential, creating an area of low pressure above the wing.

Answer (A) is incorrect. Wings create areas of low pressure, not a vacuum. A vacuum by definition is an area of zero pressure. An area of negative pressure does not exist below the wing; rather, the underside of the wing is an area of high pressure. An area of low pressure, not a vacuum, exists above the top portion of the wing. Answer (B) is incorrect. Wings create areas of low pressure, not a vacuum. A vacuum by definition is an area of zero pressure. The area of greatest pressure is located on the underside of the wing with an area of low pressure forming above the wing.

5. A rectangular wing, as compared to other wing planforms, has a tendency to stall first at the

A. wingtip, with the stall progression toward the wing root.

B. wing root, with the stall progression toward the wingtip.

C. center trailing edge, with the stall progression outward toward the wing root and tip.

Answer (B) is correct. *(AFH Chap 3)*

DISCUSSION: A rectangular wing, as compared to other wing planforms, has a tendency to stall first at the wing root, with the stall progression toward the wingtip. Because the wingtips and the ailerons stall later, the pilot can use aileron control in avoiding and recovering from the stall.

Answer (A) is incorrect. The wing root, not wingtip, will stall first. Answer (C) is incorrect. The wing root, not the center trailing edge, will stall first.

6. The angle of attack of a wing directly controls the

A. angle of incidence of the wing.

B. amount of airflow above and below the wing.

C. distribution of pressures acting on the wing.

Answer (C) is correct. *(AFH Chap 3)*
DISCUSSION: The angle of attack of an airfoil directly controls the distribution of pressure below and above it. When a wing is at a low but positive angle of attack, most of the lift is due to the wing's negative pressure (upper surface) and downwash. NOTE: Negative pressure is any pressure less than atmospheric, and positive pressure is pressure greater than atmospheric.
Answer (A) is incorrect. The angle of incidence is a fixed relationship between the wing chord line and the longitudinal axis of the airplane and is thus unrelated to the angle of attack. Answer (B) is incorrect. The same amount of air must flow above and below (over and under) the wing.

7. Frost covering the upper surface of an airplane wing usually will cause

A. the airplane to stall at an angle of attack that is higher than normal.

B. the airplane to stall at an angle of attack that is lower than normal.

C. drag factors so large that sufficient speed cannot be obtained for takeoff.

Answer (B) is correct. *(PHAK Chap 11)*
DISCUSSION: Frost on the surface of a wing interferes with the smooth flow of air over the wing surface; i.e., parasite drag is increased. The air flowing over the wing is thus disrupted and stalls at a lower angle of attack (a higher speed) when there is frost on the wing surface.
Answer (A) is incorrect. Frost on the wing surface will usually cause the airplane to stall at a lower, not higher, angle of attack. Answer (C) is incorrect. The drag created by frost usually will not be so disruptive as to prevent the aircraft from obtaining takeoff speed.

8. By changing the angle of attack of a wing, the pilot can control the airplane's

A. lift, airspeed, and drag.

B. lift, airspeed, and CG.

C. lift and airspeed, but not drag.

Answer (A) is correct. *(AFH Chap 3)*
DISCUSSION: The pilot can control the airplane's lift, airspeed, and drag by changing the angle of attack of the wing. As the angle of attack is increased, the lift increases to the critical angle of attack, airspeed decreases, and induced drag increases with the increase in lift.
Answer (B) is incorrect. The angle of attack has no effect on the CG of an airplane. Answer (C) is incorrect. Drag, as well as lift and airspeed, is determined by the angle of attack.

9. When a pilot increases the angle of attack on a symmetrical airfoil, the center of pressure will

A. move forward.

B. move aft.

C. be unchanged.

Answer (C) is correct. *(ANA Chap 1)*
DISCUSSION: An increase in the angle of attack has no effect on the center of pressure on a symmetrical wing.
Answer (A) is incorrect. The center of pressure on a symmetrical wing does not move forward with an increase in angle of attack; it is unaffected. Answer (B) is incorrect. The center of pressure on a symmetrical wing does not move aft with an increase in angle of attack; it is unaffected.

1.3 Stalls

10. The critical angle of attack is exceeded when

A. Airflow separates from the wing's trailing edge.

B. A stall occurs.

C. Indicated airspeed equals V_{SO} × 1.3.

Answer (B) is correct. *(PHAK Chap 4)*
DISCUSSION: Exceeding the critical angle of attack will result in a stall.
Answer (A) is incorrect. When an airfoil exceeds its critical angle of attack, the airflow separates from the airfoil, causing a stall. This separation affects the entire wing, not just the trailing edge. Answer (C) is incorrect. V_{SO} × 1.3 is a typical approach to landing speed; it is not the result of the critical angle of attack being exceeded.

11. The angle of attack at which a wing stalls remains constant regardless of

A. weight, dynamic pressure, bank angle, or pitch attitude.

B. dynamic pressure, but varies with weight, bank angle, and pitch attitude.

C. weight and pitch attitude, but varies with dynamic pressure and bank angle.

Answer (A) is correct. *(AFH Chap 3)*
DISCUSSION: The angle of attack at which a wing stalls is constant regardless of weight, bank, pitch, etc.
Answer (B) is incorrect. The stall speed, not angle of attack, varies with weight and bank angle. Answer (C) is incorrect. The stall speed, not angle of attack, varies with bank angle.

12. The design maneuvering speed is

A. a figure for recently designed aircraft that defines the maximum speed an airplane can be safely stalled.

B. 1.3 times V_{SO}.

C. maximum takeoff weight divided by V_{SO}.

Answer (A) is correct. *(PHAK Chap 4)*

DISCUSSION: All recently designed aircraft are required to list a design maneuvering speed (V_A) in the AFM/POH. This speed defines the maximum speed at which an airplane can be safely stalled.

Answer (B) is incorrect. For older general aviation aircraft (aircraft not recently designed), the design maneuvering speed is approximately 1.7 times the normal stalling speed. Answer (C) is incorrect. Dividing the takeoff weight by V_{SO} does not calculate design maneuvering speed.

13. The need to slow an aircraft below V_A is brought about by the following weather phenomenon:

A. High density altitude which increases the indicated stall speed.

B. Turbulence which causes an increase in stall speed.

C. Turbulence which causes a decrease in stall speed.

Answer (B) is correct. *(PHAK Chap 4)*

DISCUSSION: Turbulence, in the form of vertical air currents, can cause severe load stress on a wing. It is wise, in extremely rough air, to reduce the speed to V_A (design maneuvering speed). Yet, V_A allows a sufficient margin of safety above stall speed, which may be increased in turbulent air due to increased load factors.

Answer (A) is incorrect. Changes in density altitude do not affect indicated stall speed. Answer (C) is incorrect. Turbulence increases the load factors imposed on the aircraft, which increases, not decreases, stall speed.

14. Stall speed is affected by

A. weight, load factor, and power.

B. load factor, angle of attack, and power.

C. angle of attack, weight, and air density.

Answer (A) is correct. *(AFH Chap 3)*

DISCUSSION: Stall speed may vary under different circumstances. Factors such as weight, load factor, power, center of gravity, altitude, temperature, and the presence of snow, ice, or frost on the wings will affect an aircraft's stall speed.

Answer (B) is incorrect. Stall speed is not affected by the angle of attack. Answer (C) is incorrect. Stall speed is not affected by the angle of attack.

15. An airplane will stall at the same

A. angle of attack regardless of the attitude with relation to the horizon.

B. airspeed regardless of the attitude with relation to the horizon.

C. angle of attack and attitude with relation to the horizon.

Answer (A) is correct. *(AFH Chap 3)*

DISCUSSION: An airplane will always stall at the same angle of attack. The airplane's attitude with relation to the horizon has no significance to the stall.

Answer (B) is incorrect. The stall speed will vary with changing load factors, weight, and power. Answer (C) is incorrect. An airplane can stall in any attitude with relation to the horizon.

16. A stall will occur

A. when airspeed is no longer sufficient to generate the required lift.

B. when the wing reaches the critical angle of attack.

C. when the critical angle of attack is exceeded.

Answer (C) is correct. *(PHAK Chap 4)*

DISCUSSION: An airfoil stalls when the air can no longer flow smoothly over the top cambered surface of the wing. This phenomenon, known as early airflow separation, occurs when the wing exceeds the critical angle of attack.

Answer (A) is incorrect. A stall can occur at any airspeed, and airspeed is not a determining factor in the cause of a stall. Answer (B) is incorrect. A wing stalls when exceeding, not reaching, the critical angle of attack.

17. (Refer to Figure 3 on page 35.) Use the diagram to determine the critical angle of attack.

A. 15°

B. 16°

C. 20°

Answer (C) is correct. *(PHAK Chap 4)*

DISCUSSION: The peak point in the C_L curve is the maximum lift production point for a given airfoil, $C_{L\,MAX}$. This is also known as the critical angle of attack. Increasing the angle of attack beyond this point will cause the airfoil to stall.

Answer (A) is incorrect. The critical angle of attack is 20°, not 15°, as indicated by the peak point of the C_L curve, $C_{L\,MAX}$. Answer (B) is incorrect. The critical angle of attack is 20°, not 16°, as indicated by the peak point of the C_L curve, $C_{L\,MAX}$.

18. In a rapid recovery from a dive, the effects of load factor would cause the stall speed to

A. increase.

B. decrease.

C. not vary.

Answer (A) is correct. *(AFH Chap 3)*

DISCUSSION: In a rapid recovery from a dive, the load factor would be increased because of the rapid change in the angle of attack, since gravity and centrifugal force would prevent the airplane from immediately altering its flight path. Because the relative wind is opposite the flight path, the critical angle of attack will be reached at a higher airspeed.

Answer (B) is incorrect. As load factor increases, so does stall speed. Answer (C) is incorrect. As load factor increases, so does stall speed.

19. The stalling speed of an airplane is most affected by

A. changes in air density.

B. variations in flight altitude.

C. variations in airplane loading.

Answer (C) is correct. *(AFH Chap 3)*

DISCUSSION: Indicated stall speed is most affected by the gross weight and how it is distributed within the airplane.

Answer (A) is incorrect. Air density does not affect indicated stall speed. Answer (B) is incorrect. Flight altitude does not affect indicated stall speed.

20. (Refer to Figure 2 below.) Select the correct statement regarding stall speeds.

A. Power-off stalls occur at higher airspeeds with the gear and flaps down.

B. In a 60° bank the airplane stalls at a lower airspeed with the gear up.

C. Power-on stalls occur at lower airspeeds in shallower banks.

Answer (C) is correct. *(PHAK Chap 4)*

DISCUSSION: Using Fig. 2, work through each of the answers to determine which is true. Power-on stalls occur at lower airspeeds in shallower banks.

Answer (A) is incorrect. With power off, stall speed is lower, not higher, with gear and flaps down. Answer (B) is incorrect. In a 60° bank, the gear position alone will not affect stall speed.

GROSS WEIGHT 2750 LBS		ANGLE OF BANK			
		LEVEL	30°	45°	60°
POWER		GEAR AND FLAPS UP			
ON	MPH KTS	62 54	67 58	74 64	88 76
OFF	MPH KTS	75 65	81 70	89 77	106 92
		GEAR AND FLAPS DOWN			
ON	MPH KTS	54 47	58 50	64 56	76 66
OFF	MPH KTS	66 57	71 62	78 68	93 81

Figure 2. – Stall Speeds.

21. (Refer to Figure 2 above.) Select the correct statement regarding stall speeds. The airplane will stall

A. 10 knots higher in a power-on, 60° bank, with gear and flaps up, than with gear and flaps down.

B. 25 knots lower in a power-off, flaps-up, 60° bank, than in a power-off, flaps-down, wings-level configuration.

C. 10 knots higher in a 45° bank, power-on stall, than in a wings-level stall with flaps up.

Answer (A) is correct. *(PHAK Chap 10)*

DISCUSSION: The airplane stalls at 76 kt. with power on, gear and flaps up at 60° bank but stalls at 66 kt. with gear and flaps down (i.e., a difference of 10 knots).

Answer (B) is incorrect. The airplane stalls 35 kt. higher, not 25 kt. lower, with power off, flaps up, and a 60° bank than with power off, flaps down, and wings level. Answer (C) is incorrect. The gear position and power setting are not specified, so there is not enough information to make a proper determination.

22. Recovery from a stall in any airplane becomes more difficult when its

A. center of gravity moves aft.

B. center of gravity moves forward.

C. elevator trim is adjusted nosedown.

Answer (A) is correct. *(AFH Chap 3)*

DISCUSSION: The recovery from a stall in any airplane becomes progressively more difficult as the airplane's center of gravity moves aft. This difficulty is due to the decreasing stability in pitch, which results in the decrease of elevator effectiveness in lowering the nose.

Answer (B) is incorrect. Recovery from a stall becomes easier, not more difficult, as the center of gravity moves forward. Answer (C) is incorrect. The center of gravity, not the elevator trim adjustment, has an effect on the stall recovery characteristics of an airplane.

23. A left side slip is used to counteract a crosswind drift during the final approach for landing. An over-the-top spin would most likely occur if the controls were used in which of the following ways? Holding the stick

A. in the neutral position and applying full right rudder.

B. too far to the left and applying full left rudder.

C. too far back and applying full right rudder.

Answer (C) is correct. *(AFH Chap 4)*

DISCUSSION: The down aileron on the inside of the turn increases drag on the wing, slowing it down and decreasing its lift, which requires more aileron application. This causes the airplane to roll. This roll may occur so quickly that it is possible for the bank to be vertical or past vertical before it can be stopped. With these control inputs, the inside wing may suddenly drop and the airplane may continue to roll to an inverted position. This is usually the beginning of a spin.

Answer (A) is incorrect. If the stick were kept in the neutral position, the airplane would descend, increasing airspeed while yawing to the right. Answer (B) is incorrect. This would lead to a slipping turn.

1.4 Spins

24. In small airplanes, normal recovery from spins may become difficult if the

A. CG is too far rearward, and rotation is around the longitudinal axis.

B. CG is too far rearward, and rotation is around the CG.

C. spin is entered before the stall is fully developed.

Answer (B) is correct. *(AC 61-67C)*

DISCUSSION: Because rotation is around the CG in a spin, with a rearward CG, the control arm at the rudder is sufficiently shortened that it may make spin recovery difficult, if not impossible. Intuitively, if there is too much weight near the tail, it is also hard to get the nose down to produce an angle of attack below the critical angle.

Answer (A) is incorrect. Rotation is around the CG, not the longitudinal axis, in a spin. Answer (C) is incorrect. In order for an airplane to spin, it must first stall.

1.5 Lift and Drag

25. Which statement is true relative to changing angle of attack?

A. A decrease in angle of attack will increase pressure below the wing, and decrease drag.

B. An increase in angle of attack will increase drag.

C. An increase in angle of attack will decrease pressure below the wing, and increase drag.

Answer (B) is correct. *(PHAK Chap 4)*

DISCUSSION: As the angle of attack is increased, up to the critical angle of attack, the greater the amount of lift is developed and the greater the induced drag.

Answer (A) is incorrect. A decrease in the angle of attack will decrease, not increase, the pressure below the wing. Answer (C) is incorrect. An increase in angle of attack will increase, not decrease, the pressure below the wing.

26. A pilot who intends to maintain level flight must coordinate the angle of attack and

A. thrust.

B. drag.

C. lift.

Answer (A) is correct. *(PHAK Chap 4)*

DISCUSSION: To maintain level flight, a pilot must coordinate thrust and the angle of attack. If the angle of attack is increased, more lift will be generated so a reduction in thrust is required. If the angle of attack is reduced, lift will be reduced and less thrust will be required.

Answer (B) is incorrect. Drag is a byproduct of lift production and the basic shape of the aircraft. A change in angle of attack will change the total drag generated, but the pilot has very little control on the amount of drag produced by the aircraft in flight, especially in a clean, cruise configuration. Answer (C) is incorrect. A pilot changes the angle of attack to control the lift generated. When the total amount of lift generated is changed, a change in thrust is required to maintain straight-and-level flight.

27. To generate the same amount of lift as altitude is increased, an airplane must be flown at

A. the same true airspeed regardless of angle of attack.

B. a lower true airspeed and a greater angle of attack.

C. a higher true airspeed for any given angle of attack.

Answer (C) is correct. *(AFH Chap 3)*
DISCUSSION: At an altitude of 18,000 ft. MSL, the air has one-half the density of air at sea level. Thus, in order to maintain the same amount of lift as altitude increases, an airplane must be flown at a higher true airspeed for any given angle of attack.
Answer (A) is incorrect. True airspeed must be increased, not remain the same, as altitude increases to generate the same amount of lift. Answer (B) is incorrect. True airspeed must be increased, not decreased, as altitude increases to generate the same amount of lift.

28. As the angle of bank is increased, the vertical component of lift

A. decreases and the horizontal component of lift increases.

B. increases and the horizontal component of lift decreases.

C. decreases and the horizontal component of lift remains constant.

Answer (A) is correct. *(AFH Chap 3)*
DISCUSSION: In level flight, all lift is vertical (upwards). As bank is increased, however, a portion of the airplane's lift is transferred from a vertical component to a horizontal component. Thus, the vertical component of lift decreases and the horizontal component of lift increases as the angle of bank is increased.
Answer (B) is incorrect. The vertical component of lift decreases and the horizontal component of lift increases. Answer (C) is incorrect. The horizontal component of lift increases.

29. Which is true regarding the forces acting on an aircraft in a steady-state descent? The sum of all

A. upward forces is less than the sum of all downward forces.

B. rearward forces is greater than the sum of all forward forces.

C. forward forces is equal to the sum of all rearward forces.

Answer (C) is correct. *(AFH Chap 3)*
DISCUSSION: In any steady-state flight, whether level flight, climbs, or descents, the sum of all forward forces is equal to the sum of all rearward forces, and the upward forces equal the downward forces.
Answer (A) is incorrect. Upward forces are equal to, not less than, downward forces in steady-state flight. Answer (B) is incorrect. Rearward forces are equal to, not greater than, forward forces in steady-state flight.

30. During the transition from straight-and-level flight to a climb, the angle of attack is increased and lift

A. is momentarily decreased.

B. remains the same.

C. is momentarily increased.

Answer (C) is correct. *(AFH Chap 3)*
DISCUSSION: During the transition from straight-and-level flight to a climb, a change in lift occurs as back elevator pressure is first applied, causing an increase in the angle of attack. Lift at this moment is now greater than weight and starts the airplane's climb.
Answer (A) is incorrect. During the transition from straight-and-level flight to a climb, lift is momentarily increased, not decreased, as the angle of attack is increased. Answer (B) is incorrect. During the transition from straight-and-level flight to a climb, lift is momentarily increased, rather than remaining the same, as the angle of attack is increased.

31. What changes in airplane longitudinal control must be made to maintain altitude while the airspeed is being decreased?

A. Increase the angle of attack to produce more lift than drag.

B. Increase the angle of attack to compensate for the decreasing lift.

C. Decrease the angle of attack to compensate for the increasing drag.

Answer (B) is correct. *(AFH Chap 3)*
DISCUSSION: As airspeed decreases, the airfoils generate less lift. Accordingly, to maintain altitude, the angle of attack must be adjusted to compensate for the decrease in lift.
Answer (A) is incorrect. If the angle of attack is increased to produce more lift than weight, not drag, the airplane will begin to climb. Answer (C) is incorrect. The angle of attack must be increased, not decreased, and the objective is to compensate for the decreased lift, not increased drag.

32. Which is true regarding the force of lift in steady, unaccelerated flight?

A. At lower airspeeds the angle of attack must be less to generate sufficient lift to maintain altitude.

B. There is a corresponding indicated airspeed required for every angle of attack to generate sufficient lift to maintain altitude.

C. An airfoil will always stall at the same indicated airspeed; therefore, an increase in weight will require an increase in speed to generate sufficient lift to maintain altitude.

Answer (B) is correct. *(AFH Chap 3)*

DISCUSSION: Different angles of attack provide different lift coefficients (amounts of lift). Accordingly, any given angle of attack has a corresponding airspeed to provide sufficient lift to maintain altitude.

Answer (A) is incorrect. As airspeed is reduced, the angle of attack must be increased, not decreased, to provide sufficient lift. Answer (C) is incorrect. An airfoil will always stall at the same angle of attack, not the same indicated airspeed.

33. In theory, if the airspeed of an airplane is doubled while in level flight, parasite drag will become

A. twice as great.

B. half as great.

C. four times greater.

Answer (C) is correct. *(PHAK Chap 4)*

DISCUSSION: Tests show that lift and drag vary as the square of the velocity. The velocity of the air passing over the wing in flight is determined by the airspeed of the airplane. Thus, if an airplane doubles its airspeed, lift and drag will be four times greater (assuming that the angle of attack remains the same).

Answer (A) is incorrect. The relationship between parasite drag and airspeed is not linear. Answer (B) is incorrect. Parasite drag will increase, not decrease, with an increase in airspeed.

34. As airspeed decreases in level flight below that speed for maximum lift/drag ratio, total drag of an airplane

A. decreases because of lower parasite drag.

B. increases because of increased induced drag.

C. increases because of increased parasite drag.

Answer (B) is correct. *(AFH Chap 3)*

DISCUSSION: Total drag is at a minimum for the maximum lift/drag (L/D_{MAX}) ratio at one specific angle of attack and lift coefficient. As airspeed decreases, the induced drag will increase because a greater angle of attack is required to maintain level flight. The amount of induced drag varies inversely as the square of the airspeed.

Answer (A) is incorrect. Total drag increases, not decreases, with decreases in airspeed below L/D_{MAX} because of increased induced drag. Answer (C) is incorrect. Parasite drag changes directly, not inversely, with airspeed. Thus, below L/D_{MAX}, parasite drag decreases, not increases.

35. If airspeed remains constant, but the air density increases, what will be the effect on both lift and drag?

A. Lift will decrease and drag will decrease.

B. Drag will decrease and lift will increase.

C. Lift will increase and drag will increase.

Answer (C) is correct. *(PHAK Chap 4)*

DISCUSSION: Air density is a determining factor in lift production. The greater the density of the air, the greater the lift produced by an airfoil. Induced drag is a byproduct of lift production. As lift increases, induced drag will increase as well.

Answer (A) is incorrect. An increase in air density will result in an increase in both lift and drag, not a decrease. Answer (B) is incorrect. An increase in air density will result in an increase in both lift and drag. An increase in lift always results in an increase of drag because induced drag increases as lift production increases.

36. What performance is characteristic of flight at maximum lift/drag ratio in a propeller-driven airplane? Maximum

A. gain in altitude over a given distance.

B. range and maximum distance glide.

C. coefficient of lift and minimum coefficient of drag.

Answer (B) is correct. *(AFH Chap 3)*

DISCUSSION: If the airplane is operated in steady flight at L/D_{MAX}, the total drag is at a minimum. Many important items of airplane performance are obtained in flight at L/D_{MAX}. For a propeller-driven airplane, these items include maximum range and maximum power-off glide range.

Answer (A) is incorrect. The best angle of climb (e.g., to clear an obstacle) is at a high angle of attack with both high lift and high drag coefficients, which would not result in an L/D_{MAX} ratio. Answer (C) is incorrect. L/D_{MAX} is neither at the maximum coefficient of lift nor at the minimum coefficient of drag, but at a point somewhere in between.

37. In theory, if the angle of attack and other factors remain constant and the airspeed is doubled, the lift produced at the higher speed will be

A. the same as at the lower speed.

B. two times greater than at the lower speed.

C. four times greater than at the lower speed.

Answer (C) is correct. *(AFH Chap 3)*

DISCUSSION: If the angle of attack and other factors remain constant, lift is proportional to the square of the airplane's velocity. For example, an airplane traveling at 200 kt. has four times the lift as the same airplane traveling at 100 knots.

Answer (A) is incorrect. As airspeed is doubled, lift produced will be four times greater than, not the same as, at the lower speed. Answer (B) is incorrect. As airspeed is doubled, lift produced will be four, not two, times greater than at the lower speed.

38. An aircraft wing is designed to produce lift resulting from a difference in the

A. negative air pressure below and a vacuum above the wing's surface.

B. vacuum below the wing's surface and greater air pressure above the wing's surface.

C. higher air pressure below the wing's surface and lower air pressure above the wing's surface.

Answer (C) is correct. *(AFH Chap 3)*

DISCUSSION: An airplane's lift is produced by a pressure differential resulting from relatively lower (i.e., less than atmospheric) pressure above the wing and higher (i.e., greater than atmospheric) pressure below the wing's surface.

Answer (A) is incorrect. The air pressure below the wing is relatively higher, not negative, and the pressure above the wing is lower, not a vacuum. Answer (B) is incorrect. The air pressure below the wing is relatively higher, not a vacuum, and the pressure above the wing is lower, not higher.

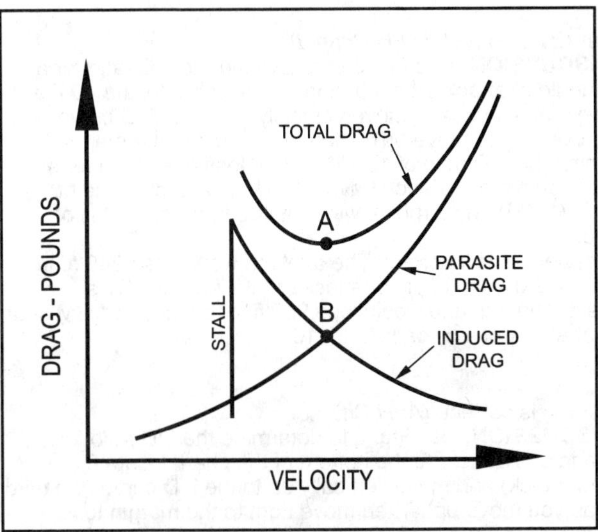

Figure 1. – Drag vs. Speed.

39. (Refer to Figure 1 above.) At an airspeed represented by point B, in steady flight, the pilot can expect to obtain the airplane's maximum

A. endurance.

B. glide range.

C. coefficient of lift.

Answer (B) is correct. *(AFH Chap 3)*

DISCUSSION: Point B (Fig. 1) is the intersection of the parasite and induced drag curves, which is the point where the total drag is at its minimum (also known as the point of maximum L/D ratio). L/D_{MAX} is the airspeed at which the pilot of either a jet or a propeller-driven airplane can expect to obtain that airplane's maximum glide range.

Answer (A) is incorrect. Only a jet-powered aircraft will obtain its maximum endurance at L/D_{MAX}. Answer (C) is incorrect. The maximum coefficient of lift is at the critical angle of attack, where total drag is also high because of an increase in induced drag.

40. (Refer to Figure 1 above.) At the airspeed represented by point A, in steady flight, the airplane will

A. have its maximum L/D ratio.

B. have its minimum L/D ratio.

C. be developing its maximum coefficient of lift.

Answer (A) is correct. *(AFH Chap 3)*

DISCUSSION: Point A (Fig. 1) is at the minimum point on the total drag curve. By definition, this is the point of maximum L/D ratio. Note that airspeed is on the horizontal axis and drag is on the vertical axis.

Answer (B) is incorrect. The minimum, not maximum, L/D ratio occurs at high airspeeds at which parasite drag is very high. Answer (C) is incorrect. The maximum coefficient of lift is produced at lower airspeeds, which have high induced drag and resulting lower L/D ratio.

41. To hold an airplane in level flight at airspeeds from very slow to very fast, a pilot must coordinate thrust and

A. angle of incidence.

B. gross weight.

C. angle of attack.

Answer (C) is correct. *(PHAK Chap 4)*

DISCUSSION: If a reduction in thrust and airspeed occurs, the force of gravity (weight) will overpower lift. A pilot must increase the angle of attack to generate more lift, thus compensating for the loss of thrust. If thrust and airspeed increase, lift will overpower gravity (weight), the aircraft will climb, and the pilot must decrease the angle of attack to maintain straight-and-level flight.

Answer (A) is incorrect. The angle of incidence defines the wing's chord line and its relationship to the longitudinal axis of the airplane. A pilot cannot change the angle of incidence. Answer (B) is incorrect. A pilot cannot alter the gross weight of an aircraft in flight.

42. Lift on a wing is most properly defined as the

A. force acting perpendicular to the relative wind.

B. differential pressure acting perpendicular to the chord of the wing.

C. reduced pressure resulting from a laminar flow over the upper camber of an airfoil, which acts perpendicular to the mean camber.

Answer (A) is correct. *(AFH Chap 3)*

DISCUSSION: Lift opposes the downward force of weight, is produced by the dynamic effect of the air acting on the wing, and acts perpendicular to the relative wind through the wing's center of lift.

Answer (B) is incorrect. Lift acts perpendicular to the relative wind, not the chord line. Answer (C) is incorrect. Lift is produced by pressure resulting from flow under as well as over the wing, and it acts perpendicular to relative wind, not the mean camber of the wing.

43. (Refer to Figure 3 on page 35.) If an airplane glides at an angle of attack of 10°, how much altitude will it lose in 1 mile?

A. 240 feet.

B. 480 feet.

C. 960 feet.

Answer (B) is correct. *(AFH Chap 3)*

DISCUSSION: Use Fig. 3 to determine the L/D ratio for a given angle of attack. At the bottom of the chart, locate 10 (i.e., 10° angle of attack) and move vertically up to the L/D curve (the third curve as you move up). Then move right to the margin to determine the L/D ratio of 11:1 (i.e., 1-ft. loss of altitude for every 11 ft. of horizontal distance traveled). Thus, at a distance of 5,280 ft. (1 SM), the airplane will lose 480 ft. (5,280 ÷ 11) of altitude.

Answer (A) is incorrect. The airplane would lose 240 ft. in 1/2, not 1, SM at an angle of attack of 10°. Answer (C) is incorrect. The airplane would lose 960 ft. of altitude in 1 SM at an angle of attack of 1.5° or 19°, not 10°.

44. (Refer to Figure 3 on page 35.) How much altitude will this airplane lose in 3 statute miles of gliding at an angle of attack of 8°?

A. 440 feet.

B. 880 feet.

C. 1,320 feet.

Answer (C) is correct. *(AFH Chap 3)*

DISCUSSION: Use Fig. 3 to determine the L/D ratio for a given angle of attack. At the bottom of the chart, locate 8 (i.e., 8° angle of attack) and move vertically up to the L/D curve (the third curve as you move up). Then move right to the margin to determine the L/D ratio of 12:1 (i.e., 1-ft. loss of altitude for every 12 ft. of horizontal distance traveled). Thus, at a distance of 15,840 ft. (5,280 ft./SM × 3 SM), the airplane will lose 1,320 ft. (15,840 ÷ 12) of altitude.

Answer (A) is incorrect. The airplane would lose 440 ft. in 1 mile. Answer (B) is incorrect. The airplane would lose 880 ft. in 2 miles.

45. (Refer to Figure 3 on page 35.) The L/D ratio at a 2° angle of attack is approximately the same as the L/D ratio for a

A. 9.75° angle of attack.

B. 10.5° angle of attack.

C. 16.5° angle of attack.

Answer (C) is correct. *(PHAK Chap 10)*

DISCUSSION: Enter the bottom of the chart in Fig. 3 at 2° angle of attack and move vertically up to the L/D curve. From this point, move right horizontally to the point where the L/D curve intersects. Then move vertically down to the bottom of the chart to determine a 16.5° angle of attack. Thus, the L/D ratio is approximately the same at both a 2° and 16.5° angle of attack.

Answer (A) is incorrect. An angle of attack of 9.75° would have the same L/D ratio as a 3.75°, not 2.0°, angle of attack. Answer (B) is incorrect. An angle of attack of 10.5° would have the same L/D ratio as a 3.5°, not 2.0°, angle of attack.

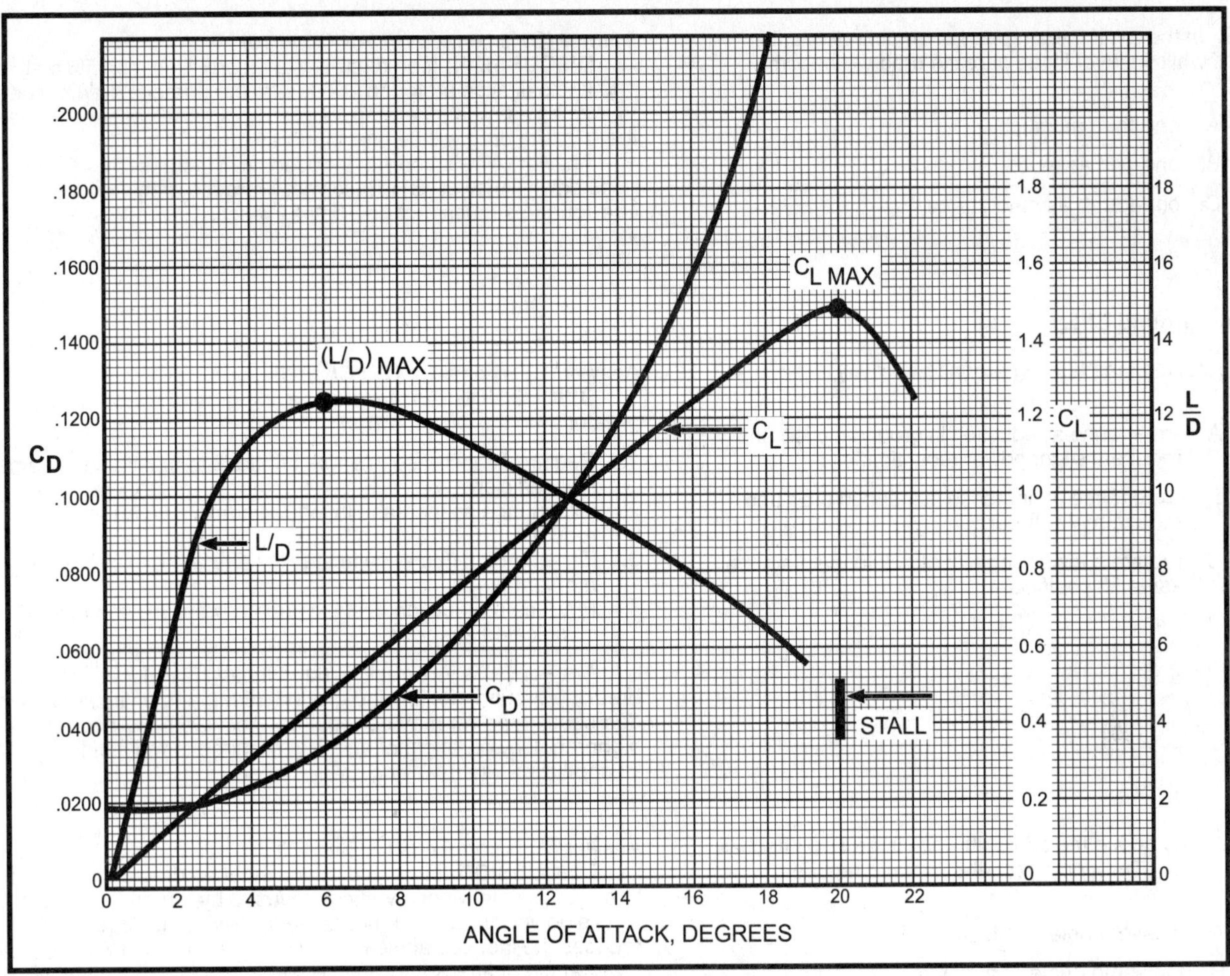

Figure 3. – Angle of Attack, Degrees.

46. On a wing, the force of lift acts perpendicular to and the force of drag acts parallel to the

A. chord line.

B. flightpath.

C. longitudinal axis.

Answer (B) is correct. *(AFH Chap 3)*

DISCUSSION: Lift acts perpendicular to the relative wind, which is opposite the flight path. Drag acts parallel to the flight path.

Answer (A) is incorrect. There is no fixed relationship between lift and drag with respect to the chord line. Answer (C) is incorrect. There is no fixed relationship between lift and drag and the longitudinal axis.

47. Which statement is true regarding the opposing forces acting on an airplane in steady-state level flight?

A. These forces are equal.

B. Thrust is greater than drag and weight and lift are equal.

C. Thrust is greater than drag and lift is greater than weight.

Answer (A) is correct. *(AFH Chap 3)*

DISCUSSION: In steady-state level flight, the sum of the opposing forces is equal to zero.

Answer (B) is incorrect. Thrust is equal to, not greater than, drag in steady-state level flight. If thrust is greater than drag, airspeed will increase. Answer (C) is incorrect. Thrust is equal to, not greater than, drag and lift is equal to, not greater than, weight in steady-state level flight. If lift is greater than weight, the airplane will enter a climb.

48. Both lift and drag would be increased when which of these devices are extended?

A. Flaps.

B. Spoilers.

C. Slats.

Answer (A) is correct. *(PHAK Chap 5)*

DISCUSSION: Flaps increase both lift and (induced) drag for any given angle of attack.

Answer (B) is incorrect. Spoilers decrease lift and increase drag. Answer (C) is incorrect. Slats increase the wing area, thereby increasing lift without increasing drag.

49. In theory, if the airspeed of an aircraft is cut in half while in level flight, parasite drag will become

A. one-third as much.

B. one-half as much.

C. one-fourth as much.

Answer (C) is correct. *(PHAK Chap 10)*

DISCUSSION: If an aircraft in a steady flight condition at 100 knots is accelerated to 200 knots, the parasite drag becomes four times as great; therefore, if you reduce the airspeed by half, the parasite drag will be one-fourth as much.

Answer (A) is incorrect. Induced drag increases as speed goes down. Answer (B) is incorrect. Parasite drag would be one-fourth as much, not one-half as much.

1.6 Ground Effect

50. An airplane leaving ground effect will

A. experience a reduction in ground friction and require a slight power reduction.

B. experience an increase in induced drag and require more thrust.

C. require a lower angle of attack to maintain the same lift coefficient.

Answer (B) is correct. *(AFH Chap 3)*

DISCUSSION: An airplane leaving ground effect (a height greater than the wingspan) will

1. Require an increase in angle of attack to maintain the same lift coefficient,
2. Experience an increase in induced drag and thrust required,
3. Experience a decrease in stability and a nose-up change in moment, and
4. Produce a reduction in static source pressure and increase in indicated airspeed.

Answer (A) is incorrect. Ground friction is reduced when breaking ground, not leaving ground effect, and an increase, not decrease, in power may be required. Answer (C) is incorrect. A higher, not lower, angle of attack is required to maintain the same lift coefficient when leaving ground effect.

51. To produce the same lift while in ground effect as when out of ground effect, the airplane requires

A. a lower angle of attack.

B. the same angle of attack.

C. a greater angle of attack.

Answer (A) is correct. *(AFH Chap 3)*

DISCUSSION: In ground effect, induced drag decreases due to a reduction in wingtip vortices (caused by a reduction in the wing's downwash), which alters the spanwise lift distribution and reduces the induced angle of attack. Thus, the wing will require a lower angle of attack in ground effect to produce the same lift as when out of ground effect.

Answer (B) is incorrect. A lower, not the same, angle of attack is required to maintain the same lift while in ground effect as when out of ground effect. Answer (C) is incorrect. A lower, not greater, angle of attack is required to maintain the same lift while in ground effect as when out of ground effect.

52. If the same angle of attack is maintained in ground effect as when out of ground effect, lift will

A. increase, and induced drag will decrease.

B. decrease, and parasite drag will increase.

C. increase, and induced drag will increase.

Answer (A) is correct. *(AFH Chap 3)*

DISCUSSION: In ground effect, induced drag decreases due to a reduction in wingtip vortices (caused by a reduction in the wing's downwash), which alters the spanwise lift distribution and reduces the induced angle of attack. Thus, if an airplane is brought into ground effect with a constant angle of attack, an increase in lift will result.

Answer (B) is incorrect. At the same angle of attack in ground effect as when out of ground effect, lift will increase, not decrease, and parasite drag does not significantly change in ground effect. Answer (C) is incorrect. Induced drag decreases, not increases, in ground effect.

1.7 Airplane Stability

53. Longitudinal stability involves the motion of the airplane controlled by its

A. rudder.

B. elevator.

C. ailerons.

Answer (B) is correct. *(AFH Chap 3)*

DISCUSSION: Longitudinal stability is the quality that makes an airplane stable about its lateral (i.e., pitch) axis. This motion is controlled by the elevators.

Answer (A) is incorrect. The rudder affects the directional, not longitudinal, stability of the airplane. Answer (C) is incorrect. The ailerons affect the lateral, not longitudinal, stability of the airplane.

54. Longitudinal dynamic instability in an airplane can be identified by

A. bank oscillations becoming progressively steeper.

B. pitch oscillations becoming progressively steeper.

C. trilatitudinal roll oscillations becoming progressively steeper.

Answer (B) is correct. *(AFH Chap 3)*

DISCUSSION: Dynamic stability is the overall tendency that the airplane displays after its equilibrium is disturbed. Negative dynamic stability (dynamic instability) is a property that causes oscillations set up by a statically stable airplane to become progressively greater. Longitudinal instability refers to pitch oscillations.

Answer (A) is incorrect. Roll (bank) oscillations refer to lateral, not longitudinal, stability. Answer (C) is incorrect. Roll (bank) oscillations refer to lateral, not longitudinal, stability.

55. If the airplane attitude remains in a new position after the elevator control is pressed forward and released, the airplane displays

A. neutral longitudinal static stability.

B. positive longitudinal static stability.

C. neutral longitudinal dynamic stability.

Answer (A) is correct. *(AFH Chap 3)*

DISCUSSION: When an airplane's attitude is momentarily displaced and it remains at its new attitude, it is said to have neutral longitudinal static stability. Longitudinal stability is the quality that makes an airplane stable about its lateral axis (pitch).

Answer (B) is incorrect. Positive longitudinal static stability is the initial tendency of the airplane to return to its original attitude after the elevator control is pressed forward and released. Answer (C) is incorrect. The longitudinal dynamic stability is the overall, not initial, tendency that the airplane displays after the elevator control is pressed forward and released. Neutral dynamic stability is indicated if the airplane attempts to return to its original state of equilibrium, but the pitch oscillations neither increase nor decrease in magnitude in time.

56. If the airplane attitude initially tends to return to its original position after the elevator control is pressed forward and released, the airplane displays

A. positive dynamic stability.

B. positive static stability.

C. neutral dynamic stability.

Answer (B) is correct. *(AFH Chap 3)*

DISCUSSION: When an airplane's elevator control is pressed forward and released and its attitude initially tends to return to its original position, the airplane displays positive static stability.

Answer (A) is incorrect. Dynamic stability is the overall, not initial, tendency the airplane displays after its equilibrium is disturbed. Positive dynamic stability means the airplane will return to its original position directly, or through a series of decreasing pitch oscillations in time. Answer (C) is incorrect. Dynamic stability is the overall, not initial, tendency the airplane displays after its equilibrium is disturbed. Neutral dynamic stability means the airplane attempts to return to its original position, but the pitch oscillations neither increase nor decrease in magnitude in time.

57. If an airplane is loaded to the rear of its CG range, it will tend to be unstable about its

A. vertical axis.

B. lateral axis.

C. longitudinal axis.

Answer (B) is correct. *(AFH Chap 3)*

DISCUSSION: As the CG is moved rearward, it may move behind the center of lift, in which case the airplane is said to have negative stability about its lateral axis. Recall that the CG should be forward of the center of lift and that the tail surface is designed to have negative lift.

Answer (A) is incorrect. The CG position has relatively little to do with the stability about the vertical axis. Answer (C) is incorrect. Stability about the longitudinal axis is not greatly affected by CG location. Remember that the airplane rolls about the longitudinal axis.

1.8 Turns

58. If airspeed is increased during a level turn, what action would be necessary to maintain altitude? The angle of attack

A. and angle of bank must be decreased.

B. must be increased or angle of bank decreased.

C. must be decreased or angle of bank increased.

Answer (C) is correct. *(AFH Chap 3)*

DISCUSSION: To compensate for the added lift that would result if the airspeed were increased during a turn, the angle of attack must be decreased, or the angle of bank increased, to maintain a constant altitude.

Answer (A) is incorrect. Either the angle of attack can be decreased or the angle of bank increased, not decreased, to maintain altitude as airspeed is increased in a turn. Answer (B) is incorrect. To maintain a constant altitude in a turn as the airspeed is decreased, not increased, the angle of attack must be increased or angle of bank decreased.

59. If a standard rate turn is maintained, how long would it take to turn 360°?

A. 1 minute.

B. 2 minutes.

C. 3 minutes.

Answer (B) is correct. *(AFH Chap 16)*

DISCUSSION: A standard rate turn is one during which the heading changes at a rate of 3°/sec. Thus, a 360° turn would take 2 min. (360° ÷ 3°/sec. = 120 sec., or 2 min.).

Answer (A) is incorrect. At standard rate, a 180°, not 360°, turn would take 1 minute. Answer (C) is incorrect. At standard rate, a 540°, not 360°, turn would take 3 minutes.

60. While holding the angle of bank constant in a level turn, if the rate of turn is varied the load factor would

A. remain constant regardless of air density and the resultant lift vector.

B. vary depending upon speed and air density provided the resultant lift vector varies proportionately.

C. vary depending upon the resultant lift vector.

Answer (A) is correct. *(PHAK Chap 4)*

DISCUSSION: For any given angle of bank, the rate of turn varies with the airspeed. For example, if the angle of bank is held constant and the airspeed is increased, the rate of turn will decrease and vice versa. Because of this, there is no change in centrifugal force while holding a constant angle of bank; thus, the load factor remains constant.

Answer (B) is incorrect. The rate of turn, not load factor, will vary depending on airspeed while holding a constant angle of bank. Answer (C) is incorrect. Load factor will vary depending on the resultant load, not lift, vector.

61. To increase the rate of turn and at the same time decrease the radius, a pilot should

A. maintain the bank and decrease airspeed.

B. increase the bank and increase airspeed.

C. increase the bank and decrease airspeed.

Answer (C) is correct. *(AFH Chap 3)*

DISCUSSION: At slower airspeeds, an airplane can make a turn in less distance (smaller radius) and at a faster rate. Thus, to decrease the radius and increase the rate, a pilot should steepen the bank and decrease airspeed.

Answer (A) is incorrect. At a given angle of bank, a decrease in airspeed will increase the rate of turn and decrease the radius, but the effect will be less than that of steepening the bank and decreasing airspeed. Answer (B) is incorrect. You decrease, not increase, airspeed to decrease the turn radius.

62. Which is correct with respect to rate and radius of turn for an airplane flown in a coordinated turn at a constant altitude?

A. For a specific angle of bank and airspeed, the rate and radius of turn will not vary.

B. To maintain a steady rate of turn, the angle of bank must be increased as the airspeed is decreased.

C. The faster the true airspeed, the faster the rate and larger the radius of turn regardless of the angle of bank.

Answer (A) is correct. *(AFH Chap 3)*

DISCUSSION: At a constant altitude in a coordinated turn, each airspeed has a specific, unvarying rate and radius of turn for each angle of bank.

Answer (B) is incorrect. You must decrease, not increase, the angle of bank when the airspeed is decreased if you are to maintain a steady rate of turn. Answer (C) is incorrect. The faster the airspeed, the slower, not faster, the rate of turn at a constant angle of bank.

63. While maintaining a constant angle of bank and altitude in a coordinated turn, an increase in airspeed will

A. decrease the rate of turn resulting in a decreased load factor.

B. decrease the rate of turn resulting in no change in load factor.

C. increase the rate of turn resulting in no change in load factor.

Answer (B) is correct. *(AFH Chap 3)*

DISCUSSION: When in a constant bank in a coordinated turn, an increase in airspeed will decrease the rate of turn. Because the bank is held constant, there will be no change in load factor.

Answer (A) is incorrect. There is no change in load factor in a coordinated turn if the angle of bank is held constant. Answer (C) is incorrect. The rate of turn decreases, not increases, with an increase in airspeed, and since the angle of bank is held constant, the load factor remains constant, not decreases.

64. Why is it necessary to increase back elevator pressure to maintain altitude during a turn? To compensate for the

A. loss of the vertical component of lift.

B. loss of the horizontal component of lift and the increase in centrifugal force.

C. rudder deflection and slight opposite aileron throughout the turn.

Answer (A) is correct. *(AFH Chap 6)*

DISCUSSION: As you enter a turn, lift is divided into horizontal and vertical components. This division reduces the amount of vertical lift, which is opposing weight, and thus the airplane loses altitude unless additional lift is created by increasing back elevator pressure to increase the angle of attack and the vertical component of lift.

Answer (B) is incorrect. When the horizontal component of lift is less than centrifugal force, the airplane is in a skidding turn, which is corrected by increasing bank or decreasing the rate of turn (or a combination of both). Answer (C) is incorrect. Slight opposite aileron pressure may be needed in a steep bank to overcome the airplane's overbanking tendency.

65. To maintain altitude during a turn, the angle of attack must be increased to compensate for the decrease in the

A. forces opposing the resultant component of drag.

B. vertical component of lift.

C. horizontal component of lift.

Answer (B) is correct. *(AFH Chap 6)*

DISCUSSION: As you enter a turn, lift is divided into horizontal and vertical components. This division reduces the amount of vertical lift, which is opposing weight, and thus the airplane loses altitude unless additional lift is created by increasing back elevator pressure to increase the angle of attack and the vertical component of lift.

Answer (A) is incorrect. The resultant component of drag is a nonsense term. Answer (C) is incorrect. As the horizontal component of lift decreases, the vertical component increases; thus, the angle of attack will need to be decreased, not increased.

1.9 Load Factor

66. The ratio between the total airload imposed on the wing and the gross weight of an aircraft in flight is known as

A. load factor and directly affects stall speed.

B. aspect load and directly affects stall speed.

C. load factor and has no relation with stall speed.

Answer (A) is correct. *(PHAK Chap 4)*

DISCUSSION: A load factor is the ratio of the total airload acting on the airplane to the gross weight of the airplane. For example, if the airload imposed on the wing is twice the actual weight of the airplane, the load factor is said to be 2 Gs, and the stall speed increases.

Answer (B) is incorrect. The ratio between the total airload imposed on the wing and the gross weight of an airplane is known as a load factor, not aspect load. Answer (C) is incorrect. The airplane's stalling speed increases in proportion to the square root of the load factor.

67. Load factor is the lift generated by the wings of an aircraft at any given time

A. divided by the total weight of the aircraft.

B. multiplied by the total weight of the aircraft.

C. divided by the basic empty weight of the aircraft.

Answer (A) is correct. *(PHAK Chap 4)*

DISCUSSION: Since the load factor is the ratio between the total airload imposed on the wing and the gross weight of the airplane, the load factor is the lift generated by the wings divided by the total weight of the airplane. For example, an airplane weighing 2,000 lb. and having a load factor of 2.0 would require 4,000 lb. of lift by the wings.

Answer (B) is incorrect. Load factor times airplane weight equals required lift. Answer (C) is incorrect. The total weight of the airplane, not the basic empty weight, is relevant.

68. For a given angle of bank, in any airplane, the load factor imposed in a coordinated constant-altitude turn

A. is constant and the stall speed increases.

B. varies with the rate of turn.

C. is constant and the stall speed decreases.

Answer (A) is correct. *(PHAK Chap 4)*

DISCUSSION: In any airplane at any airspeed, if a constant altitude is maintained during the turn, the load factor for a given degree of bank is the same, which is the resultant of weight and centrifugal force. Because of the increased load factor in a turn, the stall speed is also increased in proportion to the square root of the load factor.

Answer (B) is incorrect. The load factor is not affected by changes in the rate of turn (which is determined by airspeed when at a constant bank). Answer (C) is incorrect. When the load factor is increased as a turn is entered, the stall speed is also increased in proportion to the square root of the load factor.

69. (Refer to Figure 4 below.) What increase in load factor would take place if the angle of bank were increased from 60° to 80°?

A. 3 G's.

B. 3.5 G's.

C. 4 G's.

Answer (C) is correct. *(AFH Chap 3)*

DISCUSSION: In Fig. 4, the relationship between bank angle degrees on the horizontal axis is related to both load factor or "G" units on the vertical scale and percent increase in stall speed on the vertical axis. There are two curves on the graph. Each curve relates to the vertical scale or the vertical axis. At a 60° bank, find 60° on the horizontal axis, go up to the load factor curve, and then horizontally left to the far left vertical scale to determine approximately 2 Gs. At 80° there are approximately 6 Gs. Thus, the increase in load factor is 4 Gs (6 – 2) when the angle of bank is increased from 60° to 80°.

Answer (A) is incorrect. An additional 3 Gs would result from an increase of bank from 60° to 77°. Answer (B) is incorrect. An additional 3.5 Gs would result from an increase of bank from 60° to 78°.

70. (Refer to Figure 4 below.) What is the stall speed of an airplane under a load factor of 2.5 G's if the unaccelerated stall speed is 60 knots?

A. 62 knots.

B. 84 knots.

C. 96 knots.

Answer (C) is correct. *(AFH Chap 3)*

DISCUSSION: Use Fig. 4 to determine the percentage increase in stall speed under a load factor of 2.5 Gs. First, find 2.5 Gs on the far left vertical scale and move horizontally to the right to the load factor curve, which intersects at about a 68° bank. Then move vertically up from that point to the intersection of the stall speed increase curve. Next, move left horizontally to the vertical axis to determine a 60% increase in stall speed. If the unaccelerated stall speed is 60 kt., the accelerated stall speed is 96 kt. (60 kt. × .60 = 36, and 60 + 36 = 96).

Answer (A) is incorrect. Sixty-two knots is a 1% increase, not a 60% increase, in stall speed. Answer (B) is incorrect. Eighty-four knots is a 40% increase, not a 60% increase, in stall speed.

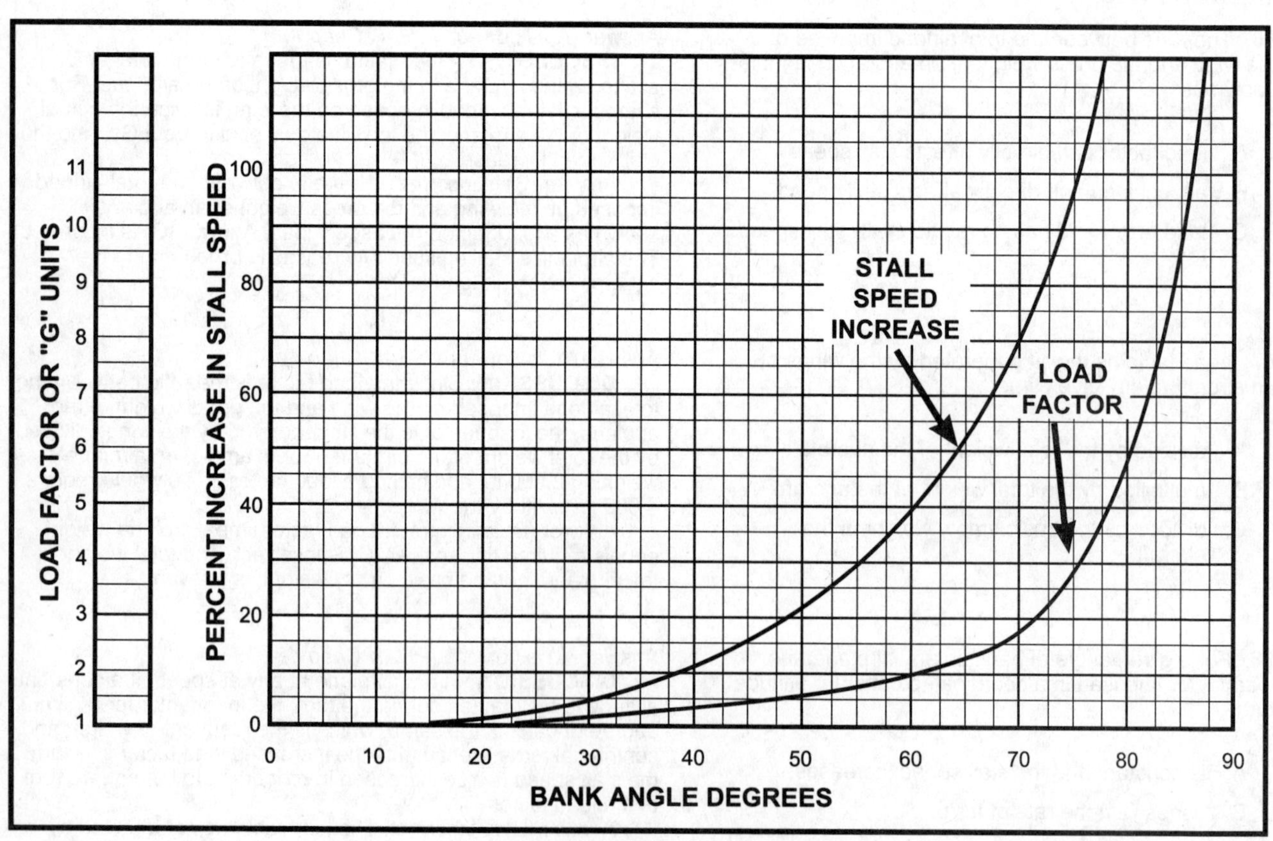

Figure 4. – Stall Speed/Load Factor.

71. (Refer to Figure 4 on page 40.) What is the stall speed of an airplane under a load factor of 2 G's if the unaccelerated stall speed is 60 knots?

A. 66 knots.

B. 74 knots.

C. 84 knots.

Answer (C) is correct. *(AFH Chap 3)*

DISCUSSION: Use Fig. 4 to determine the percentage increase in stall speed under a load factor of 2 Gs. First, find 2 Gs on the far left vertical scale and move horizontally to the right to the load factor curve, which intersects at about a 60° bank. Then move vertically up from that point to the intersection of the stall speed increase curve. Next move left horizontally to the vertical axis to determine a 40% increase in stall speed. If the unaccelerated stall speed is 60 kt., the accelerated stall speed is 84 kt. (60 kt. × 140%).

Answer (A) is incorrect. This is a 10%, not 40%, increase in stall speed. Answer (B) is incorrect. This is a 23%, not 40%, increase in stall speed.

72. Airplane wing loading during a level coordinated turn in smooth air depends upon the

A. rate of turn.

B. angle of bank.

C. true airspeed.

Answer (B) is correct. *(PHAK Chap 4)*

DISCUSSION: The load factor for a given airplane during a level coordinated turn is determined solely by the angle of bank.

Answer (A) is incorrect. In a coordinated turn, rate of turn has no impact on load factor. Answer (C) is incorrect. In a coordinated turn, true airspeed has no impact on wing loading.

73. The load factor for an airplane in a 60° banked turn is

A. 1.7 Gs.

B. 2 Gs.

C. 3 Gs.

Answer (B) is correct. *(PHAK Chap 4)*

DISCUSSION: Any airplane in a 60° banked turn has a load factor of 2 Gs.

Answer (A) is incorrect. An airplane in a 60° banked turn has a load factor of 2 Gs, not 1.7 Gs. Answer (C) is incorrect. An airplane in a 60° banked turn has a load factor of 2 Gs, not 3 Gs.

74. A load factor of 1.2 means the total load on an aircraft's structure is 1.2 times its

A. gross weight.

B. load limit.

C. gust factor.

Answer (A) is correct. *(PHAK Chap 4)*

DISCUSSION: Load factor is the ratio of an airplane's gross weight to the maximum load the airframe can support measured in Gs. Any time the aircraft's flight path is disrupted or altered, a load factor is placed on the airframe.

Answer (B) is incorrect. Load limit is the maximum load factor the airframe can withstand. Exceeding the load limit will result in severe airframe damage and structural failure. Answer (C) is incorrect. A gust factor is applied to the airplane's approach speed when landing in windy conditions.

75. If an aircraft with a gross weight of 2,000 pounds was subjected to a 60° constant-altitude bank, the total load would be

A. 3,000 pounds.

B. 4,000 pounds.

C. 12,000 pounds.

Answer (B) is correct. *(PHAK Chap 4)*

DISCUSSION: In a constant-altitude, 60° bank turn, the wings are loaded at 2 Gs. Therefore, the total load of a 2,000-lb. airplane is 4,000 lb. (2,000 × 2).

Answer (A) is incorrect. This would be the total load of a 1,500-lb. airplane in a 60° bank. Answer (C) is incorrect. This would be the total load of a 6,000-lb. airplane in a 60° bank.

76. If the airspeed is increased from 90 knots to 135 knots during a level 60° banked turn, the load factor will

A. increase as well as the stall speed.

B. decrease and the stall speed will increase.

C. remain the same but the radius of turn will increase.

Answer (C) is correct. *(AFH Chap 3)*

DISCUSSION: Since the only determinant of load factor in level, coordinated turns is the amount of bank, a change in airspeed does not change the load factor. When airspeed is increased, however, the rate of turn decreases and the radius of turn increases.

Answer (A) is incorrect. The load factor and stall speed will remain the same for a constant-altitude, constant-banked turn. Answer (B) is incorrect. The load factor and stall speed will remain the same for a constant-altitude, constant-banked turn.

77. If the airspeed is decreased from 98 knots to 85 knots during a coordinated level 45° banked turn, the load factor will

A. remain the same, but the radius of turn will decrease.

B. decrease, and the rate of turn will decrease.

C. remain the same, but the radius of turn will increase.

Answer (A) is correct. *(AFH Chap 3)*

DISCUSSION: Since the only determinant of load factor in level, coordinated turns is the amount of bank, a change in airspeed does not change the load factor. When airspeed is decreased, however, the rate of turn increases and the radius of turn decreases.

Answer (B) is incorrect. The load factor will remain the same for a constant-altitude, constant-banked turn, and the rate of turn will actually increase, not decrease. The radius of turn, however, will decrease. Answer (C) is incorrect. While the load factor will remain the same for a constant-altitude, constant-banked turn, the radius of turn will actually decrease, not increase.

78. If the airspeed is increased from 89 knots to 98 knots during a coordinated level 45° banked turn, the load factor will

A. remain the same, but the radius of turn will increase.

B. decrease, and the rate of turn will decrease.

C. increase, but the rate of turn will decrease.

Answer (A) is correct. *(AFH Chap 3)*

DISCUSSION: Since the only determinant of load factor in level, coordinated turns is the amount of bank, a change in airspeed does not change the load factor. When airspeed is increased, however, the rate of turn decreases and the radius of turn increases.

Answer (B) is incorrect. The load factor will remain the same for a constant-altitude, constant-banked turn, and the rate of turn will decrease. The radius of turn, however, will increase. Answer (C) is incorrect. The load factor will remain the same for a constant-altitude, constant-banked turn, and the rate of turn decreases. However, the radius of turn will increase.

79. Baggage weighing 90 pounds is placed in a normal category airplane's baggage compartment which is placarded at 100 pounds. If this airplane is subjected to a positive load factor of 3.5 Gs, the total load of the baggage would be

A. 315 pounds and would be excessive.

B. 315 pounds and would not be excessive.

C. 350 pounds and would not be excessive.

Answer (B) is correct. *(AFH Chap 3)*

DISCUSSION: Since 90 lb. is less than the amount of placarded weight (100 lb.), there is no problem with the weight. The positive load factor of 3.5 Gs is within the normal operational limit of 3.8 Gs of normal category airplanes. When 100 lb. was set as a baggage limit in this particular case, it was understood that it may be subjected to 3.8 Gs, i.e., 380 pounds. The baggage weight of 90 lb. is multiplied by 3.5 Gs to get a load of 315 pounds.

Answer (A) is incorrect. The baggage weight is not excessive. Load factor does not need to be figured in to determine maximum weight for any compartment. Answer (C) is incorrect. This would be the total load of 100 lb. of baggage at 3.5 Gs.

80. Which factor below is the best indication of positive or negative Gs in an aircraft?

A. Change in the amount of pressure by the pilot needed on the controls.

B. Change in how heavy or light you feel in your seat.

C. Change in control-surface effectiveness.

Answer (B) is correct. *(PHAK Chap 4)*

DISCUSSION: Positive or negative load factor is mostly easily observed by considering how heavy or light you feel in the seat. This effect is one of the primary considerations in the design of the structure for all airplanes.

Answer (A) is incorrect. Pilot pressure on the flight controls can be affected by speed and/or load factor. Answer (C) is incorrect. Control surface effectiveness can be affected by speed and/or load factor.

81. Which of the following would best indicate to the pilot that the load factor placed on the airframe has been increased?

A. An increase in the sensation of being pushed into the seat.

B. An increase in airspeed.

C. More effort is required to operate the controls.

Answer (A) is correct. *(PHAK Chap 4)*

DISCUSSION: Load factor can be judged by noting the seat pressure. Increases in load factor ("pulling Gs") result in increased pressure pushing you into the seat.

Answer (B) is incorrect. An increase in airspeed is not an indication of an increased load factor. In fact, airspeed often decreases with increases in load factor in balanced flight. Answer (C) is incorrect. The feedback provided by the flight control system will vary by aircraft type and the design of the flight control system. Some flight control systems are fly-by-wire, hydraulic, or conventional cables and pulleys. Because of these factors, the pressure applied to the controls by the pilot is not an accurate method for judging load factor.

1.10 Transonic and Supersonic Flight

82. The ratio of an airplane's true airspeed to the speed of sound in the same atmospheric conditions is

A. equivalent airspeed.

B. transonic airflow.

C. mach number.

Answer (C) is correct. *(PHAK Chap 4)*

DISCUSSION: Mach number is the ratio of an airplane's true airspeed to the speed of sound in the same atmospheric conditions. The speed of sound varies with a change of altitude and temperature. At sea level with a standard temperature of 15°C, the speed of sound is 661 knots. At 40,000 with a temperature of -55°C, the speed of sound is 574 knots.

Answer (A) is incorrect. Equivalent airspeed is the indicated airspeed corrected for position error, installation error, and adiabatic compressibility for a particular altitude. Answer (B) is incorrect. Airplanes operating between .75 and 1.20 mach experience transonic airflow over the wings and airframe. The shock wave created by transonic airflow over the wings often alters the center of pressure, resulting in a change to the airplane's pitch attitude.

83. Transonic airflow typically occurs in airplane speed regimes between Mach

A. 0.75 and 0.95.

B. 0.95 and 1.01.

C. 0.75 and 1.20.

Answer (C) is correct. *(AFNA Chap 3)*

DISCUSSION: Since there is the possibility of having both subsonic and supersonic flows existing on the aircraft, it is convenient to define certain regimes of flight. Transonic airflow is defined between Mach 0.75 and 1.20.

Answer (A) is incorrect. Transonic airflow is defined between Mach 0.75 and 1.20. Answer (B) is incorrect. Transonic airflow is defined between Mach 0.75 and 1.20.

84. Accelerating past critical Mach may result in the onset of compressibility effects such as

A. High speed stalls.

B. P factor.

C. Control difficulties.

Answer (C) is correct. *(AFNA Chap 3)*

DISCUSSION: The critical Mach number is the highest flight speed possible without supersonic flow. As critical Mach is exceeded, an area of supersonic airflow is created and a normal shockwave forms as the boundary between the supersonic flow and the subsonic flow on the aft portion of the airfoil surface. Accelerating past critical Mach is associated with trim and stability changes and a decrease in control surface effectiveness.

Answer (A) is incorrect. High-speed stalls do not necessarily result from accelerating past critical Mach. Answer (B) is incorrect. P-factor affects propeller-driven airplanes, which are not designed for Mach speeds.

85. Acceleration past critical Mach speed may cause compressibility issues such as

A. asymmetric loading.

B. propeller slippage.

C. drag increases.

Answer (C) is correct. *(AFNA Chap 3)*

DISCUSSION: The critical Mach number is the highest flight speed possible without supersonic flow. Accelerating past critical Mach is associated with a large increase in drag due to the initial formation of a weak shockwave on the wing, creating a barrier to the oncoming airflow.

Answer (A) is incorrect. Asymmetrical loading is not associated with flight near the critical Mach speed. Rather, it is most commonly referred to as P-factor – the unbalanced production of thrust created by the blades of a propeller. Answer (B) is incorrect. Propeller slippage is not associated with flight near the critical Mach speed. Rather, it has to do with the loss in efficiency inherent in the operation of any propeller-driven aircraft, particularly with fixed-pitch propellers.

END OF STUDY UNIT

STUDY UNIT TWO
AIRPLANE INSTRUMENTS, ENGINES, AND SYSTEMS

(5 pages of outline)

This study unit contains outlines of major concepts tested; sample test questions and answers regarding airplane instruments, engines, and systems; and an explanation of each answer. The table of contents above lists each subunit within this study unit, the number of questions pertaining to that particular subunit, and the pages on which the outlines and questions begin, respectively.

Recall that the **sole purpose** of this book is to expedite your passing of the FAA pilot knowledge test for the commercial pilot certificate. Accordingly, all extraneous material (i.e., topics or regulations not directly tested on the FAA pilot knowledge test) is omitted, even though much more knowledge is necessary to become a proficient commercial pilot. This additional material is presented in *Pilot Handbook* and *Commercial Pilot Flight Maneuvers and Practical Test Prep*, available from Gleim Publications, Inc. See the product listing at the back of the book and order online at www.gleim.com.

2.1 MAGNETIC COMPASS

1. The difference between direction indicated by a magnetic compass not installed in an airplane and one installed in an airplane is called compass deviation.
   a. Magnetic fields produced by metals and electrical accessories in an airplane disturb the compass needle.
   b. The compass deviation usually varies for different headings of the same aircraft.

2.2 AIRSPEED INDICATOR

1. Airspeed indicators have several color-coded markings.
   a. The white arc is the flap operating range.
      1) The lower limit is the power-off stalling speed or the minimum steady flight speed with wing flaps and landing gear in the landing position (V_{S0}).
      2) The upper limit is the maximum flap extended speed (V_{FE}).
   b. The green arc is the normal operating range.
      1) The lower limit is the power-off stalling speed with the wing flaps up and landing gear retracted (V_{S1}).
      2) The upper limit is the maximum structural cruising speed for normal operation (V_{NO}).

c. The yellow arc is the range of airspeed that is safe in smooth air only.
   1) It is known as the caution range.
d. The red line is the speed that should never be exceeded (V_{NE}).
   1) Design limit load factors could be exceeded with airspeeds in excess of V_{NE} from a variety of phenomena.

2. The most important airspeed limitation that is **not** color-coded is the maneuvering speed (V_A).
   a. The maneuvering speed is the maximum speed at which abrupt full deflection of aircraft controls can be made without causing structural damage.
   b. It is the maximum speed for flight in turbulent air.
3. The maximum landing gear extended speed (V_{LE}) is not color-coded.
   a. It is usually placarded and is included in the airplane's flight manual.
4. Types of Airspeed
   a. Indicated airspeed (IAS) is read directly off the airspeed indicator.
   b. Calibrated airspeed (CAS) is IAS corrected for installation and instrument error.
   c. True airspeed (TAS) is CAS corrected for pressure altitude and nonstandard temperature.
5. The V-G diagram (velocity versus "G" loads) shows the flight operating strength of an airplane.
   a. In the diagram on the following page, load factor is on the vertical axis with airspeed on the horizontal axis.
   b. The lines of maximum lift capability (dashed lines) are the first items of importance on the V-G diagram.
      1) The subject airplane in the diagram on the following page is capable of developing no more than one positive "G" at 64 MPH, which is the wings-level stall speed of the airplane.
      2) The maximum load factor increases dramatically with airspeed. The maximum positive lift capability of this airplane is 2 "G" at 96 MPH, 3 "G" at 116 MPH, 3.8 "G" at 126 MPH, etc.
         a) These are the "coordinates" of points on the curved line up to point C.
      3) Any load factor above this dashed line is unavailable aerodynamically. That is, the subject airplane cannot fly above the line of maximum lift capability (it will stall).
   c. Point C is the intersection of the positive limit load factor (line CDE) and the line of maximum positive lift capability (dashed line up to point C).
      1) The airspeed at this point is the minimum airspeed at which the limit load can be developed aerodynamically.
      2) Any airspeed greater than point C provides a positive lift capability sufficient to damage the airplane.
         a) Any airspeed less than point C does **not** provide positive lift capability sufficient to cause damage from excessive flight loads.
      3) The usual term given to the speed at point C is the design maneuvering speed (V_A).

d. The limit airspeed V_{NE} is a design reference point for the airplane. The subject airplane is limited to 196 MPH (line EF).

   1) If flight is attempted beyond the limit airspeed, structural damage or structural failure may result from a variety of phenomena.

e. Thus, the airplane in flight is limited to a regime of airspeeds and Gs that do not exceed

   1) The limit (or red-line) speed (line EF)
   2) Normal stall speed (line AJ)
   3) The positive and negative limit load factors (lines CDE and IHG)
   4) The maximum lift capability (dashed lines up to C, down to I)

f. A caution range is indicated between points D, E, F, and G. Within this range, certain factors must be considered to maintain flight in the envelope.

   1) Line DG represents the maximum structural cruising speed (V_{NO}).

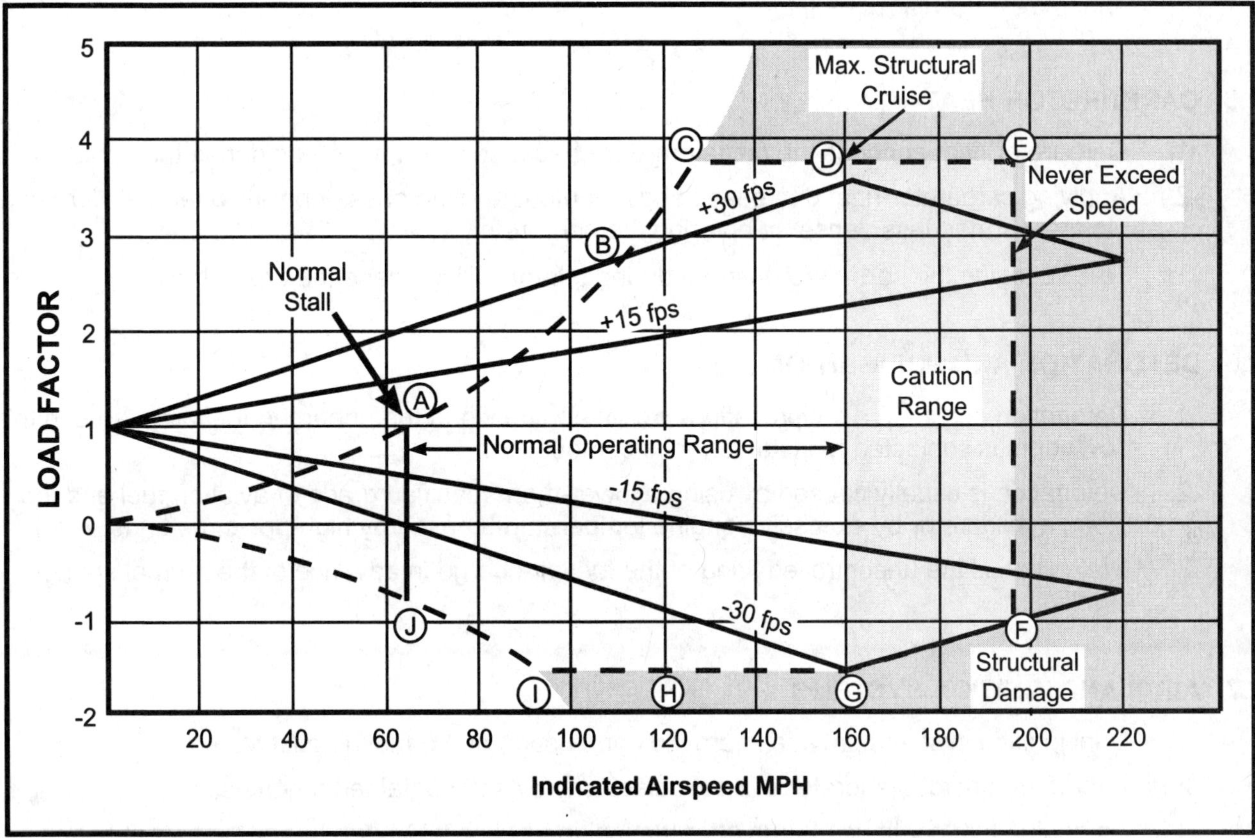

2.3 TURN COORDINATOR/TURN-AND-SLIP INDICATOR

1. The turn coordinator and the turn-and-slip indicator are usually electric-driven instruments. Each instrument has an inclinometer (i.e., ball).

   a. The turn coordinator indicates roll rate, rate of turn, and coordination.
   b. The turn-and-slip indicator indicates rate of turn and coordination.

2. The advantage of having an electric turn coordinator (or turn-and-slip indicator) is to provide bank information in case the vacuum-driven attitude indicator and heading indicator fail.

2.4 FUEL/AIR MIXTURE

1. As altitude increases, the density (weight) of air entering the carburetor decreases.
   a. If no adjustment is made, the amount of fuel remains constant and the fuel/air ratio (mixture) becomes excessively rich.
   b. Thus, the pilot adjusts the fuel flow with the mixture control to maintain the proper fuel/air ratio at all altitudes.
2. The fuel/air ratio, by definition, is the ratio between the weight of fuel and the weight of air entering the cylinder.
   a. The best power mixture refers to the fuel/air ratio that will provide the most power at any given power setting.
3. Spark plug fouling results from operating at high altitudes with an excessively rich mixture due to the below-normal temperatures in the combustion chambers.
4. In gas turbine (as well as reciprocating) engines, as temperature increases and air density decreases, thrust decreases.

2.5 CARBURETOR HEAT

1. Carburetor heat enriches the fuel/air mixture because warm air is less dense than cold air.
2. Applying carburetor heat decreases engine output and increases operating temperature due to the warmer, less dense air entering the carburetor.
   a. Leaving the carburetor heat on during takeoff will increase the ground roll.

2.6 DETONATION AND PREIGNITION

1. Detonation occurs in a reciprocating aircraft engine when the unburned fuel/air charge in the cylinders is subjected to instantaneous combustion.
2. Detonation is usually caused by using a lower-than-specified grade of aviation fuel and too lean a mixture or by excessive engine temperature caused by high-power settings.
3. Preignition is the uncontrolled firing of the fuel/air charge in advance of the normal spark ignition.

2.7 AIRPLANE IGNITION SYSTEMS

1. Dual ignition systems provide improved combustion of the fuel/air mixture.
2. Aircraft magnetos generate their own electricity by self-contained magnets.
3. An engine that continues to run after the ignition switch has been turned off probably has a broken or disconnected ground wire between the magneto and the ignition switch.
   a. Thus, a potentially dangerous situation exists because the engine could accidentally start if the propeller is moved with fuel in the cylinder.
4. A good practice before shutdown is to idle the engine and momentarily turn the ignition off.
5. Rapid opening and closing of the throttle may cause detuning of engine crankshaft counterweights (throwing the crankshaft out of balance).

2.8 ENGINE COOLING

1. Aircraft engines are largely cooled by the flow of oil through the lubrication system.
2. An excessively low oil level will prevent the oil from cooling adequately and result in an abnormally high engine oil temperature.
3. You should inspect aircraft exhaust manifold-type heating systems on a regular basis to minimize the possibility of cracks or other problems that would permit exhaust gases to leak into the cockpit.

2.9 AIRPLANE PROPELLERS

1. Propeller efficiency is the ratio of thrust horsepower to brake horsepower.
2. A fixed-pitch propeller can be most efficient only at a specified combination of airspeed and RPM.
3. The propeller's geometric pitch varies along the propeller blade because the propeller tip goes through the air faster than the section of propeller near the hub.
   a. This pitch variation permits a relatively constant angle of attack along the blade's length when in cruising flight.
4. A constant-speed (controllable-pitch) propeller adjusts the pitch angle of the propeller blade so that the engine is maintained at a selected RPM.
5. For takeoff, to develop maximum power and thrust, you should use a small angle of attack and high RPM on a controllable-pitch (constant-speed) propeller.
6. To establish climb power after takeoff in an airplane equipped with a constant-speed propeller, you should first decrease manifold pressure and then decrease RPM. When the propeller control is moved to reduce the RPM, the propeller blade angle increases.
   a. When increasing power, increase RPM first; then increase manifold pressure to avoid placing undue stress on the engine.
7. Spiraling slipstream describes the propeller blade forcing air rearward in a spiraling clockwise direction around the fuselage when the propeller rotates through the air in a clockwise direction as viewed from the rear.
   a. As a result, the airplane yaws left around the vertical axis.

QUESTIONS AND ANSWER EXPLANATIONS: All of the commercial pilot knowledge test questions chosen by the FAA for release as well as additional questions selected by Gleim relating to the material in the previous outlines are reproduced on the following pages. These questions have been organized into the same subunits as the outlines. To the immediate right of each question are the correct answer and answer explanation. You should cover these answers and answer explanations while responding to the questions. Refer to the general discussion in the Introduction on how to take the FAA knowledge test.

Remember that the questions from the FAA knowledge test bank have been reordered by topic and organized into a meaningful sequence. Also, the first line of the answer explanation gives the citation of the authoritative source for the answer.

QUESTIONS

2.1 Magnetic Compass

1. Which statement is true about magnetic deviation of a compass? Deviation

A. varies over time as the agonic line shifts.

B. varies for different headings of the same aircraft.

C. is the same for all aircraft in the same locality.

Answer (B) is correct. *(PHAK Chap 7)*

DISCUSSION: The difference between the direction indicated by a compass not installed in an airplane and one installed in an airplane is called compass deviation. Magnetic fields produced by the metal and electrical accessories in the airplane disturb the compass needle and produce errors. The amount of deviation varies with different headings.

Answer (A) is incorrect. The position of the agonic line determines magnetic variation, not compass deviation. Answer (C) is incorrect. Compass deviation varies from aircraft to aircraft.

2.2 Airspeed Indicator

2. Maximum structural cruising speed is the maximum speed at which an airplane can be operated during

A. abrupt maneuvers.

B. normal operations.

C. flight in smooth air.

Answer (B) is correct. *(PHAK Chap 7)*

DISCUSSION: The maximum structural cruising speed (V_{NO}) is the upper limit of the green arc on the airspeed indicator. It is the maximum speed for normal operations.

Answer (A) is incorrect. V_A is the design maneuvering speed, which is the rough air penetration speed and maximum speed for abrupt maneuvers. Answer (C) is incorrect. The yellow arc (V_{NO} to V_{NE}) is the caution range where flight is allowed only in smooth air.

3. Why should flight speeds above V_{NE} be avoided?

A. Excessive induced drag will result in structural failure.

B. Design limit load factors may be exceeded, if gusts are encountered.

C. Control effectiveness is so impaired that the aircraft becomes uncontrollable.

Answer (B) is correct. *(PHAK Chap 7)*

DISCUSSION: At speeds above V_{NE}, the design limit load factors for the airplane may be exceeded if gusts are encountered. Thus, this airspeed should never be exceeded, even in smooth air.

Answer (A) is incorrect. Induced drag decreases, not increases, as airspeed increases. Answer (C) is incorrect. Control effectiveness increases, not decreases, as airspeed increases.

4. (Refer to Figure 5 on page 51.) The horizontal dashed line from point C to point E represents the

A. ultimate load factor.

B. positive limit load factor.

C. airspeed range for normal operations.

Answer (B) is correct. *(AFH Chap 3)*

DISCUSSION: In Fig. 5, the line from point C to point E represents the positive limit load factor, i.e., the greatest positive load that may be placed on the aircraft without risk of structural damage.

Answer (A) is incorrect. Ultimate load factor is the limit load factor multiplied by 1.5 as a safety measure. While structural damage may occur at the limit load factor, structural failure may occur at the ultimate load factor. Answer (C) is incorrect. The airspeed range for normal operations, the green arc on the airspeed indicator, is the horizontal distance from the vertical line from point A to point J to the vertical line from point D to point G.

5. (Refer to Figure 5 on page 51.) The vertical line from point E to point F is represented on the airspeed indicator by the

A. upper limit of the yellow arc.

B. upper limit of the green arc.

C. blue radial line.

Answer (A) is correct. *(AFH Chap 3)*

DISCUSSION: In Fig. 5, the line from point E to point F is labeled as the never-exceed speed (V_{NE}). This speed is represented on the airspeed indicator by the upper limit of the yellow arc (the red radial line).

Answer (B) is incorrect. The upper limit of the green arc represents the maximum structural cruising speed (V_{NO}), which is the line from point D to point G, not E to F. Answer (C) is incorrect. The blue radial line represents the single-engine best rate-of-climb speed (V_{YSE}) in a multi-engine airplane. V_{YSE} is not shown on the V-G diagram.

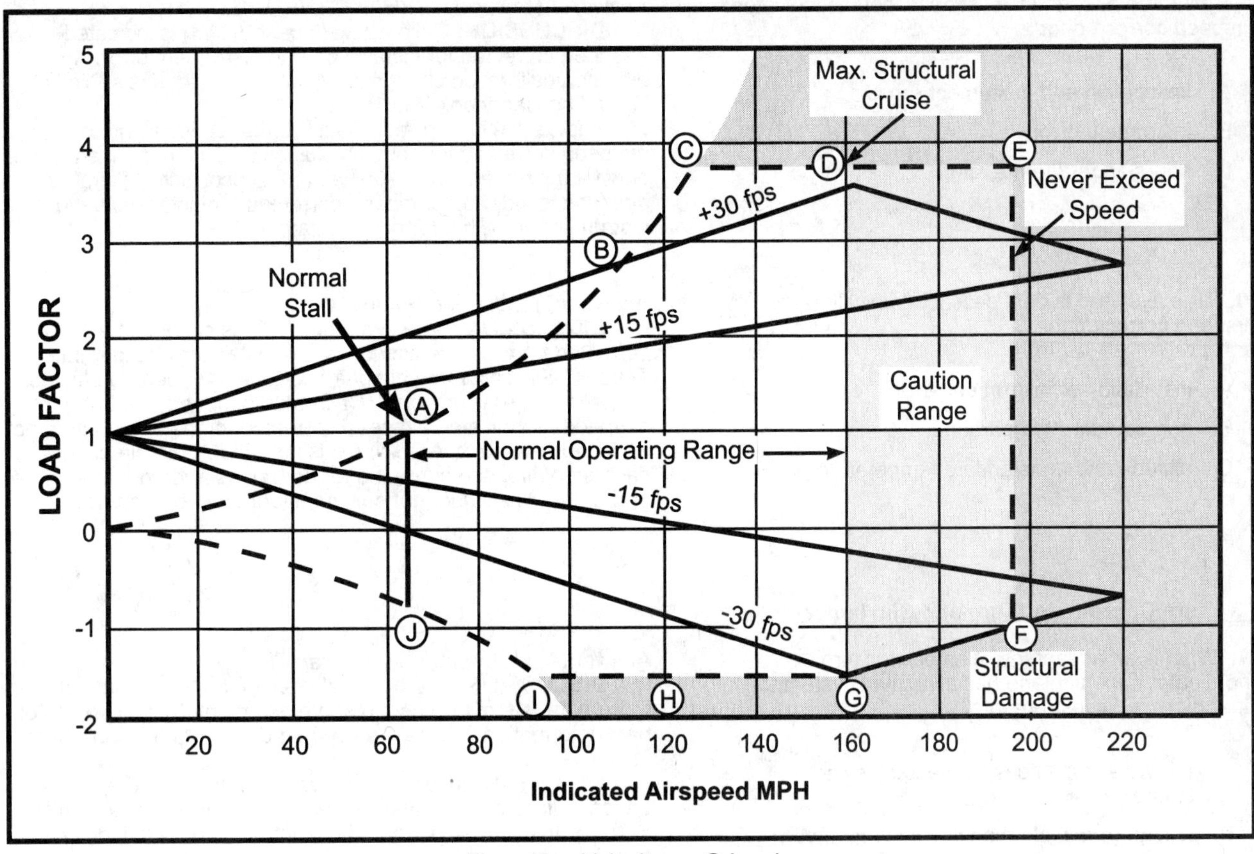

Figure 5. – Velocity vs. G-Loads.

6. (Refer to Figure 5 above.) The vertical line from point D to point G is represented on the airspeed indicator by the maximum speed limit of the

A. green arc.

B. yellow arc.

C. white arc.

Answer (A) is correct. *(AFH Chap 3)*

DISCUSSION: In Fig. 5, the line from point D to point G is labeled as the maximum structural cruising speed (V_{NO}). This speed is represented on the airspeed indicator by the upper limit of the green arc.

Answer (B) is incorrect. The upper limit of the yellow arc represents the never-exceed speed (V_{NE}), which is the line from point E to point F, not D to G. Answer (C) is incorrect. The upper limit of the white arc is the maximum flap extended speed (V_{FE}), which is not shown on the V-G diagram.

7. (Refer to Figure 5 above.) Point C references

A. V_{NE}

B. V_{NO}

C. V_A

Answer (C) is correct. *(PHAK Chap 4)*

DISCUSSION: Point C on the V-G diagram references V_A (design maneuvering speed), which is not displayed on the airspeed indicator.

Answer (A) is incorrect. V_{NE} (never-exceed speed) is represented by points E and F on the V-G diagram and by a red line on the airspeed indicator. Answer (B) is incorrect. V_{NO} (normal operating speed) is represented by point G on the V-G diagram and by the upper limit of the green arc on the airspeed indicator.

8. Which airspeed would a pilot be unable to identify by the color coding of an airspeed indicator?

A. The never-exceed speed.

B. The power-off stall speed.

C. The maneuvering speed.

Answer (C) is correct. *(PHAK Chap 7)*

DISCUSSION: The maneuvering speed (V_A) is not color coded on an airspeed indicator. It is usually placarded and included in the airplane's flight manual.

Answer (A) is incorrect. The never-exceed speed is identified by the red radial line at the top of the yellow arc. Answer (B) is incorrect. Two power-off stall speeds are represented on the airspeed indicator; the stall speeds in the landing and clean configurations are represented by the lower limits of the white and green arcs, respectively.

9. Calibrated airspeed is best described as indicated airspeed corrected for

A. installation and instrument error.

B. instrument error.

C. non-standard temperature.

Answer (A) is correct. *(PHAK Chap 7)*

DISCUSSION: Calibrated airspeed (CAS) is indicated airspeed corrected for installation and instrument error. An airspeed calibration chart is provided in the airplane's Pilot's Operating Handbook (POH).

Answer (B) is incorrect. Calibrated airspeed is indicated airspeed corrected for both installation and instrument error, not only for instrument error. Answer (C) is incorrect. Calibrated airspeed is indicated airspeed corrected for installation and instrument error, not for nonstandard temperature.

10. True airspeed is best described as calibrated airspeed corrected for

A. installation or instrument error.

B. non-standard temperature.

C. altitude and nonstandard temperature.

Answer (C) is correct. *(PHAK Chap 7)*

DISCUSSION: True airspeed (TAS) is calibrated airspeed corrected for pressure altitude and nonstandard temperature. Thus, TAS is calibrated airspeed corrected for density altitude.

Answer (A) is incorrect. Calibrated airspeed, not true airspeed, is indicated airspeed corrected for installation and, not or, instrument error. Answer (B) is incorrect. True airspeed is calibrated airspeed corrected for both nonstandard temperature and pressure altitude, not only nonstandard temperature.

2.3 Turn Coordinator/Turn-and-Slip Indicator

11. What is an advantage of an electric turn coordinator if the airplane has a vacuum system for other gyroscopic instruments?

A. It is a backup in case of vacuum system failure.

B. It is more reliable than the vacuum-driven indicators.

C. It will not tumble as will vacuum-driven turn indicators.

Answer (A) is correct. *(PHAK Chap 7)*

DISCUSSION: The principal uses of the turn coordinator are to indicate rate of turn and to serve as an emergency source of bank information in case the vacuum-driven attitude indicator fails.

Answer (B) is incorrect. The vacuum-driven and electric-driven indicators are equally reliable. Answer (C) is incorrect. Both the vacuum-driven and the electric-driven turn indicator can tumble.

12. What is an operational difference between the turn coordinator and the turn-and-slip indicator? The turn coordinator

A. is always electric; the turn-and-slip indicator is always vacuum-driven.

B. indicates bank angle only; the turn-and-slip indicator indicates rate of turn and coordination.

C. indicates roll rate, rate of turn, and coordination; the turn-and-slip indicator indicates rate of turn and coordination.

Answer (C) is correct. *(PHAK Chap 7)*

DISCUSSION: The turn-and-slip indicator indicates the rate and direction of the turn. The turn coordinator displays the movement of the aircraft along the longitudinal axis in an amount proportional to the roll rate. When the roll rate is reduced to zero (i.e., a constant bank), the instrument provides an indication of rate of turn. Both the turn coordinator and the turn indicator possess a ball that indicates rudder/aileron coordination.

Answer (A) is incorrect. The turn coordinator and the turn-and-slip indicator are usually electric-driven instruments. Answer (B) is incorrect. The turn coordinator indicates roll rate and coordination, not angle of bank.

2.4 Fuel/Air Mixture

13. Unless adjusted, the fuel/air mixture becomes richer with an increase in altitude because the amount of fuel

A. decreases while the volume of air decreases.

B. remains constant while the volume of air decreases.

C. remains constant while the density of air decreases.

Answer (C) is correct. *(PHAK Chap 6)*

DISCUSSION: As altitude increases, the density of air entering the carburetor decreases. If no leaning is done with the mixture control, the amount of fuel will remain constant, resulting in an excessively rich mixture.

Answer (A) is incorrect. The amount of fuel remains the same, not decreases, and the density, not volume, of air decreases. Answer (B) is incorrect. The density, not the volume, of air decreases.

14. Fouling of spark plugs is more apt to occur if the aircraft

A. gains altitude with no mixture adjustment.

B. descends from altitude with no mixture adjustment.

C. throttle is advanced very abruptly.

Answer (A) is correct. *(PHAK Chap 6)*

DISCUSSION: As an aircraft gains altitude, the mixture must be leaned to compensate for the decrease in air density. If the mixture is not adjusted, it becomes too rich, i.e., contains too much fuel in terms of the weight of the air. Because of excessive fuel, a cooling effect takes place, which causes below-normal temperatures in the combustion chambers, resulting in spark plug fouling.

Answer (B) is incorrect. Descending with no mixture adjustment, i.e., operating with an excessively lean mixture, results in overheating, rough engine operation, a loss of power, and detonation, not spark plug fouling. Answer (C) is incorrect. Advancing the throttle abruptly may cause the engine to sputter or stop, not foul the spark plugs.

15. What will occur if no leaning is made with the mixture control as the flight altitude increases?

A. The volume of air entering the carburetor decreases and the amount of fuel decreases.

B. The density of air entering the carburetor decreases and the amount of fuel increases.

C. The density of air entering the carburetor decreases and the amount of fuel remains constant.

Answer (C) is correct. *(PHAK Chap 6)*

DISCUSSION: As altitude increases, the density of air entering the carburetor decreases. If no leaning is done with the mixture control, the amount of fuel will remain constant, resulting in an excessively rich mixture.

Answer (A) is incorrect. The density, not volume, of air decreases, and the amount of fuel remains the same, not decreases. Answer (B) is incorrect. The amount of fuel remains the same, not decreases.

16. The basic purpose of adjusting the fuel/air mixture control at altitude is to

A. decrease the fuel flow to compensate for decreased air density.

B. decrease the amount of fuel in the mixture to compensate for increased air density.

C. increase the amount of fuel in the mixture to compensate for the decrease in pressure and density of the air.

Answer (A) is correct. *(PHAK Chap 6)*

DISCUSSION: The purpose of adjusting the fuel/air mixture control at altitude is to decrease the fuel flow to compensate for the decreased air density.

Answer (B) is incorrect. Air density decreases, not increases, at altitude. Answer (C) is incorrect. At altitude the amount of fuel is decreased, not increased, to compensate for decreased air density.

17. At high altitudes, an excessively rich mixture will cause the

A. engine to overheat.

B. fouling of spark plugs.

C. engine to operate smoother even though fuel consumption is increased.

Answer (B) is correct. *(PHAK Chap 6)*

DISCUSSION: As an aircraft gains altitude, the mixture must be leaned to compensate for the decrease in air density. If the mixture is not adjusted, it becomes too rich, i.e., contains too much fuel in terms of the weight of the air. Because of excessive fuel, a cooling effect takes place, which causes below-normal temperatures in the combustion chambers, resulting in spark plug fouling.

Answer (A) is incorrect. A lean, not rich, mixture will cause the engine to overheat. Answer (C) is incorrect. An engine runs smoothest when the mixture is appropriate, not excessively rich.

18. The pilot controls the air/fuel ratio with the

A. throttle.

B. manifold pressure.

C. mixture control.

Answer (C) is correct. *(PHAK Chap 6)*

DISCUSSION: The mixture control is used to adjust the ratio of fuel-to-air mixture entering the combustion chamber.

Answer (A) is incorrect. The throttle regulates the total volume of fuel and air, not the fuel-to-air ratio, entering the combustion chamber. Answer (B) is incorrect. The manifold pressure is an indication of an engine's power output as controlled by the throttle; it is not directly related to the air/fuel mixture.

19. Fuel/air ratio is the ratio between the

A. volume of fuel and volume of air entering the cylinder.

B. weight of fuel and weight of air entering the cylinder.

C. weight of fuel and weight of air entering the carburetor.

Answer (B) is correct. *(PHAK Chap 6)*

DISCUSSION: The fuel/air ratio, i.e., mixture, is the ratio between the weight of fuel and the weight of air entering the cylinder.

Answer (A) is incorrect. As altitude increases, the amount of air in a fixed volume (i.e., air density) decreases. Thus, the ratio is between weights, not volume. Answer (C) is incorrect. The carburetor is where the fuel/air ratio is established prior to entering the cylinders.

20. The best power mixture is that fuel/air ratio at which

A. cylinder head temperatures are the coolest.

B. the most power can be obtained for any given throttle setting.

C. a given power can be obtained with the highest manifold pressure or throttle setting.

Answer (B) is correct. *(PHAK Chap 6)*

DISCUSSION: Engines are more efficient when they are supplied the proper mixture of fuel and air. The best power mixture refers to the fuel/air ratio that provides the most power at any given throttle setting.

Answer (A) is incorrect. The engine's cylinder heads will be coolest when the mixture is richest, not when it is at its best power setting. Answer (C) is incorrect. It describes the highest power setting, not the best power mixture.

21. The mixture control can be adjusted, which

A. prevents the fuel/air combination from becoming too rich at higher altitudes.

B. regulates the amount of airflow through the carburetor's venturi.

C. prevents the fuel/air combination from becoming lean as the airplane climbs.

Answer (A) is correct. *(PHAK Chap 6)*

DISCUSSION: As an aircraft gains altitude, the mixture must be leaned to compensate for the decrease in air density. If the mixture is not adjusted, it becomes too rich, i.e., contains too much fuel in terms of the weight of the air.

Answer (B) is incorrect. The throttle, not the mixture control, regulates the airflow through the carburetor's venturi. Answer (C) is incorrect. The fuel/air ratio becomes richer, not leaner, as the airplane climbs.

22. What effect, if any, would a change in ambient temperature or air density have on gas turbine engine performance?

A. As air density decreases, thrust increases.

B. As temperature increases, thrust increases.

C. As temperature increases, thrust decreases.

Answer (C) is correct. *(AFNA Chap 2)*

DISCUSSION: A high ambient air temperature at a given pressure altitude relates to a high density altitude, or a decrease in air density. Thrust is reduced because of low air density and low mass flow. Also, thrust and fuel flow are reduced further because of high compressor inlet temperature.

Answer (A) is incorrect. As air density decreases, thrust decreases, not increases. Answer (B) is incorrect. Thrust decreases, not increases, with an increase in temperature.

2.5 Carburetor Heat

23. Which statement is true concerning the effect of the application of carburetor heat?

A. It enriches the fuel/air mixture.

B. It leans the fuel/air mixture.

C. It has no effect on the fuel/air mixture.

Answer (A) is correct. *(PHAK Chap 6)*

DISCUSSION: The application of carburetor heat reduces the density of air entering the carburetor because the air is warmer. As a result, it enriches the fuel/air mixture because there is no change in the weight of fuel being combusted.

Answer (B) is incorrect. Warmer air is less dense, so the mixture is enriched, not leaned. Answer (C) is incorrect. Warmer air is less dense, so the mixture is enriched, not unaffected.

24. Applying carburetor heat will

A. not affect the mixture.

B. lean the fuel/air mixture.

C. enrich the fuel/air mixture.

Answer (C) is correct. *(PHAK Chap 6)*

DISCUSSION: The application of carburetor heat reduces the density of air entering the carburetor because the air is warmer. As a result, it enriches the fuel/air mixture because there is no change in the weight of fuel being combusted.

Answer (A) is incorrect. Warmer air is less dense, so the mixture is enriched, not unaffected. Answer (B) is incorrect. Warmer air is less dense, so the mixture is enriched, not leaned.

25. Leaving the carburetor heat on during takeoff

A. leans the mixture for more power on takeoff.

B. will decrease the takeoff distance.

C. will increase the ground roll.

Answer (C) is correct. *(PHAK Chap 6)*

DISCUSSION: Use of carburetor heat tends to reduce the output of the engine due to the warmer, less dense air entering the carburetor. Thus, the use of carburetor heat reduces performance during critical phases of flight, e.g., takeoff and climb. During the takeoff, it will increase the ground roll.

Answer (A) is incorrect. Carburetor heat enriches, not leans, the mixture for less, not more, power. Answer (B) is incorrect. The use of carburetor heat will increase, not decrease, takeoff performance.

2.6 Detonation and Preignition

26. Detonation occurs in a reciprocating aircraft engine when

A. there is an explosive increase of fuel caused by too rich a fuel/air mixture.

B. the spark plugs receive an electrical jolt caused by a short in the wiring.

C. the unburned fuel/air charge in the cylinders is subjected to instantaneous combustion.

Answer (C) is correct. *(PHAK Chap 6)*

DISCUSSION: Detonation (or knock) is a sudden explosion, or instantaneous combustion, of the fuel/air mixture in the cylinders, producing extreme heat and severe structural stresses on the engine. It is caused by low-grade fuel, too lean a mixture, or excessively high engine temperatures.

Answer (A) is incorrect. Detonation is caused by too lean, not too rich, a mixture. Answer (B) is incorrect. Detonation is caused by excessively high engine temperatures, not a short in spark plug wiring.

27. Detonation can be caused by

A. a “rich” mixture.

B. low engine temperatures.

C. using a lower grade of fuel than recommended.

Answer (C) is correct. *(PHAK Chap 6)*

DISCUSSION: Detonation (or knock) is a sudden explosion, or instantaneous combustion, of the fuel/air mixture in the cylinders, producing extreme heat and severe structural stresses on the engine. It is caused by low-grade fuel, too lean a mixture, or excessively high engine temperatures.

Answer (A) is incorrect. Detonation is caused by the mixture being too lean, not rich. Answer (B) is incorrect. Detonation is caused by excessively high, not low, engine temperatures.

28. The uncontrolled firing of the fuel/air charge in advance of normal spark ignition is known as

A. instantaneous combustion.

B. detonation.

C. pre-ignition.

Answer (C) is correct. *(PHAK Chap 6)*

DISCUSSION: Preignition is the ignition of the fuel prior to normal ignition or ignition before the electrical arcing occurs at the spark plug. Preignition may be caused by excessively hot exhaust valves, carbon particles, or spark plugs and electrodes heated to an incandescent, or glowing, state. These hot spots are usually caused by high temperatures encountered during detonation. A significant difference between preignition and detonation is that, if the conditions for detonation exist in one cylinder, they may exist in all cylinders, but preignition could take place in only one or two cylinders.

Answer (A) is incorrect. Instantaneous combustion is detonation, which will cause extremely high engine temperatures and can result in preignition. Answer (B) is incorrect. Detonation is the instantaneous combustion of the fuel/air mixture, which can be caused by using too lean a mixture, by using too low a grade of fuel, or by operating in temperatures that are too high.

29. Detonation may occur at high-power settings when

A. the fuel mixture ignites instantaneously instead of burning progressively and evenly.

B. an excessively rich fuel mixture causes an explosive gain in power.

C. the fuel mixture is ignited too early by hot carbon deposits in the cylinder.

Answer (A) is correct. *(PHAK Chap 6)*

DISCUSSION: Detonation (or knock) is a sudden explosion, or instantaneous combustion, of the fuel/air mixture in the cylinders, producing extreme heat and severe structural stresses on the engine. It is caused by low-grade fuel, too lean a mixture, or excessively high engine temperatures.

Answer (B) is incorrect. Detonation may occur with an excessively lean, not rich, fuel mixture that causes a loss, not gain, in power. Answer (C) is incorrect. The fuel mixture being ignited too early describes preignition, not detonation.

2.7 Airplane Ignition Systems

30. Before shutdown, while at idle, the ignition key is momentarily turned OFF. The engine continues to run with no interruption; this

A. is normal because the engine is usually stopped by moving the mixture to idle cutoff.

B. should not normally happen. Indicates a magneto not grounding in OFF position.

C. is an undesirable practice, but indicates that nothing is wrong.

Answer (B) is correct. *(PHAK Chap 6)*

DISCUSSION: An engine that continues to run after the ignition switch has been turned off probably has a broken magneto ground wire. The ignition switch is not able to ground the magneto to stop the generation of electrical impulses that provide electricity to the spark plug. Thus, momentarily turning off the ignition prior to shutdown is a recommended procedure to check for a faulty ground wire.

Answer (A) is incorrect. Turning the ignition key to OFF should stop the engine. Answer (C) is incorrect. Turning off the ignition key is a recommended procedure prior to shutdown to check for a faulty ground wire.

31. A way to detect a broken magneto primary grounding lead is to

A. idle the engine and momentarily turn the ignition off.

B. add full power, while holding the brakes, and momentarily turn off the ignition.

C. run on one magneto, lean the mixture, and look for a rise in manifold pressure.

Answer (A) is correct. *(PHAK Chap 6)*

DISCUSSION: An engine that continues to run after the ignition switch has been turned off probably has a broken magneto ground wire. The ignition switch is not able to ground the magneto to stop the generation of electrical impulses that provide electricity to the spark plug. Thus, momentarily turning off the ignition prior to shutdown is a recommended procedure to check for a faulty ground wire.

Answer (B) is incorrect. It is not necessary to add full power when performing this check. Answer (C) is incorrect. This is a nonsense procedure.

32. The most probable reason an engine continues to run after the ignition switch has been turned off is

A. carbon deposits glowing on the spark plugs.

B. a magneto ground wire is in contact with the engine casing.

C. a broken magneto ground wire.

Answer (C) is correct. *(PHAK Chap 6)*

DISCUSSION: An engine that continues to run after the ignition switch has been turned off probably has a broken magneto ground wire. The ignition switch is not able to ground the magneto to stop the generation of electrical impulses that provide electricity to the spark plug. Thus, momentarily turning off the ignition prior to shutdown is a recommended procedure to check for a faulty ground wire.

Answer (A) is incorrect. Glowing carbon deposits result in preignition, not in the continued running of the engine. Answer (B) is incorrect. The magneto ground wire should be in contact with the engine casing to provide effective grounding.

33. A detuning of engine crankshaft counterweights is a source of overstress that may be caused by

A. rapid opening and closing of the throttle.

B. carburetor ice forming on the throttle valve.

C. operating with an excessively rich fuel/air mixture.

Answer (A) is correct. *(AC 20-103)*

DISCUSSION: A detuning of counterweights on balance weight-equipped crankshafts is a source of overstress for the crankshaft. The counterweights are designed to position themselves by the inertia forces generated during crankshaft rotation and to absorb and dampen crankshaft vibration effectively. If the counterweights are detuned (allowed to slam on mounts), the vibrations are not properly dampened and crankshaft failure can occur. Counterweight detuning can occur from rapid opening and closing of the throttle, excessive speed, excessive power, and operating at high RPMs and low manifold pressure.

Answer (B) is incorrect. Carburetor ice will cause the engine to stop running when the carburetor is sufficiently clogged with ice, but it will not affect the engine crankshaft counterweights. Answer (C) is incorrect. Operating with an excessively rich fuel/air mixture fouls the spark plugs but does not affect the crankshaft.

34. If the ground wire between the magneto and the ignition switch becomes disconnected, the engine

A. will not operate on one magneto.

B. cannot be started with the switch in the BOTH position.

C. could accidentally start if the propeller is moved with fuel in the cylinder.

Answer (C) is correct. *(PHAK Chap 6)*

DISCUSSION: If the magneto switch ground wire is disconnected, the magneto is ON even though the ignition switch is in the OFF position. Thus, the engine could fire if the propeller is moved from outside the airplane.

Answer (A) is incorrect. Disconnecting the ground wire causes both magnetos to remain on; i.e., they will operate even when the ignition switch is in the OFF position. The dual ignition system is designed so that, in case one magneto fails, the other magneto can operate alone. Answer (B) is incorrect. The engine can still be started; the magnetos cannot be turned OFF.

2.8 Engine Cooling

35. For internal cooling, reciprocating aircraft engines are especially dependent on

A. a properly functioning cowl flap augmenter.

B. the circulation of lubricating oil.

C. the proper freon/compressor output ratio.

Answer (B) is correct. *(PHAK Chap 6)*

DISCUSSION: An engine accomplishes much of its cooling by the flow of oil through the lubrication system. The lubrication system aids in cooling by reducing friction as well as by absorbing heat from internal engine parts. Many airplane engines also use an oil cooler, a small radiator device that cools the oil before it is recirculated through the engine.

Answer (A) is incorrect. The cowl flaps aid in controlling engine temperatures but are not the primary cooling source. Answer (C) is incorrect. The freon/compressor output ratio determines the effectiveness of cabin, not engine, cooling.

36. An abnormally high engine oil temperature indication may be caused by

A. a defective bearing.

B. the oil level being too low.

C. operating with an excessively rich mixture.

Answer (B) is correct. *(A&PM PH Chap 10)*

DISCUSSION: Operating with an excessively low oil level prevents the oil from cooling adequately; i.e., an inadequate supply of oil will not be able to transfer engine heat to the engine's oil cooler (similar to a car engine's water radiator). Insufficient oil may also damage an engine from excessive friction within the cylinders and on other metal-to-metal contact parts.

Answer (A) is incorrect. A defective bearing results in local heat and wear, which will probably increase metal particles in the oil, but it should not affect oil temperature significantly. Answer (C) is incorrect. A rich fuel/air mixture results in lower engine operating temperatures and thus does not increase engine oil temperature.

37. Frequent inspections should be made of aircraft exhaust manifold-type heating systems to minimize the possibility of

A. exhaust gases leaking into the cockpit.

B. a power loss due to back pressure in the exhaust system.

C. a cold-running engine due to the heat withdrawn by the heater.

Answer (A) is correct. *(PHAK Chap 6)*

DISCUSSION: You should inspect exhaust manifold-type heating systems regularly. Heating systems that rely on air being heated by the exhaust manifold could carry exhaust gases to the cockpit if a crack or leak develops in the exhaust manifold.

Answer (B) is incorrect. A leak in the exhaust system decreases, not increases, back pressure. Answer (C) is incorrect. Engine temperature is not affected by withdrawing heat to a cockpit heater.

2.9 Airplane Propellers

38. Propeller efficiency is the

A. ratio of thrust horsepower to brake horsepower.

B. actual distance a propeller advances in one revolution.

C. ratio of geometric pitch to effective pitch.

Answer (A) is correct. *(AFH Chap 3)*

DISCUSSION: The efficiency of any machine is the ratio of useful power output to actual power output. Thus, propeller efficiency is the ratio of thrust horsepower (amount of thrust the propeller produces) to brake horsepower (amount of torque the engine imparts on the propeller). Propeller efficiency generally varies between 50% and 85%, depending upon propeller slippage.

Answer (B) is incorrect. The distance a propeller travels in one revolution is effective pitch, not propeller efficiency. Answer (C) is incorrect. The ratio of geometric pitch to effective pitch is propeller slippage, which is related to, but is not, propeller efficiency.

39. The reason for variations in geometric pitch (twisting) along a propeller blade is that it

A. permits a relatively constant angle of incidence along its length when in cruising flight.

B. prevents the portion of the blade near the hub from stalling during cruising flight.

C. permits a relatively constant angle of attack along its length when in cruising flight.

Answer (C) is correct. *(AFH Chap 3)*

DISCUSSION: Variations in the geometric pitch of the blades permit the propeller to operate with a relatively constant angle of attack along its length when in cruising flight. Propeller blades have variations to change the blade in proportion to the differences in speed of rotation along the length of the propeller and thereby keep thrust more nearly equalized along this length.

Answer (A) is incorrect. Variations in geometric pitch permit a constant angle of attack, not incidence, along its length. Answer (B) is incorrect. If there were no variation in geometric pitch, the propeller tips, not the root, would be stalled during cruising flight.

40. A fixed-pitch propeller is designed for best efficiency only at a given combination of

A. altitude and RPM.

B. airspeed and RPM.

C. airspeed and altitude.

Answer (B) is correct. *(AFH Chap 3)*

DISCUSSION: A fixed-pitch propeller is most efficient only at a specified combination of airspeed and RPM. When designing a fixed-pitch propeller, the manufacturer usually selects a pitch that will operate most efficiently at the expected cruising speed of the airplane.

Answer (A) is incorrect. Altitude does not necessarily affect the efficiency of a fixed-pitch propeller. Answer (C) is incorrect. Altitude does not necessarily affect the efficiency of a fixed-pitch propeller.

41. Which statement best describes the operating principle of a constant-speed propeller?

A. As throttle setting is changed by the pilot, the prop governor causes pitch angle of the propeller blades to remain unchanged.

B. A high blade angle, or increased pitch, reduces the propeller drag and allows more engine power for takeoffs.

C. The propeller control regulates the engine RPM and in turn the propeller RPM.

Answer (C) is correct. *(PHAK Chap 6)*

DISCUSSION: A constant-speed propeller, as the name implies, adjusts the pitch angle of the propeller blades so that the engine is maintained at a selected RPM. This variation permits use of a blade angle that will result in the most efficient performance for each particular flight condition.

Answer (A) is incorrect. The prop governor causes pitch angle of the propeller blades to change, not remain unchanged, to maintain a specified RPM. Answer (B) is incorrect. A high blade angle increases, not reduces, propeller drag, and allows less, not more, engine power.

42. When referring to a constant speed propeller, the pitch setting is

A. varied in flight by a governor maintaining constant RPM despite varying air loads.

B. set to a specific blade angle by the pilot.

C. unchanged; the manifold pressure changes, not the propeller pitch.

Answer (A) is correct. *(PHAK Chap 6)*

DISCUSSION: A constant-speed propeller uses a governor to regulate and maintain a constant RPM. The governor changes the propeller blade pitch angles to adjust for air loads and airspeed changes.

Answer (B) is incorrect. A pilot selects a specific RPM, not a blade angle. The blade angle is constantly varied by the governor to maintain the specified RPM. Answer (C) is incorrect. Propeller pitch is always changing on aircraft fitted with a constant-speed propeller to maintain the RPM set by the pilot. The manifold pressure may be adjusted by the pilot with the throttle or may be affected by altitude change.

43. To develop maximum power and thrust, a constant-speed propeller should be set to a blade angle that will produce a

A. large angle of attack and low RPM.

B. small angle of attack and high RPM.

C. large angle of attack and high RPM.

Answer (B) is correct. *(PHAK Chap 6)*

DISCUSSION: When using a constant-speed propeller, the maximum engine power for maximum thrust can be obtained by using a small angle of attack, which results in a high RPM.

Answer (A) is incorrect. A large angle of attack and low RPM result in less, not maximum, power and thrust. Answer (C) is incorrect. Maximum power is obtained by using a small, not large, propeller angle of attack.

44. For takeoff, the blade angle of a controllable-pitch propeller should be set at a

A. small angle of attack and high RPM.

B. large angle of attack and low RPM.

C. large angle of attack and high RPM.

Answer (A) is correct. *(PHAK Chap 6)*

DISCUSSION: For takeoff with a controllable-pitch (i.e., constant-speed) propeller, the blade angle should be set for maximum power, which is a small angle of attack and high RPM.

Answer (B) is incorrect. A large angle of attack and low RPM result in low, not maximum, power. Answer (C) is incorrect. Maximum takeoff power requires a small, not large, propeller angle of attack.

45. To establish a climb after takeoff in an aircraft equipped with a constant-speed propeller, the output of the engine is reduced to climb power by decreasing manifold pressure and

A. increasing RPM by decreasing propeller blade angle.

B. decreasing RPM by decreasing propeller blade angle.

C. decreasing RPM by increasing propeller blade angle.

Answer (C) is correct. *(AFH Chap 3)*

DISCUSSION: To establish climb power after takeoff using a constant-speed propeller, you should first decrease manifold pressure and then decrease RPM. When the propeller control is moved to reduce the RPM, the propeller blade angle increases.

Answer (A) is incorrect. To reduce power, you should decrease, not increase, RPM by increasing, not decreasing, propeller blade angle. Answer (B) is incorrect. To reduce power, you should decrease RPM by increasing, not decreasing, propeller blade angle.

46. In aircraft equipped with constant-speed propellers and normally-aspirated engines, which procedure should be used to avoid placing undue stress on the engine components? When power is being

A. decreased, reduce the RPM before reducing the manifold pressure.

B. increased, increase the RPM before increasing the manifold pressure.

C. increased or decreased, the RPM should be adjusted before the manifold pressure.

Answer (B) is correct. *(PHAK Chap 6)*

DISCUSSION: To avoid placing undue stress on an engine equipped with a constant-speed propeller, you should avoid high manifold pressure settings with low RPM. Thus, when power is being increased, you should increase the RPM before increasing the manifold pressure.

Answer (A) is incorrect. When power is being decreased, you should reduce the manifold pressure before reducing the RPM, not vice versa. Answer (C) is incorrect. When power is being decreased, you should reduce the manifold pressure before reducing the RPM, not vice versa.

47. A propeller rotating clockwise as seen from the rear, creates a spiraling slipstream. The spiraling slipstream, along with torque effect, tends to rotate the airplane to the

A. right around the vertical axis, and to the left around the longitudinal axis.

B. left around the vertical axis, and to the right around the longitudinal axis.

C. left around the vertical axis, and to the left around the longitudinal axis.

Answer (B) is correct. *(PHAK Chap 4)*

DISCUSSION: As the airplane propeller rotates through the air in a clockwise direction as viewed from the rear, the propeller blade forces the air rearward in a spiraling, clockwise direction of flow around the fuselage. This clockwise flow attempts to roll the airplane to the right about the longitudinal axis. A portion of this spiraling slipstream strikes the left side of the vertical stabilizer, forcing the airplane's tail to the right, causing the airplane to rotate to the left around the vertical axis. Note that this rolling moment caused by the corkscrew flow of the slipstream is to the right, while the rolling moment caused by torque reaction is to the left, about the longitudinal axis.

Answer (A) is incorrect. The rotation is to the left, not right, around the vertical axis and to the right, not left, around the longitudinal axis. Answer (C) is incorrect. The rotation is to the right, not left, around the longitudinal axis.

END OF STUDY UNIT

GLEIM®

Garmin 530 Training Course

Master the Garmin GNS 530 with structured, easy to understand avionics training to help you.

Course Features

- Nine study units explain all functions of the GNS 530.
- Two optional study units expand your knowledge of more advanced features.
- Interactive exercises let you practice your GPS skills before you get in the airplane.
- “Portable” classroom available anywhere you have Internet access.

For 12 months access

800.874.5346 • gleim.com/aviation/g530

STUDY UNIT THREE
AIRPORTS, AIR TRAFFIC CONTROL, AND AIRSPACE

(9 pages of outline)

This study unit contains outlines of major concepts tested; sample test questions and answers regarding airports, air traffic control, and airspace; and an explanation of each answer. The table of contents above lists each subunit within this study unit, the number of questions pertaining to that particular subunit, and the pages on which the outlines and questions begin, respectively.

Recall that the **sole purpose** of this book is to expedite your passing of the FAA pilot knowledge test for the commercial pilot certificate. Accordingly, all extraneous material (i.e., topics or regulations not directly tested on the FAA pilot knowledge test) is omitted, even though much more knowledge is necessary to become a proficient commercial pilot. This additional material is presented in *Pilot Handbook* and *Commercial Pilot Flight Maneuvers and Practical Test Prep*, available from Gleim Publications, Inc. See the product listing at the back of the book and order online at www.gleim.com.

3.1 AIRSPACE

1. Flight operations in Class A airspace must be conducted under instrument flight rules (IFR).
2. All aircraft operating in Class A airspace must be equipped with an ATC transponder and altitude reporting equipment.
3. You must receive an ATC clearance before operating an airplane in Class B airspace.
4. To take off or land at an airport within Class B airspace or to operate an airplane within Class B airspace, the pilot in command must hold at least a private pilot certificate.
    a. A student pilot or a recreational pilot may fly solo in Class B airspace only if the pilot has met the requirements listed in FAR 61.95.
5. To operate in Class B airspace, the airplane must be equipped with an operating ATC (4096 code or Mode S) transponder and automatic altitude reporting equipment (Mode C).
6. The maximum indicated speed authorized when operating an airplane in the airspace underlying Class B airspace is 200 knots.
7. Unless otherwise authorized or required by ATC, the maximum indicated airspeed permitted when at or below 2,500 ft. AGL within 4 NM of the primary airport of a Class C or Class D airspace is 200 knots.
8. If the minimum safe airspeed for any particular operation is greater than the maximum airspeed prescribed in FAR Part 91, the airplane may be operated at that speed.
    a. In such cases, you are expected to advise ATC of the airspeed that will be used.
9. To operate in Class C airspace, an airplane must be equipped with an ATC transponder and automatic altitude reporting capability (Mode C).
10. Prior to entering Class C airspace, you must establish and maintain communications with the ATC facility providing air traffic services.

11. The flight requirements to operate under special VFR in Class D airspace are
    a. Remain clear of clouds, and
    b. Have flight visibility of at least 1 SM if ground visibility is not reported.
12. Flight under special VFR clearance at night is permitted only if the pilot is instrument rated and the airplane is equipped for instrument flight.
13. To take off or land under special VFR requires ground visibility of at least 1 statute mile.
    a. If ground visibility is not reported, flight visibility during landing or takeoff must be at least 1 statute mile.
14. When a part-time control tower at the primary airport in Class D airspace is not in operation, the airspace at the surface becomes either Class E or Class G with an overlying Class E area beginning at 700 ft. AGL.
15. When approaching to land at an airport in Class D airspace, you must establish communications with ATC prior to entering Class D airspace (which extends up to and includes 2,500 ft. AGL and has its lateral dimensions, such as 4 NM, set by local needs).
16. When operating in the vicinity of an airport with an operating control tower in Class E airspace, you must establish communications prior to 4 NM from the airport, up to and including 2,500 ft. AGL.
17. When approaching to land at an airport without an operating control tower in Class G airspace, you should make all turns to the left, unless otherwise indicated.
18. The Federal airways are Class E airspace areas. Unless otherwise specified, they extend upward from 1,200 ft. AGL to, but not including, 18,000 ft. MSL.

3.2 VHF/DF

1. VHF/DF, when seen in the *A/FD* for a particular airport, indicates a "very high frequency direction finder" facility at an FSS that can determine the direction of your airplane from the station.
2. To use VHF/DF facilities for assistance, you must have an operative VHF transmitter and receiver.

3.3 AIRPORT SIGNS/MARKINGS

1. Airport signs are used to provide information to pilots. (Images appear in color on the inside back cover.)
2. A no entry sign (see below) is a type of mandatory instruction sign that has a red background with a white inscription.

    a. A no entry sign prohibits an aircraft from entering an area.
    b. Typically, this sign is located on a taxiway intended to be used in only one direction or at the intersection of vehicle roadways with runways, taxiways, or aprons where the roadway may be mistaken as a taxiway or other aircraft movement surface.

3. A runway boundary sign (see below) is a type of location sign that has a yellow background with a black inscription and graphic depicting the pavement holding position marking.

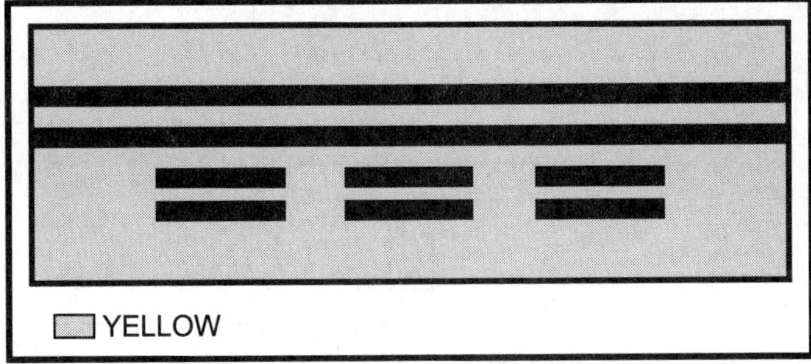

   a. This sign, which faces the runway and is visible to you when you are exiting the runway, is located adjacent to the holding position marking on the pavement.
      1) The sign is intended to provide you with another visual cue in deciding when you are clear of the runway.
   b. You are clear of the runway when your airplane is on the solid-line side of the holding position marking.
4. An ILS critical area boundary sign (see below) is another type of location sign that has a yellow background with a black inscription and graphic depicting the ILS pavement holding position marking.

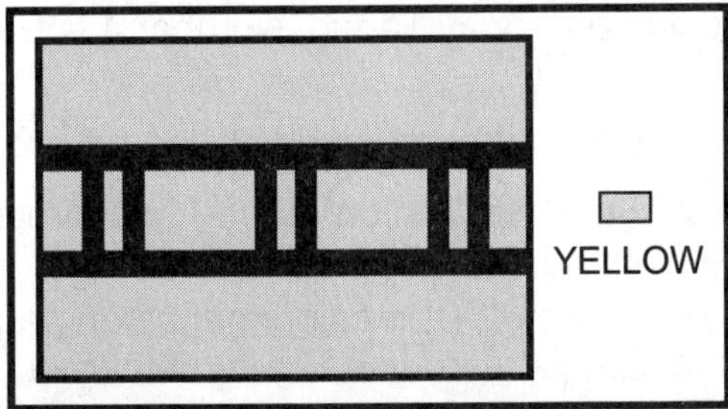

   a. This sign is located adjacent to the ILS holding position marking on the pavement. You can see it when you are leaving or approaching the critical area.
      1) The sign is intended to provide you with another visual cue to use as a guide in deciding when you are clear of, or about to enter, the ILS critical area.
5. A taxiway ending marker sign is a type of information sign that consists of alternating yellow and black diagonal stripes. Refer to Figure 60 (Sign 1) below and on page 248 (in color).
   a. This sign indicates that the taxiway does not continue beyond the sign.

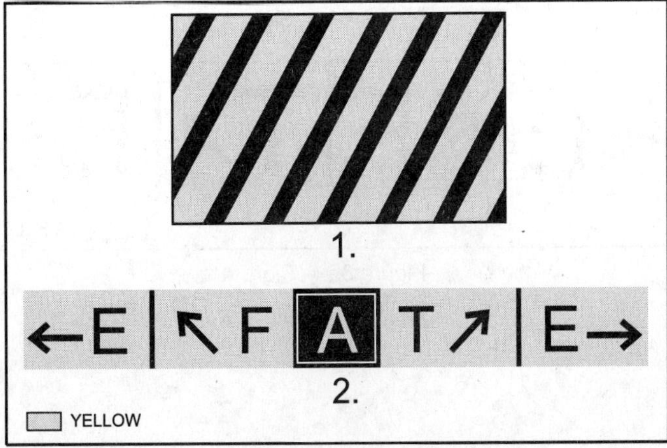

Figure 60. – Two Signs.

6. The image below is listed as Figure 59 in the Commercial FAA Test Supplement. (See color image on page 248.) It consists of a taxiway diagram and a direction sign array.

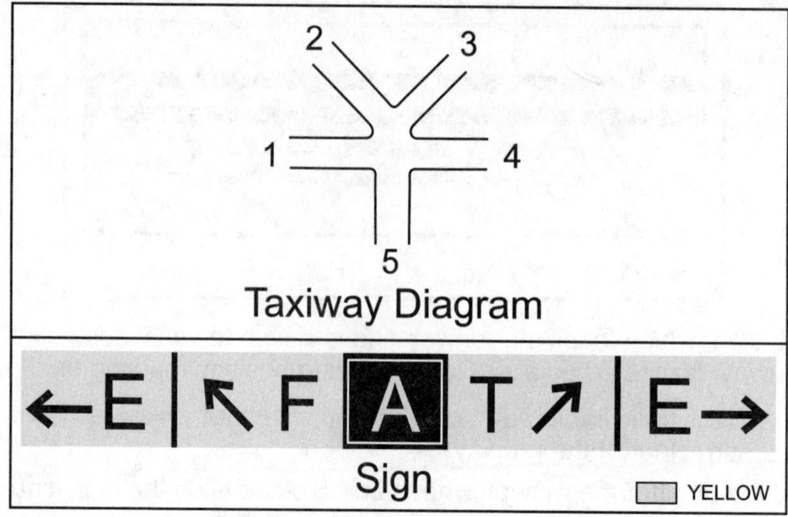

Figure 59. – Taxiway Diagram and Sign.

a. The taxiway designations and their associated arrows on the sign are arranged clockwise starting from the first taxiway on the pilot's left.

b. Therefore, at number 5, you are on taxiway Alpha, and if you turn to taxi toward number 3, it would be taxiway Tango. Number 4 is Echo, 2 is Foxtrot, and 1 is also Echo.

7. Direction signs consist of black lettering on a yellow background.

a. These signs indicate the designation (name) and direction (orientation) of taxiways leading out of an intersection.

b. Below are Figures 61 and 62 (see color images on pages 248 and 249), which are similar to the direction sign array in Figure 59 above. You may encounter pretest questions with these figures.

1) The difference between Figures 61 and 62 is that Figure 61 includes a location sign, which is the letter A. This signifies that you are on taxiway Alpha.

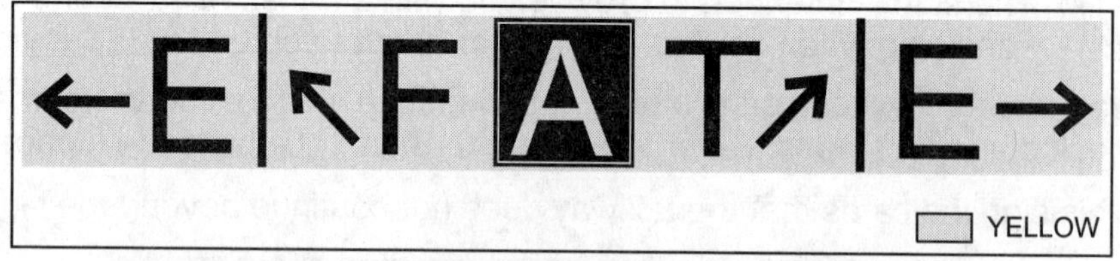

Figure 61. – Sign.

Figure 62. – Sign.

c. Figure 63 below (see color image on page 249 in this book) is very similar to Figure 59. You may encounter a question that asks which taxiway diagram is associated with the taxiway directional sign in Figure 63. The taxiway diagram labeled 2 is the correct taxiway diagram for the taxiway direction sign in Figure 63.

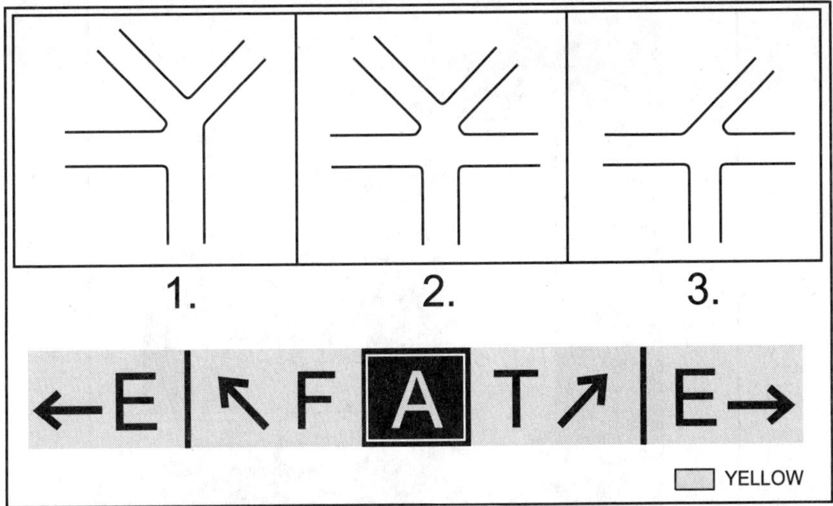

Figure 63. – Sign and Intersection Diagram.

d. Figure 57 below (and color image on page 247 in this book) is similar to the previous taxiway diagram and directional signs. However, the center of the destination sign in Figure 57 indicates a common route, straight ahead, for Runways 10 and 21. Also, if you were to use the taxiway to the left, you would encounter Runway 4. On the other hand, if you use the taxiway to the right, you would encounter Runway 22.

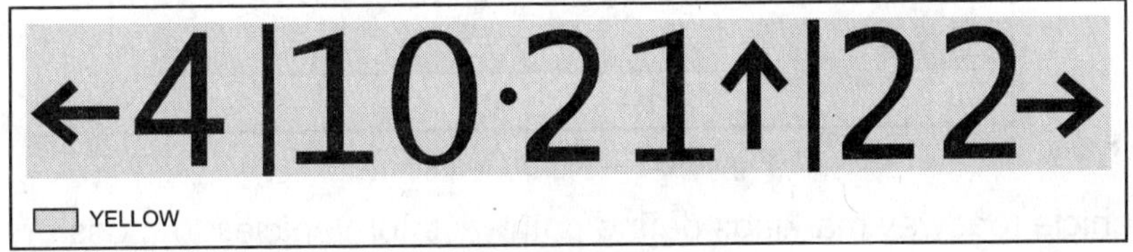

Figure 57. – Sign.

e. Figure 60 below (and color image on page 248) has two signs: (1) a taxiway ending marker and (2) a taxiway directional sign. You may encounter a pretest question referencing this figure.

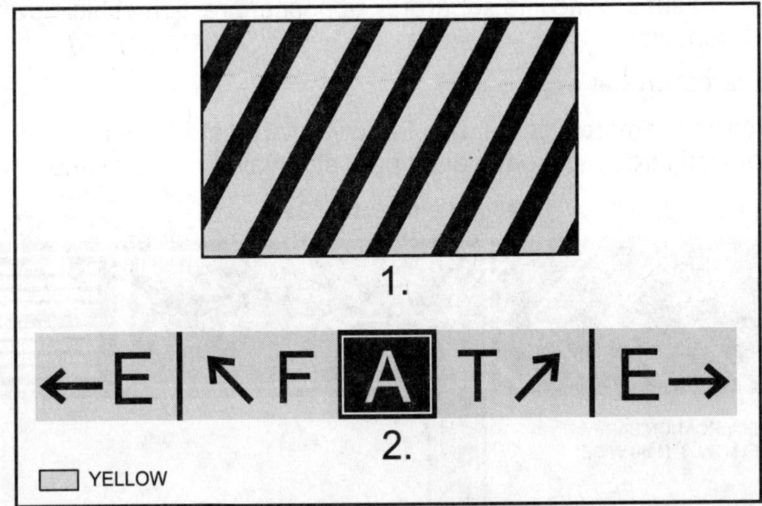

Figure 60. – Two Signs.

8. Vehicle Roadway Markings (see Figure 66 below and in color on page 250)

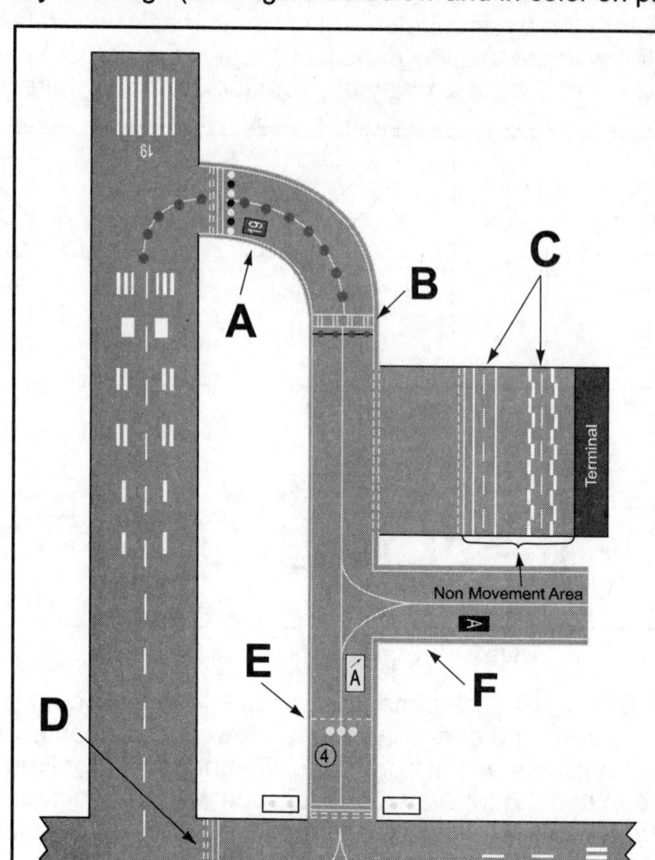

Figure 66. – Airport Markings.

a. Vehicle roadway markings define pathways for vehicles to cross areas of the airport used by aircraft.
   1) Vehicle roadway markings exist in two forms, as indicated in Letter C above.
      a) The edge of vehicle roadway markings may be defined by a solid white line or white zipper markings.
   2) A dashed white line separates opposite-direction vehicle traffic inside the roadway.

9. Yellow Demarcation Bar

a. The yellow demarcation bar is a 3-foot-wide, painted yellow bar that separates a displaced threshold from a blast pad, stopway, or taxiway that precedes the runway.

Yellow Demarcation Bar

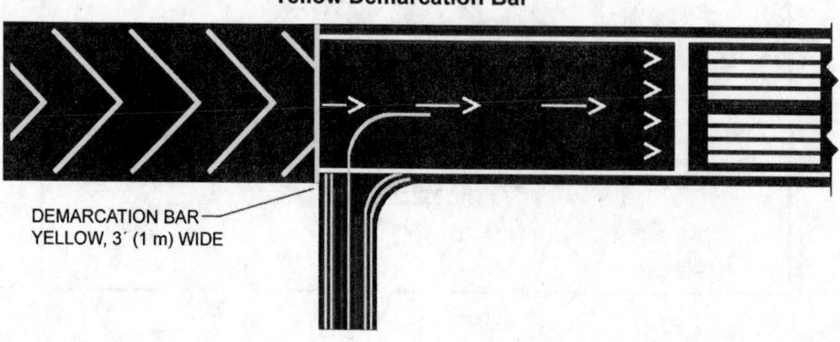

10. Figure 58 below (and color image on page 247) is an airport diagram with a runway airport sign for Runway 16-34. You will be asked where the runway hold position sign might appear on the airport diagram. The answer would be at points 10 and 11.

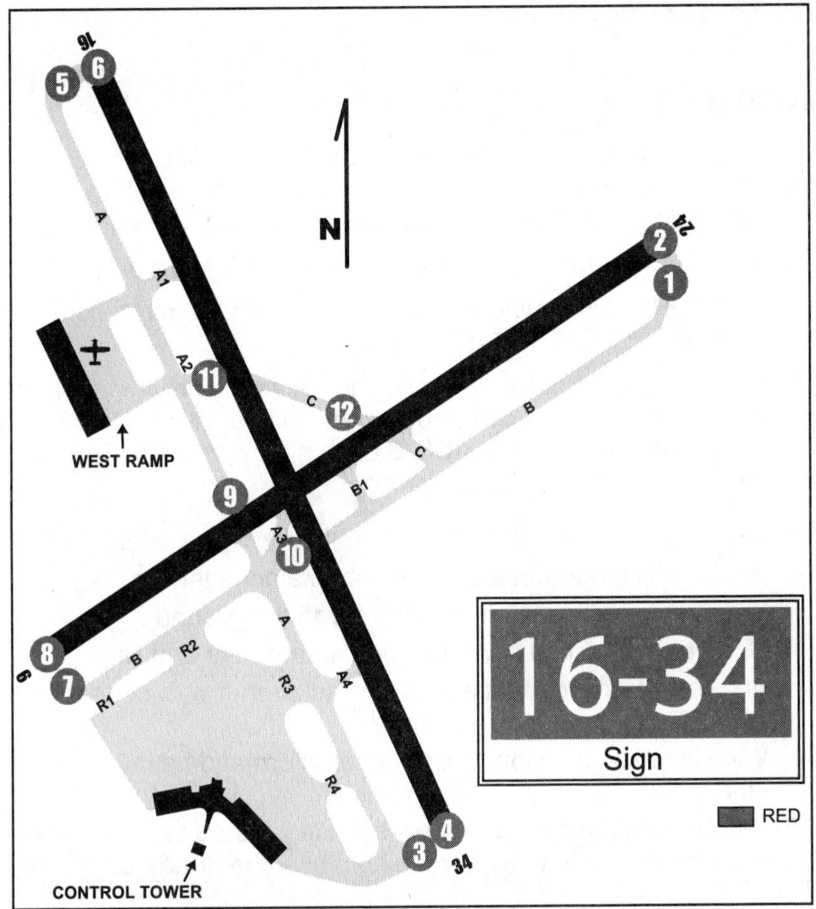

Figure 58. – Airport Diagram and Sign.

11. Figures 56 and 64 below (and in color on pages 247 and 249, respectively) contain more runway indicator signs. Figure 64 indicates that you are at an intersection of Runway 26-8. In Figure 56, Sign 1 shows that you are approaching Runway 22. Sign 2 indicates that you are holding short of Runway 4.

Figure 56. – Two Signs.

26-8

RED

Figure 64. – Sign.

a. If you were holding short at an intersection and saw the sign pictured in Figure 64, it would tell you that taking off on Runway 8 would require a left turn onto the runway and a takeoff on Runway 26 would require a right turn onto the runway.

   1) Imagine that this sign actually shows you the runway. If you were taxiing onto the end of Runway 8 for takeoff, given the runway layout shown by this sign, you would turn to the left. The sign should be used in the same manner.

12. The runway exit sign defines the direction and designation of the exit taxiway from the runway.
    a. The sign features a yellow background with a black letter and arrow that directs pilots to the appropriate exit point.

3.4 COLLISION AVOIDANCE

1. Navigation lights consist of a steady red light on the left wing, a steady green light on the right wing, and a steady white light on the tail. In night flight, when an airplane is heading away from you, you will observe a steady white light and a rotating red light.
2. Any aircraft that has no apparent relative motion is likely to be on a collision course.
3. In the vicinity of VORs, you should look carefully for other aircraft converging on the VOR from all directions.
4. ADS-B (Automatic Dependent Surveillance-Broadcast) is new technology that allows air traffic controllers (and ADS-B equipped aircraft) to see traffic with more precision. Instead of relying on old radar technology, ADS-B uses highly accurate GPS signals. Because of this, ADS-B works where radar often will not.
    a. This system
        1) Works in remote areas such as mountainous terrain
        2) Functions at low altitudes and even on the ground
        3) Can be used to monitor traffic on the taxiways and runways
        4) Allows air traffic controllers as well as aircraft with certain equipment to receive ADS-B traffic
        5) Will make subscription-free weather information available to all aircraft flying over the U.S.
    b. ADS-B will be required in 2020. This system is going to help make our skies safer. For more information, visit www.garmin.com/us/intheair/ads-b.

3.5 WAKE TURBULENCE

1. Wingtip vortices (wake turbulence) are created when airplanes develop lift.
2. The greatest wingtip vortex strength occurs behind heavy, clean (flaps and gear up), and slow aircraft.
3. When landing behind a large aircraft on the same runway, stay at or above the other aircraft's final approach flight path and land beyond that airplane's touchdown point.
    a. When taking off after a large aircraft has just landed, become airborne past the large airplane's touchdown point.
4. When taking off behind a jet, take off before the rotation point of the jet, and then climb above and stay upwind of the jet's flight path until you are able to turn clear of the wake.
5. Wingtip vortex turbulence tends to sink into the flight path of airplanes operating below the airplane generating the turbulence.
    a. Thus, you should fly above the flight path of a large jet rather than below.
6. The primary hazard of wake turbulence is loss of control because of induced roll.
7. In forward flight, helicopters produce a pair of high velocity trailing vortices similar to wing tip vortices of large fixed wing aircraft.

3.6 LAND AND HOLD SHORT OPERATIONS (LAHSO)

1. Land and hold short operations (LAHSO) take place at some airports with an operating control tower in order to increase airport capacity and improve the flow of traffic.
   a. LAHSO requires that you land and hold short of an intersecting runway, an intersecting taxiway, or some other designated point on a runway.
2. Before accepting a clearance to land and hold short, you must determine that you can safely land and stop in the available landing distance (ALD).
   a. Pilots should have readily available the published ALD and runway slope information for all LAHSO runway combinations at each airport of intended landing.
3. The pilot in command has the final authority to accept or decline any LAHSO clearance.
   a. You are expected to decline a LAHSO clearance if you determine it will compromise safety.
   b. Once a pilot in command accepts a LAHSO clearance, it must be adhered to, just as any other ATC clearance, unless an amended clearance is obtained or an emergency occurs.
   c. Once a LAHSO is accepted, it must be adhered to unless an amended clearance is obtained when an emergency occurs. A LAHSO clearance does not preclude a rejected landing.
4. You should receive a LAHSO clearance only when there is a minimum ceiling of 1,000 ft. and 3 SM visibility.
   a. The intent of having "basic" VFR weather conditions is to allow pilots to maintain visual contact with other aircraft and ground vehicle operations.

QUESTIONS AND ANSWER EXPLANATIONS: All of the commercial pilot knowledge test questions chosen by the FAA for release as well as additional questions selected by Gleim relating to the material in the previous outlines are reproduced on the following pages. These questions have been organized into the same subunits as the outlines. To the immediate right of each question are the correct answer and answer explanation. You should cover these answers and answer explanations while responding to the questions. Refer to the general discussion in the Introduction on how to take the FAA knowledge test.

Remember that the questions from the FAA knowledge test bank have been reordered by topic and organized into a meaningful sequence. Also, the first line of the answer explanation gives the citation of the authoritative source for the answer.

QUESTIONS

3.1 Airspace

1. Which is true regarding flight operations in Class A airspace?

A. Aircraft must be equipped with approved distance measuring equipment (DME).

B. Must conduct operations under instrument flight rules.

C. Aircraft must be equipped with an approved ATC transponder.

Answer (B) is correct. *(FAR 91.135)*

DISCUSSION: Each person operating an airplane in Class A airspace must conduct that operation under instrument flight rules (IFR).

Answer (A) is incorrect. If VOR navigational equipment is required, the airplane must be equipped with DME for operations at or above FL 240. Since Class A airspace begins at FL 180, DME is not required for all operations. Answer (C) is incorrect. In Class A airspace, all airplanes must be equipped with an operable transponder and altitude reporting equipment, not only an approved ATC transponder.

2. Which is true regarding flight operations in Class A airspace?

A. Aircraft must be equipped with approved distance measuring equipment (DME).

B. Aircraft must be equipped with an ATC transponder and altitude reporting equipment.

C. May conduct operations under visual flight rules.

Answer (B) is correct. *(FAR 91.135)*

DISCUSSION: All aircraft operating in Class A airspace must be equipped with an ATC transponder and altitude reporting capability, unless otherwise authorized by ATC.

Answer (A) is incorrect. If VOR navigational equipment is required, the airplane must be equipped with DME for operations at or above FL 240. Since Class A airspace begins at FL 180, DME is not required for all operations in Class A airspace. Answer (C) is incorrect. Flight operations in Class A airspace are conducted under IFR, not VFR.

3. Which is true regarding flight operations in Class B airspace?

A. Flight under VFR is not authorized unless the pilot in command is instrument rated.

B. The pilot must receive an ATC clearance before operating an aircraft in that area.

C. Solo student pilot operations are not authorized.

Answer (B) is correct. *(FAR 91.131)*

DISCUSSION: The pilot must receive an ATC clearance before operating an airplane in Class B airspace.

Answer (A) is incorrect. Flight under special VFR at night, not VFR operations in Class B airspace, requires the pilot in command to be instrument rated. Answer (C) is incorrect. Solo student pilot operations are authorized in Class B airspace, as long as the requirements of FAR 61.95 have been met.

4. What is the maximum indicated airspeed authorized in the airspace underlying Class B airspace?

A. 156 knots.

B. 200 knots.

C. 230 knots.

Answer (B) is correct. *(FAR 91.117)*

DISCUSSION: No person may operate an aircraft in the airspace underlying a Class B airspace area designated for an airport at an indicated airspeed of more than 200 kt. (230 MPH).

Answer (A) is incorrect. This is not a maximum speed associated with any type of airspace. Answer (C) is incorrect. The figure 230 MPH, not 230 kt., is the maximum indicated airspeed allowed in the airspace underlying Class B airspace.

5. Which is true regarding pilot certification requirements for operations in Class B airspace?

A. The pilot in command must hold at least a private pilot certificate with an instrument rating.

B. The pilot in command must hold at least a private pilot certificate.

C. Solo student pilot operations are not authorized.

Answer (B) is correct. *(FAR 91.131)*

DISCUSSION: No person may take off or land at an airport within Class B airspace or operate an airplane within Class B airspace unless the pilot in command holds at least a private pilot certificate. However, a student pilot or a recreational pilot seeking private pilot certification may fly solo in Class B airspace if (s)he has met the requirements listed in FAR 61.95.

Answer (A) is incorrect. There is no requirement for the pilot in command to be instrument rated if (s)he is operating under VFR in Class B airspace. Answer (C) is incorrect. Solo student pilot operations are authorized in Class B airspace, as long as the requirements of FAR 61.95 have been met.

6. What transponder equipment is required for airplane operations within Class B airspace?
A transponder

A. with 4096 code or Mode S, and Mode C capability.

B. with 4096 code capability is required except when operating at or below 1,000 feet AGL under the terms of a letter of agreement.

C. is required for airplane operations when visibility is less than 3 miles.

Answer (A) is correct. *(FAR 91.215)*

DISCUSSION: Unless otherwise authorized or directed by ATC, no person may operate an airplane within Class B airspace unless it is equipped with an operable transponder having either 4096 code capability or Mode S capability. Additionally, the airplane must be equipped with automatic pressure altitude reporting equipment having Mode C capability.

Answer (B) is incorrect. In Class B airspace, the transponder must have both 4096 code capability and Mode C capability, not only 4096 code capability. Additionally, any letter of agreement with the controlling ATC facility would be geographically specific; it would not make an exception simply for any operation below 1,000 ft. AGL. Answer (C) is incorrect. An operable transponder with 4096 code, or Mode S, capability and Mode C capability is required at all times within Class B airspace, not only at times when the visibility is less than 3 statute miles.

7. Which is true regarding flight operations in Class B airspace?

A. The aircraft must be equipped with an ATC transponder and altitude reporting equipment.

B. The pilot in command must hold at least a private pilot certificate with an instrument rating.

C. The pilot in command must hold at least a student pilot certificate.

Answer (A) is correct. *(FAR 91.131)*

DISCUSSION: To operate in Class B airspace, the airplane must be equipped with an operating ATC transponder and automatic altitude reporting equipment.

Answer (B) is incorrect. The pilot in command is not required to be instrument rated to operate in Class B airspace under VFR. Answer (C) is incorrect. To operate solo in Class B airspace, a student pilot must also have met the requirements of FAR 61.95.

8. Unless otherwise authorized or required by ATC, the maximum indicated airspeed permitted when at or below 2,500 feet AGL within 4 NM of the primary airport within Class C or D airspace is

A. 180 knots.

B. 200 knots.

C. 230 knots.

Answer (B) is correct. *(FAR 91.117)*

DISCUSSION: Unless otherwise authorized or required by ATC, the maximum airspeed permitted when at or below 2,500 ft. AGL within 4 NM of the primary airport of a Class C or Class D airspace is 200 kt. (230 MPH).

Answer (A) is incorrect. This is not a maximum indicated airspeed associated with any air space classification and/or altitude. Answer (C) is incorrect. The figure 230 MPH, not 230 kt., is the maximum indicated airspeed permitted when at or below 2,500 ft. AGL within 4 NM of the primary airport in Class C or Class D airspace.

9. The radius of the uncharted Outer Area of Class C airspace is normally

A. 20 NM.

B. 30 NM.

C. 40 NM.

Answer (A) is correct. *(AIM Chap 3)*

DISCUSSION: Class C airspace areas have a procedural outer area that normally consists of a 20-NM radius from the primary airport in the Class C airspace. This area is not charted and generally does not require action from the pilot.

Answer (B) is incorrect. A 30-NM uncharted space does not exist around Class C airspace; however, a 30-NM Mode C veil surrounds Class B airspace. Answer (C) is incorrect. A 40-NM outer area does not exist for any form of airspace.

10. At some airports located in Class D airspace where ground visibility is not reported, takeoffs and landings under special VFR are

A. not authorized.

B. authorized by ATC if the flight visibility is at least 1 SM.

C. authorized only if the ground visibility is observed to be at least 3 SM.

Answer (B) is correct. *(FAR 91.157)*

DISCUSSION: No person may take off or land an aircraft (other than a helicopter) at any airport in Class D airspace under special VFR unless ground visibility at that airport is at least 1 SM or, if ground visibility is not reported at that airport, unless flight visibility during landing or takeoff is at least 1 statute mile.

Answer (A) is incorrect. Special VFR is still authorized if flight visibility is at least 1 statute mile. Answer (C) is incorrect. The visibility requirement for special VFR is 1 SM, not 3 statute miles.

11. If the minimum safe speed for any particular operation is greater than the maximum speed prescribed in 14 CFR Part 91, the

A. operator must have a Memorandum of Agreement (MOA) with the controlling agency.

B. aircraft may be operated at that speed.

C. operator must have a Letter of Agreement with ATC.

Answer (B) is correct. *(FAR 91.117)*

DISCUSSION: If the minimum safe airspeed for any particular operation is greater than the maximum airspeed prescribed in Part 91, the aircraft may be operated at that minimum airspeed. In such cases, the pilot is expected to advise ATC of the airspeed that will be used.

Answer (A) is incorrect. If the minimum safe airspeed for any particular operation is greater than the maximum airspeed prescribed in Part 91, the aircraft may be operated at that airspeed. The pilot is expected to advise ATC of the airspeed to be used. A memorandum of agreement is not required. Answer (C) is incorrect. If the minimum safe airspeed for any particular operation is greater than the maximum airspeed prescribed in Part 91, the aircraft may be operated at that minimum airspeed. The pilot is expected to advise ATC of the airspeed to be used. A letter of agreement is not required.

12. Which is true regarding flight operations to or from a satellite airport, without an operating control tower, within the Class C airspace area?

A. Prior to entering that airspace, a pilot must establish and maintain communication with the ATC serving facility.

B. Aircraft must be equipped with an ATC transponder.

C. Prior to takeoff, a pilot must establish communication with the ATC controlling facility.

Answer (A) is correct. *(FAR 91.130)*

DISCUSSION: Prior to entering Class C airspace, a pilot must establish and maintain two-way radio communications with the ATC facility providing air traffic services.

Answer (B) is incorrect. To operate in Class C airspace, an aircraft must be equipped with an ATC transponder and altitude reporting equipment (Mode C transponder), not just a transponder. Answer (C) is incorrect. When departing from a satellite airport without an operating control tower, you must establish communication with the ATC controlling facility as soon as practicable after, not prior to, takeoff.

13. Which is true regarding flight operations to or from a satellite airport, without an operating control tower, within the Class C airspace area?

A. Prior to takeoff, a pilot must establish communication with the ATC controlling facility.

B. Aircraft must be equipped with an ATC transponder and altitude reporting equipment.

C. Prior to landing, a pilot must establish and maintain communication with an ATC facility.

Answer (B) is correct. *(FAR 91.130)*

DISCUSSION: No person may operate an airplane within Class C airspace unless the airplane is equipped with an ATC transponder and altitude reporting equipment (Mode C transponder).

Answer (A) is incorrect. When departing a satellite airport without an operating control tower, you must establish communication with the ATC controlling facility as soon as practicable after, not prior to, takeoff. Answer (C) is incorrect. Prior to entering Class C airspace, not prior to landing at a satellite airport without an operating control tower, you must establish communication with the controlling ATC facility.

14. When operating an airplane for the purpose of takeoff or landing within Class D airspace under special VFR, what minimum distance from clouds and what visibility are required?

A. Remain clear of clouds, and the ground visibility must be at least 1 SM.

B. 500 feet beneath clouds, and the ground visibility must be at least 1 SM.

C. Remain clear of clouds, and the flight visibility must be at least 1 NM.

Answer (A) is correct. *(FAR 91.157)*

DISCUSSION: Under special VFR weather minimums, you may take off or land an airplane within Class D airspace if you remain clear of clouds and if the ground visibility is at least 1 statute mile.

Answer (B) is incorrect. You must only remain clear of clouds, not 500 ft. below the clouds, when operating an airplane under special VFR in Class D airspace. Answer (C) is incorrect. If ground visibility is not reported, the flight visibility must be at least 1 SM, not 1 nautical mile.

15. To operate an airplane under SPECIAL VFR (SVFR) within Class D airspace at night, which is required?

A. The pilot must hold an instrument rating, but the airplane need not be equipped for instrument flight, as long as the weather will remain at or above SVFR minimums.

B. The Class D airspace must be specifically designated as a night SVFR area.

C. The pilot must hold an instrument rating, and the airplane must be equipped for instrument flight.

Answer (C) is correct. *(FAR 91.157)*

DISCUSSION: No person may operate an airplane in Class D airspace under special VFR at night unless that person is instrument rated and the airplane is equipped for instrument flight.

Answer (A) is incorrect. The airplane must also be equipped for instrument flight to operate under SVFR at night in Class D airspace. Answer (B) is incorrect. There is no such designation as a "night special VFR area."

16. When approaching to land at an airport with an ATC facility, in Class D airspace, the pilot must establish communications prior to

A. 10 NM, up to and including 3,000 feet AGL.

B. 30 SM, and be transponder equipped.

C. 4 NM, up to and including 2,500 feet AGL.

Answer (C) is correct. *(FAR 91.129)*

DISCUSSION: A pilot must establish communications with ATC prior to entering Class D airspace. Class D airspace extends from the surface to 2,500 ft. AGL, and the lateral dimensions are set by local needs.

Note: When approaching to land at an airport with an ATC facility in Class E or Class G airspace, the pilot must establish communications prior to 4 NM, up to and including 2,500 ft. AGL.

Answer (A) is incorrect. A pilot must establish communications with ATC prior to entering Class D airspace, not prior to 10 NM, up to and including 3,000 ft. AGL. Answer (B) is incorrect. A pilot must establish communications with ATC prior to entering Class D airspace, not prior to 30 SM, and the airplane must be transponder equipped.

17. Excluding Hawaii, the vertical limits of the Federal Low Altitude airways extend from

A. 700 feet AGL up to, but not including, 14,500 feet MSL.

B. 1,200 feet AGL up to, but not including, 18,000 feet MSL.

C. 1,200 feet AGL up to, but not including, 14,500 feet MSL.

Answer (B) is correct. *(AIM Para 3-2-6)*

DISCUSSION: Federal airways are Class E airspace, which extends upward from 1,200 ft. AGL to, but not including, 18,000 ft. MSL.

Answer (A) is incorrect. The amount of 700 ft. AGL is the floor of Class E airspace when designated in conjunction with an airport that has an IAP, not in conjunction with a Federal airway. Also, Class E airspace extends up to, but does not include, 18,000 ft. MSL, not 14,500 ft. MSL. Answer (C) is incorrect. Class E airspace that is designated as a Federal airway extends from 1,200 ft. AGL up to, but not including, 18,000 ft. MSL, not 14,500 ft. MSL.

18. When operating an aircraft in the vicinity of an airport with an operating control tower, in Class E airspace, a pilot must establish communications prior to

A. 8 NM, and up to and including 3,000 feet AGL.

B. 5 NM, and up to and including 3,000 feet AGL.

C. 4 NM, and up to and including 2,500 feet AGL.

Answer (C) is correct. *(FAR 91.127)*

DISCUSSION: When operating an airplane to, from, through, or on an airport with an operating control tower in Class E airspace, a pilot must establish communications prior to 4 NM from the airport, up to and including 2,500 ft. AGL.

Answer (A) is incorrect. When operating an airplane in the vicinity of an airport with an operating control tower in Class E airspace, a pilot must establish communications prior to 4 NM, not 8 NM, from the airport, and up to and including 2,500 ft. AGL, not 3,000 ft. AGL. Answer (B) is incorrect. When operating an airplane in the vicinity of an airport with an operating control tower in Class E airspace, a pilot must establish communications prior to 4 NM, not 5 NM, from the airport, and up to and including 2,500 ft. AGL, not 3,000 ft. AGL.

19. What designated airspace associated with an airport becomes inactive when the control tower at that airport is not in operation?

A. Class D, which then becomes Class C.

B. Class D, which then becomes Class E.

C. Class B.

Answer (B) is correct. *(AIM Para 3-2-5)*

DISCUSSION: Class D airspace is located at airports that have an operating control tower which is not associated with Class B or Class C airspace. Airspace at an airport with a part-time control tower is classified as Class D airspace when the control tower is in operation and as Class E airspace when the control tower is not in operation.

During the hours the tower is not in operation, the Class E surface area rules or a combination of Class E rules to 700 ft. AGL and Class G rules to the surface will become applicable. Check the *A/FD* for specific information about a given airspace area.

Answer (A) is incorrect. When a part-time control tower is not in operation, the Class D airspace becomes Class E, not Class C, airspace. Answer (C) is incorrect. The primary airport of Class B airspace will have a control tower that operates full-time, not part-time.

20. When approaching to land at an airport without an operating control tower, in Class G airspace, the pilot should

A. make all turns to the left, unless otherwise indicated.

B. fly a left-hand traffic pattern at 800 feet AGL.

C. enter and fly a traffic pattern at 800 feet AGL.

Answer (A) is correct. *(FAR 91.126)*

DISCUSSION: When approaching to land at an airport without an operating control tower in Class G airspace, the pilot of an airplane must make all turns to the left, unless otherwise indicated.

Answer (B) is incorrect. When approaching to land at an airport without an operating control tower in Class G airspace, the pilot should fly a left-hand traffic pattern, unless otherwise indicated by traffic pattern indicators around the segment circle. Additionally, the recommended pattern altitude is 1,000 ft. AGL, unless otherwise published. Answer (C) is incorrect. When approaching to land at an airport without an operating control tower in Class G airspace, the pilot should make all turns to the left (unless otherwise indicated), not fly any traffic pattern direction. Additionally, the recommended pattern altitude is 1,000 ft. AGL, unless otherwise published.

3.2 VHF/DF

21. To use VHF/DF facilities for assistance in locating your position, you must have an operative VHF

A. transmitter and receiver.

B. transmitter and receiver, and an operative ADF receiver.

C. transmitter and receiver, and an operative VOR receiver.

Answer (A) is correct. *(PHAK Chap 15)*

DISCUSSION: The VHF/direction finder facility is a ground-based radio receiver that displays the magnetic direction of the airplane from the station each time the airplane transmits a signal to it. Thus, to use such facilities for assistance in locating an airplane position, the airplane must have both a VHF transmitter (to send the signal) and a receiver (to communicate with the operator, who reads out the displayed magnetic direction).

Answer (B) is incorrect. An ADF is not required to use VHF/DF facilities. Answer (C) is incorrect. A VOR is not required to use VHF/DF facilities.

3.3 Airport Signs/Markings

22. (Refer to Figure 51 on page 75.) The pilot generally calls ground control after landing when the aircraft is completely clear of the runway. This is when the aircraft

A. passes the red symbol shown at the top of the figure.

B. is on the dashed-line side of the middle symbol.

C. is past the solid-line side of the middle symbol.

Answer (C) is correct. *(AIM Para 2-3-9)*

DISCUSSION: The middle symbol is a runway boundary sign that has a yellow background with a black inscription and graphic depicting the pavement holding position marking. This sign, which faces the runway and is visible to the pilot exiting the runway, is located adjacent to the holding position marking on the pavement. The sign is intended to provide you with another visual cue to use as a guide to determine when you are clear of the runway. Thus, you are clear of the runway when your entire airplane is on the solid-line side of the holding marking.

Answer (A) is incorrect. If you pass the top symbol, you will enter an area prohibited to aircraft; it does not mean that you are clear of the runway. Answer (B) is incorrect. You are considered still on, not clear of, the runway if you are on the dashed-line side of the middle symbol.

23. (Refer to Figure 51 on page 75.) The red symbol at the top would most likely be found

A. upon exiting all runways prior to calling ground control.

B. at an intersection where a roadway may be mistaken as a taxiway.

C. near the approach end of ILS runways.

Answer (B) is correct. *(AIM Para 2-3-8)*

DISCUSSION: The symbol at the top (red background with white inscription) is a mandatory instruction sign that prohibits an aircraft from entering an area. Typically, this sign is located on a taxiway intended to be used in only one direction or at an intersection of vehicle roadways with runways, taxiways, or aprons where the roadway may be mistaken as a taxiway or other aircraft movement surface.

Answer (A) is incorrect. The middle, not the top, symbol would most likely be found upon exiting all runways prior to calling ground control. Answer (C) is incorrect. The bottom, not the top, symbol would most likely be found near the approach end of ILS runways.

24. (Refer to Figure 51 on page 75.) While clearing an active runway you are most likely clear of the ILS critical area when you pass which symbol?

A. Top red.

B. Middle yellow.

C. Bottom yellow.

Answer (C) is correct. *(AIM Para 2-3-9)*

DISCUSSION: The bottom symbol is an ILS critical area boundary sign, which has a yellow background with a black inscription and graphic depicting the ILS pavement holding position marking. The sign is located adjacent to the ILS holding position marking on the pavement and can be seen by pilots leaving the critical area. The sign is intended to provide you with another visual cue to use as a guide in deciding when you are clear of the ILS critical area.

Answer (A) is incorrect. The top symbol is a sign prohibiting aircraft entry into an area, not a sign that you have cleared the ILS critical area. Answer (B) is incorrect. While clearing the active runway, you are most likely clear of the runway, not the ILS critical area, when you pass the middle symbol.

25. (Refer to Figure 51 on page 75.) The ILS Critical Area Boundary Sign indicates

A. you are about to enter, or you are clear of, the ILS critical area.

B. an area you are prohibited from entering.

C. an area in which aircraft over 30 feet tall may conflict with aircraft on the ILS approach.

Answer (A) is correct. *(AIM 2-3-8)*

DISCUSSION: This sign is located adjacent to the ILS holding position marking on the pavement. The sign is intended to provide you with a visual reference when entering the critical area while taxiing to a runway and when exiting the area while taxiing away from a runway.

Answer (B) is incorrect. You are not prohibited from entering the ILS critical area. However, you must hold short of the critical area when the ILS approach is in use or when so instructed by ATC. Answer (C) is incorrect. Aircraft on the ground, in the ILS critical area, pose no collision risk to aircraft on the ILS approach.

26. (Refer to Figure 51 on page 75.) From the cockpit, the middle marking confirms the aircraft to be

A. on a taxiway, about to enter runway zone.

B. on a runway, about to clear.

C. near an instrument approach clearance zone.

Answer (B) is correct. *(AIM Chap 4)*

DISCUSSION: When the runway holding position line is viewed from the runway side, the pilot is presented with two dashed bars. The PIC must ensure the entire aircraft has cleared the runway holding position line prior to coming to a stop.

Answer (A) is incorrect. A pilot entering a runway from a taxiway is presented with the two solid bars, not dashed lines, on the runway holding position marking. Answer (C) is incorrect. The marking depicted is a runway holding position marking and is not related to any form of clearance zone.

27. (Refer to Figure 51 below.) When taxiing up to an active runway, you are likely to be clear of the ILS critical area when short of which symbol?

A. Bottom yellow.

B. Top red.

C. Middle yellow.

Answer (A) is correct. *(AIM Para 2-3-9)*

DISCUSSION: The bottom symbol is an ILS critical area boundary sign, which has a yellow background with a black inscription depicting the ILS pavement holding position marking. The sign is located adjacent to the ILS holding position marking on the pavement and can be seen by pilots approaching the ILS critical area. Thus, you will be clear of the ILS critical area, when taxiing to an active runway, when short of the ILS critical area boundary sign.

Answer (B) is incorrect. The top red sign prohibits an aircraft from entering an area and is not used to mark the ILS critical area. Answer (C) is incorrect. The middle yellow sign is a runway boundary sign that faces toward the runway to help pilots to decide when they are clear of the runway, not the ILS critical area.

28. (Refer to Figure 51 below.) Which symbol does not directly address runway incursion with other aircraft?

A. Top red.

B. Middle yellow.

C. Bottom yellow.

Answer (A) is correct. *(AIM Para 2-3-8)*

DISCUSSION: The symbol at the top (red background with white inscription) is a mandatory instruction sign that prohibits an aircraft from entering an area. Typically, this sign would be located on a taxiway intended to be used in only one direction or at an intersection of vehicle roadways with runways, taxiways, or aprons where the roadway may be mistaken as a taxiway or other aircraft movement surface. Thus, it does not directly address runway incursion with other aircraft.

Answer (B) is incorrect. The middle symbol is used to help indicate when you are clear of the runway. If you are not clear of the active runway, you will interfere with runway operations. Answer (C) is incorrect. The bottom symbol is used to help indicate when you are clear of the ILS critical area. An aircraft that is not clear of the ILS critical area may cause ILS course distortion which will interfere with ILS approaches being conducted.

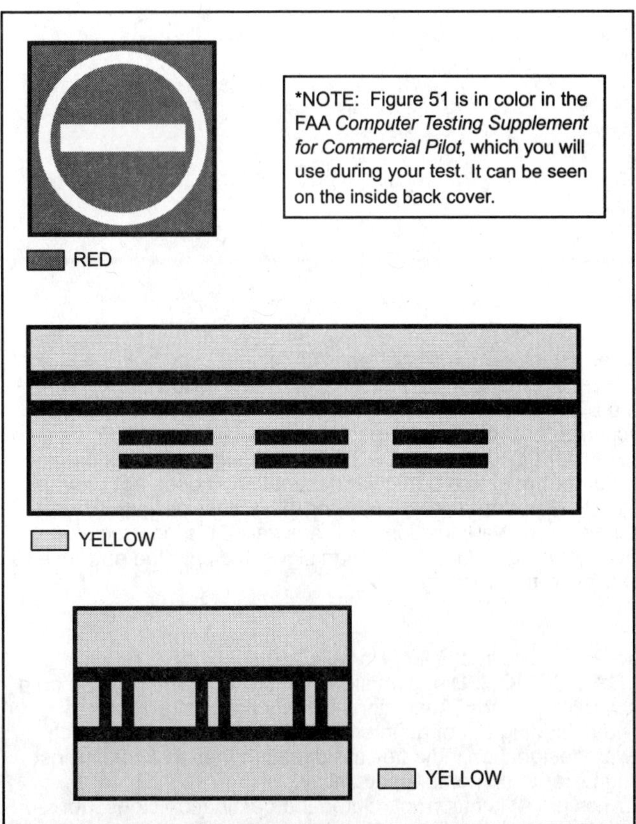

Figure 51. – Airport Signs.

29. (Refer to Figure 60 below and in color on page 248.) As you taxi you see sign 2 on the right side of the aircraft and sign 1 directly in front of you on the opposite side of the intersection. Does the taxiway continue on the opposite side of the intersection?

A. Yes, taxiway A is on the opposite side of the intersection.

B. Yes, taxiway T is on the opposite side of the intersection.

C. No, the taxiway does not continue.

Answer (C) is correct. *(AIM Para 2-3-10)*

DISCUSSION: The taxiway array sign (sign 2) shows that the pilot is currently on taxiway A. The taxiway ending sign (sign 1) indicates that taxiway A does not continue.

Answer (A) is incorrect. The pilot is on taxiway A, which ends as denoted by the taxiway ending sign. Answer (B) is incorrect. Taxiway T is to the right. The taxiway array sign shows that the pilot is currently on taxiway A. The taxiway ending sign indicates that taxiway A ends ahead of the intersection.

30. (Refer to Figure 60 below and in color on page 248.) Sign 1 is an indication

A. of an area where aircraft are prohibited.

B. that the taxiway does not continue.

C. of the general taxiing direction to a taxiway.

Answer (B) is correct. *(AIM Para 2-3-12)*

DISCUSSION: A taxiway ending marker sign consists of alternating yellow and black diagonal stripes. Taxiway ending marker signs indicate that the taxiway does not continue beyond the sign.

Answer (A) is incorrect. No entry signs, not taxiway ending marker signs, identify an area where aircraft are prohibited from entering. No entry signs consist of a white horizontal line surrounded by a white circle on a red background. Answer (C) is incorrect. A direction sign, not a taxiway ending marker sign, indicates the general taxiing direction to a taxiway. Direction signs consist of black lettering on a yellow background with an arrow indicating the direction of turn.

Figure 60. – Two Signs.

31. Which of the following best describes a destination sign?

A. Indicates a runway on which the aircraft is presently located.

B. Indicates the direction to the takeoff runway.

C. Indicates the entrance to a taxiway from a runway.

Answer (B) is correct. *(AIM Para 2-7-11)*

DISCUSSION: A destination sign has a yellow background with a black inscription. The destination sign indicates the direction of taxi required to reach a particular destination.

Answer (A) is incorrect. A destination sign indicates the direction of travel to a particular destination; it does not provide information on your present location. This answer choice best describes a runway position sign. Answer (C) is incorrect. Runway exit signs, not destination signs, indicate the entrance to a taxiway from a runway.

32. When turning onto a taxiway from another taxiway, the "taxiway directional sign" indicates

A. direction to the take-off runway.

B. designation and direction of taxiway leading out of an intersection.

C. designation and direction of exit taxiway from runway.

Answer (B) is correct. *(AIM Para 2-3-10)*

DISCUSSION: Direction signs consist of black lettering on a yellow background. These signs identify the designations of taxiways leading out of an intersection. An arrow next to each taxiway designation indicates the direction that an aircraft must turn in order to taxi onto that taxiway.

Answer (A) is incorrect. Outbound destination signs, not direction signs, indicate the direction that must be taken out of an intersection in order to follow the preferred taxi route to a runway. Answer (C) is incorrect. The question specifies that you are turning onto a taxiway from another taxiway, not from a runway.

33. (Refer to Figure 65 below and in color on page 249.) The "taxiway ending" marker

A. indicates taxiway does not continue.

B. identifies area where aircraft are prohibited.

C. provides general taxiing direction to named taxiway.

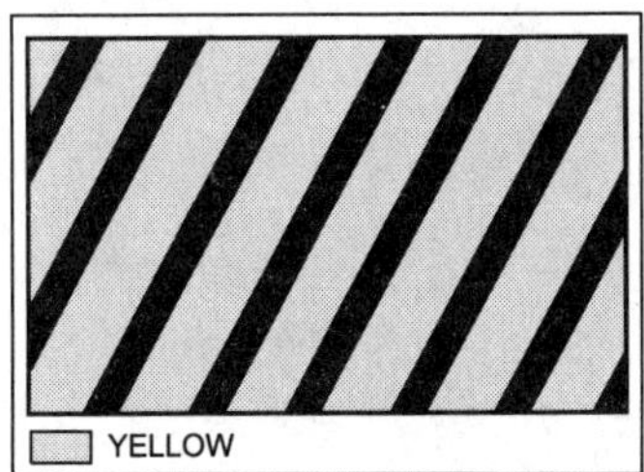

Figure 65. – Sign.

Answer (A) is correct. *(AIM Para 2-3-12)*

DISCUSSION: A taxiway ending marker sign consists of alternating yellow and black diagonal stripes. Taxiway ending marker signs indicate that the taxiway does not continue beyond the sign.

Answer (B) is incorrect. No entry signs, not taxiway ending marker signs, identify an area where aircraft are prohibited from entering. No entry signs consist of a white horizontal line surrounded by a white circle on a red background. Answer (C) is incorrect. A direction sign, not a taxiway ending marker sign, indicates the general direction to take out of an intersection in order to taxi onto the named taxiway. Direction signs consist of black lettering on a yellow background with an arrow indicating the direction of turn.

34. (Refer to Figure 59 below and in color on page 248.) Use the sign and taxiway diagram. You are approaching the intersection on taxiway 5 and see the sign at the left of the intersection. Taxiway number 2 is identified as

A. A.

B. F.

C. T.

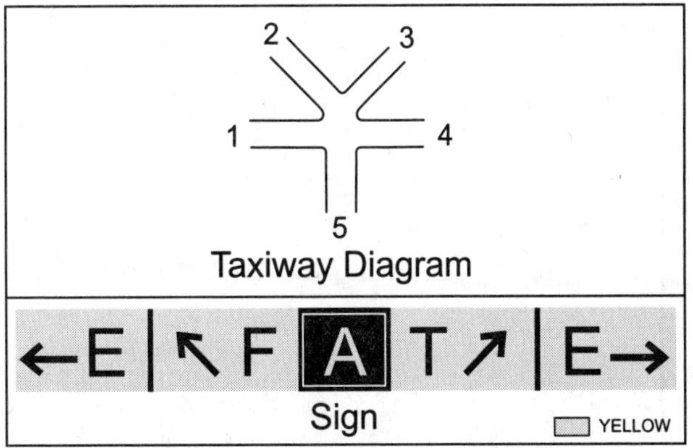

Figure 59. – Taxiway Diagram and Sign.

Answer (B) is correct. *(AIM Para 2-3-10)*

DISCUSSION: The taxiway diagram shows that taxiway 2 is forward and to the left (which is not to be confused with directly to the left). The sign shows that the taxiway to the forward left is taxiway Foxtrot (F).

Answer (A) is incorrect. The airplane is currently positioned on Taxiway Alpha (A), shown on the taxiway diagram as taxiway 5. Answer (C) is incorrect. Taxiway Tango (T) is shown as being forward and right, that is, as taxiway 3 on the taxiway diagram.

35. (Refer to Figure 61 below and in color on page 248.) This sign is a visual clue that

A. confirms the aircraft's location to be on taxiway "A."

B. warns the pilot of approaching taxiway "A."

C. indicates "A" holding area is ahead.

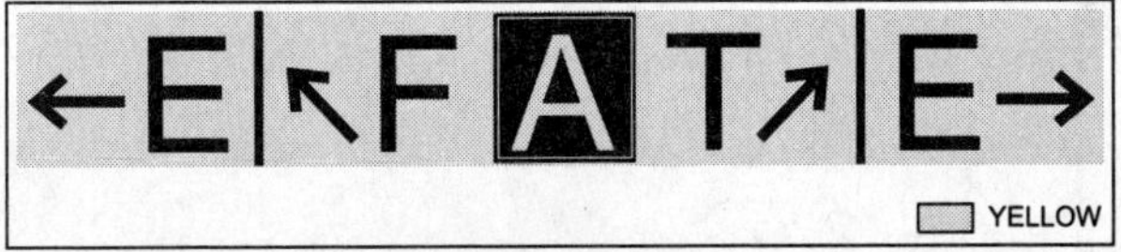

Figure 61. – Sign.

Answer (A) is correct. *(AIM Chap 3)*

DISCUSSION: The taxiway location sign consists of a yellow letter on a black background with a yellow border. This sign confirms the pilot is on taxiway "A."

Answer (B) is incorrect. A direction sign with a yellow background, a black letter, and an arrow pointing to taxiway "A" would be required to warn a pilot that (s)he is approaching taxiway "A." Answer (C) is incorrect. A taxiway location sign defines a position on a taxiway, not a holding area.

36. (Refer to Figure 57 below and in color on page 247.) You are directed to taxi to runway 10. You see this sign at a taxiway intersection while taxiing. Which way should you proceed?

A. Left.
B. Right.
C. Straight ahead.

←4 | 10·21↑ | 22→

YELLOW

Figure 57. – Sign.

Answer (C) is correct. *(AIM Chap 2)*

DISCUSSION: A direction sign has a yellow background with black numbers or letters and an arrow indicating the direction to travel. In this case, the direction sign indicates that Runway 10 is straight ahead. The sign also indicates that Runway 21 is straight ahead.

Answer (A) is incorrect. A turn to the left would take you to Runway 4, not Runway 10. Answer (B) is incorrect. A turn to the right would take you to Runway 22, not Runway 10.

37. (Refer to Figure 66 below and in color on page 250.) Which marking indicates a vehicle lane?

A. A.
B. C.
C. E.

Answer (B) is correct. *(AIM Chap 3)*

DISCUSSION: Vehicle roadway markings define pathways for vehicles to cross areas of the airport used by aircraft and exist in two forms. Vehicle roadway markings may be defined by either a solid while line or white zipper markings. A dashed white line separates opposite direction vehicle traffic inside the roadway.

Answer (A) is incorrect. The marking on the pavement defines a holding position sign at the beginning of the takeoff runway. Answer (C) is incorrect. The pavement marking delineates the movement and nonmovement surface areas.

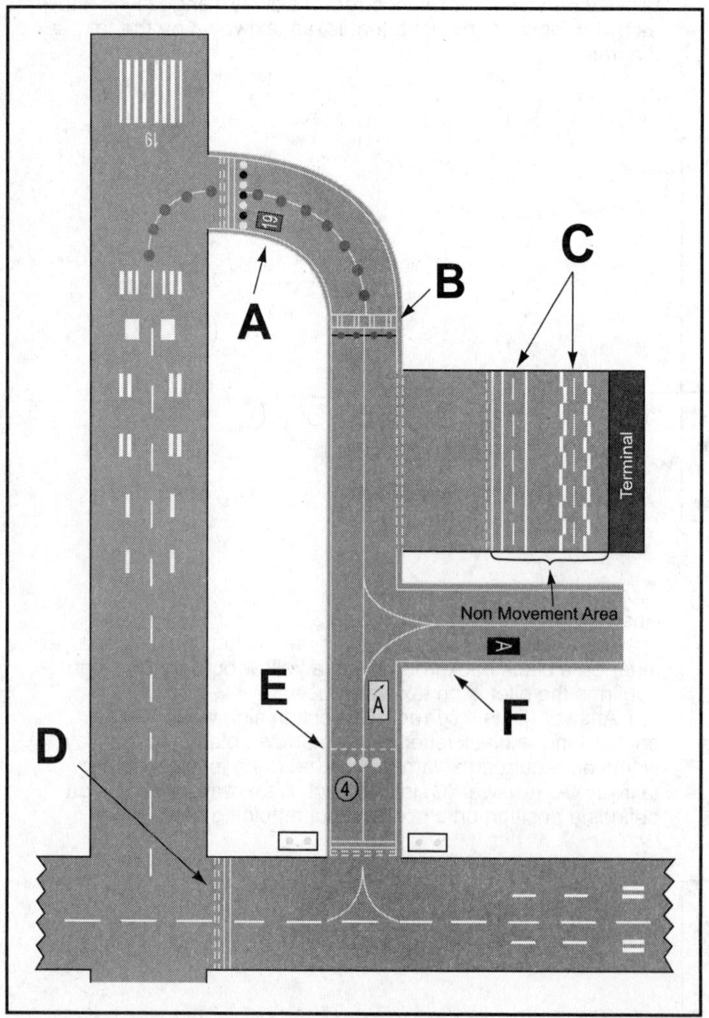

Figure 66. – Airport Markings.

38. The 'yellow demarcation bar' marking indicates

A. runway with a displaced threshold that precedes the runway.

B. a hold line from a taxiway to a runway.

C. the beginning of available runway for landing on the approach side.

Answer (A) is correct. *(AIM Chap 2)*

DISCUSSION: A demarcation bar is a 3-foot-wide yellow stripe that separates a runway with a displaced threshold from a blast pad, stopway, or taxiway that precedes the runway.

Answer (B) is incorrect. A set of solid yellow and dashed yellow lines represents the hold lines between a taxiway and runway. Answer (C) is incorrect. The yellow demarcation bar delineates the beginning of the displaced threshold, which is not a landing surface.

39. (Refer to Figure 58 below and in color on page 247.) At what point on the airport diagram could a pilot expect to see this sign?

A. 3 and 5.

B. 10 and 11.

C. 3, 5, 10, and 11.

Answer (B) is correct. *(AIM Para 2-3-8)*

DISCUSSION: The runway holding position sign will be located at the intersection of a taxiway and runway or the intersection of two runways. In this figure, you could expect to see this sign at points 10 and 11.

Answer (A) is incorrect. The runway holding position sign at the beginning of the takeoff runway may only display the designation of the takeoff runway. All other signs will have the designation of both runway directions. Answer (C) is incorrect. The runway holding position sign at the beginning of the takeoff runway may only display the designation of the takeoff runway. All other signs will have the designation of both runway directions.

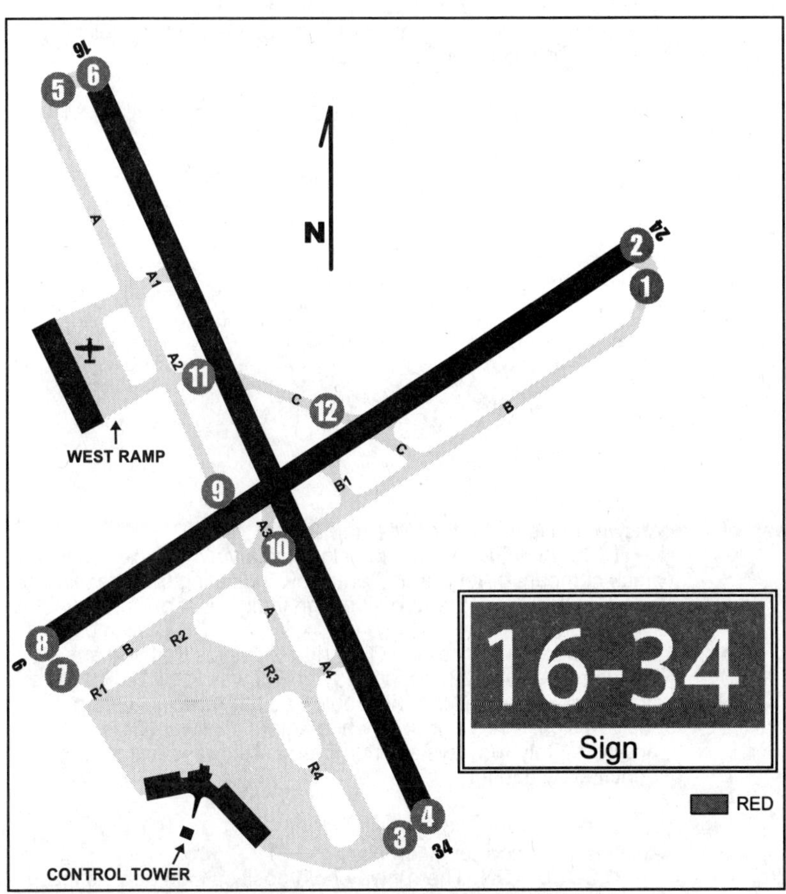

Figure 58. – Airport Diagram and Sign.

40. The runway holding position sign is located on

A. runways that intersect other runways.

B. taxiways protected from an aircraft approaching a runway.

C. runways that intersect other taxiways.

Answer (A) is correct. *(AIM Chap 2)*

DISCUSSION: The runway holding position sign is used to delineate the holding point on a taxiway that intersects a runway or on a runway that intersects another runway.

Answer (B) is incorrect. Runway holding position signs do not protect taxiways from aircraft approaching the runway. Answer (C) is incorrect. Runway holding position signs are placed on a runway to delineate intersecting runways, not taxiways.

41. 'Runway Holding Position Markings' on taxiways

A. identify where aircraft are prohibited to taxi when not cleared to proceed by ground control.

B. identify where aircraft are supposed to stop when not cleared to proceed onto the runway.

C. allow an aircraft permission onto the runway.

Answer (B) is correct. *(AIM Chap 2)*

DISCUSSION: Runway holding position markings identify where aircraft are supposed to stop when not cleared onto the runway. When told to hold short of a runway, a pilot must come to a stop prior to the runway holding position markings and ensure no portion of his or her aircraft extends beyond them. At an uncontrolled airport, a pilot must ensure the runway is clear and confirm the area is clear of arriving or departing traffic on the runway prior to crossing the runway holding position markings.

Answer (A) is incorrect. Runway holding position markings are used at both controlled and uncontrolled airports. A clearance to cross runway holding position markings will not be available from ground control at a non-towered facility. It is, however, the PIC's responsibility to ensure the area is clear of traffic prior to crossing the runway holding position markings. Answer (C) is incorrect. Access and/or a clearance onto an active runway can be granted only by ATC or the PIC at an uncontrolled airport after carefully ensuring the area is clear and (s)he is safe to cross the runway holding position markings.

42. (Refer to Figure 56 below and in color on page 247.) If you were on a taxiway approaching or leading to Runway 22, which sign would you see?

A. 1.

B. 2.

C. Neither 1 or 2.

Answer (A) is correct. *(AIM Para 2-3-11)*

DISCUSSION: Image 1 is a destination sign pointing you in the direction of Runway 22.

Answer (B) is incorrect. Image 2 is a hold position sign indicating that you are at the takeoff end of Runway 4. Answer (C) is incorrect. Image 1 is a destination sign pointing you in the direction of Runway 22.

Figure 56. – Two Signs.

43. (Refer to Figure 56 above and in color on page 247.) This sign confirms your position on

A. runway 22.

B. routing to runway 22.

C. taxiway 22.

Answer (B) is correct. *(AIM Chap 2)*

DISCUSSION: A direction sign has a yellow background with black numbers or letters and an arrow indicating the direction to travel. In this case, the direction sign indicates that Runway 22 is straight ahead.

Answer (A) is incorrect. The sign indicates that you are routing to Runway 22, not already at Runway 22. If a pilot were already at Runway 22, (s)he would see the runway holding position sign, a red sign with white letters. Answer (C) is incorrect. Only runways are numbered. Taxiways are always identified by a letter.

44. (Refer to Figure 64 on page 81 and in color on page 249.) You are viewing this sign from the cockpit as you hold short of the runway. The air traffic controller clears you to back taxi on the runway for a full length departure on Runway 8. Which way would you turn to begin the back taxi?

A. Right.

B. Left.

C. Not enough information provided.

Answer (A) is correct. *(AIM Para 2-3-8)*

DISCUSSION: The runway hold position sign depicts the runway thresholds. The "8" is on the right side of the sign, indicating the threshold for Runway 8 is to the right. A turn to the left would place you on Runway 8. To back taxi for a full length takeoff, you would turn to the right. At the end of the runway, you would perform a 180° turn and take off on Runway 8.

Answer (B) is incorrect. You would turn to the left if you intended to take off on Runway 8 for an intersection departure without a back taxi for a full length takeoff or if you intended to back taxi for a Runway 26 takeoff. Answer (C) is incorrect. There is sufficient information provided to determine the appropriate direction of turn.

45. (Refer to Figure 64 below and in color on page 249.) You are viewing this sign from the cockpit as you hold short of the runway. The air traffic controller clears you to back taxi on the runway for a full length departure on Runway 26. Which way would you turn to begin the back taxi?

A. Right.

B. Left.

C. Not enough information provided.

Answer (B) is correct. *(AIM Para 2-3-8)*

DISCUSSION: The runway hold position sign depicts the runway thresholds. The "26" is on the left side of the sign, indicating the threshold for Runway 26 is to the left. A turn to the right would place you on Runway 26. To back taxi for a full length takeoff, you would turn to the left. At the end of the runway, you would perform a 180° turn and take off on Runway 26.

Answer (A) is incorrect. You would turn to the right if you intended to take off on Runway 26 for an intersection departure without a back taxi for a full length takeoff or if you intended to back taxi for a Runway 8 take off. Answer (C) is incorrect. There is sufficient information provided to determine the appropriate direction of turn.

46. (Refer to Figure 64 below and in color on page 249.) You are holding short for an intersection departure on Runway 8 with the sign in front of you. After turning onto the runway you should

A. Turn right.

B. Turn left.

C. Insufficient information is given.

Answer (B) is correct. *(AIM Para 2-3-8)*

DISCUSSION: You would turn to the left because the runway holding position sign shown in Fig. 64 shows the actual runway layout. Therefore, you would turn away from the position of the runway designation on the sign just like you would if you were taxiing onto the end of the runway for takeoff.

Answer (A) is incorrect. Turning right would result in a takeoff from Runway 26. Answer (C) is incorrect. The runway holding position sign provides sufficient information to answer this question.

Figure 64. – Sign.

47. (Refer to Figure 64 above and in color on page 249.) If cleared for an intersection takeoff on runway 8, you see this sign at the intersection hold short position. Which way should you turn when taxiing onto the runway?

A. Left.

B. Right.

C. Need more information.

Answer (A) is correct. *(AIM Chap 2)*

DISCUSSION: The numbers on the runway holding position sign correspond to the runway threshold. In this case, the 8 is on the right side of the sign, indicating that you should turn to the left to enter Runway 8.

Answer (B) is incorrect. In this case, a turn to the right would place you on Runway 26, not Runway 8. Answer (C) is incorrect. All of the information you need to make a decision is provided by the runway holding position sign.

48. (Refer to Figure 64 above and in color on page 249.) This taxiway sign would be expected

A. at the intersection of runway 08/26 departure end and the taxiway.

B. near the intersection of runways 08 and 26.

C. at a taxiway intersecting runway 08/26.

Answer (C) is correct. *(AIM Chap 2)*

DISCUSSION: The runway holding position sign consists of white numbers on a red background. In this example, the pilot would be on a taxiway intersection of Runways 8 and 26.

Answer (A) is incorrect. The pilot would see the holding position sign if (s)he were at the departure end of the runway. The holding position sign consists of white numbers on a red background. Since the holding position sign is on the departure end of the runway, only one runway, as opposed to both, is listed. Answer (B) is incorrect. The sign indicates that the pilot is at a specific location, not nearing a location.

49. What is the purpose of the runway exit sign?

A. Defines direction and designation of runway when exiting a taxiway.

B. Defines direction and designation of exit taxiway from runway.

C. Defines a mandatory exit point from the runway during Land and Hold Short Operations (LAHSO).

Answer (B) is correct. *(AIM 2-3-10)*

DISCUSSION: A runway exit sign defines the direction and designation of an exit taxiway from the runway.

Answer (A) is incorrect. A runway exit sign is positioned on the runway, not on a taxiway. This answer choice describes a runway destination sign. Answer (C) is incorrect. Runway exit signs are not mandatory exit points during Land and Hold Short Operations (LAHSO). This answer choice partially describes runway holding position markings.

3.4 Collision Avoidance

50. How can you determine if another aircraft is on a collision course with your aircraft?

A. The nose of each aircraft is pointed at the same point in space.

B. The other aircraft will always appear to get larger and closer at a rapid rate.

C. There will be no apparent relative motion between your aircraft and the other aircraft.

Answer (C) is correct. *(AIM Para 8-1-8)*

DISCUSSION: Any aircraft that appears to have no relative motion and stays in one scan quadrant is likely to be on a collision course. Also, if a target shows no lateral or vertical movements but increases in size, take evasive action.

Answer (A) is incorrect. Even if you could determine the direction of the other airplane, you may not be able to accurately project the flight paths and speeds of the two airplanes to determine if they indeed point to the same point in space and will arrive there at the same time (i.e., collide). Answer (B) is incorrect. Aircraft on collision courses may not always appear to grow larger or to close at a rapid rate. Frequently, the degree of proximity cannot be detected.

51. What is the general direction of movement of the other aircraft if during a night flight you observe a steady white light and a rotating red light ahead and at your altitude? The other aircraft is

A. headed away from you.

B. crossing to your left.

C. approaching you head-on.

Answer (A) is correct. *(AFH Chap 10)*

DISCUSSION: A steady white light is the tail light. The other airplane is heading away from you. The rotating red light is the beacon light. The red and green wingtip position lights cannot be seen from the rear.

Answer (B) is incorrect. You would observe a steady red light if the other airplane was crossing to your left. Answer (C) is incorrect. You would see the red and green wingtip (not white) position lights if the other aircraft was approaching you head-on.

52. When in the vicinity of a VOR which is being used for navigation on VFR flight, it is important to

A. make 90° left and right turns to scan for other traffic.

B. exercise sustained vigilance to avoid aircraft that may be converging on the VOR from other directions.

C. pass the VOR on the right side of the radial to allow room for aircraft flying in the opposite direction on the same radial.

Answer (B) is correct. *(AIM Para 4-4-14)*

DISCUSSION: When operating VFR in highly congested areas, such as in the vicinity of a VOR that is being used for VFR navigation, you should exercise constant vigilance to avoid aircraft that may be converging on the VOR from other directions.

Answer (A) is incorrect. Ninety-degree turns (i.e., clearing turns) are appropriate prior to practicing stalls, etc., but not while en route. Answer (C) is incorrect. There is no convention to pass on the right side of VORs or stay on the right side of airways. The FARs require you to be on the centerline of the airway.

3.5 Wake Turbulence

53. Which is true with respect to vortex circulation in the wake turbulence generated by an aircraft?

A. Helicopters generate downwash turbulence only, not vortex circulation.

B. The vortex strength is greatest when the generating aircraft is heavy, clean, and slow.

C. When vortex circulation sinks into ground effect, it tends to dissipate rapidly and offer little danger.

Answer (B) is correct. *(PHAK Chap 4)*

DISCUSSION: Airplanes produce wingtip vortices in all phases of flight. The vortex circulation and wake turbulence is at its greatest when the airplane is heavy, clean, and slow. To compensate for a heavy, clean, and slow configuration, a pilot must operate the aircraft at a higher angle of attack to produce the required lift, resulting in greater wake turbulence. This is commonplace in and around the airport environment as aircraft are operating at a high angle of attack to generate the required lift for takeoff and landing.

Answer (A) is incorrect. A helicopter in forward flight creates strong vortices that trail the helicopter in a similar fashion to the vortices generated by a large, fixed-wing airplane. Answer (C) is incorrect. A vortex cannot sink into ground effect since ground effect is formed by the relationship of an airplane's wings to the earth's surface. It could be stated that wake turbulence generated by an airplane in ground effect is reduced.

54. During a takeoff made behind a departing large jet airplane, the pilot can minimize the hazard of wingtip vortices by

A. being airborne prior to reaching the jet's flightpath until able to turn clear of its wake.

B. maintaining extra speed on takeoff and climbout.

C. extending the takeoff roll and not rotating until well beyond the jet's rotation point.

Answer (A) is correct. *(AIM Para 7-3-6)*

DISCUSSION: When departing behind a larger aircraft, you should rotate prior to the larger aircraft's rotation point and climb above its climb path until turning clear of its wake.

Answer (B) is incorrect. Even at maximum speed, you will probably not have enough control effectiveness to counteract the induced roll of the vortices. Answer (C) is incorrect. The vortices sink below the jet's flight path, so you want to be above them, not below them.

55. To avoid possible wake turbulence from a large jet aircraft that has just landed prior to your takeoff, at which point on the runway should you plan to become airborne?

A. Past the point where the jet touched down.

B. At the point where the jet touched down, or just prior to this point.

C. Approximately 500 feet prior to the point where the jet touched down.

Answer (A) is correct. *(AIM Para 7-3-6)*

DISCUSSION: When taking off on a runway on which a large jet aircraft has just landed, plan to become airborne past the point where the jet touched down.

Answer (B) is incorrect. You should rotate past, not at or prior to, the point where the jet touched down. Answer (C) is incorrect. You should rotate past, not 500 ft. prior to, where the jet touched down.

56. Choose the correct statement regarding wake turbulence.

A. Vortex generation begins with the initiation of the takeoff roll.

B. The primary hazard is loss of control because of induced roll.

C. The greatest vortex strength is produced when the generating airplane is heavy, clean, and fast.

Answer (B) is correct. *(AIM Para 7-3-3)*

DISCUSSION: The usual hazard associated with wake turbulence is the induced rolling movements, which can exceed the rolling capability of the encountering aircraft.

Answer (A) is incorrect. Vortex generation begins at the rotation point when the airplane takes off, not the initiation of the takeoff roll. Answer (C) is incorrect. The greatest vortex strength is when the generating aircraft is slow, not fast.

57. Which procedure should you follow to avoid wake turbulence if a large jet crosses your course from left to right approximately 1 mile ahead and at your altitude?

A. Make sure you are slightly above the path of the jet.

B. Slow your airspeed to V_A and maintain altitude and course.

C. Make sure you are slightly below the path of the jet and perpendicular to the course.

Answer (A) is correct. *(AIM Para 7-3-6)*

DISCUSSION: To avoid the wake turbulence of a large jet at your altitude, you should increase your altitude slightly to get above the flight path of the jet.

Answer (B) is incorrect. The greatest danger is induced roll, not turbulence. Answer (C) is incorrect. Flight below and behind a larger aircraft's path should be avoided.

58. When landing behind a large aircraft, which procedure should be followed for vortex avoidance?

A. Stay above its final approach flightpath all the way to touchdown.

B. Stay below and to one side of its final approach flightpath.

C. Stay well below its final approach flightpath and land at least 2,000 feet behind.

Answer (A) is correct. *(AIM Para 7-3-6)*

DISCUSSION: When landing behind a large aircraft, stay above its final approach flight path all the way to touchdown; i.e., touch down beyond the touchdown point of the large aircraft.

Answer (B) is incorrect. You should stay at or above, not below, its flight path. Answer (C) is incorrect. You should stay at or above, not below, its flight path, and land beyond, not behind, its touchdown point.

59. With respect to vortex circulation, which is true?

A. Helicopters generate downwash turbulence, not vortex circulation.

B. The vortex strength is greatest when the generating aircraft is flying fast.

C. Vortex circulation generated by helicopters in forward flight trail behind in a manner similar to wingtip vortices generated by airplanes.

Answer (C) is correct. *(AIM Para 7-3-7)*

DISCUSSION: In forward flight, helicopters produce a pair of high velocity trailing vortices similar to wing tip vortices of large fixed wing aircraft.

Answer (A) is incorrect. Helicopters create both downwash turbulence and wingtip vortices. Answer (B) is incorrect. The vortex strength is greatest when flying slow, not fast.

60. Which is true with respect to vortex circulation?

A. Helicopters generate downwash turbulence only, not vortex circulation.

B. The vortex strength is greatest when the generating aircraft is heavy, clean, and slow.

C. When vortex circulation sinks into ground effect, it tends to dissipate rapidly and offer little danger.

Answer (B) is correct. *(AIM Para 7-3-3)*

DISCUSSION: The greatest vortex strength occurs when the generating aircraft is heavy, clean, and slow.

Answer (A) is incorrect. Helicopters generate both downwash turbulence and wingtip vortices. Answer (C) is incorrect. Vortices remain active in ground effect for a period of time.

3.6 Land and Hold Short Operations (LAHSO)

61. Who has the final authority to accept or decline any "land and hold short" (LAHSO) clearance?

A. ATC tower controller.

B. ATC approach controller.

C. Pilot-in-Command.

Answer (C) is correct. *(AIM Para 4-3-11)*

DISCUSSION: The pilot in command has the final authority to accept or decline any land and hold short (LAHSO) clearance. The safety and operation of the airplane remain the responsibility of the pilot. Pilots are expected to decline a LAHSO clearance if they determine it will compromise safety.

Answer (A) is incorrect. While an ATC tower controller will issue a LAHSO clearance, the pilot in command has the final authority to accept or decline the LAHSO clearance. Answer (B) is incorrect. ATC approach controllers do not issue landing or LAHSO clearances.

62. The commercial pilot operating as the pilot in command of an aircraft may accept or decline a land and hold short clearance (LAHSO)

A. when operating for hire.

B. any time.

C. at night.

Answer (B) is correct. *(AIM 4-3-11)*

DISCUSSION: The pilot in command has the final authority to accept or decline any land and hold short (LAHSO) clearance. The safety and operation of the airplane remain the responsibility of the pilot, and pilots are expected to decline a LAHSO clearance if they determine it will compromise safety.

Answer (A) is incorrect. A pilot in command may accept or decline a LAHSO clearance regardless of the mission profile. Answer (C) is incorrect. A pilot in command may accept or decline a LAHSO clearance during both day and night operations.

63. When should pilots decline a "land and hold short" (LAHSO) clearance?

A. When it will compromise safety.

B. If runway surface is contaminated.

C. Only when the tower controller concurs.

Answer (A) is correct. *(AIM Para 4-3-11)*

DISCUSSION: The pilot in command has the final authority to accept or decline a land and hold short (LAHSO) clearance. The safety and operation of the airplane remain the responsibility of the pilot. Pilots are expected to decline a LAHSO clearance if they determine it will compromise safety.

Answer (B) is incorrect. ATC should not issue a LAHSO clearance if the runway is contaminated (e.g., snow, ice, etc.), which would affect the braking action of an airplane. Answer (C) is incorrect. The pilot in command has the final authority to accept a LAHSO clearance whether or not the tower controller concurs.

64. What is the minimum visibility and ceiling required for a pilot to receive a "land and hold short" clearance?

A. 3 statute miles and 1,000 feet.

B. 3 nautical miles and 1,000 feet.

C. 3 statute miles and 1,500 feet.

Answer (A) is correct. *(AIM Para 4-3-11)*

DISCUSSION: You should only receive a LAHSO clearance when there is a minimum ceiling of 1,000 ft. and 3 SM visibility. The intent of having "basic" VFR weather conditions is to allow pilots to maintain visual contact with other aircraft and ground vehicle operations.

Answer (B) is incorrect. The minimum visibility and ceiling required for you to receive a LAHSO clearance is 3 SM, not 3 NM, and 1,000 feet. Answer (C) is incorrect. The minimum visibility and ceiling required for you to receive a LAHSO clearance is 3 SM and 1,000 ft., not 1,500 feet.

65. Once a pilot-in-command accepts a "land and hold short" (LAHSO) clearance, the clearance must be adhered to, just as any other ATC clearance, unless

A. an amended clearance is obtained or an emergency occurs.

B. the wind changes or Available Landing Distance decreases.

C. Available Landing Distance decreases or density altitude increases.

Answer (A) is correct. *(AIM Para 4-3-11)*

DISCUSSION: If, for any reason, the pilot elects to request to land on the full length of the runway, to land on another runway, or to decline LAHSO, a pilot is expected to promptly inform air traffic, ideally even before the clearance is issued. A LAHSO clearance, once accepted, must be adhered to, just as any other ATC clearance, unless an amended clearance is obtained or an emergency occurs. A LAHSO clearance does not preclude a rejected landing.

Answer (B) is incorrect. A wind shift does not cancel a LAHSO clearance and Available Landing Distance is a fixed value that cannot spontaneously change. Answer (C) is incorrect. Available Landing Distance is a fixed value that cannot spontaneously change and a density altitude increase does not cancel a LAHSO clearance.

66. To conduct LAHSO a pilot should have readily available

A. runway slope information.

B. published LAHSO procedure.

C. current ATC guide for airport runway markings, lights, signs, LAHSO, and runway safety.

Answer (A) is correct. *(AIM 4-3-11)*

DISCUSSION: To conduct LAHSO, pilots should become familiar with all available information concerning LAHSO at their destination airport. Pilots should have readily available the published Available Landing Distance (ALD) and runway slope information for all LAHSO runway combinations at each airport of intended landing.

Answer (B) is incorrect. There are no published LAHSO procedures for airports, only Available Landing Distance (ALD) information provided in the *Airport/Facility Directory*. Answer (C) is incorrect. An ATC guide on airport runway markings, lights, signs, LAHSO, and runway safety will contain information about general airport operations, not operations specific to a given airport. The PIC must use information relevant to the destination airport to determine if LAHSO is in effect and if (s)he can comply with the landing requirements.

67. What information should a pilot have available when encountering LAHSO?

A. FAA Advisory Circular on airport markings, signs, and LAHSO.

B. Published available landing distance data for the expected destination.

C. Aeronautical Information Manual content relating to LAHSO.

Answer (B) is correct. *(AIM 4-3-11)*

DISCUSSION: To conduct LAHSO, pilots should become familiar with all available information concerning LAHSO at their destination airport. Pilots should have readily available the published Available Landing Distance (ALD) and runway slope information for all LAHSO runway combinations at each airport of intended landing.

Answer (A) is incorrect. There is no FAA Advisory Circular that deals with airport markings, signs, and LAHSO. Answer (C) is incorrect. While the AIM is a useful tool for learning about LAHSO, it does not contain LAHSO information for specific airports.

68. Prior to accepting a "land and hold short" clearance (LAHSO) a pilot must confirm the aircraft can stop

A. in the Available Landing Distance.

B. prior to the intersecting taxiway.

C. prior to the intersecting runway.

Answer (A) is correct. *(AIM 4-3-11)*

DISCUSSION: To conduct LAHSO, pilots should become familiar with all available information concerning runway availability, length, and any specific LAHSO procedures at their destination airport. Pilots should have readily available the published Available Landing Distance (ALD) and runway slope information for all LAHSO runway combinations at each airport of intended landing.

Answer (B) is incorrect. Pilots must confirm the aircraft can come to a stop in the Available Landing Distance (ALD), not prior to an intersecting taxiway. While stopping prior to an intersecting taxiway might be part of your LAHSO clearance, the most accurate answer to this question is to ensure that you can stop within the ALD. Answer (C) is incorrect. Pilots must confirm the aircraft can come to a stop in the Available Landing Distance (ALD), not prior to an intersecting runway. While stopping prior to a intersecting runway might be part of your LAHSO clearance, the most accurate answer to this question is to ensure that you can stop within the ALD.

69. A 'land and hold short' (LAHSO) clearance

A. precludes a "Go Around" by ATC.

B. does not preclude a rejected landing.

C. requires a runway exit at the first taxiway.

Answer (B) is correct. *(AIM Chap 4)*

DISCUSSION: Once a LAHSO is accepted, it must be adhered to unless an amended clearance is obtained or when an emergency occurs. A LAHSO does not preclude a rejected landing.

Answer (A) is incorrect. A LAHSO clearance does not preclude a rejected landing. Answer (C) is incorrect. A LAHSO requires the aircraft to stop at the hold line or exit at any taxiway instructed to by ATC. This taxiway exit would be before the LAHSO hold line.

END OF STUDY UNIT

STUDY UNIT FOUR
FEDERAL AVIATION REGULATIONS

(11 pages of outline)

This study unit contains outlines of major concepts tested, sample test questions and answers regarding Federal Aviation Regulations, and an explanation of each answer. The table of contents above and on the previous page lists each subunit within this study unit, the number of questions pertaining to that particular subunit, and the pages on which the outlines and questions begin, respectively.

Recall that the **sole purpose** of this book is to expedite your passing of the FAA pilot knowledge test for the commercial pilot certificate. Accordingly, all extraneous material (i.e., topics or regulations not directly tested on the FAA pilot knowledge test) is omitted, even though much more knowledge is necessary to become a proficient commercial pilot. This additional material is presented in *Pilot Handbook* and *Commercial Pilot Flight Maneuvers and Practical Test Prep*, available from Gleim Publications, Inc. See the product listing at the back of the book and order online at www.gleim.com.

4.1 FAR PART 1

1.1 General Definitions

1. Airports are areas of land or water that are used or intended to be used for the landing and takeoff of aircraft, and includes its buildings and facilities, if any.
2. Commercial operators engage in carriage by aircraft in air commerce of persons or property for compensation or hire, other than as an air carrier.
3. An operator is a person who causes the aircraft to be used or authorizes its use.
4. Operational control of a flight means exercising authority over initiating, conducting, or terminating a flight.

1.2 Abbreviations and Symbols

1. V_{S1} means the stalling speed or minimum steady flight speed in a specified configuration.
2. V_S means the stalling speed or minimum steady flight speed at which the airplane is controllable.
3. V_F means the design flap speed.
4. V_{NO} means the maximum structural cruising speed.
5. V_{LE} means the maximum landing gear extended speed.
6. V_{NE} means the never-exceed speed.
7. V_Y means the best rate of climb speed.

4.2 FAR PART 23

23.3 Airplane Categories

1. The utility operational category of an airplane permits limited aerobatics, including spins (if approved for that particular type of airplane), lazy eights, chandelles, and steep turns between 60° and 90°.

4.3 FAR PART 61

61.3 Requirements for Certificates, Ratings, and Authorizations

1. A current and appropriate pilot and medical certificate is required to be in a pilot's personal possession or readily accessible in the aircraft whenever the pilot is acting as pilot in command or as a required flight crewmember.

61.5 Certificates and Ratings Issued under This Part

1. Aircraft class ratings (with respect to airmen) are single-engine land, multi-engine land, single-engine sea, and multi-engine sea.

61.15 Offenses Involving Alcohol or Drugs

1. A pilot convicted of operating a motor vehicle while either intoxicated by, impaired by, or under the influence of alcohol or a drug is required to provide a written report to the FAA Civil Aviation Security Division (AMC-700) no later than 60 days after the conviction.
2. A pilot convicted for the violation of any Federal or State statute relating to the process, manufacture, transportation, distribution, or sale of narcotic drugs is grounds for suspension or revocation of any certificate, rating, or authorization issued under Part 61.
3. A pilot convicted of operating an aircraft as a crewmember under the influence of alcohol or using drugs that affect the person's faculties (acts which are prohibited by Sec. 91.17), is grounds for denial of an application for a certificate, rating, or authorization issued under Part 61 for a period of one year after the date of that act.

61.19 Duration of Pilot and Instructor Certificates

1. Commercial pilot certificates are issued without a specific expiration date.

61.23 Medical Certificates: Requirement and Duration

1. A second-class medical certificate expires for commercial pilot purposes at the end of the last day of the 12th month after the month of the date of examination shown on the certificate.

61.31 Type Rating Requirements, Additional Training, and Authorization Requirements

1. For flights carrying passengers, the pilot must hold a category and class rating appropriate to the aircraft being flown.
2. A type rating is required when operating any turbojet-powered airplane or an airplane having a gross weight of more than 12,500 lb.
3. To act as pilot in command of a complex airplane (an airplane that has retractable landing gear, flaps, and a controllable pitch propeller), the pilot must receive and log ground and flight training in such an airplane and obtain a logbook endorsement of competence.
4. To act as pilot in command of a high-performance airplane (an airplane with an engine of more than 200 horsepower), the pilot must receive and log ground and flight training from an authorized instructor in such an airplane.
5. To act as a pilot in command of a tailwheel airplane, without prior experience, a pilot must receive and log flight training from an authorized instructor in a tailwheel airplane and receive a one-time logbook endorsement.

61.51 Pilot Logbooks

1. Pilots may log as second-in-command time all flight time when qualified and occupying a crewmember station in an aircraft that requires more than one pilot.
2. The aeronautical training and experience used to meet the requirements for a certificate, rating, or flight review and recent flight experience must be documented and recorded in a manner acceptable to the FAA, e.g., a logbook.

61.55 Second-in-Command Qualifications

1. To serve as second in command of an airplane type certificated for more than one pilot crewmember and operated under Part 91, (in part) a person, within the last 12 months, must have become familiar with the required information (systems operations, performance, limitations, etc.) and must have logged pilot time in the type of airplane for which privileges are requested.

61.56 Flight Review

1. To act as pilot in command of an aircraft, a commercial pilot must have satisfactorily completed a flight review or proficiency check within the preceding 24 months.

61.57 Recent Flight Experience: Pilot in Command

1. If a pilot does not meet the recent night experience requirements, (s)he may not carry passengers during the period from 1 hr. after sunset to 1 hr. before sunrise.
2. Prior to carrying passengers, the pilot in command must accomplish required takeoffs and landings in the same category, class, and type of aircraft (if a type rating is required).
3. To act as pilot in command under IFR or in weather conditions that are less than the minimums prescribed for VFR, a pilot must have, within the preceding 6 months, performed and logged (under actual or simulated instrument conditions) at least six instrument approaches, holding procedures, and intercepting and tracking courses through the use of navigation systems.
   a. Alternatively, the pilot may have passed an instrument proficiency check in the appropriate category of aircraft within the preceding 6 months.

61.58 Pilot-in-Command Proficiency Check: Operation of Aircraft Requiring More than One Pilot Flight Crewmember

1. To serve as pilot in command of an airplane that is certificated for more than one pilot crewmember and operated under Part 91, a person must have completed a pilot-in-command proficiency check within the preceding 12 calendar months in an airplane that is type certificated for more than one pilot.

61.60 Change of Address

1. To exercise privileges, one must report a change of permanent mailing address to the FAA Airmen Certification Branch within 30 days of moving.

61.69 Glider and Unpowered Ultralight Vehicle Towing: Experience and Training Requirements

1. To act as pilot in command of an airplane towing a glider, the tow pilot is required to hold at least a current private pilot certificate with a category rating for powered aircraft, have a logbook endorsement from an authorized glider instructor certifying receipt of ground and flight training in gliders, and be proficient with techniques and procedures for the safe towing of gliders.
2. To act as pilot in command of an airplane towing a glider, a pilot must have accomplished, within the preceding 12 months, at least three actual or simulated glider tows while accompanied by a qualified tow pilot.

61.133 Commercial Pilot Privileges and Limitations

1. Commercial pilots without an instrument rating cannot carry passengers for hire on cross-country flights during the day beyond a radius of 50 NM.
   a. Carrying passengers for hire at night is prohibited without an instrument rating.
2. A person who holds a commercial pilot certificate may act as pilot in command of an airplane that
   a. Carries persons or property for compensation or hire, provided the person is qualified in accordance with Part 61 and any other FAR Parts that apply to the operation
   b. Operates for compensation or hire, provided the person is qualified in accordance with Part 61 and any other FAR Parts that apply to the operation

4.4 FAR PART 91

91.3 Responsibility and Authority of the Pilot in Command

1. If you, as pilot in command, deviate from any rule in FAR Part 91 (due to an in-flight emergency requiring immediate action), you must submit a written report to the FAA, if requested.
2. The pilot in command is directly responsible for, and is the final authority as to, the operation of the airplane.

91.7 Civil Aircraft Airworthiness

1. You, as pilot in command, are responsible for determining whether your aircraft is in condition for safe flight.

91.9 Civil Aircraft Flight Manual, Marking, and Placard Requirements

1. You may not operate a U.S.-registered civil aircraft unless there is a current, approved Airplane Flight Manual available in the aircraft.

91.15 Dropping Objects

1. As pilot in command of a civil aircraft, you may not allow any object to be dropped from that aircraft in flight if it creates a hazard to persons or property. The dropping of an object is not prohibited if reasonable precautions are taken to avoid injury or damage to persons or property.

91.21 Portable Electronic Devices

1. Portable electronic devices that may cause interference with the navigation or communication system may not be operated on any of the following U.S.-registered civil aircraft operations:
   a. Air carrier
   b. Any other aircraft under IFR

91.23 Truth-in-Leasing Clause Requirement in Leases and Conditional Sales Contracts

1. In order to operate a large civil aircraft of U.S. registry that is subject to a lease, the lessee must have mailed a copy of the lease to the FAA in Oklahoma City within 24 hr. of its execution.

91.103 Preflight Action

1. Pilots are required to familiarize themselves with all available information concerning the flight prior to every flight, and specifically to determine
   a. For any flight, runway lengths at airports of intended use and the airplane's takeoff and landing requirements
   b. For IFR flights or those not in the vicinity of an airport
      1) Weather reports and forecasts
      2) Fuel requirements
      3) Alternatives available if the planned flight cannot be completed
      4) Any known traffic delays

91.105 Flight Crewmembers at Stations

1. Required flight crewmembers' seatbelts must be fastened while the crewmembers are at their stations.
2. Each required flight crewmember is required to keep his or her shoulder harness fastened during takeoff and landing unless
   a. The crewmember would be unable to perform required duties with the shoulder harness fastened.
   b. The seat at the crewmember's station is not equipped with a shoulder harness.

91.107 Use of Safety Belts, Shoulder Harnesses, and Child Restraint Systems

1. All occupants of airplanes must wear a safety belt and shoulder harness (if installed) during taxiing, takeoffs, and landings. The pilot in command must ensure that all passengers are briefed on how to fasten and unfasten all safety belts and harnesses.

91.109 Flight Instruction; Simulated Instrument Flight and Certain Flight Tests

1. No person may operate an airplane in simulated instrument flight conditions unless the other control seat is occupied by a safety pilot who possesses at least a private pilot certificate with category and class ratings appropriate to the airplane being flown.

91.111 Operating near Other Aircraft

1. No person may operate an aircraft so close to another aircraft as to create a collision hazard.
2. Formation flights are not authorized, except by arrangement with the pilot in command of each aircraft.
3. Formation flights are not authorized when carrying passengers for hire.

91.113 Right-of-Way Rules: Except Water Operations

1. When an airplane is overtaking another, the airplane being passed has the right-of-way.
   a. The passing (overtaking) airplane shall alter course to the right to pass well clear.
2. When aircraft of the same category are converging at approximately the same altitude (except head on, or nearly so), the aircraft to the other's right has the right-of-way.
   a. EXAMPLE: On a night flight, if the pilot of aircraft #1 sees only the green navigation light of aircraft #2, and the aircraft are converging, aircraft #1 has the right-of-way because it is to the right of aircraft #2.
   b. Airplanes and helicopters are equally maneuverable and have equal rights-of-way.
3. When two or more aircraft are approaching an airport for the purpose of landing, the aircraft at the lower altitude has the right-of-way.
   a. This rule shall not be abused by cutting in front of or overtaking another aircraft.
4. An aircraft towing or refueling another aircraft has the right-of-way over all other engine-driven aircraft.

91.121 Altimeter Settings

1. When a pilot is operating an airplane at or above 18,000 ft. MSL, the altimeter should be set to 29.92 in. Hg.

91.123 Compliance with ATC Clearances and Instructions

1. After obtaining an ATC clearance, a pilot may not deviate from that clearance unless an amended clearance is obtained, an emergency exists, or the deviation is in response to a traffic alert and collision avoidance system (TCAS) resolution advisory.

91.144 Temporary Restriction on Flight Operations during Abnormally High Barometric Pressure Conditions

1. When any information indicates that barometric pressure on the route of flight currently exceeds or will exceed 31.00 in. of mercury, no person may operate an aircraft or initiate a flight contrary to the requirements established by the FAA and published in NOTAMs.

91.155 Basic VFR Weather Minimums

1. The minimum flight visibility and cloud clearance requirements in Class C, D, or E airspace below 10,000 ft. MSL are
   a. 3-SM visibility
   b. 1,000 ft. above or 500 ft. below
2. The minimum flight visibility for VFR flight increases to 5 SM at an altitude
   a. At or above 10,000 ft. MSL and above 1,200 ft. AGL in Class G airspace or
   b. At or above 10,000 ft. MSL in Class E airspace.

91.159 VFR Cruising Altitude or Flight Level

1. Specified altitudes are required for VFR cruising flight at more than 3,000 ft. AGL and below 18,000 ft. MSL.
   a. On a magnetic course of 0° through 179°, altitudes flown must be odd thousands plus 500 feet.
      1) EXAMPLE: 3,500, 5, 500, 7,500, etc.
   b. On a magnetic course of 180° through 359°, altitudes flown must be even thousands plus 500 feet.
      1) EXAMPLE: 4,500, 6,500, 8,500, etc.

91.167 Fuel Requirements for Flight in IFR Conditions

1. When an alternate airport is required on an IFR flight plan, you must have sufficient fuel to complete the flight to the first airport of intended landing, fly to the alternate, and thereafter fly for 45 min. at normal cruising speed.

91.169 IFR Flight Plan: Information Required

1. For an airport with an approved instrument approach procedure to be listed as an alternate airport on an IFR flight plan, the forecast weather conditions at the time of arrival must be at or above the following alternate airport weather minimums:
   a. Nonprecision approach -- ceiling 800 ft. and visibility 2 SM
   b. Precision approach -- ceiling 600 ft. and visibility 2 SM
2. For an airport with no instrument approach procedure to be listed as an alternate airport, the forecast weather conditions at the time of arrival must have a ceiling and visibility that allow descent from the MEA, approach, and landing under basic VFR.

91.171 VOR Equipment Check for IFR Operations

1. To operate an airplane under IFR using the VOR, you must ensure that the VOR equipment has been operationally checked within the preceding 30 days and found to be within prescribed limits.
2. The maximum bearing error allowed for an operational VOR equipment check when using an FAA-approved ground test signal (such as a VOT) is ±4°.
   a. When performing an operational check using an airborne checkpoint, the maximum tolerance is ±6°.
3. Each person making the VOR operational check must enter the date, place, and bearing error and sign the aircraft log or other record.

91.175 Takeoff and Landing under IFR

1. One requirement for a pilot on an instrument approach to operate below the MDA or DH, or to continue the approach, is that the airplane continuously be in a position from which a descent to landing on the intended runway can be made at a normal rate using normal maneuvers.
2. A pilot is not authorized to land an airplane from an instrument approach unless the flight visibility is at, or exceeds, the visibility prescribed in the approach procedure being used.
3. In the case of a radar vector to a final approach course or fix, a timed approach from a holding fix, or an approach for which the procedure specifies "No PT," a pilot may not make a procedure turn unless cleared to do so by ATC.

91.177 Minimum Altitudes for IFR Operations

1. Except during takeoff or landing, the minimum altitude for IFR flight, within a horizontal distance of 4 NM from the course to be flown, is 2,000 ft. above the highest obstacle over designated mountainous terrain or 1,000 ft. above the highest obstacle over terrain elsewhere.

91.183 IFR Communications

1. The pilot in command of an airplane operated under IFR in controlled airspace, and not in radar contact, shall report by radio as soon as possible the time and altitude of passing each designated reporting point.

91.187 Operation under IFR in Controlled Airspace: Malfunction Reports

1. The pilot in command of an airplane operated under IFR in controlled airspace shall report to ATC, as soon as practicable, any malfunctions of navigational, approach, or communication equipment occurring in flight.

91.203 Civil Aircraft: Certifications Required

1. No person may operate a civil aircraft unless the aircraft has a U.S. airworthiness certificate displayed in a manner that makes it legible to passengers and crew.
2. To operate a civil aircraft, a valid U.S. registration issued to the owner of the aircraft must be on board.

91.205 Powered Civil Aircraft with Standard Category U.S. Airworthiness Certificates: Instrument and Equipment Requirements

1. For a flight for hire over water beyond power-off gliding distance from shore, approved flotation gear must be readily available to each occupant.
2. An anticollision light system is required for powered aircraft during VFR night flights.
3. An electric landing light is required for VFR night flights when operated for hire.

91.207 Emergency Locator Transmitters

1. ELT batteries must be replaced (or recharged, if rechargeable batteries) after 1 cumulative hour of use or after 50% of their useful life expires.

91.209 Aircraft Lights

1. Airplanes operating between sunset and sunrise must display lighted position (navigation) lights.
2. If an airplane is not equipped with an anticollision light system, no one may operate that airplane after sunset.

91.211 Supplemental Oxygen

1. At cabin pressure altitudes above 15,000 ft. MSL, each passenger of the aircraft **must be provided** with supplemental oxygen.
    a. At cabin pressure altitudes above 14,000 ft. MSL, each required crewmember **must be provided and must use** supplemental oxygen.
2. If a flight is conducted at cabin pressure altitudes above 12,500 ft. MSL to and including 14,000 ft. MSL, oxygen must be used by required crewmembers for the time in excess of 30 min. at that altitude.

91.215 ATC Transponder and Altitude Reporting Equipment and Use

1. A transponder with altitude encoding (Mode C) equipment is required in all airspace above 10,000 ft. MSL, excluding airspace at or below 2,500 ft. AGL.
2. A transponder with altitude encoding equipment is also required in Class A, Class B, and Class C airspace.

91.303 Aerobatic Flight

1. Aerobatic flight is prohibited
   a. With visibility of less than 3 SM
   b. Below 1,500 ft. AGL
   c. Within 4 NM of the center of any federal airway

91.311 Towing: Other than under Sec. 91.309

1. In order to operate an aircraft towing an advertising banner, the pilot must obtain a certificate of waiver from the administrator of the FAA.

91.313 Restricted Category Civil Aircraft: Operating Limitations

1. Persons or property cannot be transported for compensation or hire in a restricted category airplane.

91.315 Limited Category Civil Aircraft: Operating Limitations

1. Persons or property cannot be transported for compensation or hire in a limited category aircraft.

91.319 Aircraft Having Experimental Certificates: Operating Limitations

1. Persons or property cannot be transported for compensation or hire in an airplane that has an experimental certificate.

91.325 Primary Category Aircraft: Operating Limitations

1. Persons or property cannot be transported for compensation or hire in a primary category aircraft.

91.403 General

1. The owner or operator of an aircraft is primarily responsible for
   a. Maintaining that aircraft in an airworthy condition
   b. Assuring compliance with all Airworthiness Directives
2. An operator is a person who uses, causes to use, or authorizes to use an aircraft for the purpose of air navigation, including the piloting of an aircraft, with or without the right of legal control (i.e., owner, lessee, or otherwise).
   a. Thus, the pilot in command is also responsible for maintaining the aircraft in an airworthy condition and for complying with all Airworthiness Directives.

91.405 Maintenance Required

1. After an annual inspection has been completed and the aircraft has been returned to service, an appropriate notation must be made in the aircraft maintenance records.
2. A standard airworthiness certificate remains in effect as long as the airplane receives required maintenance and inspections.

91.407 Operation after Maintenance, Preventive Maintenance, Rebuilding, or Alteration

1. When aircraft alterations or repairs substantially change the flight characteristics, the aircraft documents must show that it was test flown and approved for return to service prior to carrying passengers.
   a. The pilot test flying the aircraft must be at least a private pilot and rated for the type of aircraft being tested.

91.409 Inspections

1. For commercial operations, an inspection is required every 100 hr.
   a. The 100 hr. may be exceeded by no more than 10 hr. if necessary to reach a place at which an inspection can be performed.
   b. An annual inspection may be substituted for a 100-hr. inspection but not vice versa.

91.413 ATC Transponder Tests and Inspections

1. An ATC transponder may not be used unless, within the preceding 24 calendar months, that transponder has been tested, inspected, and found to comply with appropriate regulations.

91.417 Maintenance Records

1. Each owner or operator must keep maintenance records for each airplane. The records must include
   a. Current status of life-limited parts of the airframe and each engine, propeller, rotor, and appliance
   b. Current status of each Airworthiness Directive (AD)
   c. Preventive maintenance accomplished by a pilot

91.421 Rebuilt Engine Maintenance Records

1. A new maintenance record may be used for a rebuilt (zero-time) engine, but the new records must include the status of previous Airworthiness Directives.

4.5 FAR PART 119

119.1 Applicability

1. A commercial pilot may act as pilot in command of the following operations, which are not regulated by 14 CFR Part 119 (FAR Part 119):
   a. Nonstop flights within a 25 SM radius of an airport for the purpose of carrying persons for intentional parachute jumps
   b. Crop dusting, spraying, and bird chasing

4.6 NTSB PART 830

830.2 Definitions

1. For an injury to be defined as a “serious injury” on the basis of hospitalization, the injury must require hospitalization for more than 48 hours, commencing within 7 days from the date the injury was received.

830.5 Immediate Notification

1. Even when no injuries occur to occupants, an airplane accident resulting in substantial damage must be reported to the nearest National Transportation Safety Board (NTSB) field office immediately.
   a. Damage to the landing gear, wheels, and tires are not considered "substantial damage," and thus no notification or report is required.
2. The following incidents must also be reported immediately to the NTSB:
   a. Inability of any required crewmember to perform normal flight duties because of in-flight injury or illness
   b. In-flight fire (but not a ground fire)
   c. Flight control system malfunction or failure

830.15 Reports and Statements to Be Filed

1. A written accident report is required to be filed with the nearest NTSB field office within 10 days of an accident.
2. A written incident report is required only upon request.

4.7 NEAR MIDAIR COLLISION REPORTING

1. The primary purpose of the Near Midair Collision (NMAC) Reporting Program is to provide information for use in enhancing the safety and efficiency of the National Airspace System. Data obtained from NMAC reports are used by the FAA to improve the quality of FAA services to users and to develop programs, policies, and procedures aimed at the reduction of NMAC occurrences.
2. A near midair collision is defined as an incident associated with the operation of an aircraft in which a possibility of collision occurs as a result of proximity of less than 500 feet to another aircraft, or a report is received from a pilot or a flight crew member stating that a collision hazard existed between two or more aircraft.
3. It is the responsibility of the pilot and/or flight crew to determine whether a near midair collision did actually occur and, if so, to initiate an NMAC report. Be specific, as ATC will not interpret a casual remark to mean that an NMAC is being reported. The pilot should state, "I wish to report a near midair collision."
4. Pilots and/or flight crew members involved in NMAC occurrences are urged to report each incident immediately
   a. By radio or telephone to the nearest FAA ATC facility or FSS.
   b. In writing, in lieu of the above, to the nearest Flight Standards District Office (FSDO).
5. The FSDO in whose area the incident occurred is responsible for the investigation and reporting of NMACs.

QUESTIONS AND ANSWER EXPLANATIONS: All of the commercial pilot knowledge test questions chosen by the FAA for release as well as additional questions selected by Gleim relating to the material in the previous outlines are reproduced on the following pages. These questions have been organized into the same subunits as the outlines. To the immediate right of each question are the correct answer and answer explanation. You should cover these answers and answer explanations while responding to the questions. Refer to the general discussion in the Introduction on how to take the FAA knowledge test.

Remember that the questions from the FAA knowledge test bank have been reordered by topic and organized into a meaningful sequence. Also, the first line of the answer explanation gives the citation of the authoritative source for the answer.

QUESTIONS

4.1 FAR Part 1

1.1 General Definitions

1. Which of the following terms describes an airport?

A. An area of land or water that is used or intended to be used for the landing and takeoff of aircraft, and includes its buildings and facilities, if any.

B. An area of land that is used for the takeoff and landing of aircraft, but does not include buildings since not all airports have buildings.

C. All runway, taxiway, and ramp areas created for use by aircraft.

Answer (A) is correct. *(FAR 1.1)*

DISCUSSION: Part 1.1 of the Federal Aviation Regulations defines an airport as "an area of land or water that is used or intended to be used for the landing and takeoff of aircraft, and includes its buildings and facilities, if any."

Answer (B) is incorrect. Part 1.1 of the FARs includes areas of water and any buildings and facilities in the definition of an airport. Answer (C) is incorrect. Part 1.1 of the FARs includes areas of land and water and any buildings and facilities in the definition of an airport.

2. Regulations which refer to “commercial operators” relate to that person who

A. is the owner of a small scheduled airline.

B. for compensation or hire, engages in the carriage by aircraft in air commerce of persons or property, as an air carrier.

C. for compensation or hire, engages in the carriage by aircraft in air commerce of persons or property, other than as an air carrier.

Answer (C) is correct. *(FAR 1.1)*

DISCUSSION: A commercial operator is a person who, for compensation or hire, engages in the carriage by aircraft in air commerce of persons or property, other than as an air carrier or foreign air carrier or under the authority of Part 375.

Answer (A) is incorrect. Commercial operations do not apply to airlines. Answer (B) is incorrect. Commercial operations do not apply to airlines.

3. Regulations which refer to the “operational control” of a flight are in relation to

A. the specific duties of any required crewmember.

B. acting as the sole manipulator of the aircraft controls.

C. exercising authority over initiating, conducting, or terminating a flight.

Answer (C) is correct. *(FAR 1.1)*

DISCUSSION: Operational control of a flight means the exercise of authority over initiating, conducting, or terminating a flight.

Answer (A) is incorrect. Assigning specific duties to a crewmember is only a small portion of exercising operational control. Answer (B) is incorrect. Acting as sole manipulator of an aircraft is a flight crew, not an operator, responsibility.

4. Regulations which refer to “operate” relate to that person who

A. acts as pilot in command of the aircraft.

B. is the sole manipulator of the aircraft controls.

C. causes the aircraft to be used or authorizes its use.

Answer (C) is correct. *(FAR 1.1)*

DISCUSSION: To operate an aircraft means to use, cause to use, or authorize to use aircraft for the purpose of air navigation, including the piloting of aircraft, with or without the right of legal control (as owner, lessee, or otherwise).

Answer (A) is incorrect. The pilot in command may not necessarily be the operator of the aircraft. Answer (B) is incorrect. The sole manipulator may not necessarily be the operator of the aircraft.

1.2 Abbreviations and Symbols

5. Which is the correct symbol for the stalling speed or the minimum steady flight speed in a specified configuration?

A. V_S.

B. V_{S1}.

C. V_{S0}.

Answer (B) is correct. *(FAR 1.2)*

DISCUSSION: V_{S1} means the stalling speed or the minimum steady flight speed obtained in a specified configuration. This configuration is generally specified as gear and flaps retracted.

Answer (A) is incorrect. V_S means the stalling speed or the minimum steady flight speed at which the airplane is controllable with no particular configuration specified. Answer (C) is incorrect. V_{S0} means the stalling speed or the minimum steady flight speed in the landing configuration.

6. Which is the correct symbol for the stalling speed or the minimum steady flight speed at which the airplane is controllable?

A. V_S.

B. V_{S1}.

C. V_{S0}.

Answer (A) is correct. *(FAR 1.2)*

DISCUSSION: V_S means the stalling speed or the minimum steady flight speed at which the airplane is controllable. No configuration is specified.

Answer (B) is incorrect. V_{S1} means the stalling speed or the minimum steady flight speed obtained in a specified configuration. Answer (C) is incorrect. V_{S0} means the stalling speed or the minimum steady flight speed in the landing configuration.

7. 14 CFR Part 1 defines V_F as

A. design flap speed.

B. flap operating speed.

C. maximum flap extended speed.

Answer (A) is correct. *(FAR 1.2)*

DISCUSSION: V_F means design flap speed.

Answer (B) is incorrect. The flap operating range, not speed, is indicated by the white arc on the airspeed indicator. Answer (C) is incorrect. V_{FE} means maximum flap extended speed.

8. 14 CFR Part 1 defines V_{NO} as

A. maximum structural cruising speed.

B. normal operating speed.

C. maximum operating speed.

Answer (A) is correct. *(FAR 1.2)*

DISCUSSION: V_{NO} means maximum structural cruising speed.

Answer (B) is incorrect. The normal operating range, not speed, is indicated by the green arc on the airspeed indicator. Answer (C) is incorrect. V_{MO}, not V_{NO}, means maximum operating limit speed.

9. 14 CFR Part 1 defines V_{LE} as

A. maximum landing gear extended speed.

B. maximum landing gear operating speed.

C. maximum leading edge flaps extended speed.

Answer (A) is correct. *(FAR 1.2)*

DISCUSSION: V_{LE} means maximum landing gear extended speed.

Answer (B) is incorrect. V_{LO} means maximum landing gear operating speed. Answer (C) is incorrect. Maximum leading edge flaps extended speed is not defined in FAR Part 1.

10. 14 CFR Part 1 defines V_{NE} as

A. maximum nose wheel extend speed.

B. never-exceed speed.

C. maximum landing gear extended speed.

Answer (B) is correct. *(FAR 1.2)*

DISCUSSION: V_{NE} is defined as the never-exceed speed.

Answer (A) is incorrect. V_{NE} means the never-exceed speed, not the maximum nosewheel extend speed. Answer (C) is incorrect. V_{LE}, not V_{NE}, means the maximum landing gear extended speed.

11. 14 CFR Part 1 defines V_Y as

A. speed for best rate of descent.

B. speed for best angle of climb.

C. speed for best rate of climb.

Answer (C) is correct. *(FAR 1.2)*

DISCUSSION: V_Y means the speed for the best rate of climb.

Answer (A) is incorrect. V_Y means the speed for the best rate of climb, not descent. Answer (B) is incorrect. V_X, not V_Y, means the speed for the best angle of climb.

12. 14 CFR Part 1 defines V_{NO} as

A. maximum structural cruising speed.

B. maximum operating limit speed.

C. never-exceed speed.

Answer (A) is correct. *(FAR 1.2)*

DISCUSSION: V_{NO} means maximum structural cruising speed.

Answer (B) is incorrect. V_{MO}, not V_{NO}, means maximum operating limit speed. Answer (C) is incorrect. V_{NE}, not V_{NO}, means never-exceed speed.

4.2 FAR Part 23

23.3 Airplane Categories

13. If an airplane category is listed as utility, it would mean that this airplane could be operated in which of the following maneuvers?

A. Limited acrobatics, excluding spins.

B. Any maneuver except acrobatics or spins.

C. Limited acrobatics, including spins (if approved).

Answer (C) is correct. *(FAR 23.3)*

DISCUSSION: The utility operational category of airplanes is designed to accommodate 4.4 positive Gs, which permits limited aerobatics, including spins (if approved for that particular type of airplane).

Answer (A) is incorrect. The utility category includes spins, if approved. Answer (B) is incorrect. The normal, not utility, category prohibits aerobatics and spins.

4.3 FAR Part 61

61.3 Requirements for Certificates, Ratings, and Authorizations

14. Commercial pilots are required to have a valid and appropriate pilot certificate in their physical possession or readily accessible in the aircraft when

A. piloting for hire only.

B. acting as pilot in command.

C. carrying passengers only.

Answer (B) is correct. *(FAR 61.3)*

DISCUSSION: No person may act as pilot in command or in any other capacity as a required pilot of a civil aircraft of U.S. registry unless that person has a valid and appropriate pilot certificate in that person's physical possession or readily accessible in the aircraft when exercising the privileges of that pilot certificate.

Answer (A) is incorrect. A valid and appropriate pilot certificate is required when acting as pilot in command, regardless if the flight was for hire or not. Answer (C) is incorrect. A valid and appropriate pilot certificate is required to be in your personal possession when acting as pilot in command, regardless of whether or not you are carrying passengers.

61.5 Certificates and Ratings Issued under This Part

15. Which of the following are considered aircraft class ratings?

A. Transport, normal, utility, and acrobatic.

B. Airplane, rotorcraft, glider, and lighter-than-air.

C. Single-engine land, multiengine land, single-engine sea, and multiengine sea.

Answer (C) is correct. *(FAR 61.5)*

DISCUSSION: Aircraft class ratings (with respect to airmen) are single-engine land, multiengine land, single-engine sea, and multiengine sea.

Answer (A) is incorrect. Transport, normal, utility, and acrobatic are aircraft categories with respect to the certification of aircraft, not airmen. Answer (B) is incorrect. Airplane, rotorcraft, glider, and lighter-than-air are categories, not classes, of aircraft with respect to airmen.

61.15 Offenses Involving Alcohol or Drugs

16. A pilot convicted of a motor vehicle offense involving alcohol or drugs is required to provide a written report to the

A. nearest FAA Flight Standards District Office (FSDO) within 60 days after such action.

B. FAA Civil Aeromedical Institute (CAMI) within 60 days after the conviction.

C. FAA Civil Aviation Security Division (AMC-700) within 60 days after such action.

Answer (C) is correct. *(FAR 61.15)*

DISCUSSION: A pilot convicted of a motor vehicle offense involving alcohol or drugs is required to provide a written report to the FAA Civil Aviation Security Division (AMC-700) within 60 days after such action.

Answer (A) is incorrect. A pilot convicted of a motor vehicle offense involving alcohol or drugs is required to provide a written report to the FAA Civil Aviation Security Division, not the nearest FSDO, within 60 days after such action. Answer (B) is incorrect. A pilot convicted of a motor vehicle offense involving alcohol or drugs is required to provide a written report to the FAA Civil Aviation Security Division, not the FAA Civil Aeromedical Institute (CAMI), within 60 days after the conviction.

17. A pilot convicted of operating a motor vehicle while either intoxicated by, impaired by, or under the influence of alcohol or a drug is required to provide a

A. written report to the FAA Civil Aeromedical Institute (CAMI) within 60 days after the motor vehicle action.

B. written report to the FAA Civil Aviation Security Division (AMC-700) not later than 60 days after the conviction.

C. the notification of the conviction to an FAA Aviation Medical Examiner (AME) not later than 60 days after the motor vehicle action.

Answer (B) is correct. *(FAR 61.15)*

DISCUSSION: A pilot convicted of operating a motor vehicle while either intoxicated by, impaired by, or under the influence of alcohol or a drug is required to provide a written report to the FAA Civil Aviation Security Division (AMC-700) not later than 60 days after the conviction.

Answer (A) is incorrect. A pilot convicted of operating a motor vehicle while either intoxicated by, impaired by, or under the influence of alcohol or a drug is required to provide a written report to the FAA Civil Aviation Security Division, not the FAA Civil Aeromedical Institute (CAMI), within 60 days after the motor vehicle action. Answer (C) is incorrect. A pilot convicted of operating a motor vehicle while either intoxicated by, impaired by, or under the influence of alcohol or a drug is required to provide a written report to the FAA Civil Aviation Security Division, not notify an AME, not later than 60 days after the motor vehicle action.

18. A pilot convicted for the violation of any Federal or State statute relating to the process, manufacture, transportation, distribution, or sale of narcotic drugs is grounds for

A. a written report to be filed with the FAA Civil Aviation Security Division (AMC-700) not later than 60 days after the conviction.

B. notification of this conviction to the FAA Civil Aeromedical Institute (CAMI) within 60 days after the conviction.

C. suspension or revocation of any certificate, rating, or authorization issued under 14 CFR part 61.

Answer (C) is correct. *(FAR 61.15)*

DISCUSSION: A pilot convicted for the violation of any Federal or State statute relating to the process, manufacture, transportation, distribution, or sale of narcotic drugs is grounds for suspension or revocation of any certificate, rating, or authorization issued under 14 CFR Part 61.

Answer (A) is incorrect. A written report must be filed with the FAA Civil Aviation Security Division not later than 60 days after a pilot is convicted of a motor vehicle offense involving alcohol or drugs, not for a conviction for the violation of any Federal or State statute relating to the process, manufacture, transportation, or sale of narcotic drugs. Answer (B) is incorrect. A pilot convicted for the violation of any Federal or State statute relating to the process, manufacture, transportation, distribution, or sale of narcotic drugs is grounds for suspension or revocation of any certificate, rating, or authorization issued under 14 CFR Part 61. The pilot is not required to notify CAMI of the conviction.

19. A pilot convicted of operating an aircraft as a crewmember under the influence of alcohol, or using drugs that affect the person's faculties, is grounds for a

A. written report to be filed with the FAA Civil Aviation Security Division (AMC-700) not later than 60 days after the conviction.

B. written notification to the FAA Civil Aeromedical Institute (CAMI) within 60 days after the conviction.

C. denial of an application for an FAA certificate, rating, or authorization issued under 14 CFR Part 61.

Answer (C) is correct. *(FAR 61.15)*

DISCUSSION: A pilot convicted of operating an aircraft as a crewmember under the influence of alcohol, or using drugs that affect the person's faculties (acts prohibited by Sec. 91.17), is grounds for denial of an application for a certificate or rating, or authorization issued under 14 CFR Part 61 for a period of one year after the date of that act.

Answer (A) is incorrect. A written report must be filed with the FAA Civil Aviation Security Division not later than 60 days after a pilot is convicted of a motor vehicle offense involving alcohol or drugs, not for being convicted of operating an aircraft as a crewmember under the influence of alcohol, or using drugs that affect the person's faculties. Answer (B) is incorrect. A pilot convicted of operating an aircraft as a crewmember under the influence of alcohol, or using drugs that affect a person's faculties, is grounds for denial of an application for an FAA certificate or rating. The pilot is not required to notify CAMI of the conviction.

61.19 Duration of Pilot and Instructor Certificates

20. Does a commercial pilot certificate have a specific expiration date?

A. No, it is issued without an expiration date.

B. Yes, it expires at the end of the 24th month after the month in which it was issued.

C. No, but commercial privileges expire if a flight review is not satisfactorily completed each 12 months.

Answer (A) is correct. *(FAR 61.19)*

DISCUSSION: Any pilot certificate (other than a student pilot or flight instructor certificate) issued under Part 61 is issued without a specific expiration date.

Answer (B) is incorrect. A flight instructor certificate, not a commercial pilot certificate, expires at the end of the 24th month after the month in which it was issued. Answer (C) is incorrect. A flight review is required at the end of the 24th month, not the 12th month.

61.23 Medical Certificates: Requirement and Duration

21. A second-class medical certificate issued to a commercial pilot on April 10, this year, permits the pilot to exercise which of the following privileges?

A. Commercial pilot privileges through April 30, next year.

B. Commercial pilot privileges through April 10, 2 years later.

C. Private pilot privileges through, but not after, March 31, next year.

Answer (A) is correct. *(FAR 61.23)*

DISCUSSION: A second-class medical certificate expires at the end of the last day of the 12th month after the examination for operations requiring a commercial pilot certificate (e.g., April 30, next year).

Answer (B) is incorrect. A second-class medical is valid for commercial operations for 12 months, not 24 months, and expires on the last day of the month. Answer (C) is incorrect. A second-class medical is valid for private or recreational pilot operations, not commercial pilot operations, for 24 months (if over age 40 at the time of examination) or 60 months (if under age 40 at the time of examination).

61.31 Type Rating Requirements, Additional Training, and Authorization Requirements

22. To act as pilot in command of an airplane that is equipped with retractable landing gear, flaps, and controllable pitch propeller, a person is required to

A. hold a multiengine airplane class rating.

B. make at least six takeoffs and landings in such an airplane within the preceding 6 months.

C. receive and log ground and flight training in such an airplane, and obtain a logbook endorsement certifying proficiency.

Answer (C) is correct. *(FAR 61.31)*

DISCUSSION: No person may act as pilot in command of a complex airplane (an airplane that has retractable landing gear, flaps, and a controllable pitch propeller), unless the person has received and logged ground and flight training from an authorized instructor in a complex airplane and obtained a logbook endorsement certifying proficiency.

Answer (A) is incorrect. It is not necessary to hold a multiengine rating to pilot a single-engine complex airplane. Answer (B) is incorrect. To act as pilot in command of a complex airplane, a person is required to receive and log ground and flight training in a complex airplane and obtain a logbook endorsement certifying proficiency, not just make at least six takeoffs and landings in a complex airplane within the preceding 6 months.

23. To act as pilot-in-command of an airplane with more than 200 horsepower, a person is required to

A. receive and log ground and flight training from a qualified pilot in such an airplane.

B. obtain an endorsement from a qualified pilot stating that the person is proficient to operate such an airplane.

C. receive and log ground and flight training from an authorized instructor in such an airplane.

Answer (C) is correct. *(FAR 61.31)*

DISCUSSION: To act as pilot in command of an airplane with an engine of more than 200 hp. (high-performance), a person is required to receive and log ground and flight training from an authorized instructor in a high-performance airplane, simulator, or flight training device and receive a one-time logbook endorsement from an authorized instructor who certifies the person is proficient to operate a high-performance airplane.

Answer (A) is incorrect. The ground and flight training must be given by an authorized instructor, not a qualified pilot. Additionally, a one-time logbook endorsement stating that the person is proficient to operate a high-performance airplane is required. Answer (B) is incorrect. The endorsement must be given by an authorized instructor, not any qualified pilot, and the endorsement will certify, not state, that the person is proficient to operate such an airplane.

24. To act as pilot in command of a tailwheel airplane, without prior experience, a pilot must

A. log ground and flight training from an authorized instructor.

B. pass a competency check and receive an endorsement from an authorized instructor.

C. receive and log flight training from an authorized instructor.

Answer (C) is correct. *(FAR 61.31)*

DISCUSSION: To act as pilot in command of a tailwheel airplane without prior experience, you must receive and log flight training from an authorized instructor in a tailwheel airplane and have your instructor endorse your logbook stating that you are proficient in the operation of a tailwheel airplane. This is the best answer of the choices given.

Answer (A) is incorrect. To act as pilot in command of a tailwheel airplane without prior experience, you must receive and log flight training from an authorized instructor. There is no requirement to log ground training. Answer (B) is incorrect. To act as pilot in command of a tailwheel airplane without prior experience, you must receive and log flight training and receive a logbook endorsement from an authorized instructor. There is no requirement to pass a competency check.

25. When is the pilot in command required to hold a category and class rating appropriate to the aircraft being flown?

A. On flights when carrying another person.

B. All solo flights.

C. On practical tests given by an examiner or FAA inspector.

Answer (A) is correct. *(FAR 61.31)*

DISCUSSION: To serve as pilot in command of an aircraft carrying passengers, a person must hold the appropriate category, class, and type rating (if a class rating and a type rating are required) for the aircraft to be flown.

Answer (B) is incorrect. The pilot in command must hold a category and class rating on flights when carrying passengers. Answer (C) is incorrect. The pilot in command is not required to hold a category and class rating to the aircraft being flown on a practical test.

26. Unless otherwise authorized, the pilot in command is required to hold a type rating when operating any

A. aircraft that is certificated for more than one pilot.

B. aircraft of more than 12,500 pounds maximum certificated takeoff weight.

C. multiengine airplane having a gross weight of more than 12,000 pounds.

Answer (B) is correct. *(FAR 61.31)*

DISCUSSION: A person may not act as pilot in command of any aircraft of more than 12,500 lb. maximum takeoff weight unless (s)he holds a type rating for that aircraft.

Answer (A) is incorrect. An aircraft that is certificated for more than one pilot does not necessarily require a type rating. Answer (C) is incorrect. A type rating is required for any, not only multiengine, aircraft having a maximum gross weight of more than 12,500 lb., not 12,000 lb.

27. To act as pilot in command of a tailwheel airplane, without prior experience, a pilot must

A. log ground and flight training from an authorized instructor.

B. receive and log flight training from an authorized instructor as well as receive a logbook endorsement from an authorized instructor who finds the person proficient in a tailwheel airplane.

C. pass a competency check and receive an endorsement from an authorized instructor.

Answer (B) is correct. *(FAR 61.31)*

DISCUSSION: To act as a pilot in command of a tailwheel airplane without prior experience, you must receive and log flight training from an authorized instructor in a tailwheel airplane and have your instructor endorse your logbook stating that you are proficient in the operation of a tailwheel airplane.

Answer (A) is incorrect. To act as a pilot in command of a tailwheel airplane without prior experience, you must receive and log flight training from an authorized instructor as well as receive a logbook endorsement from an authorized instructor. There is no requirement to log ground training. Answer (C) is incorrect. To act as pilot in command of a tailwheel airplane without prior experience, you must receive and log flight training and receive a logbook endorsement from an authorized instructor. There is no requirement to pass a competency check.

61.51 Pilot Logbooks

28. What flight time may a pilot log as second in command?

A. All flight time while acting as second in command in aircraft configured for more than one pilot.

B. Only that flight time during which the second in command is the sole manipulator of the controls.

C. All flight time when qualified and occupying a crewmember station in an aircraft that requires more than one pilot.

Answer (C) is correct. *(FAR 61.51)*

DISCUSSION: A person may log second-in-command flight time only for that flight time during which that person is qualified in accordance with FAR 61.55 and occupies a crewmember station in an aircraft that requires more than one pilot by the aircraft's type certificate.

Answer (A) is incorrect. A pilot may log second-in-command flight time only if (s)he is qualified and the aircraft or regulations required more than one pilot, not if the aircraft is configured for more than one pilot. Answer (B) is incorrect. A pilot may log all second-in-command flight time if (s)he is qualified and the aircraft requires more than one pilot, not just when the pilot is the sole manipulator of the controls. If the pilot is rated in that aircraft, (s)he can log PIC when (s)he is the sole manipulator of the controls.

29. What flight time must be documented and recorded by a pilot exercising the privileges of a commercial certificate?

A. All flight time flown for compensation or hire.

B. Only flight time for compensation or hire with passengers aboard which is necessary to meet the recent flight experience requirements.

C. Flight time showing training and aeronautical experience to meet requirements for a certificate, rating, or flight review.

Answer (C) is correct. *(FAR 61.51)*

DISCUSSION: Flight time showing training and aeronautical experience used to meet the requirements for a certificate, rating, or flight review must be documented and recorded in a reliable record (logbook). Additionally, the aeronautical experience required for meeting the recent flight experience requirements must also be recorded in your logbook.

Answer (A) is incorrect. You must log the training and aeronautical experience used to meet the requirements for a certificate, rating, or flight review and the recent flight experience requirements, not all flight time for compensation or hire. Answer (B) is incorrect. While you are required to log the experience required for meeting the recent flight experience requirements, it can be done at any time, not only when a flight is for compensation or hire with passengers on board.

61.55 Second-in-Command Qualifications

30. To serve as second in command of an airplane that is certificated for more than one pilot crew-member, and operated under Part 91, a person must

A. receive and log flight training from an authorized flight instructor in the type of airplane privileges are requested.

B. hold at least a commercial pilot certificate with an airplane category rating.

C. within the last 12 months become familiar with the required information, and perform and log pilot time in the type of airplane for which privileges are requested.

Answer (C) is correct. *(FAR 61.55)*

DISCUSSION: To serve as second in command of an airplane type certificated for more than one required pilot flight crewmember and operated under Part 91, a person, within the previous 12 calendar months, must become familiar with the required information (system operations, performance and limitations, normal and emergency operations, and the flight manual and placards) and have logged pilot time in the type of airplane for which privileges are requested.

Answer (A) is incorrect. To serve as second in command of an airplane that is certificated for more than one pilot flight crewmember, a person, within the previous 12 calendar months, must become familiar with the required information and must have performed and logged pilot time, not just received and logged flight training, in the type of airplane for which privileges are requested. Answer (B) is incorrect. To serve as second in command of an airplane that is certificated for more than one pilot flight crewmember under Part 91, a person must hold at least a private pilot certificate, not a commercial pilot certificate, with an airplane and appropriate class rating.

61.56 Flight Review

31. To act as pilot in command of an aircraft under 14 CFR Part 91, a commercial pilot must have satisfactorily accomplished a flight review or completed a proficiency check within the preceding

A. 24 calendar months.

B. 12 calendar months.

C. 6 calendar months.

Answer (A) is correct. *(FAR 61.56)*

DISCUSSION: No person may act as pilot in command of an aircraft unless, within the preceding 24 calendar months, (s)he has accomplished a flight review; a pilot proficiency check for a certificate, rating, or operating privilege; or one or more phases of the FAA Wings program.

Answer (B) is incorrect. A flight review or a proficiency check must have been accomplished within the preceding 24 months, not 12 months. Answer (C) is incorrect. A flight review or a proficiency check must have been accomplished within the preceding 24 months, not 6 months.

61.57 Recent Flight Experience: Pilot in Command

32. If a pilot does not meet the recency of experience requirements for night flight and official sunset is 1900 CST, the latest time passengers should be carried is

A. 1900 CST.

B. 1800 CST.

C. 1959 CST.

Answer (C) is correct. *(FAR 61.57)*

DISCUSSION: If a pilot does not meet the recent night experience requirements, (s)he may not carry passengers during the period from 1 hr. after sunset to 1 hr. before sunrise. If sunset is 1900 CST, the latest that passengers may be carried is 1959 CST.

Answer (A) is incorrect. Without recent night experience, a pilot may not carry passengers beginning 1 hr. after sunset, not at sunset. At sunset, the airplane must have lighted position lights. Answer (B) is incorrect. Without recent night experience, a pilot may not carry passengers beginning 1 hr. after, not before, sunset.

33. Prior to carrying passengers at night, the pilot in command must have accomplished the required takeoffs and landings in

A. any category aircraft.

B. the same category and class of aircraft to be used.

C. the same category, class, and type of aircraft (if a type rating is required).

Answer (C) is correct. *(FAR 61.57)*

DISCUSSION: No person may act as pilot in command of an aircraft carrying passengers at night unless that person has made at least three takeoffs and landings to a full stop within the preceding 90 days; that person was the sole manipulator of the controls; and the takeoffs and landings were performed in the same category, class, and type (if a type rating is required) of aircraft.

Answer (A) is incorrect. The takeoffs and landings must be in the same category, class, and type (if a type rating is required) of aircraft, not just the same category. Answer (B) is incorrect. If a type rating is required in a particular aircraft, then the takeoffs and landings must also be done in the same type of aircraft, not only the same category and class.

34. No pilot may act as pilot in command of an aircraft under IFR or in weather conditions less than the minimums prescribed for VFR unless that pilot has, within the past 6 months, performed and logged under actual or simulated instrument conditions, at least

A. six instrument approaches, holding procedures, intercepting and tracking courses, or passed an instrument proficiency check in an aircraft that is appropriate to the aircraft category.

B. six instrument flights and six approaches.

C. three instrument approaches and logged 3 hours of instruments.

Answer (A) is correct. *(FAR 61.57)*

DISCUSSION: No pilot may act as pilot in command when operating under IFR or in weather conditions less than the minimums prescribed for VFR unless (s)he has, within the past 6 months, logged instrument time under actual or simulated IFR conditions in the category of aircraft involved or in an appropriate flight simulator or flight training device and has performed at least six instrument approaches, holding procedures, and intercepting and tracking courses through the use of navigation systems. An alternative way to remain current is to pass an instrument proficiency check in the category of aircraft involved.

Answer (B) is incorrect. Only six approaches, not six instrument flights, are required, and holding procedures and intercepting and tracking courses must also be performed. Answer (C) is incorrect. Six, not three, instrument approaches are required, and there is no instrument time requirement.

61.58 Pilot-In-Command Proficiency Check: Operation of Aircraft Requiring More than One Pilot Flight Crewmember

35. To serve as pilot in command of an airplane that is certified for more than one pilot crewmember, and operated under Part 91, a person must

A. complete a flight review within the preceding 24 calendar months.

B. receive and log ground and flight training from an authorized flight instructor.

C. complete a pilot-in-command proficiency check within the preceding 12 calendar months in an airplane that is type certificated for more than one pilot.

Answer (C) is correct. *(FAR 61.58)*

DISCUSSION: To serve as pilot in command of an aircraft that is type certificated for more than one required pilot flight crewmember and operated under Part 91, a person must have completed a pilot-in-command proficiency check within the preceding 12 calendar months in an airplane that is type certificated for more than one required pilot flight crewmember. Additionally, that person must also have completed a pilot-in-command proficiency check within the preceding 24 calendar months in the particular type of aircraft in which that person will serve as pilot in command.

Answer (A) is incorrect. To serve as pilot in command of an airplane that is certified for more than one pilot crewmember, a person must complete a pilot-in-command proficiency check in an appropriate airplane every 12 calendar months, which meets the flight review requirement. Answer (B) is incorrect. To serve as pilot in command of an airplane that is certified for more than one pilot crewmember, a person must have completed a pilot proficiency check within the preceding 12 calendar months in an airplane that is type certificated for more than one pilot, not just receive and log ground and flight training from an authorized flight instructor.

61.60 Change of Address

36. Pilots who change their permanent mailing address and fail to notify the FAA Airmen Certification Branch of this change, are entitled to exercise the privileges of their pilot certificate for a period of

A. 30 days.

B. 60 days.

C. 90 days.

Answer (A) is correct. *(FAR 61.60)*

DISCUSSION: The holder of a pilot or flight instructor certificate who has made a change in his or her permanent mailing address may not, after 30 days from the date (s)he moved, exercise the privileges of the certificate unless (s)he has notified the FAA in writing.

NOTE: While you must notify the FAA if your address changes, you are not required to carry a certificate that shows your current address. The FAA will not issue a new certificate upon receipt of your new address unless you also send a written request and a $2 fee.

Answer (B) is incorrect. The FAA must be notified within 30, not 60, days of moving. Answer (C) is incorrect. The FAA must be notified within 30, not 90, days of moving.

61.69 Glider and Unpowered Ultralight Vehicle Towing: Experience and Training Requirements

37. To act as pilot in command of an airplane towing a glider, a pilot must have accomplished, within the preceding 12 months, at least

A. three actual glider tows under the supervision of a qualified tow pilot.

B. three actual or simulated glider tows while accompanied by a qualified tow pilot.

C. ten flights as pilot in command of an aircraft while towing a glider.

Answer (B) is correct. *(FAR 61.69)*

DISCUSSION: To act as pilot in command of an airplane towing a glider, a pilot must have accomplished, within the preceding 12 months, at least three actual or simulated glider tows while accompanied by a qualified tow pilot or must have made at least three flights as pilot in command of a glider towed by an aircraft.

Answer (A) is incorrect. The glider tows may be actual or simulated and the pilot must be accompanied by, not just under the supervision of, a qualified tow pilot. Answer (C) is incorrect. Ten flights as pilot in command of an aircraft while towing a glider is a requirement for a person to be authorized to endorse the logbook of a pilot seeking glider-towing privileges. This does not meet the 12-month requirement of three actual or simulated glider tows while accompanied by another qualified tow pilot.

38. To act as pilot in command of an airplane towing a glider, the tow pilot is required to have

A. at least a private pilot certificate with a category rating for powered aircraft, and made and logged at least three flights as pilot or observer in a glider being towed by an airplane.

B. a logbook endorsement from an authorized glider instructor certifying receipt of ground and flight training in gliders, and be proficient with techniques and procedures for safe towing of gliders.

C. a logbook record of having made at least three flights as sole manipulator of the controls of a glider being towed by an airplane.

Answer (B) is correct. *(FAR 61.69)*

DISCUSSION: No person may act as a pilot in command of an aircraft towing a glider unless (s)he has a logbook endorsement in his or her pilot logbook from an authorized glider instructor certifying that (s)he has received ground and flight training in gliders and is proficient in the techniques and procedures essential for safe towing of gliders.

Answer (A) is incorrect. To act as pilot in command of an airplane towing a glider, the pilot must have logged at least three flights as the sole manipulator of the controls of an airplane towing a glider, not as a pilot or an observer in a glider being towed by an airplane. Answer (C) is incorrect. To act as pilot in command of an airplane towing a glider, the tow pilot must have made at least three flights as pilot in command of a glider towed by an aircraft within the preceding 12 months, not just have logged three flights as sole manipulator of the controls of a glider towed by an airplane.

61.133 Commercial Pilot Privileges and Limitations

39. What limitation is imposed on a newly certificated commercial pilot-airplane, if that person does not hold an instrument rating? The carriage of passengers

A. or property for hire on cross-country flights at night is limited to a radius of 50 NM.

B. for hire on cross-country flights is limited to 50 NM for night flights, but not limited for day flights.

C. for hire on cross-country flights in excess of 50 NM, or for hire at night is prohibited.

Answer (C) is correct. *(FAR 61.133)*

DISCUSSION: If a commercial airplane pilot does not hold an instrument rating, his or her certificate will carry a limitation prohibiting the carriage of passengers for hire in airplanes on cross-country flights of more than 50 NM or at night.

Answer (A) is incorrect. The carriage of property is not restricted. Answer (B) is incorrect. The carriage of passengers is prohibited at night and is limited to 50 NM during the day.

40. A person with a Commercial Pilot certificate may act as pilot in command of an aircraft for compensation or hire, if that person

A. is qualified in accordance with 14 CFR part 61 and with the applicable parts that apply to the operation.

B. is qualified in accordance with 14 CFR part 61 and has passed a pilot competency check given by an authorized check pilot.

C. holds appropriate category, class ratings, and meets the recent flight experience requirements of 14 CFR part 61.

Answer (A) is correct. *(FAR 61.133)*

DISCUSSION: A person who holds a commercial pilot certificate may act as pilot in command of an airplane for compensation or hire, provided that person is qualified in accordance with FAR Part 61 and any other FAR Parts that apply to the operation.

Answer (B) is incorrect. A commercial pilot may act as pilot in command of an airplane operating for compensation or hire, if that person is qualified in accordance with Part 61 and any other FAR Parts that apply to the operation, not if that person passes a competency check given by an authorized check pilot. Answer (C) is incorrect. A commercial pilot may act as pilot in command of an airplane operating for compensation or hire, if that person is qualified in accordance with Part 61 and any other FAR Parts that apply to the operation, not only if that person holds the appropriate category and class ratings and meets the recent flight experience requirements.

4.4 FAR Part 91

91.3 Responsibility and Authority of the Pilot in Command

41. What action must be taken when a pilot in command deviates from any rule in 14 CFR Part 91?

A. Upon landing, report the deviation to the nearest FAA Flight Standards District Office.

B. Advise ATC of the pilot in command's intentions.

C. Upon the request of the Administrator, send a written report of that deviation to the Administrator.

Answer (C) is correct. *(FAR 91.3)*

DISCUSSION: If a pilot in command deviates from any rule in FAR Part 91 (due to an in-flight emergency requiring immediate action), (s)he must submit a written report to the Administrator (FAA), if requested.

Answer (A) is incorrect. The pilot in command must submit a written report of any rule deviation only when requested by the FAA, not upon landing. Answer (B) is incorrect. The pilot in command must inform ATC of any deviation of an ATC clearance or instruction and should advise ATC of his or her intentions, even if no rule in FAR Part 91 was violated.

42. What person is directly responsible for the final authority as to the operation of the airplane?

A. Certificate holder.

B. Pilot in command.

C. Airplane owner/operator.

Answer (B) is correct. *(FAR 91.3)*

DISCUSSION: The pilot in command of an airplane is directly responsible for, and is the final authority as to, the operation of that airplane.

Answer (A) is incorrect. The pilot in command, not the certificate holder, is directly responsible for, and is the final authority as to, the operation of that airplane. Answer (C) is incorrect. The pilot in command, not the airplane owner or operator, is directly responsible for, and the final authority as to, the operation of that airplane.

91.7 Civil Aircraft Airworthiness

43. Who is responsible for determining if an aircraft is in condition for safe flight?

A. A certificated aircraft mechanic.

B. The pilot in command.

C. The owner or operator.

Answer (B) is correct. *(FAR 91.7)*

DISCUSSION: The pilot in command is directly responsible for determining whether the airplane is in condition for safe flight.

Answer (A) is incorrect. The pilot in command, not a certificated aircraft mechanic, is responsible for determining if an airplane is in condition for safe flight. Answer (C) is incorrect. The pilot in command (who is considered the operator when piloting an airplane), not the owner, is directly responsible for determining if an airplane is in condition for safe flight.

44. An aircraft is on a stop 460 NM from base. It develops a mechanical problem. You get a technician to fix the problem. Who is responsible for the airworthiness of the aircraft?

A. Owner or operator.

B. Pilot in command.

C. Technician.

Answer (B) is the best answer. *(FAR 91.7)*

DISCUSSION: The pilot in command is directly responsible for determining whether the airplane is in condition for safe flight.

Answer (A) is incorrect. The pilot in command (who is considered the operator when piloting an airplane), not the owner, is directly responsible for determining whether an airplane is in condition for safe flight. Answer (C) is incorrect. While the technician is responsible for ensuring his or her work meets regulatory standards, it is the responsibility of the pilot in command to determine whether the aircraft is airworthy before operating it.

91.9 Civil Aircraft Flight Manual, Marking, and Placard Requirements

45. When operating a U.S.-registered civil aircraft, which document is required by regulation to be available in the aircraft?

A. A manufacturer's Operations Manual.

B. A current, approved Airplane Flight Manual.

C. An Owner's Manual.

Answer (B) is correct. *(FAR 91.9)*

DISCUSSION: No person may operate a U.S.-registered civil aircraft unless there is available in the aircraft a current, approved Airplane Flight Manual.

Answer (A) is incorrect. Anyone operating a U.S.-registered civil aircraft is required by regulation to have available in the aircraft a current, approved Airplane Flight Manual, not a manufacturer's Operations Manual. Answer (C) is incorrect. Anyone operating a U.S.-registered civil aircraft is required by regulation to have available in the aircraft a current, approved Airplane Flight Manual, not an Owner's Manual.

91.15 Dropping Objects

46. A pilot in command (PIC) of a civil aircraft may not allow any object to be dropped from that aircraft in flight

A. if it creates a hazard to persons and property.

B. unless the PIC has permission to drop any object over private property.

C. unless reasonable precautions are taken to avoid injury to property.

Answer (A) is correct. *(FAR 91.15)*

DISCUSSION: A pilot in command of a civil aircraft may not allow any object to be dropped from that aircraft in flight if it creates a hazard to persons or property. However, an object may be dropped from an aircraft if reasonable precautions are taken to avoid injury or damage to persons or property.

Answer (B) is incorrect. An object may be dropped from an aircraft if reasonable precautions are taken to avoid injury or damage to persons or property. Permission from a property owner is not required. Answer (C) is incorrect. An object may be dropped from an aircraft if reasonable precautions are taken to avoid injury or damage to persons or property, not only damage to property.

91.21 Portable Electronic Devices

47. Portable electronic devices which may cause interference with the navigation or communication system may not be operated on a U.S.-registered civil aircraft being flown

A. along Federal airways.

B. within the U.S.

C. in air carrier operations.

Answer (C) is correct. *(FAR 91.21)*

DISCUSSION: Portable electronic devices that may cause interference with the navigation or communication system may not be operated on a U.S.-registered civil aircraft being flown in air carrier operations or other operations requiring an operating certificate, or on any aircraft while it is operated under IFR.

Answer (A) is incorrect. Portable electronic devices that may cause interference with the navigation or communication system may be operated on an aircraft being flown along Federal airways, as long as the aircraft is not an air carrier or an aircraft operating under IFR. Answer (B) is incorrect. Portable electronic devices that may cause interference with the navigation or communication system may be operated within the U.S., as long as the aircraft is not an air carrier or an aircraft operating under IFR.

48. Portable electronic devices which may cause interference with the navigation or communication system may not be operated on U.S.-registered civil aircraft being operated

A. under IFR.

B. in passenger carrying operations.

C. along Federal airways.

Answer (A) is correct. *(FAR 91.21)*

DISCUSSION: Portable electronic devices that may cause interference with the navigation or communication system may not be operated on a U.S.-registered civil aircraft being operated under IFR or an aircraft being operated under an air carrier operating certificate or other operating certificate.

Answer (B) is incorrect. Portable electronic devices that may cause interference with the navigation or communication system may be operated on an aircraft in passenger-carrying operations, as long as the aircraft is not operated under an air carrier or other operating certificate or under IFR. Answer (C) is incorrect. Portable electronic devices that may cause interference with the navigation or communication system may be operated on an aircraft operating along Federal airways, as long as the airplane is not operated under IFR.

91.23 Truth-in-Leasing Clause Requirement in Leases and Conditional Sales Contracts

49. No person may operate a large civil aircraft of U.S.-registry which is subject to a lease, unless the lessee has mailed a copy of the lease to the FAA Aircraft Registration Branch, Oklahoma City, OK, within how many hours of its execution?

A. 24.

B. 48.

C. 72.

Answer (A) is correct. *(FAR 91.23)*

DISCUSSION: A copy of the lease or contract to a large civil aircraft must be mailed to the FAA within 24 hr. of its execution.

Answer (B) is incorrect. The lease must be mailed within 24 hr., not 48 hr. Answer (C) is incorrect. The lease must be mailed within 24 hr., not 72 hr.

91.103 Preflight Action

50. When is preflight action required, relative to alternatives available, if the planned flight cannot be completed?

A. IFR flights only.

B. Any flight not in the vicinity of an airport.

C. Any flight conducted for hire or compensation.

Answer (B) is correct. *(FAR 91.103)*

DISCUSSION: Each pilot in command shall, before beginning a flight, familiarize himself or herself with all available information concerning that flight. This information must include, for a flight under IFR or a flight not in the vicinity of an airport, weather reports and forecasts, fuel requirements, alternatives available if the planned flight cannot be completed, and any known traffic delays of which (s)he has been advised by ATC. For any flight, runway lengths at airports of intended use and certain takeoff and landing distance information should be obtained.

Answer (A) is incorrect. Preflight action relative to alternate airports is required for all flights not in the vicinity of an airport, not just IFR flights. Answer (C) is incorrect. Preflight action relative to alternate airports is required for all flights not in the vicinity of an airport, not just commercial flights.

51. The required preflight action relative to weather reports and fuel requirements is applicable to

A. any flight conducted for compensation or hire.

B. any flight not in the vicinity of an airport.

C. IFR flights only.

Answer (B) is correct. *(FAR 91.103)*

DISCUSSION: A required preflight action by the pilot in command of a flight not in the vicinity of an airport or a flight under IFR is to become familiar with all available information concerning that flight, including weather reports and forecasts and fuel requirements. Additional preflight information for the flight includes alternatives available, runway length at airports of intended use, and takeoff and landing distance information.

Answer (A) is incorrect. Preflight action relative to weather reports and fuel requirements is applicable to a flight under IFR or a flight not in the vicinity of an airport, not just any flight conducted for compensation or hire. Answer (C) is incorrect. Preflight action relative to weather reports and fuel requirements is applicable to a flight under IFR or a flight not in the vicinity of an airport, not IFR flights only.

52. Before beginning any flight under IFR, the pilot in command must become familiar with all available information concerning that flight. In addition, the pilot must

A. be familiar with all instrument approaches at the destination airport.

B. list an alternate airport on the flight plan, and confirm adequate takeoff and landing performance at the destination airport.

C. be familiar with the runway lengths at airports of intended use, and the alternatives available, if the flight cannot be completed.

Answer (C) is correct. *(FAR 91.103)*

DISCUSSION: Each pilot in command shall, before beginning a flight, familiarize himself or herself with all available information concerning that flight. For a flight under IFR or a flight not in the vicinity of an airport, this information should include weather reports and forecasts, fuel requirements, alternatives available if the planned flight cannot be completed, and any known traffic delays of which (s)he has been advised by ATC. For any flight, the preflight information should include runway lengths at airports of intended use and takeoff and landing distance information.

Answer (A) is incorrect. IFR pilots should carry instrument approach charts for their destination airports and possible alternates. Answer (B) is incorrect. An alternate is not always required.

53. Before beginning any flight under IFR, the pilot in command must become familiar with all available information concerning that flight. In addition, the pilot must

A. list an alternate airport on the flight plan, and confirm adequate takeoff and landing performance at the destination airport.

B. be familiar with all instrument approaches at the destination airport.

C. be familiar with the runway lengths at airports of intended use, weather reports, fuel requirements, and alternatives available, if the planned flight cannot be completed.

Answer (C) is correct. *(FAR 91.103)*

DISCUSSION: Before beginning any flight under IFR, the pilot in command must become familiar with all available information concerning the flight. This information must include the runway lengths at airports of intended use, weather reports and forecasts, alternatives available if the planned flight cannot be completed, and any known traffic delays that have been advised by ATC.

Answer (A) is incorrect. An alternate airport may not be required for the flight, based on the weather reports and forecast at the destination. Answer (B) is incorrect. While the pilot in command should be familiar with the instrument approaches at the destination airport (especially if (s)he should expect to conduct an instrument approach), it is not a required preflight action for any flight under IFR.

54. A pilot in command is required to be aware of all of the information pertinent to the flight. This should include what information about the destination airport?

A. Customs availability at an airport of entry.

B. Land and hold short operations (LAHSO).

C. Available airport services.

Answer (B) is correct. *(FAR 91.103)*

DISCUSSION: Prior to a flight, the PIC of the aircraft must be aware of all of the information available for the flight, including takeoff and landing distances, which may be affected by land and hold short operations (LAHSO).

Answer (A) is incorrect. Customs availability at an airport of entry would only be required for international flights arriving in the United States. Answer (C) is incorrect. While is it certainly good operating practice, pilots are not required to know the services available at an airport.

91.105 Flight Crewmembers at Stations

55. Required flight crewmembers' seatbelts must be fastened

A. only during takeoff and landing.

B. while the crewmembers are at their stations.

C. only during takeoff and landing when passengers are aboard the aircraft.

Answer (B) is correct. *(FAR 91.105)*

DISCUSSION: During takeoff and landing, and while en route, each required flight crewmember shall keep his or her seatbelt fastened while at his or her station.

Answer (A) is incorrect. Crewmembers are required to keep their seatbelts fastened while at their stations, not only during takeoff and landing. Answer (C) is incorrect. Crewmembers are required to keep their seatbelts fastened while at their stations, not only during takeoff and landing when passengers are aboard.

56. Each required flight crewmember is required to keep his or her shoulder harness fastened

A. during takeoff and landing only when passengers are aboard the aircraft.

B. while the crewmembers are at their stations, unless he or she is unable to perform required duties.

C. during takeoff and landing, unless he or she is unable to perform required duties.

Answer (C) is correct. *(FAR 91.105)*

DISCUSSION: Each required flight crewmember is required to keep his or her shoulder harness fastened during takeoff or landing while at his or her assigned duty station, unless (s)he would be unable to perform required duties or the seat is not equipped with a shoulder harness.

Answer (A) is incorrect. A required flight crewmember is required to keep his or her shoulder harness fastened during takeoff and landing, regardless of whether or not passengers are aboard the airplane. Answer (B) is incorrect. Each required flight crewmember is required to keep his or her shoulder harness fastened during takeoff and landing while at their stations, not all the time while at their stations.

91.107 Use of Safety Belts, Shoulder Harnesses, and Child Restraint Systems

57. Operating regulations for U.S.-registered civil airplanes require that during movement on the surface, takeoffs, and landings, a seat belt and shoulder harness (if installed) must be properly secured about each

A. flight crewmember only.

B. person on board.

C. flight and cabin crewmembers.

Answer (B) is correct. *(FAR 91.107)*

DISCUSSION: Each person on board a U.S.-registered civil airplane must occupy an approved seat or berth with a safety belt and, if installed, shoulder harness properly secured about him or her during movement on the surface, takeoffs, and landings.

Answer (A) is incorrect. Each person on board, not only the flight crewmembers, must have a safety belt and, if installed, shoulder harness properly secured about him or her during movement on the surface, takeoffs, and landings. Answer (C) is incorrect. Each person on board, not only the flight and cabin crewmembers, must have a safety belt and, if installed, a shoulder harness properly secured about him or her during movement on the surface, takeoffs, and landings.

58. With U.S.-registered civil airplanes, the use of safety belts is required during movement on the surface, takeoffs, and landings for

A. safe operating practice, but not required by regulations.

B. each person over 2 years of age on board.

C. commercial passenger operations only.

Answer (B) is correct. *(FAR 91.107)*

DISCUSSION: Each person over 2 years of age on a U.S.-registered civil airplane must occupy an approved seat or berth with a safety belt and, if installed, shoulder harness properly secured about him or her during movement on the surface, takeoff, and landing.

Answer (A) is incorrect. While the use of safety belts is a safe operating practice, it is also required by regulations during movement on the surface, takeoffs, and landings for each person over 2 years of age on board. Answer (C) is incorrect. The use of safety belts is required on all U.S.-registered civil airplanes, not only commercial passenger airplanes, during movement on the surface, takeoffs, and landings for each person over 2 years of age on board.

91.109 Flight Instruction; Simulated Instrument Flight and Certain Flight Tests

59. No person may operate an aircraft in simulated instrument flight conditions unless the

A. other control seat is occupied by at least an appropriately rated commercial pilot.

B. pilot has filed an IFR flight plan and received an IFR clearance.

C. other control seat is occupied by a safety pilot, who holds at least a private pilot certificate and is appropriately rated.

Answer (C) is correct. *(FAR 91.109)*

DISCUSSION: No person may operate an aircraft in simulated instrument flight conditions unless the other control seat is occupied by a safety pilot who possesses at least a private pilot certificate with category and class ratings appropriate to the aircraft being flown.

Answer (A) is incorrect. The safety pilot must hold at least a private, not commercial, pilot certificate with the category and class ratings appropriate to the aircraft being flown. Answer (B) is incorrect. There is no requirement that a person file an IFR flight plan and receive an IFR clearance to operate in simulated flight conditions. Normally, a person will be operating under VFR while operating in simulated instrument flight conditions.

91.111 Operating near Other Aircraft

60. Which is true with respect to formation flights? Formation flights are

A. authorized when carrying passengers for hire, with prior arrangement with the pilot in command of each aircraft in the formation.

B. not authorized when visibilities are less than 3 SM.

C. not authorized when carrying passengers for hire.

Answer (C) is correct. *(FAR 91.111)*

DISCUSSION: No person may operate an aircraft carrying passengers for hire in formation flight.

Answer (A) is incorrect. Formation flights are prohibited when carrying passengers for hire. Answer (B) is incorrect. Formation flights are authorized when visibility is less than 3 SM.

61. Which is true with respect to operating near other aircraft in flight? They are

A. not authorized, when operated so close to another aircraft they can create a collision hazard.

B. not authorized, unless the pilot in command of each aircraft is trained and found competent in formation.

C. authorized when carrying passengers for hire, with prior arrangement with the pilot in command of each aircraft in the formation.

Answer (A) is correct. *(FAR 91.111)*

DISCUSSION: No person may operate an aircraft so close to another aircraft as to create a collision hazard.

Answer (B) is incorrect. Formation flights are authorized when an arrangement is made with the pilot in command of each aircraft in the formation. There is no regulatory requirement for any type of training in formation flying. Answer (C) is incorrect. Formation flight is not authorized when carrying passengers for hire.

62. Which is true with respect to formation flights? Formation flights are

A. not authorized, except by arrangement with the pilot in command of each aircraft.

B. not authorized, unless the pilot in command of each aircraft is trained and found competent in formation.

C. authorized when carrying passengers for hire, with prior arrangement with the pilot in command of each aircraft in the formation.

Answer (A) is correct. *(FAR 91.111)*

DISCUSSION: Formation flights are not authorized, except by arrangement with the pilot in command of each aircraft in the formation.

Answer (B) is incorrect. Formation flights are not authorized, except by arrangement with the pilot in command of each aircraft in the formation. There is no regulatory requirement for any specific training in formation flying. Answer (C) is incorrect. Formation flights are not authorized when carrying passengers for hire.

91.113 Right-of-Way Rules: Except Water Operations

63. Airplane A is overtaking airplane B. Which airplane has the right-of-way?

A. Airplane A; the pilot should alter course to the right to pass.

B. Airplane B; the pilot should expect to be passed on the right.

C. Airplane B; the pilot should expect to be passed on the left.

Answer (B) is correct. *(FAR 91.113)*

DISCUSSION: Each aircraft that is being overtaken has the right-of-way, and each pilot of an overtaking aircraft shall alter course to the right to pass well clear.

Answer (A) is incorrect. The airplane being overtaken has the right-of-way. Answer (C) is incorrect. When overtaking another aircraft, you pass to the right, not left.

64. An airplane is overtaking a helicopter. Which aircraft has the right-of-way?

A. Helicopter; the pilot should expect to be passed on the right.

B. Airplane; the airplane pilot should alter course to the left to pass.

C. Helicopter; the pilot should expect to be passed on the left.

Answer (A) is correct. *(FAR 91.113)*

DISCUSSION: Each aircraft that is being overtaken (the helicopter) has the right-of-way, and each pilot of an overtaking aircraft (the airplane) shall alter course to the right to pass well clear.

Answer (B) is incorrect. The helicopter has the right-of-way because it is being overtaken and the airplane should alter course to the right, not left, to pass well clear. Answer (C) is incorrect. The airplane should alter course to the right, not left, to pass well clear.

65. Two aircraft of the same category are approaching an airport for the purpose of landing. The right-of-way belongs to the aircraft

A. at the higher altitude.

B. at the lower altitude, but the pilot shall not take advantage of this rule to cut in front of or to overtake the other aircraft.

C. that is more maneuverable, and that aircraft may, with caution, move in front of or overtake the other aircraft.

Answer (B) is correct. *(FAR 91.113)*

DISCUSSION: When two or more aircraft are approaching an airport for the purpose of landing, the aircraft at the lower altitude has the right-of-way, but it shall not take advantage of this rule to cut in front of another that is on final approach to land, or to overtake that aircraft.

Answer (A) is incorrect. The right-of-way belongs to the aircraft at the lower, not higher, altitude. Answer (C) is incorrect. The right-of-way belongs to the aircraft at the lower altitude, not to the more maneuverable aircraft.

66. During a night operation, the pilot of aircraft #1 sees only the green light of aircraft #2. If the aircraft are converging, which pilot has the right-of-way? The pilot of aircraft

A. #2; aircraft #2 is to the left of aircraft #1.

B. #2; aircraft #2 is to the right of aircraft #1.

C. #1; aircraft #1 is to the right of aircraft #2.

Answer (C) is correct. *(FAR 91.113)*

DISCUSSION: When aircraft of the same category are converging at approximately the same altitude (except head-on or nearly so), the aircraft to the other's right has the right-of-way. Since the green position light is on aircraft #2's right wing, aircraft #1 is to the right of aircraft #2 and thus has the right-of-way.

Answer (A) is incorrect. When two aircraft are converging, the aircraft to the right, not left, has the right-of-way. Since aircraft #2 is to the left of aircraft #1, aircraft #1 has the right-of-way. Answer (B) is incorrect. The green position light is on the right wing of aircraft #2. Since aircraft #1 can see only the green position light, aircraft #1 is to the right, not left, of aircraft #2, and aircraft #1 has the right-of-way.

67. A pilot flying a single-engine airplane observes a multiengine airplane approaching from the left. Which pilot should give way?

A. The pilot of the multiengine airplane should give way; the single-engine airplane is to its right.

B. The pilot of the single-engine airplane should give way; the other airplane is to the left.

C. Each pilot should alter course to the right.

Answer (A) is correct. *(FAR 91.113)*

DISCUSSION: When aircraft of the same category are converging at the same altitude (except head-on, or nearly so), the aircraft to the other's right has the right-of-way. Since the single-engine airplane is to the right of the multiengine airplane, the pilot of the multiengine airplane should give way to the single-engine airplane.

Answer (B) is incorrect. The airplane to the right, not left, has the right-of-way. Thus, the pilot of the multiengine airplane should give way to the single-engine airplane. Answer (C) is incorrect. Each pilot should alter course to the right if the airplanes are approaching each other head-on, not converging.

68. While in flight a helicopter and an airplane are converging at a 90° angle, and the helicopter is located to the right of the airplane. Which aircraft has the right-of-way, and why?

A. The helicopter, because it is to the right of the airplane.

B. The helicopter, because helicopters have the right-of-way over airplanes.

C. The airplane, because airplanes have the right-of-way over helicopters.

Answer (A) is correct. *(FAR 91.113)*

DISCUSSION: When aircraft are converging at approximately the same altitude, the aircraft to the other's right has the right-of-way. Since the helicopter is to the airplane's right, it has the right-of-way. Since helicopters and airplanes are considered equally maneuverable, neither has the right-of-way over the other.

Answer (B) is incorrect. Helicopters do not have the right-of-way over airplanes. Answer (C) is incorrect. Airplanes do not have the right-of-way over helicopters.

91.121 Altimeter Settings

69. What altimeter setting is required when operating an aircraft at 18,000 feet MSL?

A. Current reported altimeter setting of a station along the route.

B. 29.92" Hg.

C. Altimeter setting at the departure or destination airport.

Answer (B) is correct. *(FAR 91.121)*

DISCUSSION: When operating an airplane at or above 18,000 ft. MSL, the altimeter should be set to 29.92 in. Hg.

Answer (A) is incorrect. The altimeter is set to the current reported altimeter setting of a station along the route when below 18,000 ft. MSL, not at or above 18,000 ft. MSL. Answer (C) is incorrect. The altimeter is set to 29.92 in. Hg when operating at or above 18,000 ft. MSL, not to the altimeter setting at the departure or destination airport.

91.123 Compliance with ATC Clearances and Instructions

70. After an ATC clearance has been obtained, a pilot may not deviate from that clearance, unless the pilot

A. requests an amended clearance.

B. is operating VFR on top.

C. receives an amended clearance or has an emergency.

Answer (C) is correct. *(FAR 91.123)*

DISCUSSION: After an ATC clearance has been obtained, a pilot may not deviate from that clearance unless an amended clearance is obtained, an emergency exists, or the deviation is in response to a traffic alert and collision avoidance system (TCAS) resolution advisory.

Answer (A) is incorrect. A pilot may not deviate from an ATC clearance until an amended clearance has been received, not when the pilot requests an amended clearance. Answer (B) is incorrect. Operating VFR-on-top is an IFR clearance; thus, a pilot may not deviate from VFR-on-top unless an amended clearance is received or an emergency exists.

91.144 Temporary Restriction on Flight Operations during Abnormally High Barometric Pressure Conditions

71. When weather information indicates that abnormally high barometric pressure exists, or will be above ___ inches of mercury, flight operations will not be authorized contrary to the requirements published in NOTAMs.

A. 31.00

B. 32.00

C. 30.50

Answer (A) is correct. *(FAR 91.144)*

DISCUSSION: When weather information indicates that barometric pressure on the route of flight exceeds 31.00 in. of mercury, no person may operate an aircraft or initiate a flight contrary to the requirements published in NOTAMs.

Answer (B) is incorrect. Flight operations will not be authorized contrary to the requirements published in NOTAMs when barometric pressure exceeds, or will exceed, 31.00 in., not 32.00 in., of mercury. Answer (C) is incorrect. Flight operations will not be authorized contrary to the requirements published in NOTAMs when barometric pressure exceeds, or will exceed, 31.00 in., not 30.50 in., of mercury.

91.155 Basic VFR Weather Minimums

72. What is the minimum flight visibility and proximity to cloud requirements for VFR flight, at 6,500 feet MSL, in Class C, D, and E airspace?

A. 1 mile visibility; clear of clouds.

B. 3 miles visibility; 1,000 feet above and 500 feet below.

C. 5 miles visibility; 1,000 feet above and 1,000 feet below.

Answer (B) is correct. *(FAR 91.155)*

DISCUSSION: At 6,500 ft. MSL in Class C, D, or E airspace, the basic VFR flight visibility requirement is 3 SM. The distance from clouds requirement is 500 ft. below, 1,000 ft. above, and 2,000 ft. horizontal.

Answer (A) is incorrect. One SM visibility and clear of clouds is the basic VFR weather minimums when at or below 1,200 ft. AGL (regardless of MSL altitude) in Class G airspace during the day, not at 6,500 ft. MSL in Class C, D, or E airspace. Answer (C) is incorrect. Five SM visibility and a distance from clouds of 1,000 ft. above or below is the basic VFR weather minimums in Class E airspace at or above, not below, 10,000 ft. MSL.

73. The minimum flight visibility for VFR flight increases to 5 statute miles beginning at an altitude of

A. 14,500 feet MSL.

B. 10,000 feet MSL if above 1,200 feet AGL.

C. 10,000 feet MSL regardless of height above ground.

Answer (B) is correct. *(FAR 91.155)*

DISCUSSION: The minimum flight visibility for VFR flight increases to 5 SM beginning at an altitude of 10,000 ft. MSL if above 1,200 ft. AGL in Class G airspace. In Class E airspace, the minimum flight visibility for VFR flight increases to 5 SM beginning at an altitude of 10,000 ft. MSL regardless of height above ground. This is the best answer because it includes both Class E and Class G airspace.

Answer (A) is incorrect. This is not an altitude associated with basic VFR minimums. Answer (C) is incorrect. While the minimum flight visibility for VFR flight increases to 5 SM at an altitude of 10,000 ft. MSL regardless of the height above ground for Class E airspace, it does not include that in Class G airspace. The minimum flight visibility increases to 5 SM when at 10,000 ft. MSL and above 1,200 ft. AGL.

91.159 VFR Cruising Altitude or Flight Level

74. VFR cruising altitudes are required to be maintained when flying

A. at 3,000 feet or more AGL; based on true course.

B. more than 3,000 feet AGL; based on magnetic course.

C. at 3,000 feet or more above MSL; based on magnetic heading.

Answer (B) is correct. *(FAR 91.159)*

DISCUSSION: VFR cruising altitudes are prescribed for level flight above 3,000 ft. AGL and are based on magnetic course.

Answer (A) is incorrect. VFR cruising altitudes are based upon magnetic (not true) course. Answer (C) is incorrect. VFR cruising altitudes apply for flight above 3,000 ft. AGL (not MSL) and are based on magnetic course (not heading).

91.167 Fuel Requirements for Flight in IFR Conditions

75. If weather conditions are such that it is required to designate an alternate airport on your IFR flight plan, you should plan to carry enough fuel to arrive at the first airport of intended landing, fly from that airport to the alternate airport, and fly thereafter for

A. 30 minutes at slow cruising speed.

B. 45 minutes at normal cruising speed.

C. 1 hour at normal cruising speed.

Answer (B) is correct. *(FAR 91.167)*

DISCUSSION: No person may operate a civil aircraft in IFR conditions unless it carries enough fuel (considering weather reports, forecasts, and conditions) to complete the flight to the first airport of intended landing; fly from that airport to the alternate airport; and fly after that for 45 min. at normal cruising speed.

Answer (A) is incorrect. Enough fuel must be carried to fly for 45 (not 30) min. at normal (not slow) cruising speed after reaching the alternate airport. Answer (C) is incorrect. Enough fuel must be carried to fly for 45 min. (not 1 hr.) at normal cruising speed after reaching the alternate airport.

91.169 IFR Flight Plan: Information Required

76. For an airport with an approved instrument approach procedure to be listed as an alternate airport on an IFR flight plan, the forecasted weather conditions at the time of arrival must be at or above the following weather minimums.

A. Ceiling 600 feet and visibility 2 NM for precision.

B. Ceiling 800 feet and visibility 2 SM for nonprecision.

C. Ceiling 800 feet and visibility 2 NM for nonprecision.

Answer (B) is correct. *(FAR 91.169)*

DISCUSSION: For an airport with an approved instrument approach procedure to be listed as an alternate airport on an IFR flight plan, the forecasted weather conditions at the time of arrival for a nonprecision approach must be at or above a ceiling of 800 ft. and visibility of 2 SM.

Answer (A) is incorrect. For a precision approach, the weather minimums are a ceiling of 600 ft. and visibility of 2 SM, not 2 NM. Answer (C) is incorrect. For a nonprecision approach, the weather minimums are a ceiling of 800 ft. and visibility of 2 SM, not 2 NM.

77. For an airport without an approved instrument approach procedure to be listed as an alternate airport on an IFR flight plan, the forecasted weather conditions at the time of arrival must have at least a

A. ceiling of 2,000 feet and visibility 3 SM.

B. ceiling and visibility that allows for a descent, approach, and landing under basic VFR.

C. ceiling of 1,000 feet and visibility 3 NM.

Answer (B) is correct. *(FAR 91.169)*

DISCUSSION: For an airport without an approved instrument approach procedure to be listed as an alternate airport on an IFR flight plan, the forecasted weather conditions at the time of arrival must have ceiling and visibility minimums that allow for descent from the MEA, approach, and landing under basic VFR.

Answer (A) is incorrect. The weather minimums for an alternate airport without an approved instrument approach must allow for a descent from the MEA, approach, and landing under basic VFR, not a ceiling of 2,000 ft. and visibility of 3 SM. Answer (C) is incorrect. The weather minimums for an alternate airport without an approved instrument approach must allow for a descent from the MEA, approach, and landing under basic VFR, not a ceiling of 1,000 ft. and visibility of 3 SM.

91.171 VOR Equipment Check for IFR Operations

78. When must an operational check on the aircraft VOR equipment be accomplished to operate under IFR? Within the preceding

A. 30 days or 30 hours of flight time.

B. 10 days or 10 hours of flight time.

C. 30 days.

Answer (C) is correct. *(FAR 91.171)*

DISCUSSION: To use the aircraft VOR equipment under IFR, the VOR equipment must have been operationally checked within the preceding 30 days.

Answer (A) is incorrect. Prior to operating under IFR, an operational check of the VOR must have been accomplished within the preceding 30 days, regardless of the flight time. Answer (B) is incorrect. Prior to operating under IFR, an operational check of the VOR must have been accomplished within the preceding 30 days, not 10 days, regardless of the flight time.

79. What is the maximum bearing error (+ or –) allowed for an operational VOR equipment check when using an FAA-approved ground test signal?

A. 4 degrees.

B. 6 degrees.

C. 8 degrees.

Answer (A) is correct. *(FAR 91.171)*

DISCUSSION: When using an FAA-approved ground test signal (such as a VOT) for an operational VOR equipment check, the maximum allowable bearing error is ±4°.

Answer (B) is incorrect. The permissible bearing error when using an airborne checkpoint, not a ground test signal, is ±6°. Answer (C) is incorrect. This is not a permissible bearing error on VOR checks.

80. Which data must be recorded in the aircraft logbook or other record by a pilot making a VOR operational check for IFR operations?

A. VOR name or identification, place of operational check, amount of bearing error, and date of check.

B. Date of check, place of operational check, bearing error, and signature.

C. VOR name or identification, amount of bearing error, date of check, and signature.

Answer (B) is correct. *(FAR 91.171)*

DISCUSSION: When you make a VOR operational check, you must enter the date of check, place of operational check, and bearing error, and sign the airplane logbook or other record.

Answer (A) is incorrect. When you make a VOR operational check, you must enter in the airplane logbook or other record the date, place, and bearing error. The VOR name or identification is not required, but you must sign the airplane logbook or other record. Answer (C) is incorrect. When you make a VOR operational check, you must enter in the airplane logbook or other record the date, bearing error, and your signature. Additionally, the place of the operational check, not the VOR name or identification, must be entered.

91.175 Takeoff and Landing under IFR

81. On an instrument approach where a DH or MDA is applicable, the pilot may not operate below, or continue the approach unless the

A. aircraft is continuously in a position from which a descent to a normal landing, on the intended runway, can be made.

B. approach and runway lights are distinctly visible to the pilot.

C. flight visibility and ceiling are at, or above, the published minimums for that approach.

Answer (A) is correct. *(FAR 91.175)*

DISCUSSION: On an instrument approach when a DH or MDA is applicable, the pilot may not operate below the DH or MDA, or continue the approach, unless (among other items) the airplane is continuously in a position from which a descent to a landing on the intended runway can be made at a normal rate of descent using normal maneuvers.

Answer (B) is incorrect. To operate below the DH or MDA, or to continue the approach, a pilot needs only to (among other requirements) maintain visual reference to either the approach lights or the runway lights, not both. Answer (C) is incorrect. A pilot may not operate below the DH or MDA, or continue the approach, unless the flight visibility, not the ceiling, is at or above the published minimums for that approach.

82. Pilots are not authorized to land an aircraft from an instrument approach unless the

A. flight visibility is at, or exceeds, the visibility prescribed in the approach procedure being used.

B. flight visibility and ceiling are at, or exceed, the minimums prescribed in the approach being used.

C. visual approach slope indicator and runway references are distinctly visible to the pilot.

Answer (A) is correct. *(FAR 91.175)*

DISCUSSION: Pilots are not authorized to land an airplane from an instrument approach unless the flight visibility is at, or exceeds, the visibility prescribed in the instrument approach procedure being used.

Answer (B) is incorrect. A pilot may not land an airplane from an instrument approach unless the flight visibility, not the ceiling, is at, or exceeds, the visibility prescribed for that instrument approach. Answer (C) is incorrect. A pilot may not descend below the DH or MDA unless runway references or the VASI is available. To land, the flight visibility must be at, or must exceed, the visibility minimum prescribed in the instrument approach procedure being used.

83. A pilot performing a published instrument approach is not authorized to perform a procedure turn when

A. receiving a radar vector to a final approach course or fix.

B. maneuvering at minimum safe altitudes.

C. maneuvering at radar vectoring altitudes.

Answer (A) is correct. *(FAR 91.175)*

DISCUSSION: In the case of a radar vector to a final approach or fix, a timed approach from a holding fix, or an approach for which the procedure specifies “No PT,” a pilot may not make a procedure turn unless cleared to do so by ATC.

Answer (B) is incorrect. A pilot performing a published instrument approach is not authorized to perform a procedure turn when receiving a radar vector to a final approach course or fix, rather than when maneuvering at minimum safe altitudes. Answer (C) is incorrect. A pilot performing a published instrument approach is not authorized to perform a procedure turn when receiving a radar vector to a final approach course or fix, rather than when maneuvering at minimum radar vector altitudes.

91.177 Minimum Altitudes for IFR Operations

84. Except when necessary for takeoff or landing or unless otherwise authorized by the Administrator, the minimum altitude for IFR flight is

A. 2,000 feet over all terrain.

B. 3,000 feet over designated mountainous terrain; 2,000 feet over terrain elsewhere.

C. 2,000 feet above the highest obstacle over designated mountainous terrain; 1,000 feet above the highest obstacle over terrain elsewhere.

Answer (C) is correct. *(FAR 91.177)*

DISCUSSION: No one may operate an aircraft under IFR below the published minimum altitudes or, if none are prescribed, below an altitude of 2,000 ft. above the highest obstacle in a mountainous area or an altitude of 1,000 ft. above the highest obstacle over terrain elsewhere.

Answer (A) is incorrect. This is the minimum altitude for IFR operations over mountainous terrain; elsewhere the minimum altitude is 1,000 ft. Answer (B) is incorrect. The minimum altitude is 2,000 ft., not 3,000 ft., over mountainous terrain and 1,000 ft., not 2,000 ft., over terrain elsewhere.

91.183 IFR Communications

85. The pilot in command of an aircraft operated under IFR, in controlled airspace, not in radar contact, shall report by radio as soon as possible when

A. passing FL 180.

B. passing each designated reporting point, to include time and altitude.

C. changing control facilities.

Answer (B) is correct. *(FAR 91.183)*

DISCUSSION: The pilot in command of an airplane operated under IFR in controlled airspace and not in radar contact shall report by radio as soon as possible the time and altitude of passing each designated reporting point.

Answer (A) is incorrect. When operating under IFR in controlled airspace and not in radar contact, the pilot must report passing each designated reporting point, not passing FL 180. Answer (C) is incorrect. When operating under IFR in controlled airspace and not in radar contact, the pilot must report passing each designated reporting point, not changing control facilities. When changing control facilities, the pilot will check in with the new facility whether operating in radar contact or not.

91.187 Operation under IFR in Controlled Airspace: Malfunction Reports

86. The pilot in command of an aircraft operated under IFR, in controlled airspace, shall report as soon as practical to ATC when

A. climbing or descending to assigned altitudes.

B. experiencing any malfunctions of navigational, approach, or communications equipment, occurring in flight.

C. requested to contact a new controlling facility.

Answer (B) is correct. *(FAR 91.187)*

DISCUSSION: The pilot in command of an airplane operated under IFR in controlled airspace shall report as soon as practicable to ATC any malfunctions of navigational, approach, or communication equipment occurring in flight.

Answer (A) is incorrect. A pilot should inform ATC that (s)he is climbing or descending to an assigned altitude only on initial contact with an ATC facility, not at all times. The reports that the pilot shall (must) make while operating under IFR are found in FAR Part 91, while the reports the pilot should make (established general procedures) are found in the *AIM*. Answer (C) is incorrect. As a general procedure, the pilot should acknowledge and select the new frequency as soon as possible and make the initial call as soon as practical. The reports that the pilot shall (must) make while operating under IFR are found in FAR Part 91; established general IFR procedures are found in the *AIM* and include acknowledging ATC directives, clearances, etc.

91.203 Civil Aircraft: Certifications Required

87. Which list accurately reflects some of the documents required to be current and carried in a U.S. registered civil airplane flying in the United States under day Visual Flight Rules (VFR)?

A. Proof of insurance certificate, VFR flight plan or flight itinerary, and the aircraft logbook.

B. VFR sectional(s) chart(s) for the area in which the flight occurs, aircraft logbook, and engine logbook.

C. Airworthiness certificate, approved airplane flight manual, and aircraft registration certificate.

Answer (C) is correct. *(FAR 91.9/91.203)*

DISCUSSION: No person may operate a civil aircraft unless it has within it an appropriate and current airworthiness certificate and an effective U.S. registration certificate. No person may operate a U.S. registered civil aircraft unless there is available in the aircraft a current and approved Airplane Flight Manual.

Answer (A) is incorrect. A proof of insurance certificate, VFR flight plan or flight itinerary, and aircraft logbook are not required for flight in day VFR conditions. Answer (B) is incorrect. Sectional charts, aircraft logbook, and engine logbook are not requirements for flight in day VFR conditions.

88. Which of the following preflight actions is the pilot in command required to take in order to comply with the United States Code of Federal Regulations regarding day Visual Flight Rules (VFR)?

A. File a VFR flight plan with a Flight Service Station.

B. Verify the airworthiness certificate is legible to passengers.

C. Verify approved position lights are not burned out.

Answer (B) is correct. *(FAR 91.203)*

DISCUSSION: No person may operate a civil aircraft unless the airworthiness certificate or a special flight authorization is displayed at the cabin or cockpit entrance so that it is legible to passengers and crew.

Answer (A) is incorrect. A VFR flight plan is not required to conduct VFR flight operations. Answer (C) is incorrect. A pilot is only required to have approved position lights for night VFR operations.

89. A commercial pilot is preparing for a VFR flight that will involve carrying passengers 150 NM at night. Prior to the flight what action must the PIC perform?

A. Confirm the Airworthiness Certificate is on board and visible to passengers.

B. File a flight plan.

C. Confirm the proof of insurance is on board.

Answer (A) is correct. *(FAR 91.203)*

DISCUSSION: No person may operate a civil aircraft unless an airworthiness certificate or special flight authorization is displayed at the cabin or cockpit entrance so it is visible to passengers and crew.

Answer (B) is incorrect. A flight plan is not required for VFR night cross-country flying. Answer (C) is incorrect. Proof of insurance is not required to be on board U.S.-registered civil aircraft while operating within the National Airspace System.

90. Prior to departing on a VFR cross country flight over mountainous terrain, what action must the pilot in command perform?

A. Confirm the Airworthiness certificate is visible to passengers and crew.

B. Perform a VOR check.

C. Take a mountain flying awareness course (MFAC).

Answer (A) is correct. *(FAR 91.203)*

DISCUSSION: No person may operate a civil aircraft unless an airworthiness certificate or special flight authorization is displayed at the cabin or cockpit entrance so it is visible to passengers and crew.

Answer (B) is incorrect. A VOR check is required every 30 days for flight under instrument flight rules. A VFR cross-country flight does not require the use of a VOR. Answer (C) is incorrect. A mountain flying awareness course (MFAC) is not required to operate over mountainous terrain.

91. You are taking a 123 nautical mile VFR flight from one airport to another. Which of the following actions must the pilot in command take?

A. Ensure each passenger has a legible photo identification.

B. Verify the airworthiness certificate is legible to passengers.

C. File a VFR flight plan with a Flight Service Station.

Answer (B) is correct. *(FAR 91.203)*

DISCUSSION: No person may operate a civil aircraft unless the airworthiness certificate or a special flight authorization is displayed at the cabin or cockpit entrance so that it is legible to passengers and crew.

Answer (A) is incorrect. It is not required for the pilot in command to ensure that each passenger has photo identification. Answer (C) is incorrect. A VFR flight plan is not required to conduct VFR flight operations.

92. You are taking a 196 nautical mile VFR cross country flight in mountainous terrain. Which of the following actions must the pilot in command take?

A. Verify the airworthiness certificate is legible to passengers.

B. File a VFR flight plan with a Flight Service Station.

C. Ensure all items in the baggage area are strapped down.

Answer (A) is correct. *(FAR 91.203)*

DISCUSSION: No person may operate a civil aircraft unless the airworthiness certificate or a special flight authorization is displayed at the cabin or cockpit entrance so that it is legible to passengers and crew.

Answer (B) is incorrect. A VFR flight plan is not required to conduct VFR flight operations. Answer (C) is incorrect. This is not the best answer because most baggage areas use cargo nets to keep baggage in place and not necessarily strapped down.

91.205 Powered Civil Aircraft with Standard Category U.S. Airworthiness Certificates: Instrument and Equipment Requirements

93. Which is required equipment for powered aircraft during VFR night flights?

A. Flashlight with red lens, if the flight is for hire.

B. An electric landing light, if the flight is for hire.

C. Sensitive altimeter adjustable for barometric pressure.

Answer (B) is correct. *(FAR 91.205)*

DISCUSSION: For VFR flights at night, the required equipment includes one electric landing light if the aircraft is operated for hire.

Answer (A) is incorrect. No specific requirement concerns flashlights and the color of the lens. Answer (C) is incorrect. Sensitive altimeters are required only for IFR flight.

94. Which is required equipment for powered aircraft during VFR night flights?

A. Anticollision light system.

B. Gyroscopic direction indicator.

C. Gyroscopic bank-and-pitch indicator.

Answer (A) is correct. *(FAR 91.205)*

DISCUSSION: For VFR flight at night, the required instruments and equipment include an approved aviation red or aviation white anticollision light system on all U.S.-registered civil aircraft.

Answer (B) is incorrect. A gyroscopic direction indicator is required for IFR, not VFR night, flight. Answer (C) is incorrect. A gyroscopic bank-and-pitch indicator is required for IFR, not VFR night, flight.

95. Approved flotation gear, readily available to each occupant, is required on each airplane if it is being flown for hire over water,

A. in amphibious aircraft beyond 50 NM from shore.

B. beyond power-off gliding distance from shore.

C. more than 50 statute miles from shore.

Answer (B) is correct. *(FAR 91.205)*

DISCUSSION: If an airplane is operated for hire over water and beyond power-off gliding distance from shore, approved flotation gear, readily available to each occupant, and at least one pyrotechnic signaling device are required.

Answer (A) is incorrect. The flotation gear requirement applies to all aircraft operated for hire when flying beyond power-off gliding distance, not 50 NM, from shore. Answer (C) is incorrect. Flotation gear is required for each occupant if the airplane is flown beyond the power-off gliding distance from shore, not more than 50 SM from shore.

91.207 Emergency Locator Transmitters

96. The maximum cumulative time that an emergency locator transmitter may be operated before the rechargeable battery must be recharged is

A. 30 minutes.

B. 45 minutes.

C. 60 minutes.

Answer (C) is correct. *(FAR 91.207)*

DISCUSSION: ELT batteries must be replaced or recharged when the transmitter has been in use for more than 1 cumulative hr. or when 50% of their useful life (or useful life of charge) has expired.

Answer (A) is incorrect. An ELT battery must be replaced or recharged after 1 hr. (not 30 min.) of cumulative use. Answer (B) is incorrect. An ELT battery must be replaced or recharged after 1 hr. (not 45 min.) of cumulative use.

91.209 Aircraft Lights

97. If not equipped with required position lights, an aircraft must terminate flight

A. at sunset.

B. 30 minutes after sunset.

C. 1 hour after sunset.

Answer (A) is correct. *(FAR 91.209)*

DISCUSSION: No person may, during the period from sunset to sunrise, operate an aircraft unless it has lighted position lights.

Answer (B) is incorrect. Position lights are required at, not 30 min. after, sunset. Answer (C) is incorrect. Position lights are required at, not 1 hr. after, sunset.

98. If an aircraft is not equipped with an electrical or anticollision light system, no person may operate that aircraft

A. after dark.

B. 1 hour after sunset.

C. after sunset to sunrise.

Answer (C) is correct. *(FAR 91.209)*

DISCUSSION: If an aircraft is not equipped with an electrical or anticollision light system, you may not operate that aircraft during the period from sunset to sunrise.

Answer (A) is incorrect. You may not operate an aircraft that is not equipped with an electrical or anticollision light system after sunset, not after dark. Answer (B) is incorrect. You may not operate an aircraft that is not equipped with an electrical or anticollision light system after sunset, not 1 hr. after sunset. The logging of night flight time, to meet recent experience requirements for carrying passengers at night, begins 1 hr. after sunset.

91.211 Supplemental Oxygen

99. What are the oxygen requirements when operating at cabin pressure altitudes above 15,000 feet MSL?

A. Oxygen must be available for the flightcrew.

B. Oxygen is not required at any altitude in a balloon.

C. The flightcrew and passengers must be provided with supplemental oxygen.

Answer (C) is correct. *(FAR 91.211)*

DISCUSSION: No person may operate a civil aircraft of U.S. registry at cabin pressure altitudes above 15,000 ft. MSL unless each occupant of the aircraft is provided with supplemental oxygen.

Answer (A) is incorrect. The flightcrew must use oxygen (not just have it available) above 14,000 ft. MSL. Answer (B) is incorrect. Each occupant, not only the flightcrew, must be provided with supplemental oxygen at cabin pressure altitudes above 15,000 ft. MSL.

100. In accordance with 14 CFR Part 91, supplemental oxygen must be used by the required minimum flightcrew for that time exceeding 30 minutes while at cabin pressure altitudes of

A. 10,500 feet MSL up to and including 12,500 feet MSL.

B. 12,000 feet MSL up to and including 18,000 feet MSL.

C. 12,500 feet MSL up to and including 14,000 feet MSL.

Answer (C) is correct. *(FAR 91.211)*

DISCUSSION: No one may operate a U.S. civil aircraft at cabin pressure altitudes above 12,500 ft. MSL up to and including 14,000 ft. MSL, unless the required minimum flight crew is provided with and uses supplemental oxygen for that part of the flight at those altitudes that is of more than 30 min. duration.

Answer (A) is incorrect. Supplemental oxygen is not required below 12,500 ft. MSL. Answer (B) is incorrect. Supplemental oxygen is not required below 12,500 ft. MSL and is required at all times above 14,000 ft. MSL.

91.215 ATC Transponder and Altitude Reporting Equipment and Use

101. A coded transponder equipped with altitude reporting equipment is required for

A. Class A, Class B, and Class C airspace areas.

B. all airspace of the 48 contiguous U.S. and the District of Columbia at and above 10,000 feet MSL (including airspace at and below 2,500 feet above the surface).

C. both of the other answers.

Answer (A) is correct. *(FAR 91.215)*

DISCUSSION: An operable coded transponder with altitude reporting capability (i.e., Mode C) is required in Class A, Class B, and Class C airspace areas.

Answer (B) is incorrect. An operable coded transponder equipped with altitude reporting capability is required in all airspace of the 48 contiguous U.S. and the District of Columbia at and above 10,000 ft. MSL excluding, not including, airspace at and below 2,500 ft. AGL. Answer (C) is incorrect. An operable coded transponder equipped with altitude reporting capability is required in all airspace of the 48 contiguous U.S. and the District of Columbia at and above 10,000 ft. MSL excluding, not including, airspace at and below 2,500 ft. AGL.

102. In the contiguous U.S., excluding the airspace at and below 2,500 feet AGL, an operable coded transponder equipped with Mode C capability is required in all airspace above

A. 10,000 feet MSL.

B. 12,500 feet MSL.

C. 14,500 feet MSL.

Answer (A) is correct. *(FAR 91.215)*

DISCUSSION: An operable transponder with altitude reporting capability (i.e., Mode C) is required for all operations above 10,000 ft. MSL, excluding the airspace at and below 2,500 ft. AGL.

Answer (B) is incorrect. The altitude above which crewmembers are required to use oxygen after 30 min. in an unpressurized aircraft is 12,500 ft. MSL. Answer (C) is incorrect. The base of Class E airspace is 14,500 ft. MSL.

91.303 Aerobatic Flight

103. What is the minimum altitude and flight visibility required for acrobatic flight?

A. 1,500 feet AGL and 3 miles.

B. 2,000 feet MSL and 2 miles.

C. 3,000 feet AGL and 1 mile.

Answer (A) is correct. *(FAR 91.303)*

DISCUSSION: No person may operate an aircraft in acrobatic flight below an altitude of 1,500 ft. AGL or with flight visibility of less than 3 SM.

Answer (B) is incorrect. The minimum altitude and visibility are 1,500 ft. AGL, not 2,000 ft. MSL, and 3 SM, not 2 SM. Answer (C) is incorrect. The minimum altitude and visibility are 1,500 ft. AGL, not 3,000 ft., AGL and 3 SM, not 1 SM.

91.311 Towing: Other than under Sec. 91.309

104. Which is required to operate an aircraft towing an advertising banner?

A. Approval from ATC to operate in Class E airspace.

B. A certificate of waiver issued by the Administrator.

C. A safety link at each end of the towline which has a breaking strength not less than 80 percent of the aircraft's gross weight.

Answer (B) is correct. *(FAR 91.311)*

DISCUSSION: No pilot of a civil aircraft may tow anything with that aircraft (other than a glider) except in accordance with the terms of a certificate of waiver issued by the Administrator of the FAA.

Answer (A) is incorrect. ATC approval for flight in Class E airspace is required only during IFR conditions. Answer (C) is incorrect. The breaking strength of the safety link applies to towing gliders, not banners.

91.313 Restricted Category Civil Aircraft: Operating Limitations

105. Which is true with respect to operating limitations of a "restricted" category airplane?

A. A pilot of a "restricted" category airplane is required to hold a commercial pilot certificate.

B. A "restricted" category airplane is limited to an operating radius of 25 miles from its home base.

C. No person may operate a "restricted" category airplane carrying passengers or property for compensation or hire.

Answer (C) is correct. *(FAR 91.313)*

DISCUSSION: Persons or property cannot be transported for compensation or hire in a restricted category airplane.

Answer (A) is incorrect. With respect to operating limitations of a restricted category airplane, there is no minimum pilot certification level. If the pilot is receiving compensation, then, due to that type of operation, a commercial pilot certificate may be required. Answer (B) is incorrect. With respect to operating limitations of a restricted category airplane, there is no limitation as to how far from the airplane's home base it may be operated.

91.315 Limited Category Civil Aircraft: Operating Limitations

106. The carriage of passengers for hire by a commercial pilot is

A. not authorized in limited category aircraft.

B. not authorized in utility category airplane.

C. authorized in restricted category aircraft.

Answer (A) is correct. *(FAR 91.315)*

DISCUSSION: Persons or property cannot be transported for compensation or hire in a limited category civil aircraft.

Answer (B) is incorrect. Carriage of passengers for hire is permitted in utility category aircraft. Answer (C) is incorrect. Carriage of passengers for hire is not permitted in restricted category aircraft.

91.319 Aircraft Having Experimental Certificates: Operating Limitations

107. No person may operate an aircraft that has an experimental airworthiness certificate

A. under instrument flight rules (IFR).

B. when carrying property for hire.

C. when carrying persons or property for hire.

Answer (C) is correct. *(FAR 91.319)*

DISCUSSION: No person may operate an aircraft that has an experimental airworthiness certificate when carrying persons or property for hire.

Answer (A) is incorrect. While an experimental aircraft is to be flown only VFR-day weather conditions, the FAA may specifically authorize IFR operations. Answer (B) is incorrect. No person may operate an aircraft that has an experimental certificate when carrying persons or property for hire, not only property.

91.325 Primary Category Aircraft: Operating Limitations

108. Which is true with respect to operating limitations of a "primary" category airplane?

A. A "primary" category airplane is limited to a specified operating radius from its home base.

B. No person may operate a "primary" category airplane carrying passengers or property for compensation or hire.

C. A pilot of a "primary" category airplane must hold a commercial pilot certificate when carrying passengers for compensation or hire.

Answer (B) is correct. *(FAR 91.325)*

DISCUSSION: With respect to operating limitations of a primary category airplane, no person may operate a primary category airplane carrying persons or property for compensation or hire.

Answer (A) is incorrect. With respect to operating limitations of a primary category airplane, there is no limitation as to how far from the airplane's home base it may be operated. Answer (C) is incorrect. With respect to operating limitations of a primary category airplane, there is no minimum level of pilot certification required.

91.403 General

109. Assuring compliance with an Airworthiness Directive is the responsibility of the

A. pilot in command and the FAA certificated mechanic assigned to that aircraft.

B. pilot in command of that aircraft.

C. owner or operator of that aircraft.

Answer (C) is correct. *(FAR 91.403)*

DISCUSSION: The owner or operator of an aircraft is primarily responsible for maintaining that aircraft in an airworthy condition, including compliance with all Airworthiness Directives. The term "operator" includes the pilot in command.

Answer (A) is incorrect. Although a mechanic will perform the maintenance required to comply with an Airworthiness Directive, assuring compliance is the responsibility of the owner or operator. Answer (B) is incorrect. The owner or operator, not only the pilot in command, is responsible for assuring compliance with all Airworthiness Directives.

110. Who is primarily responsible for maintaining an aircraft in an airworthy condition?

A. The lead mechanic responsible for that aircraft.

B. Pilot in command or operator.

C. Owner or operator of the aircraft.

Answer (C) is correct. *(FAR 91.403)*

DISCUSSION: The owner or operator of an aircraft is primarily responsible for maintaining that aircraft in an airworthy condition. The term "operator" includes the pilot in command.

Answer (A) is incorrect. Mechanics work at the direction of the owner or operator. Answer (B) is incorrect. The owner or operator, not only the operator, of an aircraft is primarily responsible for an aircraft's airworthiness. The term "operator" includes the pilot in command.

91.405 Maintenance Required

111. After an annual inspection has been completed and the aircraft has been returned to service, an appropriate notation should be made

A. on the airworthiness certificate.

B. in the aircraft maintenance records.

C. in the FAA-approved flight manual.

Answer (B) is correct. *(FAR 91.405)*

DISCUSSION: Each owner or operator shall ensure that maintenance personnel make appropriate entries in the aircraft maintenance records indicating that an annual inspection has been completed and that the aircraft has been approved for return to service.

Answer (A) is incorrect. Annual inspections are recorded in maintenance records, not on the Airworthiness Certificate. Answer (C) is incorrect. Annual inspections are recorded in maintenance records, not in the flight manual.

112. A standard airworthiness certificate remains in effect as long as the aircraft receives

A. required maintenance and inspections.

B. an annual inspection.

C. an annual inspection and a 100-hour inspection prior to their expiration dates.

Answer (A) is correct. *(FAR 91.405)*

DISCUSSION: A standard airworthiness certificate remains in effect as long as the aircraft receives the required maintenance and inspections. This includes compliance with Airworthiness Directives, annual inspections, 100-hr. inspections, repairs between inspections, etc.

Answer (B) is incorrect. A standard airworthiness certificate remains in effect as long as the aircraft receives the required maintenance and inspections. An annual inspection is just one part of the inspections and maintenance requirements, and some aircraft have an inspection program, which means an annual inspection is not required. Answer (C) is incorrect. A standard airworthiness certificate remains in effect as long as the aircraft receives the required maintenance and inspections. Not all aircraft require an annual and a 100-hr. inspection.

91.407 Operation after Maintenance, Preventive Maintenance, Rebuilding, or Alteration

113. If an aircraft's operation in flight was substantially affected by an alteration or repair, the aircraft documents must show that it was test flown and approved for return to service by an appropriately-rated pilot prior to being operated

A. under VFR or IFR rules.

B. with passengers aboard.

C. for compensation or hire.

Answer (B) is correct. *(FAR 91.407)*

DISCUSSION: No person may carry any person (other than crewmembers) in an altered aircraft that may have appreciably changed its flight characteristics or substantially affected its operation in flight until an appropriately rated pilot with at least a private pilot certificate flies the aircraft, makes an operational check of the maintenance performed or alteration made, and logs the flight in the aircraft records.

Answer (A) is incorrect. An altered aircraft must be test flown before passengers are carried. A maintenance logbook entry by an appropriate maintenance person returns the aircraft to service, which allows the airplane to be flown under VFR or IFR. Answer (C) is incorrect. An altered aircraft must be test flown before passengers are carried regardless of whether the flight is for compensation or hire.

91.409 Inspections

114. Which is true concerning required maintenance inspections?

A. A 100-hour inspection may be substituted for an annual inspection.

B. An annual inspection may be substituted for a 100-hour inspection.

C. An annual inspection is required even if a progressive inspection system has been approved.

Answer (B) is correct. *(FAR 91.409)*

DISCUSSION: No person may operate an aircraft within the preceding 12 calendar months unless it has had an annual inspection. If the aircraft is required to have a 100-hr. inspection, an annual inspection may be substituted for a 100-hr. inspection.

Answer (A) is incorrect. An annual inspection may be substituted for a 100-hr. inspection (not vice versa). Answer (C) is incorrect. An annual inspection is not required if a progressive inspection system has been approved.

115. An aircraft carrying passengers for hire has been on a schedule of inspection every 100 hours of time in service. Under which condition, if any, may that aircraft be operated beyond 100 hours without a new inspection?

A. The aircraft may be flown for any flight as long as the time in service has not exceeded 110 hours.

B. The aircraft may be dispatched for a flight of any duration as long as 100 hours has not been exceeded at the time it departs.

C. The 100-hour limitation may be exceeded by not more than 10 hours if necessary to reach a place at which the inspection can be done.

Answer (C) is correct. *(FAR 91.409)*

DISCUSSION: The 100-hr. limitation may be exceeded by not more than 10 hr. if necessary to reach a place at which the inspection can be done. The excess time, however, is included in computing the next 100 hr. of time in service.

Answer (A) is incorrect. The 10-hr. leeway is applicable only if necessary to reach a place to perform the 100-hr. inspection. Answer (B) is incorrect. There is a 10-hr. leeway in excess of the 100-hr. limitation, and the 10-hr. leeway is applicable only if necessary to reach a place to perform the 100-hr. inspection.

91.413 ATC Transponder Tests and Inspections

116. If an ATC transponder installed in an aircraft has not been tested, inspected, and found to comply with regulations within a specified period, what is the limitation on its use?

A. Its use is not permitted.

B. It may be used when in Class G airspace.

C. It may be used for VFR flight only.

Answer (A) is correct. *(FAR 91.413)*

DISCUSSION: No person may use an ATC transponder unless, within the preceding 24 calendar months, that ATC transponder has been tested and inspected and found to comply with the appropriate regulations.

Answer (B) is incorrect. There are no exceptions. Answer (C) is incorrect. There are no exceptions.

117. An ATC transponder is not to be used unless it has been tested, inspected, and found to comply with regulations within the preceding

A. 30 days.

B. 12 calendar months.

C. 24 calendar months.

Answer (C) is correct. *(FAR 91.413)*

DISCUSSION: No person may use an ATC transponder unless, within the preceding 24 calendar months, that ATC transponder has been tested and inspected and found to comply with the appropriate regulations.

Answer (A) is incorrect. A VOR (not a transponder) must be checked every 30 days. Answer (B) is incorrect. A transponder must be inspected every 24 (not 12) calendar months.

91.417 Maintenance Records

118. Aircraft maintenance records must include the current status of the

A. applicable airworthiness certificate.

B. life-limited parts of only the engine and airframe.

C. life-limited parts of each airframe, engine, propeller, rotor, and appliance.

Answer (C) is correct. *(FAR 91.417)*

DISCUSSION: Each owner or operator must keep certain records for each airplane:

1. Records of maintenance, preventive maintenance, and alteration, and of the 100-hr., annual, progressive, and other required of approved inspections for each aircraft
2. Records containing total time in service of the airframe, each engine, and each propeller; current status of life-limited parts of each airframe, engine, propeller, rotor, and appliance; all items which are required to be overhauled on a specified time basis; the current inspection of the aircraft; airworthiness directives; and copies of forms prescribed for major alterations

Answer (A) is incorrect. Airworthiness certificates are issued only at the time of manufacture. Answer (B) is incorrect. The current status of the life-limited parts of the propeller, rotor, and appliance is required as well.

119. Which is correct concerning preventive maintenance, when accomplished by a pilot?

A. A record of preventive maintenance is not required.

B. A record of preventive maintenance must be entered in the maintenance records.

C. Records of preventive maintenance must be entered in the FAA-approved flight manual.

Answer (B) is correct. *(FAR 91.417)*

DISCUSSION: Each owner or operator must keep certain records for each airplane:

1. Records of maintenance, preventive maintenance, and alteration, and of the 100-hr., annual, progressive, and other required of approved inspections for each aircraft
2. Records containing total time in service of the airframe, each engine, and each propeller; current status of life-limited parts of each airframe, engine, propeller, rotor, and appliance; all items which are required to be overhauled on a specified time basis; the current inspection of the aircraft; airworthiness directives; and copies of forms prescribed for major alterations

Answer (A) is incorrect. Preventive maintenance records are required. Answer (C) is incorrect. Maintenance must be recorded in the maintenance records, not the flight manual.

120. Which is true relating to Airworthiness Directives (AD's)?

A. AD's are advisory in nature and are, generally, not addressed immediately.

B. Noncompliance with AD's renders an aircraft unairworthy.

C. Compliance with AD's is the responsibility of maintenance personnel.

Answer (B) is correct. *(FAR 91.417)*

DISCUSSION: FAR 91.405 requires annual inspections with appropriate entries in the airplane maintenance records. FAR 91.417 requires that the current status of applicable Airworthiness Directives (ADs) and the method of compliance be specified. Noncompliance means the airplane is unairworthy and may not be flown.

Answer (A) is incorrect. ADs are regulatory in nature, i.e., mandatory. Answer (C) is incorrect. Compliance with ADs as well as maintenance is the responsibility of the operator/owner, not maintenance personnel.

91.421 Rebuilt Engine Maintenance Records

121. A new maintenance record being used for an aircraft engine rebuilt by the manufacturer must include previous

A. operating hours of the engine.

B. annual inspections performed on the engine.

C. changes as required by Airworthiness Directives.

Answer (C) is correct. *(FAR 91.421)*

DISCUSSION: Each manufacturer or agency that grants zero time to an engine rebuilt by it shall enter, in the new record, a signed statement of the date the engine was rebuilt; each change made as required by AD; and each change made in compliance with manufacturer's service bulletins, if the entry is specifically requested in that bulletin.

Answer (A) is incorrect. A rebuilt engine is considered to have zero operating hours. Answer (B) is incorrect. A record of previous inspections is not required on a rebuilt engine.

4.5 FAR Part 119

119.1 Applicability

122. In what type of operation, not regulated by 14 CFR Part 119, may a commercial pilot act as pilot in command and receive compensation for services?

A. Part-time contract pilot.

B. Nonstop flights within a 25 SM radius of an airport to carry persons for intentional parachute jumps.

C. Nonstop flights within a 25 SM radius of an airport to carry cargo only.

Answer (B) is correct. *(FAR 119.1)*

DISCUSSION: Certification of air carriers and commercial operators is regulated by 14 CFR Part 119. FAR 119.1 lists several types of operations to which Part 119 does not apply, including nonstop flights within a 25 SM radius of an airport to carry persons for intentional parachute jumps.

Answer (A) is incorrect. Part 119 regulates the types of operations which need an operating certificate, not how a pilot is employed. A commercial pilot may act as PIC (and receive compensation for services) as a part-time contract pilot for any of the operations regulated or not regulated under Part 119, provided the pilot complies with all applicable regulations for those operations. Answer (C) is incorrect. Operators conducting nonstop cargo-only flights within a 25 SM radius of an airport are regulated by Part 119.

123. In what type of operation, not regulated by 14 CFR Part 119, may a commercial pilot act as pilot in command and receive compensation for services?

A. Crop dusting, spraying, and bird chasing.

B. On-demand, nine or less passenger, charter flights.

C. On-demand cargo flights.

Answer (A) is correct. *(FAR 119.1)*

DISCUSSION: FAR Part 119 regulates the certification of air carriers and commercial operators. FAR 119.1 lists several types of operations to which Part 119 does not apply, including crop dusting, seeding, spraying, and bird chasing.

Answer (B) is incorrect. Operators of on-demand charter flights are regulated by Part 119. Answer (C) is incorrect. Operators of on-demand cargo flights are regulated by Part 119.

4.6 NTSB Part 830

830.2 Definitions

124. What period of time must a person be hospitalized before an injury may be defined by the NTSB as a "serious injury"?

A. 10 days, with no other extenuating circumstances.

B. 48 hours; commencing within 7 days after date of the injury.

C. 72 hours; commencing within 10 days after date of the injury.

Answer (B) is correct. *(NTSB 830.2)*

DISCUSSION: A serious injury is defined as an injury which: requires hospitalization for more than 48 hours, commencing within 7 days from the date of the injury; results in the fracture of any bone, other than simple fractures of the fingers, toes, or nose; causes severe hemorrhages, nerve, muscle, or tendon damage; involves any internal organ; or involves second- or third-degree burns, or any burns affecting more than 5% of the body surface.

Answer (A) is incorrect. For an injury to be considered a serious injury on the basis of hospitalization, the injury must require hospitalization for more than 48 hours, not 10 days, commencing within 7 days from the date of the injury, not without other extenuating circumstances or requirements. Answer (C) is incorrect. For an injury to be considered a serious injury on the basis of hospitalization, the injury must require hospitalization for more than 48 hours, not 72 hours, commencing within 7 days, not 10 days, from the date of the injury.

830.5 Immediate Notification

125. When should notification of an aircraft accident be made to the NTSB if there was substantial damage and no injuries?

A. Immediately.

B. Within 10 days.

C. Within 30 days.

Answer (A) is correct. *(NTSB 830.5)*

DISCUSSION: An accident is an occurrence associated with the operation of an aircraft that takes place between the time any person boards the aircraft with the intention of flight and all such persons have disembarked, and in which any person suffers death or serious injury, or in which the aircraft receives substantial damage. The operator of an aircraft must immediately notify the nearest NTSB field office when an accident occurs.

Answer (B) is incorrect. Ten days is the time specified to file a detailed aircraft accident report with the NTSB. Answer (C) is incorrect. Thirty days is not a deadline specified in NTSB Part 830.

126. NTSB Part 830 requires an immediate notification as a result of which incident?

A. Engine failure for any reason during flight.

B. Damage to the landing gear as a result of a hard landing.

C. Any required flight crewmember being unable to perform flight duties because of illness.

Answer (C) is correct. *(NTSB 830.5)*

DISCUSSION: Immediate notification is required when an aircraft accident or any of the following listed incidents occurs: flight control system malfunction or failure; inability of any required flight crewmember to perform normal flight duties as a result of injury or illness; failure of structural components of a turbine engine excluding compressor and turbine blades and vanes; in-flight fire; or aircraft collision in flight. Immediate notice is also required when an aircraft is overdue and is believed to have been involved in an accident.

Answer (A) is incorrect. Engine failure, in itself, is not considered "substantial damage" requiring immediate notification. Answer (B) is incorrect. Damage to landing gear is not considered "substantial damage" requiring immediate notification.

127. Which incident would require that the nearest NTSB field office be notified immediately?

A. In-flight fire.

B. Ground fire resulting in fire equipment dispatch.

C. Fire of the primary aircraft while in a hangar which results in damage to other property of more than $25,000.

Answer (A) is correct. *(NTSB 830.5)*

DISCUSSION: Immediate notification is required when an aircraft accident or any of the following listed incidents occurs: flight control system malfunction or failure; inability of any required flight crewmember to perform normal flight duties as a result of injury or illness; failure of structural components of a turbine engine excluding compressor and turbine blades and vanes; in-flight fire; or aircraft collision in flight. Immediate notice is also required when an aircraft is overdue and is believed to have been involved in an accident.

Answer (B) is incorrect. Only in-flight incidents require immediate notification. Answer (C) is incorrect. Only in-flight incidents require immediate notification.

128. Which airborne incident would require that the nearest NTSB field office be notified immediately?

A. Cargo compartment door malfunction or failure.

B. Cabin door opened in-flight.

C. Flight control systems malfunction or failure.

Answer (C) is correct. *(NTSB 830.5)*

DISCUSSION: Immediate notification is required when an aircraft accident or any of the following listed incidents occurs: flight control system malfunction or failure; inability of any required flight crewmember to perform normal flight duties as a result of an injury or illness; failure of structural components of a turbine engine excluding compressor and turbine blades and vanes; in-flight fire; or aircraft collision in flight. Immediate notification is also required when an aircraft is overdue and believed to have been involved in an accident.

Answer (A) is incorrect. A flight control system, not a cargo compartment door, malfunction or failure requires immediate notification. Answer (B) is incorrect. A cabin door that comes open in flight is not considered an incident that requires immediate notification.

129. While taxiing for takeoff, a small fire burned the insulation from a transceiver wire. What action would be required to comply with NTSB Part 830?

A. No notification or report is required.

B. A report must be filed with the avionics inspector at the nearest FAA field office within 48 hours.

C. An immediate notification must be filed by the operator of the aircraft with the nearest NTSB field office.

Answer (A) is correct. *(NTSB 830.5)*

DISCUSSION: An in-flight fire is an incident that requires immediate notification. The minor fire described did not occur in flight, however. Moreover, it did not cause substantial damage and was thus not classifiable as an accident. No report or notification is required unless an accident or a specified incident has occurred or unless an aircraft is overdue and believed to have been in an accident.

Answer (B) is incorrect. An immediate report is required only if certain items occur such as an in-flight fire. Also, the reports are to go to the NTSB, not the FAA offices. Answer (C) is incorrect. An immediate report is required only if certain items occur such as an in-flight fire.

130. While taxiing on the parking ramp, the landing gear, wheel, and tire are damaged by striking ground equipment. What action would be required to comply with NTSB Part 830?

A. An immediate notification must be filed by the operator of the aircraft with the nearest NTSB field office.

B. A report must be filed with the nearest FAA field office within 7 days.

C. No notification or report is required.

Answer (C) is correct. *(NTSB 830.5)*

DISCUSSION: No report or notification is required unless an accident or a specified incident has occurred or unless an aircraft is overdue and believed to have been in an accident. The described incident is not one specified that requires notification or a report, and it is not considered an accident under NTSB Part 830. One requirement of an accident is substantial damage. Under NTSB Part 830.2, damage to landing gear, wheels, and tires is not considered "substantial damage."

Answer (A) is incorrect. Immediate notification is required only for accidents or certain incidents. Damage to the landing gear, wheel, and tire is not considered an accident or an incident that requires immediate notification under NTSB Part 830. Answer (B) is incorrect. No report is required to be filed under NTSB Part 830. Additionally, NTSB Part 830 deals with notification and reports to the NTSB only, not the FAA.

131. Notification to the NTSB is required when there has been substantial damage

A. which requires repairs to landing gear.

B. to an engine caused by engine failure in flight.

C. which adversely affects structural strength or flight characteristics.

Answer (C) is correct. *(NTSB 830.5)*

DISCUSSION: An accident is an occurrence associated with the operation of an aircraft that takes place between the time any person boards the aircraft with the intention of flight and all such persons have disembarked, and in which any person suffers death or serious injury, or in which the aircraft receives substantial damage. Substantial damage means damage or failure that adversely affects the structural strength, performance, or flight characteristics of the aircraft and that would normally require major repair or replacement of the affected component. An accident causing substantial damage requires immediate notification to the NTSB.

Answer (A) is incorrect. Damage to landing gear is not considered "substantial damage" requiring immediate notification. Answer (B) is incorrect. Damage to an engine caused by engine failure is not considered "substantial damage" requiring immediate notification.

132. During flight a fire, which was extinguished, burned the insulation from a transceiver wire. What action is required by regulations?

A. No notification or report is required.

B. A report must be filed with the avionics inspector at the nearest FAA Flight Standards District Office within 48 hours.

C. An immediate notification by the operator of the aircraft to the nearest NTSB field office.

Answer (C) is correct. *(NTSB 830.5)*

DISCUSSION: Immediate notification is required when an aircraft accident or any of the following listed incidents occurs: flight control system malfunction or failure, inability of any required flight crewmember to perform normal flight duties as a result of injury or illness, failure of structural components of a turbine engine excluding compressor and turbine blades and vanes, in-flight fire, or aircraft collision in flight. Immediate notice is also required when an aircraft is overdue and is believed to have been involved in an accident.

Answer (A) is incorrect. An in-flight fire (in contrast to an on-ground fire) does require immediate notification. Answer (B) is incorrect. No report to the avionics inspector is required.

830.15 Reports and Statements to Be Filed

133. How many days after an accident is a report required to be filed with the nearest NTSB field office?

A. 2.

B. 7.

C. 10.

Answer (C) is correct. *(NTSB 830.15)*

DISCUSSION: The operator of an aircraft must file a report within 10 days after an accident, or after 7 days if an overdue aircraft is still missing. A report on an incident for which notification is required should be filed only as requested by an authorized representative of the NTSB.

Answer (A) is incorrect. Two days is not a reporting requirement in NTSB Part 830. Answer (B) is incorrect. Seven days is the limitation with respect to an overdue aircraft that is missing.

134. The operator of an aircraft that has been involved in an incident is required to submit a report to the nearest field office of the NTSB

A. within 7 days.

B. within 10 days.

C. only if requested to do so.

Answer (C) is correct. *(NTSB 830.15)*

DISCUSSION: The operator of an aircraft must file a report within 10 days after an accident, or after 7 days if an overdue aircraft is still missing. A report on an incident for which notification is required shall be filed only as requested by an authorized representative of the Board.

Answer (A) is incorrect. Seven days is the time limitation for reporting overdue (missing) aircraft. Answer (B) is incorrect. Ten days is the limitation on filing a report for accidents.

4.7 Near Midair Collision Reporting

135. Who is responsible for filing a Near Midair Collision (NMAC) Report?

A. A passenger on board the involved aircraft.

B. Local law enforcement.

C. Pilot and/or Flight Crew of aircraft involved in the accident.

Answer (C) is correct. *(AIM Chap 7)*

DISCUSSION: The primary purpose of the Near Midair Collision (NMAC) Reporting Program is to provide information for use in enhancing the safety and efficiency of the National Airspace System. Data obtained from NMAC reports are used by the FAA to improve the quality of FAA services to users and to develop programs, policies, and procedures aimed at the reduction of NMAC occurrences. A near midair collision is defined as an incident associated with the operation of an aircraft in which a possibility of collision occurs as a result of proximity of less than 500 feet to another aircraft, or a report is received from a pilot or a flight crew member stating that a collision hazard existed between two or more aircraft. It is the responsibility of the pilot and/or flight crew to determine whether a near midair collision did actually occur and, if so, to initiate an NMAC report. Be specific, as ATC will not interpret a casual remark to mean that an NMAC is being reported. The pilot should state, “I wish to report a near midair collision.”

Answer (A) is incorrect. A passenger is not responsible because it is the responsibility of the pilot and/or flight crew to determine whether a near midair collision did actually occur and, if so, to initiate an NMAC report. Answer (B) is incorrect. While the FSDO in whose area the incident occurred is responsible for the investigation and reporting of NMACs, it is the responsibility of the pilot and/or flight crew to determine whether a near midair collision did actually occur and, if so, to initiate an NMAC report. Be specific, as ATC will not interpret a casual remark to mean that an NMAC is being reported. The pilot should state, “I wish to report a near midair collision.”

136. Pilots and/or Flight Crew members involved in NMAC occurrences are urged to report each incident immediately:

A. By radio or telephone to the nearest FAA ATC Facility or FSS.

B. To local law enforcement.

C. By cell phone to the nearest Flight Standards District Office (FSDO) as this is an emergency.

Answer (A) is correct. *(AIM Chap 7)*

DISCUSSION: Pilots and/or Flight Crew members involved in NMAC occurrences are urged to report each incident immediately by radio or telephone to the nearest FAA ATC Facility or FSS.

Answer (B) is incorrect. The *AIM* states to report each incident immediately by radio or telephone to the nearest FAA ATC Facility or FSS. Answer (C) is incorrect. Contacting the nearest FSDO is in lieu of contacting the nearest FAA ATC Facility or FSS, and an NMAC is not deemed an emergency.

END OF STUDY UNIT

STUDY UNIT FIVE
AIRPLANE PERFORMANCE AND WEIGHT AND BALANCE

(10 pages of outline)

This study unit contains outlines of major concepts tested, sample test questions and answers regarding airplane performance and weight and balance, and an explanation of each answer. The table of contents above lists each subunit within this study unit, the number of questions pertaining to that particular subunit, and the pages on which the outlines and questions begin, respectively.

Recall that the **sole purpose** of this book is to expedite your passing of the FAA pilot knowledge test for the commercial pilot certificate. Accordingly, all extraneous material (i.e., topics or regulations not directly tested on the FAA pilot knowledge test) is omitted, even though much more knowledge is necessary to become a proficient commercial pilot. This additional material is presented in *Pilot Handbook* and *Commercial Pilot Flight Maneuvers and Practical Test Prep*, available from Gleim Publications, Inc. See the product listing at the back of the book and order online at www.gleim.com.

5.1 DENSITY ALTITUDE

1. Density altitude is a measurement of the density of the air in terms of altitude on a standard day.
   a. Air density varies inversely with altitude and temperature and varies directly with barometric pressure.
      1) Humidity also affects air density.
   b. The scale of air density to altitude was made using a constant (standard) temperature and barometric pressure.
      1) Standard temperature at sea level is 15°C.
      2) Standard pressure at sea level is 29.92" Hg.
   c. Pressure altitude is the height above the standard pressure plane.
      1) To determine pressure altitude, the altimeter is set to 29.92 and the altimeter indication is noted.
   d. Density altitude is pressure altitude corrected for nonstandard temperature.

2. The performance tables of an aircraft are based on pressure/density altitude.
   a. High density altitude reduces an airplane's performance.
      1) Climb performance is lower.
      2) Takeoff distance is longer.
      3) Propellers also have less efficiency because there is less air for the propeller to grip.
   b. However, the same indicated airspeed is used for takeoffs and landings, regardless of altitude or air density, because the airspeed indicator is also directly affected by air density.

5.2 DENSITY ALTITUDE COMPUTATIONS

1. Density altitude is determined by finding the pressure altitude (the indicated altitude when your altimeter is set to 29.92) and adjusting for the temperature.
   a. This adjustment is made using your flight computer or a density altitude chart. This part of the FAA knowledge test requires you to use your flight computer.
   b. On your flight computer, set the air temperature (°C) over the pressure altitude in the center right.
      1) In the adjacent density altitude window, read the density altitude.
   c. Note that humidity affects air density and aircraft performance slightly but is not taken into account on performance charts.
2. To convert °F to °C, you may use a conversion chart (on most flight computers) or calculate by using the following formula:

$$°C = \frac{5}{9} \times (°F - 32)$$

3. EXAMPLE: Pressure altitude 12,000 ft.
   True air temperature +50°F

   From the conditions given, the approximate density altitude is 14,130 feet. This is determined as follows:
   a. Convert +50°F to °C by using the formula

$$°C = \frac{5}{9} \times (°F - 32)$$

$$\text{Thus, } \frac{5}{9} \times (50 - 32) = +10°C$$

   b. Under the "True Airspeed and Density Altitude" window on your flight computer, put the pressure altitude of 12,000 ft. under the true air temperature of +10°C.
   c. In the window above ("Density Altitude"), read the density altitude above the index mark to be approximately 14,130 feet.

5.3 TAKEOFF DISTANCE

1. Takeoff distance is displayed in the airplane operating manual in graph form or on a chart. The variables are
   a. Pressure altitude and temperature
   b. Airplane weight
   c. Headwind component
2. In either case, it is usually presented in terms of pressure altitude and temperature. Thus, one must first adjust the airport elevation for barometric pressure. Associated conditions are often listed in legends, e.g., paved runway, sloping runway, etc.
   a. An upslope runway increases takeoff distance.
3. In the graph used on this exam (see Figure 32 on page 145), the first section on the left uses outside air temperature and pressure altitude to obtain density altitude.
   a. The line labeled "ISA" is standard atmosphere, which you use when the question calls for standard temperature.
   b. The second section of the graph, to the right of the first reference line, takes the weight in pounds into account.
   c. The third section of the graph, to the right of the second reference line, takes the headwind into account.
4. EXAMPLE: Given an outside air temperature of 75°F, an airport pressure altitude of 4,000 ft., a takeoff weight of 3,100 lb., and a headwind component of 20 kt., find the ground roll.
   a. The solution to the example problem is marked with arrows on the graph. Move straight up from 75°F to the pressure altitude of 4,000 ft. and then horizontally to the right. From the first reference line (2,400 lb.), you must proceed up and to the right, parallel to the guide lines, to 3,100 pounds. From that point, continue horizontally to the right to the second reference line. The headwind component of 20 kt. requires you to move down and to the right parallel to the guide lines to the 20-kt. point. Finally, moving horizontally to the right gives the total takeoff distance over a 50-ft. obstacle of 1,350 feet.
   b. A note above the graph states that the ground roll is approximately 73% of the total takeoff distance over a 50-ft. obstacle. Thus, the ground roll is 986 ft. (1,350 ft. × .73).
   c. You may be asked the maximum weight that may be carried under specified conditions to meet a certain takeoff distance requirement.
      1) To solve this, simply work backwards on the chart to find the maximum weight.

5.4 TIME, FUEL, AND DISTANCE TO CLIMB

1. Performance data concerning time, fuel, and distance to climb are often presented in operating handbooks for both normal conditions (Figure 14 on page 148) and maximum rate of climb (Figure 13 on page 147). The variables involved are
   a. Airplane weight
   b. Pressure altitude and temperature
   c. Climb speed (indicated airspeed)
   d. Rate of climb in feet per minute (fpm)
   e. Data from sea level
      1) Time in minutes
      2) Pounds of fuel used
      3) Distance in nautical miles
2. See Figure 13.
   a. EXAMPLE: At 4,000 lb., to climb from sea level to a pressure altitude of 8,000 ft., the indicated climb speed is 100 kt., and the average rate of climb is 845 fpm, requiring 9 min. using 24 lb. of fuel and covering a distance of 16 nautical miles.
      1) Note that, frequently, one starts at a pressure altitude other than sea level, so the computation must be done twice, and the difference between the two calculations is the time, fuel, and distance to climb. For example, if you depart with a pressure altitude of 4,000 ft. and are going to cruise at a pressure altitude of 8,000 ft., you must compute the values for both and then subtract the values at 4,000 ft. from those at 8,000 ft. to determine the time, fuel, and distance for climbing from a pressure altitude of 4,000 ft. to 8,000 feet.
   b. Adjust for differences from standard temperature, if necessary.
      1) Recall that the formula for computing standard temperature at altitude is 15°C – (N × 2°C), where N is the altitude divided by 1,000.
      2) EXAMPLE: At 8,000 ft. MSL, standard temperature is –1°C [15°C – (8 × 2°C)].
   c. Note 1 in Figure 13 states that you must add 16 lb. of fuel for engine start, taxi, and takeoff allowance.
   d. You may need to interpolate to find the values for an altitude that is not specifically shown in the table.
3. As an alternative to a table, the fuel, time, and distance to climb may be presented in graph form, as in Figure 15 on page 150. The same variables are involved.
   a. Note the example in Figure 15 for computing fuel, time, and distance for departing an airport with a pressure altitude of 1,400 ft. with an OAT of 15°C to a cruise pressure altitude of 12,000 ft. that has an OAT of 0°C.
      1) Here again, note that the solution is the difference between calculations at the airport elevation and at the desired cruise altitude.

5.5 MAXIMUM RATE OF CLIMB

1. The rate of climb for maximum climb is dependent upon
   a. Pressure altitude and temperature
   b. Airplane weight
   c. Use of the best rate of climb speed
2. The maximum rate of climb can be presented in a table such as Figure 33 on page 156.
   a. EXAMPLE: At 3,700 lb., the rate of climb at an 8,000-ft. pressure altitude at +20°C is 815 fpm.
   b. You may need to interpolate to find the value for an altitude that is not specifically shown in the table.

5.6 CRUISE AND RANGE PERFORMANCE

1. Cruise performance is based upon the pressure altitude and temperature, the manifold pressure, and the engine RPM setting.
2. Given these variables, charts provide the following information:
   a. The percentage of brake horsepower (%BHP)
   b. True airspeed (TAS)
   c. Pounds of fuel per hour (PPH) or gallons of fuel per hour (GPH)
3. Also used is a cruise and range performance chart, as in Figure 11 on page 158.
   a. Note that the range assumes a zero wind component.
   b. Note each of the nine columns in the chart (Figure 11).
   c. Given altitude and RPM in the first two columns, the last seven columns are the results.
   d. EXAMPLE: At a gross weight of 2,300 lb., 5,000-ft. pressure altitude, and 2300 RPM, you are operating at 55% power and will achieve a true airspeed of 108 mph, burn 6.5 GPH, and have a range with a 38-gal. tank of 5.9 hr., or 635 statute miles.
4. See the cruise performance chart, Figure 12, on page 160.
   a. Note each of the columns in the chart.
   b. Given the pressure altitude of 18,000 ft. and the manifold pressure (MP) and RPM, the last nine columns are the results.
   c. EXAMPLE: At 2500 RPM, 28" MP, –41°C, you are using 80% power, will achieve a true airspeed of 184 kt., and will burn 105 PPH.
      1) If you have 315 lb. of usable fuel on board, you have a total available flight time of 3 hr. (315 ÷ 105).
      2) Allowing for day-VFR reserve, your maximum endurance is 2 hr. 30 min. (3 hr. – 30 minutes).
5. Finally, a fuel consumption versus brake horsepower graph is sometimes available. It relates the fuel flow in GPH (vertical scale) to brake horsepower (horizontal scale), based upon various power settings at various altitudes, as illustrated in Figure 8 on page 164.
   a. EXAMPLE: If you want to determine the amount of fuel consumed when climbing at 75% power for 10 min., find the intersection of the takeoff and climb curve with the 75% brake horsepower line, and from that intersection proceed horizontally to the left to the margin to read a fuel flow of 18.3 GPH.
      1) Since 10 min. is 1/6 hr., divide 18.3 by 6 to determine the amount consumed in 10 minutes.
6. As gross weight decreases, maximum range airspeed decreases.

5.7 CROSSWIND/HEADWIND COMPONENT

1. Many airplanes have an upper limit as to the amount of direct crosswind in which they can land. Crosswinds of less than 90° (i.e., direct) can be converted into a 90° component by the use of charts. Variables on the crosswind component charts are
   a. Angle between wind and runway
   b. Knots of total wind velocity
2. The variables are plotted on the graph; tracing the coordinates to the vertical and horizontal axes indicates the headwind and crosswind components of a quartering headwind.
3. An example crosswind component chart appears below.

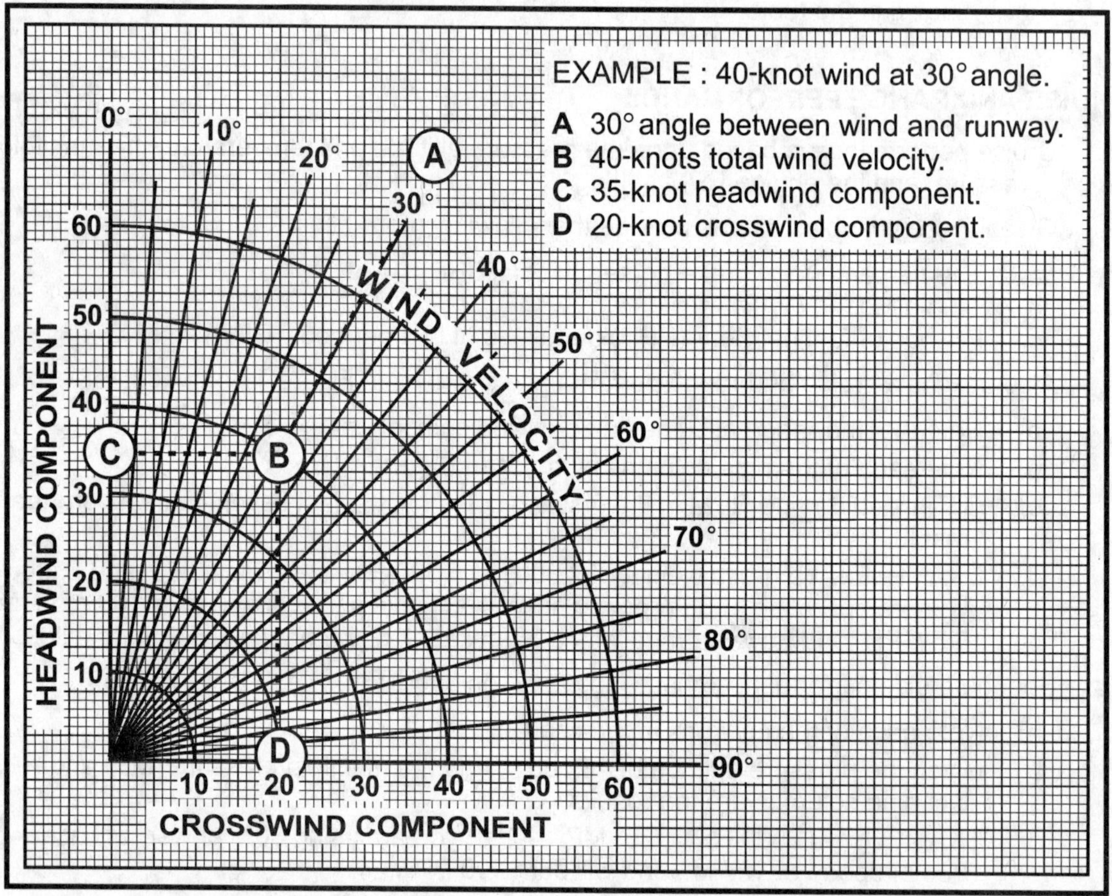

   a. Note the example on the chart of a 40-kt. wind at a 30° angle.
   b. Find the 30° wind angle line. This is the angle between the wind direction and runway direction, e.g., runway 16 and wind from 190°.
   c. Find the 40-kt. wind velocity arc. Note the intersection of the wind arc and the 30° angle line (point B).
   d. Drop straight down from point B to determine the crosswind component of 20 kt.; i.e., landing in this situation is like having a direct crosswind of 20 knots.
   e. Move horizontally to the left from point B to determine the headwind component of 35 kt.; i.e., landing in this situation is like having a headwind component of 35 knots.
   f. Note whether you are being asked for the headwind or the crosswind component.
4. An airplane's crosswind capability may be expressed in terms of a fraction of its V_{S0}.
   a. EXAMPLE: Given a .2-V_{S0} crosswind capability and V_{S0} of 65 kt., the crosswind capability is 13 kt. (65 × .2).

5.8 LANDING DISTANCE

1. Required landing distances differ at various altitudes and temperatures due to changes in air density.
   a. However, indicated airspeed for landing is the same at all altitudes.
2. Landing distance information is given in airplane operating manuals in chart or graph form to adjust for headwind, temperature, and dry grass runways.
3. You must distinguish between the distance for clearing a 50-ft. obstacle and the distance without a 50-ft. obstacle at the beginning of the runway (the latter is described as the ground roll).
4. A landing distance graph is used on this exam (see Figure 35 on page 168).
   a. The first section on the left uses outside air temperature and pressure altitude to obtain density altitude.
   b. The second section of the graph, to the right of the first reference line, takes the weight in pounds into account.
   c. The third section of the graph, to the right of the second reference line, takes the headwind into account.
   d. A note above the graph states that the ground roll is approximately 53% of the total landing distance over a 50-ft. obstacle.
   e. EXAMPLE: Given an outside air temperature of 75°F, a pressure altitude of 4,000 ft., a landing weight of 3,200 lb., and a headwind component of 10 kt., find the ground roll for landing.
      1) The solution to the example problem is marked with the dotted arrows on the graph. Move straight up from 75°F to the pressure altitude of 4,000 ft. and then horizontally to the right. Then move up and to the right, parallel to the guide lines, to 3,200 lb. and then horizontally to the next reference line. Continuing to the right, the headwind component of 10 kt. means moving down and to the right (parallel to the guide lines to 10 knots). Finally, moving to the right horizontally gives the total landing distance over a 50-ft. obstacle of 1,475 feet. Ground roll is 53% of this amount, or 782 ft. (1,475 × .53).

5.9 WEIGHT AND BALANCE

1. Empty weight consists of the airframe, the engine, and all installed optional equipment, including fixed ballast, unusable fuel, full operating fluids, and full oil.
2. The center of gravity (CG) by definition is total moments divided by total weight.
   a. Total moment is the position of weight (measured in index units) from some fixed point (called the datum) times that weight.
3. If all index units (arms) are positive when computing weight and balance, the location of the datum is at the nose or out in front of the airplane.

5.10 WEIGHT AND MOMENT COMPUTATIONS

1. Airplanes must be loaded in a manner such that the CG is in front of the center of lift. This placement provides airplane stability about the lateral axis (for pitch).
2. The CG is a point of balance in an airplane determined in relation to the weight of objects put into the airplane times their distance from a specified point in the airplane (either positive or negative). This distance is called the arm. The CG determination can be made by calculation or by chart.

3. The basic formula for weight and balance is

$$Weight \times Arm = Moment$$

a. Arm is the distance from the datum (a fixed position on the longitudinal axis of the airplane).
b. The weight/arm/moment calculation computes the location of the CG.
   1) Multiply the weight of each item loaded into the airplane by its arm (distance from datum) to determine "moment."
   2) Add moments.
   3) Divide total weight into total moments to obtain CG (expressed in distance from the datum).
c. EXAMPLE: You have placed items A, B, and C into the airplane. Note that the airplane's empty weight is given as 1,500 lb. with a 20-in. arm.

	Weight		Arm		Moment
Empty airplane	1,500	×	20	=	30,000
A (pilot and passenger?)	300	×	25	=	7,500
B (25 gal. of fuel?)	150	×	30	=	4,500
C (baggage?)	100	×	40	=	4,000
	2,050				46,000

The total loaded weight of the airplane is 2,050 pounds. Divide the total moments of 46,000 in.-lb. by the total weight of 2,050 lb. to obtain the CG of 22.44 inches. Then check to see whether the weight and the CG are within allowable limits.

4. Some manufacturers provide a loading graph (see Figure 38 page 172) that is used to plot weight vs. moment of various items. The graph can save you the steps of multiplying and dividing to obtain moments and CG.

a. The load weight in pounds is listed on the left side. Using Figure 38, move horizontally to the right across the chart from the amount of weight to intersect the line indicating where the weight is located; e.g., different diagonal lines usually exist for fuel, baggage, pilot and front seat passengers, and center seat and back seat passengers.
b. From the point of intersection of the weight with the appropriate diagonal line, drop straight down to the bottom of the chart where the moments are located.
   1) Note that you may have to estimate some moments when it is not clear exactly where the diagonal line intersects. For instance, the pilot and copilot diagonal at 300 lb. on Figure 38 intersects somewhere between 27.0 and 28.0 in.-lb. of moment. Do not let this worry you, as using 27.0 in.-lb. will be close enough.
c. Total the weights and moments.
d. EXAMPLE: Determine the center of gravity moment/1,000 in.-lb. given the following situation. The "/1,000" reduces the number to manageable proportions by eliminating a lot of zeros. First, set up a schedule of what you are given and what you must find (see below).

	Weight (lb.)	Moment/1000 in.-lb.
Empty weight	1,271	102.04
Pilot and copilot	340	?
Rear-seat passengers	140	?
Cargo	60	?
Fuel (25 gal. × 6 lb./gal.)	150	?

1) Compute the moment of the pilot and copilot by referring to the loading graph (Figure 38 on page 172). Locate 340 lb. on the weight scale. Move horizontally across the graph to intersect the diagonal line representing the pilot and front passenger. Then move vertically to the bottom scale, which indicates a moment of approximately 31.0 inch-pounds.
2) Locate 140 lb. on the weight scale for the rear-seat passengers. Move horizontally across the graph to intersect the diagonal line that represents rear-seat passengers. Then move down vertically to the bottom scale, which indicates a moment of approximately 18.0 inch-pounds.
3) Use the graph in the same manner to locate moments for cargo and fuel.
4) Now add the weights and the moments.

	Weight (lb.)	Moment/1000 in.-lb.
Empty weight	1,271	102.04
Pilot and copilot	340	31.0
Rear-seat passengers	140	18.0
Cargo	60	7.0
Fuel (25 gal. × 6 lb./gal.)	150	13.5
	1,961	171.54

5) Use the center-of-gravity envelope graph to see whether the total weight and the CG are within acceptable limits.
6) Find the total weight of 1,961 lb. on the weight scale (left margin) and draw a horizontal line from it across the graph.
7) Find the total moment of 171.54 in.-lb. on the moment scale (bottom of graph) and draw a vertical line from it up the graph.
8) Because the lines intersect inside the normal-category envelope, the airplane is loaded within acceptable limits for normal-category operations.

5.11 WEIGHT CHANGE AND WEIGHT SHIFT COMPUTATIONS

1. Authors' note: The following is an effective, intuitively appealing handout used by Dr. Melville R. Byington at Embry-Riddle Aeronautical University (used with permission).
   a. **Background** -- Center of gravity shift problems can be intimidating when an organized approach is not followed. If one goes to the usual texts for assistance, the result is often either
      1) "Just plug this/these formulas" (without adequate rationale), or
      2) Follow a set of (up to six) formulas to solve the problems, or
      3) Follow a tabular approach, which is often lengthy and tedious.
   b. **Basic theory** -- The foregoing "methods" obscure what can and should be a logical, straightforward approach. The standard question is, **"If the CG started out there, and certain changes occurred, where is it now?"** It can be answered directly using a SINGLE, UNIVERSAL, UNCOMPLICATED FORMULA.
      1) At **any** time, the CG is simply the sum of all moments (ΣM) divided by the sum of all weights (ΣW).

$$CG = \frac{\sum M}{\sum W}$$

2) Since CG was known at some previous (#1) loading condition (with moment = M_1 and weight = W_1), it is logical that this become the point of departure. Due to weight addition, removal, or shift, the moment has changed by some amount, ΔM. The total weight has also changed **if**, and only if, weight has been added or removed. Therefore, the current CG is merely the current total moment divided by the current total weight. In equation format,

$$CG = \text{Current Moment/Current Weight becomes } CG = \frac{M_1 \pm \Delta M}{W_1 \pm \Delta W}$$

c. **Application** -- This universal formula will accommodate any CG shift problem! Before proceeding, certain conventions deserve review:

1) Any weight added causes a + moment change (Weight removed is –).
2) Weight **shifted** rearward causes a + moment change (Forward is –).
3) A weight **shift** changes only the moment ($\Delta W = 0$).

d. **Example 1** -- An airplane takes off at 3,000 lb. with CG at station 60. Since takeoff, 25 gal. (150 lb.) of fuel has been consumed. Fuel cell CG is station 65. Find the new CG.

$$CG = \frac{M_1 \pm \Delta M}{W_1 \pm \Delta W} = \frac{(3{,}000 \times 60) - (150 \times 65)}{3{,}000 - 150} = 59.74 \text{ in.}$$

e. **Example 2** -- An airplane has a gross weight of 10,000 pounds. Five hundred lb. of cargo is shifted 50 inches. How far does the CG shift? (Note that the original CG and direction of shift are unspecified. Since datum is undefined, why not define it, temporarily, as the initial CG location, even though it is unknown? This causes M_1 to become zero! Incidentally, the **direction** of CG shift corresponds precisely to the **direction** of the weight shift.)

$$CG = \frac{M_1 \pm \Delta M}{W_1 \pm \Delta W} = \frac{500 \times 50}{10{,}000} = 2.5 \text{ in.}$$

QUESTIONS AND ANSWER EXPLANATIONS: All of the commercial pilot knowledge test questions chosen by the FAA for release as well as additional questions selected by Gleim relating to the material in the previous outlines are reproduced on the following pages. These questions have been organized into the same subunits as the outlines. To the immediate right of each question are the correct answer and answer explanation. You should cover these answers and answer explanations while responding to the questions. Refer to the general discussion in the Introduction on how to take the FAA knowledge test.

Remember that the questions from the FAA knowledge test bank have been reordered by topic and organized into a meaningful sequence. Also, the first line of the answer explanation gives the citation of the authoritative source for the answer.

QUESTIONS

5.1 Density Altitude

1. The performance tables of an aircraft for takeoff and climb are based on

A. pressure/density altitude.

B. cabin altitude.

C. true altitude.

Answer (A) is correct. *(AFH Chap 3)*

DISCUSSION: Performance tables of an aircraft for takeoff, climb, cruise, and landing are based on pressure and/or density altitude. They are an index to the efficiency of airplane performance at various air densities. Pressure altitude is the indicated altitude when the altimeter is set to 29.92 (the standard datum plane). Density altitude is pressure altitude adjusted for nonstandard temperature.

Answer (B) is incorrect. Cabin altitude is the altitude that corresponds to the pressure within the cabin of a pressurized airplane. Answer (C) is incorrect. True altitude is the height above sea level. Airport, terrain, and obstacle elevations found on aeronautical charts are true altitudes.

2. Density altitude is the vertical distance above mean sea level in the standard atmosphere at which

A. pressure altitude is corrected for standard temperature.

B. a given atmospheric density is to be found.

C. temperature, pressure, altitude, and humidity are considered.

Answer (B) is correct. *(PHAK Chap 3)*

DISCUSSION: Density altitude is defined as the vertical distance above mean sea level at which a given atmospheric density is to be found.

Answer (A) is incorrect. Density altitude is pressure altitude corrected for nonstandard temperature, not standard temperature. Answer (C) is incorrect. Temperature, pressure, altitude, and humidity all can affect density altitude, but they do not define density altitude.

3. To determine pressure altitude prior to takeoff, the altimeter should be set to

A. the current altimeter setting.

B. 29.92" Hg and the altimeter indication noted.

C. the field elevation and the pressure reading in the altimeter setting window noted.

Answer (B) is correct. *(AFH Chap 3)*

DISCUSSION: Pressure altitude can be determined by either of two methods: (1) Set the barometric scale of the altimeter to 29.92 and read the indicated altitude, or (2) apply a correction factor to the airport elevation according to the reported altimeter setting.

Answer (A) is incorrect. With the current altimeter setting in the altimeter, the altimeter should indicate the airport elevation (i.e., true altitude), not pressure altitude. Answer (C) is incorrect. The pressure reading in the altimeter setting window should be the current altimeter setting, which should indicate the airport elevation (i.e., true, not pressure, altitude).

4. At higher elevation airports the pilot should know that indicated airspeed

A. will be unchanged, but groundspeed will be faster.

B. will be higher, but groundspeed will be unchanged.

C. should be increased to compensate for the thinner air.

Answer (A) is correct. *(AFH Chap 3)*

DISCUSSION: If an airplane of given weight and configuration is operated at greater heights above standard sea level, the airplane will still require the same dynamic pressure to become airborne at the takeoff lift coefficient. Thus, the airplane at altitude will take off at the same indicated airspeed as at sea level, but because of the reduced air density, the true airspeed (and groundspeed) will be greater.

Answer (B) is incorrect. The indicated airspeed will remain the same, not higher, and the groundspeed will be higher, not unchanged. Answer (C) is incorrect. The true, not indicated, airspeed will increase at higher elevation airports due to the thinner (i.e., reduced air density) air.

5.2 Density Altitude Computations

5. GIVEN:

Pressure altitude . . . . 12,000 ft
True air temperature . . . . +50°F

From the conditions given, the approximate density altitude is

A. 11,900 feet.

B. 14,130 feet.

C. 18,150 feet.

Answer (B) is correct. *(AFH Chap 3)*

DISCUSSION: To convert from °F to °C, use the formula

$$°C = \frac{5}{9} \times (°F - 32)$$

Thus, convert +50°F to °C as follows:

$$\frac{5}{9} \times (50 - 32) = +10°C$$

On the center of the computer side of your flight computer, put the pressure altitude of 12,000 ft. under the true air temperature of +10°C. The density altitude is indicated in the window as 14,130 feet.

Answer (A) is incorrect. This is the density altitude for –10°C, not +10°C. Answer (C) is incorrect. This is the density for +50°C, not +50°F.

6. GIVEN:

Pressure altitude. . . . . 5,000 ft
True air temperature . . . . +30°C

From the conditions given, the approximate density altitude is

A. 7,800 feet.

B. 7,200 feet.

C. 9,000 feet.

Answer (A) is correct. *(AFH Chap 3)*

DISCUSSION: On the center of the computer side of your flight computer, put the pressure altitude of 5,000 ft. under the true air temperature of +30°C. The density altitude is indicated in the window as 7,800 feet.

Answer (B) is incorrect. This is the approximate density altitude at a temperature of 25°C, not 30°C. Answer (C) is incorrect. This is the approximate density altitude at a temperature of 42°C, not 30°C.

7. GIVEN:

Pressure altitude. . . . . 6,000 ft
True air temperature . . . . +30°F

From the conditions given, the approximate density altitude is

A. 9,000 feet.

B. 5,500 feet.

C. 5,000 feet.

Answer (B) is correct. *(AFH Chap 3)*

DISCUSSION: To convert from °F to °C, use the formula

$$°C = \frac{5}{9} \times (°F - 32)$$

Thus, convert +30°F to °C as follows:

$$\frac{5}{9} \times (30 - 32) = -1°C$$

On the center of the computer side of your flight computer, put the pressure altitude of 6,000 ft. under the true air temperature of –1°C. The density altitude is indicated in the window as 5,500 ft.

Answer (A) is incorrect. This is the density altitude for +30°C, not +30°F. Answer (C) is incorrect. This is the density altitude for –5°C, not –1°C.

8. GIVEN:

Pressure altitude . . . . 12,000 feet
True air temperature . . . . +15°F

From the conditions given, the approximate density altitude is

A. 11,900 feet.

B. 14,130 feet.

C. 18,150 feet.

Answer (A) is correct. *(AFH Chap 3)*

DISCUSSION: To convert from °F to °C, use the bottom of the computer side of the E6B flight computer, where the temperature conversion scale is located. The bottom of the conversion scale is °F and the top of the scale is °C. Find +15 on the °F side of the scale and you will see it is lined up about halfway between the first tick mark to the right of -10 of the °C scale. This is about -9.5°C. Therefore, +15°F = -9.5°C.
On the center of the computer side of your flight computer, in the window to the right, put the pressure altitude of 12,000 ft. under the air temperature of -9.5°C. The density altitude is indicated in the window as about 12,000 feet. The best and closest answer is 11,900 feet.

Answer (B) is incorrect. This is the density altitude for +50°F, not -9.5°C. Answer (C) is incorrect. This is the density altitude for +50°C, not +15°F.

9. GIVEN:

Pressure altitude. . . . . 7,000 ft
True air temperature . . . . +15°C

From the conditions given, the approximate density altitude is

A. 5,000 feet.

B. 8,500 feet.

C. 9,500 feet.

Answer (B) is correct. *(AFH Chap 3)*

DISCUSSION: On the center of the computer side of your flight computer, put the pressure altitude of 7,000 ft. under the true air temperature of +15°C. The density altitude is indicated in the window as 8,500 ft.

Answer (A) is incorrect. This is the density altitude for –15°C, not +15°C. Answer (C) is incorrect. This is the density altitude for +23°C, not +15°C.

Page Intentionally Left Blank

5.3 Takeoff Distance

10. (Refer to Figure 32 on page 145.)

GIVEN:

Temperature . . . . 30°F
Pressure altitude. 6,000 ft
Weight. . . . . 3,300 lb
Headwind . . . . 20 kts

What is the total takeoff distance over a 50-foot obstacle?

A. 1,100 feet.

B. 1,300 feet.

C. 1,500 feet.

Answer (C) is correct. *(PHAK Chap 10)*

DISCUSSION: Fig. 32 presents the takeoff distance graph. Find the total takeoff distance over a 50-ft. obstacle as follows:

1. Move up vertically from 30°F to the 6,000-ft. pressure altitude line.
2. Move to the right horizontally to the first reference line.
3. Move up and to the right, parallel to the guideline, to the weight of 3,300 pounds.
4. Move to the right horizontally to the second reference line.
5. Move down and to the right, parallel to the guideline, to the headwind of 20 knots.
6. Move to the right horizontally to the right margin of the graph and read the distance, which is 1,500 feet.

Answer (A) is incorrect. The figure of 1,100 ft. (73% of 1,500 ft.) is the approximate ground roll, not total takeoff, distance. Answer (B) is incorrect. The figure of 1,300 ft. is required for an aircraft weighing 3,000 lb., not 3,300 pounds.

11. (Refer to Figure 32 on page 145.)

GIVEN:

Temperature . . . . 100°F
Pressure altitude. 4,000 ft
Weight. . . . . 3,200 lb
Wind . . . . Calm

What is the ground roll required for takeoff over a 50-foot obstacle?

A. 1,180 feet.

B. 1,350 feet.

C. 1,850 feet.

Answer (B) is correct. *(PHAK Chap 10)*

DISCUSSION: Fig. 32 presents the takeoff distance graph. Find the ground roll required for takeoff over a 50-ft. obstacle as follows:

1. Move up vertically from 100°F to the 4,000-ft. pressure altitude line.
2. Move to the right horizontally to the first reference line.
3. Move up and to the right, parallel to the guideline, to the weight of 3,200 pounds.
4. Since the wind is calm, move right horizontally to the right margin to determine the total takeoff distance of 1,850 feet.
5. Ground roll is approximately 73% of the total takeoff distance (as stated in the note below the Associated Conditions). Thus, the ground roll is approximately 1,350 ft. (1,850 × .73).

Answer (A) is incorrect. This is the required ground roll for a 2,950-lb., not 3,200-lb., aircraft. Answer (C) is incorrect. This is the total takeoff, not ground roll, distance to clear a 50-ft. obstacle.

12. (Refer to Figure 32 on page 145.)

GIVEN:

Temperature . . . . 50°F
Pressure altitude. 2,000 ft
Weight. . . . . 2,700 lb
Wind . . . . Calm

What is the total takeoff distance over a 50-foot obstacle?

A. 800 feet.

B. 650 feet.

C. 1,050 feet.

Answer (A) is correct. *(PHAK Chap 10)*

DISCUSSION: Fig. 32 presents the takeoff distance graph. Find the total takeoff distance over a 50-ft. obstacle as follows:

1. Move up vertically from 50°F to the 2,000 ft. pressure altitude line.
2. Move to the right horizontally to the first reference line.
3. Move up and to the right, parallel to the guideline, to the weight of 2,700 pounds.
4. Since the wind is calm, move right horizontally to the right margin of the graph to determine the total takeoff distance, which is 800 feet.

Answer (B) is incorrect. This is required for a pressure altitude of sea level, not 2,000 feet. Answer (C) is incorrect. This is required for an aircraft weighing 2,900 lb., not 2,700 pounds.

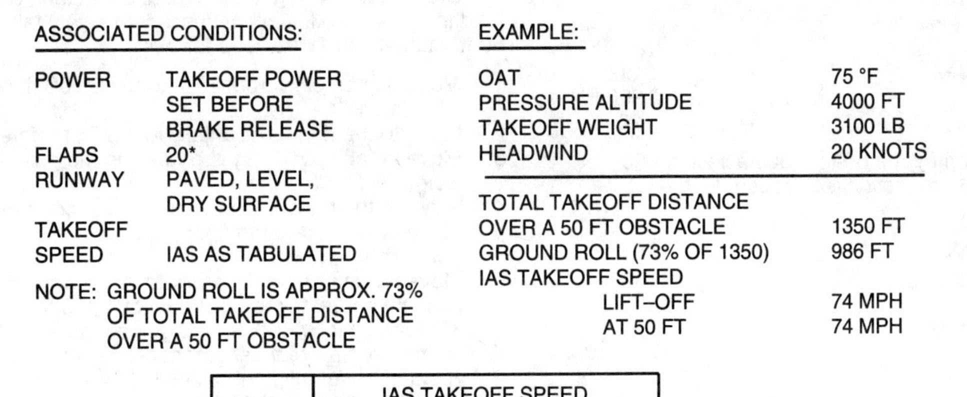

WEIGHT POUNDS	IAS TAKEOFF SPEED (ASSUMES ZERO INSTR. ERROR)			
	LIFT–OFF		50 FEET	
	MPH	KNOTS	MPH	KNOTS
3400	77	67	77	67
3200	75	65	75	65
3000	72	63	72	63
2800	69	60	69	60
2600	66	57	66	57
2400	63	55	63	55

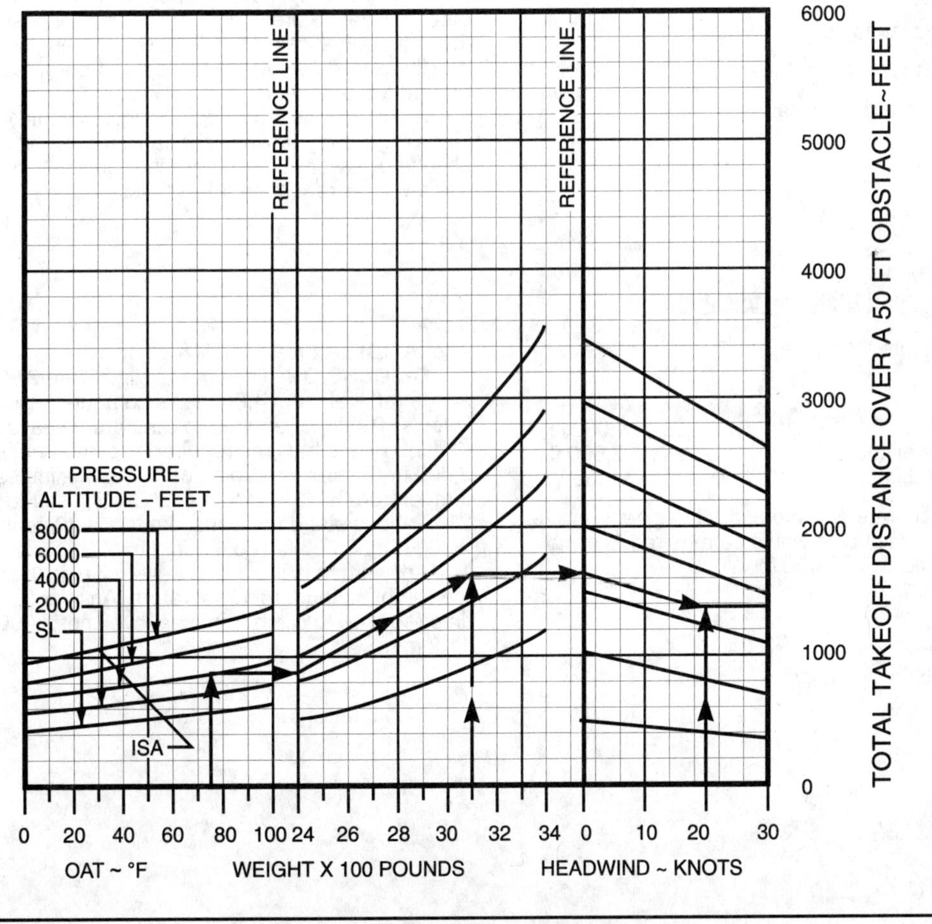

Figure 32. – Obstacle Take-off Chart.

13. (Refer to Figure 32 on page 145.)

GIVEN:

Temperature . . . . 75°F
Pressure altitude. . . . . 6,000 ft
Weight. . . . . 2,900 lb
Headwind . . . . 20 kts

To safely take off over a 50-foot obstacle in 1,000 feet, what weight reduction is necessary?

A. 50 pounds.

B. 100 pounds.

C. 300 pounds.

Answer (C) is correct. *(PHAK Chap 10)*

DISCUSSION: Fig. 32 presents the takeoff distance graph. Find the weight reduction necessary to safely take off over a 50-ft. obstacle in 1,000 ft. as follows:

1. Move up vertically from 75°F to the 6,000-ft. pressure altitude line.
2. Move to the right horizontally to the first reference line.
3. Move up and to the right, parallel to the guideline, to the weight of 2,900 pounds.
4. Move to the right horizontally to the second reference line.
5. Move down and to the right, parallel to the guideline, to the headwind of 20 knots.
6. Move to the right horizontally to the margin of the graph to indicate a total takeoff distance of 1,400 ft. This exceeds the 1,000-ft. limit by 400 ft., or 2 grid squares on the graph.
7. Return to the weight segment of the graph.
8. From the original point of 2,900 lb., move down and to the left, parallel to the guideline, to a point that is 3 grid squares less than 2,900 lb. This would be 2,600 pounds.
9. The total weight reduction required is 300 lb. (2,900 – 2,600).

Answer (A) is incorrect. A 50-lb. reduction requires a takeoff distance of 1,350 ft., not 1,000 feet. Answer (B) is incorrect. A 100-lb. reduction requires a takeoff distance of 1,300 ft., not 1,000 feet.

14. What effect does an uphill runway slope have on takeoff performance?

A. Increases takeoff speed.

B. Increases takeoff distance.

C. Decreases takeoff distance.

Answer (B) is correct. *(PHAK Chap 10)*

DISCUSSION: The upslope or downslope of the runway (runway gradient) is quite important when runway length and takeoff distance are critical. Upslope provides a retarding force that impedes acceleration because the engine has to overcome gravity as well as surface friction and drag, resulting in a longer ground run or takeoff.

Answer (A) is incorrect. The indicated takeoff speed is the same on a level, downhill, or uphill runway at a given density altitude. Answer (C) is incorrect. A downhill, not an uphill, runway slope will decrease the takeoff distance.

5.4 Time, Fuel, and Distance to Climb

15. (Refer to Figure 13 on page 147.)

GIVEN:

Aircraft weight . . . . 4,000 lb
Airport pressure altitude. . . . . 2,000 ft
Temperature at 2,000 ft. . . . . 32°C

Using a maximum rate of climb under the given conditions, how much time would be required to climb to a pressure altitude of 8,000 feet?

A. 7 minutes.

B. 8.4 minutes.

C. 11.2 minutes.

Answer (B) is correct. *(PHAK Chap 10)*

DISCUSSION: The time to climb from 2,000 ft. to 8,000 ft. at an aircraft weight of 4,000 lb. is computed using Fig. 13 as follows: The time required to climb from sea level to 8,000 ft. (9 min.) minus the time required to climb from sea level to 2,000 ft. (2 min., interpolated) equals 7 minutes. Standard temperature is 11°C [15°C – (2°C × 2)], so the temperature is 21°C above standard. Thus, the total time required to climb from 2,000 ft. to 8,000 ft. is 8.4 min. (7 × 1.21).

Answer (A) is incorrect. Seven min. is the time required for the climb at standard temperature. Answer (C) is incorrect. The time required to climb from sea level, not 2,000 ft., to 8,000 ft. is 11.2 min.

16. (Refer to Figure 13 below.)

GIVEN:

Aircraft weight . . . . 3,400 lb
Airport pressure altitude. . . . . 6,000 ft
Temperature at 6,000 ft . . . . 10°C

Using a maximum rate of climb under the given conditions, how much fuel would be used from engine start to a pressure altitude of 16,000 feet?

A. 43 pounds.

B. 45 pounds.

C. 49 pounds.

Answer (A) is correct. *(PHAK Chap 10)*

DISCUSSION: The procedure is to note the difference on Fig. 13 between fuel usage on a climb to 16,000 ft. and on a climb to 6,000 feet. Also note that the temperature is not standard. Standard temperature at sea level is 15°C, and there is a lapse rate of 2°C per 1,000 ft., so the standard temperature at 6,000 ft. would be 3°C [15°C – (6 × 2°C)]. On a climb from sea level to 16,000 ft. with an aircraft weight of 3,400 lb., the amount of fuel used is 39 pounds. For a climb from sea level to 6,000 ft., interpolate to find a fuel burn of 14 pounds. The difference between the two altitudes is 25 lb. (39 – 14), but this difference must be increased by 7%, which is 1.75 lb., to allow for the 7°C above standard. Do not forget the 16 lb. for engine start, taxi, and takeoff. Thus, the total fuel used is approximately 43 lb. (25 + 1.75 + 16).

Answer (B) is incorrect. Forty-five lb. of fuel is required to climb from approximately 5,000 ft., not 6,000 ft., to 16,000 feet.

Answer (C) is incorrect. Forty-nine lb. of fuel is required to climb from approximately 3,000 ft., not 6,000 ft., to 16,000 feet.

MAXIMUM RATE OF CLIMB

CONDITIONS:
Flaps Up
Gear Up
2600 RPM
Cowl Flaps Open
Standard Temperature

PRESS ALT	MP	PPH
S.L. TO 17,000	35	162
18,000	34	156
20,000	32	144
22,000	30	132
24,000	28	120

NOTES:
1. Add 16 pounds of fuel for engine start, taxi and takeoff allowance.
2. Increase time, fuel and distance by 10% for each 10°C above standard temperature.
3. Distances shown are based on zero wind.

WEIGHT LBS	PRESS ALT FT	CLIMB SPEED KIAS	RATE OF CLIMB FPM	FROM SEA LEVEL		
				TIME MIN	FUEL USED POUNDS	DISTANCE NM
4000	S.L.	100	930	0	0	0
	4000	100	890	4	12	7
	8000	100	845	9	24	16
	12,000	100	790	14	38	25
	16,000	100	720	19	52	36
	20,000	99	515	26	69	50
	24,000	97	270	37	92	74
3700	S.L.	99	1060	0	0	0
	4000	99	1020	4	10	6
	8000	99	975	8	21	13
	12,000	99	915	12	33	21
	16,000	99	845	17	45	30
	20,000	97	630	22	59	42
	24,000	95	370	30	77	60
3400	S.L.	97	1205	0	0	0
	4000	97	1165	3	9	5
	8000	97	1120	7	19	12
	12,000	97	1060	11	29	18
	16,000	97	985	15	39	26
	20,000	96	760	19	51	36
	24,000	94	485	26	65	50

Figure 13. – Fuel, Time, and Distance to Climb.

NORMAL CLIMB - 110 KIAS

CONDITIONS:
Flaps Up
Gear Up
2500 RPM
30 Inches Hg
120 PPH Fuel Flow
Cowl Flaps Open
Standard Temperature

NOTES:
1. Add 16 pounds of fuel for engine start, taxi and takeoff allowance.
2. Increase time, fuel and distance by 10% for each 7°C above standard temperature.
3. Distances shown are based on zero wind.

WEIGHT LBS	PRESS ALT FT	RATE OF CLIMB FPM	FROM SEA LEVEL		
			TIME MIN	FUEL USED POUNDS	DISTANCE NM
4000	S.L.	605	0	0	0
	4000	570	7	14	13
	8000	530	14	28	27
	12,000	485	22	44	43
	16,000	430	31	62	63
	20,000	365	41	82	87
3700	S.L.	700	0	0	0
	4000	665	6	12	11
	8000	625	12	24	23
	12,000	580	19	37	37
	16,000	525	26	52	53
	20,000	460	34	68	72
3400	S.L.	810	0	0	0
	4000	775	5	10	9
	8000	735	10	21	20
	12,000	690	16	32	31
	16,000	635	22	44	45
	20,000	565	29	57	61

Figure 14. – Fuel, Time, and Distance to Climb.

17. (Refer to Figure 14 on page 148.)

GIVEN:

Aircraft weight . . . . 3,700 lb
Airport pressure altitude. . . . . 4,000 ft
Temperature at 4,000 ft . . . . 21°C

Using a normal climb under the given conditions, how much fuel would be used from engine start to a pressure altitude of 12,000 feet?

A. 30 pounds.

B. 37 pounds.

C. 46 pounds.

Answer (C) is correct. *(PHAK Chap 10)*

DISCUSSION: The amount of fuel needed to climb from 4,000 ft. (airport pressure altitude) to 12,000 ft. pressure altitude with a weight of 3,700 lb. is calculated as the amount needed to climb from sea level to 12,000 ft. (37 lb.) minus the amount to climb to 4,000 ft. (12 pounds). The difference is 25 pounds. However, you must adjust (add) 10% for every 7°C above standard. Here, standard temperature at the 4,000-ft. pressure altitude is 7°C [15°C – (2°C × 4)], so OAT of 21°C is 14°C above standard. If you increase time, fuel, and distance by 10% for each 7°C above standard, multiply standard conditions usage by 120% for 14°C over standard. Fuel needed to climb is thus 30 lb. (25 lb. × 1.20). Finally, you must add 16 lb. for engine start, taxi, and takeoff. Total fuel needed to climb from engine start is thus 46 lb. (30 + 16).

Answer (A) is incorrect. Thirty lb. is the fuel required for the climb without taking into consideration the 16 lb. for engine start, taxi, and takeoff. Answer (B) is incorrect. Thirty-seven lb. is the fuel required for a climb from sea level to 12,000 ft. at standard temperature.

18. (Refer to Figure 14 on page 148.)

GIVEN:

Weight. . . . . 3,400 lb
Airport pressure altitude. . . . . 4,000 ft
Temperature at 4,000 ft . . . . 14°C

Using a normal climb under the given conditions, how much time would be required to climb to a pressure altitude of 8,000 feet?

A. 4.8 minutes.

B. 5 minutes.

C. 5.5 minutes.

Answer (C) is correct. *(PHAK Chap 10)*

DISCUSSION: The time to climb to 8,000 ft. from 4,000 ft. with a weight of 3,400 lb. is calculated as the time to climb from sea level to 8,000 ft. (10 min.) minus the time to climb to 4,000 ft. (5 minutes). The difference is 5 minutes. However, you must adjust (add) 10% for every 7°C above standard. Here, standard temperature at the 4,000-ft. pressure altitude is 7°C [15°C – (2°C × 4)], so OAT of 14°C at 4,000 ft. is 7°C above standard. Time to climb is thus 5.5 min. (5 min. × 1.10).

Answer (A) is incorrect. This figure was not arrived at by subtracting the climb from sea level to 4,000 ft. from the climb from sea level to 8,000 ft. and factoring in nonstandard temperature. Answer (B) is incorrect. Five min. would be the time required for the climb before the correction for nonstandard temperature is made.

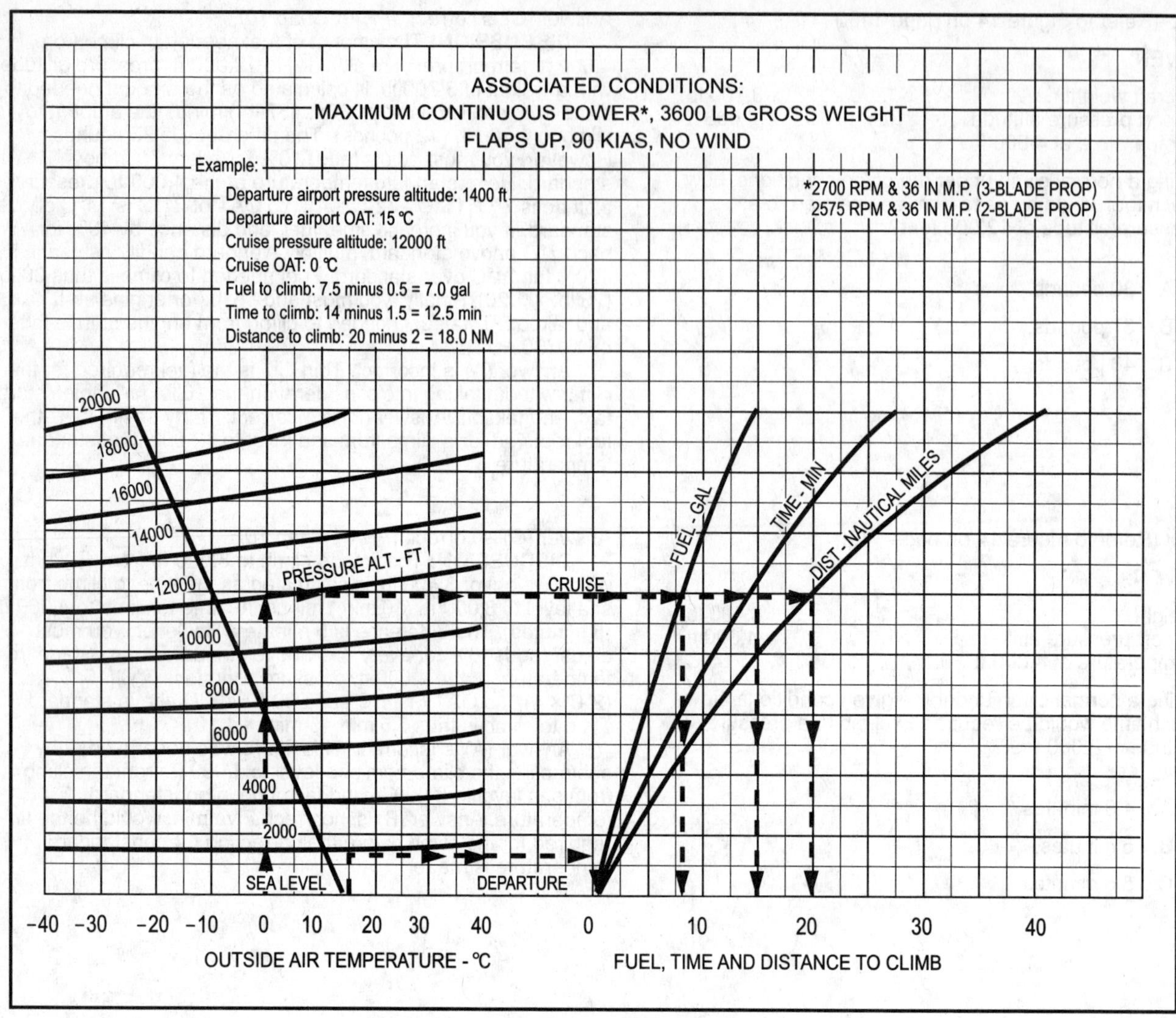

Figure 15. – Fuel, Time, and Distance to Climb.

19. (Refer to Figure 15 on page 150.)

GIVEN:

Airport pressure altitude. . . . . 4,000 ft
Airport temperature . . . . 12°C
Cruise pressure altitude . . . . 9,000 ft
Cruise temperature . . . . – 4°C

What will be the distance required to climb to cruise altitude under the given conditions?

A. 6 miles.

B. 8.5 miles.

C. 11 miles.

Answer (B) is correct. *(PHAK Chap 10)*

DISCUSSION: Start at the lower left corner of Fig. 15. Go up from –4°C cruise temperature to the 9,000-ft. cruise pressure altitude. From there, proceed horizontally to the right to the intersection of the third curve (distance). Then proceed down to the bottom of the chart, which is at 14 nautical miles. Note that this is the distance from sea level to 9,000 feet.

Since the airport pressure altitude is 4,000 ft., go back to the left lower corner and go up from the airport temperature of 12°C to the pressure altitude line of 4,000 feet. Then proceed horizontally to the third curve (distance) and move downward to determine the distance of 5.5 NM to climb to 4,000 ft. from sea level. Thus, the distance to climb from 4,000 ft. to 9,000 ft. is 8.5 NM (14 – 5.5).

Answer (A) is incorrect. This is approximately the distance required to climb from sea level to 4,000 ft., not from 4,000 ft. to 9,000 feet. Answer (C) is incorrect. The distance required to climb from 4,000 ft. to 9,000 ft. is 8.5 NM, not 11 nautical miles.

20. (Refer to Figure 15 on page 150.)

GIVEN:

Airport pressure altitude. . . . . 2,000 ft
Airport temperature . . . . 20°C
Cruise pressure altitude . . . . 10,000 ft
Cruise temperature . . . . 0°C

What will be the fuel, time, and distance required to climb to cruise altitude under the given conditions?

A. 5 gallons, 9 minutes, 13 NM.

B. 6 gallons, 11 minutes, 16 NM.

C. 7 gallons, 12 minutes, 18 NM.

Answer (A) is correct. *(PHAK Chap 10)*

DISCUSSION: Start at the lower left corner of Fig. 15. Go up from 0°C cruise temperature to the 10,000-ft. cruise pressure altitude. From there, proceed horizontally to the right to the intersection of each of the curves (fuel, time, and distance). From there, proceed down to 6 gal., 11 min., and 16 nautical miles. Note that these are the fuel, time, and distance from sea level to 10,000 feet.

Since the airport pressure altitude is 2,000 ft., go back to the left lower corner and go up from the airport temperature of 20°C to the pressure altitude line of 2,000 feet. Then proceed horizontally to each of the curves and move downward to determine the fuel of 1 gal., time of 2 min., and distance of 3 NM to climb to 2,000 ft. from sea level.

Thus, to climb from 2,000 ft. to 10,000 ft. requires 5 gal. (6 – 1), 9 min. (11 – 2), and 13 NM (16 – 3).

Answer (B) is incorrect. Six gal., 11 min., and 16 NM are required for a climb from sea level, not 2,000 ft., to 10,000 feet. Answer (C) is incorrect. To climb from 2,000 ft. to 10,000 ft. requires 5 gal., not 7 gal.; 9 min., not 12 min.; and 13 NM, not 18 nautical miles.

NORMAL CLIMB - 100 KIAS

CONDITIONS:
Flaps Up
Gear Up
2550 RPM
25 Inches MP or Full Throttle
Cowl Flaps Open
Standard Temperature

MIXTURE SETTING	
PRESS ALT	PPH
S.L. to 4000	108
8000	96
12,000	84

NOTES:
1. Add 12 pounds of fuel for engine start, taxi and takeoff allowance.
2. Increase time, fuel and distance by 10% for each 10°C above standard temperature.
3. Distances shown are based on zero wind.

WEIGHT LBS	PRESS ALT FT	RATE OF CLIMB FPM	FROM SEA LEVEL		
			TIME MIN	FUEL USED POUNDS	DISTANCE NM
3800	S.L.	580	0	0	0
	2000	580	3	6	6
	4000	570	7	12	12
	6000	470	11	19	19
	8000	365	16	27	28
	10,000	265	22	37	40
	12,000	165	32	51	59
3500	S.L.	685	0	0	0
	2000	685	3	5	5
	4000	675	6	11	10
	6000	565	9	16	16
	8000	455	13	23	23
	10,000	350	18	31	33
	12,000	240	25	41	46
3200	S.L.	800	0	0	0
	2000	800	2	4	4
	4000	795	5	9	8
	6000	675	8	14	13
	8000	560	11	19	19
	10,000	445	15	25	27
	12,000	325	20	33	37

Figure 9. – Fuel, Time, and Distance to Climb.

21. (Refer to Figure 9 on page 152.) Using a normal climb, how much fuel would be used from engine start to 12,000 feet pressure altitude?

Aircraft weight	3,800 lb
Airport pressure altitude.	4,000 ft
Temperature	26°C

A. 46 pounds.

B. 51 pounds.

C. 58 pounds.

Answer (C) is correct. *(PHAK Chap 10)*

DISCUSSION: At 3,800 lb., 51 lb. of fuel is required to climb from sea level to 12,000 ft., according to Fig. 9. From sea level to 4,000 ft., only 12 lb. is required. The net difference is 39 lb. to climb from 4,000 ft. pressure altitude to 12,000 ft. pressure altitude. The air temperature of 26°C, however, is 19°C over standard temperature (standard at 4,000 ft. is 7°C, which is 15°C at sea level minus 8°C for the lapse rate). Note that there is an increase of 1% for each 1°C above standard. Accordingly, you must increase the 39 lb. by 19% (39 × 1.19) to get 46.41 lb. Then add 12 lb. to taxi, takeoff, etc., which is approximately 58 lb.

Answer (A) is incorrect. This is the fuel required to make the climb without factoring in the 12 lb. required for engine start, taxi, and takeoff. Answer (B) is incorrect. This amount of fuel is required for the climb from sea level to 12,000 ft. before adjustments are made for nonstandard temperature; the 4,000-ft. airport altitude; and engine start, taxi, and takeoff.

22. (Refer to Figure 9 on page 152.) Using a normal climb, how much fuel would be used from engine start to 10,000 feet pressure altitude?

Aircraft weight	3,500 lb
Airport pressure altitude.	4,000 ft
Temperature	21°C

A. 23 pounds.

B. 31 pounds.

C. 35 pounds.

Answer (C) is correct. *(PHAK Chap 10)*

DISCUSSION: At 3,500 lb., 31 lb. of fuel is required to climb from sea level to 10,000 ft., per Fig. 9. From sea level to 4,000 ft., only 11 lb. is required. The net difference is 20 lb. to climb from 4,000 ft. pressure altitude to 10,000 ft. pressure altitude. The air temperature of 21°C, however, is 14°C over standard temperature (standard at 4,000 ft. is 7°C, which is 15°C at sea level minus 8°C for the lapse rate). Note that there is an increase of 1% for each 1° above standard. Accordingly, you must increase the 20 lb. by 14% (20 × 1.14) to get 22.8 lb. Then add 12 lb. to taxi, takeoff, etc., which is approximately 35 lb.

Answer (A) is incorrect. This amount of fuel is required for the climb itself. The fuel required for engine start, taxi, and takeoff must be factored in. Answer (B) is incorrect. This amount of fuel is required to climb from sea level to 10,000 ft. Adjustments must be made for nonstandard temperature; a 4,000-ft. airport altitude; and the engine start, taxi, and takeoff.

MAXIMUM RATE OF CLIMB

CONDITIONS:
Flaps Up
Gear Up
2700 RPM
Full Throttle
Mixture Set at Placard Fuel Flow
Cowl Flaps Open
Standard Temperature

MIXTURE SETTING	
PRESS ALT	PPH
S.L.	138
4000	126
8000	114
12,000	102

NOTES:
1. Add 12 pounds of fuel for engine start, taxi and takeoff allowance.
2. Increase time, fuel and distance by 10% for each 10°C above standard temperature.
3. Distances shown are based on zero wind.

WEIGHT LBS	PRESS ALT FT	CLIMB SPEED KIAS	RATE OF CLIMB FPM	FROM SEA LEVEL		
				TIME MIN	FUEL USED POUNDS	DISTANCE NM
3800	S.L.	97	860	0	0	0
	2000	95	760	2	6	4
	4000	94	660	5	12	9
	6000	93	565	9	18	14
	8000	91	465	13	26	21
	10,000	90	365	18	35	29
	12,000	89	265	24	47	41
3500	S.L.	95	990	0	0	0
	2000	94	885	2	5	3
	4000	93	780	5	10	7
	6000	91	675	7	16	12
	8000	90	570	11	22	17
	10,000	89	465	15	29	24
	12,000	87	360	20	38	32
3200	S.L.	94	1135	0	0	0
	2000	92	1020	2	4	3
	4000	91	910	4	9	6
	6000	90	800	6	14	10
	8000	88	685	9	19	14
	10,000	87	575	12	25	20
	12,000	86	465	16	32	26

Figure 10. – Fuel, Time, and Distance to Climb.

23. (Refer to Figure 10 on page 154.) Using a maximum rate of climb, how much fuel would be used from engine start to 6,000 feet pressure altitude?

Aircraft weight	3,200 lb
Airport pressure altitude	2,000 ft
Temperature	27°C

A. 10 pounds.

B. 14 pounds.

C. 24 pounds.

Answer (C) is correct. *(PHAK Chap 10)*

DISCUSSION: At 3,200 lb., 14 lb. of fuel is required to climb from sea level to 6,000 ft. per Fig. 10. From sea level to 2,000 ft., only 4 lb. is required. The net difference is 10 lb. to climb from 2,000 ft. pressure altitude to 6,000 ft. pressure altitude. The air temperature of 27°C, however, is 16°C over standard temperature (standard at 2,000 ft. is 11°C, which is 15°C at sea level minus 4°C for the lapse rate). Note that there is an increase of 1% for each 1° above standard. Accordingly, you must increase the 10 lb. by 16% (10 × 1.16) to get 11.6 lb. Then add 12 lb. to taxi, takeoff, etc., which is approximately 24 lb.

Answer (A) is incorrect. This is required for the climb from 2,000 ft. to 6,000 ft. without factoring in nonstandard temperature or the fuel required for the engine start, taxi, and takeoff adjustment. Answer (B) is incorrect. This is required for a climb from sea level, not 2,000 ft., to 6,000 ft.

24. (Refer to Figure 10 on page 154.) Using a maximum rate of climb, how much fuel would be used from engine start to 10,000 feet pressure altitude?

Aircraft weight	3,800 lb
Airport pressure altitude	4,000 ft
Temperature	30°C

A. 28 pounds.

B. 35 pounds.

C. 40 pounds.

Answer (C) is correct. *(PHAK Chap 10)*

DISCUSSION: At 3,800 lb., 35 lb. of fuel is required to climb from sea level to 10,000 ft., per Fig. 10. From sea level to 4,000 ft., only 12 lb. is required. The net difference is 23 lb. to climb from 4,000 ft. pressure altitude to 10,000 ft. pressure altitude. The air temperature of 30°C, however, is 23°C over standard temperature (standard at 4,000 ft. is 7°C, which is 15°C at sea level minus 8°C for the lapse rate). Note that there is an increase of 1% for each 1° above standard. Accordingly, you must increase the 23 lb. by 23% (23 × 1.23) to get 28.29 lb. Then add 12 lb. to taxi, takeoff, etc., which is approximately 40 lb.

Answer (A) is incorrect. This amount of fuel is required to climb from 4,000 ft. to 10,000 ft., but the 12 lb. of fuel required for engine start, taxi, and takeoff has not been added to the total. Answer (B) is incorrect. This amount of fuel is required to climb from sea level, not 4,000 ft., to 10,000 ft.

CONDITIONS:
Flaps Up
Gear Up
2600 RPM
Cowl Flaps Open

PRESS ALT	MP	PPH
S.L. TO 17,000	35	162
18,000	34	156
20,000	32	144
22,000	30	132
24,000	28	120

WEIGHT LBS	PRESS ALT FT	CLIMB SPEED KIAS	RATE OF CLIMB - FPM			
			-20 °C	0 °C	20 °C	40 °C
4000	S.L.	100	1170	1035	895	755
	4000	100	1080	940	800	655
	8000	100	980	840	695	555
	12,000	100	870	730	590	---
	16,000	100	740	605	470	---
	20,000	99	485	355	---	---
	24,000	97	190	70	---	---
3700	S.L.	99	1310	1165	1020	875
	4000	99	1215	1070	925	775
	8000	99	1115	965	815	670
	12,000	99	1000	855	710	---
	16,000	99	865	730	590	---
	20,000	97	600	470	---	---
	24,000	95	295	170	---	---
3400	S.L.	97	1465	1320	1165	1015
	4000	97	1370	1220	1065	910
	8000	97	1265	1110	955	795
	12,000	97	1150	995	845	---
	16,000	97	1010	865	725	---
	20,000	96	730	595	---	---
	24,000	94	405	275	---	---

Figure 33. – Maximum Rate-of-Climb Chart.

5.5 Maximum Rate of Climb

25. (Refer to Figure 33 on page 156.)

GIVEN:

Weight. . . . . 3,700 lb
Pressure altitude. . . . . 22,000 ft
Temperature . . . . –10°C

What is the maximum rate of climb under the given conditions?

A. 305 ft/min.

B. 320 ft/min.

C. 384 ft/min.

Answer (C) is correct. *(PHAK Chap 10)*

DISCUSSION: The maximum rate of climb at a pressure altitude of 22,000 ft., temperature of –10°C, and 3,700 lb. is found by using the 3,700 lb. weight section of Fig. 33. Note that you must interpolate for both 22,000 ft. and –10°C.

First, interpolate for 22,000 ft. At 0°C, the difference between 20,000 ft. and 24,000 ft. is 300 fpm (470 – 170). One-half of 300 added to 170 is 320 (170 + 150).

At –20°C, the difference is 305 (600 – 295). Adding one-half of 305 to 295 is 447.5 (295 + 152.5).

The next step is to interpolate the 22,000 ft. values for –10°C: 320 at 0° and 447.5 at –20°. The difference is 127.5 (447.5 – 320). Adding one-half of 127.5 to 320 to split the difference between 0° and –20° gives 384 fpm (320 + 64).

Answer (A) is incorrect. The difference in rate of climb between 20,000 ft. and 24,000 ft. at –20°C is 305 fpm. Answer (B) is incorrect. The maximum rate of climb at 22,000 ft. and a temperature of 0°C, not –10°C, is 320 fpm.

26. (Refer to Figure 33 on page 156.)

GIVEN:

Weight. . . . . 4,000 lb
Pressure altitude. . . . . 5,000 ft
Temperature . . . . 30°C

What is the maximum rate of climb under the given conditions?

A. 655 ft/min.

B. 702 ft/min.

C. 774 ft/min.

Answer (B) is correct. *(PHAK Chap 10)*

DISCUSSION: The maximum rate of climb at a pressure altitude of 5,000 ft., temperature of 30°C, and 4,000 lb. is found by using the 4,000 lb. weight section of Fig. 33. Note that you must interpolate for both 5,000 ft. and 30°C.

First, interpolate for 5,000 ft. At 20°C, the difference between 4,000 ft. and 8,000 ft. is 105 fpm (800 – 695). Five thousand ft. is 1/4 of the way between 4,000 ft. and 8,000 feet; 105 × .25 = 26.25, and 800 – 26.25 = 773.75. At 40°C, the difference is 100 (655 – 555). Subtracting one-fourth of 100 from 655 gives 630 (655 – 25).

Using these values, interpolate for 30°C between 773.75 at 20° and 630 at 40°. The difference is 143.75 fpm (773.75 – 630). Subtracting one-half of 143.75 (about 72) from 773.75 to split the difference between 40° and 30° gives about 702 fpm.

Answer (A) is incorrect. This is the maximum rate of climb at 4,000 ft., not 5,000 ft., at 40°C, not 30°C. Answer (C) is incorrect. This is the maximum rate of climb at 5,000 ft. at 20°C, not 30°C.

Gross Weight - 2300 Lbs.
Standard Conditions
Zero Wind   Lean Mixture

NOTE: Maximum cruise is normally limited to 75% power.

					38 GAL (NO RESERVE)		48 GAL (NO RESERVE)	
ALT.	RPM	% BHP	TAS MPH	GAL/ HOUR	ENDR. HOURS	RANGE MILES	ENDR. HOURS	RANGE MILES
2500	2700	86	134	9.7	3.9	525	4.9	660
	2600	79	129	8.6	4.4	570	5.6	720
	2500	72	123	7.8	4.9	600	6.2	760
	2400	65	117	7.2	5.3	620	6.7	780
	2300	58	111	6.7	5.7	630	7.2	795
	2200	52	103	6.3	6.1	625	7.7	790
5000	2700	82	134	9.0	4.2	565	5.3	710
	2600	75	128	8.1	4.7	600	5.9	760
	2500	68	122	7.4	5.1	625	6.4	790
	2400	61	116	6.9	5.5	635	6.9	805
	2300	55	108	6.5	5.9	635	7.4	805
	2200	49	100	6.0	6.3	630	7.9	795
7500	2700	78	133	8.4	4.5	600	5.7	755
	2600	71	127	7.7	4.9	625	6.2	790
	2500	64	121	7.1	5.3	645	6.7	810
	2400	58	113	6.7	5.7	645	7.2	820
	2300	52	105	6.2	6.1	640	7.7	810
10,000	2650	70	129	7.6	5.0	640	6.3	810
	2600	67	125	7.3	5.2	650	6.5	820
	2500	61	118	6.9	5.5	655	7.0	830
	2400	55	110	6.4	5.9	650	7.5	825
	2300	49	100	6.0	6.3	635	8.0	800

Figure 11. – Cruise and Range Performance.

5.6 Cruise and Range Performance

27. (Refer to Figure 11 on page 158.) If the cruise altitude is 7,500 feet, using 64 percent power at 2,500 RPM, what would be the range with 48 gallons of usable fuel?

A. 635 miles.

B. 645 miles.

C. 810 miles.

Answer (C) is correct. *(PHAK Chap 10)*

DISCUSSION: On Fig. 11 at 7,500 ft. and 2500 RPM, which is 64% power, go to the far right-hand column to determine range of 810 mi. with 48 gal. of usable fuel.

Answer (A) is incorrect. The range at 7,500 ft. and 2500 RPM is found in the far right column to be 810 mi., not 635 miles. Answer (B) is incorrect. This is the range at 7,500 ft. and 2,500 RPM with 38 gal., not 48 gal., of usable fuel.

28. (Refer to Figure 11 on page 158.) What would be the endurance at an altitude of 7,500 feet, using 52 percent power?

NOTE: (With 48 gallons of fuel – no reserve.)

A. 6.1 hours.

B. 7.7 hours.

C. 8.0 hours.

Answer (B) is correct. *(PHAK Chap 10)*

DISCUSSION: On Fig. 11 at 7,500 ft. and 2300 RPM, which is 52% power, go to the endurance column at 48 gal. of usable fuel to determine 7.7 hours.

Answer (A) is incorrect. The endurance for 38 gal., not 48 gal., of usable fuel is 6.1 hr. Answer (C) is incorrect. The endurance at 10,000 ft., not 7,500 ft., and 49%, not 52%, power is 8.0 hr.

29. (Refer to Figure 11 on page 158.) What would be the approximate true airspeed and fuel consumption per hour at an altitude of 7,500 feet, using 52 percent power?

A. 103 MPH TAS, 6.3 GPH.

B. 105 MPH TAS, 6.6 GPH.

C. 105 MPH TAS, 6.2 GPH.

Answer (C) is correct. *(PHAK Chap 10)*

DISCUSSION: On Fig. 11 at 7,500 ft. and 2300 RPM, which is 52% power, the TAS is 105 mph and the fuel consumption is 6.2 GPH.

Answer (A) is incorrect. At 52% power, a TAS of 103 mph and a fuel consumption of 6.3 GPH are for an altitude of 2,500 ft., not 7,500 ft. Answer (B) is incorrect. The figure of 6.6 is not a performance value (i.e., fuel consumption or endurance) that appears on the chart.

PRESSURE ALTITUDE 18,000 FEET

CONDITIONS:
4000 Pounds
Recommended Lean Mixture
Cowl Flaps Closed

NOTE

For best fuel economy at 70% power or less, operate at 6 PPH leaner than shown in this chart or at peak EGT.

		20°C BELOW STANDARD TEMP -41°C			STANDARD TEMPERATURE -21°C			20°C ABOVE STANDARD TEMP -1°C		
RPM	MP	% BHP	KTAS	PPH	% BHP	KTAS	PPH	% BHP	KTAS	PPH
2500	30	---	---	---	81	188	106	76	185	100
	28	80	184	105	76	182	99	71	178	93
	26	75	178	99	71	176	93	67	172	88
	24	70	171	91	66	168	86	62	164	81
	22	63	162	84	60	159	79	56	155	75
2400	30	81	185	107	77	183	101	72	180	94
	28	76	179	100	72	177	94	67	173	88
	26	71	172	93	67	170	88	63	166	83
	24	66	165	87	62	163	82	58	159	77
	22	61	158	80	57	155	76	54	150	72
2300	30	79	182	103	74	180	97	70	176	91
	28	74	176	97	70	174	91	65	170	86
	26	69	170	91	65	167	86	61	163	81
	24	64	162	84	60	159	79	56	155	75
	22	58	154	77	55	150	73	51	145	65
2200	26	66	166	87	62	163	82	58	159	77
	24	61	158	80	57	154	76	54	150	72
	22	55	148	73	51	144	69	48	138	66
	20	49	136	66	46	131	63	43	124	59

Figure 12. – Cruise Performance.

30. (Refer to Figure 12 on page 160.)

GIVEN:

Pressure altitude . . . . 18,000 ft
Temperature . . . . –21°C
Power. . . . . 2,400 RPM – 28" MP
Recommended lean
mixture usable fuel . . . . 425 lb

What is the approximate flight time available under the given conditions? (Allow for VFR day fuel reserve.)

A. 3 hours 46 minutes.

B. 4 hours 1 minute.

C. 4 hours 31 minutes.

Answer (B) is correct. *(PHAK Chap 10)*

DISCUSSION: Given 2400 RPM and manifold pressure of 28", use Fig. 12 to find 94 lb. of fuel per hr. at –21°C. Since you have 425 lb. of usable fuel, you can cruise for 4 hr. 31 min., less the 30-min. VFR-day fuel reserve, or 4 hr. 1 minute. The time, calculated as 425 lb. of fuel divided by 94 lb./hr., equals 4.52 hr. Sixty min./hr. times .52 hr. equals 31 min.

Alternatively, you can use your flight computer. Put 94 over 60 min. on the time index (dark triangle). Then look to 425 on the outer scale and find that it corresponds to 4 hr. 31 min. on the inner scale. Note that the question asks for the flight time, not flight time plus VFR-day reserve; i.e., compute 4 hr. 31 min. and subtract 30 min. to get 4 hr. 1 min.

Answer (A) is incorrect. The flight time available with a VFR-night, not VFR-day, fuel reserve of 45 minutes is 3 hr. 46 min. Answer (C) is incorrect. The flight time available with no reserve is 4 hr. 31 min.

31. (Refer to Figure 12 on page 160.)

GIVEN:

Pressure altitude. . . . . 18,000 ft
Temperature . . . . –41°C
Power . . . . 2,500 RPM – 26" MP
Recommended lean
mixture usable fuel . . . . 318 lb

What is the approximate flight time available under the given conditions? (Allow for VFR night fuel reserve.)

A. 2 hours 27 minutes.

B. 3 hours 12 minutes.

C. 3 hours 42 minutes.

Answer (A) is correct. *(PHAK Chap 10)*

DISCUSSION: Given 2500 RPM and manifold pressure of 26", use Fig. 12 to find 99 lb. of fuel per hr. at –41°C. Since you have 318 lb. of usable fuel, you can cruise for 3 hr. 12 min., less the 45-min. VFR-night fuel reserve, or 2 hr. 27 min.

Calculate the time as 318 lb. of fuel divided by 99 lb./hr., which equals 3.21 hr. Sixty min./hr. times .21 hr. equals about 12 min.

Answer (B) is incorrect. The flight time available with no fuel reserve is 3 hr. 12 min. Answer (C) is incorrect. The flight time with no reserve at a fuel consumption of 86 PPH, not 99 PPH, is 3 hr. 42 min.

32. (Refer to Figure 12 on page 160.)

GIVEN:

Pressure altitude. . . . . 18,000 ft
Temperature . . . . –1°C
Power . . . . 2,200 RPM – 20" MP
Best fuel economy
usable fuel. . . . . 344 lb

What is the approximate flight time available under the given conditions? (Allow for VFR day fuel reserve.)

A. 4 hours 50 minutes.

B. 5 hours 20 minutes.

C. 5 hours 59 minutes.

Answer (C) is correct. *(PHAK Chap 10)*

DISCUSSION: Given 2200 RPM and manifold pressure of 20", use Fig. 12 to find 59 lb. of fuel per hr. at –1°C. The "Note" indicates to use 6 lb./hr. less for "best fuel economy." Thus, use 53 lb./hr. (59 – 6). Since you have 344 lb. of usable fuel, you can cruise for 6 hr. 29 min. (344 lb./53 lb. per hr.), less the 30-min. VFR-day fuel reserve, or 5 hr. 59 min.

Answer (A) is incorrect. Using 53 PPH, the flight time available is 5 hr. 59 min., not 4 hr. 50 min. Answer (B) is incorrect. This is the endurance, with a VFR-day reserve, using the recommended lean mixture, not the best fuel economy, fuel flow.

PRESSURE ALTITUDE 6,000 FEET

CONDITIONS:
Recommended Lean Mixture
3800 Pounds
Cowl Flaps Closed

		20 °C BELOW STANDARD TEMP -17 °C			STANDARD TEMPERATURE 3 °C			20 °C ABOVE STANDARD TEMP 23 °C		
RPM	MP	% BHP	KTAS	PPH	% BHP	KTAS	PPH	% BHP	KTAS	PPH
2550	24	---	---	---	78	173	97	75	174	94
	23	76	167	96	74	169	92	71	171	89
	22	72	164	90	69	166	87	67	167	84
	21	68	160	85	65	162	82	63	163	80
2500	24	78	169	98	75	171	95	73	172	91
	23	74	166	93	71	167	90	69	169	87
	22	70	162	88	67	164	85	65	165	82
	21	66	158	83	63	160	80	61	160	77
2400	24	73	165	91	70	166	88	68	167	85
	23	69	161	87	67	163	84	64	164	81
	22	65	158	82	63	159	79	61	160	77
	21	61	154	77	59	155	75	57	155	73
2300	24	68	161	86	66	162	83	64	163	80
	23	65	158	82	62	159	79	60	159	76
	22	61	154	77	59	155	75	57	155	72
	21	57	150	73	55	150	71	53	150	68
2200	24	63	156	80	61	157	77	59	158	75
	23	60	152	76	58	153	73	56	154	71
	22	57	149	72	54	149	70	53	149	67
	21	53	144	68	51	144	66	49	143	64
	20	50	139	64	48	138	62	46	137	60
	19	46	133	60	44	132	58	43	131	57

Figure 34. – Cruise Performance Chart.

33. (Refer to Figure 34 on page 162.)

GIVEN:

Pressure altitude. 6,000 ft
Temperature . . . . +3°C
Power . . . . 2,200 RPM – 22" MP
Usable fuel available . . . . 465 lb

What is the maximum available flight time under the conditions stated?

A. 6 hours 27 minutes.
B. 6 hours 39 minutes.
C. 6 hours 56 minutes.

Answer (B) is correct. *(PHAK Chap 10)*

DISCUSSION: Using Fig. 34 at 2,200 RPM, find the 22" MP line. Then go across to the PPH column in the middle section for standard temperatures and find 70 PPH. Divide 465 lb. of usable fuel by 70 PPH to determine a time of 6.64 hr., which translates to about 6 hr. 39 min.

Alternatively, use your flight computer. Put 70 PPH on the outer scale over the time index on the inner scale. Then find 465 on the outer scale and read about 6 hr. 40 min. on the inner scale.

Answer (A) is incorrect. The maximum available flight time at 2,200 RPM, 22" MP, and –17°C, not +3°C, is 6 hr. 27 min. Answer (C) is incorrect. The maximum available flight time at 2,200 RPM, 22" MP, and +23°C, not +3°C, is 6 hr. 56 min.

34. (Refer to Figure 34 on page 162.)

GIVEN:

Pressure altitude. 6,000 ft
Temperature . . . . –17 °C
Power . . . . 2,300 RPM – 23" MP
Usable fuel available . . . . 370 lb

What is the maximum available flight time under the conditions stated?

A. 4 hours 20 minutes.
B. 4 hours 30 minutes.
C. 4 hours 50 minutes.

Answer (B) is correct. *(PHAK Chap 10)*

DISCUSSION: Using Fig. 34 at 2300 RPM, find the 23" MP line. Then go across to the PPH column in the section for 20° below standard temperature and find 82 PPH. Divide 370 lb. of usable fuel by 82 PPH to determine a time of 4.51 hr., which translates to about 4 hr. 30 min.

Alternatively, use your flight computer. Put 82 PPH on the outer scale over the time index on the inner scale. Then find 370 on the outer scale and find about 4 hr. 30 min. on the inner scale.

Answer (A) is incorrect. The maximum available flight time of 4 hr. 20 min. is achieved by using an MP of 24 in., not 23 in. Answer (C) is incorrect. The maximum flight time of 4 hr. 50 min. is achieved by using an MP of 22 in., not 23 in.

35. (Refer to Figure 34 on page 162.)

GIVEN:

Pressure altitude. 6,000 ft
Temperature . . . . +13°C
Power . . . . 2,500 RPM – 23" MP
Usable fuel available . . . . 460 lb

What is the maximum available flight time under the conditions stated?

A. 4 hours 58 minutes.
B. 5 hours 7 minutes.
C. 5 hours 12 minutes.

Answer (C) is correct. *(PHAK Chap 10)*

DISCUSSION: Using Fig. 34 at 2500 RPM, find the 23" MP line. Then, notice that 13°C, 10° above standard temperature (ST), is not given. You must interpolate between standard temperature and 20° above ST. At standard temperature, fuel flow equals 90 PPH; at 20° above ST, fuel flow equals 87 PPH, a difference of 3 PPH. Since the required 10° above ST is exactly halfway between ST and ST + 20°, half of 3 PPH, or 1.5, should be added to the value of 87 PPH, giving 88.5 PPH. Divide 460 lb. of usable fuel by 88.5 PPH to determine a time of 5.19 hr., which translates to about 5 hr. 12 min.

Answer (A) is incorrect. The maximum flight time of 4 hr. 58 min. is at a temperature of –17°C, not +13°C. Answer (B) is incorrect. The maximum flight time of 5 hr. 7 min. is at a temperature of +3°C, not +13°C.

36. Which maximum range factor decreases as weight decreases?

A. Altitude.
B. Airspeed.
C. Angle of attack.

Answer (B) is correct. *(AFH Chap 3)*

DISCUSSION: As weight decreases, the maximum range is achieved when the airplane is flown at the airspeed which maximizes the lift/drag ratio. As weight decreases, the L/D_{MAX} airspeed decreases.

Answer (A) is incorrect. Maximum range altitude may increase, not decrease, with weight decrease. Answer (C) is incorrect. Angle of attack is not a maximum range factor (as are weight, altitude, and power setting).

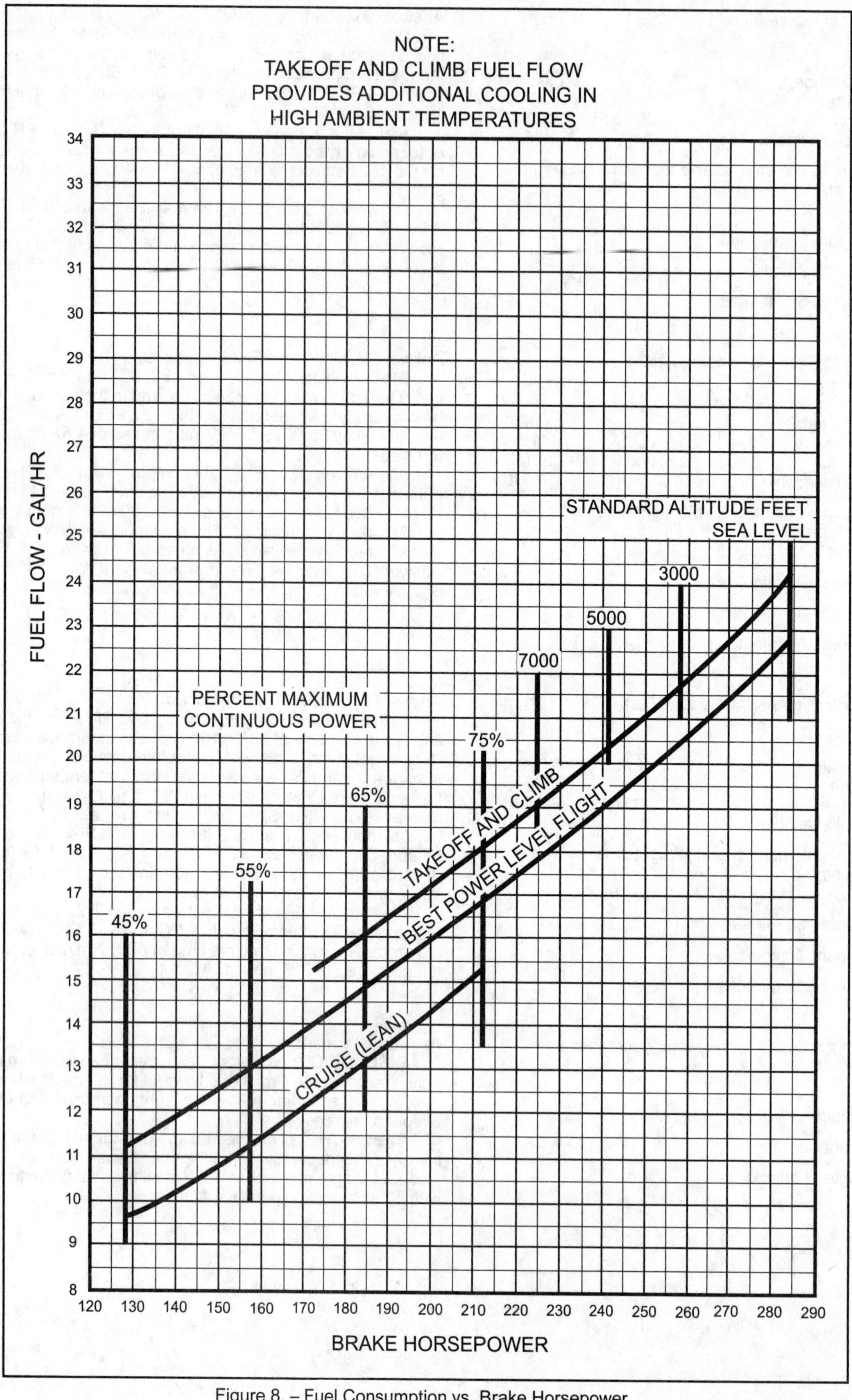

Figure 8. – Fuel Consumption vs. Brake Horsepower.

37. (Refer to Figure 8 on page 164.)

GIVEN:

Fuel quantity . . . . 47 gal
Power-cruise (lean) . . . . 55 percent

Approximately how much flight time would be available with a night VFR fuel reserve remaining?

A. 3 hours 8 minutes.

B. 3 hours 22 minutes.

C. 3 hours 43 minutes.

Answer (B) is correct. *(PHAK Chap 10)*

DISCUSSION: Given 47 gal. of fuel available at cruise power (55%), how much time is available, not counting a 45-min. fuel reserve? On Fig. 8, find the intersection of the cruise (lean) curve and 55% power. From the intersection, proceed horizontally to the left to determine 11.4 GPH. Divide 47 gal. usable fuel by 11.4 GPH to determine 4.122 hr., which translates to 4 hr. 7 min. Subtract 45 min. to determine 3 hr. 22 min.

Alternatively, use your flight computer. Put 11.4 over the true index. Then, on the outer scale, find 47, which gives you about 4 hr. 7 min. Subtract 45 min. to get 3 hr. 22 min.

Answer (A) is incorrect. This is the flight time at best power, not cruise, and with a VFR-day, not VFR-night (i.e., 45-min.), reserve. Answer (C) is incorrect. The flight time with a VFR-night reserve (45 min.) at cruise (lean) power is 3 hr. 22 min., not 3 hr. 43 min.

38. (Refer to Figure 8 on page 164.)

GIVEN:

Fuel quantity . . . . 65 gal
Best power (level flight) . . . . 55 percent

Approximately how much flight time would be available with a day VFR fuel reserve remaining?

A. 4 hours 17 minutes.

B. 4 hours 30 minutes.

C. 5 hours 4 minutes.

Answer (B) is correct. *(PHAK Chap 10)*

DISCUSSION: Given 65 gal. of fuel available at best power (55%), how much time is available, not counting a 30-min. fuel reserve? On Fig. 8, find the intersection of the level flight curve and 55% power. From the intersection, proceed horizontally to the left to determine 13 GPH. Divide 65 gal. usable fuel by 13 GPH to determine 5 hr. Subtract 30 min. to determine 4 hr. 30 min.

Answer (A) is incorrect. This is the approximate flight time with a VFR-night, not VFR-day, fuel reserve. Answer (C) is incorrect. The approximate flight time with no fuel reserve is 5 hr. 4 min.

39. (Refer to Figure 8 on page 164.) Approximately how much fuel would be consumed when climbing at 75 percent power for 7 minutes?

A. 1.82 gallons.

B. 1.97 gallons.

C. 2.12 gallons.

Answer (C) is correct. *(PHAK Chap 10)*

DISCUSSION: To determine the amount of fuel to be burned in 7 min., on Fig. 8, find the intersection of the takeoff and climb curve with 75% power. From the intersection, proceed horizontally to the left to determine about 18.2 GPH. Multiply this by 7/60 to determine 2.12 gallons.

Answer (A) is incorrect. The amount of 1.8 gal. is used with a fuel flow of 15.6 GPH, not 18.2 GPH. Answer (B) is incorrect. The amount of 1.97 gal. is used with a fuel flow of 16.8 GPH, not 18.2 GPH.

40. (Refer to Figure 8 on page 164.) Determine the amount of fuel consumed during takeoff and climb at 70 percent power for 10 minutes.

A. 2.66 gallons.

B. 2.88 gallons.

C. 3.2 gallons.

Answer (B) is correct. *(PHAK Chap 10)*

DISCUSSION: To determine the amount of fuel to be burned in 10 min., on Fig. 8, find the intersection of the takeoff and climb curve with 70% power (the 70% power line is approximately one-half of the way between 65% and 75%), which is about 17.3 GPH. One-sixth of this is 2.88 gallons.

Answer (A) is incorrect. The amount of 2.66 gal. is used with a fuel flow of 16 GPH, not 17.3 GPH. Answer (C) is incorrect. The amount of 3.2 gal. is used with a fuel flow of 19.2 GPH, not 17.3 GPH.

41. (Refer to Figure 8 on page 164.) With 38 gallons of fuel aboard at cruise power (55 percent), how much flight time is available with night VFR fuel reserve still remaining?

A. 2 hours 34 minutes.

B. 2 hours 49 minutes.

C. 3 hours 18 minutes.

Answer (A) is correct. *(PHAK Chap 10)*

DISCUSSION: On Fig. 8, find the intersection of the cruise (lean) curve and 55% power. From the intersection, proceed horizontally to the left to determine 11.4 GPH. Divide 38 gal. usable fuel by 11.4 GPH to determine 3 hr. 19 minutes. Subtract 45 min. to determine 2 hr. 34 min.

Answer (B) is incorrect. This time requires a fuel flow of 10.7 GPH, not 11.4 GPH. Answer (C) is incorrect. This time is the approximate flight time without considering the 45-min. VFR-night fuel reserve.

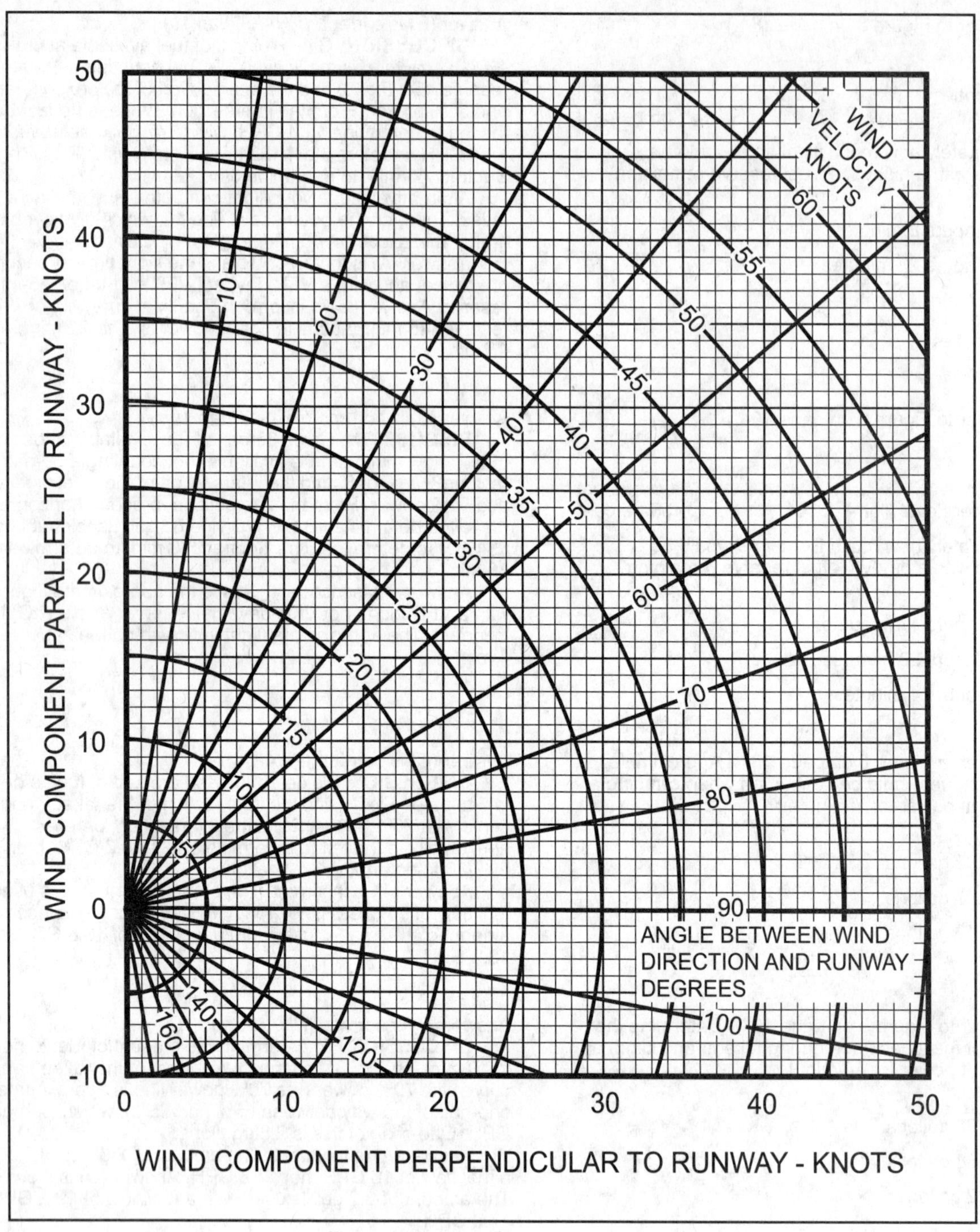

Figure 31. – Wind Component Chart.

5.7 Crosswind/Headwind Component

42. (Refer to Figure 31 on page 166.) Rwy 30 is being used for landing. Which surface wind would exceed the airplane's crosswind capability of 0.2 V_{S0}, if V_{S0} is 60 knots?

A. 260° at 20 knots.

B. 275° at 25 knots.

C. 315° at 35 knots.

Answer (A) is correct. *(PHAK Chap 10)*

DISCUSSION: The crosswind capability of .2 V_{S0} with a V_{S0} of 60 kt. means a crosswind capability of 12 kt. (60 × .2). Thus, you must go through each of the situations to determine which crosswind component is in excess of 12 knots.

With a wind of 260° and a landing on Rwy 30 (i.e., at 300°), the crosswind angle is 40° (300° – 260°). Go out to the 20-kt. arc and then down vertically to determine a 13-kt. crosswind component, which exceeds the 12-kt. capability.

Answer (B) is incorrect. The crosswind angle is 25° (300° – 275°). Go out to the 25-kt. arc and then down vertically to determine a 10.5-kt. crosswind component, which is less than the airplane's 12-kt. crosswind capability. Answer (C) is incorrect. The crosswind angle is 15° (315° – 300°). Go out to the 35-kt. arc and then down vertically to determine a 9-kt. crosswind component, which is less than the airplane's 12-kt. crosswind capability.

43. (Refer to Figure 31 on page 166.) The surface wind is 180° at 25 knots. What is the crosswind component for a Rwy 13 landing?

A. 19 knots.

B. 21 knots.

C. 23 knots.

Answer (A) is correct. *(PHAK Chap 10)*

DISCUSSION: When landing on Rwy 13 with a surface wind of 180°, the crosswind will be at 50° (180° – 130°). On Fig. 31, go out the 50° line to the 25-kt. wind arc. From that intersection, go vertically down to the horizontal scale at the bottom of the graph and find a 19-kt. crosswind component.

Answer (B) is incorrect. A 21-kt. crosswind component requires a surface wind of 180° at 28 kt., not 25 knots. Answer (C) is incorrect. A 23-kt. crosswind component requires a surface wind of 180° at 30 kt., not 25 knots.

44. (Refer to Figure 31 on page 166.) What is the headwind component for a Rwy 13 takeoff if the surface wind is 190° at 15 knots?

A. 7 knots.

B. 13 knots.

C. 15 knots.

Answer (A) is correct. *(PHAK Chap 10)*

DISCUSSION: When landing on Rwy 13 with a surface wind of 190°, the crosswind will be at 60° (190° – 130°). On Fig. 31, go out the 60° line to the 15-kt. wind arc. From that intersection, go horizontally across to the left to the vertical scale at the side of the graph and find a 7-kt. headwind component.

Answer (B) is incorrect. This is the crosswind, not headwind, component. Answer (C) is incorrect. This is the surface wind, not headwind, component.

45. (Refer to Figure 31 on page 166.) If the tower-reported surface wind is 010° at 18 knots, what is the crosswind component for a Rwy 08 landing?

A. 7 knots.

B. 15 knots.

C. 17 knots.

Answer (C) is correct. *(PHAK Chap 10)*

DISCUSSION: When landing on Rwy 08 with a surface wind of 10° the crosswind will be at 70° (80° – 10°). On Fig. 31, go out the 70° line to the 18-kt. wind arc. From that intersection, go vertically down to the horizontal scale at the bottom of the graph and find a 17-kt. crosswind component.

Answer (A) is incorrect. A 7-kt. crosswind component requires a 7-kt., not an 18-kt., surface wind at 010°. Answer (B) is incorrect. A 15-kt. crosswind component requires a 16-kt., not an 18-kt., surface wind at 010°.

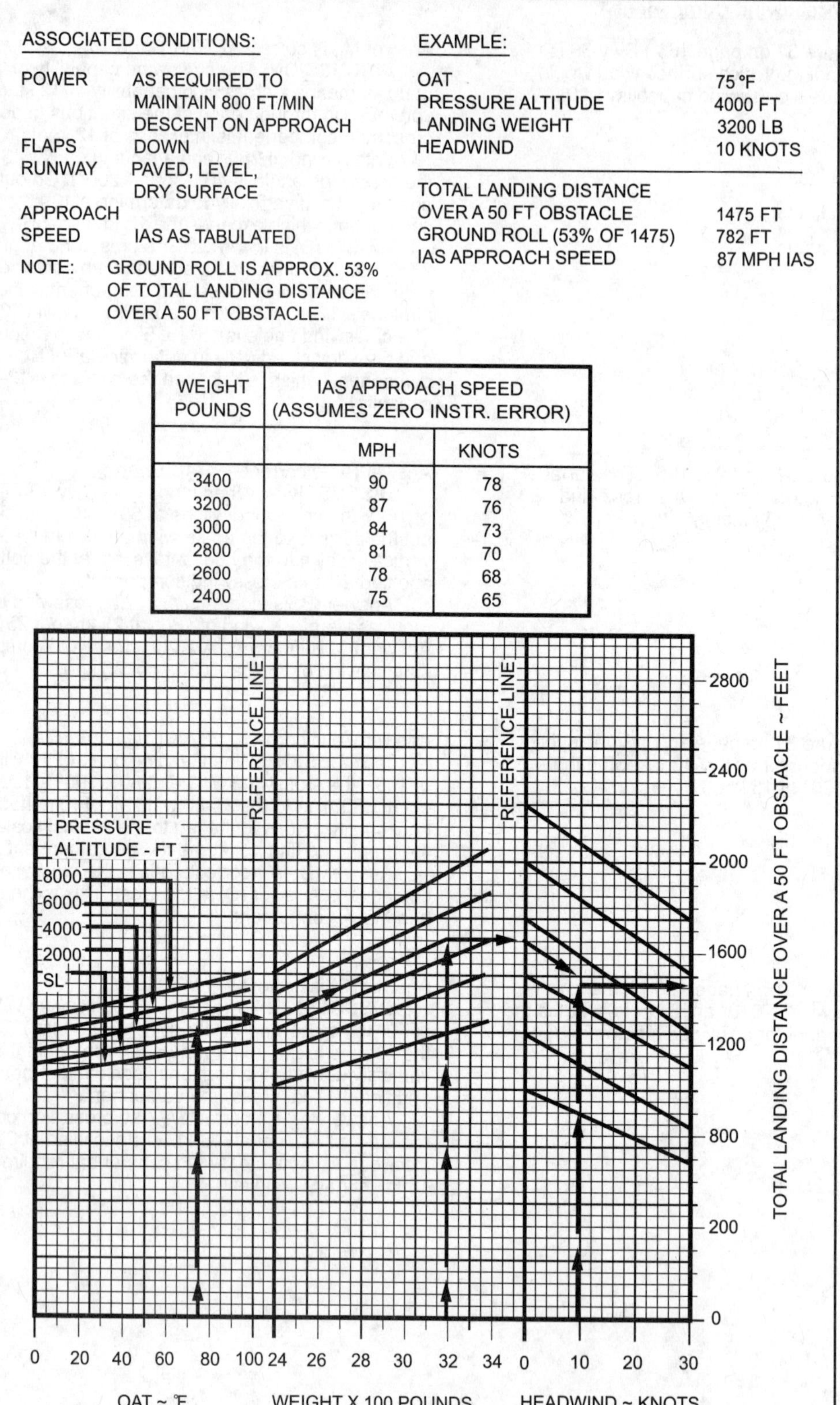

WEIGHT POUNDS	IAS APPROACH SPEED (ASSUMES ZERO INSTR. ERROR)	
	MPH	KNOTS
3400	90	78
3200	87	76
3000	84	73
2800	81	70
2600	78	68
2400	75	65

Figure 35. – Normal Landing Chart.

5.8 Landing Distance

46. (Refer to Figure 35 on page 168.)

GIVEN:

Temperature . . . . 50°F
Pressure altitude. . . . . Sea level
Weight. . . . . 3,000 lb
Headwind . . . . 10 kts

Determine the approximate ground roll.

A. 425 feet.

B. 636 feet.

C. 836 feet.

Answer (B) is correct. *(PHAK Chap 10)*

DISCUSSION: Determine the ground roll on Fig. 35 by computing 53% of the total landing distance over a 50-ft. obstacle, which is listed on the right-hand side of the figure. Begin with the temperature of 50°F at the lower left. Proceed upward to the sea-level line. From that intersection, proceed horizontally to the right to the first reference line. From that point, proceed up and to the right, parallel to the guidelines, to the 3,000-lb. point, as shown at the bottom of the graph. From that point, proceed horizontally to the second reference line. Then proceed to the right and down, parallel to the headwind guidelines, until you intersect the 10-kt. line. From that point, proceed horizontally to the right to determine about 1,200 ft. to clear a 50-ft. obstacle. Multiply this amount by .53 to get the ground roll of 636 feet.

Answer (A) is incorrect. This is the ground roll for a total landing distance over a 50-ft. obstacle of 802 feet. Answer (C) is incorrect. This is the ground roll for a total landing distance over a 50-ft. obstacle of 1,577 feet.

47. (Refer to Figure 35 on page 168.)

GIVEN:

Temperature . . . . 80°F
Pressure altitude. 4,000 ft
Weight. . . . . 2,800 lb
Headwind . . . . 24 kts

What is the total landing distance over a 50-foot obstacle?

A. 1,125 feet.

B. 1,250 feet.

C. 1,325 feet.

Answer (B) is correct. *(PHAK Chap 10)*

DISCUSSION: Begin with the temperature of 80°F at the lower left on Fig. 35. Proceed upward to the 4,000-ft. line. From that intersection, proceed horizontally to the right to the first reference line. From that point, proceed up and to the right, parallel to the guidelines, to the 2,800-lb. point, as shown at the bottom of the graph. From that point, proceed horizontally to the second reference line. From that point on the second reference line, proceed to the right and down, parallel to the headwind guidelines, until you intersect the 24-kt. line. From that point, proceed horizontally to the right to determine about 1,250 ft. to clear a 50-ft. obstacle.

Answer (A) is incorrect. This figure requires a headwind of 28 kt., not 24 knots. Answer (C) is incorrect. This figure requires a headwind of 10 kt., not 24 knots.

48. (Refer to Figure 35 on page 168.)

GIVEN:

Temperature . . . . 70°F
Pressure altitude. . . . . Sea level
Weight. . . . . 3,400 lb
Headwind . . . . 16 kts

Determine the approximate ground roll.

A. 689 feet.

B. 716 feet.

C. 1,275 feet.

Answer (A) is correct. *(PHAK Chap 10)*

DISCUSSION: Determine the ground roll on Fig. 35 by computing 53% of the total landing distance over a 50-ft. obstacle, which is listed on the right-hand side of the figure. Begin with the temperature of 70°F at the lower left. Proceed upward to the sea-level line. From that intersection, proceed horizontally to the right to the first reference line. From that point, proceed up and to the right, parallel to the guidelines, to the 3,400-lb. point, as shown at the bottom of the graph. From that point, proceed horizontally to the second reference line. Then proceed to the right and down, parallel to the headwind guidelines, until you intersect the 16-kt. line. From that point, proceed horizontally to the right to determine a total landing distance of 1,300 ft. to clear a 50-ft. obstacle. Multiply this amount by .53 to get the ground roll of 689 feet.

Answer (B) is incorrect. A ground roll of 716 ft. requires a headwind of 14 kt., not 16 knots. Answer (C) is incorrect. This is the total landing distance over a 50-ft. obstacle, not ground roll, with a 19-kt., not 16-kt., headwind.

49. (Refer to Figure 35 on page 168.)

GIVEN:

Temperature . . . . 85°F
Pressure altitude. . . . . 6,000 ft
Weight. . . . . 2,800 lb
Headwind . . . . 14 kts

Determine the approximate ground roll.

A. 742 feet.

B. 1,280 feet.

C. 1,480 feet.

Answer (A) is correct. *(PHAK Chap 10)*

DISCUSSION: Determine the ground roll on Fig. 35 by computing 53% of the total landing distance over a 50-ft. obstacle, which is listed on the right-hand side of the figure. Begin with the temperature of 85°F at the lower left. Proceed upward to the 6,000-ft. line. From that intersection, proceed horizontally to the right to the first reference line. From that point, proceed up and to the right, parallel to the guidelines, to the 2,800-lb. point, as shown at the bottom of the graph. From that point, proceed horizontally to the second reference line. Then proceed to the right and down, parallel to the headwind guidelines, until you intersect the 14-kt. line. From that point, proceed horizontally to the right to determine about 1,400 ft. to clear a 50-ft. obstacle. Multiply this amount by .53 to get the ground roll of 742 feet.

Answer (B) is incorrect. A 1,280-ft. ground roll requires a 2,415-ft. total landing distance. Answer (C) is incorrect. This is the total landing distance, not the ground roll, with a 10-kt., not 14-kt., headwind.

5.9 Weight and Balance

50. When computing weight and balance, the basic empty weight includes the weight of the airframe, engine(s), and all installed optional equipment. Basic empty weight also includes

A. the unusable fuel, full operating fluids, and full oil.

B. all usable fuel, full oil, hydraulic fluid, but does not include the weight of pilot, passengers, or baggage.

C. all usable fuel and oil, but does not include any radio equipment or instruments that were installed by someone other than the manufacturer.

Answer (A) is correct. *(PHAK Chap 9)*

DISCUSSION: Empty weight consists of the airframe, the engine, and all installed optional equipment, including fixed ballast, unusable fuel, full operating fluids, and full oil.

Answer (B) is incorrect. Empty weight does not include usable fuel. Answer (C) is incorrect. Empty weight does not include usable fuel, but it does include all installed equipment.

51. The CG of an aircraft can be determined by which of the following methods?

A. Dividing total arms by total moments.

B. Multiplying total arms by total weight.

C. Dividing total moments by total weight.

Answer (C) is correct. *(PHAK Chap 9)*

DISCUSSION: The center of gravity, by definition, is the total moment of the airplane divided by its total weight. Moment is the position of weight from some fixed point (called the datum) multiplied by that weight.

Answer (A) is incorrect. Arms are the distances of weight from the datum; each arm is individually multiplied by its respective weight to determine an individual moment. Answer (B) is incorrect. Arms are the distances of weight from the datum; each arm is individually multiplied by its respective weight to determine an individual moment.

52. The CG of an aircraft may be determined by

A. dividing total arms by total moments.

B. dividing total moments by total weight.

C. multiplying total weight by total moments.

Answer (B) is correct. *(PHAK Chap 9)*

DISCUSSION: The center of gravity, by definition, is the total moment of the airplane divided by its total weight. Moment is the position of weight from some fixed point (called the datum) multiplied by that weight.

Answer (A) is incorrect. Arms are the distances of weight from the datum; each arm is individually multiplied by its respective weight to determine an individual moment. Answer (C) is incorrect. You must divide total moments by total weight (not vice versa).

53. If all index units are positive when computing weight and balance, the location of the datum would be at the

A. centerline of the main wheels.

B. nose, or out in front of the airplane.

C. centerline of the nose or tailwheel, depending on the type of airplane.

Answer (B) is correct. *(AWBH Chap 3)*

DISCUSSION: Index units refer to arms. If all the arms are positive in computing weight and balance, the datum (or starting point) must be at the nose or out in front of the nose of the airplane. If it is somewhere between the nose and the tail, some items (those between the datum and the nose) would be negative.

Answer (A) is incorrect. If the datum were at the centerline of the main wheels, the engine would have a negative arm (or index unit). Answer (C) is incorrect. If the datum were at the centerline of the nose or tailwheel, at least the propeller would have a negative arm (or index unit).

5.10 Weight and Moment Computations

54. GIVEN:

Weight A -- 155 pounds at 45 inches aft of datum
Weight B -- 165 pounds at 145 inches aft of datum
Weight C -- 95 pounds at 185 inches aft of datum

Based on this information, where would the CG be located aft of datum?

A. 86.0 inches.

B. 116.8 inches.

C. 125.0 inches.

Answer (B) is correct. *(AWBH Chap 4)*

DISCUSSION: To determine the CG, use a three-step process:

1. First, multiply the individual weights by their arms to get the individual moments.

		W	×	A	=	M
A	=	155	×	45	=	6,975
B	=	165	×	145	=	23,925
C	=	95	×	185	=	17,575
		415				48,475

2. Compute total weight and total moments.
3. Divide total moments by total weight to get the CG.

$$CG = \frac{48,475}{415} = 116.8 \text{ in.}$$

Answer (A) is incorrect. The CG is 116.8 in., not 86.0 in. Answer (C) is incorrect. The CG is 116.8 in., not 125.0 in.

55. GIVEN:

Weight A -- 140 pounds at 17 inches aft of datum
Weight B -- 120 pounds at 110 inches aft of datum
Weight C -- 85 pounds at 210 inches aft of datum

Based on this information, the CG would be located how far aft of datum?

A. 89.11 inches.

B. 96.89 inches.

C. 106.92 inches.

Answer (B) is correct. *(AWBH Chap 4)*

DISCUSSION: To determine the CG, use a three-step process:

1. First, multiply the individual weights by their arms to get the individual moments.

		W	×	A	=	M
A	=	140	×	17	=	2,380
B	=	120	×	110	=	13,200
C	=	85	×	210	=	17,850
		345				33,430

2. Compute total weight and total moments.
3. Divide total moments by total weight to get the CG.

$$CG = \frac{33,430}{345} = 96.89 \text{ in.}$$

Answer (A) is incorrect. The CG is 96.89 in., not 89.11 in. Answer (C) is incorrect. The CG is 96.89 in., not 106.92 in.

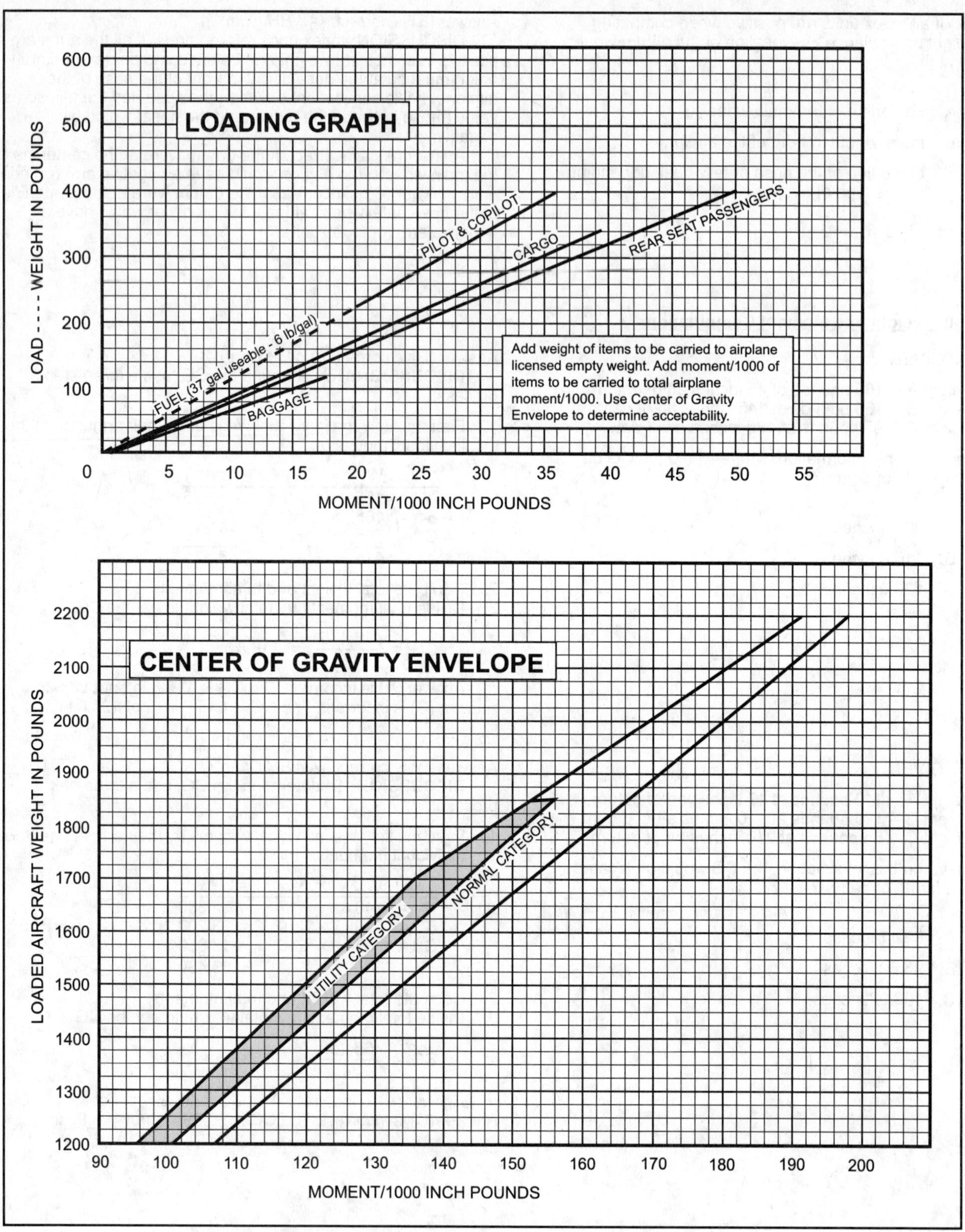

Figure 38. – Loading Graph and Center-of-Gravity Envelope.

56. (Refer to Figure 38 on page 172.)

GIVEN:

Empty weight (oil is included)	1,271 lb
Empty weight moment (in-lb/1,000)	102.04
Pilot and copilot	400 lb
Rear seat passenger	140 lb
Cargo	100 lb
Fuel	37 gal

Is the airplane loaded within limits?

A. Yes, the weight and CG is within limits.

B. No, the weight exceeds the maximum allowable.

C. No, the weight is acceptable, but the CG is aft of the aft limit.

Answer (A) is correct. *(AWBH Chap 4)*

DISCUSSION: Use the loading graph at the top of Fig. 38 to determine the moment for each individual weight.

	Weight	Moment/ 1,000 in.-lb.
Empty weight	1,271	102.04
Pilot and copilot	400	36.0
Rear-seat passenger	140	18.0
Cargo	100	11.5
Fuel (37 gal. × 6 lb./gal.)	222	20.0
	2,133	187.54

The intersection of total weight of 2,133 lb. and total moment of 187.54 in.-lb. is within the CG moment envelope in Fig. 38.

Answer (B) is incorrect. A weight of 2,133 lb. is less than the maximum allowable weight of 2,200 lb. Answer (C) is incorrect. The amount of 187.54 in.-lb. is less than the aft limit at 2,133 lb. of 193 in.-lb.

57. (Refer to Figure 38 on page 172.)

GIVEN:

Empty weight (oil is included)	1,271 lb
Empty weight moment (in-lb/1,000)	102.04
Pilot and copilot	260 lb
Rear seat passenger	120 lb
Cargo	60 lb
Fuel	37 gal

Under these conditions, the CG is determined to be located

A. within the CG envelope.

B. on the forward limit of the CG envelope.

C. within the shaded area of the CG envelope.

Answer (A) is correct. *(AWBH Chap 4)*

DISCUSSION: Use the loading graph at the top of Fig. 38 to determine the moment for each individual weight.

	Weight	Moment/ 1,000 in.-lb.
Empty weight	1,271	102.04
Pilot and copilot	260	23.5
Rear-seat passenger	120	15.0
Cargo	60	7.0
Fuel (37 gal. × 6 lb./gal.)	222	20.0
	1,933	167.54

The intersection of total weight of 1,933 lb. and total moment of 167.54 in.-lb. is within the CG moment envelope in Fig. 38.

Answer (B) is incorrect. A total moment of approximately 160.5 in.-lb., not 167.54 in.-lb., would put the CG at the forward limit of the CG envelope at a weight of 1,933 lb. Answer (C) is incorrect. Both the weight and the moment are outside the shaded (utility category) area.

58. (Refer to Figure 38 on page 172.)

GIVEN:

Empty weight (oil is included)	1,271 lb
Empty weight moment (in-lb/1,000)	102.04
Pilot and copilot	360 lb
Cargo	340 lb
Fuel	37 gal

Will the CG remain within limits after 30 gallons of fuel has been used in flight?

A. Yes, the CG will remain within limits.

B. No, the CG will be located aft of the aft CG limit.

C. Yes, but the CG will be located in the shaded area of the CG envelope.

Answer (A) is correct. *(AWBH Chap 4)*

DISCUSSION: Use the loading graph at the top of Fig. 38 to determine the moment for each individual weight. Fuel remaining is determined by 37 gal. to start – 30 gal. burned = 7 gal. left × 6 lb. per gallon.

	Weight	Moment/ 1,000 in.-lb.
Empty weight	1,271	102.04
Pilot and copilot	360	32.5
Cargo	340	39.5
Fuel (7 gal. × 6 lb./gal.)	42	4.0
	2,013	178.04

The intersection of total weight of 2,013 lb. and total moment of 178.04 in.-lb. is within the CG moment envelope in Fig. 38.

Answer (B) is incorrect. The amount of 178.04 in.-lb. is less than the aft CG limit at 2,013 lb. of 180 in.-lb. Answer (C) is incorrect. Both the weight and the moment are outside the shaded (utility category) area.

59. GIVEN:

	WEIGHT	ARM	MOMENT
Empty weight	957	29.07	?
Pilot (fwd seat)	140	–45.30	?
Passenger (aft seat)	170	+1.60	?
Ballast	15	–45.30	?
TOTALS	?	?	?

The CG is located at station

A. –6.43.

B. +16.43.

C. +27.38.

Answer (B) is correct. *(AWBH Chap 4)*

DISCUSSION: To determine the CG, use a three-step process:

1. Multiply the individual weights by individual arms to get individual moments.

	W ×	A =	M
A =	957 ×	29.07 =	27,819.99
B =	140 ×	–45.30 =	–6,342.00
C =	170 ×	1.60 =	272.00
D =	15 ×	–45.30 =	–679.50
	1,282		21,070.49

2. Compute total weight and total moments.
3. Divide total moments by total weight to get the CG.

$$CG = \frac{21,070.49}{1,282} = +16.43$$

Answer (A) is incorrect. The CG is +16.43, not –6.43.
Answer (C) is incorrect. The CG is +16.43, not +27.38.

60. GIVEN:

Weight A -- 135 pounds at 15 inches aft of datum
Weight B -- 205 pounds at 117 inches aft of datum
Weight C -- 85 pounds at 195 inches aft of datum

Based on this information, the CG would be located how far aft of datum?

A. 100.2 inches.

B. 109.0 inches.

C. 121.7 inches.

Answer (A) is correct. *(AWBH Chap 4)*

DISCUSSION: To determine the CG, use a three-step process:

1. Multiply the individual weights by their arms to get the individual moments.

	W ×	A =	M
A =	135 ×	15 =	2,025
B =	205 ×	117 =	23,985
C =	85 ×	195 =	16,575
	425		42,585

2. Compute total weight and total moments.
3. Divide total moments by total weight to get the CG.

$$CG = \frac{42,585}{425} = 100.2 \text{ in.}$$

Answer (B) is incorrect. The CG is 100.2 in., not 109.0 in.
Answer (C) is incorrect. The CG is 100.2 in., not 121.7 in.

61. GIVEN:

Weight A -- 175 pounds at 135 inches aft of datum
Weight B -- 135 pounds at 115 inches aft of datum
Weight C -- 75 pounds at 85 inches aft of datum

The CG for the combined weights would be located how far aft of datum?

A. 91.76 inches.

B. 111.67 inches.

C. 118.24 inches.

Answer (C) is correct. *(AWBH Chap 4)*

DISCUSSION: To determine the CG, use a three-step process:

1. Multiply the individual weights by their arms to get the individual moments.

	W ×	A =	M
A =	175 ×	135 =	23,625
B =	135 ×	115 =	15,525
C =	75 ×	85 =	6,375
	385		45,525

2. Compute total weight and total moments.
3. Divide total moments by total weight to get the CG.

$$CG = \frac{45,525}{385} = 118.24 \text{ in.}$$

Answer (A) is incorrect. The CG is 118.24 in., not 91.76 in.
Answer (B) is incorrect. The CG is 118.24 in., not 111.67 in.

5.11 Weight Change and Weight Shift Computations

62. GIVEN:

Total weight. . . . . 4,137 lb
CG location. . . . . Station 67.8
Fuel consumption. . . . . 13.7 GPH
Fuel CG. . . . . Station 68.0

After 1 hour 30 minutes of flight time, the CG would be located at station

A. 67.79

B. 68.79

C. 70.78

Answer (A) is correct. *(AWBH Chap 2)*

DISCUSSION: To determine the new CG, complete the following steps:

1. Weight change = Fuel consumption (GPH) × flight time × 6 lb./gal.
   = 13.7 × 1.5 × 6
   = 123.3 lb.
2. Use the following formula to determine the new CG:

$$New\ CG = \frac{M_1 \pm \Delta M}{W_1 \pm \Delta W}$$

where M_1 = original moment and W_1 = original weight.

$$\text{New CG} = \frac{(4{,}137 \times 67.8) - (123.3 \times 68.0)}{4{,}137 - 123.3}$$

$$= \frac{280{,}488.6 - 8{,}384.4}{4{,}013.7}$$

$$= \frac{272{,}104.2}{4{,}013.7} = 67.79$$

Answer (B) is incorrect. The new CG is 67.79, not 68.79.
Answer (C) is incorrect. The new CG is 67.79, not 70.78.

63. GIVEN:

Total weight. . . . . 3,037 lb
CG location. . . . . Station 68.8
Fuel consumption. . . . . 12.7 GPH
Fuel CG. . . . . Station 68.0

After 1 hour 45 minutes of flight time, the CG would be located at station

A. 68.77

B. 68.83

C. 69.77

Answer (B) is correct. *(AWBH Chap 2)*

DISCUSSION: To determine the new CG, complete the following steps:

1. Weight change = Fuel consumption (GPH) × flight time × 6 lb./gal.
   = 12.7 × 1.75 × 6
   = 133.35 lb.
2. Use the following formula to determine the new CG:

$$New\ CG = \frac{M_1 \pm \Delta M}{W_1 \pm \Delta W}$$

where M_1 = original moment and W_1 = original weight.

$$\text{New CG} = \frac{(3{,}037 \times 68.8) - (133.35 \times 68.0)}{3{,}037 - 133.35}$$

$$= \frac{208{,}945.6 - 9{,}067.8}{2{,}903.65}$$

$$= \frac{199{,}877.8}{2{,}903.65} = 68.83$$

Answer (A) is incorrect. The new CG is 68.83, not 68.77.
Answer (C) is incorrect. The new CG is 68.83, not 69.77.

64. An airplane is loaded to a gross weight of 4,800 pounds, with three pieces of luggage in the rear baggage compartment. The CG is located 98 inches aft of datum, which is 1 inch aft of limits. If luggage which weighs 90 pounds is moved from the rear baggage compartment (145 inches aft of datum) to the front compartment (45 inches aft of datum), what is the new CG?

A. 96.13 inches aft of datum.

B. 95.50 inches aft of datum.

C. 99.87 inches aft of datum.

Answer (A) is correct. *(AWBH Chap 2)*

DISCUSSION: To determine the new CG, use the following formula:

$$New\ CG = \frac{M_1 \pm \Delta M}{W_1 \pm \Delta W}$$

where M_1 = original moment and W_1 = original weight.

Since there is no change in weight, $\Delta W = 0$ and weight shifted forward causes a "–" moment change.

$$\text{New CG} = \frac{(4{,}800 \times 98) - 90(145 - 45)}{4{,}800}$$

$$= \frac{470{,}400 - 9{,}000}{4{,}800}$$

$$= \frac{461{,}400}{4{,}800} = 96.13$$

Answer (B) is incorrect. The new CG is 96.13, not 95.50.
Answer (C) is incorrect. The new CG is 96.13, not 99.87.

65. An aircraft is loaded with a ramp weight of 3,650 pounds and having a CG of 94.0, approximately how much baggage would have to be moved from the rear baggage area at station 180 to the forward baggage area at station 40 in order to move the CG to 92.0?

A. 52.14 pounds.

B. 62.24 pounds.

C. 78.14 pounds.

Answer (A) is correct. *(AWBH Chap 2)*

DISCUSSION: To determine how much weight needs to be shifted forward (causing a "–" moment change), use the following formula:

$$New\ CG = \frac{M_1 \pm \Delta M}{W_1 \pm \Delta W}$$

where M_1 = original moment and W_1 = original weight, and since there is no change in weight, $\Delta W = 0$.

$$92.0 = \frac{(3{,}650 \times 94.0) - x(180 - 40)}{3{,}650}$$

$$335{,}800 = 343{,}100 - 140x$$

$$140x = 343{,}100 - 335{,}800$$

$$140x = 7{,}300$$

$$x = 52.14 \text{ lb.}$$

Answer (B) is incorrect. Only 52.14 lb., not 62.24 lb., of baggage needs to be shifted. Answer (C) is incorrect. Only 52.14 lb., not 78.14 lb., of baggage needs to be shifted.

END OF STUDY UNIT

STUDY UNIT SIX
AEROMEDICAL FACTORS AND AERONAUTICAL DECISION MAKING (ADM)

(4 pages of outline)

This study unit contains outlines of major concepts tested, sample test questions and answers regarding aeromedical factors and aeronautical decision making (ADM), and an explanation of each answer. The table of contents above lists each subunit within this study unit, the number of questions pertaining to that particular subunit, and the pages on which the outlines and questions begin, respectively.

Recall that the **sole purpose** of this book is to expedite your passing of the FAA pilot knowledge test for the commercial pilot certificate. Accordingly, all extraneous material (i.e., topics or regulations not directly tested on the FAA pilot knowledge test) is omitted, even though much more knowledge is necessary to become a proficient commercial pilot. This additional material is presented in *Pilot Handbook* and *Commercial Pilot Flight Maneuvers and Practical Test Prep*, available from Gleim Publications, Inc. See the product listing at the back of the book and order online at www.gleim.com.

6.1 HYPOXIA AND ALCOHOL

1. Hypoxia is a state of oxygen deficiency in the body sufficient to impair functions of the brain and other organs.
2. The following are four types of hypoxia based on their causes:
    a. **Hypoxic hypoxia** is a result of insufficient oxygen available to the body as a whole.
        1) EXAMPLE: Reduction of partial pressure at high altitude, a blocked airway, or drowning
    b. **Hypemic hypoxia** occurs when the blood is not able to take up and transport a sufficient amount of oxygen to the cells in the body. The result is oxygen deficiency in the blood rather than a lack of inhaled oxygen.
        1) EXAMPLE: Carbon monoxide poisoning
    c. **Stagnant hypoxia** results when oxygen-rich blood in the lungs is not moving.
        1) EXAMPLE: Shock, reduced circulation due to extreme cold, or pulling excessive Gs in flight
    d. **Histotoxic hypoxia** is the inability of cells to effectively use oxygen.
        1) EXAMPLE: Impairment due to alcohol and drugs
3. Symptoms of hypoxia include an initial feeling of euphoria but lead to more serious concerns such as headache, decreased reaction time, visual impairment, and eventual unconsciousness.
4. The correct response to counteract feelings of hypoxia is to lower altitude or use supplemental oxygen.

5. Alcohol is a central nervous system depressant that interferes with the brain's ability to use oxygen.
    a. Even small amounts of alcohol in the body adversely affect judgment and decision-making abilities.
6. Altitude multiplies the effects of alcohol on the brain; at higher altitudes, alcohol from two drinks may have the same effect as three or four drinks at lower altitudes.
7. 14 CFR 91.17 requires that the blood alcohol level be less than 0.04% and that 8 hours pass between consuming alcohol and piloting an aircraft.
    a. The body requires about 3 hours to rid itself of all the alcohol contained in one mixed drink, one beer, or one glass of wine.

6.2 HYPERVENTILATION

1. Hyperventilation occurs when an excessive amount of air is breathed in and out of the lungs, e.g., when you become excited or undergo stress, tension, fear, or anxiety.
    a. This results in insufficient carbon dioxide in the body.
    b. Symptoms include lightheadedness, suffocation, drowsiness, tingling in the extremities, and coolness. Incapacitation and finally unconsciousness can occur.
    c. To overcome hyperventilation, a pilot should slow the breathing rate.

6.3 SPATIAL DISORIENTATION

1. Spatial disorientation, e.g., not knowing whether you are going up, going down, or turning, is a state of temporary confusion resulting from misleading information being sent to the brain by various sensory organs.
2. If you lose outside visual references and become disoriented, you are experiencing spatial disorientation. This occurs when you rely on the sensations of muscles and the inner ear to tell you what the airplane's attitude is.
    a. This might occur during a night flight, in clouds, or in dust.
    b. Examples of spatial disorientation in flight could include the following:
        1) **Graveyard spiral.** An observed loss of altitude during a coordinated constant-rate turn that has ceased stimulating the motion-sensing system can create the illusion of being in a descent with the wings level. The disoriented pilot will pull back on the controls, tightening the spiral and increasing the loss of altitude.
        2) **False horizon.** Sloping cloud formations, an obscured horizon, or certain geometric patterns of ground lights can create the illusion of not being correctly aligned with the true horizon. Without reference to instruments, a pilot may place the airplane in a dangerous attitude based on incorrect visual cues.
3. Ways to overcome the effects of spatial disorientation include relying on the airplane instruments, avoiding sudden head movements, and ensuring that outside visual references are fixed points on the surface.

6.4 PILOT VISION

1. Scanning for traffic is best accomplished by bringing small portions of the sky into the central field of vision slowly and in succession.
    a. Each movement should not exceed 10°, and each area should be observed for at least 1 second.

2. Haze can create the illusion of traffic or terrain being farther away than they actually are.
3. Visual illusions may affect a pilot's ability to properly judge a landing.
   a. Rain on a windscreen can create the illusion of greater height from the runway.
   b. Haze can create the illusion of greater distance from the runway.
   c. Landing errors from these illusions can be overcome by knowledge and anticipation of the illusions.

6.5 AERONAUTICAL DECISION MAKING (ADM)

1. **Aeronautical decision making (ADM)** is a systematic approach to the mental process used by pilots to consistently determine the best course of action in response to a given set of circumstances.
2. **Risk management** is the part of the ADM process that relies on situational awareness, problem recognition, and good judgment to reduce risks associated with each flight.
3. The ADM process addresses all aspects of decision making in the cockpit and identifies the steps involved in good decision making.
   a. One of the steps for good decision making is for you to identify personal hazardous attitudes to safe flight.
      1) This is accomplished by taking a Self-Assessment Hazardous Attitude Inventory Test.
4. There are a number of classical behavioral traps into which pilots have been known to fall.
   a. Experienced pilots, as a rule, always try to complete a flight as planned, please passengers, meet schedules, and generally demonstrate that they have the "right stuff."
   b. The basic drive to demonstrate the "right stuff" can have an adverse effect on safety and can impose an unrealistic assessment of piloting skills under stressful conditions.
      1) These tendencies ultimately may lead to practices that are dangerous and often illegal and that may result in a mishap.
5. Most pilots have fallen prey to dangerous tendencies or behavioral problems at some time. Some of these dangerous tendencies or behavioral patterns, which must be identified and eliminated, include
   a. Peer pressure
   b. Get-there-itis
   c. Loss of positional or situational awareness
   d. Operating without adequate fuel reserves
6. ADM addresses the following five hazardous attitudes:
   a. Antiauthority -- "Don't tell me!"
      1) EXAMPLE: The passengers for a charter flight have arrived almost an hour late for a flight that requires a reservation. An antiauthority attitude (reaction) by the pilot would be to think that those reservation rules do not apply to this flight.
   b. Impulsivity -- "Do something quickly without thinking!"
      1) EXAMPLE: The pilot and the passengers are anxious to get to their destination for a business presentation, but level 4 thunderstorms are reported to be in a line across their intended route of flight. An impulsivity attitude (reaction) would be for the pilot to "hurry and get going" before things get worse.

c. Invulnerability -- "It won't happen to me."

   1) EXAMPLE: During an operational check of the cabin pressurization system, the pilot discovers that the rate control feature is inoperative. Since the pilot knows that (s)he can manually control the system, the pilot elects to disregard the discrepancy. An invulnerability attitude (reaction) would be to think, "What is the worst that could happen? (Problems happen to other people.)"

d. Macho -- "I can do it!"

   1) EXAMPLE: While on an IFR flight, a pilot emerges from a cloud to find himself within 300 ft. of a helicopter. A macho attitude (reaction) by the pilot would be to fly a little closer to the helicopter, just to "show" the other pilot.

e. Resignation -- "What's the use?"

   1) EXAMPLE: A pilot and friends are going to fly to an out-of-town football game. When the passengers arrive, the pilot determines that the loaded airplane will be over the maximum gross weight for takeoff with the existing fuel load. A resignation attitude (reaction) by the pilot would be to think, "Well, nobody told me about the extra weight."

7. Hazardous attitudes that contribute to poor pilot judgment can be effectively counteracted by redirecting those hazardous attitudes so that appropriate action can be taken.
8. Recognition of hazardous thoughts is the first step in neutralizing them in the ADM process.
9. When you recognize a hazardous thought, you should label it as hazardous and then correct it by stating the corresponding antidote.
10. The hazardous attitude antidotes shown below should be learned thoroughly and practiced.

Hazardous Attitude	**Antidote**
Antiauthority: *Don't tell me!*	Follow the rules. They are usually right.
Impulsivity: *Do something quickly!*	Not so fast. Think first.
Invulnerability: *It won't happen to me.*	It could happen to me.
Macho: *I can do it.*	Taking chances is foolish.
Resignation: *What's the use?*	I'm not helpless. I can make a difference.

11. Good cockpit stress management begins with good life stress management.

    a. Since many of the stress coping techniques practiced for life stress management are not usually practiced in flight, you must condition yourself to relax and think rationally when stress occurs.

12. The Decide Model is comprised of a six-step process to provide pilots with a logical way of approaching ADM. The six steps (in order) are

    a. **D**etect. The decision maker detects the fact that change has occurred.
    b. **E**stimate. The decision maker estimates the need to counter or react to the change.
    c. **C**hoose. The decision maker chooses a desirable outcome (in terms of success) for the flight.
    d. **I**dentify. The decision maker identifies actions that could successfully control the change.
    e. **D**o. The decision maker takes the necessary action.
    f. **E**valuate. The decision maker evaluates the effect(s) of his or her action countering the change.

QUESTIONS AND ANSWER EXPLANATIONS: All of the commercial pilot knowledge test questions chosen by the FAA for release as well as additional questions selected by Gleim relating to the material in the previous outlines are reproduced on the following pages. These questions have been organized into the same subunits as the outlines. To the immediate right of each question are the correct answer and answer explanation. You should cover these answers and answer explanations while responding to the questions. Refer to the general discussion in the Introduction on how to take the FAA knowledge test.

Remember that the questions from the FAA knowledge test bank have been reordered by topic and organized into a meaningful sequence. Also, the first line of the answer explanation gives the citation of the authoritative source for the answer.

QUESTIONS

6.1 Hypoxia and Alcohol

1. Which is not a type of hypoxia?

A. Histotoxic.

B. Hypoxic.

C. Hypertoxic.

Answer (C) is correct. *(PHAK Chap 16)*

DISCUSSION: There is no such thing as hypertoxic hypoxia. The four types of hypoxia are histotoxic, hypoxic, hypemic, and stagnant hypoxia.

Answer (A) is incorrect. The four types of hypoxia are histotoxic, hypoxic, hypemic, and stagnant hypoxia. Answer (B) is incorrect. The four types of hypoxia are histotoxic, hypoxic, hypemic, and stagnant hypoxia.

2. Which of the following is a correct response to counteract the feelings of hypoxia in flight?

A. Promptly descend altitude.

B. Increase cabin air flow.

C. Avoid sudden inhalations.

Answer (A) is correct. *(PHAK Chap 16)*

DISCUSSION: The correct response to counteract feelings of hypoxia is to lower altitude or use supplemental oxygen, if the aircraft is so equipped.

Answer (B) is incorrect. Increasing the amount of air flowing inside an aircraft will not help counteract hypoxia. Because of the reduction of partial pressure at higher altitudes, there is less oxygen in the air to draw from. Answer (C) is incorrect. Breathing deeply or suddenly will not counteract feelings of hypoxia.

3. Hypoxia susceptibility due to inhalation of carbon monoxide increases as

A. altitude increases.

B. humidity decreases.

C. oxygen demand increases.

Answer (A) is correct. *(PHAK Chap 16)*

DISCUSSION: The inhalation of carbon monoxide reduces body's ability to transport oxygen. The red blood cells will pick up carbon monoxide molecules instead of oxygen. This problem is compounded by increasing altitude, which also limits the body's ability to transport oxygen.

Answer (B) is incorrect. A change in humidity does not change the body's susceptibility to hypoxia due to the inhalation of carbon monoxide. Answer (C) is incorrect. An increase in altitude, not an increase in oxygen demand, increases the susceptibility to hypoxia when carbon monoxide is inhaled.

4. If a pilot has not consumed a drink in 12 hours, and has a blood alcohol level of .04 percent, can (s)he fly?

A. Yes, if it has been in excess of 8 hours since the pilot last consumed alcohol.

B. No, the pilot has a blood alcohol level of .04.

C. Yes, the FAA requires at least 12 hours and a blood alcohol level of .04.

Answer (B) is correct. *(FAR 91.17)*

DISCUSSION: Pilots are required to have a blood alcohol level that is less than .04%, and at least 8 hours must have passed since the last alcoholic beverage was consumed.

Answer (A) is incorrect. The FAA requires pilots to wait at least 8 hours from the time an alcoholic beverage is consumed to the time flight is attempted. In addition to the 8 hours, pilots must also have a blood alcohol level that is less than .04%. Answer (C) is incorrect. The FAA requires that at least 8 hours pass between the last consumption of alcohol and the beginning of a flight. Further, the blood alcohol level must be less than .04%.

5. 14 CFR 91.17 requires that blood alcohol level be less than

A. 0.40% when piloting an aircraft.

B. 0.08% when piloting an aircraft.

C. 0.04% when piloting an aircraft.

Answer (C) is correct. *(PHAK Chap 16)*

DISCUSSION: Current regulations require that a pilot's blood alcohol level be less than 0.04% and that 8 hours pass between consuming alcohol and piloting an aircraft.

Answer (A) is incorrect. Pilots should have a blood alcohol level of less than 0.04%, not 0.40%. Answer (B) is incorrect. Pilots should have a blood alcohol level of less than 0.04%, not 0.08%.

6. According to current regulations, how many hours must elapse between consuming alcohol and piloting an aircraft?

A. 4 hours.

B. 8 hours.

C. 16 hours.

Answer (B) is correct. *(PHAK Chap 16)*

DISCUSSION: According to 14 CFR 91.17, 8 hours must pass between consuming alcohol and flying an aircraft.

Answer (A) is incorrect. Regulations require that 8 hours, not 4, must pass between consuming alcohol and flying an aircraft. Answer (C) is incorrect. While considerable amounts of alcohol may remain in the body for over 16 hours, and it is good to be cautious about flying too soon after drinking, the regulations state that only 8 hours must elapse between consuming alcohol and flying.

7. Which of the following statements concerning the combination of alcohol and altitude is true?

A. Judgment and decision-making abilities will only be affected at altitudes greater than 2,000 ft. MSL.

B. Altitude multiplies the effects of alcohol.

C. Increases in altitude do not change how alcohol affects individuals.

Answer (B) is correct. *(PHAK Chap 16)*

DISCUSSION: Altitude multiplies the effects of alcohol on the brain; at higher altitudes, alcohol from two drinks may have the same effect as three or four drinks at lower altitudes.

Answer (A) is incorrect. An increase in altitude, no matter how small, can multiply the effects of alcohol on the body. Answer (C) is incorrect. Increasing altitude multiplies the effects alcohol will have on the body.

8. Hypoxia is the result of which of these conditions?

A. Excessive oxygen in the bloodstream.

B. Insufficient oxygen reaching the brain.

C. Excessive carbon dioxide in the bloodstream.

Answer (B) is correct. *(AIM Para 8-1-2)*

DISCUSSION: Hypoxia is a state of oxygen deficiency in the bloodstream sufficient to impair function of the brain and other organs.

Answer (A) is incorrect. The problem is insufficient oxygen, not excessive oxygen. Answer (C) is incorrect. It is a nonsense answer. Insufficient, not excessive, carbon dioxide in the bloodstream is the result of hyperventilation, not hypoxia.

9. Which is true regarding the presence of alcohol within the human body?

A. A small amount of alcohol increases vision acuity.

B. An increase in altitude decreases the adverse effect of alcohol.

C. Judgment and decision-making abilities can be adversely affected by even small amounts of alcohol.

Answer (C) is correct. *(AIM Para 8-1-1)*

DISCUSSION: As little as 1 ounce of liquor, 12 ounces of beer, or 4 ounces (one glass) of wine can impair flying skills, with the alcohol consumed in these drinks being detectable in the breath and blood for at least 3 hr.

Answer (A) is incorrect. Any amount of alcohol decreases, not increases, virtually all mental and physical activities. Answer (B) is incorrect. Increases in altitude increase, not decrease, the adverse effects of alcohol.

10. It takes how long for the alcohol from one drink to completely leave the body?

A. 1 hour.

B. 2 hours.

C. 3 hours.

Answer (C) is correct. *(PHAK Chap 16)*

DISCUSSION: The body requires about 3 hours to rid itself of all the alcohol contained in one mixed drink, one beer, or one glass of wine.

Answer (A) is incorrect. The body requires 3 hours, not 1 hour, to rid itself of all the alcohol contained in one mixed drink, one beer, or one glass of wine. Answer (B) is incorrect. The body requires 3 hours, not 2 hours, to rid itself of all the alcohol contained in one mixed drink, one beer, or one glass of wine.

11. To rid itself of all the alcohol contained in one beer, the human body requires about

A. 1 hour.

B. 2 hours.

C. 3 hours.

Answer (C) is correct. *(PHAK Chap 16)*

DISCUSSION: The body requires about 3 hours to rid itself of all the alcohol contained in one mixed drink, one beer, or one glass of wine.

Answer (A) is incorrect. The body requires 3 hours, not 1 hour, to rid itself of all the alcohol contained in one mixed drink, one beer, or one glass of wine. Answer (B) is incorrect. The body requires 3 hours, not 2 hours, to rid itself of all the alcohol contained in one mixed drink, one beer, or one glass of wine.

12. With a blood alcohol level below .04 percent, a pilot cannot fly sooner than

A. 4 hours after drinking alcohol.

B. 12 hours after drinking alcohol.

C. 8 hours after drinking alcohol.

Answer (C) is correct. *(PHAK Chap 16)*

DISCUSSION: According to 14 CFR 91.17, 8 hours must pass between consuming alcohol and flying an aircraft.

Answer (A) is incorrect. A pilot who has consumed alcohol must wait more than 4 hours before flying. Answer (B) is incorrect. While considerable amounts of alcohol may remain in the body for over 12 hours and it is good to be cautious about flying too soon after drinking, the regulations state that only 8 hours must elapse between consuming alcohol and flying.

6.2 Hyperventilation

13. Which is a common symptom of hyperventilation?

A. Drowsiness.

B. Decreased breathing rate.

C. Euphoria - sense of well-being.

Answer (A) is correct. *(AIM Para 8-1-3)*

DISCUSSION: Hyperventilation is an abnormal increase in breathing, which can occur subconsciously when a stressful situation is encountered. It can cause lightheadedness, drowsiness, suffocation, tingling in the extremities, and coolness.

Answer (B) is incorrect. Hyperventilation usually occurs from an increased, not a decreased, breathing rate. Answer (C) is incorrect. Euphoria is a potential symptom of hypoxia, not hyperventilation.

14. As hyperventilation progresses a pilot can experience

A. decreased breathing rate and depth.

B. heightened awareness and feeling of well-being.

C. symptoms of suffocation and drowsiness.

Answer (C) is correct. *(AIM Para 8-1-3)*

DISCUSSION: Hyperventilation is an abnormal increase in breathing, which can occur subconsciously when a stressful situation is encountered. It can cause lightheadedness, drowsiness, suffocation, tingling in the extremities, and coolness.

Answer (A) is incorrect. Hyperventilation is an increase, not a decrease, of the breathing rate and depth. Answer (B) is incorrect. Heightened awareness and euphoria are potential symptoms of hypoxia, not hyperventilation.

15. To overcome the symptoms of hyperventilation, a pilot should

A. swallow or yawn.

B. slow the breathing rate.

C. increase the breathing rate.

Answer (B) is correct. *(AIM Para 8-1-3)*

DISCUSSION: A pilot should be able to overcome the symptoms of hyperventilation by slowing the breathing rate or breathing into a bag.

Answer (A) is incorrect. Swallowing or yawning helps to equalize ear pressures, not overcome hyperventilation. Answer (C) is incorrect. Increasing the breathing rate aggravates hyperventilation.

16. Which would most likely result in hyperventilation?

A. Insufficient oxygen.

B. Excessive carbon monoxide.

C. Insufficient carbon dioxide.

Answer (C) is correct. *(AIM Para 8-1-3)*

DISCUSSION: Hyperventilation occurs when an excessive amount of carbon dioxide is passed out of the body and too much oxygen is retained.

Answer (A) is incorrect. It describes hypoxia. Answer (B) is incorrect. It describes carbon monoxide poisoning.

6.3 Spatial Disorientation

17. A state of temporary confusion resulting from misleading information being sent to the brain by sensory organs is know as

A. visual illusion.

B. spatial disorientation.

C. spatial miscue.

Answer (B) is correct. *(PHAK Chap 16)*

DISCUSSION: Spatial disorientation is the state of temporary confusion resulting from misleading information being sent to the brain by various sensory organs.

Answer (A) is incorrect. Visual illusions, while affecting judgment, only take into account one sensory receptor: the eyes. Answer (C) is incorrect. Spatial disorientation, not a spatial miscue, is the state of temporary confusion resulting from misleading information being sent to the brain by various sensory organs.

18. How may a pilot overcome spatial disorientation?

A. By relying on his flight instruments.

B. By decreasing the amount of time spent looking inside.

C. By relying on all outside visual references.

Answer (A) is correct. *(PHAK Chap 16)*
DISCUSSION: Ways to overcome the effects of spatial disorientation include relying on the airplane instruments, avoiding sudden head movements, and ensuring that outside visual references are fixed points on the surface.
Answer (B) is incorrect. Decreasing the amount of time spent looking inside is not a remedy for overcoming spatial disorientation. Answer (C) is incorrect. Not all visual references can be relied on, as some may be moving. A pilot must ensure that any outside visual references are fixed points on the surface.

19. Which of the following flight conditions would indicate a pilot is experiencing spatial disorientation?

A. Steep turn.

B. Graveyard spiral.

C. Turns around a point.

Answer (B) is correct. *(PHAK Chap 16)*
DISCUSSION: A graveyard spiral is an example of a pilot being adversely affected by spatial disorientation.
Answer (A) is incorrect. Steep turns are common maneuvers performed during training and do not indicate that a pilot is experiencing spatial disorientation. Answer (C) is incorrect. Turns around a point are maneuvers performed during training and do not indicate that a pilot is experiencing spatial disorientation.

20. A pilot who needs to overcome the effects of spatial disorientation should

A. breathe rapidly.

B. ignore the instruments and rely on body sensations.

C. place a greater emphasis on the flight instruments.

Answer (C) is correct. *(PHAK Chap 16)*
DISCUSSION: A pilot can overcome the effects of spatial disorientation by placing a greater emphasis on the flight instruments. Doing this will help the pilot ignore the kinesthetic sensations encountered during spatial disorientation.
Answer (A) is incorrect. Increasing the rate of respiration will not help the pilot overcome spatial disorientation and can subsequently lead to hyperventilation. Answer (B) is incorrect. Relying on the sensations of the body will further increase the effects of spatial disorientation, not decrease the symptoms.

6.4 Pilot Vision

21. To scan properly for traffic, a pilot should

A. slowly sweep the field of vision from one side to the other at intervals.

B. concentrate on any peripheral movement detected.

C. use a series of short, regularly spaced eye movements that bring successive areas of the sky into the central visual field.

Answer (C) is correct. *(AIM Para 8-1-6)*
DISCUSSION: The most effective way to scan for other aircraft during the day is to use a series of short, regularly spaced eye movements that bring successive areas of the sky into your central vision. Each movement should not exceed 10°, and each area should be observed for at least 1 sec. to facilitate detection.
Answer (A) is incorrect. You must concentrate on different segments systematically. Answer (B) is incorrect. Peripheral movement will not be detected easily, especially under adverse conditions such as haze.

22. Which technique should a pilot use to scan for traffic to the right and left during straight-and-level flight?

A. Systematically focus on different segments of the sky for short intervals.

B. Concentrate on relative movement detected in the peripheral vision area.

C. Continuous sweeping of the windshield from right to left.

Answer (A) is correct. *(AIM Para 8-1-6)*
DISCUSSION: Due to the fact that eyes can focus only on a narrow viewing area, effective scanning is accomplished with a series of short, regularly spaced eye movements that bring successive areas of the sky into the central vision field.
Answer (B) is incorrect. It concerns scanning for traffic at night. Answer (C) is incorrect. A pilot must continually scan successive, small portions of the sky. The eyes can focus only on a narrow viewing area and require at least 1 sec. to detect a faraway object.

23. What effect does haze have on the ability to see traffic or terrain features during flight?

A. Haze causes the eyes to focus at infinity.

B. The eyes tend to overwork in haze and do not detect relative movement easily.

C. All traffic or terrain features appear to be farther away than their actual distance.

Answer (C) is correct. *(AIM Para 8-1-5)*

DISCUSSION: Atmospheric haze can create the illusion of being at a greater distance from traffic or terrain than you actually are. This is especially prevalent on landings.

Answer (A) is incorrect. In haze, the eyes focus at a comfortable distance, which may be only 10 to 30 ft. outside of the cockpit. Answer (B) is incorrect. In haze, the eyes relax and tend to stare outside without focusing or looking for common visual cues.

24. Haze creates which of the following atmospheric illusions?

A. Being at a greater distance from the runway.

B. Being at a closer distance from the runway.

C. Haze creates no atmospheric illusions.

Answer (A) is correct. *(AIM Para 8-1-5)*

DISCUSSION: Rain on a windscreen can create the illusion of greater height from the runway, and haze can create the illusion of greater distance from the runway; landing errors from these illusions can be overcome by knowledge and anticipation of the illusions.

Answer (B) is incorrect. Haze creates the illusion of being further from, not closer to, the runway. Answer (C) is incorrect. Haze creates the illusion of being at a greater distance from the runway.

6.5 Aeronautical Decision Making (ADM)

25. Aeronautical Decision Making (ADM) is a

A. systematic approach to the mental process used by pilots to consistently determine the best course of action for a given set of circumstances.

B. decision making process which relies on good judgment to reduce risks associated with each flight.

C. mental process of analyzing all information in a particular situation and making a timely decision on what action to take.

Answer (A) is correct. *(AC 60-22)*

DISCUSSION: ADM is a systematic approach to the mental process used by pilots to consistently determine the best course of action in response to a given set of circumstances.

Answer (B) is incorrect. Risk management, not ADM, is the part of the decision-making process that relies on situational awareness, problem recognition, and good judgment to reduce risks associated with each flight. Answer (C) is incorrect. Judgment, not ADM, is the mental process of recognizing and analyzing all pertinent information in a particular situation, rationally evaluating alternative actions in response to it, and making a timely decision on which action to take.

26. Risk management, as part of the aeronautical decision making (ADM) process, relies on which features to reduce the risks associated with each flight?

A. Application of stress management and risk element procedures.

B. The mental process of analyzing all information in a particular situation and making a timely decision on what action to take.

C. Situational awareness, problem recognition, and good judgment.

Answer (C) is correct. *(AC 60-22)*

DISCUSSION: Risk management is that part of the ADM process that relies on situational awareness, problem recognition, and good judgment to reduce risks associated with each flight.

Answer (A) is incorrect. Risk management relies on situational awareness, problem recognition, and good judgment, not the application of stress management and risk-element procedures, to reduce the risks associated with each flight. Answer (B) is incorrect. Judgment, not risk management, is the mental process of analyzing all information in a particular situation and making a timely decision on what action to take.

27. The Aeronautical Decision Making (ADM) process identifies the steps involved in good decision making. One of these steps includes a pilot

A. making a rational evaluation of the required actions.

B. developing the "right stuff" attitude.

C. identifying personal attitudes hazardous to safe flight.

Answer (C) is correct. *(AC 60-22)*

DISCUSSION: The ADM process addresses all aspects of decision making in the cockpit and identifies the steps involved in good decision making. One step in good decision making is to identify personal attitudes hazardous to safe flight.

Answer (A) is incorrect. Making a rational evaluation of the required actions is a part of judgment, not a step in good decision making. Answer (B) is incorrect. A step in the ADM process is to identify, not develop, a behavioral trap.

28. An early part of the Aeronautical Decision Making (ADM) process involves

A. taking a self-assessment hazardous attitude inventory test.

B. understanding the drive to have the "right stuff."

C. obtaining proper flight instruction and experience during training.

Answer (A) is correct. *(AC 60-22)*

DISCUSSION: An early part of the ADM process includes identifying personal attitudes hazardous to safe flight by taking a self-assessment hazardous attitude inventory test.

Answer (B) is incorrect. Taking a self-assessment hazardous attitude inventory test, not just understanding the drive to have the "right stuff," is an early part of the ADM process. Answer (C) is incorrect. Obtaining proper flight instruction and experience during training is critical in the development of a safe pilot but is not a part of the ADM process itself.

29. Examples of classic behavioral traps that experienced pilots may fall into are: trying to

A. assume additional responsibilities and assert PIC authority.

B. promote situational awareness and then necessary changes in behavior.

C. complete a flight as planned, please passengers, meet schedules, and demonstrate the "right stuff."

Answer (C) is correct. *(AC 60-22)*

DISCUSSION: There are a number of classic behavioral traps into which pilots have been known to fall. Pilots, particularly those with considerable experience, as a rule always try to complete a flight as planned, please passengers, meet schedules, and generally demonstrate that they have the "right stuff."

Answer (A) is incorrect. Classical behavioral traps include trying to complete a flight as planned, please passengers, meet schedules, and demonstrate the "right stuff," not trying to assume additional responsibilities and assert PIC authority. Answer (B) is incorrect. Classical behavioral traps include trying to complete a flight as planned, please passengers, meet schedules, and demonstrate the "right stuff," not trying to promote situational awareness and then necessary changes in behavior.

30. The basic drive for a pilot to demonstrate the "right stuff" can have an adverse effect on safety, by

A. a total disregard for any alternative course of action.

B. generating tendencies that lead to practices that are dangerous, often illegal, and may lead to a mishap.

C. allowing events, or the situation, to control his or her actions.

Answer (B) is correct. *(AC 60-22)*

DISCUSSION: The basic drive to demonstrate the "right stuff" can have an adverse effect on safety and can impose an unrealistic assessment of piloting skills under stressful conditions. These tendencies ultimately may lead to practices that are dangerous and often illegal and may result in a mishap.

Answer (A) is incorrect. "Get-there-itis," not a basic drive to demonstrate the "right stuff," has an adverse effect on safety when a pilot totally disregards any alternative course of action. Answer (C) is incorrect. Getting behind the aircraft, not a basic drive to demonstrate the "right stuff," has an adverse effect on safety by allowing events or the situation to control the pilot's actions.

31. Most pilots have fallen prey to dangerous tendencies or behavior problems at some time. Some of these dangerous tendencies or behavior patterns which must be identified and eliminated include:

A. Deficiencies in instrument skills and knowledge of aircraft systems or limitations.

B. Performance deficiencies from human factors such as fatigue, illness, or emotional problems.

C. Peer pressure, get-there-itis, loss of positional or situational awareness, and operating without adequate fuel reserves.

Answer (C) is correct. *(AC 60-22)*

DISCUSSION: Peer pressure, get-there-itis, loss of positional or situational awareness, operating without an adequate fuel reserve, and others are dangerous tendencies or behavior patterns that must be identified and eliminated.

Answer (A) is incorrect. Deficiencies in skills and/or knowledge may be overcome by conventional training and do not represent dangerous tendencies or behavior problems. Answer (B) is incorrect. Performance deficiencies caused by fatigue may be overcome by rest, and those caused by illness or emotional problems may be overcome by medical intervention. These deficiencies are physiological; they do not result from dangerous tendencies or behavior patterns.

32. What are some of the hazardous attitudes dealt with in Aeronautical Decision Making (ADM)?

A. Antiauthority (don't tell me), impulsivity (do something quickly without thinking), macho (I can do it).

B. Risk management, stress management, and risk elements.

C. Poor decision making, situational awareness, and judgment.

Answer (A) is correct. *(AC 60-22)*

DISCUSSION: ADM addresses five hazardous attitudes: antiauthority ("Don't tell me"), impulsivity ("Do something quickly without thinking"), invulnerability ("It won't happen to me"), macho ("I can do it"), and resignation ("What's the use?").

Answer (B) is incorrect. Risk management, stress management, and risk elements are all part of the ADM process, not hazardous attitudes dealt with in ADM. Answer (C) is incorrect. Situational awareness and judgment are part of the mental process in ADM to prevent or stop poor judgment, not hazardous attitudes in ADM.

33. The passengers for a charter flight have arrived almost an hour late for a flight that requires a reservation. Which of the following alternatives best illustrates the ANTIAUTHORITY reaction?

A. Those reservation rules do not apply to this flight.

B. If the pilot hurries, he or she may still make it on time.

C. The pilot can't help it that the passengers are late.

Answer (A) is correct. *(AC 60-22)*

DISCUSSION: By demonstrating the attitude that rules do not apply to his or her flight, the pilot is illustrating the antiauthority hazardous attitude.

Answer (B) is incorrect. If the pilot chooses the alternative to hurry in the belief that (s)he may make it on time, the pilot is illustrating the impulsivity reaction, not the antiauthority reaction. Answer (C) is incorrect. If the pilot feels that (s)he cannot help that the passengers are late, (s)he is illustrating the resignation reaction, not the antiauthority reaction.

34. The pilot and passengers are anxious to get to their destination for a business presentation. Level IV thunderstorms are reported to be in a line across their intended route of flight. Which of the following alternatives best illustrates the IMPULSIVITY reaction?

A. They want to hurry and get going, before things get worse.

B. A thunderstorm won't stop them.

C. They can't change the weather, so they might as well go.

Answer (A) is correct. *(AC 60-22)*

DISCUSSION: The pilot and passengers are anxious to get to their destination for a business presentation, but level 4 thunderstorms are reported to be in a line across their intended route of flight. An impulsivity hazardous attitude ("Act now; there is no time") would be to "hurry and get going" before things get worse.

Answer (B) is incorrect. A thought of "a thunderstorm will not stop them" is an invulnerability, not impulsivity, hazardous attitude. Answer (C) is incorrect. A thought of "they cannot change the weather, so they might as well go" is a resignation, not impulsivity, hazardous attitude.

35. While conducting an operational check of the cabin pressurization system, the pilot discovers that the rate control feature is inoperative. He knows that he can manually control the cabin pressure, so he elects to disregard the discrepancy. Which of the following alternatives best illustrates the INVULNERABILITY reaction?

A. What is the worst that could happen?

B. He can handle a little problem like this.

C. It's too late to fix it now.

Answer (A) is correct. *(AC 60-22)*

DISCUSSION: A pilot discovers that the rate control feature is inoperative on the cabin pressurization system, but he elects to disregard the discrepancy since he knows he can manually control the pressurization. An invulnerability ("Nothing bad will happen") reaction would be, "What is the worst that could happen?"

Answer (B) is incorrect. "He can handle a little problem like this" is a macho reaction, not an invulnerability reaction. Answer (C) is incorrect. "It is too late to fix it now" is an impulsivity reaction, not an invulnerability reaction.

36. While on an IFR flight, a pilot emerges from a cloud to find himself within 300 feet of a helicopter. Which of the following alternatives best illustrates the "MACHO" reaction?

A. He is not too concerned; everything will be alright.

B. He flies a little closer, just to show him.

C. He quickly turns away and dives, to avoid collision.

Answer (B) is correct. *(AC 60-22)*

DISCUSSION: While on an IFR flight, a pilot emerges from a cloud to find himself within 300 ft. of a helicopter. A hazardous macho reaction would be to fly a little closer, just to "show" the other pilot. Macho hazardous thoughts include "I will show you."

Answer (A) is incorrect. A reaction of "not too concerned; everything will be all right" is one of invulnerability, not macho. Answer (C) is incorrect. A reaction of quickly turning away and diving to avoid a collision is an impulsivity reaction, not a macho reaction.

37. What is the first step in neutralizing a hazardous attitude in the ADM process?

A. Dealing with improper judgment.

B. Recognition of hazardous thoughts.

C. Recognition of invulnerability in the situation.

Answer (B) is correct. *(AC 60-22)*

DISCUSSION: The first step in neutralizing hazardous attitudes is recognizing hazardous thoughts. When a pilot recognizes a hazardous thought, (s)he then should correct it by stating the corresponding antidote.

Answer (A) is incorrect. Recognizing hazardous thoughts, not dealing with improper judgment, is the first step in neutralizing hazardous attitudes. Answer (C) is incorrect. Recognizing hazardous thoughts, not the invulnerability in the situation, is the first step in neutralizing hazardous attitudes.

38. A pilot and friends are going to fly to an out-of-town football game. When the passengers arrive, the pilot determines that they will be over the maximum gross weight for takeoff with the existing fuel load. Which of the following alternatives best illustrates the RESIGNATION reaction?

A. Well, nobody told him about the extra weight.

B. Weight and balance is a formality forced on pilots by the FAA.

C. He can't wait around to de-fuel, they have to get there on time.

Answer (A) is correct. *(AC 60-22)*

DISCUSSION: A pilot and his friends are going on a flight, but when the passengers arrive, the pilot determines the loaded airplane will be over maximum gross weight for takeoff with the existing fuel load. A resignation reaction by the pilot would be that nobody told him about the extra weight. When the responsibility is assumed to be someone else's, a pilot is in the hazardous thinking pattern of resignation.

Answer (B) is incorrect. Considering weight and balance to be a formality forced on pilots by the FAA (ignoring the rules) is a hazardous attitude of antiauthority, not resignation. Answer (C) is incorrect. The pilot who cannot wait around to defuel because of a need to get somewhere on time illustrates the impulsivity ("I must act now; there is no time"), not the resignation, hazardous attitude.

39. Hazardous attitudes which contribute to poor pilot judgment can be effectively counteracted by

A. early recognition of hazardous thoughts.

B. taking meaningful steps to be more assertive with attitudes.

C. redirecting that hazardous attitude so that appropriate action can be taken.

Answer (C) is correct. *(AC 60-22)*

DISCUSSION: Hazardous attitudes that contribute to poor pilot judgment can be effectively counteracted by redirecting those hazardous attitudes so that appropriate action can be taken.

Answer (A) is incorrect. While early recognition of hazardous thoughts is important as an initial step in dealing with hazardous attitudes, they can be effectively counteracted only by redirecting them so that appropriate action can be taken. Answer (B) is incorrect. Being more assertive with attitudes, if those attitudes are hazardous, would be counterproductive to safety, while redirecting the hazardous attitudes will allow appropriate action to be taken in dealing with them.

40. What should a pilot do when recognizing a thought as hazardous?

A. Avoid developing this hazardous thought.

B. Develop this hazardous thought and follow through with modified action.

C. Label that thought as hazardous, then correct that thought by stating the corresponding learned antidote.

Answer (C) is correct. *(AC 60-22)*

DISCUSSION: When a pilot recognizes a hazardous thought, the pilot should label it as hazardous and then correct it by stating the corresponding learned antidote.

Answer (A) is incorrect. Once a hazardous thought is recognized, it is too late to avoid developing the thought. The pilot should label the thought as hazardous and then correct it by stating the corresponding learned antidote. Answer (B) is incorrect. Once a hazardous thought is recognized, it should not be developed. Instead, the pilot should label the thought as hazardous and then correct it by stating the corresponding learned antidote.

41. When a pilot recognizes a hazardous thought, he or she then should correct it by stating the corresponding antidote. Which of the following is the antidote for antiauthority?

A. Not so fast. Think first.

B. It could happen to me.

C. Follow the rules. They are usually right.

Answer (C) is correct. *(AC 60-22)*

DISCUSSION: When you recognize a hazardous thought, you should then correct it by stating the corresponding antidote. The antidote for an antiauthority ("Do not tell me") attitude is "Follow the rules. They are usually right."

Answer (A) is incorrect. "Not so fast. Think first" is the antidote for the impulsivity, not the antiauthority, attitude. Answer (B) is incorrect. "It could happen to me" is the antidote for the invulnerability ("It will not happen to me"), not the antiauthority, attitude.

42. When a pilot recognizes a hazardous thought, he or she then should correct it by stating the corresponding antidote. Which of the following is the antidote for MACHO?

A. Follow the rules. They are usually right.

B. Not so fast. Think first.

C. Taking chances is foolish.

Answer (C) is correct. *(AC 60-22)*

DISCUSSION: The antidote for the macho hazardous attitude is: "Taking chances is foolish."

Answer (A) is incorrect. "Taking chances is foolish" is the antidote for macho, not "Follow the rules. They are usually right," which is the antidote for antiauthority. Answer (B) is incorrect. "Taking chances is foolish" is the antidote for macho, rather than "Not so fast. Think first," which is the antidote for impulsivity.

43. What does good cockpit stress management begin with?

A. Knowing what causes stress.

B. Eliminating life and cockpit stress issues.

C. Good life stress management.

Answer (C) is correct. *(AC 60-22)*

DISCUSSION: Good cockpit stress management begins with good life stress management, since you will bring the stress in your life into the cockpit with you.

Answer (A) is incorrect. Knowing what causes stress is required to reduce stress associated with crisis management in the air, but it is not the beginning of cockpit stress management. Answer (B) is incorrect. Eliminating life and cockpit stress issues is impossible. In fact, stress is a necessary part of life that increases motivation and heightens your response to meet a challenge.

44. To help manage cockpit stress, pilots must

A. be aware of life stress situations that are similar to those in flying.

B. condition themselves to relax and think rationally when stress appears.

C. avoid situations that will degrade their abilities to handle cockpit responsibilities.

Answer (B) is correct. *(AC 60-22)*

DISCUSSION: To help manage cockpit stress, pilots must condition themselves to relax and think rationally when stress occurs.

Answer (A) is incorrect. Pilots must condition themselves to relax and think rationally when stress occurs since many of the stress coping techniques practiced for life stress management are not usually practical in flight. Answer (C) is incorrect. Pilots must condition themselves to relax and think rationally when unavoidable situations occur that could increase stress and degrade their abilities.

45. The Decide Model is comprised of a 6-step process to provide a pilot a logical way of approaching Aeronautical Decision Making. These steps are:

A. Detect, estimate, choose, identify, do, and evaluate.

B. Determine, evaluate, choose, identify, do, and eliminate.

C. Determine, eliminate, choose, identify, detect, and evaluate.

Answer (A) is correct. *(AC 60-22)*

DISCUSSION: The Decide Model, comprised of a six-step process, is intended to provide you with a logical way of approaching decision making. The six steps (in order) are detect, estimate, choose, identify, do, and evaluate.

Answer (B) is incorrect. Detect, not determine, and estimate, not eliminate, are steps in the Decide Model. Answer (C) is incorrect. Do, not determine, and estimate, not eliminate, are steps in the Decide Model.

46. Which of the following is the first step of the DECIDE Model for effective risk management and Aeronautical Decision Making (ADM)?

A. Detect.

B. Identify.

C. Evaluate.

Answer (A) is correct. *(AC 60-22)*

DISCUSSION: The DECIDE Model, comprised of a six-step process, is intended to provide you with a logical way of approaching decision making. The six steps (in order) are detect, estimate, choose, identify, do, and evaluate.

Answer (B) is incorrect. Identify is the fourth step, not the first step, in the DECIDE Model. Answer (C) is incorrect. Evaluate is the final step, not the first step, in the DECIDE Model.

47. Which of the following is the final step of the Decide Model for effective risk management and Aeronautical Decision Making?

A. Estimate.

B. Evaluate.

C. Eliminate.

Answer (B) is correct. *(AC 60-22)*

DISCUSSION: The Decide Model, comprised of a six-step process, is intended to provide you with a logical way of approaching decision making. The six steps (in order) are detect, estimate, choose, identify, do, and evaluate.

Answer (A) is incorrect. Estimate is the second step, not the final step, in the Decide Model. Answer (C) is incorrect. Eliminate is not a step in the Decide Model.

END OF STUDY UNIT

“Just for the record I previously used only Gleim study guides for my instrument, commercial, and instructor tests, with first time high passing scores on all of them! Thanks again! You can quote me and my belief that the Gleim Study Guides are the best in the industry.”

Jay Rickmeyer

“Your courses are incredible. I tried "the other guys" and made them send me my money back after completion.”

HRSIII

“Keep up the fabulous work; your customer awareness is exemplary! I am a committed Gleim customer.”

Ken Norris

“I have used the Gleim flight training products for private, instrument, commercial, and multi-engine. They have been very thorough in preparing me for my testing. My wife will use their instrument course as she adds on this rating.”

David

“I passed the FAA exam successfully (88%) a few weeks ago. Many thanks to you. Your online learning program was an essential tool to success. Thank you 1000x. The ATP kit is very good because it allows needed transfer of knowledge in a very efficient & structural way.”

Michel Mesmaekers

What our customers are saying

STUDY UNIT SEVEN
AVIATION WEATHER

(5 pages of outline)

This study unit contains outlines of major concepts tested, sample test questions and answers regarding aviation weather, and an explanation of each answer. The table of contents above lists each subunit within this study unit, the number of questions pertaining to that particular subunit, and the pages on which the outlines and questions begin, respectively.

Recall that the **sole purpose** of this book is to expedite your passing of the FAA pilot knowledge test for the commercial pilot certificate. Accordingly, all extraneous material (i.e., topics or regulations not directly tested on the FAA pilot knowledge test) is omitted, even though much more knowledge is necessary to become a proficient commercial pilot. This additional material is presented in *Pilot Handbook* and *Commercial Pilot Flight Maneuvers and Practical Test Prep*, available from Gleim Publications, Inc. See the product listing at the back of the book and order online at www.gleim.com.

7.1 CAUSES OF WEATHER

1. Every physical process of weather is accompanied by, or is a result of, heat exchange.
2. Moisture is added to a parcel of air by evaporation and sublimation.
3. Wind is caused by pressure differences with wind flowing from high-pressure areas to low-pressure areas.
   a. When the isobars are close together, the pressure gradient force is greater, which results in a stronger wind.
4. The Coriolis force deflects wind to the right in the Northern Hemisphere.
   a. Coriolis force tends to counterbalance the horizontal pressure gradient, causing wind to flow parallel to the isobars.
5. A cold front occlusion occurs when the air ahead of the warm front is warmer than the air behind the overtaking cold front.

7.2 HIGH/LOW PRESSURE AREAS

1. A high-pressure area or ridge is an area of descending air.
   a. The general circulation of air in a high-pressure area in the Northern Hemisphere is outward, downward, and clockwise.
2. A low-pressure area or trough is an area of rising air.
   a. The circulation of air (wind system) in a low-pressure area in the Northern Hemisphere is cyclonic, i.e., counterclockwise.
   b. Thus, when flying into such a low-pressure area, the wind direction and velocity will be from the left and increasing.
   c. A low-pressure area is generally an area of unfavorable weather conditions.
3. The Coriolis force prevents wind from flowing directly from high-pressure areas to low-pressure areas and produces the associated circulations.

7.3 JET STREAM

1. In the middle latitudes during the winter months, the jet stream shifts south and the wind speed increases.
   a. It is normally weaker and farther north in the summer.
2. Clear air turbulence (CAT) is typically found in an upper trough on the polar side of the jet stream.
3. The jet stream and associated CAT can sometimes be visually identified by long streaks of cirrus clouds.
4. Strong wind shears can be expected on the low-pressure side of a jet stream core where the wind speed at the core is greater than 110 kt.
5. A curving jet stream means there are abrupt weather system changes, which lend themselves to more violent turbulence.
6. The tropopause is the layer of air above the troposphere and is characterized by an abrupt change in the temperature lapse rate.

7.4 TEMPERATURE

1. Standard temperature is 15°C (59°F) at sea level; the standard lapse rate is 2°C per 1,000 ft.
   a. Thus, the standard temperature at any altitude is 15°C minus (2 times the altitude in thousands of feet).
   b. EXAMPLE: Standard temperature at 20,000 ft. is 15°C – (2 × 20) = –25°C.
2. Standard sea level pressure is 29.92 in. Hg or 1013.2 mb.
3. The temperature/dew point spread decreases as relative humidity increases.

7.5 CLOUDS

1. When air is being forced to ascend, the stability of air before lifting occurs determines the structure or type of clouds which will form.
2. When a cold air mass moves over a warm surface, the result is unstable air.
   a. Unstable conditions, moist air, and a lifting action provide cumuliform clouds, good visibility, showery rain, and possible clear icing in clouds.
   b. Towering cumulus clouds indicate convective turbulence.

3. The altitude of cumuliform cloud bases can be estimated using surface temperature/dew point spread.
   a. Unsaturated air in a convective current cools at about 3.0°C per 1,000 ft., and dew point decreases about 0.5°C per 1,000 ft.
   b. Thus, temperature and dew point converge at about 2.5°C per 1,000 ft.
   c. Cloud bases are at the altitude where the temperature and dew point are the same.
4. Standing lenticular altocumulus clouds are a good indication of very strong turbulence.
5. Virga describes streamers of precipitation trailing beneath clouds but evaporating before reaching the ground.

7.6 FOG

1. Evaporation or precipitation-induced fog arises from drops of warm rain or drizzle falling through cool air.
   a. This kind of fog is produced by frontal activity.
   b. Precipitation-induced fog is an in-flight hazard most commonly associated with warm fronts.
2. A situation in which advection fog forms is when an air mass moves inland from the coastline during winter.
   a. It is most common along coastal areas.
   b. Wind stronger than 15 kt. dissipates or lifts the fog into low stratus clouds.
   c. It is usually more persistent than radiation fog and can appear suddenly during day or night.
3. Radiation fog is the result of a surface-based temperature inversion that occurs on clear, cool nights with calm or light wind.
   a. It is restricted to land areas.
4. Steam fog occurs when cold air moves over relatively warm water or wet ground.

7.7 STABILITY

1. The stability of the atmosphere is determined by the ambient lapse rate, which is the decrease in temperature with altitude.
2. Warming from below decreases the stability of an air mass.
   a. Cooling from below increases the stability of an air mass.
3. The formation of either predominantly stratiform or cumuliform clouds is dependent upon the stability of the air being lifted.
   a. If clouds form as a result of stable, moist air ascending a mountain slope, the clouds will be stratus type.
4. The lifted index is computed as if a parcel of air near the surface were lifted to the 500-mb level (18,000 ft. MSL).
5. Convective circulation is caused by unequal heating of air by the Earth's surface.
   a. An example is sea and land breezes created by land absorbing and radiating heat faster than water.
   b. Cool air sinks because it is denser than warm air. The sinking cool air displaces the warmer, less dense air, which then rises.

Characteristics of Stable and Unstable Air

	Stable	Unstable
Temperature decreases as altitude increases	Little or none	More than normal so air rises as soon as lifting action occurs
Clouds	Stratiform Flat, layered	Cumuliform Billowy, cumulus
Turbulence	Relatively little	Turbulent, strong updrafts
Visibility	Poor	Good
Precipitation	Steady	Showery, intermittent

7.8 THUNDERSTORMS AND ICING

1. Extreme turbulence in a thunderstorm is indicated by very frequent lightning and roll clouds on the leading edge of cumulonimbus clouds.
   a. A lifting action and unstable, moist air are necessary for the formation of cumulonimbus clouds.
2. The life of a thunderstorm can be divided into three stages:
   a. The cumulus stage is associated with continuous updraft.
   b. The mature stage is indicated by the start of rain at the Earth's surface.
   c. The dissipating stage is characterized predominantly by downdrafts.
3. Outside thunderstorm clouds, shear turbulence can be encountered 20 NM laterally from severe storms.
4. A squall line is a non-frontal, narrow band of active thunderstorms.
   a. It often contains severe steady-state thunderstorms and presents the single most intense weather hazard to aircraft.
   b. It is also associated with destructive winds, heavy hail, and tornadoes.
5. Airborne weather avoidance radar is designed to identify areas of precipitation, especially heavy precipitation, which may signify an active thunderstorm.
   a. Instrument weather conditions can be caused by clouds that are not indicated on radar screens.
   b. Intense radar echoes should be avoided by at least 20 NM.
      1) Thus, 40 NM should exist between intense echoes before you attempt to fly between them.
6. Hail, an in-flight hazard, is likely to be associated with cumulonimbus clouds.
   a. Hailstones may be encountered in clear air several miles from a thunderstorm.
7. When a warm front (or a cold front) is about to pass, any rain freezes as it falls from the warmer air into air having a temperature of 32°F or less.
   a. As the freezing rain continues to fall, it turns into ice pellets.
   b. Thus, ice pellets indicate freezing rain at a higher altitude.

7.9 TURBULENCE

1. Light turbulence momentarily causes slight, erratic changes in altitude and/or attitude.
2. Moderate turbulence causes changes in altitude and/or attitude, but aircraft control remains positive.
   a. Moderate turbulence should be expected where vertical wind shear exceeds 6 kt. per 1,000 ft.
3. Clear air turbulence (CAT) is a higher-level phenomenon, i.e., above 15,000 ft. AGL, not associated with cumuliform cloudiness.
4. When wind flows over ridges or mountain ranges, it flows up the windward side and down the leeward side.
   a. A pilot who approaches mountainous terrain from the leeward side may be forced into the side of the mountain by the downward-flowing air.
   b. Wave formation should be expected with stable air at mountaintop altitude and winds of at least 20 kt. across the mountaintop.
      1) The most dangerous feature of mountain waves is the turbulent areas in and below rotor clouds.
5. Convective currents are most active on warm summer afternoons when winds are light.

7.10 WIND SHEAR

1. Wind shear is a change in wind direction and/or speed within a very short distance in the atmosphere.
   a. It can be present at any level and can exist in both a horizontal and vertical direction.
2. Hazardous wind shear is commonly encountered during periods of strong temperature inversion and near thunderstorms.
   a. Low-level wind shear may occur when there is a low-level temperature inversion with strong winds above the inversion.
3. During an approach, possible wind shear is indicated by changes in the power and vertical velocity required to remain on the proper glide path.
   a. A sudden decrease in headwind results in a loss of indicated airspeed equal to the decrease in wind velocity.
4. While approaching for landing when either possible wind shear or convective turbulence is indicated, you should increase approach airspeed slightly above normal to avoid stalling.

QUESTIONS AND ANSWER EXPLANATIONS: All of the commercial pilot knowledge test questions chosen by the FAA for release as well as additional questions selected by Gleim relating to the material in the previous outlines are reproduced on the following pages. These questions have been organized into the same subunits as the outlines. To the immediate right of each question are the correct answer and answer explanation. You should cover these answers and answer explanations while responding to the questions. Refer to the general discussion in the Introduction on how to take the FAA knowledge test.

Remember that the questions from the FAA knowledge test bank have been reordered by topic and organized into a meaningful sequence. Also, the first line of the answer explanation gives the citation of the authoritative source for the answer.

QUESTIONS

7.1 Causes of Weather

1. Every physical process of weather is accompanied by or is the result of

A. a heat exchange.

B. the movement of air.

C. a pressure differential.

Answer (A) is correct. *(AvW Chap 1)*

DISCUSSION: Every physical process of weather is accompanied by, or is the result of, a heat exchange. A heat differential (difference between the temperatures of two air masses) causes a differential in pressure, which in turn causes movement of air. Heat exchanges occur constantly, e.g., melting, cooling, evaporation, condensation, updrafts, downdrafts, wind, etc.

Answer (B) is incorrect. Movement of air is caused by heat exchanges. Answer (C) is incorrect. Pressure differentials are caused by heat exchanges.

2. Moisture is added to a parcel of air by

A. sublimation and condensation.

B. evaporation and condensation.

C. evaporation and sublimation.

Answer (C) is correct. *(AvW Chap 5)*

DISCUSSION: Moisture is added to a parcel of air when liquid water or ice are changed into water vapor. Evaporation is the change from liquid water to water vapor. Sublimation is the change from ice directly to water vapor, without the intervening liquid stage.

Answer (A) is incorrect. Condensation is the changing of water vapor into liquid water, which removes (not adds) moisture from the air. Answer (B) is incorrect. Condensation is the changing of water vapor into liquid water, which removes (not adds) moisture from the air.

3. In the Northern Hemisphere, the wind is deflected to the

A. right by Coriolis force.

B. right by surface friction.

C. left by Coriolis force.

Answer (A) is correct. *(AvW Chap 4)*

DISCUSSION: Coriolis force, caused by the Earth's rotation, deflects air movements to the right in the Northern Hemisphere and to the left in the Southern Hemisphere. Coriolis force is at a right angle to wind direction and is directly proportional to wind speed.

Answer (B) is incorrect. Surface friction slows wind speed, which lessens the deflection to the right caused by Coriolis force. Answer (C) is incorrect. Wind is deflected to the left by Coriolis force in the Southern (not Northern) Hemisphere.

4. Why does the wind have a tendency to flow parallel to the isobars above the friction level?

A. Coriolis force tends to counterbalance the horizontal pressure gradient.

B. Coriolis force acts perpendicular to a line connecting the highs and lows.

C. Friction of the air with the Earth deflects the air perpendicular to the pressure gradient.

Answer (A) is correct. *(AvW Chap 4)*

DISCUSSION: Normally, wind flows from areas of high pressure to areas of low pressure. Wind is deflected by the Coriolis force, however. This force, which is the result of the Earth's rotation, deflects wind to the right in the Northern Hemisphere, counterbalancing the horizontal pressure gradient. Its effects are lessened by friction with the Earth's surface at altitudes closer to the surface.

Answer (B) is incorrect. The Coriolis force acts at a right angle to wind direction in direct proportion to wind speed. Also, the Coriolis force varies with latitude from zero at the equator to maximum at the poles. Answer (C) is incorrect. Surface friction tends to diminish the Coriolis force and permits the wind to follow the pressure gradient force.

5. With regard to windflow patterns shown on surface analysis charts; when the isobars are

A. close together, the pressure gradient force is slight and wind velocities are weaker.

B. not close together, the pressure gradient force is greater and wind velocities are stronger.

C. close together, the pressure gradient force is greater and wind velocities are stronger.

Answer (C) is correct. *(AvW Chap 4)*

DISCUSSION: Pressure differences create a force, the pressure gradient force, which drives the wind from higher pressure to lower pressure. This force is perpendicular to isobars, or pressure contours. The closer the spacing of isobars, the stronger the pressure gradient force and the stronger the wind.

Answer (A) is incorrect. When the isobars are close together, the pressure gradient force and wind are stronger (not weaker). Answer (B) is incorrect. When the isobars are not close together, the pressure gradient force and wind are weaker (not stronger).

6. What causes wind?

A. The Earth's rotation.

B. Air mass modification.

C. Pressure differences.

Answer (C) is correct. *(AvW Chap 4)*

DISCUSSION: Wind is caused by pressure differences with wind flowing from high-pressure areas to low-pressure areas. These pressure differences arise from the different heating of the Earth's surface.

Answer (A) is incorrect. The Earth's rotation results in Coriolis force, which deflects wind but does not cause wind. It deflects it to the right in the Northern Hemisphere. Answer (B) is incorrect. Air mass modification refers to air masses taking on the properties of the underlying region(s) after it leaves its source region.

7. Which is true regarding a cold front occlusion? The air ahead of the warm front

A. is colder than the air behind the overtaking cold front.

B. is warmer than the air behind the overtaking cold front.

C. has the same temperature as the air behind the overtaking cold front.

Answer (B) is correct. *(AvW Chap 8)*

DISCUSSION: An occluded front, or occlusion, occurs when a cold front overtakes a warm front. A cold front occlusion occurs when the cool air ahead of the warm front is warmer than the cold air behind the overtaking cold front, lifting the warm front aloft.

Answer (A) is incorrect. When the cool air ahead of the warm front is colder than that behind the cold front, a warm front (not cold front) occlusion occurs. Answer (C) is incorrect. When the cool air ahead of the warm front has the same temperature as that behind the cold front, a temperature inversion (not a cold front occlusion) is likely to occur.

8. On Surface Analysis Charts, widely spaced isobars indicate a

A. weak pressure gradient.

B. strong pressure gradient.

C. relatively turbulent wind.

Answer (A) is correct. *(PHAK Chap 11)*

DISCUSSION: Weak pressure gradients are represented by isobars that are spaced far apart and are indicative of light winds.

Answer (B) is incorrect. Strong pressure gradients are represented by isobars that are spaced close together and are indicative of strong winds. Answer (C) is incorrect. The Surface Analysis Charts do not give direct information about turbulent winds.

7.2 High/Low Pressure Areas

9. Which is true with respect to a high- or low-pressure system?

A. A high-pressure area or ridge is an area of rising air.

B. A low-pressure area or trough is an area of descending air.

C. A high-pressure area or ridge is an area of descending air.

Answer (C) is correct. *(AvW Chap 4)*

DISCUSSION: High-pressure air descends because it is heavier than low-pressure air. Ridge refers to an elongated area of high pressure.

Answer (A) is incorrect. High-pressure air descends, not rises. Answer (B) is incorrect. Low-pressure air rises, not descends.

10. Which is true regarding high- or low-pressure systems?

A. A high-pressure area or ridge is an area of rising air.

B. A low-pressure area or trough is an area of rising air.

C. Both high- and low-pressure areas are characterized by descending air.

Answer (B) is correct. *(AvW Chap 4)*

DISCUSSION: Low-pressure air rises because it weighs less than high-pressure air. Trough refers to an elongated area of low pressure.

Answer (A) is incorrect. High-pressure air descends, not rises. Answer (C) is incorrect. High-pressure air descends, and low-pressure air rises, not descends.

11. While flying cross-country in the Northern Hemisphere, you experience a continuous left crosswind which is associated with a major wind system. This indicates that you

A. are flying toward an area of generally unfavorable weather conditions.

B. have flown from an area of unfavorable weather conditions.

C. cannot determine weather conditions without knowing pressure changes.

Answer (A) is correct. *(AvW Chap 4)*

DISCUSSION: Due to the counterclockwise circulation around a low pressure area in the Northern Hemisphere, a continuous left crosswind indicates that you are flying into such an area. Low pressure areas are areas of rising air that are conducive to cloudiness and precipitation -- generally unfavorable weather conditions.

Answer (B) is incorrect. When flying away from unfavorable weather, you are generally flying out of a low, which means you should have a right, not left, crosswind. Answer (C) is incorrect. The wind can give you a general indication of pressure changes and thus weather.

12. When flying into a low-pressure area in the Northern Hemisphere, the wind direction and velocity will be from the

A. left and decreasing.

B. left and increasing.

C. right and decreasing.

Answer (B) is correct. *(AvW Chap 4)*

DISCUSSION: When flying into a low-pressure area, the wind is flowing counterclockwise and thus will be from the left. Also, winds tend to be greater in low-pressure systems than in high-pressure systems, so the velocity will increase as you fly into the area.

Answer (A) is incorrect. The wind is usually increasing, not decreasing, as you fly into a low-pressure area. Answer (C) is incorrect. The wind will be from the left, not right, and the wind is usually increasing, not decreasing, as you fly into a low pressure area.

13. What prevents air from flowing directly from high-pressure areas to low-pressure areas?

A. Coriolis force.

B. Surface friction.

C. Pressure gradient force.

Answer (A) is correct. *(AvW Chap 4)*

DISCUSSION: Coriolis force, caused by the Earth's rotation, deflects air movements to the right in the Northern Hemisphere and to the left in the Southern Hemisphere. Coriolis force is at a right angle to wind direction and is directly proportional to wind speed. Thus, air is deflected to the right as it flows from high-pressure areas to low-pressure areas.

Answer (B) is incorrect. Surface friction encourages air movement directly from highs to lows by decreasing wind speed, which decreases the Coriolis force effect. Answer (C) is incorrect. The pressure gradient force causes the initial movement from high-pressure areas to low-pressure areas.

14. The general circulation of air associated with a high-pressure area in the Northern Hemisphere is

A. outward, downward, and clockwise.

B. outward, upward, and clockwise.

C. inward, downward, and clockwise.

Answer (A) is correct. *(AvW Chap 4)*

DISCUSSION: Air flows outward from a high-pressure area, causing a descending column of air within the high. As the air moves outward, it is deflected to the right by Coriolis force, resulting in a clockwise rotation.

Answer (B) is incorrect. Air flows downward (not upward) in a high-pressure area. Answer (C) is incorrect. Air flows outward (not inward) from a high-pressure area.

15. The wind system associated with a low-pressure area in the Northern Hemisphere is

A. an anticyclone and is caused by descending cold air.

B. a cyclone and is caused by Coriolis force.

C. an anticyclone and is caused by Coriolis force.

Answer (B) is correct. *(AvW Chap 4)*

DISCUSSION: Air flowing into a low-pressure area is deflected to the right in the Northern Hemisphere, resulting in a counterclockwise (or cyclonic) circulation.

Answer (A) is incorrect. An anticyclone and descending air describes a high- (not low-) pressure area. Answer (C) is incorrect. An anticyclone caused by Coriolis force describes a high- (not low-) pressure area.

7.3 Jet Stream

16. During the winter months in the middle latitudes, the jet stream shifts toward the

A. north and speed decreases.

B. south and speed increases.

C. north and speed increases.

Answer (B) is correct. *(AvW Chap 13)*

DISCUSSION: The jet stream is a narrow band of strong winds meandering through the atmosphere at an altitude near the tropopause. In the mid-latitudes, the wind speed in the jet stream is considerably stronger in winter than in summer. Also, the jet stream shifts farther south in winter than in summer.

Answer (A) is incorrect. The jet stream shifts south (not north) and speed increases (not decreases) in the winter months. Answer (C) is incorrect. The jet stream shifts south (not north) in the winter months.

17. The strength and location of the jet stream is normally

A. weaker and farther north in the summer.

B. stronger and farther north in the winter.

C. stronger and farther north in the summer.

Answer (A) is correct. *(AvW Chap 13)*

DISCUSSION: The jet stream is a narrow band of strong winds meandering through the atmosphere at an altitude near the tropopause. In the mid-latitudes, the wind speed in the jet stream is considerably stronger in winter than in summer. Also, the jet stream shifts farther south in winter than in summer.

Answer (B) is incorrect. The jet stream is normally farther south (not north) in the winter. Answer (C) is incorrect. The jet stream is normally weaker in the summer.

18. A common location of clear air turbulence is

A. in an upper trough on the polar side of a jet stream.

B. near a ridge aloft on the equatorial side of a high-pressure flow.

C. south of an east/west oriented high-pressure ridge in its dissipating stage.

Answer (A) is correct. *(AvW Chap 13)*

DISCUSSION: The typical location of clear air turbulence is an upper trough on the cold (polar) side of the jet stream.

Answer (B) is incorrect. Most clear air turbulence is on the northern or polar (not equatorial) side of contrasting air masses. Answer (C) is incorrect. Most clear air turbulence is on the northern or polar (not southern) side of contrasting air masses.

19. The jet stream and associated clear air turbulence can sometimes be visually identified in flight by

A. dust or haze at flight level.

B. long streaks of cirrus clouds.

C. a constant outside air temperature.

Answer (B) is correct. *(AvW Chap 13)*

DISCUSSION: Streamlined, windswept cirrus clouds always indicate very strong upper winds.

Answer (A) is incorrect. The presence of dust or haze means there is not much wind or air movement to dissipate the particles. Answer (C) is incorrect. Clear air turbulence is caused by mixing cold and warm air at different pressure levels.

20. A strong wind shear can be expected

A. in the jetstream front above a core having a speed of 60 to 90 knots.

B. if the 5°C isotherms are spaced between 7° to 10° of latitude.

C. on the low-pressure side of a jetstream core where the speed at the core is stronger than 110 knots.

Answer (C) is correct. *(AC 00-30B)*

DISCUSSION: When the speed of the jet stream is in excess of 110 kt., strong wind shears can be expected on the lower-pressure side.

Answer (A) is incorrect. Wind speeds of less than 100 kt. are not dramatic in the jet stream. Also, the turbulence is usually to the sides or beneath the core. Answer (B) is incorrect. This does not indicate abrupt temperature or wind changes (which cause wind shear).

21. Which type of jetstream can be expected to cause the greater turbulence?

A. A straight jetstream associated with a low-pressure trough.

B. A curving jetstream associated with a deep low-pressure trough.

C. A jetstream occurring during the summer at the lower latitudes.

Answer (B) is correct. *(AvW Chap 13)*

DISCUSSION: A curving jet stream indicates abrupt weather system changes, which lend themselves to more violent turbulence. In general, the more pronounced the difference in weather systems, the greater the potential for very strong turbulence.

Answer (A) is incorrect. A straight jet stream normally produces less turbulence than a curving jet stream. Answer (C) is incorrect. The jet stream is weaker in the summer, when it usually does not get to the lower latitudes.

22. Which feature is associated with the tropopause?

A. Constant height above the Earth.
B. Abrupt change in temperature lapse rate.
C. Absolute upper limit of cloud formation.

Answer (B) is correct. *(AvW Chap 13)*
DISCUSSION: The tropopause is the transition layer of atmosphere between the troposphere and the stratosphere. Height of the tropopause varies from about 65,000 ft. over the Equator to 20,000 ft. or lower over the poles. A characteristic of the tropopause is an abrupt change in the temperature lapse rate, i.e., the rate at which temperature decreases with height.
Answer (A) is incorrect. The tropopause is considerably closer to the Earth's surface at the poles than at the equator. Answer (C) is incorrect. Clouds may form above the tropopause.

7.4 Temperature

23. What is the standard temperature at 10,000 feet?

A. –5°C.
B. –15°C.
C. +5°C.

Answer (A) is correct. *(AvW Chap 2)*
DISCUSSION: Standard temperature is 15°C at sea level, and the standard lapse rate is 2°C per 1,000 ft. Thus, at 10,000 ft., the standard temperature would be 20°C colder than at sea level, or –5°C (15°C – 20°C).
Answer (B) is incorrect. The standard temperature at 15,000 ft. (not 10,000 ft.) is –15°C. Answer (C) is incorrect. The standard temperature at 5,000 ft. (not 10,000 ft.) is +5°C.

24. What are the standard temperature and pressure values for sea level?

A. 15°C and 29.92" Hg.
B. 59°F and 1013.2" Hg.
C. 15°C and 29.92 Mb.

Answer (A) is correct. *(AvW Chap 1)*
DISCUSSION: Standard temperature at sea level is defined as 15°C, or 59°F. Standard sea-level pressure is 29.92 in. Hg, or 1013.2 mb.
Answer (B) is incorrect. Standard sea-level pressure is 1013.2 mb (not in. Hg). Answer (C) is incorrect. Standard sea-level pressure is 29.92 in. Hg (not mb).

25. What is the standard temperature at 20,000 feet?

A. –15°C.
B. –20°C.
C. –25°C.

Answer (C) is correct. *(AvW Chap 2)*
DISCUSSION: Standard temperature is 15°C at sea level and the standard lapse rate is 2°C per 1,000 ft. Thus, at 20,000 ft., the standard temperature would be 40°C colder than at sea level, or –25°C (15°C – 40°C).
Answer (A) is incorrect. The standard temperature at 15,000 ft. (not 20,000 ft.) is –15°C. Answer (B) is incorrect. The standard temperature at 17,500 ft. (not 20,000 ft.) is –20°C.

26. Which is true regarding actual air temperature and dew point temperature spread? The temperature spread

A. decreases as the relative humidity decreases.
B. decreases as the relative humidity increases.
C. increases as the relative humidity increases.

Answer (B) is correct. *(AvW Chap 5)*
DISCUSSION: Dew point refers to the temperature to which air must be cooled to become saturated by the water vapor already present in the air. Thus, as the relative humidity increases, the dew point-temperature spread decreases. As relative humidity increases to 100%, the dew point approaches the temperature and the spread approaches zero.
Answer (A) is incorrect. As relative humidity decreases, the temperature/dew point spread increases (not decreases). Answer (C) is incorrect. The temperature/dew point spread decreases (not increases) as relative humidity increases.

27. What is the standard temperature at 6,500 feet?

A. 15°C.
B. 2°C.
C. 38°F.

Answer (B) is correct. *(AvW Chap 2)*
DISCUSSION: Standard temperature is 15°C at sea level, and the standard lapse rate is 2°C per 1,000 ft. Thus, at 6,500 ft., the standard temperature would be 13°C colder than at sea level, or 2°C (15°C – 13°C).
Answer (A) is incorrect. The standard temperature at sea level is 15°C. Answer (C) is incorrect. At 6,000 feet, the temperature would be approximately 3.4°C or 38.1°F.

7.5 Clouds

28. Which cloud types would indicate convective turbulence?

A. Cirrus clouds.

B. Nimbostratus clouds.

C. Towering cumulus clouds.

Answer (C) is correct. *(AvW Chap 7)*

DISCUSSION: Towering cumulus clouds signify a relatively deep layer of unstable air, thus indicating very strong convective turbulence.

Answer (A) is incorrect. Cirrus clouds are high, thin, feathery ice crystal clouds in patches and narrow bands that are not generated by any convective activity. Answer (B) is incorrect. Nimbostratus are gray or dark, massive clouds, usually producing continuous rain or ice pellets. They form in stable air and do not produce convective activity or turbulence.

29. Which combination of weather-producing variables would likely result in cumuliform-type clouds, good visibility, and showery rain?

A. Stable, moist air and orographic lifting.

B. Unstable, moist air and orographic lifting.

C. Unstable, moist air and no lifting mechanism.

Answer (B) is correct. *(AvW Chap 8)*

DISCUSSION: Unstable, moist air accompanied by lifting usually results in showery rain, good visibility, and cumuliform clouds. Orographic lifting is caused by mountain forces, mountain winds, etc.

Answer (A) is incorrect. If air is stable, stratiform rather than cumuliform type clouds will form, and the rain will be steady (not showery). Answer (C) is incorrect. Cumuliform clouds and showery rain cannot exist without a lifting mechanism.

30. Which are characteristics of a cold air mass moving over a warm surface?

A. Cumuliform clouds, turbulence, and poor visibility.

B. Cumuliform clouds, turbulence, and good visibility.

C. Stratiform clouds, smooth air, and poor visibility.

Answer (B) is correct. *(AvW Chap 6)*

DISCUSSION: When a cold air mass moves over a warm surface, the warm air near the surface rises and creates an unstable condition. These convective currents give rise to cumuliform clouds, turbulence, and good visibility.

Answer (A) is incorrect. Unstable air lifts and blows haze away, resulting in good (not poor) visibility. Answer (C) is incorrect. Unstable conditions produce cumuliform (not stratiform) clouds.

31. What is the approximate base of the cumulus clouds if the temperature at 2,000 feet MSL is 10°C and the dew point is 1°C?

A. 3,000 feet MSL.

B. 4,000 feet MSL.

C. 6,000 feet MSL.

Answer (C) is correct. *(AvW Chap 6)*

DISCUSSION: The height of cumuliform cloud bases can be estimated using the surface temperature/dew point spread. Unsaturated air in a convective current cools at about 3°C per 1,000 ft., and dew point decreases about 0.5°C per 1,000 ft. Thus, temperature and dew point converge at about 2.5°C per 1,000 ft. Since the temperature/dew point spread was 9°C (10 – 1), temperature and dew point will converge at 3,600 ft. AGL (9 ÷ 2.5 = 3.6 or 3,600). The base of the cumulus clouds is approximately 5,600 ft. MSL (3,600 + 2,000).

Answer (A) is incorrect. This is the approximate base of the cumulus clouds if the dew point of 1°C, not the temperature/dew point spread of 9°C, is divided by 2.5. Answer (B) is incorrect. The base of the cumulus clouds is approximately 4,000 ft. AGL, not 4,000 ft. MSL.

32. What determines the structure or type of clouds which will form as a result of air being forced to ascend?

A. The method by which the air is lifted.

B. The stability of the air before lifting occurs.

C. The relative humidity of the air after lifting occurs.

Answer (B) is correct. *(AvW Chap 6)*

DISCUSSION: The structure of cloud types that form as a result of air being forced to ascend is determined by the stability of the air before lifting occurs. The difference between the existing lapse rate (the actual decrease in temperature with altitude) and the adiabatic rate of cooling in upward-moving air (cooling of air as a result of expansion as it ascends) determines the stability of the air. If the upward-moving air remains warmer than the surrounding air, the air is accelerated upward as a convective current. The air is considered unstable, and these conditions provide for the vertical development of cumulus clouds. If, on the other hand, the upward-moving air becomes colder than the surrounding air, it sinks. The air is considered stable, and stratiform clouds will form.

Answer (A) is incorrect. The stability of the air (not the lifting method) determines the type of clouds that will form. Answer (C) is incorrect. The relative humidity of the air determines the amount (not type) of clouds that will form.

33. The presence of standing lenticular altocumulus clouds is a good indication of

A. lenticular ice formation in calm air.

B. very strong turbulence.

C. heavy icing conditions.

Answer (B) is correct. *(AvW Chaps 7, 9)*

DISCUSSION: When stable air crosses a mountain barrier, turbulence usually results. Air flowing up the windward side is relatively smooth. Windflow across the barrier is laminar; i.e., it tends to flow in layers. The barrier may set up waves in these layers, much as waves develop on a disturbed water surface. Wave crests extend well above the highest mountain tops. Under each wave crest is a rotary circulation in which turbulence can be quite violent. Updrafts and downdrafts in the waves can also create very violent turbulence.

Answer (A) is incorrect. Standing lenticular clouds indicate turbulence (not calm air). Answer (C) is incorrect. Standing lenticular clouds indicate turbulence (not icing conditions).

34. Virga is best described as

A. streamers of precipitation trailing beneath clouds which evaporate before reaching the ground.

B. wall cloud torrents trailing beneath cumulonimbus clouds which dissipate before reaching the ground.

C. turbulent areas beneath cumulonimbus clouds.

Answer (A) is correct. *(AvW Chap 5)*

DISCUSSION: Virga is streamers of precipitation, either water or ice particles, falling from a cloud in wisps or streaks and evaporating before reaching the ground.

Answer (B) is incorrect. Virga is generally thin and wispy (not a torrential wall). Answer (C) is incorrect. Virga is precipitation (not turbulence).

7.6 Fog

35. Fog produced by frontal activity is a result of saturation due to

A. nocturnal cooling.

B. adiabatic cooling.

C. evaporation of precipitation.

Answer (C) is correct. *(AvW Chap 12)*

DISCUSSION: Fog produced by frontal activity is known as precipitation-induced fog. It arises from drops of warm rain or drizzle falling through cool air. The evaporation from the precipitation saturates the cool air and forms fog.

Answer (A) is incorrect. Nocturnal cooling forms radiation (not precipitation-induced) fog. Answer (B) is incorrect. Adiabatic cooling forms upslope (not precipitation-induced) fog.

36. Which in-flight hazard is most commonly associated with warm fronts?

A. Advection fog.

B. Radiation fog.

C. Precipitation-induced fog.

Answer (C) is correct. *(AvW Chap 6)*

DISCUSSION: Precipitation-induced fog arises from drops of warm rain or drizzle evaporating as it falls through cool air. This evaporation saturates the cool air and forms fog. This kind of fog can become quite dense and continue for an extended period of time. It is most commonly associated with warm fronts.

Answer (A) is incorrect. Advection fog results from the movement of warm, humid air over a cold water surface. Answer (B) is incorrect. Radiation fog results from terrestrial cooling of the Earth's surface on calm, clear nights.

37. A situation most conducive to the formation of advection fog is

A. a light breeze moving colder air over a water surface.

B. an air mass moving inland from the coastline during the winter.

C. a warm, moist air mass settling over a cool surface under no-wind conditions.

Answer (B) is correct. *(AvW Chap 12)*

DISCUSSION: Advection fog forms when moist air moves over colder ground or water. This type of fog is common when comparatively warm, moist oceanic air moves inland from the coastline during winter.

Answer (A) is incorrect. A light breeze moving colder air over a warmer water surface describes steam fog. Answer (C) is incorrect. A warm, moist air mass settling over a cool surface under no-wind conditions describes radiation fog.

38. Advection fog has drifted over a coastal airport during the day. What may tend to dissipate or lift this fog into low stratus clouds?

A. Nighttime cooling.

B. Surface radiation.

C. Wind 15 knots or stronger.

Answer (C) is correct. *(AvW Chap 12)*

DISCUSSION: Advection fog deepens as wind speed increases up to 15 kt. Wind much stronger than 15 kt. will lift the fog into a layer of low stratus or stratocumulus.

Answer (A) is incorrect. Nighttime cooling forms radiation fog (not low stratus clouds). Answer (B) is incorrect. Surface radiation forms radiation fog (not low stratus clouds).

39. What lifts advection fog into low stratus clouds?

A. Nighttime cooling.

B. Dryness of the underlying land mass.

C. Surface winds of approximately 15 knots or stronger.

Answer (C) is correct. *(AvW Chap 12)*

DISCUSSION: Advection fog deepens as wind speed increases up to 15 kt. Wind much stronger than 15 kt. lifts the fog into a layer of low stratus or stratocumulus.

Answer (A) is incorrect. Nighttime cooling forms radiation fog (not low stratus clouds). Answer (B) is incorrect. Dryness of the underlying land mass forms radiation fog (not low stratus clouds).

40. Which conditions are favorable for the formation of a surface based temperature inversion?

A. Clear, cool nights with calm or light wind.

B. Area of unstable air rapidly transferring heat from the surface.

C. Broad areas of cumulus clouds with smooth, level bases at the same altitude.

Answer (A) is correct. *(AvW Chap 12)*

DISCUSSION: A temperature inversion occurs when warm air exists over cooler air. When ground heat radiates out on clear nights, the cool ground surface cools still air at the surface to a temperature below the air above it.

Answer (B) is incorrect. The air near the surface must be stable both horizontally and vertically to permit the cool ground to cool the air near the surface. Answer (C) is incorrect. Cumulus clouds are well above the surface.

41. In what ways do advection fog, radiation fog, and steam fog differ in their formation or location?

A. Radiation fog is restricted to land areas; advection fog is most common along coastal areas; steam fog forms over a water surface.

B. Advection fog deepens as windspeed increases up to 20 knots; steam fog requires calm or very light wind; radiation fog forms when the ground or water cools the air by radiation.

C. Steam fog forms from moist air moving over a colder surface; advection fog requires cold air over a warmer surface; radiation fog is produced by radiational cooling of the ground.

Answer (A) is correct. *(AvW Chap 12)*

DISCUSSION: Radiation fog is restricted to land because water surfaces cool little from nighttime radiation. Advection fog forms when moist air moves over colder ground or water. It is most common along coastal areas. Steam fog occurs when cold air moves over relatively warm water or wet ground.

Answer (B) is incorrect. Advection fog breaks up (not deepens) when wind speed increases to 15 kt. or more; steam fog requires wind to move cold air over warm, moist surfaces; and radiation fog does not form over water. Answer (C) is incorrect. Steam fog occurs when cold air moves over warm, moist surfaces, and advection fog is caused by warm air moving over a cool surface.

42. With respect to advection fog, which statement is true?

A. It is slow to develop and dissipates quite rapidly.

B. It forms almost exclusively at night or near daybreak.

C. It can appear suddenly during day or night, and it is more persistent than radiation fog.

Answer (C) is correct. *(AvW Chap 12)*

DISCUSSION: Advection fog is usually more extensive and much more persistent than radiation fog. Advection fog can move in rapidly regardless of the time of day or night.

Answer (A) is incorrect. Advection fog can move in rapidly regardless of the time of day or night and is persistent. Answer (B) is incorrect. It describes radiation fog.

7.7 Stability

43. What are the characteristics of stable air?

A. Good visibility; steady precipitation; stratus clouds.

B. Poor visibility; steady precipitation; stratus clouds.

C. Poor visibility; intermittent precipitation; cumulus clouds.

Answer (B) is correct. *(AvW Chap 8)*

DISCUSSION: Stable air is still or moving horizontally but without vertical movement. As a result, the pollutants in the air are not swept away and visibility is poor. Also, stable air forms layer-like clouds since the air is moving in layers. Relatedly, precipitation spreads over a wide area and is relatively steady and the air is smooth.

Answer (A) is incorrect. The visibility is poor (not good) in stable air. Answer (C) is incorrect. The precipitation is steady (not intermittent) and the clouds are stratiform (not cumulus) in stable air.

44. Which would decrease the stability of an air mass?

A. Warming from below.

B. Cooling from below.

C. Decrease in water vapor.

Answer (A) is correct. *(AvW Chap 8)*

DISCUSSION: When air is warmed from below, it tends to rise, resulting in instability; i.e., vertical movement occurs.

Answer (B) is incorrect. Cooling from below keeps the air from rising, resulting in increased (not decreased) stability. Answer (C) is incorrect. A decrease in water vapor lowers the dew point of the air, which does not affect the stability.

45. What is a characteristic of stable air?

A. Stratiform clouds.

B. Fair weather cumulus clouds.

C. Temperature decreases rapidly with altitude.

Answer (A) is correct. *(AvW Chap 6)*

DISCUSSION: Stable air is still or moving horizontally but without vertical movement. As a result, the pollutants in the air are not swept away and visibility is poor. Also, stable air forms layer-like clouds since the air is moving in layers. Relatedly, precipitation spreads over a wide area and is relatively steady and the air is smooth.

Answer (B) is incorrect. Cumulus clouds are a characteristic of unstable (not stable) air. Answer (C) is incorrect. A rapid temperature decrease with altitude (high lapse rate) is a characteristic of unstable (not stable) air.

46. Which would increase the stability of an air mass?

A. Warming from below.

B. Cooling from below.

C. Decrease in water vapor.

Answer (B) is correct. *(AvW Chap 8)*

DISCUSSION: When air is cooled from below, it does not rise, resulting in stability, i.e., no vertical movement.

Answer (A) is incorrect. Warming from below causes the air to rise, resulting in decreased (not increased) stability. Answer (C) is incorrect. A decrease in water vapor lowers the dew point of the air, which does not affect stability.

47. Which is a characteristic of stable air?

A. Cumuliform clouds.

B. Excellent visibility.

C. Restricted visibility.

Answer (C) is correct. *(AvW Chap 6)*

DISCUSSION: Stable air is still or moving horizontally but without vertical movement. As a result, the pollutants in the air are not swept away and visibility is poor. Also, stable air forms layer-like clouds since the air is moving in layers. Relatedly, precipitation spreads over a wide area and is relatively steady and the air is smooth.

Answer (A) is incorrect. Cumuliform clouds are a characteristic of unstable (not stable) air. Answer (B) is incorrect. Excellent visibility is a characteristic of unstable (not stable) air.

48. Which is a characteristic typical of a stable air mass?

A. Cumuliform clouds.

B. Showery precipitation.

C. Continuous precipitation.

Answer (C) is correct. *(AvW Chap 6)*

DISCUSSION: Stable air is still or moving horizontally but without vertical movement. As a result, the pollutants in the air are not swept away and visibility is poor. Also, stable air forms layer-like clouds since the air is moving in layers. Relatedly, precipitation spreads over a wide area and is relatively steady, and the air is smooth.

Answer (A) is incorrect. Cumuliform clouds are a characteristic of unstable (not stable) air. Answer (B) is incorrect. Showery precipitation is a characteristic of unstable (not stable) air.

49. What type weather can one expect from moist, unstable air, and very warm surface temperature?

A. Fog and low stratus clouds.

B. Continuous heavy precipitation.

C. Strong updrafts and cumulonimbus clouds.

Answer (C) is correct. *(AvW Chap 8)*

DISCUSSION: Unstable air is air that is being heated from below, producing updrafts. As a result, pollutants in the air are swept away and visibility is good. Also, unstable air forms cumulus clouds because the air is moving vertically. Relatedly, precipitation is showery and turbulence may be present.

Answer (A) is incorrect. Fog and stratus clouds are characteristics of stable (not unstable) air. Answer (B) is incorrect. Continuous precipitation is a characteristic of stable (not unstable) air.

50. A moist, unstable air mass is characterized by

A. poor visibility and smooth air.

B. cumuliform clouds and showery precipitation.

C. stratiform clouds and continuous precipitation.

Answer (B) is correct. *(AvW Chap 8)*

DISCUSSION: Unstable air is air that is being heated from below, producing updrafts. As a result, pollutants in the air are swept away and visibility is good. Also, unstable air forms cumulus clouds because the air is moving vertically. Relatedly, precipitation is showery and turbulence may be present.

Answer (A) is incorrect. Poor visibility and smooth air are characteristics of stable (not unstable) air. Answer (C) is incorrect. Stratiform clouds and continuous precipitation are characteristics of stable (not unstable) air.

51. If clouds form as a result of very stable, moist air being forced to ascend a mountain slope, the clouds will be

A. cirrus type with no vertical development or turbulence.

B. cumulus type with considerable vertical development and turbulence.

C. stratus type with little vertical development and little or no turbulence.

Answer (C) is correct. *(AvW Chap 8)*

DISCUSSION: Moist, stable air flowing upslope produces stratified clouds as it cools. Stable air resists upward movement.

Answer (A) is incorrect. Cirrus are high clouds, usually consisting of ice crystals. Answer (B) is incorrect. There would be vertical development only if the air were unstable. Also, there is little or no turbulence in stable air.

52. The formation of either predominantly stratiform or predominantly cumuliform clouds is dependent upon the

A. source of lift.

B. stability of the air being lifted.

C. temperature of the air being lifted.

Answer (B) is correct. *(AvW Chap 6)*

DISCUSSION: The structure of cloud types that form as a result of air being forced to ascend is determined by the stability of the air before lifting occurs. Stability refers to the relationship of the lapse rate to the adiabatic cooling rate. If the temperature that decreases with altitude (lapse rate) is warmer than the adiabatic cooling rate (cooling of air as a result of expansion as it ascends), the air that is lifted will continue to rise, which provides for the vertical development of cumulus clouds. That is, unstable conditions exist. If, on the other hand, the lapse rate is less than (cooler than) the adiabatic rate, the air that is lifted will be as cool as or cooler than the air around it, will not lift further, and stratiform clouds will form; i.e., stable conditions exist.

Answer (A) is incorrect. The stability of the air (not the source of lift) determines the type of clouds that will form. Answer (C) is incorrect. The temperature of the air (along with the dew point) determines the altitude (not type) of cloud formation.

53. When an air mass is stable, which of these conditions is most likely to exist?

A. Numerous towering cumulus and cumulonimbus clouds.

B. Moderate to severe turbulence at the lower levels.

C. Smoke, dust, haze, etc., concentrated at the lower levels with resulting poor visibility.

Answer (C) is correct. *(AvW Chap 8)*

DISCUSSION: Stable air is still or moving horizontally but without vertical movement. As a result, the pollutants in the air are not swept away and visibility is poor. Also, stable air forms layer-like clouds since the air is moving in layers. Relatedly, precipitation spreads over a wide area and is relatively steady, and the air is smooth.

Answer (A) is incorrect. Towering cumulus and cumulonimbus clouds are characteristics of unstable (not stable) air. Answer (B) is incorrect. Turbulence is a characteristic of unstable (not stable) air.

54. Which is true regarding the development of convective circulation?

A. Cool air must sink to force the warm air upward.

B. Warm air is less dense and rises on its own accord.

C. Warmer air covers a larger surface area than the cool air; therefore, the warmer air is less dense and rises.

Answer (A) is correct. *(AvW Chap 4)*

DISCUSSION: When two surfaces are heated unequally, they heat the overlying air unevenly. The warmer air expands and becomes lighter or less dense than the cool air. The more dense, cool air is drawn to the ground by its greater gravitational force lifting or forcing the warm air upward much as oil is forced to the top of water when the two are mixed.

Answer (B) is incorrect. Cool air sinking forces the warm air up (without the cool air, the warm air would be stationary). Answer (C) is incorrect. Convective circulation is based on unequal heating of the Earth's surface, not the relative size of surface.

55. When conditionally unstable air with high-moisture content and very warm surface temperature is forecast, one can expect what type of weather?

A. Strong updrafts and stratonimbus clouds.

B. Restricted visibility near the surface over a large area.

C. Strong updrafts and cumulonimbus clouds.

Answer (C) is correct. *(AvW Chap 8)*

DISCUSSION: Unstable air is air that is being heated from below, producing updrafts. As a result, pollutants in the air are swept away and visibility is good. Also, unstable air forms cumulus clouds because the air is moving vertically. Relatedly, precipitation is showery and turbulence may be present.

Answer (A) is incorrect. Stratonimbus clouds are a characteristic of stable (not unstable) air. Answer (B) is incorrect. Restricted visibility is a characteristic of stable (not unstable) air.

56. Convective circulation patterns associated with sea breezes are caused by

A. water absorbing and radiating heat faster than the land.

B. land absorbing and radiating heat faster than the water.

C. cool and less dense air moving inland from over the water, causing it to rise.

Answer (B) is correct. *(AvW Chap 4)*

DISCUSSION: Sea breezes are caused by cool and denser air moving inland off of the water. Once over the warmer land, the air heats up and rises. Currents push the hot air over the water where it cools and descends, starting the cycle over again. The temperature differential between land and water is caused by land absorbing and radiating heat faster than water.

Answer (A) is incorrect. Water absorbs and radiates heat slower (not faster) than land. Answer (C) is incorrect. The cool air moving inland is more (not less) dense, and it rises after it is warmed, not while it is cool.

57. From which measurement of the atmosphere can stability be determined?

A. Atmospheric pressure.

B. The ambient lapse rate.

C. The dry adiabatic lapse rate.

Answer (B) is correct. *(AvW Chap 6)*

DISCUSSION: The stability of the atmosphere is determined by vertical movements of air. Warm air rises when the air above is cooler. The lapse rate, which is the decrease of temperature with altitude, is therefore a measure of stability.

Answer (A) is incorrect. While atmospheric pressure may have some effect on temperature changes and air movements, it is the actual lapse rate that determines the stability of the atmosphere. Answer (C) is incorrect. The dry adiabatic lapse rate is a constant rate.

58. The difference found by subtracting the temperature of a parcel of air theoretically lifted from the surface to 500 millibars and the existing temperature at 500 millibars is called the

A. lifted index.

B. negative index.

C. positive index.

Answer (A) is correct. *(AWS Sect 9)*

DISCUSSION: The lifted index is computed as if a parcel of air near the surface were lifted to 500 mb (18,000 ft. MSL). As the air is lifted, it cools by expansion. The temperature the parcel would have at 500 mb is then subtracted from the environmental 500-mb temperature. The difference is the lifted index, which may be positive, zero, or negative. Thus, the lifted index indicates stability at 500 mb (18,000 ft. MSL).

Answer (B) is incorrect. A negative index means that a parcel of air, if lifted, would be warmer than existing air at 500 mb, and thus the air is unstable. Answer (C) is incorrect. A positive index means that a parcel of air, if lifted, would be colder than existing air at 500 mb, and thus the air is stable.

59. The conditions necessary for the formation of stratiform clouds are a lifting action and

A. unstable, dry air.

B. stable, moist air.

C. unstable, moist air.

Answer (B) is correct. *(AvW Chap 6)*

DISCUSSION: Stable, moist air and adiabatic cooling, e.g., upslope flow or lifting over colder air, are needed to form stratiform clouds.

Answer (A) is incorrect. Stable (not unstable), moist (not dry) air is required. Answer (C) is incorrect. Stable (not unstable) air is required.

7.8 Thunderstorms and Icing

60. What visible signs indicate extreme turbulence in thunderstorms?

A. Base of the clouds near the surface, heavy rain, and hail.

B. Low ceiling and visibility, hail, and precipitation static.

C. Cumulonimbus clouds, very frequent lightning, and roll clouds.

Answer (C) is correct. *(AvW Chap 11)*

DISCUSSION: Cumulonimbus clouds are thunderstorms by definition. Their intensity can be gauged by the presence of roll clouds on the lower leading edge of the storm, which mark the eddies in the shear. Roll clouds are prevalent with cold frontal or squall line thunderstorms and signify an extremely turbulent zone. Also, the more frequent the lightning, the more severe the storm.

Answer (A) is incorrect. Cloud bases and precipitation are not, in themselves, definite indicators of extreme turbulence. Answer (B) is incorrect. Low ceilings, hail, and precipitation static are not, in themselves, definite indicators of extreme turbulence.

61. What feature is normally associated with the cumulus stage of a thunderstorm?

A. Roll cloud.

B. Continuous updraft.

C. Beginning of rain at the surface.

Answer (B) is correct. *(AvW Chap 11)*

DISCUSSION: The cumulus stage of a thunderstorm has continuous updrafts that build the cloud up. The water droplets are carried up until they become too heavy. Once they begin falling and creating downdrafts, the storm changes from the cumulus to the mature stage.

Answer (A) is incorrect. The roll cloud is the cloud near the ground, which is formed by the downrushing cold air pushing out from below the thunderstorm, usually in the mature stage. Answer (C) is incorrect. The beginning of rain at the surface indicates the start of the mature stage, which follows the cumulus stage.

62. The conditions necessary for the formation of cumulonimbus clouds are a lifting action and

A. unstable, dry air.

B. stable, moist air.

C. unstable, moist air.

Answer (C) is correct. *(AvW Chap 6)*

DISCUSSION: Unstable, moist air and a lifting action, i.e., convective activity, are needed to form cumulonimbus clouds.

Answer (A) is incorrect. Moist (not dry) air is required. Answer (B) is incorrect. Unstable (not stable) air is required.

63. The most severe weather conditions, such as destructive winds, heavy hail, and tornadoes, are generally associated with

A. slow-moving warm fronts which slope above the tropopause.

B. squall lines.

C. fast-moving occluded fronts.

Answer (B) is correct. *(AvW Chap 11)*

DISCUSSION: A squall line is a non-frontal, narrow band of thunderstorms that often develops ahead of a cold front. It often contains severe steady-state thunderstorms and presents the single most intense weather hazard to aircraft.

Answer (A) is incorrect. Warm fronts generally do not produce severe weather. Answer (C) is incorrect. Although occluded fronts have some associated instability, the weather they produce is not nearly as severe as a squall line.

64. Of the following, which is accurate regarding turbulence associated with thunderstorms?

A. Outside the clouds, shear turbulence can be encountered 50 miles laterally from a severe storm.

B. Shear turbulence is encountered only inside cumulonimbus clouds or within a 5-mile radius of them.

C. Outside the cloud, shear turbulence can be encountered 20 miles laterally from a severe storm.

Answer (C) is correct. *(AvW Chap 11)*

DISCUSSION: Hazardous turbulence is present in and around all thunderstorms. Outside the cloud, shear turbulence has been encountered several thousand feet above and 20 NM laterally from a severe storm. The roll cloud signifies an extremely turbulent zone.

Answer (A) is incorrect. Shear turbulence can be encountered to 20 NM (not 50 NM) laterally from a severe storm. Answer (B) is incorrect. Shear turbulence can be encountered above and 20 NM (not 5 NM) laterally (not just inside) severe thunderstorms.

65. Which statement is true concerning squall lines?

A. They form slowly, but move rapidly.

B. They are associated with frontal systems only.

C. They offer the most intense weather hazards to aircraft.

Answer (C) is correct. *(AvW Chap 11)*

DISCUSSION: A squall line is a non-frontal narrow band of active thunderstorms. It often contains severe steady-state thunderstorms and presents the single most intense weather hazard to aircraft.

Answer (A) is incorrect. Squall lines usually form rapidly, generally reaching maximum intensity during the late afternoon and the first few hours of darkness. Answer (B) is incorrect. It may develop ahead of a cold front in moist and unstable air or in unstable air far removed from a front.

66. Which statement is true regarding squall lines?

A. They are always associated with cold fronts.

B. They are slow in forming, but rapid in movement.

C. They are nonfrontal and often contain severe, steady-state thunderstorms.

Answer (C) is correct. *(AvW Chap 11)*

DISCUSSION: A squall line is a non-frontal, narrow band of active thunderstorms that frequently develops ahead of a cold front. It can, however, occur in any area of moist, unstable air. It often contains severe steady-state thunderstorms and presents the single most intense weather hazard to aircraft.

Answer (A) is incorrect. While squall lines usually precede cold fronts, they can form in any area of unstable air. Answer (B) is incorrect. Squall lines usually form rapidly.

67. Select the true statement pertaining to the life cycle of a thunderstorm.

A. Updrafts continue to develop throughout the dissipating stage of a thunderstorm.

B. The beginning of rain at the Earth's surface indicates the mature stage of the thunderstorm.

C. The beginning of rain at the Earth's surface indicates the dissipating stage of the thunderstorm.

Answer (B) is correct. *(AvW Chap 11)*

DISCUSSION: Thunderstorms have three stages in their life cycle: cumulus, mature, and dissipating. The beginning of rain at the Earth's surface indicates the mature stage, which is characterized by numerous updrafts and downdrafts.

Answer (A) is incorrect. Updrafts do not continue during the dissipating stage of the thunderstorm; only downdrafts are present. Answer (C) is incorrect. The beginning of rain at the Earth's surface is the beginning of the mature (not dissipating) stage.

68. Which is true regarding the use of airborne weather-avoidance radar for the recognition of certain weather conditions?

A. The radarscope provides no assurance of avoiding instrument weather conditions.

B. The avoidance of hail is assured when flying between and just clear of the most intense echoes.

C. The clear area between intense echoes indicates that visual sighting of storms can be maintained when flying between the echoes.

Answer (A) is correct. *(AvW Chap 11)*

DISCUSSION: Airborne weather avoidance radar is designed to identify areas of precipitation, especially heavy precipitation, which may signify an active thunderstorm. Instrument weather conditions are restricted visibility due to clouds or fog which are not indicated on radar screens.

Answer (B) is incorrect. Hail is often thrown from the tops of thunderstorms for several miles away from the cloud itself. Answer (C) is incorrect. Clouds without precipitation may exist between the intense echoes.

69. Which weather phenomenon signals the beginning of the mature stage of a thunderstorm?

A. The start of rain.

B. The appearance of an anvil top.

C. Growth rate of cloud is maximum.

Answer (A) is correct. *(AvW Chap 11)*

DISCUSSION: Thunderstorms have three stages in their life cycle: cumulus, mature, and dissipating. The beginning of rain at the Earth's surface indicates the mature stage, which is characterized by numerous updrafts and downdrafts.

Answer (B) is incorrect. The anvil top generally appears during (not necessarily at the beginning of) the mature stage. Answer (C) is incorrect. Maximum cloud growth rate occurs further into the mature stage of a thunderstorm (not at the beginning).

70. During the life cycle of a thunderstorm, which stage is characterized predominately by downdrafts?

A. Mature.

B. Developing.

C. Dissipating.

Answer (C) is correct. *(AvW Chap 11)*

DISCUSSION: Thunderstorms have three stages in their life cycle: cumulus, mature, and dissipating. In the dissipating stage, the storm is characterized by downdrafts as the storm rains itself out.

Answer (A) is incorrect. The mature stage has both updrafts and downdrafts, which creates tremendous wind shears. Answer (B) is incorrect. Cumulus is the developing stage when there are primarily updrafts.

71. What minimum distance should exist between intense radar echoes before any attempt is made to fly between these thunderstorms?

A. 20 miles.

B. 30 miles.

C. 40 miles.

Answer (C) is correct. *(AvW Chap 11)*

DISCUSSION: Wind shear turbulence has been encountered as far as 20 NM laterally from a severe thunderstorm. Thus, a minimum distance of 40 NM should exist between intense radar echoes before any attempt is made to fly between them.

Answer (A) is incorrect. Shear turbulence may be encountered 20 NM (not 10 NM) laterally from intense echoes. Answer (B) is incorrect. Shear turbulence may be encountered 20 NM (not 15 NM) laterally from intense echoes.

72. Which situation would most likely result in freezing precipitation? Rain falling from air which has a temperature of

A. 32°F or less into air having a temperature of more than 32°F.

B. 0°C or less into air having a temperature of 0°C or more.

C. more than 32°F into air having a temperature of 32°F or less.

Answer (C) is correct. *(AvW Chap 10)*

DISCUSSION: A condition favorable for rapid accumulation of clear icing is freezing rain. Rain forms at temperatures warmer than freezing, then falls through air at temperatures below freezing and becomes supercooled. The supercooled drops freeze on impact with an aircraft surface.

Answer (A) is incorrect. The rain must begin in temperatures of 32°F or warmer and fall through a layer of below-freezing temperatures. Answer (B) is incorrect. The rain must begin in temperatures of 0°C or warmer and fall through a layer of below-freezing temperatures.

73. If airborne radar is indicating an extremely intense thunderstorm echo, this thunderstorm should be avoided by a distance of at least

A. 20 miles.

B. 10 miles.

C. 5 miles.

Answer (A) is correct. *(AvW Chap 11)*

DISCUSSION: Wind shear turbulence has been encountered as far as 20 NM laterally from a severe thunderstorm.

Answer (B) is incorrect. The danger of shear turbulence exists 20 NM (not 10 NM) laterally from a severe storm. Answer (C) is incorrect. The danger of shear turbulence exists 20 NM (not 5 NM) laterally from a severe storm.

74. Which statement is true concerning the hazards of hail?

A. Hail damage in horizontal flight is minimal due to the vertical movement of hail in the clouds.

B. Rain at the surface is a reliable indication of no hail aloft.

C. Hailstones may be encountered in clear air several miles from a thunderstorm.

Answer (C) is correct. *(AvW Chap 11)*

DISCUSSION: Hail competes with turbulence as the greatest thunderstorm hazard to aircraft. Hail has been observed in clear air several miles from the parent thunderstorm. You should anticipate possible hail with any thunderstorm, especially beneath the anvil of a large cumulonimbus cloud.

Answer (A) is incorrect. Hail, along with turbulence, presents one of the greatest hazards to aircraft in thunderstorms; hail damages the leading edges and windshields of aircraft. Answer (B) is incorrect. Rain at the surface does not mean the absence of hail aloft; i.e., hail vs. rain is a function of temperature.

75. Hail is most likely to be associated with

A. cumulus clouds.

B. cumulonimbus clouds.

C. stratocumulus clouds.

Answer (B) is correct. *(AvW Chap 11)*

DISCUSSION: Hail competes with turbulence as the greatest thunderstorm hazard to aircraft. Hail has been observed in clear air several miles from the parent thunderstorm. You should anticipate possible hail with any thunderstorm, especially beneath the anvil of a large cumulonimbus cloud.

Answer (A) is incorrect. Hail is usually associated with cumulonimbus (not cumulus) clouds. Answer (C) is incorrect. Hail is usually associated with cumulonimbus (not stratocumulus) clouds.

76. Ice pellets encountered during flight normally are evidence that

A. a warm front has passed.

B. a warm front is about to pass.

C. there are thunderstorms in the area.

Answer (B) is correct. *(AvW Chap 10)*

DISCUSSION: Ice pellets form as a result of rain freezing at a higher altitude. This indicates that there is a layer of warm air above in which it is raining and the rain freezes as it falls through the colder air. Thus, either a warm front or a cold front is about to pass.

Answer (A) is incorrect. The layer of warm air above cold air necessary for the formation of ice pellets occurs when a warm front is about to pass (not after it has passed). Answer (C) is incorrect. Ice pellets are a result of rain freezing at a higher altitude (not necessarily from a thunderstorm).

77. Ice pellets encountered during flight are normally evidence that

A. a cold front has passed.

B. there are thunderstorms in the area.

C. freezing rain exists at higher altitude.

Answer (C) is correct. *(AvW Chap 10)*

DISCUSSION: Rain falling through subfreezing cold air may become supercooled, freezing on impact as freezing rain, or it may freeze during its descent, falling as ice pellets. Ice pellets always indicate freezing rain at higher altitude.

Answer (A) is incorrect. Ice pellets may indicate that either a warm front is about to pass OR a cold front has passed, not only that a cold front has passed. Answer (B) is incorrect. Ice pellets always indicate freezing rain at higher altitudes (not necessarily that a thunderstorm is in the area).

78. What is indicated if ice pellets are encountered at 8,000 feet?

A. Freezing rain at higher altitude.

B. You are approaching an area of thunderstorms.

C. You will encounter hail if you continue your flight.

Answer (A) is correct. *(AvW Chap 10)*

DISCUSSION: Ice pellets form as a result of rain freezing at a higher altitude. There is a layer of warm air above in which it is raining, and the rain freezes as it falls through the colder air. Thus, either a warm front is about to pass or a cold front has passed.

Answer (B) is incorrect. Freezing rain can be encountered even where there are no thunderstorms. Answer (C) is incorrect. Ice pellets are a form of hail.

79. Thunderstorms identified as severe or giving an intense radar echo should be avoided by what distance?

A. 5 miles.

B. At least 25 miles.

C. At least 20 miles.

Answer (C) is correct. *(AvW Chap 11)*

DISCUSSION: Wind shear turbulence has been encountered as far as 20 NM laterally from a severe thunderstorm.

Answer (A) is incorrect. The danger of shear turbulence exists 20 NM (not 5 NM) laterally from a severe storm. Answer (B) is incorrect. The danger of shear turbulence exists 20 NM (not 25 NM) laterally from a severe storm.

80. The greatest threats to an aircraft operating in the vicinity of thunderstorms are:

A. thunder and heavy rain.

B. hail and turbulence.

C. precipitation static and low visibility.

Answer (B) is correct. *(AvW Chap 11)*

DISCUSSION: Hail competes with turbulence as the greatest thunderstorm hazard to aircraft. Hail has been observed in clear air several miles from the parent thunderstorm. You should anticipate possible hail with any thunderstorm, especially beneath the anvil of a large cumulonimbus cloud.

Answer (A) is incorrect. Hail, along with turbulence, presents one of the greatest hazards to aircraft in thunderstorms; hail damages the leading edges and windshields of aircraft. Answer (C) is incorrect. Precipitation static may cause communications or navigational aids to fail, but neither precipitation static and low visibility are not considered as hazardous to aircraft as hail and turbulence Precipitation static can be active in any rain or cloud conditions an aircraft flies in, not just thunderstorms.

7.9 Turbulence

81. A pilot reporting turbulence that momentarily causes slight, erratic changes in altitude and/or attitude should report it as

A. light chop.

B. light turbulence.

C. moderate turbulence.

Answer (B) is correct. *(AWS Sect 14)*

DISCUSSION: Light turbulence momentarily causes slight, erratic changes in altitude and/or attitude.

Answer (A) is incorrect. Light chop is rapid, somewhat rhythmic bumpiness. Answer (C) is incorrect. Moderate turbulence causes changes in altitude and/or attitude, and variations in indicated airspeed.

82. When turbulence causes changes in altitude and/or attitude, but aircraft control remains positive, that should be reported as

A. light.

B. severe.

C. moderate.

Answer (C) is correct. *(AWS Sect 14)*

DISCUSSION: Moderate turbulence is similar to light turbulence but of greater intensity. Changes in altitude and/or attitude occur, but the aircraft remains in positive control at all times.

Answer (A) is incorrect. Light turbulence momentarily causes slight, erratic changes in altitude and/or attitude. Answer (B) is incorrect. Severe turbulence causes large, abrupt changes in altitude and/or attitude and the aircraft may be momentarily out of control.

83. Turbulence that is encountered above 15,000 feet AGL not associated with cumuliform cloudiness, including thunderstorms, should be reported as

A. severe turbulence.

B. clear air turbulence.

C. convective turbulence.

Answer (B) is correct. *(AWS Sect 14)*

DISCUSSION: CAT (clear air turbulence) is turbulence encountered in air where no clouds (or only occasional cirrus clouds) are present. The name is properly applied to high-level turbulence associated with wind shear, i.e., above 15,000 ft. AGL.

Answer (A) is incorrect. Severe is a degree of turbulence not related to altitude. CAT may be light, moderate, or severe. Answer (C) is incorrect. Convective turbulence refers to cumulus clouds and the lifting action related to turbulence.

84. The minimum vertical wind shear value critical for probable moderate or greater turbulence is

A. 4 knots per 1,000 feet.

B. 6 knots per 1,000 feet.

C. 8 knots per 1,000 feet.

Answer (B) is correct. *(AWS Sect 14)*

DISCUSSION: Moderate or greater turbulence should be expected where vertical wind shears exceed 6 kt. per 1,000 ft.

Answer (A) is incorrect. Moderate or greater turbulence should be expected where vertical wind shears exceed 6 kt. (not 4 kt.) per 1,000 ft. Answer (C) is incorrect. Moderate or greater turbulence should be expected where vertical wind shears exceed 6 kt. (not 8 kt.) per 1,000 ft.

85. One of the most dangerous features of mountain waves is the turbulent areas in and

A. below rotor clouds.

B. above rotor clouds.

C. below lenticular clouds.

Answer (A) is correct. *(AvW Chap 16)*

DISCUSSION: When stable air flows across a mountain range, large waves occur downwind from the mountains. Underneath each wave crest is a rotary circulation called a rotor. Turbulence is most frequent and most severe in and below the rotor clouds.

Answer (B) is incorrect. The turbulent areas of a mountain wave are in and below (not above) the rotor clouds. Answer (C) is incorrect. The most turbulent areas of a mountain wave are in and below the rotor (not lenticular) clouds.

86. The conditions most favorable to wave formation over mountainous areas are a layer of

A. stable air at mountaintop altitude and a wind of at least 20 knots blowing across the ridge.

B. unstable air at mountaintop altitude and a wind of at least 20 knots blowing across the ridge.

C. moist, unstable air at mountaintop altitude and a wind of less than 5 knots blowing across the ridge.

Answer (A) is correct. *(AvW Chap 16)*

DISCUSSION: A mountain wave requires a layer of stable air at mountaintop altitude and a wind of at least 20 kt. blowing across the ridge.

Answer (B) is incorrect. The air at the mountaintop must be stable (not unstable). Unstable air tends to deter wave formation. Answer (C) is incorrect. The air at the mountaintop must be stable (not unstable). Unstable air tends to deter wave formation. Also, a wind of at least 20 kt. (not 5 kt.) must be blowing across the ridge.

87. When flying low over hilly terrain, ridges, or mountain ranges, the greatest potential danger from turbulent air currents will usually be encountered on the

A. leeward side when flying with a tailwind.

B. leeward side when flying into the wind.

C. windward side when flying into the wind.

Answer (B) is correct. *(AvW Chap 9)*

DISCUSSION: When wind flows over ridges or mountain ranges, it flows up the windward side and down the leeward side. Thus, a pilot who approaches mountainous terrain from the leeward side may be forced into the side of the mountain by the downward-flowing air.

Answer (A) is incorrect. You are flying away from the mountain when you fly with the wind. Answer (C) is incorrect. You are flying in air rising up the mountain on the windward side.

88. Convective currents are most active on warm summer afternoons when winds are

A. light.

B. moderate.

C. strong.

Answer (A) is correct. *(AvW Chap 9)*

DISCUSSION: Convective currents are localized vertical air movements, both ascending and descending. They are most active on warm summer afternoons when winds are light. Heated air at the surface creates a shallow, unstable layer, and the warm air is forced upward. Convection increases in strength and to greater heights as surface heating increases.

Answer (B) is incorrect. Moderate wind disrupts the vertical movement of convective currents. Answer (C) is incorrect. Strong wind disrupts the vertical movement of convective currents.

7.10 Wind Shear

89. During departure under conditions of suspected low-level wind shear, a sudden decrease in headwind will cause

A. a loss in airspeed equal to the decrease in wind velocity.

B. a gain in airspeed equal to the decrease in wind velocity.

C. no change in airspeed, but groundspeed will decrease.

Answer (A) is correct. *(AvW Chap 9)*

DISCUSSION: In such low-airspeed operations, wind shears causing a sudden decrease in headwind are critical. A sudden decrease in headwind will decrease airspeed equal to the decrease in the wind velocity.

Answer (B) is incorrect. There is a loss (not gain) in airspeed. Answer (C) is incorrect. Initially, there is a loss of airspeed followed by an increase (not decrease) of groundspeed.

90. During an approach, the most important and most easily recognized means of being alerted to possible wind shear is monitoring the

A. amount of trim required to relieve control pressures.

B. heading changes necessary to remain on the runway centerline.

C. power and vertical velocity required to remain on the proper glidepath.

Answer (C) is correct. *(AvW Chap 9)*

DISCUSSION: If substantial power and vertical speed adjustments are required to remain on the proper glidepath during an approach, wind shear factors exist.

Answer (A) is incorrect. Trim adjustments are a function of power settings, airspeeds, and flap-gear configurations. Answer (B) is incorrect. Heading changes necessary to remain on the runway centerline are related to crosswind direction rather than headwind/tailwind wind shears.

91. What is an important characteristic of wind shear?

A. It is present at only lower levels and exists in a horizontal direction.

B. It is present at any level and exists in only a vertical direction.

C. It can be present at any level and can exist in both a horizontal and vertical direction.

Answer (C) is correct. *(AvW Chap 9)*

DISCUSSION: Wind shear occurs because of changes in wind direction and wind velocity, both horizontal and vertical. It may be present at any flight level.

Answer (A) is incorrect. Wind shear occurs at all altitudes and can be both vertical and horizontal. Answer (B) is incorrect. Wind shear occurs at all altitudes and can be both vertical and horizontal.

92. Low-level wind shear may occur when

A. surface winds are light and variable.

B. there is a low-level temperature inversion with strong winds above the inversion.

C. surface winds are above 15 knots and there is no change in wind direction and windspeed with height.

Answer (B) is correct. *(AvW Chap 9)*

DISCUSSION: A low-level temperature inversion forms on a clear night with calm or light surface winds. When the wind just above the inversion is relatively strong, a wind shear zone develops between the calm and the stronger winds above.

Answer (A) is incorrect. Light surface winds alone would not cause wind shear. Answer (C) is incorrect. By definition, wind shear refers to abrupt changes in wind speed and/or direction.

93. Hazardous wind shear is commonly encountered

A. near warm or stationary frontal activity.

B. when the wind velocity is stronger than 35 knots.

C. in areas of temperature inversion and near thunderstorms.

Answer (C) is correct. *(AvW Chap 9)*

DISCUSSION: Hazardous wind shear is found near thunderstorms and also near strong temperature inversions.

Answer (A) is incorrect. Although frontal activity implies a change in wind, i.e., wind shear, the most hazardous wind shear is found specifically near inversions and thunderstorms. Answer (B) is incorrect. A strong wind does not by itself result in wind shear; it occurs only if there are strong winds in another direction.

94. If a temperature inversion is encountered immediately after takeoff or during an approach to a landing, a potential hazard exists due to

A. wind shear.

B. strong surface winds.

C. strong convective currents.

Answer (A) is correct. *(AvW Chap 9)*

DISCUSSION: A wind shear develops in a zone between cold, calm air covered by warm air with a strong wind. This often occurs during a temperature inversion.

Answer (B) is incorrect. Strong surface winds by themselves do not create the potential hazard that wind shear does. Answer (C) is incorrect. Temperature inversion precludes (not generates) strong convective currents.

95. GIVEN:

Winds at 3,000 feet AGL . . . . 30 kts
Surface winds . . . . Calm

While on approach for landing, under clear skies with convective turbulence a few hours after sunrise, one should

A. increase approach airspeed slightly above normal to avoid stalling.

B. keep the approach airspeed at or slightly below normal to compensate for floating.

C. not alter the approach airspeed, these conditions are nearly ideal.

Answer (A) is correct. *(AvW Chap 9)*

DISCUSSION: When landing in calm wind under clear skies within a few hours after sunrise, you should be prepared for a temperature inversion near the ground. Wind shear can be expected if the winds at 2,000 to 4,000 ft. are 25 kt. or more (30 kt. at 3,000 ft. in this question). Additionally, the convective turbulence on approach can cause abrupt changes in airspeed and may result in a stall at a low altitude. The corrective action for both of these conditions is to increase approach airspeed slightly above normal to avoid stalling.

Answer (B) is incorrect. The danger in this situation is low-level wind shear and convective turbulence, both of which may cause an abrupt loss of airspeed during the approach. Thus, you should slightly increase, not maintain or reduce, airspeed above the normal approach speed. Answer (C) is incorrect. Low-level wind shear and convective turbulence are not ideal landing conditions. Thus, you should increase approach airspeed slightly above normal to avoid stalling.

96. The Low Level Wind Shear Alert System (LLWAS) provides wind data and software process to detect the presence of a

A. rotating column of air extending from a cumulonimbus cloud.

B. change in wind direction and/or speed within a very short distance above the airport.

C. downward motion of the air associated with continuous winds blowing with an easterly component due to the rotation of the Earth.

Answer (B) is correct. *(AIM Para 7-1-27)*

DISCUSSION: The LLWAS provides wind data and software process to detect the presence of hazardous wind shear and microbursts in the vicinity of the airport. Wind sensors mounted on poles as high as 150 ft., are located 2,000 to 3,500 ft. from the runway centerline.

Wind shear is defined as a change in wind speed and/or direction in a short distance and can exist in either, or both, horizontal or vertical direction.

Answer (A) is incorrect. A rotating column of air extending from a cumulonimbus cloud describes a funnel cloud or tornado, which is a phenomenon that the LLWAS cannot detect. Answer (C) is incorrect. The downward motion of air associated with continuous winds blowing with an easterly component due to the rotation of the Earth is describing a general circulation pattern of air in the north polar region, not something a LLWAS is designed to detect.

END OF STUDY UNIT

STUDY UNIT EIGHT
AVIATION WEATHER SERVICES

(6 pages of outline)

This study unit contains outlines of major concepts tested, sample test questions and answers regarding aviation weather services, and an explanation of each answer. The table of contents above lists each subunit within this study unit, the number of questions pertaining to that particular subunit, and the pages on which the outlines and questions begin, respectively.

Recall that the **sole purpose** of this book is to expedite your passing of the FAA pilot knowledge test for the commercial pilot certificate. Accordingly, all extraneous material (i.e., topics or regulations not directly tested on the FAA pilot knowledge test) is omitted, even though much more knowledge is necessary to become a proficient commercial pilot. This additional material is presented in *Pilot Handbook* and *Commercial Pilot Flight Maneuvers and Practical Test Prep*, available from Gleim Publications, Inc. See the product listing at the back of the book and order online at www.gleim.com.

8.1 SOURCES OF WEATHER INFORMATION

1. Current en route and destination flight information for an IFR flight should be obtained from an FSS or an FAA-approved online source such as DUAT or DUATS.
   a. Weather report forecasts that are not routinely available at the FSS can best be obtained by contacting an NWS weather forecast office (WFO).
2. En Route Flight Advisory Service (EFAS) is available by contacting flight watch using the name of the ARTCC facility in your area, your airplane identification, and the name of the nearest VOR on 122.0 MHz, when operating below 17,500 ft. MSL.
3. Telephone Information Briefing Service (TIBS), provided by an FSS, is a continuous recording of meteorological and aeronautical information available by telephone.
4. Hazardous Inflight Weather Advisory Service (HIWAS) is a continuous broadcast over selected VORs of convective SIGMETs, SIGMETs, AIRMETs, severe weather forecast alerts (AWWs), and center weather advisories (CWAs).
5. Weather advisory broadcasts, including AWWs, convective SIGMETs, and SIGMETs, are provided by ARTCCs on all frequencies, except emergency, when any part of the area described is within 150 mi. of the airspace under their jurisdiction.

8.2 AVIATION ROUTINE WEATHER REPORT (METAR)

1. Aviation routine weather reports (METARs) are actual weather observations at the time indicated on the report. There are two types of reports:
   a. METAR is an hourly routine observation (scheduled).
   b. SPECI is a special METAR observation (unscheduled).
2. Following the type of report are the elements listed below:
   a. The four-letter ICAO station identifier
   b. Date and time of report
   c. Modifier (if required)
   d. Wind
   e. Visibility
   f. Runway visual range
   g. Weather phenomena
      1) **RA** means rain.
      2) **BR** means mist.
   h. Sky conditions
      1) Cloud bases are reported with three digits in hundreds of feet AGL.
         a) EXAMPLE: **OVC005** means overcast cloud layer at 500 ft. AGL.
      2) To determine the thickness of a cloud layer, first add the field elevation to the reported cloud base to determine the height of the cloud base in feet MSL and then subtract this from the reported cloud layer top.
   i. Temperature/dewpoint
   j. Altimeter
   k. Remarks (RMK)
      1) **RAB12** means rain began at 12 min. past the hour.
         a) If the time of the observation was at 1854 UTC, the rain began at 1812 UTC.
      2) **WSHFT 30 FROPA** means wind shift, 30 min. past the hour, due to frontal passage.
3. EXAMPLE: METAR KAUS 301651Z 12008KT 4SM -RA HZ BKN010 BKN023 OVC160 21/17 A3005 RMK RAB25
   a. METAR is a routine weather observation.
   b. KAUS is Austin, TX.
   c. 301651Z is the date (30th day) and time (1651 UTC) of the observation.
   d. 12008KT means the wind is from 120° true at 8 kt.
   e. 4SM means the visibility is 4 statute miles.
   f. –RA HZ means light rain and haze.
   g. BKN010 BKN023 OVC160 means ceiling 1,000 ft. broken, 2,300 ft. broken, 16,000 ft. overcast.
   h. 21/17 means the temperature is 21°C and the dewpoint is 17°C.
   i. A3005 means the altimeter setting is 30.05 in. of Hg.
   j. RMK RAB25 means remarks, rain began at 25 min. past the hour.

4. **Pilot Report (PIREP).** In a PIREP, reported sky cover begins with **/SK**, followed by
   a. Height of cloud base in hundreds of feet MSL
   b. Cloud cover contraction
   c. Height of cloud tops in hundreds of feet MSL
   d. Cloud layers separated by a solidus (/)
   e. EXAMPLE: **/SK OVC 025/045 OVC 090** means the top of the lower overcast cloud layer is 2,500 ft. MSL and the base and top of the second overcast cloud layer is 4,500 ft. MSL and 9,000 ft. MSL, respectively.
5. To determine the bases of convective-type cumulus clouds in thousands of feet, divide the temperature/dewpoint spread by 2.5.

8.3 RADAR WEATHER REPORT (SD/ROB)

1. Thunderstorms and general areas of precipitation can be observed by radar. An SD/ROB may be transmitted as a separate report, or it may be included in a scheduled weather broadcast by Flight Service Stations.
2. EXAMPLE:

   LZK 1133 AREA 4TRW +/+ 22/100 88/170 196/180 220/115 C2425 MT 310 AT 162/110

   Little Rock (Arkansas) radar weather observation at 1133 UTC. An area of echoes, four-tenths coverage, containing thunderstorms and heavy rainshowers, increasing in intensity.

   The AREA is defined by points (referenced from LZK radar site) at 22°, 100 NM; 88°, 170 NM; 196°, 180 NM; and 220°, 115 NM. Cells moving from 240° at 25 kt. (These points are plotted on a map. Connecting the points with straight lines outlines the area of echoes.)

   Maximum top (MT) is 31,000 ft. MSL located at 162° and 110 NM from LZK.

8.4 SURFACE ANALYSIS CHART

1. The Surface Analysis Chart, often referred to as a surface weather map, is the basic observed weather chart.
   a. It provides a ready means of locating observed frontal positions and pressure centers.
   b. The Surface Analysis Chart displays weather information, such as
      1) Surface wind direction and speed
      2) Temperature
      3) Dewpoint
      4) Position of fronts
      5) Areas of high or low pressure
      6) Obstructions to vision
   c. It does not show cloud heights and coverage.
2. Solid lines depicting the pressure pattern are called isobars. They denote lines of equal pressure.
   a. Isobars are placed at 4-mb intervals.
   b. When the pressure gradient is weak, dashed isobars are sometimes inserted at 2-mb intervals to more clearly define the pressure pattern.
   c. Close spacing of isobars indicates a strong pressure gradient.

8.5 CONSTANT PRESSURE CHARTS

1. Constant pressure charts provide information about the observed temperature, wind, and temperature/dewpoint spread at a specified altitude.
2. Areas of strong winds (70 to 110 kt.) are denoted by hatching.

8.6 TERMINAL AERODROME FORECAST (TAF)

1. A terminal aerodrome forecast (TAF) is a concise statement of the expected meteorological conditions at an airport during a specified period.
   a. TAFs are issued four times daily and are usually valid for a 24-hr. period.
2. The elements of a TAF are listed below:
   a. Type of report
      1) TAF is a routine forecast.
      2) TAF AMD is an amended forecast.
   b. ICAO station identifier
   c. Date and time the forecast is actually prepared
   d. Valid period of the forecast
   e. Forecast meteorological conditions -- the body of the forecast, which includes
      1) Wind
         a) **VRB** means a variable wind direction.
      2) Visibility
         a) **P6SM** means the forecast visibility is greater than 6 SM.
      3) Weather
      4) Sky condition
         a) **SKC** means no clouds or less than 1/8 cloud coverage, i.e., sky clear.
3. A PROB40 group in a TAF indicates a 40% probability of occurrence of thunderstorms or other precipitation events.
   a. EXAMPLE: **PROB40 2102 +TSRA** means there is a 40% probability between 2100Z and 0200Z of thunderstorms with heavy rain.

8.7 AVIATION AREA FORECAST (FA)

1. An aviation area forecast (FA) is a forecast of general weather conditions over an area the size of several states. It is used to determine forecast en route weather and to interpolate conditions at airports that do not have TAFs issued.
   a. FAs are issued three times a day by the Aviation Weather Center.
2. The FA is comprised of four sections:
   a. Product header
   b. Precautionary statements
   c. Synopsis
   d. VFR clouds and weather (VFR CLDS/WX)

3. VFR CLDS/WX section contains a 12-hr. specific forecast followed by a 6-hr. categorical outlook.
    a. The specific forecast section gives a general description of clouds and weather that cover an area greater than 3,000 square miles and are significant to VFR operations.
        1) Surface visibility and obstructions to vision are included when the forecast visibility is 6 SM or less.
        2) Precipitation, thunderstorms, and sustained winds of 20 kt. or greater are always included when forecast.

8.8 IN-FLIGHT WEATHER ADVISORIES

1. In-flight aviation weather advisories, designated as severe weather forecast alerts (AWWs), convective SIGMETs, SIGMETs, AIRMETs, and center weather advisories (CWAs), are forecasts to advise en route aircraft of development of potentially hazardous weather.
    a. A SIGMET contains information regarding a volcanic eruption that is occurring or expected to occur.
    b. AIRMETs and CWAs are issued for the possibility of moderate icing, moderate turbulence, sustained surface winds of 30 kt. or more, and extensive mountain obscurement.
2. SIGMET advisories are issued as a warning of weather phenomena that are potentially hazardous to all aircraft.
3. Convective SIGMETs contain both an observation and a forecast or just a forecast for
    a. Tornadoes
    b. Lines of thunderstorms
    c. Embedded thunderstorms
    d. Thunderstorm areas greater than or equal to thunderstorm intensity level 4 with an area coverage of 40% or more
    e. Hail greater than or equal to 3/4 in. in diameter
4. A squall is a sudden increase in wind speed of at least 16 kt. to a sustained speed of 22 kt. or more and lasting for at least 1 min.
5. Transcribed Weather Broadcasts (TWEBs) provide recorded meteorological and aeronautical information to pilots over selected low/medium frequency (L/MF) and VOR facilities in Alaska.
    a. Information contained in a TWEB is dependent on the type of equipment installed at the broadcast facility. The TWEB may contain some or all of the following:
        1) Summary of adverse conditions
        2) Surface weather observations
        3) Pilot weather reports (PIREPs)
        4) Winds aloft forecast
        5) En route and terminal forecast data
        6) Radar reports

8.9 LOW-LEVEL AND HIGH-LEVEL PROGNOSTIC CHARTS

1. Low-Level Significant Weather Prognostic Charts depict conditions expected to exist 12 and 24 hr. in the future.
   a. The upper limit of the Low-Level Significant Weather Prognostic Chart is 24,000 ft. MSL.
2. High-Level Significant Weather Prognostic Charts are also published.
   a. They forecast significant weather between 24,000 ft. MSL and 63,000 ft. MSL.
   b. Small scalloped lines are used in high-level significant weather prognostic charts to indicate cumulonimbus clouds.
      1) The presence of these clouds automatically implies moderate or greater turbulence and icing.

8.10 OTHER CHARTS AND FORECASTS

1. To best determine observed weather conditions between weather reporting stations, the pilot should refer to pilot reports.
2. The Weather Depiction Chart provides a graphic display of both VFR and IFR weather.
   a. When the sky cover is few or scattered, the height on the chart is the base of the lowest layer.
3. The Radar Summary Chart shows lines and cells of significant thunderstorms.
4. The freezing level panel found on the Composite Moisture Stability Chart is an analysis of observed freezing level data from upper air observations.
5. In the Winds Aloft Forecast, the winds are given in true direction and in knots.

QUESTIONS AND ANSWER EXPLANATIONS: All of the commercial pilot knowledge test questions chosen by the FAA for release as well as additional questions selected by Gleim relating to the material in the previous outlines are reproduced on the following pages. These questions have been organized into the same subunits as the outlines. To the immediate right of each question are the correct answer and answer explanation. You should cover these answers and answer explanations while responding to the questions. Refer to the general discussion in the Introduction on how to take the FAA knowledge test.

Remember that the questions from the FAA knowledge test bank have been reordered by topic and organized into a meaningful sequence. Also, the first line of the answer explanation gives the citation of the authoritative source for the answer.

QUESTIONS

8.1 Sources of Weather Information

1. The Telephone Information Briefing Service (TIBS) provided by FSSs includes

A. weather information service on a common frequency (122.0 mHz).

B. recorded weather briefing service for the local area, usually within 50 miles and route forecasts.

C. continuous recording of meteorological and/or aeronautical information available by telephone.

Answer (C) is correct. *(AWS Sect 1)*

DISCUSSION: Telephone Information Briefing Service (TIBS) is provided by FSSs and provides continuous telephone recordings of meteorological and/or aeronautical information. Specifically, TIBS provides area and/or route briefings, airspace procedures, and special announcements, if applicable, concerning aviation interests.

Answer (A) is incorrect. En Route Flight Advisory Service (EFAS), not TIBS, is a weather service on a common frequency of 122.0 mHz. Answer (B) is incorrect. Pilot's Automatic Telephone Weather Answering System (PATWAS), not TIBS, is a recorded telephone briefing service for the local area, usually within a 50-NM radius of the station. A few selected stations also provide route forecasts.

2. The most current en route and destination weather information for an instrument flight should be obtained from the

A. FSS.

B. ATIS broadcast.

C. Notices to Airmen (class II).

Answer (A) is correct. *(AWS Sect 1)*

DISCUSSION: FSSs are the primary source for obtaining en route and destination weather information.

Answer (B) is incorrect. The ATIS broadcast includes information pertaining only to landing and departing operations at one airport and is thus not sufficient for en route information. Answer (C) is incorrect. Notices to Airmen (class II) do not contain weather information.

3. The Hazardous Inflight Weather Advisory Service (HIWAS) is a broadcast service over selected VORs that provides

A. SIGMETs and AIRMETs at 15 minutes and 45 minutes past the hour for the first hour after issuance.

B. continuous broadcast of inflight weather advisories.

C. SIGMETs, CONVECTIVE SIGMETs and AIRMETs at 15 minutes and 45 minutes past the hour.

Answer (B) is correct. *(AWS Sect 1)*

DISCUSSION: The Hazardous Inflight Weather Advisory Service (HIWAS) is a continuous broadcast service over selected VORs of in-flight weather advisories, i.e., SIGMETs, convective SIGMETs, AIRMETs, severe weather forecast alerts (AWWs), and center weather advisories (CWAs).

Answer (A) is incorrect. An FSS, not HIWAS, may broadcast SIGMETs and AIRMETs in their entirety upon receipt and at 15 min. and 45 min. past the hour for the first hour after issuance if there is no local HIWAS outlet. Answer (C) is incorrect. An FSS, not HIWAS, may broadcast a summarized alert notice at 15 min. and 45 min. past the hour of any in-flight weather advisory, including SIGMETs, convective SIGMETs, and AIRMETs, if there is no HIWAS outlet.

4. En route Flight Advisory Service (EFAS) is a service that provides en route aircraft with timely and meaningful weather advisories pertinent to the type of flight intended, route, and altitude. This information is received by

A. listening to en route VORs at 15 and 45 minutes past the hour.

B. contacting flight watch, using the name of the ARTCC facility identification in your area, your aircraft identification, and name of nearest VOR, on 122.0 MHz below 17,500 feet MSL.

C. contacting the FSS facility in your area, using your airplane identification, and the name of the nearest VOR.

Answer (B) is correct. *(AIM Para 7-1-5)*

DISCUSSION: En route Flight Advisory Service (EFAS) is a service specifically designed to provide en route aircraft with timely and meaningful weather advisories pertinent to the type of flight intended, route of flight, and altitude. This information is received by contacting flight watch, using the name of the ARTCC facility identification in your area, followed by your aircraft identification, and the name of the nearest VOR to your position on 122.0 MHz, when below 17,500 ft. MSL.

Answer (A) is incorrect. In some areas, in-flight weather advisories, not EFAS, are broadcasted on VORs at 15 and 45 min. past the hour. Answer (C) is incorrect. Only selected, not all, FSSs have specially trained Flight Watch (EFAS) specialists.

5. During preflight preparation, weather report forecasts which are not routinely available at the local service outlet (FSS) can best be obtained by means of contacting

A. weather forecast office (WFO).

B. air route traffic control center.

C. pilot's automatic telephone answering service.

Answer (A) is correct. *(AWS Sect 1)*

DISCUSSION: Weather report forecasts that are not routinely available at an FSS can be obtained by contacting a weather forecast office (WFO).

Answer (B) is incorrect. ARTCC is concerned with air traffic control, not weather briefings. Answer (C) is incorrect. PATWAS contains the weather products available at an FSS.

6. Weather Advisory Broadcasts, including Severe Weather Forecast Alerts (AWWs), Convective SIGMETs, and SIGMETs, are provided by

A. ARTCCs on all frequencies, except emergency, when any part of the area described is within 150 miles of the airspace under their jurisdiction.

B. FSSs on 122.2 MHz and adjacent VORs, when any part of the area described is within 200 miles of the airspace under their jurisdiction.

C. selected VOR navigational aids.

Answer (A) is correct. *(AIM Para 7-1-10)*

DISCUSSION: ARTCCs broadcast a Severe Weather Forecast Alert (AWW), convective SIGMET, SIGMET, or center weather advisory (CWA) alert once on all frequencies, except emergency, when any part of the area described is within 150 mi. of the airspace under their jurisdiction.

Answer (B) is incorrect. Weather advisory broadcasts are provided by ARTCCs on all frequencies (except emergency), not by FSSs on 122.2 MHz and adjacent VORs, when any part of the area described is within 150 mi., not 200 mi., of the airspace under their jurisdiction. Answer (C) is incorrect. Weather Advisory Broadcasts are provided by ARTCCs while Hazardous Inflight Advisory Service (HIWAS) is broadcast over selected VOR navigational aids.

8.2 Aviation Routine Weather Report (METAR)

7. Refer to the excerpt from the following METAR report:

KTUS.....08004KT 4SM HZ .....26/04 A2995 RMK RAE36

At approximately what altitude AGL should bases of convective-type cumuliform clouds be expected?

A. 4,400 feet.

B. 8,800 feet.

C. 17,600 feet.

Answer (B) is correct. *(AvW Chap 6)*

DISCUSSION: To determine the approximate height of the cloud bases, you need the temperature and dewpoint. In the METAR report, the temperature is 26°C and the dewpoint is 4°C (26/04).

In a convective current, temperature and dewpoint converge at a rate of 2.5°C per 1,000 ft.

We can estimate the cumuliform cloud base in thousands of feet by dividing the temperature/dewpoint spread by 2.5. Given a temperature/dewpoint spread of 22°C (26° – 4°), the base of the convective-type cumuliform clouds is approximately 8,800 ft. AGL (22 ÷ 2.5).

Answer (A) is incorrect. This is the approximate height of the base of cumuliform clouds if the temperature/dewpoint spread is 11°C, not 22°C. Answer (C) is incorrect. This is the approximate height of the base of cumuliform clouds if the temperature/dewpoint spread is 44°C, not 22°C.

8. What significant cloud coverage is reported by this pilot report?

KMOB
UA/OV 15NW MOB 1340Z/SK OVC 025/045 OVC 090

A. Three (3) separate overcast layers exist with bases at 250, 7,500, and 9,000 feet.

B. The top of the lower overcast is 2,500 feet; base and top of second overcast layer is 4,500 and 9,000 feet, respectively.

C. The base of the second overcast layer is 2,500 feet; top of second overcast layer is 7,500 feet; base of third layer is 9,000 feet.

Answer (B) is correct. *(AWS Sect 3)*

DISCUSSION: In a PIREP, the significant cloud coverage is located in the sky cover (/SK) element. This PIREP states the top of the lower overcast cloud layer is 2,500 ft. (OVC 025/) and the base and top of the second overcast cloud layer is 4,500 ft. and 9,000 ft., respectively (045 OVC 090).

Answer (A) is incorrect. There are two, not three, overcast cloud layers. Answer (C) is incorrect. There are two, not three, overcast cloud layers.

9. The remarks section of the Aviation Routine Weather Report (METAR) contains the following coded information. What does it mean?

RMK FZDZB42 WSHFT 30 FROPA

A. Freezing drizzle with cloud bases below 4,200 feet.

B. Freezing drizzle below 4,200 feet and wind shear.

C. Wind shift at three zero due to frontal passage.

Answer (C) is correct. *(AIM Para 7-1-31)*

DISCUSSION: The remark is decoded as freezing drizzle that began at 42 min. past the hour (FZDZB42) and a wind shift at 30 min. past the hour due to frontal passage (WSHFT 30 FROPA).

Answer (A) is incorrect. FZDZB42 means that freezing drizzle began at 42 min. past the hour, not that the cloud bases are below 4,200 feet. Answer (B) is incorrect. Freezing drizzle began at 42 min. past the hour, not below 4,200 ft., and there was a wind shift, not wind shear, reported at 30 min. past the hour due to frontal passage.

10. The station originating the following METAR observation has a field elevation of 3,500 feet MSL. If the sky cover is one continuous layer, what is the thickness of the cloud layer? (Top of overcast reported at 7,500 feet MSL.)

METAR KHOB 151250Z 17006KT 4SM OVC005 13/11 A2998

A. 2,500 feet.

B. 3,500 feet.

C. 4,000 feet.

Answer (B) is correct. *(AIM Para 7-1-31)*

DISCUSSION: In the METAR report, the base of the overcast cloud layer is reported as 500 ft. AGL (OVC005) or 4,000 ft. MSL (3,500 ft. field elevation plus 500 ft. AGL). If the overcast cloud layer top is reported at 7,500 ft. MSL, the cloud layer is 3,500 ft. thick (7,500 – 4,000).

Answer (A) is incorrect. The cloud layer would be 2,500 ft. thick if the base of the overcast cloud layer was reported at 1,500 ft. (OVC015), not 500 ft. (OVC005). Answer (C) is incorrect. The top of the overcast cloud layer, not the thickness of the cloud layer, is 4,000 ft. AGL.

11. The station originating the following METAR observation has a field elevation of 5,000 feet MSL. If the sky cover is one continuous layer, what is the thickness of the cloud layer? (Top of overcast reported at 8,000 feet MSL.)

METAR KHOB 151250Z 17006KT 4SM OVC005 13/11 A2998

A. 2,500 feet.

B. 3,500 feet.

C. 4,000 feet.

Answer (A) is correct. *(AIM Para 7-1-31)*

DISCUSSION: In the METAR report, the base of the overcast cloud layer is reported as 500 ft. AGL (OVC005) or 5,500 ft. MSL (5,000 ft. field elevation plus 500 ft. AGL). If the overcast cloud layer top is reported at 8,000 ft. MSL, the cloud layer is 2,500 ft. thick (8,000 – 5,500).

Answer (B) is incorrect. To arrive at the cloud layer thickness, do not add the overcast cloud layer (OVC005) height (500 ft.) to the distance between the top of the cloud layer (8,000 ft.) and the field elevation (5,000 ft.). Answer (C) is incorrect. The top of the overcast cloud layer, not the thickness of the cloud layer, is 4,000 ft. AGL.

12. What is meant by the Special METAR weather observation for KBOI?

SPECI KBOI 091854Z 32005KT 1 1/2SM RA BR OVC007 17/16 A2990 RMK RAB12

A. Rain and fog obscuring two-tenths of the sky; rain began at 1912Z.

B. Rain and mist obstructing visibility; rain began at 1812Z.

C. Rain and overcast at 1,200 feet AGL.

Answer (B) is correct. *(AIM Para 7-1-31)*

DISCUSSION: The SPECI report for KBOI is reporting a visibility of 1 1/2 SM in rain and mist (1 1/2SM RA BR), and the remarks indicate that the rain began at 12 min. past the hour, or 1812Z (RMK RAB12). Note the time of the SPECI is 1854Z.

Answer (A) is incorrect. The obscuration is reported as mist (BR), not fog (FG), since the visibility is between 5/8 to 6 SM. Additionally, the rain began at 12 min. past the hour, or 1812Z, not 1912Z. Answer (C) is incorrect. The base of the overcast layer is reported at 700 ft. AGL (OVC007), not 1,200 ft. AGL.

13. What is meant by the Special METAR weather observation for KBOI?

SPECI KBOI 091854Z 32005KT 1 1/2SM RA BR OVC007 17/16 A2990 RMK RAB12

A. Rain and fog are creating an overcast at 700 feet AGL; rain began at 1912Z.

B. The temperature-dew point spread is 1°C; rain began at 1812Z.

C. Rain and overcast at 1,200 feet AGL.

Answer (B) is correct. *(AIM Para 7-1-31)*

DISCUSSION: The SPECI report for KBOI is reporting a visibility of 1 1/2 SM in rain and mist (1 1/2SM RA BR), and the remarks indicate that the rain began at 12 min. past the hour, or 1812Z (RMK RAB12). Also, the report states temperature is 16°C and dew point is 17°C, which implies a temperature-dew point spread of 1°C. Note the time of the SPECI is 1854Z.

Answer (A) is incorrect. The obscuration is reported as mist (BR), not fog (FG), since the visibility is between 5/8 to 6 SM. Additionally, the rain began at 12 min. past the hour, or 1812Z, not 1912Z. Answer (C) is incorrect. The base of the overcast layer is reported at 700 ft. AGL (OVC007), not 1,200 ft. AGL.

8.3 Radar Weather Report (SD/ROB)

14. Which is true concerning the radar weather report (SD) for KOKC?

KOKC 1934 LN 8TRW++/+ 86/40 164/60 199/115 15W L2425 MT 570 AT 159/65 2 INCH HAIL RPRTD THIS CELL

A. There are three cells with tops at 11,500, 40,000, and 60,000 feet.

B. The line of cells is moving 060° with winds reported up to 40 knots.

C. The maximum tops of the cells is 57,000 feet located 65 NM southeast of the station.

Answer (C) is correct. *(AWS Sect 3)*

DISCUSSION: In the SD/ROB for KOKC, the coded information **MT 570 AT 159/65** means the maximum tops of the cells are 57,000 ft. MSL, located on 159° from KOKC (i.e., southeast) at 65 NM.

Answer (A) is incorrect. The coded information **86/40 164/60 199/115** is the azimuth, referenced to true north, and range (NM) of points defining the echo pattern, not the tops of three cells. Answer (B) is incorrect. The coded information **L2425** means the line (L) echo pattern movement is from 240° at 25 kt., not winds reported up to 40 knots.

8.4 Surface Analysis Chart

15. The Surface Analysis Chart depicts

A. frontal locations and expected movement, pressure centers, cloud coverage, and obstructions to vision at the time of chart transmission.

B. actual frontal positions, pressure patterns, temperature, dewpoint, wind, weather, and obstructions to vision at the valid time of the chart.

C. actual pressure distribution, frontal systems, cloud heights and coverage, temperature, dewpoint, and wind at the time shown on the chart.

Answer (B) is correct. *(AWS Sect 5)*

DISCUSSION: The Surface Analysis Chart depicts actual frontal positions, pressure patterns, temperature, dewpoint, wind, weather, and obstructions to vision at the valid time of the chart.

Answer (A) is incorrect. The Surface Analysis Chart reports actual surface weather as it exists at the time of observation, i.e., no forecasts. Answer (C) is incorrect. Surface Analysis Charts do not indicate cloud heights.

16. On a Surface Analysis Chart, the solid lines that depict sea level pressure patterns are called

A. isobars.

B. isogons.

C. millibars.

Answer (A) is correct. *(AWS Sect 5)*

DISCUSSION: Isobars are solid lines on the Surface Analysis Chart depicting the sea level pressure pattern. They are usually spaced at 4-mb intervals and connect points of equal or constant pressure.

Answer (B) is incorrect. Isogons are lines of magnetic variation found on navigational charts. Answer (C) is incorrect. Millibars are units of pressure, not lines that depict pressure patterns.

17. Dashed lines on a Surface Analysis Chart, if depicted, indicate that the pressure gradient is

A. weak.

B. strong.

C. unstable.

Answer (A) is correct. *(AWS Sect 5)*

DISCUSSION: When the pressure gradient is weak, dashed isobars are sometimes inserted at 2-mb intervals on the Surface Analysis Chart to more clearly define the pressure pattern.

Answer (B) is incorrect. Strong pressure gradients are depicted by closely spaced solid isobars at 4-mb intervals, not by dashed isobars at 2-mb intervals. Answer (C) is incorrect. Stability has to do with temperature lapse rates, not pressure levels.

18. On a Surface Analysis Chart, close spacing of the isobars indicates

A. weak pressure gradient.

B. strong pressure gradient.

C. strong temperature gradient.

Answer (B) is correct. *(AWS Sect 5)*

DISCUSSION: On a Surface Analysis Chart, close spacing of the isobars indicates a strong pressure gradient. Each line represents a 4-mb change. If the lines are close together, the pressure is changing more rapidly over a given area.

Answer (A) is incorrect. The isobars will be widely, not closely, spaced when there is a weak pressure gradient. Answer (C) is incorrect. Isotherms, not isobars, indicate changing temperatures.

19. Which chart provides a ready means of locating observed frontal positions and pressure centers?

A. Surface Analysis Chart.

B. Constant Pressure Analysis Chart.

C. Weather Depiction Chart.

Answer (A) is correct. *(AWS Sect 5)*

DISCUSSION: The Surface Analysis Chart provides a ready means of locating pressure systems and fronts. It also gives an overview of winds, temperatures, and dewpoint temperatures at chart time.

Answer (B) is incorrect. Constant Pressure Analysis Charts have to do with observed moisture content, temperatures, and winds aloft. Answer (C) is incorrect. The Weather Depiction Chart shows frontal location, cloud coverage and height, VFR-MVFR-IFR, etc., but not pressure centers.

8.5 Constant Pressure Charts

20. What flight planning information can a pilot derive from Constant Pressure Analysis Charts?

A. Winds and temperatures aloft.

B. Clear air turbulence and icing conditions.

C. Frontal systems and obstructions to vision aloft.

Answer (A) is correct. *(AWS Sect 5)*

DISCUSSION: Constant Pressure Analysis Charts provide information about the observed upper-air temperature, wind, and temperature/dewpoint spread along your proposed route.

Answer (B) is incorrect. Clear air turbulence is shown on prognostic charts and is included in area forecasts. Answer (C) is incorrect. Frontal systems and obstructions to vision aloft are shown on Surface Analysis and Weather Depiction Charts.

21. From which of the following can the observed temperature, wind, and temperature/dewpoint spread be determined at a specified altitude?

A. Stability Charts.

B. Winds Aloft Forecasts.

C. Constant Pressure Analysis Charts.

Answer (C) is correct. *(AWS Sect 5)*

DISCUSSION: Constant Pressure Analysis Charts provide pilots with information about observed temperature, wind, and temperature/dewpoint spread at specified pressure altitudes. The altitudes are 850 mb (5,000 ft.), 700 mb (10,000 ft.), 500 mb (18,000 ft.), 300 mb (30,000 ft.), and 200 mb (approximately 39,000 ft.).

Answer (A) is incorrect. Stability Charts provide information about stability, freezing level, precipitable water, and average relative humidity, but they do not contain the temperature/dewpoint spread. Answer (B) is incorrect. Winds Aloft Forecasts do not give the temperature/dewpoint spread aloft.

22. Hatching on a Constant Pressure Analysis Chart indicates

A. hurricane eye.

B. windspeed 70 knots to 110 knots.

C. windspeed 110 knots to 150 knots.

Answer (B) is correct. *(AWS Sect 5)*

DISCUSSION: On Constant Pressure Analysis Charts, areas of strong winds are indicated by hatching, or shading, which indicates winds of 70 to 110 kt.

Answer (A) is incorrect. Hurricane eyes have very low winds. Answer (C) is incorrect. Wind speeds between 110 and 150 kt. are shown by a clear area within a hatched area.

8.6 Terminal Aerodrome Forecast (TAF)

23. What is the meaning of the terms PROB40 2102 +TSRA as used in a Terminal Aerodrome Forecast (TAF)?

A. Probability of heavy thunderstorms with rain showers below 4,000 feet at time 2102.

B. Between 2100Z and 0200Z there is a forty percent (40%) probability of thunderstorms with heavy rain.

C. Beginning at 2102Z forty percent (40%) probability of heavy thunderstorms and rain showers.

Answer (B) is correct. *(AIM Para 7-1-31)*

DISCUSSION: A PROB40 group in a TAF indicates the probability of occurrence of thunderstorms or other precipitation events in the 40% to 49% range; thus the value 40% is appended to the PROB contraction. The forecast **PROB40 2102 +TSRA** means that between 2100Z and 0200Z there is a 40% probability of thunderstorms with heavy rain.

Answer (A) is incorrect. There is a 40% probability of thunderstorms with heavy rain (+RA), not rain showers (SHRA), between 2100Z and 0200Z, not at 2102Z. The intensity symbol (+) refers to the precipitation, not the descriptor. Answer (C) is incorrect. There is a 40% probability of thunderstorms with heavy rain (+RA), not rain showers (SHRA), between 2100Z and 0200Z, not beginning at 2102Z. The intensity symbol (+) refers to the precipitation (RA), not the descriptor (TS).

24. What does the contraction VRB in the Terminal Aerodrome Forecast (TAF) mean?

A. Wind speed is variable throughout the period.

B. Cloud base is variable.

C. Wind direction is variable.

Answer (C) is correct. *(AWS Sect 7)*

DISCUSSION: A variable wind direction forecast is noted by the contraction VRB where the three-digit wind direction usually appears.

Answer (A) is incorrect. The contraction VRB indicates that the wind direction, not wind speed, is variable. Answer (B) is incorrect. The contraction VRB indicates that the wind direction, not cloud base, is variable.

25. Which statement pertaining to the following Terminal Aerodrome Forecast (TAF) is true?

TAF
KMEM 091135Z 0915 15005KT 5SM HZ BKN060
FM1600 VRB04KT P6SM SKC

A. Wind in the valid period implies surface winds are forecast to be greater than 5 KTS.

B. Wind direction is from 160° at 4 KTS and reported visibility is 6 statute miles.

C. SKC in the valid period indicates no significant weather and sky clear.

Answer (C) is correct. *(AIM Para 7-1-31)*

DISCUSSION: The TAF indicates that from 1600Z the wind is forecast variable at 4 kt., visibility greater than 6 SM, no significant weather (implied since the weather element is omitted), and sky clear.

Answer (A) is incorrect. Prior to 1600 UTC, the forecast wind is 150° at 5 kt., not greater than 5 knots. Answer (B) is incorrect. The wind direction is forecast to be variable, not 160°, and visibility is forecast to be greater than 6 SM (P6SM), not 6 SM (6SM).

26. The visibility entry in a Terminal Aerodrome Forecast (TAF) of P6SM implies that the prevailing visibility is expected to be greater than

A. 6 nautical miles.

B. 6 statute miles.

C. 6 kilometers.

Answer (B) is correct. *(AWS Sect 7)*

DISCUSSION: The visibility entry in a TAF of P6SM implies that the prevailing visibility is expected to be more than 6 statute miles (SM).

Answer (A) is incorrect. The units of measure is statute miles (SM), not nautical miles (NM). Answer (C) is incorrect. The unit of measure is statute miles (SM), not kilometers.

27. Terminal Aerodrome Forecasts (TAF) are issued how many times a day and cover what period of time?

A. Four times daily and are usually valid for a 24 hour period.

B. Six times daily and are usually valid for a 24 hour period including a 4-hour categorical outlook.

C. Six times daily and are valid for 12 hours including a 6-hour categorical outlook.

Answer (A) is correct. *(AIM Para 7-1-31)*

DISCUSSION: TAFs are issued four times daily and are usually valid for a 24-hr. period.

Answer (B) is incorrect. TAFs are issued four, not six, times daily, and TAFs do not have a categorical outlook. Answer (C) is incorrect. TAFs are valid for a 24-hr., not 12-hr., period, and TAFs do not have a categorical outlook.

8.7 Aviation Area Forecast (FA)

28. The Aviation Weather Center (AWC) prepares FA's for the contiguous U.S.

A. twice each day.

B. three times each day.

C. every 6 hours unless significant changes in weather require it more often.

Answer (B) is correct. *(AWS Sect 7)*

DISCUSSION: The Aviation Weather Center (AWC) prepares Area Forecasts (FAs) for the contiguous United States three times each day. They cover an 18-hr. period, including a 6-hr. outlook.

Answer (A) is incorrect. FAs are issued three, not two, times each day. Answer (C) is incorrect. FAs are issued three times each day, not every 6 hours.

29. Aviation Area Forecasts (FAs) for the contiguous U.S. are used in conjunction with inflight aviation weather advisories to interpolate

A. temperatures and winds at altitude.

B. conditions at airports for which no TAFs are issued.

C. radar echo precipitation types and intensity levels.

Answer (B) is correct. *(AWS Section 4)*

DISCUSSION: The Aviation Area Forecast (FA) is a forecast of visual meteorological conditions (VMC), clouds, and general weather conditions over an area the size of several states. To understand the complete weather picture, the FA must be used in conjunction with in-flight aviation weather advisories. Together, they are used to determine forecast en route weather and to interpolate conditions at airports for which TAFs are not issued.

Answer (A) is incorrect. A pilot would use a Forecast Winds and Temperatures Aloft (FD) chart to gather information about temperature and winds at altitude. Answer (C) is incorrect. A pilot would use a Radar Summary Chart to gather information about radar echo, precipitation types, and intensity levels.

30. Which information section is contained in the Aviation Area Forecast (FA)?

A. Winds aloft, speed and direction.

B. VFR Clouds and Weather (VFR CLDS/WX).

C. In-Flight Aviation Weather Advisories.

Answer (B) is correct. *(AWS Sect 7)*

DISCUSSION: The FA is comprised of four sections: a communications and product header section, a precautionary statement section, and two weather sections – a SYNOPSIS section and a VFR CLDS/WX section.

Answer (A) is incorrect. Winds aloft, speed, and direction are contained in the winds and temperatures aloft forecast (FD), not the FA. Answer (C) is incorrect. In-flight aviation weather advisories include convective SIGMETs, SIGMETs, AIRMETs, severe weather forecast alerts (AWWs), and center weather advisories (CWAs), none of which are included in the FA.

31. The section of the Aviation Area Forecast (FA) entitled VFR Clouds and Weather contains a summary of

A. forecast sky cover, cloud tops, visibility, and obstructions to vision along specific routes.

B. only those weather systems producing liquid or frozen precipitation, fog, thunderstorms, or IFR ceilings.

C. sky condition, cloud heights, visibility, obstructions to vision, precipitation, and sustained surface winds of 20 knots or greater.

Answer (C) is correct. *(AWS Sect 7)*

DISCUSSION: The VFR Clouds and Weather (VFR CLDS/WX) section is usually several paragraphs long. The specific forecast section gives a general description of clouds and weather that cover an area greater than 3,000 sq. mi. and is significant to VFR operations. Surface visibility and obstructions to vision are included when the forecast visibility is 6 SM or less. Precipitation, thunderstorms, and sustained winds of 20 kt. or greater are always included when forecast.

Answer (A) is incorrect. A TWEB Route Forecast, not an FA, contains a forecast of sky cover, cloud tops, visibility, and obstructions to vision along specific routes. Answer (B) is incorrect. Hazardous weather, e.g., IMC and icing, is found in the in-flight aviation weather advisories, not an FA.

<u>8.8 In-Flight Weather Advisories</u>

32. What single reference contains information regarding a volcanic eruption, that is occurring or expected to occur?

A. In-Flight Weather Advisories.

B. Terminal Area Forecasts (TAF).

C. Weather Depiction Chart.

Answer (A) is correct. *(AIM Para 7-1-6)*

DISCUSSION: A SIGMET, which is a type of in-flight weather advisory, will contain information regarding a volcanic eruption that is occurring or expected to occur.

Answer (B) is incorrect. A SIGMET, not a TAF, is the single reference containing information regarding a volcanic eruption that is occurring or expected to occur. Answer (C) is incorrect. A weather depiction chart is prepared from METAR reports and does not provide information regarding a volcanic eruption.

33. In-Flight Aviation Weather Advisories include what type of information?

A. Forecasts for potentially hazardous flying conditions for en route aircraft.

B. State and geographic areas with reported ceilings and visibilities below VFR minimums.

C. IFR conditions, turbulence, and icing within a valid period for the listed states.

Answer (A) is correct. *(AIM Para 7-1-6)*

DISCUSSION: In-flight aviation weather advisories serve to notify en route pilots of the possibility of encountering hazardous flying conditions that may not have been forecast at the time of the preflight briefing. Whether or not the condition described is potentially hazardous to a particular flight is for the pilot to evaluate on the basis of experience and the operational limits of the aircraft.

Answer (B) is incorrect. In-flight aviation weather advisories are forecasts, not reported or observed conditions. Answer (C) is incorrect. In-flight aviation weather advisories have a defined maximum forecast period and do not necessarily cover the entire time that IFR weather conditions, turbulence, and icing may be experienced.

34. What type of In-Flight Weather Advisories provides an en route pilot with information regarding the possibility of moderate icing, moderate turbulence, winds of 30 knots or more at the surface and extensive mountain obscurement?

A. Convective SIGMETs and SIGMETs.

B. Severe Weather Forecast Alerts (AWWs) and SIGMETs.

C. AIRMETs and Center Weather Advisories (CWAs).

Answer (C) is correct. *(AIM Para 7-1-6)*

DISCUSSION: AIRMETs are issued for the possibility of moderate icing, moderate turbulence, sustained winds of 30 kt. or more at the surface, widespread area of ceilings less than 1,000 ft. and/or visibility less than 3 SM, and extensive mountain obscurement. A center weather advisory (CWA) may be issued to supplement an AIRMET or to inform pilots when existing conditions meet AIRMET criteria but an AIRMET has not been issued.

Answer (A) is incorrect. Convective SIGMETs concern only thunderstorms and related phenomena and imply the associated occurrence of turbulence and icing. A SIGMET is issued for severe, not moderate, icing and severe to extreme, not moderate, turbulence. Answer (B) is incorrect. A severe weather forecast alert (AWW) defines an area of possible severe thunderstorms or tornado activity. A SIGMET is issued for severe, not moderate, icing and severe to extreme, not moderate, turbulence.

35. SIGMETs are issued as a warning of weather conditions which are hazardous

A. to all aircraft.

B. particularly to heavy aircraft.

C. particularly to light airplanes.

Answer (A) is correct. *(AWS Sect 6)*

DISCUSSION: SIGMETs (significant meteorological information) advise of weather potentially hazardous to all aircraft other than convective activity (which is reported in a convective SIGMET). SIGMETs cover severe icing; severe or extreme turbulence; or duststorms, sandstorms, or volcanic ash lowering visibility to less than 3 SM.

Answer (B) is incorrect. SIGMETs pertain to all, not just heavy, aircraft. Answer (C) is incorrect. SIGMETs pertain to all, not just light, aircraft.

36. Which correctly describes the purpose of convective SIGMETs (WST)?

A. They consist of an hourly observation of tornadoes, significant thunderstorm activity, and large hailstone activity.

B. They contain both an observation and a forecast of all thunderstorm and hailstone activity. The forecast is valid for 1 hour only.

C. They consist of either an observation and a forecast or just a forecast for tornadoes, significant thunderstorm activity, or hail greater than or equal to 3/4 inch in diameter.

Answer (C) is correct. *(AWS Sect 6)*

DISCUSSION: Convective SIGMETs are issued for severe thunderstorms resulting in surface winds greater than 50 kt., hail at the surface, hail of 3/4 in. diameter, tornadoes, embedded thunderstorms, lines of thunderstorms, and very severe thunderstorms.

Answer (A) is incorrect. A WST is an unscheduled, not a scheduled, forecast. Answer (B) is incorrect. WSTs are issued only for severe thunderstorms and hail 3/4 in. or larger. Also, WSTs can be for periods up to 2 hr., not 1 hr.

37. What wind conditions would you anticipate when squalls are reported at your destination?

A. Rapid variations in windspeed of 15 knots or more between peaks and lulls.

B. Peak gusts of at least 35 knots combined with a change in wind direction of 30° or more.

C. Sudden increases in windspeed of at least 16 knots to a sustained speed of 22 knots or more for at least 1 minute.

Answer (C) is correct. *(AvW Glossary)*

DISCUSSION: A squall is a sudden increase in wind speed of at least 16 kt. to a sustained speed of 22 kt. or more and lasting for at least 1 minute.

Answer (A) is incorrect. Rapid variations in wind speed describe gusts (not squalls). Answer (B) is incorrect. Abrupt changes in both direction and speed describe wind shear (not squalls).

38. By which of the following methods may a pilot obtain a TWEB (Transcribed Weather Briefing)?

A. By tuning to a low or medium frequency VOR broadcasting TWEBs as indicated in the identifier boxes on your navigational charts.

B. By monitoring AWOS.

C. By monitoring TRACON.

Answer (A) is correct. *(AWS Chap 6)*

DISCUSSION: Transcribed weather broadcasts, such as TWEB or HIWAS, are available on certain VOR and NDB frequencies, as indicated in the identifier boxes on your navigational charts. TWEB broadcasts are currently only available in Alaska.

Answer (B) is incorrect. AWOS provides pilots with up-to-date weather information for a particular airport, not for a given geographic area. Further, TWEBs are not broadcast over AWOS frequencies. Answer (C) is incorrect. TRACON (Terminal Radar Approach Control) provides traffic separation services in Class B and Class C terminal areas, not TWEBs.

8.9 Low-Level and High-Level Prognostic Charts

39. Which weather chart depicts conditions forecast to exist at a specific time in the future?

A. Freezing Level Chart.

B. Weather Depiction Chart.

C. 12-hour Significant Weather Prognostic Chart.

Answer (C) is correct. *(AWS Sect 8)*

DISCUSSION: U.S. Low-Level Significant Weather Prog Charts are issued four times daily. They contain 12- and 24-hr. forecasts indicating forecast weather at 00Z, 06Z, 12Z, and 18Z.

Answer (A) is incorrect. There is no Freezing Level Weather Chart, per se. Answer (B) is incorrect. Weather Depiction Charts report current observed, not forecast, weather.

40. What is the upper limit of the Low Level Significant Weather Prognostic Chart?

A. 30,000 feet.

B. 24,000 feet.

C. 18,000 feet.

Answer (B) is correct. *(AWS Sect 8)*

DISCUSSION: The upper limit of the Low-Level Significant Weather Prognostic Chart is 24,000 ft. MSL. The lower limit is the surface.

Answer (A) is incorrect. The upper limit of the Low-Level Significant Weather Prognostic Chart is 24,000 ft. MSL, not 30,000 ft. MSL. Answer (C) is incorrect. The upper limit of the Low-Level Significant Weather Prognostic Chart is 24,000 ft. MSL (not 18,000 ft. MSL).

41. What weather phenomenon is implied within an area enclosed by small scalloped lines on a U.S. High-Level Significant Weather Prognostic Chart?

A. Cirriform clouds, light to moderate turbulence, and icing.

B. Cumulonimbus clouds, icing, and moderate or greater turbulence.

C. Cumuliform or standing lenticular clouds, moderate to severe turbulence, and icing.

Answer (B) is correct. *(AWS Sect 8)*

DISCUSSION: Small scalloped lines are used on High-Level Significant Weather Prognostic Charts to indicate expected cumulonimbus clouds. This automatically implies moderate or greater turbulence and icing (which are not depicted separately).

Answer (A) is incorrect. Cumulonimbus, not cirriform, clouds are indicated by small scalloped lines. Answer (C) is incorrect. Standing lenticular clouds would be indicated as clear air turbulence by heavy dashed lines encircling the forecast area.

42. The U.S. High-Level Significant Weather Prognostic Chart forecasts significant weather for what airspace?

A. 18,000 feet to 45,000 feet.

B. 24,000 feet to 45,000 feet.

C. 24,000 feet to 63,000 feet.

Answer (C) is correct. *(AWS Sect 8)*

DISCUSSION: High-Level Significant Weather Prognostic Charts forecast significant weather for the altitudes from 24,000 ft. MSL to 63,000 ft. MSL.

Answer (A) is incorrect. The base is 24,000 ft. MSL, not 18,000 ft. MSL, and the ceiling is 63,000 ft. MSL, not 45,000 ft. MSL. Answer (B) is incorrect. The ceiling is 63,000 ft. MSL, not 45,000 ft. MSL.

8.10 Other Charts and Forecasts

43. What significant cloud coverage is reported by this pilot report?

KMOB
UA/OV 15NW MOB 1340Z/SK 025 OVC 045/075 OVC 080/090 OVC

A. Three (3) separate overcast layers exist with bases at 2,500, 7,500 and 9,000 feet.

B. The top of the lower overcast is 2,500 feet; base and top of second overcast layer are 4,500 and 9,000 feet, respectively.

C. The base of the second overcast layer is 2,500 feet; top of second overcast layer is 7,500 feet; base of third layer is 9,000 feet.

Answer (A) is correct. *(AIM Chap 7)*

DISCUSSION: The PIREP describes three overcast layers. The first layer has a base of 2,500 feet and a ceiling of 4,500 feet. The second layer has a base of 7,500 feet and a ceiling of 8,000 feet. The third layer begins at 9,000 feet.

Answer (B) is incorrect. The base of the lowest layer is 2,500 feet. The base and top of the second overcast layer are 7,500 feet and 8,000 feet, respectively. Answer (C) is incorrect. The base of the second layer is 4,500 feet. The top of the second overcast layer is 8,000 feet. The last portion, which states a base for the third layer at 9,000 feet, is correct.

44. To best determine observed weather conditions between weather reporting stations, the pilot should refer to

A. pilot reports.

B. Area Forecasts.

C. prognostic charts.

Answer (A) is correct. *(AWS Sect 3)*

DISCUSSION: Pilot Weather Reports (PIREP) are observed weather conditions usually between weather reporting stations.

Answer (B) is incorrect. Area forecasts are forecasts, not observed weather. Answer (C) is incorrect. Prognostic charts are forecasts, not observed weather.

45. When total sky cover is few or scattered, the height on the Weather Depiction Chart is the

A. top of the lowest layer.

B. base of the lowest layer.

C. base of the highest layer.

Answer (B) is correct. *(AWS Sect 6)*

DISCUSSION: On the Weather Depiction Chart, cloud height above ground level is entered under the station circle in hundreds of feet, similar to hourly weather reports. If the total sky cover is scattered, the height entered is the base of the lowest layer. If total sky cover is broken or greater, the cloud height entered is the ceiling.

Answer (A) is incorrect. The base, not the top, of the lowest layer is indicated. Answer (C) is incorrect. The base of the lowest, not the highest, layer is indicated.

46. Which provides a graphic display of both VFR and IFR weather?

A. Surface Weather Map.

B. Radar Summary Chart.

C. Weather Depiction Chart.

Answer (C) is correct. *(AWS Sect 5)*

DISCUSSION: The Weather Depiction Chart is computer-prepared from METAR reports to give a broad overview of observed flying category conditions as of the valid time of the chart. It provides information concerning cloud heights and ceilings, weather, and obstructions to vision on a national map. Areas that are marginal VFR are indicated by an unshaded contour line, while areas of IFR conditions are depicted by shading within the contour area. Frontal systems are also depicted.

Answer (A) is incorrect. A Surface Weather Map, also known as a Surface Analysis Chart, shows pressure systems rather than VFR vs. FR areas due to visibilities and ceilings. Answer (B) is incorrect. A Radar Summary Chart graphically depicts a collection of radar reports. It is a national map that displays the kind of precipitation echoes, their intensity, trends, configurations, and coverage, i.e., not VFR vs. IFR.

47. What information is provided by the Radar Summary Chart that is not shown on other weather charts?

A. Lines and cells of hazardous thunderstorms.

B. Ceilings and precipitation between reporting stations.

C. Areas of cloud cover and icing levels within the clouds.

Answer (A) is correct. *(AWS Sect 3)*

DISCUSSION: The Radar Summary Chart shows lines and cells of significant thunderstorms. It is a national map displaying a collection of radar reports, including the type of precipitation echoes, their intensity, trend, configuration, coverage, echo tops and bases, and movement.

Answer (B) is incorrect. Ceilings and precipitation between reporting stations must be inferred from the Weather Depiction Chart, not the Radar Summary Chart. Answer (C) is incorrect. Areas of cloud cover and icing levels are forecast on the prog charts, not shown on the Radar Summary Chart.

48. What values are used for Winds Aloft Forecasts?

A. True direction and MPH.

B. True direction and knots.

C. Magnetic direction and knots.

Answer (B) is correct. *(AWS Sect 7)*

DISCUSSION: In the Winds Aloft Forecast, the temperature is in degrees Celsius, and the winds are the true direction and in knots.

Answer (A) is incorrect. The wind measurement is in knots, not MPH. Answer (C) is incorrect. The wind direction is true, not magnetic.

49. A freezing level panel of the composite moisture stability chart is an analysis of

A. forecast freezing level data from surface observations.

B. forecast freezing level data from upper air observations.

C. observed freezing level data from upper air observations.

Answer (C) is correct. *(AWS Sect 10)*

DISCUSSION: The freezing level panel found on the Composite Moisture Stability Chart is an analysis of observed freezing level data from upper air observations.

Answer (A) is incorrect. The freezing level panel contains observed, not forecast, freezing level data from upper, not surface, air observations. Answer (B) is incorrect. The freezing level panel contains observed, not forecast, freezing level data.

END OF STUDY UNIT

STUDY UNIT NINE
NAVIGATION: CHARTS, PUBLICATIONS, FLIGHT COMPUTERS

(6 pages of outline)

This study unit contains outlines of major concepts tested; sample test questions and answers regarding navigation charts, publications, and flight computers; and an explanation of each answer. The table of contents above lists each subunit within this study unit, the number of questions pertaining to that particular subunit, and the pages on which the outlines and questions begin, respectively.

Recall that the **sole purpose** of this book is to expedite your passing of the FAA pilot knowledge test for the commercial pilot certificate. Accordingly, all extraneous material (i.e., topics or regulations not directly tested on the FAA pilot knowledge test) is omitted, even though much more knowledge is necessary to become a proficient commercial pilot. This additional material is presented in *Pilot Handbook* and *Commercial Pilot Flight Maneuvers and Practical Test Prep*, available from Gleim Publications, Inc. See the product listing at the back of the book and order online at www.gleim.com.

9.1 SECTIONAL CHARTS

Important Note about FAA Charts

The FAA prints the charts published in their Airman Knowledge Testing Supplements to the wrong scale. If you were to measure a distance on one of these charts with the plotter, do the calculations based on that information, and enter that answer, you would be wrong every time.

Accurately calculating distance is a part of the testing process. By printing the charts to the wrong scale, the FAA is testing to see if you checked your plotter to the scale printed on the chart to make sure the chart is accurate. Because our goal at Gleim is to prepare you for your Knowledge Test, our reproductions of the charts are also not to scale.

To answer questions related to these charts, you must transfer the chart's scale to a scrap of paper, which is supplied to you at the testing site. You will use this scale as an accurate measuring tool in place of your plotter.

1. Blue airport symbols indicate airports with at least a part-time control tower.
   a. Magenta airport symbols indicate airports without a control tower.
2. True course measurements on a sectional chart should be made along a meridian (line of longitude) near the midpoint of the course because the angles formed by lines of longitude and the course line vary from point to point.
   a. Lines of longitude are not parallel because they go from pole to pole.

3. Each rectangular area bounded by lines of latitude and longitude contains a pair of numbers in large, bold print to indicate the height of the maximum elevation of terrain or obstructions within that area of latitude and longitude. This is called the **maximum elevation figure (MEF)**.
   a. The larger number to the left indicates thousands of feet.
   b. The smaller number to the right indicates hundreds of feet.
4. Obstructions on sectional charts are marked as shown below:

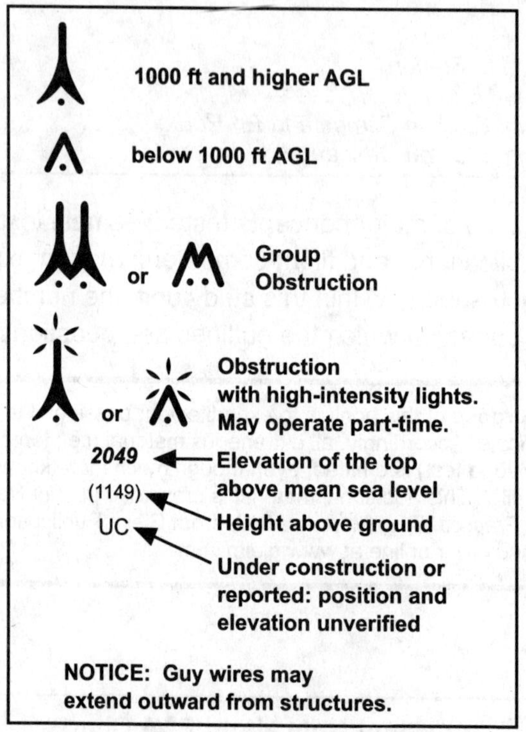

   a. The elevation (MSL) of the terrain at the base of the obstruction is the bold figure minus the light figure.
      1) Use this computation to compute terrain elevation.
      2) Airport elevation is also given in the airport identifier for each airport.
5. Airport identifiers include the following information:
   a. The name of the airport.
   b. The elevation of the airport, followed by the length of the longest hard-surfaced runway. An L between the altitude and length indicates lighting.
      1) EXAMPLE: "1008 L 70" means an airport elevation of 1,008 ft. MSL, lighting sunset to sunrise, and a length of 7,000 ft. for the longest hard-surfaced runway.
      2) If the L has an asterisk beside it (*L), it means part-time or pilot-controlled lighting.
   c. Private, or **"(Pvt),"** indicating a nonpublic-use airport having emergency or landmark value.

6. Class E airspace is controlled airspace that is not defined as Class A, Class B, Class C, or Class D.
   a. The lower limits of Class E airspace are specified by markings on terminal and sectional charts.
      1) The surface in areas marked by segmented (dashed) magenta lines.
      2) 700 ft. AGL in areas marked by shaded magenta lines.
      3) 1,200 ft. AGL in areas marked by shaded blue lines.
      4) 1,200 ft. AGL in areas defined as Federal Airways. Blue lines between VOR facilities labeled with the letter "V" followed by numbers, e.g., V-120.
      5) A specific altitude depicted in En Route Domestic Areas denoted by blue "zipper" marks.
   b. If not defined, the floor of Class E airspace begins at 14,500 ft. MSL or 1,200 ft. AGL, whichever is higher.
   c. Class E airspace extends up to, but does not include, 18,000 ft. MSL.
7. In Class G airspace at or below 1,200 ft. AGL during the day, the minimum flight visibility for VFR operations is 1 SM.
   a. In Class E airspace below 10,000 ft. MSL, the minimum flight visibility for VFR operations is 3 SM.
8. An **Alert Area** is airspace within which there is a high volume of pilot training or an unusual type of aerial activity. Pilots should be particularly alert when flying in these areas.
   a. Alert Areas are depicted on sectional charts by a magenta box.
9. **Military training routes** are depicted on sectional charts by a thin gray line.
10. **Class D airspace** is an area of controlled airspace surrounding an airport with an operating control tower, not associated with Class B or Class C airspace areas.
   a. Class D airspace is depicted by a segmented (dashed) blue line on sectional charts.
   b. The height of the Class D airspace is shown in a broken box and is expressed in hundreds of feet MSL.
      1) EXAMPLE: [31] means the height of the Class D airspace is 3,100 ft. MSL.
   c. Two-way radio communication is not required to take off or land at the primary Class D airport if weather conditions are at or above basic VFR weather minimums and you received the appropriate clearance from the tower, i.e., light signals.
      1) A transponder is not required in Class D airspace.
11. **Class C airspace** areas are depicted by solid magenta lines on sectional charts.
   a. The vertical limits are indicated on the chart within each area and are expressed in hundreds of feet MSL. The top limit is shown above a straight line and the bottom limit beneath the line.
      1) EXAMPLE: The Metropolitan Oakland International (OAK) Class C airspace is shown on Fig. 54, point 6, on page 245.
         a) $\frac{T}{SFC}$ over OAK means the Class C airspace extends from the surface to the base of the overlying Class B airspace.
            i) Note the blue line depicting Class B airspace is drawn over OAK. Thus, the top of Class C airspace is at 2,100 ft. MSL to the left of OAK and 3,000 ft. MSL to the right of OAK.

9.2 INSTRUMENT APPROACH CHARTS

1. The minimum navigation equipment required for a VOR/DME approach is one VOR receiver and DME.

9.3 FUEL CONSUMPTION

1. To determine the time en route, divide the number of miles by your groundspeed.
2. To determine the fuel consumed, multiply the time en route by the fuel consumed per hour.
3. EXAMPLE: If an airplane uses 10.5 GPH and has a TAS (or groundspeed) of 145 kt., you may be asked to estimate the fuel burn on a 460 NM trip. First, determine the time en route by dividing the distance of 460 NM by 145 kt. to arrive at 3.17 hr. Second, multiply the time of 3.17 hr. by 10.5 GPH to arrive at 33 gal.

9.4 TIME, DISTANCE, AND FUEL TO STATION

1. The time/distance to station can also be found by application of the isosceles triangle principle (i.e., if two angles of a triangle are equal, two of the sides are also equal).
   a. The formula may be applied as follows:
      1) With the aircraft established on a radial, inbound, rotate the OBS 10° to the left (90° – 10° = 80°, i.e., now using 260° radial).
      2) Turn 10° to the right and note the time.
      3) Maintain constant heading until the CDI centers, and note the elapsed time.
      4) Time to station is the same as the time taken to complete the 10° change of bearing.

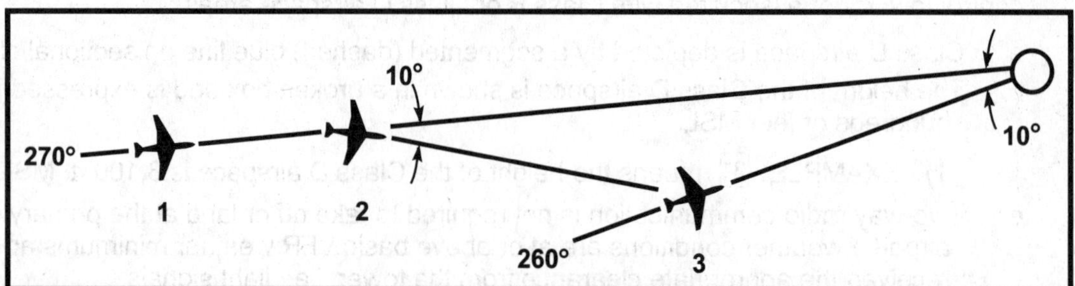

Figure 21. – Isosceles Triangle.

   b. This same formula can also be used for left turns, as well as varying angles (i.e., 5°, 10°, 15°, etc.).
2. When tracking inbound to a VOR or an NDB, you can determine the time and distance to the station using the following method:
   a. Note the radial or bearing you are on.
   b. Turn 90° to the left or right.
   c. Note the time elapsed between bearings.

$$\text{Time to station (min.)} = \frac{60 \times \text{Min. flown between bearing change}}{\text{Degrees of bearing change}}$$

$$\text{Distance to station (NM)} = \frac{\text{TAS} \times \text{Min. flown between bearing change}}{\text{Degrees of bearing change}}$$

d. EXAMPLE: The ADF indicates a 5° wingtip bearing change in 2.5 min. If the TAS is 125 kt., what is the time and distance to the station?

$$\text{Time to station} = \frac{60 \times 2.5}{5} = \frac{150}{5} = 30 \text{ min.}$$

$$\text{Distance to station} = \frac{125 \times 2.5}{5} = \frac{312.5}{5} = 62.5 \text{ NM}$$

3. To determine the fuel required, convert the time to station into hours and multiply by the fuel consumption as shown.

$$\textit{Fuel required} = \frac{\textit{Rate of fuel consumption} \times \textit{Min. to station}}{60}$$

a. EXAMPLE: You are 20 min. from the station and your fuel burn is 15 GPH.

$$\text{Fuel required} = \frac{15 \times 20}{60} = \frac{300}{60} = 5 \text{ gal.}$$

4. When a relative bearing doubles in a specific time, the time to the station is that time (the time to double the relative bearing); e.g., if it takes 5 min. to double your relative bearing, you are 5 min. from the station.

9.5 WIND DIRECTION AND SPEED

1. To estimate your wind given true heading and a true course, simply use the wind side of your flight computer backwards.
   a. Place the groundspeed under the grommet (the hole in the center) with the true course under the true index.
   b. Then on the true airspeed arc, place a pencil mark reflecting the right or left wind correction angle you are holding.
   c. Rotate the inner scale so the pencil mark is on the centerline and read the wind direction under the true index.
   d. The distance up from the grommet is the wind speed.
2. To determine the total course correction needed to converge on (fly direct to) your destination, use the following steps:
   a. Since 1° off course equals 1 NM per 60 NM from the station, the following formula applies:

$$\frac{\textit{NM off}}{\textit{NM flown}} \times 60 = \textit{Degrees off course from departure point}$$

      1) Turning back this number of degrees will parallel the original course.

   b. To fly direct to your destination, calculate the number of degrees off course.

$$\frac{\textit{NM off}}{\textit{NM remaining}} \times 60 = \textit{Degrees off course to destination}$$

      1) Turning this number of degrees farther will take you direct to your destination.

c. EXAMPLE: You are 140 NM from your departure point and have determined that you are 11 NM off course. If 71 NM remain to be flown, the approximate total correction to be made to converge on the destination is 14°, as computed below.

$$\frac{11 \text{ NM}}{140 \text{ NM}} \times 60 = 4.7°$$

$$\frac{11 \text{ NM}}{71 \text{ NM}} \times 60 = \underline{9.3°}$$

$$\underline{\underline{14.0°}}$$

9.6 TIME, COMPASS HEADING, ETC., ON CLIMBS AND EN ROUTE

1. You may be asked to determine the minutes, compass heading, distance, and fuel consumed during a climb or en route.
2. The first step is to determine the number of minutes to climb.
   a. Divide the amount of climb required by the rate of climb.
      1) EXAMPLE: If you must climb 5,000 ft. at 500 fpm, the climb takes 10 min. (5,000 ÷ 500).
3. If there are several alternative answers with the correct number of minutes, you may be able to determine the correct answer based upon the amount of fuel burned.
   a. Convert the time required to climb into hours by dividing by 60.
   b. Then multiply by the rate of fuel consumption to determine the amount of fuel used.
4. Finally, if you must determine the compass heading, begin by converting the true course to true heading by adjusting for wind effect using the wind side of your flight computer.
   a. Align the wind direction on the inner scale under the true index (top of the computer) on the outer scale.
   b. Measure up the vertical line the amount of wind speed in kt., and put a pencil mark on the plastic.
   c. Rotate the inner scale so the true course is under the true index.
   d. Slide the grid so that your pencil dot is superimposed over the true airspeed. The location of the grommet will indicate the groundspeed.
   e. The pencil mark will indicate the wind correction angle (if to the left, it is a negative wind correction, and if to the right, a positive wind correction).
   f. True heading is found by adjusting the true course for the wind correction.
   g. Magnetic heading is found by adjusting the true heading for magnetic variation.
      1) Subtract easterly variation ("east is least").
      2) Add westerly variation ("west is best").
   h. Convert magnetic heading to compass heading by adjusting for the compass deviation, which is given in these questions as + or –.

9.7 TIME, COMPASS HEADING, ETC., ON DESCENTS

1. These questions are calculated the same as for climbs (Subunit 9.6), except you are descending.
2. Note that the questions require you to arrive at some elevation AGL above the airport, not the airport elevation.
   a. Add the airport elevation to the altitude AGL required; then subtract that amount from the cruising altitude.

QUESTIONS AND ANSWER EXPLANATIONS: All of the commercial pilot knowledge test questions chosen by the FAA for release as well as additional questions selected by Gleim relating to the material in the previous outlines are reproduced on the following pages. These questions have been organized into the same subunits as the outlines. To the immediate right of each question are the correct answer and answer explanation. You should cover these answers and answer explanations while responding to the questions. Refer to the general discussion in the Introduction on how to take the FAA knowledge test.

Remember that the questions from the FAA knowledge test bank have been reordered by topic and organized into a meaningful sequence. Also, the first line of the answer explanation gives the citation of the authoritative source for the answer.

QUESTIONS

9.1 Sectional Charts

1. Which is true concerning the blue and magenta colors used to depict airports on Sectional Aeronautical Charts?

A. Airports with control towers underlying Class A, B, and C airspace are shown in blue; Class D and E airspace are magenta.

B. Airports with control towers underlying Class C, D, and E airspace are shown in magenta.

C. Airports with control towers underlying Class B, C, D, and E airspace are shown in blue.

Answer (C) is correct. *(ACL)*

DISCUSSION: On sectional charts, airports with control towers underlying Class B, C, D, E, or G airspace are shown in blue. Airports with no control towers are shown in magenta.

Answer (A) is incorrect. There are no airports in Class A airspace. Airports with control towers are shown in blue, all others in magenta. Answer (B) is incorrect. Airports with control towers are shown in blue, not magenta.

2. True course measurements on a Sectional Aeronautical Chart should be made at a meridian near the midpoint of the course because the

A. values of isogonic lines change from point to point.

B. angles formed by isogonic lines and lines of latitude vary from point to point.

C. angles formed by lines of longitude and the course line vary from point to point.

Answer (C) is correct. *(PHAK Chap 15)*

DISCUSSION: Because meridians (lines of longitude) converge toward the poles, the angles formed by meridians and the course line may vary from point to point. Thus, course measurement should be taken at a meridian near the midpoint of the course rather than at the departure point.

Answer (A) is incorrect. Isogonic lines are used to calculate magnetic (not true) course. Answer (B) is incorrect. Isogonic lines are used to calculate magnetic (not true) course.

3. When a dashed blue circle surrounds an airport on a sectional aeronautical chart, it will depict the boundary of

A. Special VFR airspace.

B. Class B airspace.

C. Class D airspace.

Answer (C) is correct. *(AIM Para 3-2-5)*

DISCUSSION: On a sectional aeronautical chart, the boundary of Class D airspace is depicted by a dashed (segmented) blue circle around an airport.

Answer (A) is incorrect. There is no airspace designated as special VFR. Answer (B) is incorrect. On a sectional chart, a solid, not dashed, blue circle that surrounds an airport depicts the boundary of Class B airspace.

4. (Refer to Figure 52 on page 243.) (Refer to point 6.) Mosier Airport is

A. an airport restricted to use by private and recreational pilots.

B. a restricted military stage field within restricted airspace.

C. a nonpublic use airport.

Answer (C) is correct. *(ACL)*

DISCUSSION: Mosier Airport (west of 6) is a private, i.e., nonpublic-use, airport as indicated by the term "(Pvt)" after the airport name. Private airports that are shown on the sectional charts have an emergency or landmark value.

Answer (A) is incorrect. The airport symbol with the letter "R" in the center means it is a nonpublic-use airport, not that only private and recreational pilots may use the airport. Answer (B) is incorrect. Military airfields are labeled as AFB, NAS, AAF, NAAS, NAF, MCAS, or DND.

5. (Refer to Figure 52 on page 243.) (Refer to point 9.) The alert area depicted within the magenta lines is an area in which

A. there is a high volume of pilot training activities or an unusual type of aerial activity, neither of which is hazardous to aircraft.

B. the flight of aircraft is prohibited.

C. the flight of aircraft, while not prohibited, is subject to restriction.

Answer (A) is correct. *(ACL)*

DISCUSSION: Alert Areas are depicted on charts to inform nonparticipating pilots of areas that may contain a high volume of pilot training or an unusual type of aerial activity, neither of which is hazardous to aircraft.

Answer (B) is incorrect. A Prohibited Area, not an Alert Area, is airspace within which the flight of aircraft is prohibited. Answer (C) is incorrect. A Restricted Area, not an Alert Area, is airspace within which the flight of aircraft, while not prohibited, is subject to restriction.

---

6. (Refer to Figure 52 on page 243.) (Refer to point 7.) The floor of Class E airspace over the town of Woodland is

A. 700 feet AGL over part of the town and no floor over the remainder.

B. 1,200 feet AGL over part of the town and no floor over the remainder.

C. both 700 feet and 1,200 feet AGL.

Answer (C) is correct. *(ACL)*

DISCUSSION: The town of Woodland (right of point 7) has magenta shading over part of the town. To the inside of the shading, Class E airspace begins at 700 ft. AGL. Where the outer edge of the magenta area ends, Class E airspace begins at 1,200 ft. AGL. One can assume the town of Woodland is to the inside of a shaded blue line not depicted on the chart excerpt.

Answer (A) is incorrect. No floor would imply Class E airspace begins at the surface. Class E airspace at the surface is depicted with a dashed magenta line. Answer (B) is incorrect. The area to the inside of the magenta shading indicates the floor of Class E airspace is at 700 ft. AGL.

7. (Refer to Figure 52 on page 243.) (Refer to point 8.) The floor of the Class E airspace over the town of Auburn is

A. 1,200 feet MSL.

B. 700 feet AGL.

C. 1,200 feet AGL.

Answer (B) is correct. *(ACL)*

DISCUSSION: The town of Auburn (southeast of point 8) is located inside the magenta-shaded area, which means the floor of Class E airspace is 700 ft. AGL.

Answer (A) is incorrect. The floor of Class E airspace over the town of Auburn is 700 ft. AGL, not 1,200 ft. MSL. The town of Auburn is within the magenta shading. Answer (C) is incorrect. The floor of Class E airspace inside the magenta-shaded area is 700 ft. AGL, not 1,200 ft. AGL.

8. (Refer to Figure 52 on page 243.) (Refer to point 1.) The floor of the Class E airspace above Georgetown Airport (Q61) is at

A. the surface.

B. 3,823 feet MSL.

C. 700 feet AGL.

Answer (B) is correct. *(ACL)*

DISCUSSION: Georgetown Airport is located within 4 NM of the blue shaded area representing a federal airway, which means the floor of Class E airspace is at 1,200 ft. AGL. The airport elevation is given in the first line of the airport data as 2,623 ft. MSL. Thus, the floor of Class E airspace above Georgetown Airport is 3,823 ft. MSL (2,623 + 1,200).

Answer (A) is incorrect. Class E airspace would begin at the surface only if the airport were surrounded by a magenta segmented circle. Answer (C) is incorrect. The floor of Class E airspace would begin at 700 ft. AGL if Georgetown Airport were inside, not outside, the magenta-shaded areas.

9. (Refer to Figure 52 on page 243.) (Refer to point 4.) The highest obstruction with high intensity lighting within 10 NM of Lincoln Regional Airport (LHM) is how high above the ground?

A. 1,254 feet.

B. 662 feet.

C. 299 feet.

Answer (C) is correct. *(ACL)*

DISCUSSION: Obstructions with high-intensity lights are depicted by lightning bolt symbols around the top of the obstruction symbol. The only symbol having high-intensity lights within 10 NM of Lincoln Airport is located approximately 3.5 NM south of the airport. The height above ground of this obstruction is the number in parentheses, which is 299 ft. AGL.

Answer (A) is incorrect. This is the height of the obstruction above sea level, not the ground, located approximately 8.5 NM east of the airport. This obstruction does not have high-intensity lights. Answer (B) is incorrect. This is the height above ground of the group of obstructions located approximately 8 NM southwest of the airport. While these obstructions are the highest above ground, they do not have high-intensity lighting.

10. (Refer to Figure 52 on page 243.) (Refer to point 5.) The floor of the Class E airspace over University Airport (0O5) is

A. the surface.

B. 700 feet AGL.

C. 1,200 feet AGL.

Answer (B) is correct. *(ACL)*

DISCUSSION: University Airport (east of point 5) is located within the magenta shading, which means the floor of Class E airspace is at 700 ft. AGL.

Answer (A) is incorrect. Class E airspace would begin at the surface only if the airport were surrounded by a magenta segmented circle. Answer (C) is incorrect. Class E airspace would begin at 1,200 ft. only if the airport were surrounded by a shaded blue line.

11. (Refer to Figure 52 on page 243.) (Refer to point 4.) The terrain at the obstruction approximately 8 NM east southeast of the Lincoln Airport is approximately how much higher than the airport elevation?

A. 376 feet.

B. 835 feet.

C. 1,135 feet.

Answer (B) is correct. *(ACL)*

DISCUSSION: The obstruction approximately 8 NM east-southeast of the Lincoln Airport (point 4) is marked as having an elevation of 1,254 ft. MSL, and a height of 300 ft. AGL. Thus, the terrain elevation at that point is 954 ft. MSL (1,254 – 300). The Lincoln Airport elevation is shown to be 119 ft. MSL, which is 835 ft. (954 – 119) lower than the terrain elevation at the obstruction.

Answer (A) is incorrect. The terrain at the obstruction is 835 ft., not 376 ft., higher than the Lincoln Airport elevation. Answer (C) is incorrect. This is the height of the obstruction above the airport elevation.

12. (Refer to Figure 53 on page 244.) (Refer to point 1.) This thin black shaded line is most likely

A. an arrival route.

B. a military training route.

C. a state boundary line.

Answer (B) is correct. *(ACL)*

DISCUSSION: The thin black shaded line is most likely a military training route (MTR). Generally, MTRs are established below 10,000 ft. MSL for operations at speeds in excess of 250 kt. MTRs are normally labeled on sectional charts with either IR (IFR operations) or VR (VFR operations) and followed by either three or four number characters.

Answer (A) is incorrect. Arrival routes are not depicted on sectional charts. Answer (C) is incorrect. A state boundary line is depicted on sectional charts by a thin black broken line, not a thin black shaded line.

13. (Refer to Figure 53 on page 244.)

GIVEN:

Location	Madera Airport (MAE)
Altitude	1,000 ft. AGL
Position	7 NM north of Madera (MAE)
Time	3 p.m. local
Flight visibility	1 SM

You are VFR approaching Madera Airport for a landing from the north. You

A. are in violation of the CFR's; you need 3 miles of visibility under VFR.

B. are required to descend to below 700 feet AGL to remain clear of Class E airspace and may continue for landing.

C. may descend to 800 feet AGL (Pattern Altitude) after entering Class E airspace and continue to the airport.

Answer (B) is correct. *(ACL)*

DISCUSSION: If you are 7 NM north of Madera Airport (middle of Fig. 53), you are outside of the magenta shaded area, which means the floor of Class E airspace is at 1,200 ft. AGL. Since you are flying at 1,000 ft. AGL (i.e., Class G airspace) during daylight hours, the minimum flight visibility required for VFR flight is 1 SM. At the edge of the magenta shading the floor of Class E is at 700 ft. AGL. Thus, to maintain VFR you must remain in Class G airspace and descend below 700 ft. AGL to remain clear of Class E airspace, and you may continue for landing.

Answer (A) is incorrect. You are currently in Class G airspace at 1,000 ft. AGL during daylight hours, and thus you need only 1 SM, not 3 SM, visibility. Answer (C) is incorrect. In order to remain VFR, you must descend below 700 ft. AGL, not the pattern altitude of 800 ft. AGL, to remain clear of Class E airspace.

14. (Refer to Figure 53 on page 244.) (Refer to point 2.) The 16 indicates

A. an antenna top at 1,600 feet AGL.

B. the maximum elevation figure for that quadrangle.

C. the minimum safe sector altitude for that quadrangle.

Answer (B) is correct. *(ACL)*

DISCUSSION: The large bold 1 and somewhat smaller 6 (point 2) refer to the maximum elevation figure (MEF) in feet MSL of the highest obstruction or terrain in the quadrangle bounded by tick lines of longitude and latitude. On sectional charts, the MEF is provided in each square bounded by lines of longitude and latitude.

Answer (A) is incorrect. An antenna is shown by an obstruction symbol (as shown to the southeast of 2) and the height above ground is the number in parentheses, not large, bold numbers. Answer (C) is incorrect. Minimum safe altitudes are depicted on IAP, not sectional, charts.

15. (Refer to Figure 54 on page 245.) (Refer to point 6.) The Class C airspace at Metropolitan Oakland International (OAK) which extends from the surface upward has a ceiling of

A. both 2,100 feet and 3,000 feet MSL.

B. 8,000 feet MSL.

C. 2,100 feet AGL.

Answer (A) is correct. *(ACL)*

DISCUSSION: The Class C airspace at OAK (point 6) is shown in solid magenta lines. The surface area over the airport indicates the Class C airspace extends from the surface (SFC) upward to T, which means the ceiling ends at the base of the San Francisco Class B airspace. The base of the Class B airspace changes over OAK. To the left of OAK the base is 2,100 ft. MSL and to the right of OAK the base is 3,000 ft. MSL.

Answer (B) is incorrect. This is the ceiling of the Class B, not the Class C, airspace over OAK. Answer (C) is incorrect. This is the approximate ceiling of the Class C airspace on the west side of OAK, but the ceiling on the east side is 3,000 ft. MSL.

16. (Refer to Figure 54 on page 245.) (Refer to point 1.) What minimum altitude is required to avoid the Livermore Airport (LVK) Class D airspace?

A. 2,503 feet MSL.

B. 2,901 feet MSL.

C. 3,297 feet MSL.

Answer (B) is correct. *(AIM Para 3-2-5)*

DISCUSSION: The Class D airspace at Livermore Airport extends from the surface to 2,900 ft. MSL, as indicated by the [29] within the blue segmented circle. Thus, the minimum altitude to fly over and avoid the Livermore Airport Class D airspace is 2,901 ft. MSL.

Answer (A) is incorrect. At 2,503 ft. MSL, you would be in Class D airspace. Answer (C) is incorrect. Although at 3,297 ft. MSL you would be above the Class D airspace, it is not the minimum altitude at which you could avoid the airspace.

17. (Refer to Figure 54 on page 245.) What is the ceiling of the Class D Airspace of the Byron (C83) airport (Area 2)?

A. 2,900 feet.

B. 7,600 feet.

C. Class D Airspace does not exist at Byron (C83).

Answer (C) is correct. *(PHAK Chap 14 and Sectional Chart)*

DISCUSSION: Class D airspace is depicted on the Sectional Chart with a dashed blue line surrounding the airport. There is no dashed blue line surrounding Byron (C83) airport.

Answer (A) is incorrect. The magenta shaded circle around Byron (C83) indicates Class E airspace with the floor being at 700 feet and Class G below that, not 2,900 feet. Answer (B) is incorrect. The shaded magenta surrounding Byron (C83) indicates Class E airspace with the floor being at 700 feet with Class G below that, not 7,600 feet.

18. (Refer to Figure 54 on page 245.) (Refer to point 4.) The thin magenta line represents

A. the outer limits of the San Jose (SJC) Class C airspace.

B. the San Francisco (SFO) Mode C veil, which requires a mode C transponder from 1,200 feet AGL up to 10,000 feet MSL.

C. the San Francisco Mode C veil, which requires the use of an appropriate transponder.

Answer (C) is correct. *(ACL)*

DISCUSSION: Every Class B airspace area is surrounded by a 30 NM halo referred to as a Mode C veil and represented by a thin magenta line. Operations inside the Mode C veil require the use of an altitude-encoding transponder.

Answer (A) is incorrect. The magenta line represents the Mode C veil, not the SJC Class C boundary. Answer (B) is incorrect. The requirement for an altitude-encoding transponder within the Mode C veil begins at the surface, not 1,200 feet AGL.

Figure 52. – Sectional Chart Excerpt.

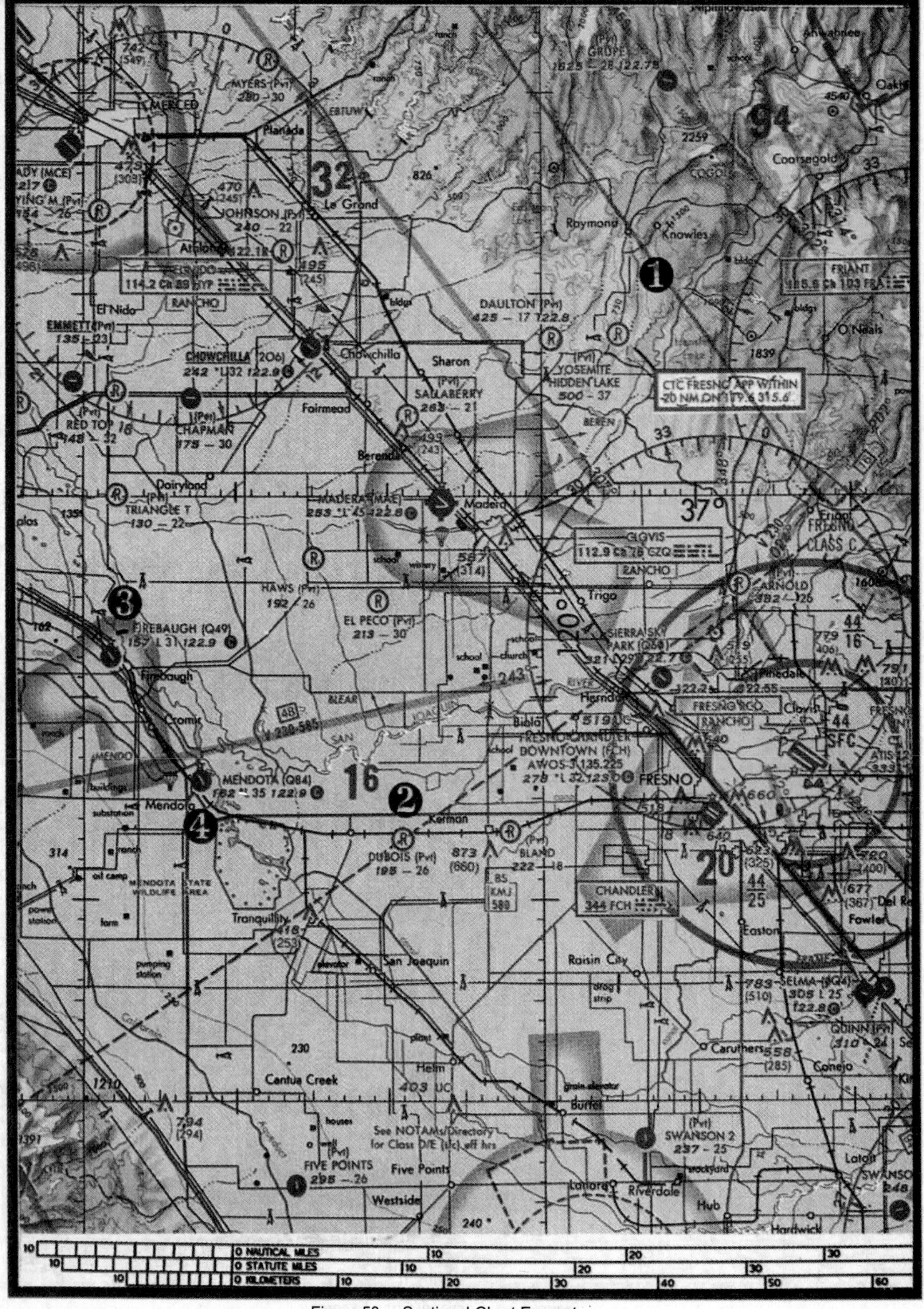

Figure 53. – Sectional Chart Excerpt.

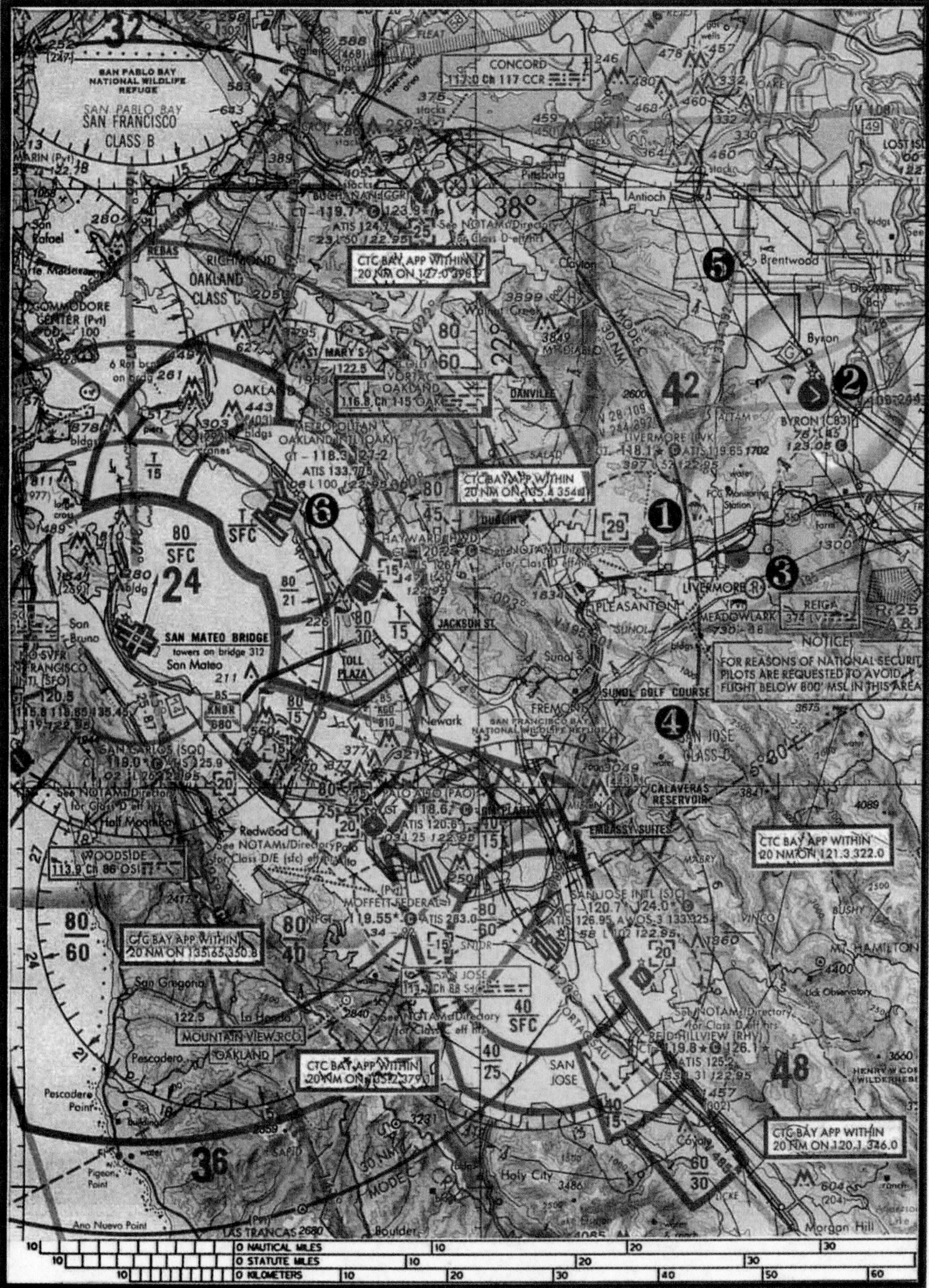

Figure 54. – Sectional Chart Excerpt.

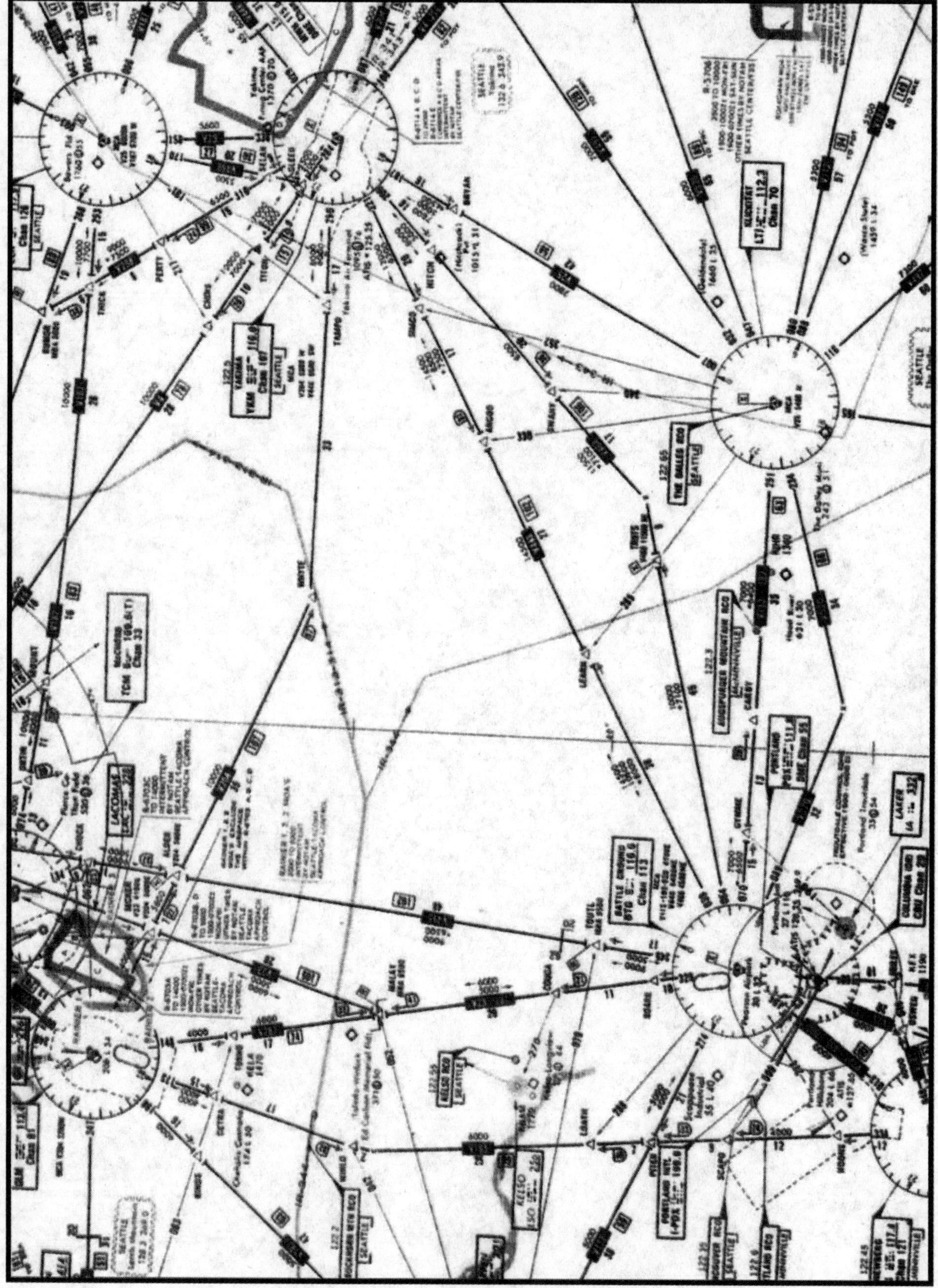

Figure 55. – En Route Low Altitude Chart Segment.

Figure 56. – Two Signs.

Figure 57. – Sign.

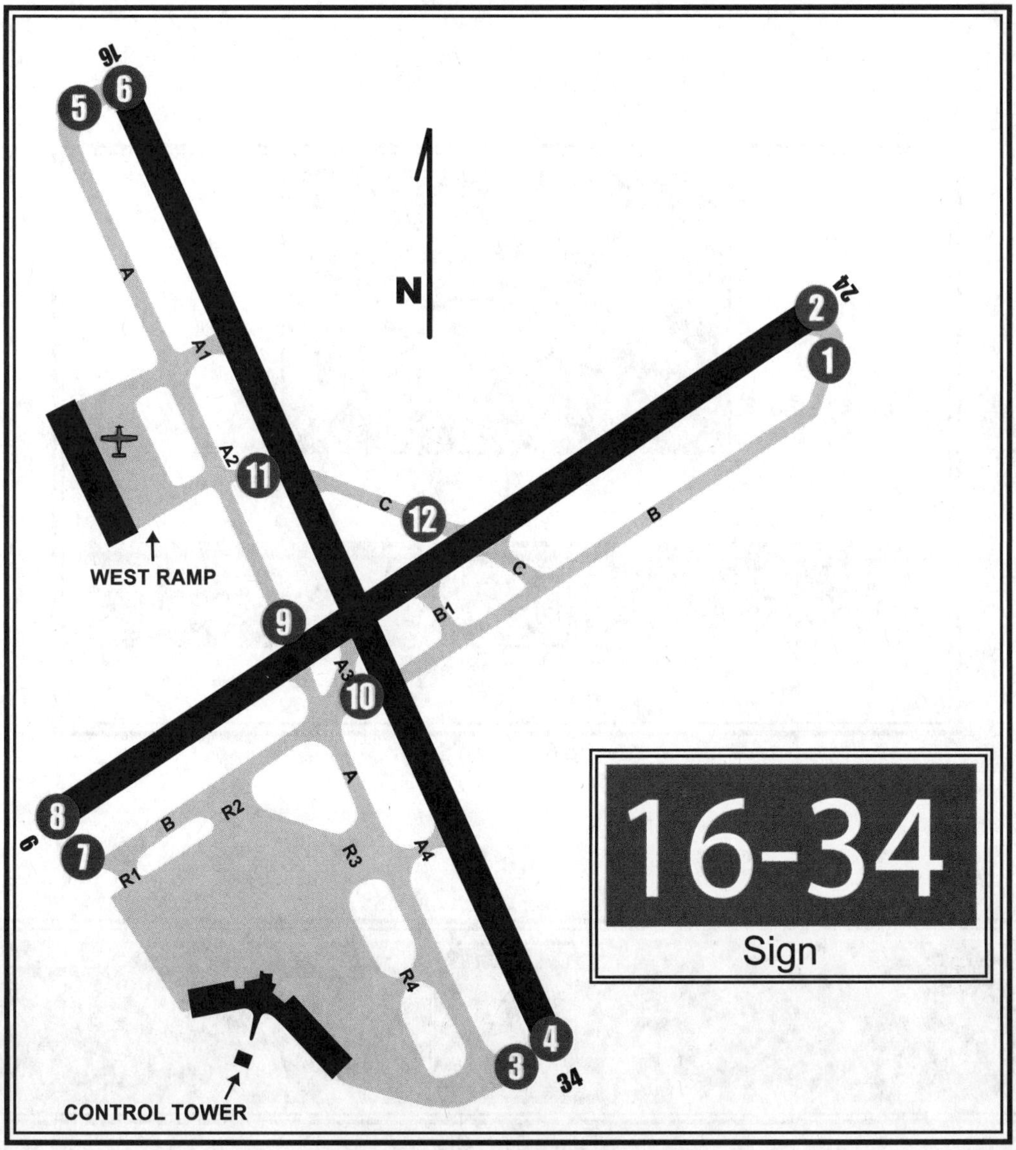

Figure 58. – Airport Diagram and Sign.

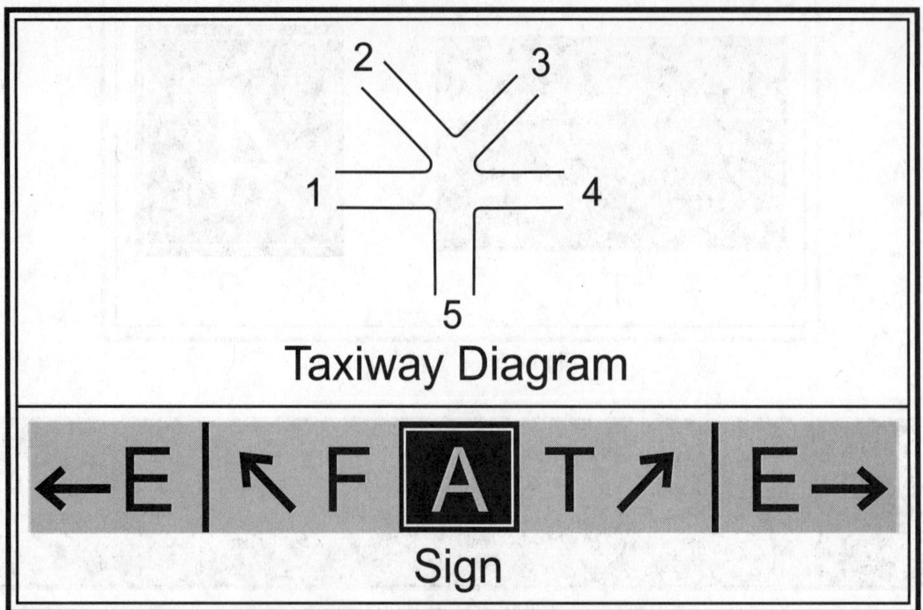

Figure 59. – Taxiway Diagram and Sign.

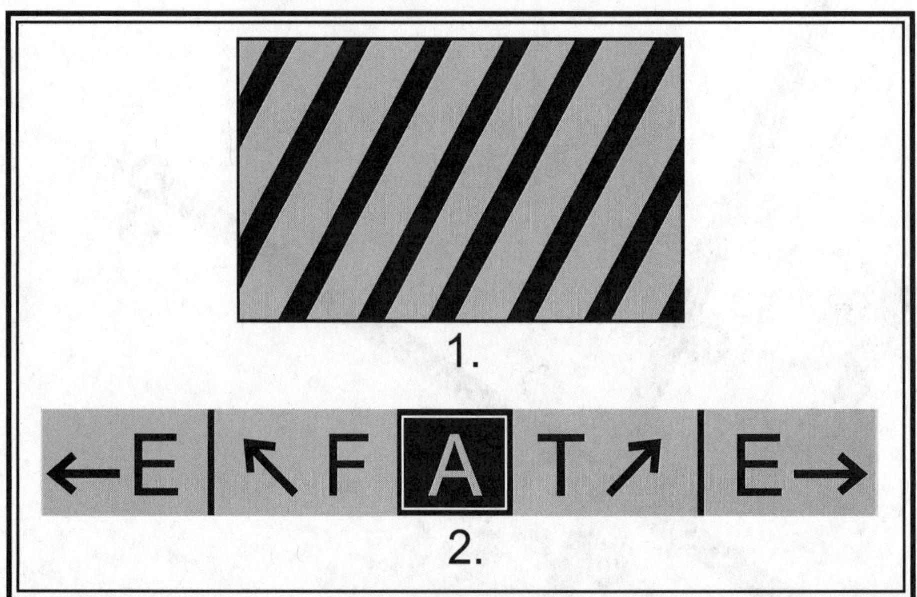

Figure 60. – Two Signs.

Figure 61. – Sign.

Figure 62. – Sign.

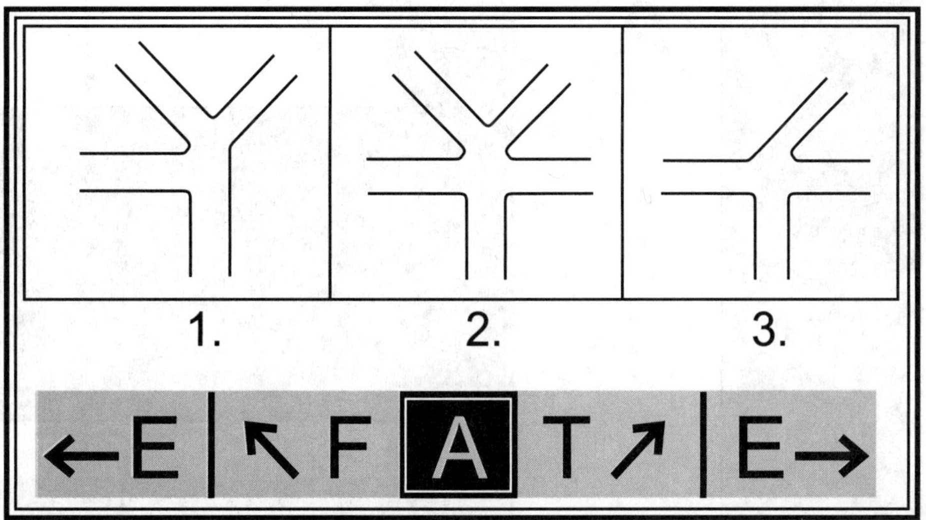

Figure 63. – Sign and Intersection Diagram.

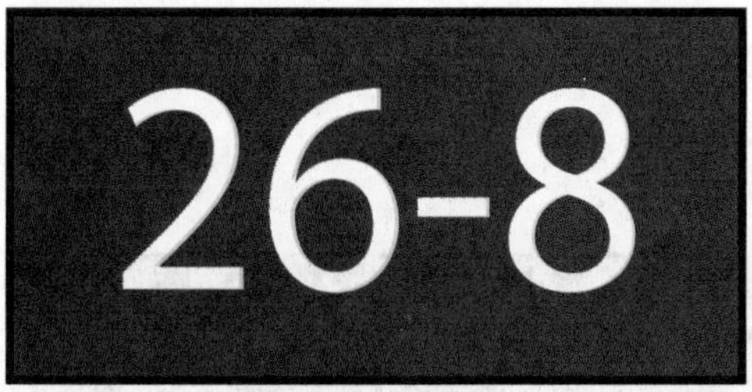

26-8

Figure 64. – Sign.

Figure 65. – Sign.

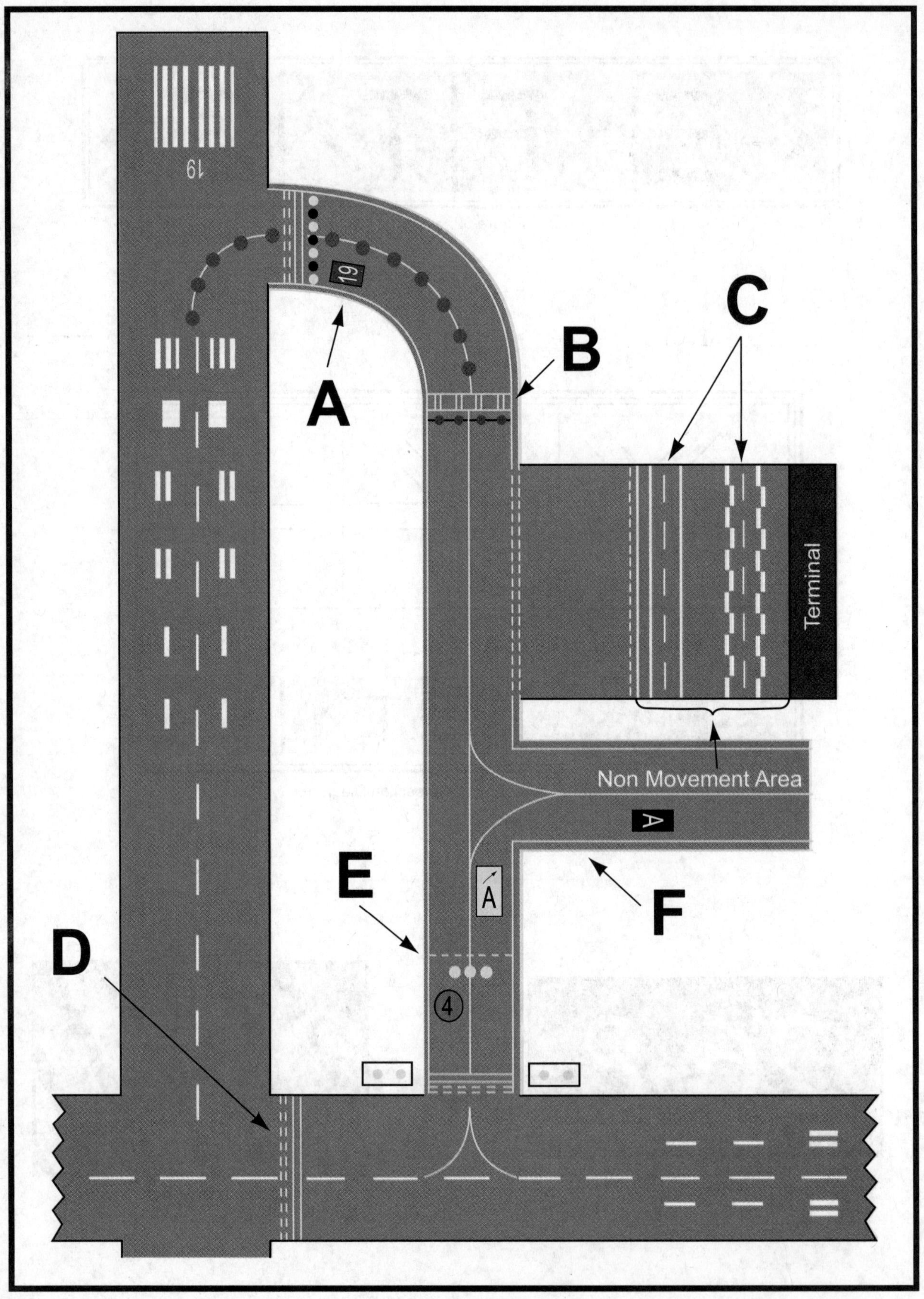

Figure 66. – Airport Markings.

9.2 Instrument Approach Charts

19. (Refer to Figure 30 below.) What minimum navigation equipment is required to complete the VOR/DME-A procedure?

A. One VOR receiver.

B. One VOR receiver and DME.

C. Two VOR receivers and DME.

Answer (B) is correct. *(IFH Chap 10)*

DISCUSSION: The minimum navigation equipment required for a VOR/DME approach is one VOR receiver and DME.

Answer (A) is incorrect. The minimum equipment required for a VOR/DME approach includes DME. Answer (C) is incorrect. The approach requires one VOR receiver, not two.

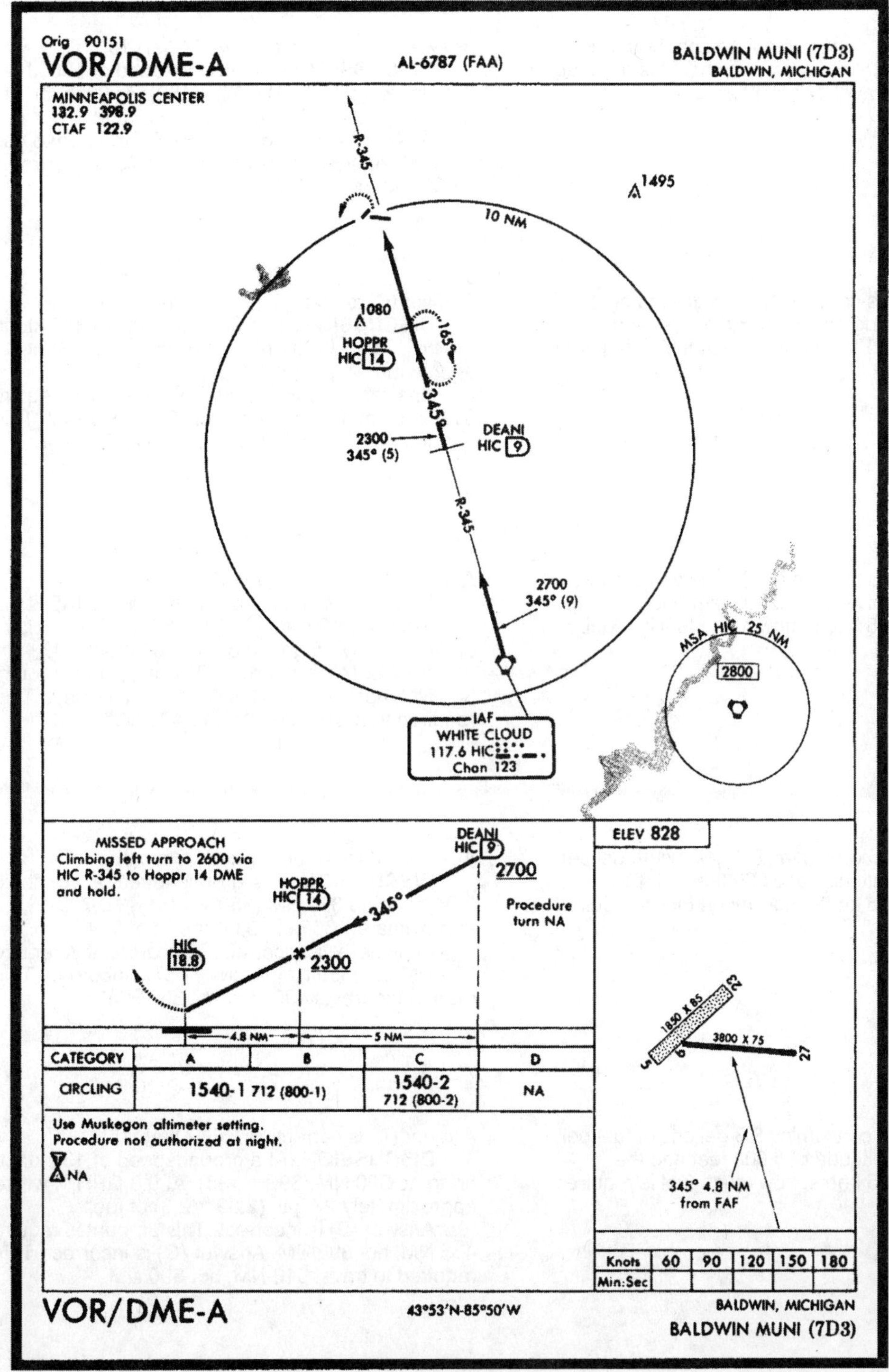

Figure 30. – VOR/DME-A (7D3).

9.3 Fuel Consumption

20. If an airplane is consuming 95 pounds of fuel per hour at a cruising altitude of 6,500 feet and the groundspeed is 173 knots, how much fuel is required to travel 450 NM?

A. 248 pounds.

B. 265 pounds.

C. 284 pounds.

Answer (A) is correct. *(PHAK Chap 15)*

DISCUSSION: At a groundspeed of 173 kt., it will take 2.60 hr. to go 450 NM (450 ÷ 173). At 95 lb./hr., it will take approximately 248 lb. (2.60 × 95) of fuel.

Answer (B) is incorrect. This is required to travel 483 NM, not 450 NM. Answer (C) is incorrect. This is required to travel 517 NM, not 450 NM.

21. If fuel consumption is 80 pounds per hour and groundspeed is 180 knots, how much fuel is required for an airplane to travel 477 NM?

A. 205 pounds.

B. 212 pounds.

C. 460 pounds.

Answer (B) is correct. *(PHAK Chap 15)*

DISCUSSION: At a groundspeed of 180 kt., it will take 2.39 hr. to go 477 NM (477 ÷ 180). At 80 lb./hr., it will take approximately 212 lb. (2.39 × 80) of fuel.

Answer (A) is incorrect. This is required to travel 461 NM, not 477 NM. Answer (C) is incorrect. This is required to travel 1,035 NM, not 477 NM.

22. If an airplane is consuming 12.5 gallons of fuel per hour at a cruising altitude of 8,500 feet and the groundspeed is 145 knots, how much fuel is required to travel 435 NM?

A. 27 gallons.

B. 34 gallons.

C. 38 gallons.

Answer (C) is correct. *(PHAK Chap 15)*

DISCUSSION: At a groundspeed of 145 kt., it will take 3.0 hr. to go 435 NM (435 ÷ 145). At 12.5 GPH, it will take approximately 38 gal. (3 × 12.5) of fuel.

Answer (A) is incorrect. This amount is required to travel 313 NM, not 435 NM. Answer (B) is incorrect. This amount is required to travel 394 NM, not 435 NM.

23. If an airplane is consuming 9.5 gallons of fuel per hour at a cruising altitude of 6,000 feet and the groundspeed is 135 knots, how much fuel is required to travel 490 NM?

A. 27 gallons.

B. 30 gallons.

C. 35 gallons.

Answer (C) is correct. *(PHAK Chap 15)*

DISCUSSION: At a groundspeed of 135 kt., it will take 3.63 hr. to go 490 NM (490 ÷ 135). At 9.5 GPH, it will take approximately 35 gal. (3.63 × 9.5) of fuel.

Answer (A) is incorrect. This amount is required to travel 384 NM, not 490 NM. Answer (B) is incorrect. This amount is required to travel 426 NM, not 490 NM.

24. If an aircraft is consuming 9.7 gallons of fuel per hour at a cruising altitude of 6,000 feet and the groundspeed is 115 knots, how much fuel is required to travei 350 NM?

A. 36 gallons.

B. 30 gallons.

C. 41 gallons.

Answer (B) is correct. *(PHAK Chap 15)*

DISCUSSION: At a groundspeed of 115 kt., it will take 3.04 hr. to go 350 NM (350 ÷ 115). At 9.7 GPH, it will take approximately 30 gal. (3.04 × 9.7) of fuel.

Answer (A) is incorrect. This amount is required to travel 426 NM, not 350 NM. Answer (C) is incorrect. This amount is required to travel 490 NM, not 350 NM.

25. If an aircraft is consuming 9.3 gallons of fuel per hour at a cruising altitude of 6,000 feet and the groundspeed is 135 knots, how much fuel is required to travel 390 NM?

A. 27 gallons.

B. 30 gallons.

C. 35 gallons.

Answer (A) is correct. *(PHAK Chap 15)*

DISCUSSION: At a groundspeed of 135 kt., it will take 2.89 hr. to go 390 NM (390 ÷ 135). At 9.3 GPH, it will take approximately 27 gal. (2.89 × 9.3) of fuel.

Answer (B) is incorrect. This amount is required to travel 435 NM, not 390 NM. Answer (C) is incorrect. This amount is required to travel 510 NM, not 390 NM.

26. If an airplane is consuming 14.8 gallons of fuel per hour at a cruising altitude of 7,500 feet and the groundspeed is 167 knots, how much fuel is required to travel 560 NM?

A. 50 gallons.

B. 53 gallons.

C. 57 gallons.

Answer (A) is correct. *(PHAK Chap 15)*

DISCUSSION: At a groundspeed of 167 kt., it will take 3.35 hr. to go 560 NM (560 ÷ 167). At 14.8 GPH, it will take approximately 50 gal. (3.35 × 14.8) of fuel.

Answer (B) is incorrect. This amount is required to travel 598 NM, not 560 NM. Answer (C) is incorrect. This amount is required to travel 643 NM, not 560 NM.

27. If fuel consumption is 14.7 gallons per hour and groundspeed is 157 knots, how much fuel is required for an airplane to travel 612 NM?

A. 58 gallons.

B. 60 gallons.

C. 64 gallons.

Answer (A) is correct. *(PHAK Chap 15)*

DISCUSSION: At a groundspeed of 157 kt., it will take 3.90 hr. to go 612 NM (612 ÷ 157). At 14.7 GPH, it will take approximately 58 gal. (3.90 × 14.7) of fuel.

Answer (B) is incorrect. This amount is required to travel 641 NM, not 612 NM. Answer (C) is incorrect. This amount is required to travel 684 NM, not 612 NM.

9.4 Time, Distance, and Fuel to Station

28. (Refer to Figure 21 below.) If the time flown between aircraft positions 2 and 3 is 13 minutes, what is the estimated time to the station?

A. 13 minutes.

B. 17 minutes.

C. 26 minutes.

Answer (A) is correct. *(IFH Chap 9)*

DISCUSSION: The time/distance to station can be found by application of the isosceles triangle principle (i.e., if two angles of a triangle are equal, two of the sides are also equal), as follows:

1. With the aircraft established on a radial (here 270°), inbound, rotate the OBS 10° to the left, i.e., 260°.
2. Turn 10° to the right and note the time.
3. Maintain constant heading until the CDI centers, and note the elapsed time.
4. Time to station is the same as the time taken to complete the 10° change of bearing.

Thus, if the time flown between aircraft positions 2 and 3 is 13 min., the estimated time to the station is also 13 min.

Answer (B) is incorrect. The time between positions 2 and 3 and between position 3 and the station should be equal, i.e., 13 min. Answer (C) is incorrect. The time between positions 2 and 3 and between position 3 and the station should be equal, i.e., 13 min.

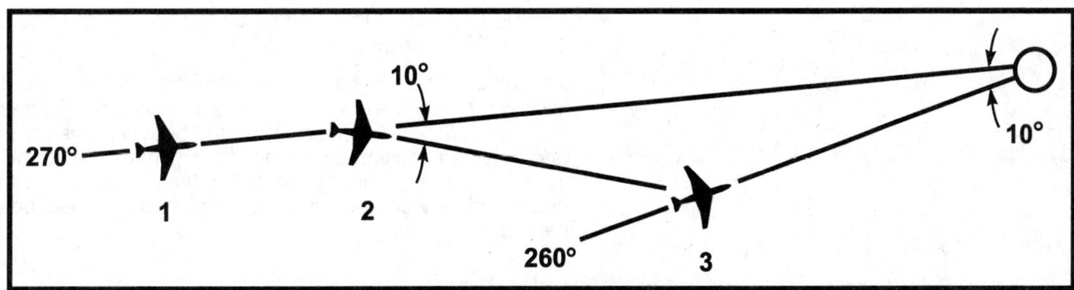

Figure 21. – Isosceles Triangle.

29. (Refer to Figure 24 below.) If the time flown between aircraft positions 2 and 3 is 15 minutes, what is the estimated time to the station?

A. 15 minutes.

B. 30 minutes.

C. 60 minutes.

Answer (A) is correct. *(IFH Chap 9)*

DISCUSSION: The time/distance to station can be found by application of the isosceles triangle principle (i.e., if two angles of a triangle are equal, two of the sides are also equal), as follows:

1. With the aircraft established on a radial (here 105°) inbound, rotate the OBS 15° to the left, i.e., 90°.
2. Turn 15° to the right and note the time.
3. Maintain constant heading until the CDI centers, and note the elapsed time.
4. Time to station is the same as the time taken to complete the 15° change of bearing.

Thus, if the time flown between aircraft positions 2 and 3 is 15 min., the estimated time to the station is also 15 min.

Answer (B) is incorrect. The time between positions 2 and 3 and between position 3 and the station should be equal, i.e., 15 min. Answer (C) is incorrect. The time between positions 2 and 3 and between position 3 and the station should be equal, i.e., 15 min.

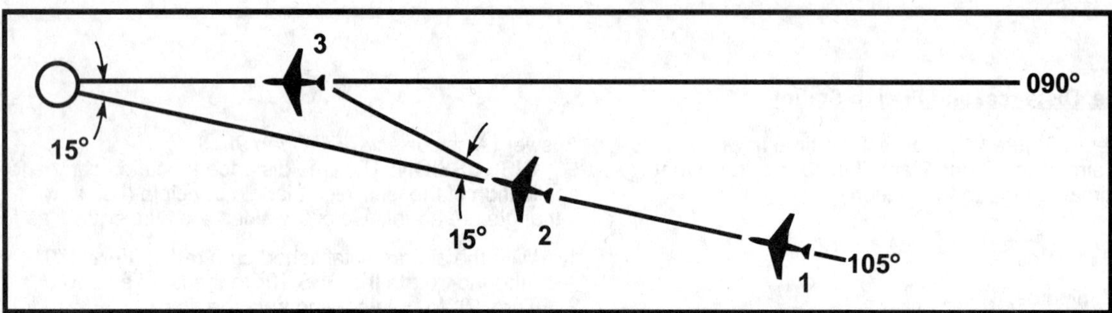

Figure 24. – Isosceles Triangle.

30. (Refer to Figure 23 below.) If the time flown between aircraft positions 2 and 3 is 13 minutes, what is the estimated time to the station?

A. 7.8 minutes.

B. 13 minutes.

C. 26 minutes.

Answer (B) is correct. *(IFH Chap 9)*

DISCUSSION: The time/distance to station can be found by application of the isosceles triangle principle (i.e., if two angles of a triangle are equal, two of the sides are also equal), as follows:

1. With the aircraft established on a radial (here 90°) inbound, rotate the OBS 20° to the right, i.e., 110°.
2. Turn 20° to the left and note the time.
3. Maintain constant heading until the CDI centers, and note the elapsed time.
4. Time to station is the same as the time taken to complete the 20° change of bearing.

Thus, if the time flown between aircraft positions 2 and 3 is 13 min., the estimated time to the station is also 13 min.

Answer (A) is incorrect. The time between positions 2 and 3 and between position 3 and the station should be equal, i.e., 13 min. Answer (C) is incorrect. The time between positions 2 and 3 and between position 3 and the station should be equal, i.e., 13 min.

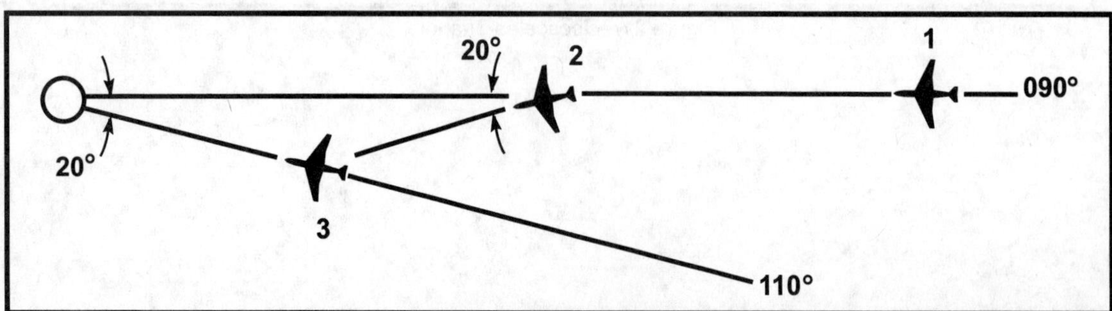

Figure 23. – Isosceles Triangle.

31. (Refer to Figure 22 below.) If the time flown between aircraft positions 2 and 3 is 8 minutes, what is the estimated time to the station?

A. 8 minutes.

B. 16 minutes.

C. 48 minutes.

Answer (A) is correct. *(IFH Chap 9)*

DISCUSSION: The time/distance to station can be found by application of the isosceles triangle principle (i.e., if two angles of a triangle are equal, two of the sides are also equal), as follows:

1. With the aircraft established on a radial (here 270°) inbound, rotate the OBS 5° to the left, i.e., 265°.
2. Turn 5° to the right and note the time.
3. Maintain constant heading until the CDI centers, and note the elapsed time.
4. Time to station is the same as the time taken to complete the 5° change of bearing.

Thus, if the time flown between aircraft positions 2 and 3 is 8 min., the estimated time to the station is also 8 min.

Answer (B) is incorrect. The time between positions 2 and 3 and between position 3 and the station should be equal, i.e., 8 min. Answer (C) is incorrect. The time between positions 2 and 3 and between position 3 and the station should be equal, i.e., 8 min.

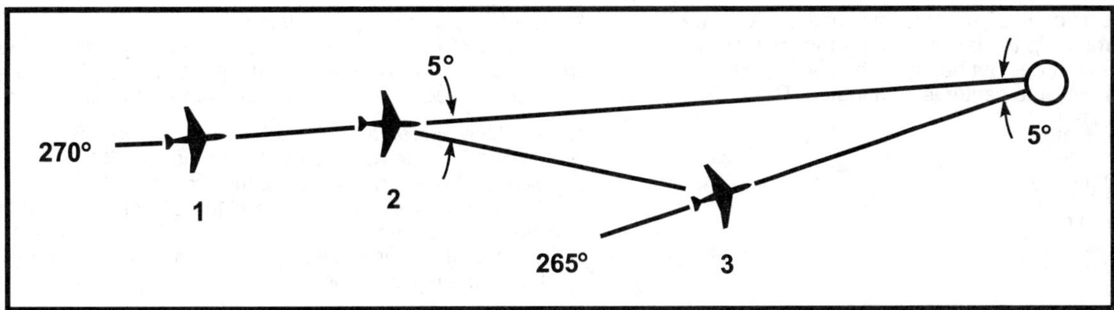

Figure 22. – Isosceles Triangle.

32. Inbound on the 040 radial, a pilot selects the 055 radial, turns 15° to the left, and notes the time. While maintaining a constant heading, the pilot notes the time for the CDI to center is 15 minutes. Based on this information, the ETE to the station is

A. 8 minutes.

B. 15 minutes.

C. 30 minutes.

Answer (B) is correct. *(IFH Chap 9)*

DISCUSSION: The time/distance to station can be found by application of the isosceles triangle principle (i.e., if two angles of a triangle are equal, two of the sides are also equal), as follows:

1. With the aircraft established on a radial (here 40°) inbound, rotate the OBS 15° (to 55° in this case).
2. Turn 15° (to the left in this example) and note the time.
3. Maintain constant heading until the CDI centers, and note the elapsed time.
4. Time to station is the same as the time taken to complete the 15° change of bearing.

Thus, if it takes 15 min. for the CDI to center, the estimated time to the station is also 15 min.

Answer (A) is incorrect. The time to the station is the same as the time between bearings, i.e., 15 min. Answer (C) is incorrect. The time to the station is the same as the time between bearings, i.e., 15 min.

33. Inbound on the 090 radial, a pilot rotates the OBS 010° to the left, turns 010° to the right, and notes the time. While maintaining a constant heading, the pilot determines that the elapsed time for the CDI to center is 8 minutes. Based on this information, the ETE to the station is

A. 8 minutes.

B. 16 minutes.

C. 24 minutes.

Answer (A) is correct. *(IFH Chap 9)*

DISCUSSION: The time/distance to station can be found by application of the isosceles triangle principle (i.e., if two angles of a triangle are equal, two of the sides are also equal), as follows:

1. With the aircraft established on a radial (here 90°) inbound, rotate the OBS 10° to the left, i.e., 80°.
2. the time to the station is the same as the time to the right and note the time.
3. Maintain constant heading until the CDI centers, and note the elapsed time.
4. Time to station is the same as the time taken to complete the 10° change of bearing.

Thus, if it takes 8 min. for the CDI to center, the estimated time to the station is also 8 min.

Answer (B) is incorrect. The time to the station is the same as the time between bearings, i.e., 8 min. Answer (C) is incorrect. The time to the station is the same as the time between bearings, i.e., 8 min.

34. Inbound on the 315 radial, a pilot selects the 320 radial, turns 5° to the left, and notes the time. While maintaining a constant heading, the pilot notes the time for the CDI to center is 12 minutes. The ETE to the station is

A. 10 minutes.

B. 12 minutes.

C. 24 minutes.

Answer (B) is correct. *(IFH Chap 9)*

DISCUSSION: The time/distance to station can be found by application of the isosceles triangle principle (i.e., if two angles of a triangle are equal, two of the sides are also equal), as follows:

1. With the aircraft established on a radial (here 315°) inbound, rotate the OBS 5° to the left, i.e., 80°.
2. Turn 5° to the right and note the time.
3. Maintain constant heading until the CDI centers, and note the elapsed time.
4. Time to station is the same as the time taken to complete the 5° change of bearing.

Thus, if it takes 12 min. for the CDI to center, the estimated time to the station is also 12 min.

Answer (A) is incorrect. The time to the station is the same as the time between bearings, i.e., 12 min. Answer (C) is incorrect. The time to the station is the same as the time between bearings, i.e., 12 min.

35. Inbound on the 190 radial, a pilot selects the 195 radial, turns 5° to the left, and notes the time. While maintaining a constant heading, the pilot notes the time for the CDI to center is 10 minutes. The ETE to the station is

A. 10 minutes.

B. 15 minutes.

C. 20 minutes.

Answer (A) is correct. *(IFH Chap 9)*

DISCUSSION: The time/distance to station can be found by application of the isosceles triangle principle (i.e., if two angles of a triangle are equal, two of the sides are also equal), as follows:

1. With the aircraft established on a radial inbound (190° in this example), rotate the OBS 5° to the left (to 185° for this problem).
2. Turn 5° to the right and note the time.
3. Maintain constant heading until the CDI centers, and note the elapsed time.
4. Time to station is the same as the time taken to complete the 5° change of bearing.

Thus, if it takes 10 min. for the CDI to center, the estimated time to the station is also 10 min.

Answer (B) is incorrect. The time to the station is the same as the time between bearings, i.e., 10 min. Answer (C) is incorrect. The time to the station is the same as the time between bearings, i.e., 10 min.

36. While maintaining a magnetic heading of 270° and a true airspeed of 120 knots, the 360 radial of a VOR is crossed at 1237 and the 350 radial is crossed at 1244. The approximate time and distance to this station are

A. 42 minutes and 84 NM.

B. 42 minutes and 91 NM.

C. 44 minutes and 96 NM.

Answer (A) is correct. *(IFH Chap 9)*

DISCUSSION: To determine the time and distance to the station, use the following formulas:

$$\text{Time to station} = \frac{60 \times \text{Min. flown between bearing change}}{\text{Degrees of bearing change}}$$

$$= \frac{60 \times 7}{10} = \frac{420}{10} = 42 \text{ min.}$$

$$\text{Distance to station} = \frac{\text{TAS} \times \text{Min. flown between bearing change}}{\text{Degrees of bearing change}}$$

$$= \frac{120 \times 7}{10} = \frac{840}{10} = 84 \text{ NM}$$

Answer (B) is incorrect. The distance would be 91 NM if the TAS were 132 kt., not 120 kt. Answer (C) is incorrect. The time to the station is 42 min., not 44 min., and the distance is 84 NM, not 96 NM.

37. The relative bearing on an ADF changes from 265° to 260° in 2 minutes of elapsed time. If the groundspeed is 145 knots, the distance to that station would be

A. 26 NM.

B. 37 NM.

C. 58 NM.

Answer (C) is correct. *(IFH Chap 9)*

DISCUSSION: To determine the distance to the station, use the following formula:

$$\text{Distance to station} = \frac{\text{TAS} \times \text{Min. flown between bearing change}}{\text{Degrees of bearing change}}$$

$$= \frac{145 \times 2}{5} = \frac{290}{5} = 58 \text{ NM}$$

Note the FAA incorrectly uses groundspeed instead of TAS to calculate the distance to the station.

Answer (A) is incorrect. A distance of 26 NM to the station would require a TAS of 65 kt., not 145 kt. Answer (B) is incorrect. A distance of 37 NM to the station would require a TAS of 93 kt., not 145 kt.

38. The ADF indicates a wingtip bearing change of 10° in 2 minutes of elapsed time, and the TAS is 160 knots. What is the distance to the station?

A. 15 NM.

B. 32 NM.

C. 36 NM.

Answer (B) is correct. *(IFH Chap 9)*

DISCUSSION: To determine the distance to the station, use the following formula:

$$\text{Distance to station} = \frac{\text{TAS} \times \text{Min. flown between bearing change}}{\text{Degrees of bearing change}}$$

$$= \frac{160 \times 2}{10} = \frac{320}{10} = 32 \text{ NM}$$

Answer (A) is incorrect. A distance of 15 NM to the station would require a TAS of 75 kt., not 160 kt. Answer (C) is incorrect. A distance of 36 NM to the station would require a TAS of 180 kt., not 160 kt.

39. With a TAS of 115 knots, the relative bearing on an ADF changes from 090° to 095° in 1.5 minutes of elapsed time. The distance to the station would be

A. 12.5 NM.

B. 24.5 NM.

C. 34.5 NM.

Answer (C) is correct. *(IFH Chap 9)*

DISCUSSION: To determine the distance to the station, use the following formula:

$$\text{Distance to station} = \frac{\text{TAS} \times \text{Min. flown between bearing change}}{\text{Degrees of bearing change}}$$

$$= \frac{115 \times 1.5}{5} = \frac{172.5}{5} = 34.5 \text{ NM}$$

Answer (A) is incorrect. A distance of 12.5 NM to the station would require a TAS of 42 kt., not 115 kt. Answer (B) is incorrect. A distance of 24.5 NM to the station would require a TAS of 82 kt., not 115 kt.

40. GIVEN:

Wingtip bearing change . . . . 5°
Time elapsed between bearing change . . . . 5 min.
True airspeed . . . . 115 kts

The distance to the station is

A. 36 NM.

B. 57.5 NM.

C. 115 NM.

Answer (C) is correct. *(IFH Chap 9)*

DISCUSSION: To determine the distance to the station, use the following formula:

$$\text{Distance to station} = \frac{\text{TAS} \times \text{Min. flown between bearing change}}{\text{Degrees of bearing change}}$$

$$= \frac{115 \times 5}{5} = \frac{575}{5} = 115 \text{ NM}$$

Answer (A) is incorrect. A distance of 36 NM to the station would require a TAS of 36 kt., not 115 kt. Answer (B) is incorrect. A distance of 57.5 NM to the station would require a TAS of 57.5 kt., not 115 kt.

41. The ADF is tuned to a nondirectional radiobeacon and the relative bearing changes from 095° to 100° in 1.5 minutes of elapsed time. The time en route to that station would be

A. 18 minutes.

B. 24 minutes.

C. 30 minutes.

Answer (A) is correct. *(IFH Chap 9)*

DISCUSSION: The time to the station is determined by the following formula:

$$\text{Time to station} = \frac{60 \times \text{Min. flown between bearing change}}{\text{Degrees of bearing change}}$$

$$= \frac{60 \times 1.5}{5} = \frac{90}{5} = 18 \text{ min.}$$

Answer (B) is incorrect. Two min., not 1.5 min., of elapsed time between 5° of bearing change would indicate 24 min. to the station. Answer (C) is incorrect. Elapsed time of 2.5 min., not 1.5 min., between 5° of bearing change would indicate 30 min. to the station.

42. While maintaining a constant heading, a relative bearing of 10° doubles in 5 minutes. If the true airspeed is 105 knots, the time and distance to the station being used is approximately

A. 5 minutes and 8.7 miles.

B. 10 minutes and 17 miles.

C. 15 minutes and 31.2 miles.

Answer (A) is correct. *(IFH Chap 9)*

DISCUSSION: When a relative bearing doubles in a specific time, the time to the station is that time (the time to double the relative bearing). Thus, the time to the station is 5 min. Since the TAS is 105 kt., the distance would be 8.7 NM (5 ÷ 60 × 105).

Answer (B) is incorrect. The time to the station is the same as the time to double the relative bearing, i.e., 5 min. Answer (C) is incorrect. The time to the station is the same as the time to double the relative bearing, i.e., 5 min.

43. GIVEN:

Wingtip bearing change . . . . 15°
Elapsed time between bearing change . . . . . 6 min.
Rate of fuel consumption . . . . 8.6 gal/hr

Calculate the approximate fuel required to fly to the station.

A. 3.44 gallons.

B. 6.88 gallons.

C. 17.84 gallons.

Answer (A) is correct. *(IFH Chap 9)*

DISCUSSION: To determine the time and fuel required to fly to the station, use the following steps:

1. $$\text{Time to station} = \frac{60 \times \text{Min. flown between bearing change}}{\text{Degrees of bearing change}}$$

$$= \frac{60 \times 6}{15} = \frac{360}{15} = 24 \text{ min.}$$

2. Use your flight computer or your calculator to determine the fuel required.

$$\text{Fuel required} = \frac{\text{Rate of fuel consumption} \times \text{Min. to station}}{60}$$

$$= \frac{8.6 \times 24}{60} = \frac{206.4}{60} = 3.44 \text{ gal.}$$

Answer (B) is incorrect. This would be required if the fuel consumption were 17.2 gal./hr., not 8.6 gal./hr. Answer (C) is incorrect. This would be required if the fuel consumption were 44.6 gal./hr., not 8.6 gal./hr.

44. GIVEN:

Wingtip bearing change . . . . 15°
Elapsed time between bearing change . . . . 7.5 min
True airspeed . . . . 85 kts
Rate of fuel consumption . . . . 9.6 gal/hr

The time, distance, and fuel required to fly to the station is

A. 30 minutes; 42.5 miles; 4.80 gallons.

B. 32 minutes; 48 miles; 5.58 gallons.

C. 48 minutes; 48 miles; 4.58 gallons.

Answer (A) is correct. *(IFH Chap 9)*

DISCUSSION: To determine the time, distance, and fuel required to fly to the station, use the following steps:

1. Time to station $= \dfrac{60 \times \text{Min. flown between bearing change}}{\text{Degrees of bearing change}}$

$$= \frac{60 \times 7.5}{15} = \frac{450}{15} = 30 \text{ min.}$$

2. Distance to station $= \dfrac{\text{TAS} \times \text{Min. flown between bearing change}}{\text{Degrees of bearing change}}$

$$= \frac{85 \times 7.5}{15} = \frac{637.5}{15} = 42.5 \text{ NM, and}$$

3. Fuel required $= \dfrac{\text{Rate of fuel consumption} \times \text{Min. to station}}{60}$

$$= \frac{9.6 \times 30}{60} = \frac{288}{60} = 4.80 \text{ gal.}$$

Answer (B) is incorrect. Eight min., not 7.5 min., of elapsed time between 15° of bearing change would indicate 32 min. to the station. Answer (C) is incorrect. Twelve min., not 7.5 min., of elapsed time between 15° of bearing change would indicate 48 min. to the station.

45. While maintaining a constant heading, a relative bearing of 15° doubles in 6 minutes. The time to the station being used is

A. 3 minutes.

B. 6 minutes.

C. 12 minutes.

Answer (B) is correct. *(IFH Chap 9)*

DISCUSSION: When a relative bearing doubles in a specific time, the time to the station is that time (the time to double the relative bearing). Thus, the time to the station is 6 min.

Answer (A) is incorrect. The time to the station is the same as the time to double the relative bearing, i.e., 6 min. Answer (C) is incorrect. The time to the station is the same as the time to double the relative bearing, i.e., 6 min.

46. While maintaining a constant heading, the ADF needle increases from a relative bearing of 045° to 090° in 5 minutes. The time to the station being used is

A. 5 minutes.

B. 10 minutes.

C. 15 minutes.

Answer (A) is correct. *(IFH Chap 9)*

DISCUSSION: When a relative bearing doubles in a specific time, the time to the station is that time (the time to double the relative bearing). Thus, the time to the station is 5 min.

Answer (B) is incorrect. The time to the station is the same as the time to double the relative bearing, i.e., 5 min. Answer (C) is incorrect. The time to the station is the same as the time to double the relative bearing, i.e., 5 min.

47. While cruising at 135 knots and on a constant heading, the ADF needle decreases from a relative bearing of 315° to 270° in 7 minutes. The approximate time and distance to the station being used is

A. 7 minutes and 16 miles.

B. 14 minutes and 28 miles.

C. 19 minutes and 38 miles.

Answer (A) is correct. *(IFH Chap 9)*

DISCUSSION: When a relative bearing doubles in a specific time, the time to the station is that time (the time to double the relative bearing). Thus, the time to the station is 7 min. Since the TAS is 135 kt., the distance to the station is 15.7 NM (7 ÷ 60 × 135).

Answer (B) is incorrect. The time to the station is the same as the time to double the relative bearing, i.e., 7 min. Answer (C) is incorrect. The time to the station is the same as the time to double the relative bearing, i.e., 7 min.

48. The ADF is tuned to a nondirectional radiobeacon and the relative bearing changes from 270° to 265° in 2.5 minutes of elapsed time. The time en route to that beacon would be

A. 9 minutes.

B. 18 minutes.

C. 30 minutes.

Answer (C) is correct. *(IFH Chap 9)*

DISCUSSION: To determine the time to the station, use the following formula:

$$\text{Time to station} = \frac{60 \times \text{Min. flown between bearing change}}{\text{Degrees of bearing change}}$$

$$= \frac{60 \times 2.5}{5} = \frac{150}{5} = 30 \text{ min.}$$

Answer (A) is incorrect. Elapsed time of 45 sec., not 2.5 min., between 5° of bearing change would indicate 9 min. to the station. Answer (B) is incorrect. Elapsed time of 1.5 min., not 2.5 min., between 5° of bearing change would indicate 18 min. to the station.

49. The ADF is tuned to a nondirectional radiobeacon and the relative bearing changes from 090° to 100° in 2.5 minutes of elapsed time. If the true airspeed is 90 knots, the distance and time en route to that radiobeacon would be

A. 15 miles and 22.5 minutes.

B. 22.5 miles and 15 minutes.

C. 32 miles and 18 minutes.

Answer (B) is correct. *(IFH Chap 9)*

DISCUSSION: To determine the time and distance to the station, use the following formulas:

$$\text{Time to station} = \frac{60 \times \text{Min. flown between bearing change}}{\text{Degrees of bearing change}}$$

$$= \frac{60 \times 2.5}{10} = \frac{150}{10} = 15 \text{ min.}$$

$$\text{Distance to station} = \frac{\text{TAS} \times \text{Min. flown between bearing change}}{\text{Degrees of bearing change}}$$

$$= \frac{90 \times 2.5}{10} = \frac{225}{10} = 22.5 \text{ NM}$$

Answer (A) is incorrect. The time, not distance, is 15 min., and the distance, not time, is 22.5 NM. Answer (C) is incorrect. Three min., not 2.5 min., of elapsed time between 10° of bearing change would indicate 18 min. to the station.

50. The ADF is tuned to a nondirectional radiobeacon and the relative bearing changes from 085° to 090° in 2 minutes of elapsed time. The time en route to the station would be

A. 15 minutes.

B. 18 minutes.

C. 24 minutes.

Answer (C) is correct. *(IFH Chap 9)*

DISCUSSION: To determine the time to the station, use the following formula:

$$\text{Time to station} = \frac{60 \times \text{Min. flown between bearing change}}{\text{Degrees of bearing change}}$$

$$= \frac{60 \times 2}{5} = \frac{120}{5} = 24 \text{ min.}$$

Answer (A) is incorrect. Elapsed time of 1.25 min., not 2 min., between 5° of bearing change would indicate 15 min. to the station. Answer (B) is incorrect. Elapsed time of 1.5 min., not 2 min., between 5° of bearing change would indicate 18 min. to the station.

51. If the relative bearing changes from 090° to 100° in 2.5 minutes of elapsed time, the time en route to the station would be

A. 12 minutes.

B. 15 minutes.

C. 18 minutes.

Answer (B) is correct. *(IFH Chap 9)*

DISCUSSION: To determine the time to the station, use the following formula:

$$\text{Time to station} = \frac{60 \times \text{Min. flown between bearing change}}{\text{Degrees of bearing change}}$$

$$= \frac{60 \times 2.5}{10} = \frac{150}{10} = 15 \text{ min.}$$

Answer (A) is incorrect. Two min., not 2.5 min., of elapsed time between 10° of bearing change would indicate 12 min. to the station. Answer (C) is incorrect. Three min., not 2.5 min., of elapsed time between 10° of bearing change would indicate 18 min. to the station.

52. GIVEN:

Wingtip bearing change . . . . 10°
Elapsed time between bearing change . . . . 4 min.
Rate of fuel consumption . . . . 11 gal/hr

Calculate the fuel required to fly to the station.

A. 4.4 gallons.

B. 8.4 gallons.

C. 12 gallons.

Answer (A) is correct. *(IFH Chap 9)*

DISCUSSION: To calculate the fuel required to fly to the station, use the following steps:

1. Time to station $= \dfrac{60 \times \text{Min. flown between bearing change}}{\text{Degrees of bearing change}}$

$$= \frac{60 \times 4}{10} = \frac{240}{10} = 24 \text{ min.}$$

2. Fuel required $= \dfrac{\text{Rate of fuel consumption} \times \text{Min. to station}}{60}$

$$= \frac{11 \times 24}{60} = \frac{264}{60} = 4.4 \text{ gal.}$$

Answer (B) is incorrect. The amount of 8.4 gal. would be required if the fuel consumption were 21 gal./hr., not 11 gal./hr. Answer (C) is incorrect. The amount of 12 gal. would be required if the fuel consumption were 30 gal./hr., not 11 gal./hr.

53. GIVEN:

Wingtip bearing change . . . . 5°
Elapsed time between bearing change . . . . . 6 min.
Rate of fuel consumption . . . . 12 gal/hr

The fuel required to fly to the station is

A. 8.2 gallons.

B. 14.4 gallons.

C. 18.7 gallons.

Answer (B) is correct. *(IFH Chap 9)*

DISCUSSION: To calculate the fuel required to fly to the station, use the following steps:

1. Time to station $= \dfrac{60 \times \text{Min. flown between bearing change}}{\text{Degrees of bearing change}}$

$$= \frac{60 \times 6}{5} = \frac{360}{5} = 72 \text{ min.}$$

2. Fuel required $= \dfrac{\text{Rate of fuel consumption} \times \text{Min. to station}}{60}$

$$= \frac{12 \times 72}{60} = \frac{864}{60} = 14.4 \text{ gal.}$$

Answer (A) is incorrect. The amount of 8.2 gal. would be required if the fuel consumption were 6.8 gal./hr., not 12 gal./hr. Answer (C) is incorrect. The amount of 18.7 gal. would be required if the fuel consumption were 15.6 gal./hr., not 12 gal./hr.

9.5 Wind Direction and Speed

54. GIVEN:

Distance off course . . . . 9 mi
Distance flown . . . . 95 mi
Distance to fly . . . . 125 mi

To converge at the destination, the total correction angle would be

A. 4°.

B. 6°.

C. 10°.

Answer (C) is correct. *(IFH Chap 9)*

DISCUSSION: To determine the total correction angle to converge on your destination, use the following steps:

1. Since 1° off course equals 1 NM per 60 NM from the station, the following formula applies:

$$\frac{\text{NM off}}{\text{NM flown}} \times 60 = \text{Degrees off course from departure point}$$

$$\frac{9 \text{ NM}}{95 \text{ NM}} \times 60 = 5.68°$$

Turning back this number of degrees will parallel the original course.

2. To converge on your destination, calculate the number of degrees off it:

$$\frac{\text{NM off}}{\text{NM remaining}} \times 60 = \text{Degrees off course to destination}$$

$$\frac{9 \text{ NM}}{125 \text{ NM}} \times 60 = 4.32°$$

3. Turning this number of degrees farther will take you to your destination. Thus, the total correction angle is approximately 10° (5.68 + 4.32).

Answer (A) is incorrect. Turning 4° would converge you on your destination if you were already paralleling the original course. Answer (B) is incorrect. Six degrees is the amount of correction required to parallel the original course.

55. You have flown 52 miles, are 6 miles off course, and have 118 miles yet to fly. To converge on your destination, the total correction angle would be

A. 3°.

B. 6°.

C. 10°.

Answer (C) is correct. *(IFH Chap 9)*

DISCUSSION: To determine the total correction angle to converge on your destination use the following steps:

1. Since 1° off course equals 1 NM per 60 NM from the station, the following formula applies:

$$\frac{\text{NM off}}{\text{NM flown}} \times 60 = \text{Degrees off course from departure point}$$

$$\frac{6\text{ NM}}{52\text{ NM}} \times 60 = 6.92°$$

Turning back this number of degrees will parallel the original course.

2. To converge on your destination, calculate the number of degrees off it:

$$\frac{\text{NM off}}{\text{NM remaining}} \times 60 = \text{Degrees off course to destination}$$

$$\frac{6\text{ NM}}{118\text{ NM}} \times 60 = 3.05°$$

3. Turning this number of degrees farther will take you to your destination. Thus, the total correction angle is approximately 10° (6.92 + 3.05).

Answer (A) is incorrect. Turning 3° would converge you on your destination if you were already paralleling the original course. Answer (B) is incorrect. Six degrees is the amount of correction required to parallel the original course.

56. GIVEN:

True course	105°
True heading	085°
True airspeed	95 kts
Groundspeed	87 kts

Determine the wind direction and speed.

A. 020° and 32 knots.

B. 030° and 38 knots.

C. 200° and 32 knots.

Answer (A) is correct. *(FI Comp)*

DISCUSSION: To estimate your wind, given a true heading and a true course, simply use the wind side of your flight computer backwards. First, place your groundspeed of 87 kt. under the grommet with your true course of 105° under the true index. Since your true heading is 085°, you are holding a 20° left wind correction angle. Next, place a pencil mark on the 95-kt. true airspeed arc, 20° left of the centerline. Finally, rotate the wheel until the pencil mark is on the centerline, and read a wind of 020° (under the true index) at 32 kt. (up from the grommet).

Answer (B) is incorrect. A wind from 030° at 38 kt. would result in less wind correction and a slower groundspeed. Answer (C) is incorrect. A wind from 200° at 32 kt. would result in a higher, not lower, groundspeed than airspeed.

57. GIVEN:

True course	345°
True heading	355°
True airspeed	85 kts
Groundspeed	95 kts

Determine the wind direction and speed.

A. 095° and 19 knots.

B. 113° and 19 knots.

C. 238° and 18 knots.

Answer (B) is correct. *(FI Comp)*

DISCUSSION: To estimate your wind, given a true heading and a true course, simply use the wind side of your flight computer backwards. First, place your groundspeed of 95 kt. under the grommet with your true course of 345° under the true index. Since your true heading is 355°, you are holding a 10° right wind correction angle. Next, place a pencil mark on the 85-kt. true airspeed arc, 10° right of centerline. Finally, rotate the wheel until the pencil mark is on the centerline, and read a wind of 113° (under the true index) at 19 kt. (up from the grommet).

Answer (A) is incorrect. A wind from 095° at 19 kt. would result in more wind correction angle and a slower groundspeed. Answer (C) is incorrect. A wind from 238° at 18 kt. would require a left, not right, wind correction angle.

9.6 Time, Compass Heading, Etc., on Climbs and En Route

58. An airplane departs an airport under the following conditions:

Airport elevation . . . . 1000 ft
Cruise altitude . . . . 9,500 ft
Rate of climb . . . . 500 ft/min
Average true airspeed . . . . 135 kts
True course . . . . 215°
Average wind velocity . . . . 290° at 20 kts
Variation . . . . 3° W
Deviation . . . . –2°
Average fuel consumption . . . . 13 gal/hr

Determine the approximate time, compass heading, distance, and fuel consumed during the climb.

A. 14 minutes, 234°, 26 NM, 3.9 gallons.

B. 17 minutes, 224°, 36 NM, 3.7 gallons.

C. 17 minutes, 242°, 31 NM, 3.5 gallons.

Answer (B) is correct. *(FI Comp)*

DISCUSSION: The requirement is the time, compass heading, distance, and fuel consumed during the climb. The airport elevation is 1,000 ft. and the climb is to 9,500 ft., which is a climb of 8,500 ft. At 500 fpm, this requires 17 min. In 17 min., the fuel burned would be 3.7 gal. [(17 ÷ 60) × 13].

To determine the compass heading, first determine the true heading using the wind side of your flight computer. Then adjust the true heading to magnetic heading, and then to compass heading.

To determine the distance, multiply the time by the groundspeed also found on the wind side of the computer.

Answer (A) is incorrect. The time required to climb is 17 min., not 14 min. Answer (C) is incorrect. The fuel used during 17 min. of climb is 3.7 gal., not 3.5 gal.

59. An airplane departs an airport under the following conditions:

Airport elevation . . . . 1,500 ft
Cruise altitude . . . . 9,500 ft
Rate of climb . . . . 500 ft/min
Average true airspeed . . . . 160 kts
True course . . . . 145°
Average wind velocity . . . . 080° at 15 kts
Variation . . . . 5° E
Deviation . . . . –3°
Average fuel consumption . . . . 14 gal/hr

Determine the approximate time, compass heading, distance, and fuel consumed during the climb.

A. 14 minutes, 128°, 35 NM, 3.2 gallons.

B. 16 minutes, 132°, 41 NM, 3.7 gallons.

C. 16 minutes, 128°, 32 NM, 3.8 gallons.

Answer (B) is correct. *(FI Comp)*

DISCUSSION: The requirement is the time, compass heading, distance, and fuel consumed during the climb. The airport elevation is 1,500 ft. and the climb is to 9,500 ft., which is a climb of 8,000 ft. At 500 fpm, this requires 16 min., which narrows the answer choices down to two. In 16 min. at 14 gal./hr., just over one-fourth of 14 gal. would be burned, which is approximately 3.7 gal. To determine the compass heading, first determine the true heading using the wind side of your flight computer. Then adjust the true heading to magnetic heading, and then to compass heading. To determine the distance, multiply the time by the groundspeed also found on the wind side of the computer.

Answer (A) is incorrect. The time required to climb is 16 min., not 14 min. Answer (C) is incorrect. The fuel used during 16 min. of climb is 3.7 gal., not 3.8 gal.

60. GIVEN

Wind . . . . 175° at 20 kts
Distance . . . . 135 NM
True course . . . . 075°
True airspeed . . . . 80 kts
Fuel consumption . . . . 105 lb/hr

Determine the time en route and fuel consumption.

A. 1 hour 28 minutes and 73.2 pounds.

B. 1 hour 38 minutes and 158 pounds.

C. 1 hour 40 minutes and 175 pounds.

Answer (C) is correct. *(FI Comp)*

DISCUSSION: Using the wind side of your flight computer, follow these steps:

1. Place the wind direction under the true index (175°).
2. Mark the wind velocity up from the grommet (+20 kt.).
3. Place the true course under the true index (75°).
4. Slide the wind velocity mark to the (80-kt.) TAS line, and the groundspeed is under the grommet which is 81 kt.

Using the computer side, determine the time it takes to travel 135 NM by placing the index under 81 kt. and locating 135 NM on the outer scale. Under it is the time of 1 hr. 40 min. Next, place the index under 105 lb./hr. and locate 1 hr. 40 min. on the inner scale, and determine the fuel consumption on the outer scale to be 175 lb.

Answer (A) is incorrect. To travel 135 NM in 1 hr. and 28 min. would require a groundspeed of 92 kt., not 81 kt. Answer (B) is incorrect. In 1 hr. and 38 min. at 105 lb./hr., the fuel consumption would be 171 lb., not 158 lb.

9.7 Time, Compass Heading, Etc., on Descents

61. An airplane descends to an airport under the following conditions:

Cruising altitude . . . . 6,500 ft
Airport elevation . . . . 700 ft
Descends to. . . . . 800 ft AGL
Rate of descent . . . . 500 ft/min
Average true airspeed . . . . 110 kts
True course . . . . 335°
Average wind velocity . . . . 060° at 15 kts
Variation . . . . 3°W
Deviation . . . . +2°
Average fuel consumption . . . . 8.5 gal/hr

Determine the approximate time, compass heading, distance, and fuel consumed during the descent.

A. 10 minutes, 348°, 18 NM, 1.4 gallons.

B. 10 minutes, 355°, 17 NM, 2.4 gallons.

C. 12 minutes, 346°, 18 NM, 1.6 gallons.

Answer (A) is correct. *(FI Comp)*

DISCUSSION: A descent is to be made from 6,500 ft. to 1,500 ft. MSL (airport elevation of 700 ft. + 800 ft. AGL), which is a 5,000-ft. descent. At 500 fpm, it would take 10 min. Thus, the correct answer must either be 10 minutes, 348°, 18 NM, 1.4 gallons or 10 minutes, 355°, 17 NM, 2.4 gallons. At 8.5 gal./hr., 1.4 gal. would be burned in 10 min. (10/60 × 8.5). Thus, 10 minutes, 348°, 18 NM, 1.4 gallons is correct.

Compute the compass heading by using the wind side of your flight computer. Convert true course to true heading based upon the wind effect. Then convert the true heading to magnetic heading by adjusting for the magnetic variation. The compass heading is determined by adjusting the magnetic heading for the compass deviation.

Answer (B) is incorrect. At 8.5 gal./hr., 1.4 gal., not 2.4 gal., would be used in 10 min. Answer (C) is incorrect. It would take approximately 12 min. to descend from 6,500 ft. MSL to the surface of the airport, not the level altitude of 1,500 ft. MSL (800 ft. AGL).

62. An airplane descends to an airport under the following conditions:

Cruising altitude . . . . 7,500 ft
Airport elevation . . . . 1,300 ft
Descends to. . . . . 800 ft AGL
Rate of descent . . . . 300 ft/min
Average true airspeed . . . . 120 kts
True course . . . . 165°
Average wind velocity . . . . 240° at 20 kts
Variation . . . . 4°E
Deviation . . . . –2°
Average fuel consumption . . . . 9.6 gal/hr

Determine the approximate time, compass heading, distance, and fuel consumed during the descent.

A. 16 minutes, 168°, 30 NM, 2.9 gallons.

B. 18 minutes, 164°, 34 NM, 3.2 gallons.

C. 18 minutes, 168°, 34 NM, 2.9 gallons.

Answer (C) is correct. *(FI Comp)*

DISCUSSION: A descent is to be made from 7,500 ft. to 2,100 ft. MSL (airport elevation of 1,300 ft. + 800 ft. AGL), which is a 5,400-ft. descent. At 300 fpm, it would take 18 min. Thus, the correct answer must either be 18 minutes, 164°, 34 NM, 3.2 gallons or 18 minutes, 168°, 34 NM, 2.9 gallons. Based on fuel consumption of 9.6 gal./hr., the fuel consumption would be 2.9 gal. (18/60 × 9.6), which makes the answer 18 minutes, 168°, 34 NM, 2.9 gallons correct.

Compute the compass heading by using the wind side of your flight computer. Convert true course to true heading based upon the wind effect. Then convert the true heading to magnetic heading by adjusting for the magnetic variation. The compass heading is determined by adjusting the magnetic heading for the compass deviation.

Answer (A) is incorrect. The time to descend is 18 min., not 16 min. Answer (B) is incorrect. At 9.6 gal./hr., 2.9 gal., not 3.2 gal., would be used in 18 min.

63. An airplane descends to an airport under the following conditions:

Cruising altitude . . . . 10,500 ft
Airport elevation . . . . 1,700 ft
Descends to. . . . . 1,000 ft AGL
Rate of descent . . . . 600 ft/min
Average true airspeed . . . . 135 kts
True course . . . . 263°
Average wind velocity . . . . 330° at 30 kts
Variation . . . . 7°E
Deviation . . . . +3°
Average fuel consumption . . . . 11.5 gal/hr

Determine the approximate time, compass heading, distance, and fuel consumed during the descent.

A. 9 minutes, 274°, 26 NM, 2.8 gallons.

B. 13 minutes, 274°, 28 NM, 2.5 gallons.

C. 13 minutes, 271°, 26 NM, 2.5 gallons.

Answer (C) is correct. *(FI Comp)*

DISCUSSION: A descent is to be made from 10,500 ft. to 2,700 ft. MSL (airport elevation of 1,700 ft. + 1,000 ft. AGL), which is a 7,800-ft. descent. At 600 fpm, it would take 13 min. Thus, the correct answer must either be 13 minutes, 274°, 28 NM, 2.5 gallons or 13 minutes, 271°, 26 NM, 2.5 gallons and you must compute the compass heading.

Place the wind direction of 330° under the true index. With a pencil, mark the wind velocity of 30 kt. above the grommet. Then turn the inner scale so that the true course of 263° is under the true index. Next, slide the wind scale such that the pencil mark is on the true airspeed of 135 kt., and note that the groundspeed is 121 kt. Also note that a 12 right correction is required. Thus, the true heading will be 275° (263° + 12°). To convert to magnetic, subtract the 7 easterly variation to get 268° (275° – 7°). Then add the compass deviation of 3° to determine the compass heading of 271° (268° + 3°). Thus, 13 minutes, 271°, 26 NM, 2.5 gallons is correct.

Answer (A) is incorrect. The time to descend is 13 min., not 9 min. Answer (B) is incorrect. The compass heading is 271°, not 274°.

END OF STUDY UNIT

STUDY UNIT TEN
NAVIGATION SYSTEMS

(5 pages of outline)

This study unit contains outlines of major concepts tested, sample test questions and answers regarding navigation systems, and an explanation of each answer. The table of contents above lists each subunit within this study unit, the number of questions pertaining to that particular subunit, and the pages on which the outlines and questions begin, respectively.

Recall that the **sole purpose** of this book is to expedite your passing of the FAA pilot knowledge test for the commercial pilot certificate. Accordingly, all extraneous material (i.e., topics or regulations not directly tested on the FAA pilot knowledge test) is omitted, even though much more knowledge is necessary to become a proficient commercial pilot. This additional material is presented in *Pilot Handbook* and *Commercial Pilot Flight Maneuvers and Practical Test Prep*, available from Gleim Publications, Inc. See the product listing at the back of the book and order online at www.gleim.com.

10.1 AUTOMATIC DIRECTION FINDER (ADF)

1. The ADF indicator always has its needle pointing toward the NDB station (nondirectional beacon, also known as a radio beacon).
   a. If the NDB is directly in front of the airplane, the needle will point straight up.
   b. If the NDB is directly off the right wing, i.e., at 3 o'clock, the needle will point directly to the right.
   c. If the NDB is directly behind the airplane, the needle will point straight down, etc.
2. Homing to a station is accomplished by keeping the needle centered on the top index of your ADF.
   a. A wind will cause you to drift on your inbound course and fly a curved path to the station.
3. When properly correcting for crosswind while heading to the NDB, the needle will point (not straight up) to the side the crosswind is blowing to. The amount of deflection depends on the amount of crosswind correction.
   a. When tracking away from the station, the head of the needle will point to the side from which the crosswind is blowing.
4. To compute magnetic heading, relative bearing, or magnetic bearing, use the formula

   MH + RB = MB

   a. Magnetic heading (MH) is the magnetic heading of the airplane.
   b. Relative bearing (RB) is the direction of the magnetic bearing relative to the airplane.
   c. Magnetic bearing (MB) is the relative direction from north.
   d. In order to obtain answers ranging between 0° and 360°, you may need to add or subtract 360° to or from your answer.
   e. The preceding formula is for magnetic bearing TO the station. If magnetic bearing FROM the station is desired, add or subtract 180°.

5. EXAMPLE: Given a 300° magnetic heading and a relative bearing of 30°, the magnetic bearing is 300° + 30° = 330° (MH + RB = MB).
   a. If you know your MH is 300° and the MB is 330°, the ADF would indicate 30°, which is the RB.
6. There is a series of questions referring to the interception of a magnetic bearing from an ADF at a specified angle.
   a. Remember, a bearing from an ADF is the same as a VOR radial, e.g., spokes FROM the axle of a wheel.
      1) Bearings TO are the opposite direction. A 90° bearing FROM is to the east. A 90° bearing TO is west of the station.
   b. Begin by constructing a diagram.
      1) Start with a point indicating the ADF station.
      2) Extend the "desired" bearing FROM or TO the station.
      3) Draw your airplane based on your relative bearing (indicated by an ADF indicator or stated in the question) and your magnetic heading (also given).
      4) Trace your current ground track on the diagram and compute your angle of interception with the "desired" bearing.
      5) If a revised MH is required, first compute your present angle of interception and then determine the amount of MH change needed to obtain the desired angle of interception.

10.2 VOR USE AND RECEIVER CHECKS

1. When checking the course sensitivity of a VOR receiver, the OBS should be rotated 10° to 12° to move the CDI from the center to the last dot.
   a. One-fifth deflection represents 2° off course, or 2 NM at 60 NM from the VOR station.
2. When using a VOT to make a VOR receiver check, the CDI should be centered and the OBS should indicate that the aircraft is on the 360° radial.
   a. To use a designated checkpoint on an airport surface, set the OBS on the designated radial.
      1) The CDI must center within ±4° of that radial with a FROM indication.
   b. When the CDI is centered during an airborne check, the OBS and the TO/FROM indicator should read within ±6° of the selected radial.
3. To track outbound on a VOR radial, set the OBS to the desired radial, and make heading corrections toward the CDI.
   a. To track inbound on a VOR radial, set the OBS to the reciprocal of the desired radial, and make heading corrections toward the CDI.
   b. Flying a heading that is reciprocal to the bearing selected on the OBS would result in reverse sensing of the VOR receiver.
4. For IFR operations off established airways, VORs that are no more than 80 NM apart should be listed in the "route of flight" portion of an IFR flight plan.

10.3 RADIO MAGNETIC INDICATOR (RMI)

1. The radio magnetic indicator (RMI) consists of a rotating compass card (heading indicator) and one or more navigation indicators that point to stations.

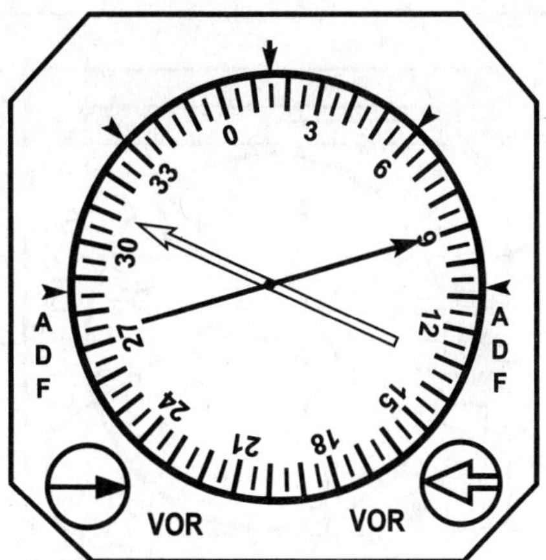

2. The magnetic heading of the airplane is always directly under the index at the top of the instrument.
3. The bearing pointer displays magnetic bearings to selected navigation stations.
   a. The tail of the indicator tells you which radial you are on.
   b. For example, the RMI above indicates a 015° magnetic heading, crossing the R-270 of VOR 1 (thin needle) and crossing the R-130 of VOR 2 (wide needle).

10.4 HORIZONTAL SITUATION INDICATOR (HSI)

1. The horizontal situation indicator (HSI) is a combination of a heading indicator and a VOR/ILS indicator, as illustrated and described below.

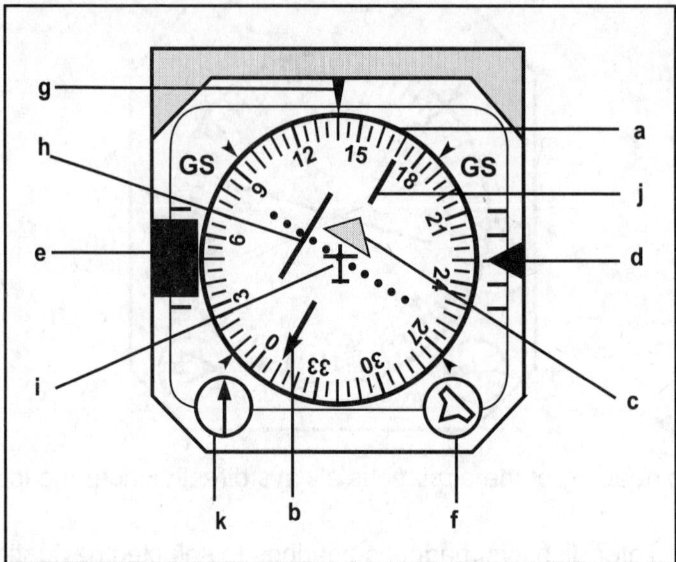

a. The azimuth card, which rotates so that the heading is shown under the index at the top of the instrument.
    1) The azimuth card may be part of a remote indicating compass (RIC).
    2) The azimuth card must be checked against the magnetic compass and reset with a heading set knob.
b. The course indicating arrow, which is the VOR (OBS) indicator.
c. The TO/FROM indicator for the VOR.
d. Glide slope deviation pointer. It indicates above or below the glide slope, which is the longer center line.
e. Glide slope warning flag, which comes out when reliable signals are not received by the glide slope deviation pointer.
f. Heading set knob, which is used to coordinate the heading indicator (directional gyro, etc.) with the actual compass.
    1) If the azimuth card is part of an RIC, normally a heading bug (pointer) set knob moves a bug around the periphery of the azimuth card.
g. Lubber line, which shows the current heading.
h. Course deviation bar, which indicates the direction one would have to turn to intercept the desired radial if one were on the approximate heading of the OBS selection.
i. The airplane symbol, which is fixed, showing the airplane relative to the selected course if seen from above the airplane looking down.
j. The tail of the course-indicating arrow shows the reciprocal of the OBS heading.
k. The course setting knob, which is used to adjust the OBS.

10.5 GLOBAL POSITIONING SYSTEM (GPS)

1. To effectively navigate by means of GPS, pilots should
   a. Determine the GPS unit is approved for their planned flight
   b. Determine the status of the databases
      1) The current status of navigational databases, weather databases, NOTAMs, and signal availability should be ensured prior to takeoff.
   c. Understand how to make and cancel all appropriate entries
      1) Stressful situations, heavy workloads, and turbulence make data entry errors real problems, and pilots should know how to recover basic aircraft controls quickly.
   d. Program and review the planned route
      1) Because each GPS layout can vary widely in type and function (knobs, switches, etc.), programming of the units should be verified for accuracy.
      2) Name changes or spelling mistakes contribute to errors in flying appropriate routes.
   e. Ensure the track flown is approved by ATC
2. One of the primary benefits of GPS navigation is that it permits aircraft to fly optimum routes and altitudes.
   a. The "Direct To," or D▸, key is a primary function key on most GPS units. A user hits the button and, using a series of knobs or switches, programs the intended waypoint or airport using the proper identifier. This feature shows the quickest way to fly to any given point, which is usually in a straight line.
   b. The "nearest" button, abbreviated on most units as NRST, will show the closest airports in relation to the aircraft's current location.
      1) The "nearest" function is very beneficial in emergency situations. A pilot simply presses this button to see the name, location, and direction to the nearest airport for landing.
      2) Information such as navigation and communication frequencies, runway numbers and lengths, and other pertinent data is also provided.
3. Due to the use of and reliance on GPS systems for navigation, it is easy for pilots to lose proficiency in performing manual calculations on courses, times, distances, headings, etc.
   a. Emergency situations (e.g., electrical failures) make it important to maintain proficiency in these calculations.

QUESTIONS AND ANSWER EXPLANATIONS: All of the commercial pilot knowledge test questions chosen by the FAA for release as well as additional questions selected by Gleim relating to the material in the previous outlines are reproduced on the following pages. These questions have been organized into the same subunits as the outlines. To the immediate right of each question are the correct answer and answer explanation. You should cover these answers and answer explanations while responding to the questions. Refer to the general discussion in the Introduction on how to take the FAA knowledge test.

Remember that the questions from the FAA knowledge test bank have been reordered by topic and organized into a meaningful sequence. Also, the first line of the answer explanation gives the citation of the authoritative source for the answer.

QUESTIONS

10.1 Automatic Direction Finder (ADF)

1. Which is true about homing when using ADF during crosswind conditions? Homing

A. to a radio station results in a curved path that leads to the station.

B. is a practical navigation method for flying both to and from a radio station.

C. to a radio station requires that the ADF have an automatically or manually rotatable azimuth.

Answer (A) is correct. *(IFH Chap 9)*

DISCUSSION: Homing to a station is accomplished by keeping the needle centered on the top index of your ADF. As a result, any wind will cause you to drift on your inbound course and fly a curved path to the station.

Answer (B) is incorrect. Homing is an impractical means of navigating to the station and an absolutely faulty means of navigating from the station. Answer (C) is incorrect. Homing can be accomplished with any ADF by keeping the needle pointed to the top of your ADF dial, regardless if the ADF has an automatically or manually rotatable azimuth.

2. Which is true regarding tracking on a desired bearing when using ADF during crosswind conditions?

A. To track outbound, heading corrections should be made away from the ADF pointer.

B. When on the desired track outbound with the proper drift correction established, the ADF pointer will be deflected to the windward side of the tail position.

C. When on the desired track inbound with the proper drift correction established, the ADF pointer will be deflected to the windward side of the nose position.

Answer (B) is correct. *(IFH Chap 9)*

DISCUSSION: When tracking outbound from an NDB station, the nose of the aircraft will be crabbed into the wind. As a result of this crab and flying away from the station, the ADF needle will be deflected towards the windward side (the side the wind is coming from).

Answer (A) is incorrect. When tracking outbound, corrections should be made towards, not away from, the ADF pointer. Answer (C) is incorrect. When inbound, the pointer is deflected to the leeward (the side the wind is blowing toward), not the windward side.

3. The magnetic heading is 315° and the ADF shows a relative bearing of 140°. The magnetic bearing FROM the radiobeacon would be

A. 095°.

B. 175°.

C. 275°.

Answer (C) is correct. *(IFH Chap 9)*

DISCUSSION: To compute the magnetic bearing to an NDB, you use the formula below. The MH is given as 315°, and the RB is given as 140°.

MH + RB = MB (TO)
315° + 140° = MB (TO) 455° – 360° = 095°

You adjust by 180° to get MB (FROM)

095° + 180° = 275°

Answer (A) is incorrect. This is the MB TO the station, not FROM the station. Answer (B) is incorrect. This is not a related direction in this problem.

4. The magnetic heading is 350° and the relative bearing to a radiobeacon is 240°. What would be the magnetic bearing TO that radiobeacon?

A. 050°.

B. 230°.

C. 295°.

Answer (B) is correct. *(IFH Chap 9)*

DISCUSSION: To compute the magnetic bearing to an NDB, you use the formula below. The MH is given as 350°, and the RB is given as 240°.

MH + RB = MB (TO)
350° + 240° = MB (TO)
MB (TO) = 590° – 360° = 230°

Answer (A) is incorrect. This is the MB FROM the station, not TO the station. Answer (C) is incorrect. This is not a related direction in this problem.

5. The ADF is tuned to a radiobeacon. If the magnetic heading is 040° and the relative bearing is 290°, the magnetic bearing TO that radiobeacon would be

A. 150°.

B. 285°.

C. 330°.

Answer (C) is correct. *(IFH Chap 9)*

DISCUSSION: To compute the magnetic bearing to an NDB, you use the formula below. The MH is given as 040°, and the RB is 290°.

MH + RB = MB (TO)
040° + 290° = 330°

Answer (A) is incorrect. This is the MB FROM the station, not TO the station. Answer (B) is incorrect. This is not a related direction in this problem.

6. If the relative bearing to a nondirectional radiobeacon is 045° and the magnetic heading is 355°, the magnetic bearing TO that radiobeacon would be

A. 040°.

B. 065°.

C. 220°.

Answer (A) is correct. *(IFH Chap 9)*

DISCUSSION: To compute the magnetic bearing to an NDB, you use the formula below. The MH is given as 355°, and the RB is given as 045°.

MH + RB = MB (TO)
355° + 045° = MB (TO)
MB (TO) = 400° – 360° = 040°

Answer (B) is incorrect. This is not a related direction in this problem. Answer (C) is incorrect. This is the MB FROM the station, not TO the station.

7. An aircraft is maintaining a magnetic heading of 265° and the ADF shows a relative bearing of 065°. This indicates that the aircraft is crossing the

A. 065° magnetic bearing FROM the radiobeacon.

B. 150° magnetic bearing FROM the radiobeacon.

C. 330° magnetic bearing FROM the radiobeacon.

Answer (B) is correct. *(IFH Chap 9)*

DISCUSSION: To compute the magnetic bearing to an NDB, you use the formula below. The MH is given as 265°, and the RB is given as 065°.

MH + RB = MB (TO)
265° + 065° = 330°

You adjust by 180° to get MB (FROM)

330° – 180° = 150°

Answer (A) is incorrect. The RB TO the station, not MB FROM the station, is 065°. Answer (C) is incorrect. The MB TO the station, not MB FROM the station, is 330°.

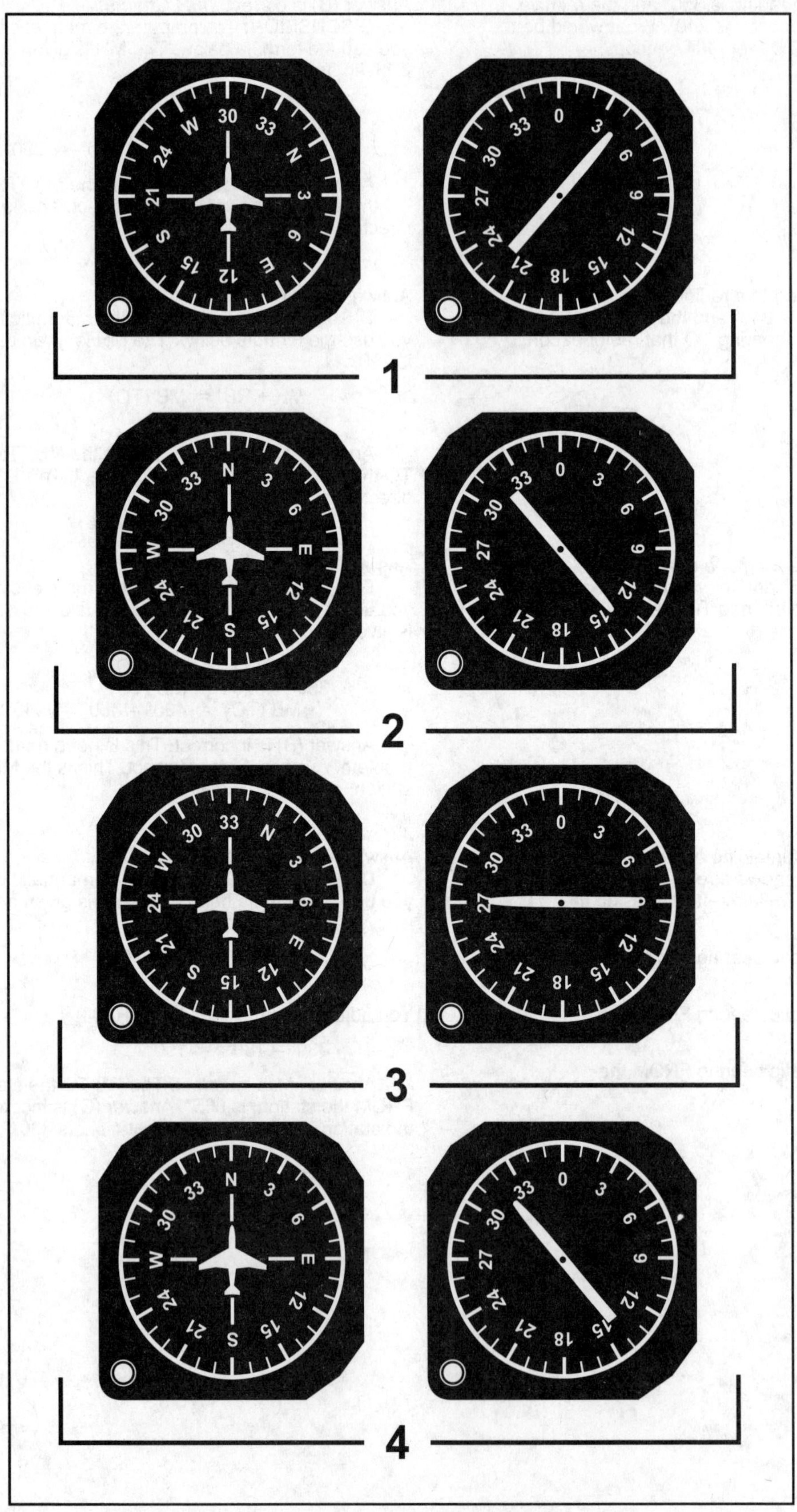

Figure 16. – Magnetic Compass/ADF.

8. (Refer to Figure 16 on page 272.) At the position indicated by instrument group 1, to intercept the 330° magnetic bearing to the NDB at a 30° angle, the aircraft should be turned

A. left to a heading of 270°.

B. right to a heading of 330°.

C. right to a heading of 360°.

Answer (C) is correct. *(IFH Chap 9)*

DISCUSSION: Draw a diagram as illustrated below.

Note you are west of the 330° MB because your RB is greater than 30° (on the 330° MB, you will have a 30° RB). Thus, you need to turn right. Since you wish a 30° intersection angle with the 330° MB, your heading should be 360°.

Answer (A) is incorrect. A MH of 270° will take you farther from the 330° MB TO the station. Answer (B) is incorrect. A MH of 330° will parallel, not intercept, the 330° MB TO the station.

9. (Refer to Figure 16 on page 272.) If the aircraft continues its present heading as shown in instrument group 3, what will be the relative bearing when the aircraft reaches the magnetic bearing of 030° FROM the NDB?

A. 030°.

B. 060°.

C. 240°.

Answer (C) is correct. *(IFH Chap 9)*

DISCUSSION: Draw a diagram as illustrated below.

Recall the formula

$$\begin{aligned} MH + RB &= MB\ (TO) \\ MH + RB &= MB\ (FROM) + 180° \\ 330° + RB &= 30° + 180° + 360° \\ RB &= 240° \end{aligned}$$

Answer (A) is incorrect. A 030° RB would mean that the NDB is north of the airplane. Answer (B) is incorrect. A 060° RB would mean that the NDB is northeast of the airplane.

10. (Refer to Figure 16 on page 272.) At the position indicated by instrument group 1, what would be the relative bearing if the aircraft were turned to a magnetic heading of 090°?

A. 150°.

B. 190°.

C. 250°.

Answer (C) is correct. *(IFH Chap 9)*

DISCUSSION: The requirement is your new RB if you change your MH from 300° to 90°. Begin by solving for your MB.

$$\begin{aligned} MH + RB &= MB \\ 300° + 40° &= MB = 340° \end{aligned}$$

Note your MB will remain the same, but your MH changes. Resolve the above equation.

$$\begin{aligned} MH + RB &= MB \\ 90° + RB &= 340° \\ RB &= 250° \end{aligned}$$

Answer (A) is incorrect. To have a RB of 150° after a turn to a MH of 090° would mean the airplane is on the 240°, not 340°, MB TO the station. Answer (B) is incorrect. To have a RB of 190° after a turn to a MH of 090° would mean the airplane is on the 280°, not 340°, MB TO the station.

11. (Refer to Figure 16 on page 272.) At the position indicated by instrument group 1, what would be the relative bearing if the aircraft were turned to a magnetic heading of 150°?

A. 150°.

B. 190°.

C. 250°.

Answer (B) is correct. *(IFH Chap 9)*

DISCUSSION: The requirement is your new RB if you change your MH from 300° to 150°. Begin by solving for your MB.

$$\begin{aligned} MH + RB &= MB \\ 300° + 40° &= MB = 340° \end{aligned}$$

Note your MB will remain the same, but your MH changes. Resolve the above equation.

$$\begin{aligned} MH + RB &= MB \\ 150° + RB &= 340° \\ RB &= 190° \end{aligned}$$

Answer (A) is incorrect. To have a RB of 150° after a turn to a MH of 150° would mean the airplane is on the 300°, not 340°, MB TO the station. Answer (C) is incorrect. To have a RB of 190° after a turn to a MH of 090° would mean the airplane is on the 40°, not 340°, MB TO the station.

12. (Refer to Figure 18 below.) To intercept a magnetic bearing of 240° FROM at a 030° angle (while outbound), the airplane should be turned

A. left 065°.

B. left 125°.

C. right 270°.

Answer (B) is correct. *(IFH Chap 9)*

DISCUSSION: Draw a diagram as illustrated below. Read the illustration from right to left. You are on a 35° MH. Your RB is 310°. That identifies where the NDB is. Finally, you want to draw the 240° MB outbound. To intercept the 240° MB at a 30° angle, you need a left turn from 35° to 270° which is 125°.

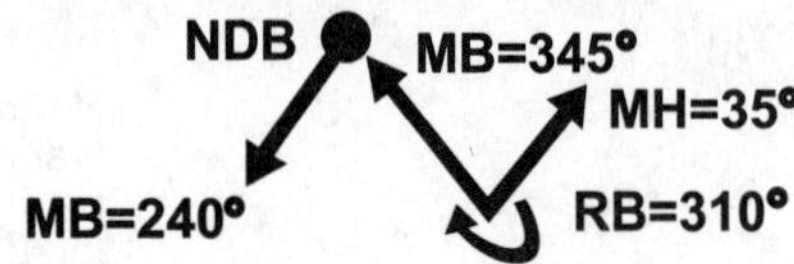

MH + RB = MB
035° + 310° = MB (TO) = 345°

Answer (A) is incorrect. A left 65° turn brings the airplane to a 330° MH, which will intercept the 240° MB FROM the station at a 90° angle, not a 30° angle. Answer (C) is incorrect. A right 270° turn brings the airplane to a 305° MH, which will intercept the 240° MB FROM the station at a 65° angle, not a 30° angle.

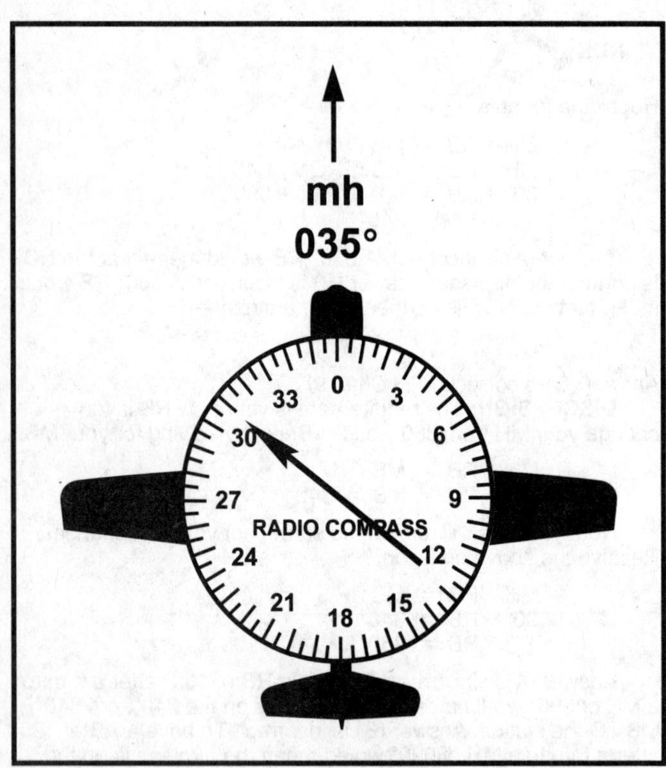

Figure 18. – Magnetic Heading/Radio Compass.

13. (Refer to Figure 18 above.) If the airplane continues to fly on the heading as shown, what magnetic bearing FROM the station would be intercepted at a 35° angle outbound?

A. 035°.

B. 070°.

C. 215°.

Answer (B) is correct. *(IFH Chap 9)*

DISCUSSION: You are currently on the 165° MB (FROM). With a 35° MH, you will cross the 70° MB (FROM) at a 35° intersection angle (70° – 35° = 35°). Note that the 70° MB (FROM) is in front of you when you are northeast bound currently crossing the 165° MB (FROM).

Answer (A) is incorrect. With a 35° MH, you will parallel the 35° MB (FROM). Answer (C) is incorrect. You will not cross the 215° MB (FROM) the station.

14. (Refer to Figure 19 below.) If the airplane continues to fly on the magnetic heading as illustrated, what magnetic bearing FROM the station would be intercepted at a 35° angle?

A. 090°.

B. 270°.

C. 305°.

Answer (C) is correct. *(IFH Chap 9)*

DISCUSSION: Draw a diagram as illustrated below. Begin by determining your present MB.

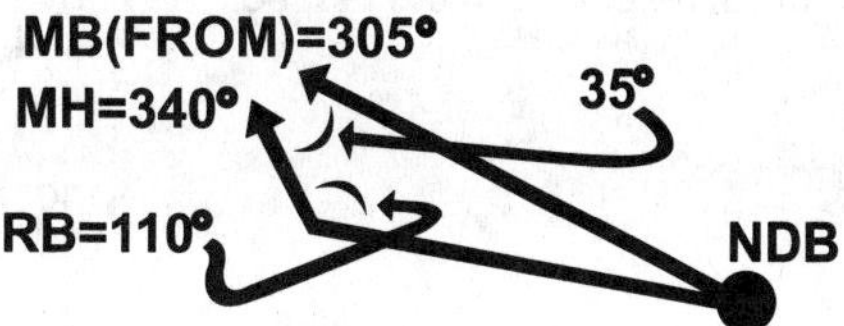

MH + RB = MB (TO)

ADD 180° for MB (FROM)

340° + 110° + 180° = MB (FROM) = 630° – 360° = 270°

You are now on the 270° MB (FROM). When you cross the 305° MB (FROM) of the NDB, you will have a 35° interception angle (340° – 305° = 35°).

Answer (A) is incorrect. On this heading, you will never cross the 090° MB (FROM). Answer (B) is incorrect. You are already on the 270° MB (FROM).

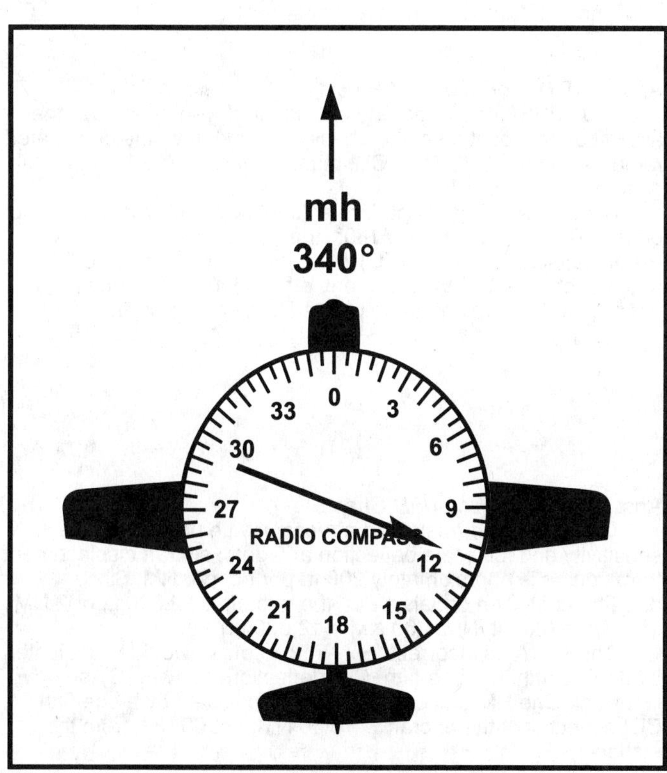

Figure 19. – Magnetic Heading/Radio Compass.

15. (Refer to Figure 19 above.) If the airplane continues to fly on the magnetic heading as illustrated, what magnetic bearing FROM the station would be intercepted at a 30° angle?

A. 090°.

B. 270°.

C. 310°.

Answer (C) is correct. *(IFH Chap 9)*

DISCUSSION: Refer to the diagram in question 14 above. Begin by determining your present MB.

MH + RB = MB (TO)

Add 180° for MB (FROM)

340° + 110° + 180° = MB (FROM) = 630° – 360° = 270°

When you cross the 310° MB (FROM) of the NDB, you will have a 30° interception angle (340° – 310° = 30°).

Answer (A) is incorrect. On this heading, you will never cross the 090° MB (FROM). Answer (B) is incorrect. You are already on the 270° MB (FROM).

10.2 VOR Use and Receiver Checks

16. When checking the course sensitivity of a VOR receiver, how many degrees should the OBS be rotated to move the CDI from the center to the last dot on either side?

A. 5° to 10°.

B. 10° to 12°.

C. 18° to 20°.

Answer (B) is correct. *(IFH Chap 9)*

DISCUSSION: Course sensitivity may be checked on a VOR by noting the number of degrees of change in the course selected as you rotate the OBS to move the CDI from center to the last dot on either side. This should be between 10° and 12°.

Answer (A) is incorrect. Normal VOR sensitivity is 10° to 12°, not 5° to 10°. Answer (C) is incorrect. Normal VOR sensitivity is 10° to 12°, not 18° to 20°.

17. When using VOT to make a VOR receiver check, the CDI should be centered and the OBS should indicate that the aircraft is on the

A. 090 radial.

B. 180 radial.

C. 360 radial.

Answer (C) is correct. *(AIM Para 1-1-4)*

DISCUSSION: To use a VOT, tune in the published VOT frequency on your VOR receiver. With the course deviation indicator (CDI) centered, the omnibearing selector (OBS) should read 0° with the TO-FROM indicator showing FROM or the OBS should read 180° with the TO-FROM indicator showing TO. This indicates you are on the 360° radial.

Answer (A) is incorrect. A VOT sends out a 360°, not 090°, radial in all directions. Answer (B) is incorrect. A VOT sends out a 360°, not 180°, radial in all directions.

18. How should the pilot make a VOR receiver check when the aircraft is located on the designated checkpoint on the airport surface?

A. Set the OBS on 180° plus or minus 4°; the CDI should center with a FROM indication.

B. Set the OBS on the designated radial. The CDI must center within plus or minus 4° of that radial with a FROM indication.

C. With the aircraft headed directly toward the VOR and the OBS set to 000°, the CDI should center within plus or minus 4° of that radial with a TO indication.

Answer (B) is correct. *(AIM Para 1-1-4)*

DISCUSSION: On ground checkpoints, you must have the aircraft on the location of the checkpoint and have the designated radial set on the OBS. The CDI must center within ±4° of the designated radial.

Answer (A) is incorrect. It relates to VOT receiver checks, but on a VOT, with the OBS on 180°, there should be a TO, not a FROM, indication. Answer (C) is incorrect. It relates to VOT receiver checks, but VOTs, or any other VOR receiver check, do not require the airplane to be pointed in a particular direction.

19. An aircraft 60 miles from a VOR station has a CDI indication of one-fifth deflection, this represents a course centerline deviation of approximately

A. 6 miles.

B. 2 miles.

C. 1 mile.

Answer (B) is correct. *(IFH Chap 9)*

DISCUSSION: Assuming a receiver with normal course sensitivity and full-scale deflection at 5 dots, aircraft displacement from course is approximately 200 ft. per dot per NM. Since one-fifth deflection equals 1 dot, the aircraft is 12,000 ft. or 2 NM off course (200 ft./NM × 60 NM = 12,000 ft.).

Answer (A) is incorrect. Six NM off course would be indicated by a three-fifth, not one-fifth, CDI deflection. Answer (C) is incorrect. One NM off course would be indicated by a one-fifth CDI deflection if the aircraft were 30 NM, not 60 NM, from the station.

20. When the CDI needle is centered during an airborne VOR check, the omnibearing selector and the TO/FROM indicator should read

A. within 4° of the selected radial.

B. within 6° of the selected radial.

C. 0° TO, only if you are due south of the VOR.

Answer (B) is correct. *(AIM Para 1-1-4)*

DISCUSSION: For an airborne VOR receiver check, the maximum permissible bearing error of a VOR is ±6°.

Answer (A) is incorrect. The airborne check tolerance is 6°, not 4°. Answer (C) is incorrect. The airborne check is performed over points designated by the FAA or over specific landmarks, not just due south of the VOR.

21. Which situation would result in reverse sensing of a VOR receiver?

A. Flying a heading that is reciprocal to the bearing selected on the OBS.

B. Setting the OBS to a bearing that is 90° from the bearing on which the aircraft is located.

C. Failing to change the OBS from the selected inbound course to the outbound course after passing the station.

Answer (A) is correct. *(IFH Chap 9)*

DISCUSSION: By flying a heading that is a reciprocal of the course set in the OBS, you will have two situations: You will be flying to the station with a FROM indication, or you will fly from the station with a TO indication. Either will result in reverse sensing.

Answer (B) is incorrect. It will result in the TO/FROM flag indicating the "cone of confusion." Answer (C) is incorrect. Although it may put you off course, it would not cause reverse sensing.

22. To track outbound on the 180 radial of a VOR station, the recommended procedure is to set the OBS to

A. 360° and make heading corrections toward the CDI needle.

B. 180° and make heading corrections away from the CDI needle.

C. 180° and make heading corrections toward the CDI needle.

Answer (C) is correct. *(IFH Chap 9)*

DISCUSSION: The recommended procedure is to set 180° on the OBS (your outbound course). This will give you a FROM indication while flying away from the station. This is normal sensing and you correct towards the needle.

Answer (A) is incorrect. It would give you reverse sensing. Thus, corrections are made away from, not toward, the needle. Answer (B) is incorrect. It would take you away from your course (it is the way you navigate when using reverse sensing, e.g., on the back course of a localizer approach).

23. To track inbound on the 215 radial of a VOR station, the recommended procedure is to set the OBS to

A. 215° and make heading corrections toward the CDI needle.

B. 215° and make heading corrections away from the CDI needle.

C. 035° and make heading corrections toward the CDI needle.

Answer (C) is correct. *(IFH Chap 9)*

DISCUSSION: Since radials emanate outward from the VOR, tracking inbound on R-215 means you are flying the reciprocal course of 035°. Thus, you should set 035° on the OBS, and make heading corrections toward the needle.

Answer (A) is incorrect. It would result in reverse sensing by the CDI. Answer (B) is incorrect. It would result in reverse sensing by the CDI.

24. For IFR operations off established airways, ROUTE OF FLIGHT portion of an IFR flight plan should list VOR navigational aids which are no more than

A. 80 miles apart.

B. 70 miles apart.

C. 40 miles apart.

Answer (A) is correct. *(AIM Para 5-1-8)*

DISCUSSION: The *Aeronautical Information Manual* indicates that, in order to facilitate the use of VOR signals, the distance between VORs defining a direct route of flight in controlled air space off established airways below 18,000 ft. MSL should not exceed 80 NM.

Answer (B) is incorrect. The recommended maximum distance between VOR navigational aids is 80 NM, not 70 NM. Answer (C) is incorrect. The recommended maximum distance between VOR navigational aids is 80 NM, not 40 NM.

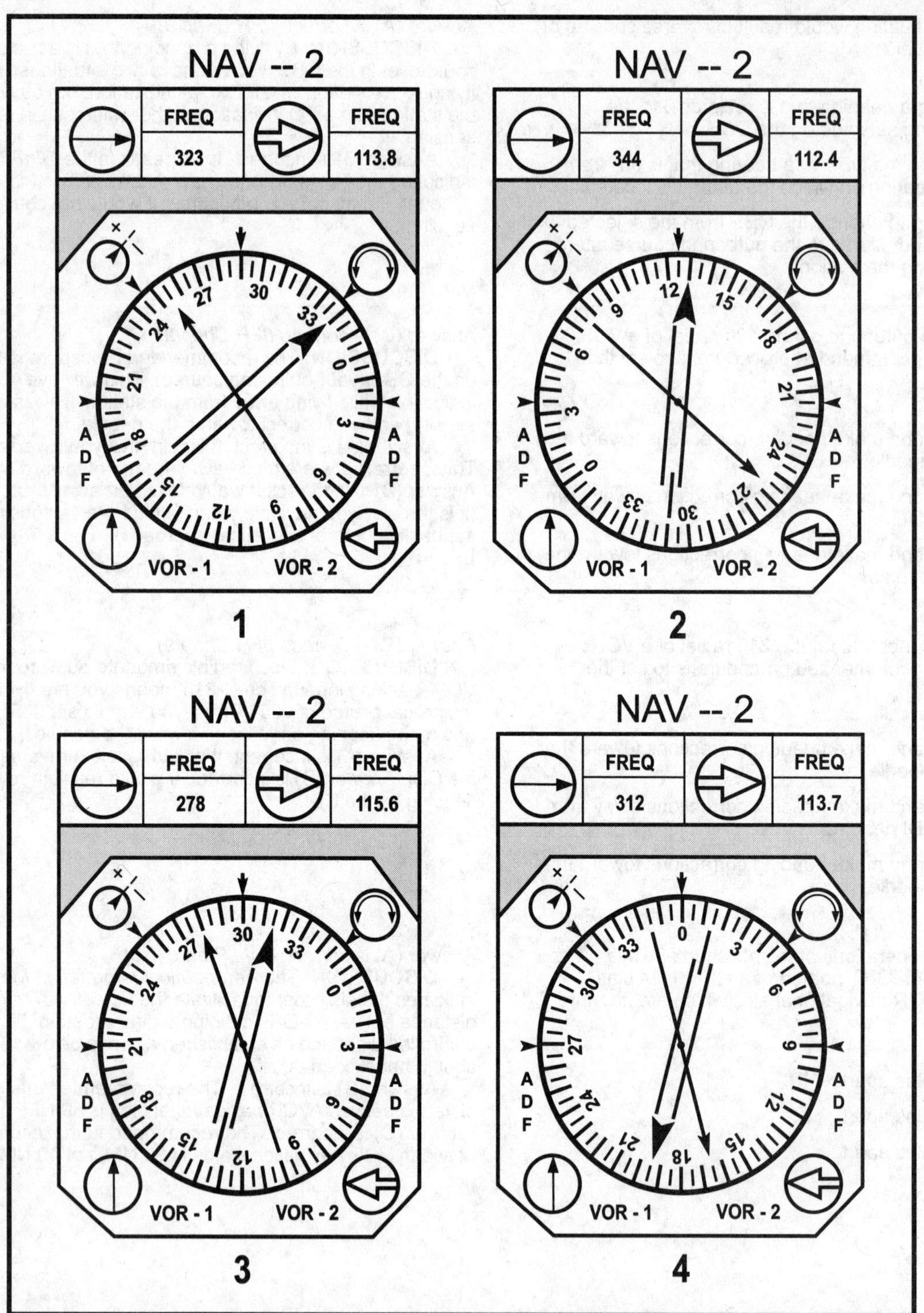

Figure 20. – Radio Magnetic Indicator (RMI).

10.3 Radio Magnetic Indicator (RMI)

25. (Refer to Figure 20 on page 278.) Using instrument group 3, if the aircraft makes a 180° turn to the left and continues straight ahead, it will intercept which radial?

A. 135 radial.

B. 270 radial.

C. 360 radial.

Answer (A) is correct. *(IFH Chap 9)*

DISCUSSION: RMI 3 is on R-135 of the VOR, based on the tail of the wide needle. It has a heading of 300° (under the arrow at the top). A 180° turn to the left will result in a 120° course. The left turn takes the airplane southwest of the R-135 and the 120° heading takes the airplane back through R-135.

Answer (B) is incorrect. R-270 is west of the VOR, so an airplane southeast of the VOR that turns to a southeast heading would not cross this radial. Answer (C) is incorrect. R-360 is north of the VOR, so an airplane southeast of the VOR that turns to a southeast heading would not cross this radial.

26. (Refer to Figure 20 on page 278.) Which instrument shows the aircraft in a position where a straight course after a 90° left turn would result in intercepting the 180 radial?

A. 2.

B. 3.

C. 4.

Answer (B) is correct. *(IFH Chap 9)*

DISCUSSION: RMI 3 shows the airplane on R-135 of the VOR, i.e., southeast, and on a heading of 300°. A 90° left turn to 210° would cause the airplane to fly southwest and thus intercept R-180.

Answer (A) is incorrect. RMI 2 shows the airplane on R-310 (northwest) and heading 125°. A 90° left turn to 035° would not intercept R-180. Answer (C) is incorrect. RMI 4 shows the airplane on R-015 (northeast) and heading 360°. A 90° left turn to 270° would intercept R-360, not R-180.

27. (Refer to Figure 20 on page 278.) Which instrument shows the aircraft in a position where a 180° turn would result in the aircraft intercepting the 150 radial at a 30° angle?

A. 2.

B. 3.

C. 4.

Answer (C) is correct. *(IFH Chap 9)*

DISCUSSION: RMI 4 is on R-015 of the VOR, i.e., north-northeast, and on a heading of 360°. A 180° turn to 180° would cause the airplane to intercept R-150 at a 30° angle (180° – 150° = 30°).

Answer (A) is incorrect. RMI 2 shows the airplane on R-310 (northwest) and heading 125°. A 180° turn to 305° would not intercept R-150. Answer (B) is incorrect. On the present heading of 300°, not after a 180° turn to 120°, you would intercept the R-150 at a 30° angle.

28. (Refer to Figure 20 on page 278.) Which instrument shows the aircraft to be northwest of the VORTAC?

A. 1.

B. 2.

C. 3.

Answer (B) is correct. *(IFH Chap 9)*

DISCUSSION: RMI 2 shows the aircraft to be on R-310 of the VORTAC, i.e., northwest.

Answer (A) is incorrect. RMI 1 shows R-160, which is southeast. Answer (C) is incorrect. RMI 3 shows R-135, which is southeast.

29. (Refer to Figure 20 on page 278.) Which instrument(s) show(s) that the aircraft is getting further from the selected VORTAC?

A. 4.

B. 1 and 4.

C. 2 and 3.

Answer (A) is correct. *(IFH Chap 9)*

DISCUSSION: On an RMI, the head of the needle points to the selected station. Thus, RMI 4 shows the aircraft flying away from the VORTAC.

Answer (B) is incorrect. RMI 1 shows the aircraft flying toward, not away from, the VORTAC. Answer (C) is incorrect. RMIs 2 and 3 show the aircraft flying toward, not away from, the VORTAC.

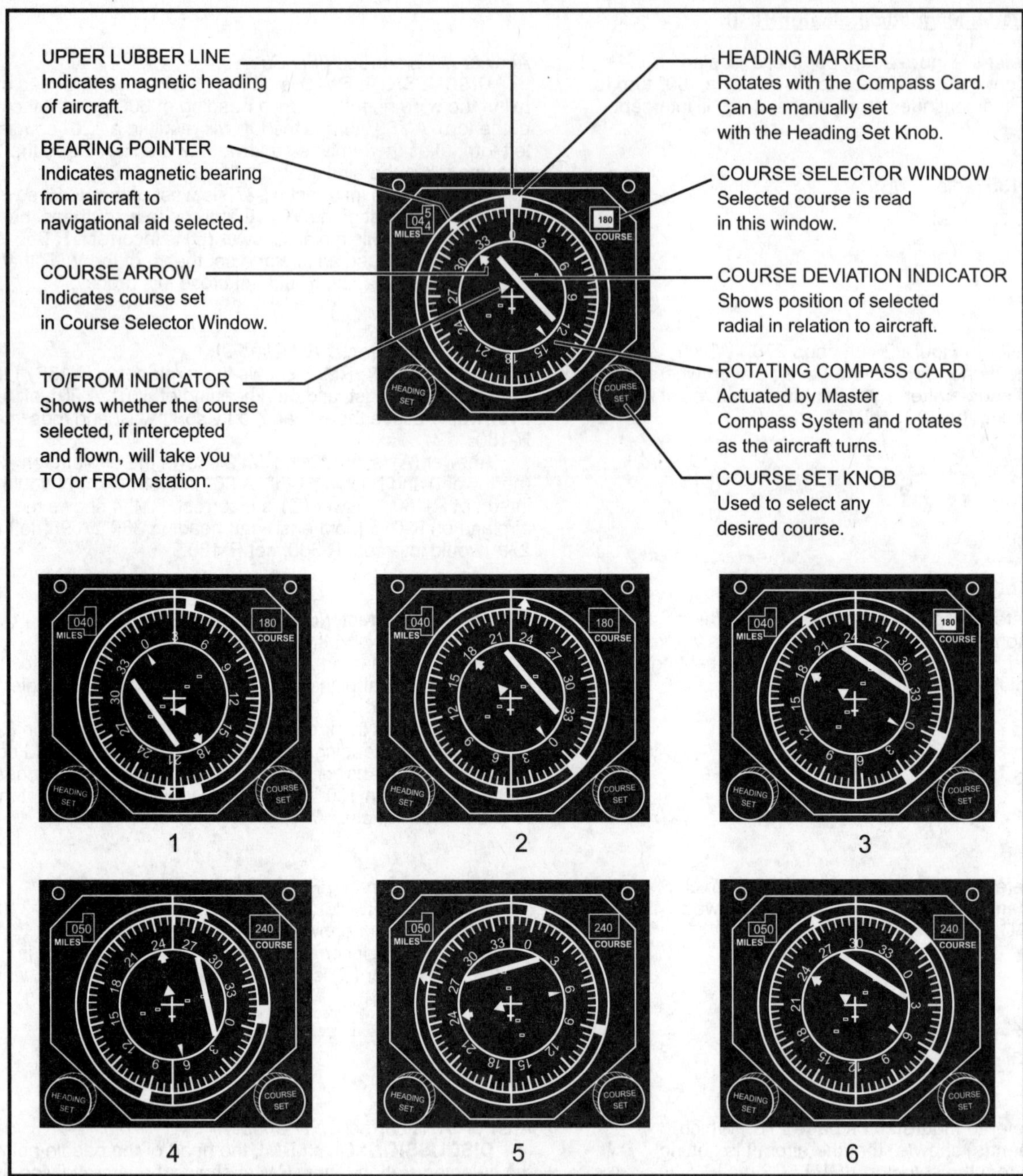

Figure 17. – Horizontal Situation Indicator (HSI).

10.4 Horizontal Situation Indicator (HSI)

30. (Refer to Figure 17 above.) Which illustration indicates that the airplane will intercept the 060 radial at a 75° angle outbound, if the present heading is maintained?

A. 4.

B. 5.

C. 6.

Answer (B) is correct. *(IFH Chap 9)*

DISCUSSION: The present magnetic heading of the airplane in illustration 5 is 345°, so you will cross R-060 at a 75° angle. The TO indication indicates you are east of the 330° – 150° radials. The right deflection on the 240° OBS selection means you are south of the 060° radial.

Answer (A) is incorrect. Illustration 4 shows the airplane intercepting R-060 at a 15° angle (255° – 240°). Answer (C) is incorrect. Illustration 6 shows the airplane intercepting R-060 at a 60° angle (300° – 240°).

31. (Refer to Figure 17 on page 280.) Which statement is true regarding illustration 2, if the present heading is maintained? The airplane will

A. cross the 180 radial at a 45° angle outbound.

B. intercept the 225 radial at a 45° angle.

C. intercept the 360 radial at a 45° angle inbound.

Answer (A) is correct. *(IFH Chap 9)*

DISCUSSION: Illustration 2 indicates that the airplane is heading approximately 227°. The bearing pointer indicates that a heading of 235° will take you to the station; thus, you are on the 055 radial (i.e., east-northeast of the station heading southwest). If you maintain the present heading, the station will remain to the right of the aircraft, and you will cross the 180 radial at approximately a 45° angle outbound (227 – 180 = 47).

Answer (B) is incorrect. You would intercept the 180 radial, not the 225 radial, at a 45° angle outbound. Answer (C) is incorrect. The bearing point is currently to the right of the airplane's heading; thus, the station would remain to the right. The airplane would fly south, not north, of the station and would cross the 180, not the 360, radial at a 45° angle outbound, not inbound.

32. (Refer to Figure 17 on page 280.) Which illustration indicates that the airplane will intercept the 060 radial at a 60° angle inbound, if the present heading is maintained?

A. 6.

B. 4.

C. 5.

Answer (A) is correct. *(IFH Chap 9)*

DISCUSSION: Illustration 6 indicates that the airplane is east of the station on a heading of 300°. The course selector is set to 240 and a TO indication. On a heading of 300°, the airplane will intercept the 060 radial inbound, which is 240° TO the station, at a 60° angle (300 – 240 = 60).

Answer (B) is incorrect. In illustration 4, the airplane is east of the station heading 255°. The airplane will intercept the 240 radial, not the 060 radial, at a 15° angle outbound. Answer (C) is incorrect. In illustration 5, the airplane is east of the station heading 345°. The airplane will intercept the 060 radial at a 105° angle inbound (345 – 240 = 105), not a 60° angle inbound.

33. (Refer to Figure 17 on page 280.) Which illustration indicates that the airplane should be turned 150° left to intercept the 360 radial at a 60° angle inbound?

A. 1.

B. 2.

C. 3.

Answer (A) is correct. *(IFH Chap 9)*

DISCUSSION: By turning the airplane as indicated in illustration 1, 150° left you would be heading 240°. This would be a 60° interception to the 360° radial.

Note the TO indication on a 180° OBS means you are north. The right deflection on the 180° OBS means you are east of the 360° radial. A 240° MH will intercept the 360° radial at a 60° angle.

Answer (B) is incorrect. Airplane 2 is inbound from the northeast. If you turn 150° left from 227°, your new heading will be 077°. You will fly away from the 360° radial. Answer (C) is incorrect. Airplane 3 is inbound from the northeast. If you make a 150° left turn from 244°, your new heading will be 094°. You will fly east, away from the 360° radial.

34. (Refer to Figure 17 on page 280.) Which is true regarding illustration 4, if the present heading is maintained? The airplane will

A. cross the 060 radial at a 15° angle.

B. intercept the 240 radial at a 30° angle.

C. cross the 180 radial at a 75° angle.

Answer (C) is correct. *(IFH Chap 9)*

DISCUSSION: Illustration 4 indicates that the airplane is heading 255°. The bearing pointer indicates that a heading of 275° will take you to the station; thus, you are on the 095 radial (i.e., east of the station heading southwest). If you maintain the present heading, you will cross the R-180 at a 75° angle (255 – 180 = 75).

Answer (A) is incorrect. You will cross the 240 radial, not the 060 radial, at a 15° angle. Answer (B) is incorrect. You will cross the 240 radial at a 15°, not 30°, angle.

10.5 Global Positioning System (GPS)

35. Effective navigation by means of GPS includes

A. determining the current status of all databases.

B. ensuring that ATC approves your planned route.

C. relying solely on the GPS for course information.

Answer (A) is correct. *(AAH Chap 3)*

DISCUSSION: A pilot must determine the status of all appropriate databases. If a database is not current, the pilot must use an alternate means of navigation as a primary form.

Answer (B) is incorrect. Pilots may be, and frequently are, given changes to their requested planned route by ATC. A pilot must ensure that the route flown is approved by ATC whether it is his or her requested plan or not. Answer (C) is incorrect. All systems have the possibility of failing at some point, and it would not be effective to rely solely on a GPS unit for navigation. It is wise to have another means (paper chars, approach plates, etc.) from which to navigate.

36. Why should pilots understand how to cancel entries made on a GPS?

A. Because GPS units frequently provide wrong or false information.

B. Because heavy workloads and turbulence can increase data entry errors.

C. Because published route names commonly change.

Answer (B) is correct. *(AAH Chap 3)*

DISCUSSION: Stressful situations, heavy workloads, and turbulence make data entry errors real problems, and pilots should know how to recover basic aircraft controls quickly.

Answer (A) is incorrect. GPS units provide a high degree of accuracy and are unreliable very infrequently. Answer (C) is incorrect. It is not common for names of published routes to change.

37. Reliance on GPS units

A. can cause pilots to lose proficiency in performing manual calculations of time, distance, and heading.

B. will increase a pilot's skill in navigating by visual reference.

C. does not decrease pilot workload.

Answer (A) is correct. *(AAH Chap 3)*

DISCUSSION: Due to the reliance on GPS systems for navigation, it is easy for pilots to lose proficiency in performing manual calculations on courses, times, distances, headings, etc.

Answer (B) is incorrect. Reliance on GPS units for navigation does not increase skill in navigating by outside references. Answer (C) is incorrect. Navigation by GPS does decrease pilot workload.

38. The primary purpose of the direct-to button is to

A. provide waypoints to a given runway.

B. give routing to the nearest airport.

C. show the quickest way to fly to any given point.

Answer (C) is correct. *(AAH Chap 3)*

DISCUSSION: The "direct-to" feature shows the quickest way to fly to any given point, whether an airport or waypoint.

Answer (A) is incorrect. A pilot would not use the "direct-to" function to see all the waypoints to a given airport. The "flight plan" feature should be used to see this information. Answer (B) is incorrect. The "nearest," or NRST, button provides information about the closest airport at any given time.

39. Which button/feature provides information on the closest airport at any given time?

A. Direct-to.

B. Nearest.

C. Flight plan.

Answer (B) is correct. *(AAH Chap 3)*

DISCUSSION: The "nearest," or NRST, button will provide information including frequencies, direction, and distance to the closest airport. It is especially beneficial in emergency situations because very few keystrokes are needed to gather information.

Answer (A) is incorrect. The "direct-to" button shows the quickest way to fly to any given point, whether an airport or waypoint, but does not necessarily provide airport information. Answer (C) is incorrect. The "flight plan" button shows all waypoints to a given airport. A pilot has to program all this information manually.

END OF STUDY UNIT

STUDY UNIT ELEVEN
FLIGHT OPERATIONS

(3 pages of outline)

This study unit contains outlines of major concepts tested, sample test questions and answers regarding flight operations, and an explanation of each answer. The table of contents above lists each subunit within this study unit, the number of questions pertaining to that particular subunit, and the pages on which the outlines and questions begin, respectively.

Recall that the **sole purpose** of this book is to expedite your passing of the FAA pilot knowledge test for the commercial pilot certificate. Accordingly, all extraneous material (i.e., topics or regulations not directly tested on the FAA pilot knowledge test) is omitted, even though much more knowledge is necessary to become a proficient commercial pilot. This additional material is presented in *Pilot Handbook* and *Commercial Pilot Flight Maneuvers and Practical Test Prep*, available from Gleim Publications, Inc. See the product listing at the back of the book and order online at www.gleim.com.

11.1 FLIGHT FUNDAMENTALS

1. The four flight fundamentals involved in maneuvering an airplane are
   a. Straight-and-level flight
   b. Turns
   c. Climbs
   d. Descents

11.2 TAXIING

1. When taxiing in a strong quartering tailwind, the aileron control should be opposite the direction from which the wind is blowing.
   a. This keeps the aileron down on the side from which the wind is blowing.
2. On crosswind takeoffs,
   a. The rudder is used to maintain directional control,
   b. The aileron pressure should be into the wind to keep the upwind wing down, and
   c. There should be a higher-than-normal liftoff speed so the airplane does not skip sideways during liftoff.

11.3 LANDINGS

1. During gusty wind conditions, a power-on approach and power-on landing should be conducted.
2. On crosswind landings, at the moment of touchdown, the direction of motion of the airplane and its longitudinal axis should be parallel to the runway, i.e., not skipping sideways, which would impose side loads on the landing gear.
3. When turbulence is encountered during the approach to a landing, you should increase the airspeed slightly above normal approach speed to attain more positive control.

11.4 EMERGENCIES

1. The vital and most immediate concern in the event of complete power failure after becoming airborne on takeoff is maintaining a safe, i.e., best glide, airspeed so as to avoid stalls/spins.
2. When diverting to an alternate airport in an emergency, time is usually of the essence. Accordingly, you should divert to the new course as soon as possible. Rule of thumb computations, estimates, and any other shortcuts are appropriate.

11.5 ANTI-COLLISION LIGHT SYSTEM

1. Pilots are required to have the aircraft's anti-collision lighting system operating during all operations, night and day, unless the pilot in command determines that it should be turned off for safety reasons.

11.6 COLD WEATHER OPERATION

1. The cabin area as well as the engine should be preheated for cold weather operation.
2. In cold weather, crankcase breather lines should be inspected to determine whether they are clogged with ice from crankcase vapors that have condensed and frozen.
3. When taking off from a slushy runway, you can minimize the freezing of landing gear mechanisms by recycling the gear several times after takeoff.

11.7 TURBULENCE

1. In severe turbulence, set power for the design maneuvering airspeed (V_A) and maintain a level flight attitude.
   a. Accept changes in airspeed and altitude.
2. Flight at or below V_A means the airplane will stall before excessive loads can be imposed on the wings.
3. When entering an area where significant clear air turbulence (CAT) has been reported, reduce the airspeed to that recommended for rough air at the first indication of turbulence.

11.8 NIGHT FLYING OPERATIONS

1. For night flying operations, the best night vision is achieved when the rods in the eyes become adjusted to the darkness in approximately 30 min.
2. When planning a night cross-country flight, you should check the availability and status of en route and destination airport lighting systems.

3. Light beacons producing red flashes indicate obstructions or areas considered hazardous to aerial navigation.
4. When flying VFR at night, the first indication of flying into restricted visibility conditions is the gradual disappearance of lights on the ground.
5. When planning for an emergency landing at night, two of the primary considerations should include
    a. Planning the emergency approach and landing to an unlighted portion of an area
    b. Selecting a landing close to public access, if possible

QUESTIONS AND ANSWER EXPLANATIONS: All of the commercial pilot knowledge test questions chosen by the FAA for release as well as additional questions selected by Gleim relating to the material in the previous outlines are reproduced on the following pages. These questions have been organized into the same subunits as the outlines. To the immediate right of each question are the correct answer and answer explanation. You should cover these answers and answer explanations while responding to the questions. Refer to the general discussion in the Introduction on how to take the FAA knowledge test.

Remember that the questions from the FAA knowledge test bank have been reordered by topic and organized into a meaningful sequence. Also, the first line of the answer explanation gives the citation of the authoritative source for the answer.

QUESTIONS

11.1 Flight Fundamentals

1. Name the four fundamentals involved in maneuvering an aircraft.

A. Power, pitch, bank, and trim.

B. Thrust, lift, turns, and glides.

C. Straight-and-level flight, turns, climbs, and descents.

Answer (C) is correct. *(AFH Chap 3)*

DISCUSSION: Maneuvering the airplane is generally divided into four flight fundamentals: straight-and-level flight, turns, climbs, and descents. All controlled flight consists of either one or a combination of more than one of these basic maneuvers.

Answer (A) is incorrect. Power, pitch, bank, and trim are the components of aircraft control by which the four fundamental maneuvers are performed. Answer (B) is incorrect. Thrust and lift are two of the forces that act on an airplane, and glides are a type of descent.

11.2 Taxiing

2. While taxiing a light, high-wing airplane during strong quartering tailwinds, the aileron control should be positioned

A. neutral at all times.

B. toward the direction from which the wind is blowing.

C. opposite the direction from which the wind is blowing.

Answer (C) is correct. *(AFH Chap 2)*

DISCUSSION: When taxiing with a quartering tailwind, the aileron control should be positioned opposite the direction from which the wind is blowing so that the aileron is down on the side from which the wind is blowing. This will prevent the wind from lifting the wing or getting under it and blowing the airplane over.

Answer (A) is incorrect. The ailerons can assist in keeping the wind from blowing the airplane over in strong crosswinds. Answer (B) is incorrect. You position the aileron control toward the direction from which the wind is blowing when taxiing with a quartering headwind, not tailwind.

3. When taxiing during strong quartering tailwinds, which aileron positions should be used?

A. Neutral.

B. Aileron up on the side from which the wind is blowing.

C. Aileron down on the side from which the wind is blowing.

Answer (C) is correct. *(AFH Chap 2)*

DISCUSSION: When taxiing with a quartering tailwind, the aileron control should be positioned opposite the direction from which the wind is blowing so that the aileron is down on the side from which the wind is blowing. This will prevent the wind from lifting the wing or getting under it and blowing the airplane over.

Answer (A) is incorrect. The ailerons can assist in keeping the wind from blowing the airplane over in strong crosswinds. Answer (B) is incorrect. You should position the aileron up on the side from which the wind is blowing in a quartering headwind, not tailwind.

4. With regard to the technique required for a crosswind correction on takeoff, a pilot should use

A. aileron pressure into the wind and initiate the lift-off at a normal airspeed in both tailwheel- and nosewheel-type airplanes.

B. right rudder pressure, aileron pressure into the wind, and higher than normal lift-off airspeed in both tricycle- and conventional-gear airplanes.

C. rudder as required to maintain directional control, aileron pressure into the wind, and higher than normal lift-off airspeed in both conventional- and nosewheel-type airplanes.

Answer (C) is correct. *(AFH Chap 5)*

DISCUSSION: For crosswind takeoffs, the aileron control must be held into the crosswind, which raises the aileron on the upwind wing to impose a downward force on the wing to counteract the lifting force of the crosswind and prevents that wing from rising. The rudder is used to maintain directional control. Finally, a higher than normal lift-off airspeed is appropriate in both conventional and nosewheel-type airplanes to keep the airplane from skipping sideways during a possible slow transition from the directional control down the runway to crabbing into the wind once you are airborne.

Answer (A) is incorrect. The lift-off speed should be increased slightly and rudder pressure should be applied as necessary to maintain directional control. Answer (B) is incorrect. The amount of rudder pressure required to maintain directional control of the airplane should be applied, not necessarily only right rudder pressure.

11.3 Landings

5. A proper crosswind landing on a runway requires that, at the moment of touchdown, the

A. direction of motion of the airplane and its lateral axis be perpendicular to the runway.

B. direction of motion of the airplane and its longitudinal axis be parallel to the runway.

C. downwind wing be lowered sufficiently to eliminate the tendency for the airplane to drift.

Answer (B) is correct. *(AFH Chap 8)*

DISCUSSION: At the moment of touchdown, the upwind wing must be held down and opposite rudder applied so that the direction of motion of the airplane and its longitudinal axis are both parallel to the runway. Failure to accomplish this results in severe sideloads being imposed on the landing gear and imparts ground looping tendencies.

Answer (A) is incorrect. The direction of motion of the airplane must be parallel, not perpendicular, to the runway. Answer (C) is incorrect. You lower the upwind wing, not the downwind wing, to eliminate drift.

6. Which type of approach and landing is recommended during gusty wind conditions?

A. A power-on approach and power-on landing.

B. A power-off approach and power-on landing.

C. A power-on approach and power-off landing.

Answer (A) is correct. *(AFH Chap 8)*

DISCUSSION: Power-on approaches at airspeeds slightly above normal should be used for landing in gusty or turbulent wind conditions. To maintain good control in a gusty crosswind, the use of partial wing flaps may be necessary. The touchdown will be at a higher airspeed to ensure more positive control. An adequate amount of power should be used to maintain the proper airspeed throughout the approach, and the throttle should be retarded to idling position only after the main wheels contact the landing surface.

Answer (B) is incorrect. A power-on, not power-off, approach should be used during gusty conditions. Answer (C) is incorrect. A power-on, not power-off, landing should be used during gusty conditions.

7. When turbulence is encountered during the approach to a landing, what action is recommended and for what primary reason?

A. Increase the airspeed slightly above normal approach speed to attain more positive control.

B. Decrease the airspeed slightly below normal approach speed to avoid overstressing the airplane.

C. Increase the airspeed slightly above normal approach speed to penetrate the turbulence as quickly as possible.

Answer (A) is correct. *(AFH Chap 8)*

DISCUSSION: Power-on approaches at airspeeds slightly above normal should be used for landing in gusty or turbulent wind conditions. To maintain good control in a gusty crosswind, the use of partial wing flaps may be necessary. The touchdown will be at a higher airspeed to ensure more positive control. An adequate amount of power should be used to maintain the proper airspeed throughout the approach, and the throttle should be retarded to idling position only after the main wheels contact the landing surface.

Answer (B) is incorrect. Since normal approach speed is generally well below V_A, a slightly higher approach speed will improve control effectiveness without overstressing the airplane. Answer (C) is incorrect. The increased approach speed is for improved control effectiveness. In general, turbulence should be penetrated slowly, not as quickly as possible.

11.4 Emergencies

8. A pilot's most immediate and vital concern in the event of complete engine failure after becoming airborne on takeoff is

A. maintaining a safe airspeed.

B. landing directly into the wind.

C. turning back to the takeoff field.

Answer (A) is correct. *(AFH Chap 8)*

DISCUSSION: The most immediate concern in the event of complete engine failure while airborne in all phases of flight is establishing and maintaining a safe (i.e., best glide) airspeed. This is especially true when an engine failure occurs after becoming airborne on takeoff since the airplane is in a nose-up attitude and a relatively slow airspeed, which may be near the stall speed.

Answer (B) is incorrect. Landing into the wind may not always be the best choice, given available landing areas and obstructions. Answer (C) is incorrect. Turning back to the takeoff field will not be possible until sufficient altitude has been gained.

9. When diverting to an alternate airport because of an emergency, pilots should

A. rely upon radio as the primary method of navigation.

B. climb to a higher altitude because it will be easier to identify checkpoints.

C. apply rule-of-thumb computations, estimates, and other appropriate shortcuts to divert to the new course as soon as possible.

Answer (C) is correct. *(PHAK Chap 15)*

DISCUSSION: When diverting to an alternate airport because of an emergency, time is usually of the essence. Accordingly, you should divert to the new course as soon as possible. Rule of thumb computations, estimates, and any other shortcuts are appropriate.

Answer (A) is incorrect. Any appropriate means of navigation is satisfactory. Answer (B) is incorrect. Climbs may consume valuable time and/or fuel.

11.5 Anti-Collision Light System

10. Pilots are required to have the anti-collision light system operating

A. during all types of operations, both day and night.

B. anytime the pilot is in the cockpit.

C. anytime an engine is in operation.

Answer (A) is correct. *(AIM Para 4-3-23)*

DISCUSSION: Aircraft equipped with an anti-collision lighting system are required to have that system operating during all types of operations, both day and night, except when the pilot in command determines that it should be turned off for safety reasons.

Answer (B) is incorrect. The anti-collision light system need not be operated if the pilot is in the cockpit of an aircraft that is not performing an operation (e.g., the system does not have to be on while the pilot preflights the cockpit). Answer (C) is incorrect. The anti-collision light system is required to be operational during all types of operations, day and night, not just when an engine is in operation (e.g., a motor-glider equipped with anti-collision lights must use them during power-off soaring as well as during powered flight).

11.6 Cold Weather Operation

11. Which is true regarding preheating an aircraft during cold weather operations?

A. The cabin area as well as the engine should be preheated.

B. The cabin area should not be preheated with portable heaters.

C. Hot air should be blown directly at the engine through the air intakes.

Answer (A) is correct. *(AC 91-13C)*

DISCUSSION: Low temperatures may cause a change in the viscosity of engine oils, batteries to lose a high percentage of their effectiveness, and instruments to stick. Thus, preheating of the engine as well as the cabin area is desirable during cold weather operations.

Answer (B) is incorrect. The cockpit area can be preheated with portable heaters if they are available and appropriate. Answer (C) is incorrect. The engine should be heated by blowing warm air on the entire engine surface, not through the air intake areas.

12. During preflight in cold weather, crankcase breather lines should receive special attention because they are susceptible to being clogged by

A. congealed oil from the crankcase.

B. moisture from the outside air which has frozen.

C. ice from crankcase vapors that have condensed and subsequently frozen.

Answer (C) is correct. *(AC 91-13C)*

DISCUSSION: Frozen crankcase breather lines prevent oil from circulating adequately in the engine and may even result in broken oil lines or oil being pumped out of the crankcase. Accordingly, you must always visually inspect to make sure that the crankcase breather lines are free of ice. The ice may have formed as a result of the crankcase vapors freezing in the lines after the engine has been turned off.

Answer (A) is incorrect. Oil in the crankcase virtually never gets into the breather lines, but rather remains in the bottom of the crankcase. Answer (B) is incorrect. Very cold outside air usually has a low moisture content.

13. If necessary to take off from a slushy runway, the freezing of landing gear mechanisms can be minimized by

A. recycling the gear.

B. delaying gear retraction.

C. increasing the airspeed to V_{LE} before retraction.

Answer (A) is correct. *(AC 91-13C)*

DISCUSSION: When taking off from a slushy runway, recycling the landing gear several times after takeoff will ensure that any ice in the process of forming will be broken off and blown away before it completely freezes within the landing gear mechanisms.

Answer (B) is incorrect. Delaying the landing gear retraction will impede the climbout and also may result in freezing the landing gear in the extended position. Answer (C) is incorrect. The landing gear should always be retracted well below V_{LE}.

11.7 Turbulence

14. If severe turbulence is encountered during flight, the pilot should reduce the airspeed to

A. minimum control speed.

B. design-maneuvering speed.

C. maximum structural cruising speed.

Answer (B) is correct. *(PHAK Chap 7)*

DISCUSSION: Flight at or below design maneuvering speed (V_A) means the airplane will stall before excess loads can be imposed on the wings and cause structural damage.

Answer (A) is incorrect. Minimum control speed is just above stall speed. In turbulence, the changing airspeeds would result in the airplane stalling and/or significant control problems. Answer (C) is incorrect. The maximum structural cruising speed (V_{NO}) is considerably above V_A.

15. Which is the best technique for minimizing the wing-load factor when flying in severe turbulence?

A. Change power settings, as necessary, to maintain constant airspeed.

B. Control airspeed with power, maintain wings level, and accept variations of altitude.

C. Set power and trim to obtain an airspeed at or below maneuvering speed, maintain wings level, and accept variations of airspeed and altitude.

Answer (C) is correct. *(AvW Chap 11)*

DISCUSSION: In severe turbulence, you should set power and trim to obtain an airspeed at or below maneuvering speed (V_A), maintain a level pitch and bank attitude, and accept variations of airspeed and altitude.

Answer (A) is incorrect. Maintaining a constant airspeed in severe turbulence is impossible. Answer (B) is incorrect. Maintaining a constant airspeed in severe turbulence is impossible.

16. A pilot is entering an area where significant clear air turbulence has been reported. Which action is appropriate upon encountering the first ripple?

A. Maintain altitude and airspeed.

B. Adjust airspeed to that recommended for rough air.

C. Enter a shallow climb or descent at maneuvering speed.

Answer (B) is correct. *(PHAK Chap 7)*

DISCUSSION: When entering an area where significant air turbulence has been reported, you should adjust the airspeed to that recommended for rough air (V_A) at the first indication of turbulence.

Answer (A) is incorrect. You should reduce your airspeed to V_A. Answer (C) is incorrect. You do not need to adjust altitude; just slow to V_A.

11.8 Night Flying Operations

17. For night flying operations, the best night vision is achieved when the

A. pupils of the eyes have become dilated in approximately 10 minutes.

B. rods in the eyes have become adjusted to the darkness in approximately 30 minutes.

C. cones in the eyes have become adjusted to the darkness in approximately 5 minutes.

Answer (B) is correct. *(AFH Chap 10)*

DISCUSSION: In the eye's adaptation to darkness process, the pupils of the eyes first enlarge (dilate) to receive as much of the available light as possible. After about 5 to 10 min., the cones become adjusted and the eyes become 100 times more sensitive to the light than they were before the process began. The best night vision is achieved when the rods in the eyes have become adjusted to the darkness, which takes about 30 min. At this time, the eyes are about 100,000 times more sensitive to light than they were in a lighted area.

Answer (A) is incorrect. The eyes dilate (enlarge) at the beginning of the eye's adaptation to darkness. Additionally, the cones become adjusted after 10 min., but the best night vision is achieved when the rods become adjusted in approximately 30 min. Answer (C) is incorrect. The best night vision is achieved when the rods, not cones, in the eyes become adjusted to the darkness in approximately 30 min., not 5 min.

18. When planning a night cross-country flight, a pilot should check for

A. availability and status of en route and destination airport lighting systems.

B. red en route course lights.

C. location of rotating light beacons.

Answer (A) is correct. *(AFH Chap 10)*

DISCUSSION: When planning a night cross-country flight, you should check the availability and status of lighting systems at en route and destination airports. Information about their availability can be found on aeronautical charts and in the *Airport/Facility Directory*. The status of each facility can be determined by reviewing pertinent NOTAMs.

Answer (B) is incorrect. Red lights indicate obstructions or areas considered hazardous to aircraft. There are no red en route course lights. Answer (C) is incorrect. While knowing the location of rotating light beacons will assist you during night navigation, it is more important that you know the availability and status of en route and destination airport lighting systems. These lighting systems include runway lights, taxiway lights, and rotating beacons.

19. When planning a night cross-country flight, a pilot should check for the availability and status of

A. all VORs to be used en route.

B. airport rotating light beacons.

C. destination airport lighting systems

Answer (C) is correct. *(AFH Chap 10)*

DISCUSSION: When planning a night cross-country flight, you should check the availability and status of lighting systems at the destination airport. These lighting systems include runway lights, taxiway lights, and rotating beacons. Information about their availability can be found on aeronautical charts and in the *Airport/Facility Directory*. The status of each facility can be determined by reviewing pertinent Notices to Airmen (NOTAMs).

Answer (A) is incorrect. While knowing the availability and status of VORs to be used en route will assist you in night navigation, it is more important that you know the availability and status of lighting systems at the destination airport. Answer (B) is incorrect. While knowing the availability and status of rotating light beacons at airports along your route will assist you in night navigation, it is more important that you know the availability and status of the entire lighting system, not just the rotating beacon, at your destination airport.

20. Light beacons producing red flashes indicate

A. end of runway warning at departure end.

B. a pilot should remain clear of an airport traffic pattern and continue circling.

C. obstructions or areas considered hazardous to aerial navigation.

Answer (C) is correct. *(AFH Chap 10)*

DISCUSSION: Light beacons producing red flashes indicate obstructions or areas considered hazardous to aerial navigation.

Answer (A) is incorrect. End of runway lights are steady, not flashing, red lights. Answer (B) is incorrect. In the case of ATC light signals to an airplane in flight, a steady red, not a flashing red, light signal means to give way to other aircraft and continue circling.

21. When operating VFR at night, what is the first indication of flying into restricted visibility conditions?

A. Ground lights begin to take on an appearance of being surrounded by a halo or glow.

B. A gradual disappearance of lights on the ground.

C. Cockpit lights begin to take on an appearance of a halo or glow around them.

Answer (B) is correct. *(AFH Chap 10)*

DISCUSSION: When operating VFR at night, the first indication of flying into restricted visibility conditions is the gradual disappearance of lights on the ground.

Answer (A) is incorrect. Ground fog, not flying into restricted visibility, is indicated when ground lights begin to take on an appearance of being surrounded by a halo or glow. Caution should be used in attempting further flight in that same direction. Answer (C) is incorrect. Ground fog, not flying into restricted visibility, is indicated when ground lights, not cockpit lights, begin to take on an appearance of a halo or glow around them.

22. After experiencing a powerplant failure at night, one of the primary considerations should include

A. turning off all electrical switches to save battery power for landing.

B. planning the emergency approach and landing to an unlighted portion of an area.

C. maneuvering to, and landing on a lighted highway or road.

Answer (B) is correct. *(AFH Chap 10)*

DISCUSSION: After experiencing an engine failure at night, one of the primary considerations should include that you plan the emergency approach and landing to an unlighted portion of an area. This is to avoid the possibility of landing in an area where you could hurt people on the ground and/or avoiding buildings on the ground during landing.

Answer (A) is incorrect. Turning off all electrical switches to save battery power for the landing is a procedure to use for an alternator failure, not an engine failure, at night. Answer (C) is incorrect. After experiencing an engine failure at night, one of the primary considerations should include turning away from, not maneuvering toward, a lighted highway or road. Highways or roads are hazardous to you and people on the ground.

23. When planning for an emergency landing at night, one of the primary considerations should include

A. turning off all electrical switches to save battery power for the landing.

B. selecting a landing area close to public access, if possible.

C. landing without flaps to ensure a nose-high landing attitude at touchdown.

Answer (B) is correct. *(AFH Chap 10)*

DISCUSSION: When planning for an emergency landing at night, one of the primary considerations should include selecting an emergency landing area close to public access, if possible. This may facilitate rescue or help, if needed.

Answer (A) is incorrect. Turning off all electrical switches to save battery power for landing is a procedure to use for an alternator failure, not an engine failure, at night. Answer (C) is incorrect. When planning for an emergency landing at night, you should plan to land in the normal landing configuration. The flaps should be extended to ensure to land at the slowest possible speed in a nose-high attitude at touchdown.

END OF STUDY UNIT

APPENDIX A
COMMERCIAL PILOT PRACTICE TEST

The following 100 questions have been randomly selected from the airplane-related questions in our commercial pilot test bank. You will be referred to figures (charts, tables, etc.) throughout this book. Be careful not to consult the answers or answer explanations when you look for and at the figures. Topical coverage in this practice test is similar to that of the FAA commercial pilot knowledge test. Use the correct answer listing on page 300 to grade your practice test.

1. (Refer to Figure 17 on page 280.) Which illustration indicates that the airplane will intercept the 060 radial at a 60° angle inbound, if the present heading is maintained?

A— 6.
B— 4.
C— 5.

2. (Refer to Figure 9 on page 152.) Using a normal climb, how much fuel would be used from engine start to 10,000 feet pressure altitude?

Aircraft weight . . . . 3,500 lb
Airport pressure altitude. . . . . 4,000 ft
Temperature . . . . 21°C

A— 23 pounds.
B— 31 pounds.
C— 35 pounds.

3. An airplane descends to an airport under the following conditions:

Cruising altitude . . . . 6,500 ft
Airport elevation . . . . 700 ft
Descends to. . . . . 800 ft AGL
Rate of descent . . . . 500 ft/min
Average true airspeed . . . . 110 kts
True course . . . . 335°
Average wind velocity . . . . 060° at 15 kts
Variation . . . . 3°W
Deviation . . . . +2°
Average fuel consumption . . . . 8.5 gal/hr

Determine the approximate time, compass heading, distance, and fuel consumed during the descent.

A— 10 minutes, 348°, 18 NM, 1.4 gallons.
B— 10 minutes, 355°, 17 NM, 2.4 gallons.
C— 12 minutes, 346°, 18 NM, 1.6 gallons.

4. (Refer to Figure 35 on page 168.)

GIVEN:

Temperature . . . . 80°F
Pressure altitude. . . . . 4,000 ft
Weight. . . . . 2,800 lb
Headwind . . . . 24 kts

What is the total landing distance over a 50-foot obstacle?

A— 1,125 feet.
B— 1,250 feet.
C— 1,325 feet.

5. (Refer to Figure 14 on page 148.)

GIVEN:

Aircraft weight . . . . 3,700 lb
Airport pressure altitude. . . . . 4,000 ft
Temperature at 4,000 ft . . . . 21°C

Using a normal climb under the given conditions, how much fuel would be used from engine start to a pressure altitude of 12,000 feet?

A— 30 pounds.
B— 37 pounds.
C— 46 pounds.

6. (Refer to Figure 12 on page 160.)

GIVEN:

Pressure altitude. . . . . 18,000 ft
Temperature . . . . –1°C
Power . . . . 2,200 RPM – 20" MP
Best fuel economy
usable fuel. . . . . 344 lb

What is the approximate flight time available under the given conditions? (Allow for VFR day fuel reserve.)

A— 4 hours 50 minutes.
B— 5 hours 20 minutes.
C— 5 hours 59 minutes.

7. (Refer to Figure 8 on page 164.)

GIVEN:

Fuel quantity . . . . 47 gal
Power-cruise (lean). . . . . 55 percent

Approximately how much flight time would be available with a night VFR fuel reserve remaining?

A— 3 hours 8 minutes.
B— 3 hours 22 minutes.
C— 3 hours 43 minutes.

8. If an airplane is consuming 14.8 gallons of fuel per hour at a cruising altitude of 7,500 feet and the groundspeed is 167 knots, how much fuel is required to travel 560 NM?

A— 50 gallons.
B— 53 gallons.
C— 57 gallons.

9. (Refer to Figure 22 on page 255.) If the time flown between aircraft positions 2 and 3 is 8 minutes, what is the estimated time to the station?

A— 8 minutes.
B— 16 minutes.
C— 48 minutes.

10. Inbound on the 315 radial, a pilot selects the 320 radial, turns 5° to the left, and notes the time. While maintaining a constant heading, the pilot notes the time for the CDI to center is 12 minutes. The ETE to the station is

A— 10 minutes.
B— 12 minutes.
C— 24 minutes.

11. While maintaining a constant heading, the ADF needle increases from a relative bearing of 045° to 090° in 5 minutes. The time to the station being used is

A— 5 minutes.
B— 10 minutes.
C— 15 minutes.

12. You have flown 52 miles, are 6 miles off course, and have 118 miles yet to fly. To converge on your destination, the total correction angle would be

A— 3°.
B— 6°.
C— 10°.

13. (Refer to Figure 31 on page 166.) Rwy 30 is being used for landing. Which surface wind would exceed the airplane's crosswind capability of 0.2 V_{S0}, if V_{S0} is 60 knots?

A— 260° at 20 knots.
B— 275° at 25 knots.
C— 315° at 35 knots.

14. While maintaining a magnetic heading of 270° and a true airspeed of 120 knots, the 360 radial of a VOR is crossed at 1237 and the 350 radial is crossed at 1244. The approximate time and distance to this station are

A— 42 minutes and 84 NM.
B— 42 minutes and 91 NM.
C— 44 minutes and 96 NM.

15. The ADF is tuned to a nondirectional radiobeacon and the relative bearing changes from 095° to 100° in 1.5 minutes of elapsed time. The time en route to that station would be

A— 18 minutes.
B— 24 minutes.
C— 30 minutes.

16. The ADF is tuned to a nondirectional radiobeacon and the relative bearing changes from 090° to 100° in 2.5 minutes of elapsed time. If the true airspeed is 90 knots, the distance and time en route to that radiobeacon would be

A— 15 miles and 22.5 minutes.
B— 22.5 miles and 15 minutes.
C— 32 miles and 18 minutes.

17. The magnetic heading is 315° and the ADF shows a relative bearing of 140°. The magnetic bearing FROM the radiobeacon would be

A— 095°.
B— 175°.
C— 275°.

18. (Refer to Figure 16 on page 272.) If the aircraft continues its present heading as shown in instrument group 3, what will be the relative bearing when the aircraft reaches the magnetic bearing of 030° FROM the NDB?

A— 030°.
B— 060°.
C— 240°.

19. (Refer to Figure 18 on page 274.) To intercept a magnetic bearing of 240° FROM at a 030° angle (while outbound), the airplane should be turned

A— left 065°.
B— left 125°.
C— right 270°.

20. (Refer to Figure 11 on page 158.) If the cruise altitude is 7,500 feet, using 64 percent power at 2,500 RPM, what would be the range with 48 gallons of usable fuel?

A— 635 miles.
B— 645 miles.
C— 810 miles.

21. The CG of an aircraft may be determined by

A — dividing total arms by total moments.
B — dividing total moments by total weight.
C — multiplying total weight by total moments.

22. GIVEN:

	WEIGHT	ARM	MOMENT
Empty weight	957	29.07	?
Pilot (fwd seat)	140	–45.30	?
Passenger (aft seat)	170	+1.60	?
Ballast	15	–45.30	?
TOTALS	?	?	?

The CG is located at station

A — –6.43.
B — +16.43.
C — +27.38.

23. Which is true concerning the radar weather report (SD) for KOKC?

KOKC 1934 LN 8TRW++/+ 86/40 164/60 199/115
15W L2425 MT 570 AT 159/65 2 INCH HAIL RPRTD
THIS CELL

A — There are three cells with tops at 11,500, 40,000, and 60,000 feet.
B — The line of cells is moving 060° with winds reported up to 40 knots.
C — The maximum tops of the cells is 57,000 feet located 65 NM southeast of the station.

24. (Refer to Figure 54 on page 245.) (Refer to point 1.) What minimum altitude is required to avoid the Livermore Airport (LVK) Class D airspace?

A — 2,503 feet MSL.
B — 2,901 feet MSL.
C — 3,297 feet MSL.

25. (Refer to Figure 3 on page 35.) If an airplane glides at an angle of attack of 10°, how much altitude will it lose in 1 mile?

A — 240 feet.
B — 480 feet.
C — 960 feet.

26. (Refer to Figure 53 on page 244.) (Refer to point 1.) This thin black shaded line is most likely

A — an arrival route.
B — a military training route.
C — a state boundary line.

27. (Refer to Figure 32 on page 145.)

GIVEN:

Temperature . . . . 100°F
Pressure altitude. . . . . 4,000 ft
Weight. . . . . 3,200 lb
Wind . . . . Calm

What is the ground roll required for takeoff over a 50-foot obstacle?

A — 1,180 feet.
B — 1,350 feet.
C — 1,850 feet.

28. (Refer to Figure 38 on page 172.)

GIVEN:

Empty weight (oil is included) . . . . 1,271 lb
Empty weight moment (in-lb/1,000) 102.04
Pilot and copilot. . . . . 400 lb
Rear seat passenger . . . . 140 lb
Cargo. . . . . 100 lb
Fuel . . . . 37 gal

Is the airplane loaded within limits?

A — Yes, the weight and CG is within limits.
B — No, the weight exceeds the maximum allowable.
C — No, the weight is acceptable, but the CG is aft of the aft limit.

29. The angle of attack of a wing directly controls the

A — angle of incidence of the wing.
B — amount of airflow above and below the wing.
C — distribution of pressures acting on the wing.

30. True course measurements on a Sectional Aeronautical Chart should be made at a meridian near the midpoint of the course because the

A — values of isogonic lines change from point to point.
B — angles formed by isogonic lines and lines of latitude vary from point to point.
C — angles formed by lines of longitude and the course line vary from point to point.

31. Detonation may occur at high-power settings when

A — the fuel mixture ignites instantaneously instead of burning progressively and evenly.
B — an excessively rich fuel mixture causes an explosive gain in power.
C — the fuel mixture is ignited too early by hot carbon deposits in the cylinder.

32. An airplane is loaded to a gross weight of 4,800 pounds, with three pieces of luggage in the rear baggage compartment. The CG is located 98 inches aft of datum, which is 1 inch aft of limits. If luggage which weighs 90 pounds is moved from the rear baggage compartment (145 inches aft of datum) to the front compartment (45 inches aft of datum), what is the new CG?

A — 96.13 inches aft of datum.
B — 95.50 inches aft of datum.
C — 99.87 inches aft of datum.

33. Which is true regarding the forces acting on an aircraft in a steady-state descent? The sum of all

A — upward forces is less than the sum of all downward forces.
B — rearward forces is greater than the sum of all forward forces.
C — forward forces is equal to the sum of all rearward forces.

34. If the same angle of attack is maintained in ground effect as when out of ground effect, lift will

A — increase, and induced drag will decrease.
B — decrease, and parasite drag will increase.
C — increase, and induced drag will increase.

35. During preflight in cold weather, crankcase breather lines should receive special attention because they are susceptible to being clogged by

A — congealed oil from the crankcase.
B — moisture from the outside air which has frozen.
C — ice from crankcase vapors that have condensed and subsequently frozen.

36. What is the minimum flight visibility and proximity to cloud requirements for VFR flight, at 6,500 feet MSL, in Class C, D, and E airspace?

A — 1 mile visibility; clear of clouds.
B — 3 miles visibility; 1,000 feet above and 500 feet below.
C — 5 miles visibility; 1,000 feet above and 1,000 feet below.

37. Which is a characteristic typical of a stable air mass?

A — Cumuliform clouds.
B — Showery precipitation.
C — Continuous precipitation.

38. Applying carburetor heat will

A — not affect the mixture.
B — lean the fuel/air mixture.
C — enrich the fuel/air mixture.

39. Which cloud types would indicate convective turbulence?

A — Cirrus clouds.
B — Nimbostratus clouds.
C — Towering cumulus clouds.

40. When in the vicinity of a VOR which is being used for navigation on VFR flight, it is important to

A — make 90° left and right turns to scan for other traffic.
B — exercise sustained vigilance to avoid aircraft that may be converging on the VOR from other directions.
C — pass the VOR on the right side of the radial to allow room for aircraft flying in the opposite direction on the same radial.

41. The general circulation of air associated with a high-pressure area in the Northern Hemisphere is

A — outward, downward, and clockwise.
B — outward, upward, and clockwise.
C — inward, downward, and clockwise.

42. Which statement is true about magnetic deviation of a compass? Deviation

A — varies over time as the agonic line shifts.
B — varies for different headings of the same aircraft.
C — is the same for all aircraft in the same locality.

43. A pilot's most immediate and vital concern in the event of complete engine failure after becoming airborne on takeoff is

A — maintaining a safe airspeed.
B — landing directly into the wind.
C — turning back to the takeoff field.

44. Fog produced by frontal activity is a result of saturation due to

A — nocturnal cooling.
B — adiabatic cooling.
C — evaporation of precipitation.

45. Lift on a wing is most properly defined as the

A — force acting perpendicular to the relative wind.
B — differential pressure acting perpendicular to the chord of the wing.
C — reduced pressure resulting from a laminar flow over the upper camber of an airfoil, which acts perpendicular to the mean camber.

46. In theory, if the airspeed of an airplane is doubled while in level flight, parasite drag will become

A — twice as great.
B — half as great.
C — four times greater.

47. In small airplanes, normal recovery from spins may become difficult if the

A — CG is too far rearward, and rotation is around the longitudinal axis.
B — CG is too far rearward, and rotation is around the CG.
C — spin is entered before the stall is fully developed.

48. The stalling speed of an airplane is most affected by

A — changes in air density.
B — variations in flight altitude.
C — variations in airplane loading.

49. If an airplane is loaded to the rear of its CG range, it will tend to be unstable about its

A — vertical axis.
B — lateral axis.
C — longitudinal axis.

50. Fuel/air ratio is the ratio between the

A — volume of fuel and volume of air entering the cylinder.
B — weight of fuel and weight of air entering the cylinder.
C — weight of fuel and weight of air entering the carburetor.

51. Which statement is true concerning the hazards of hail?

A — Hail damage in horizontal flight is minimal due to the vertical movement of hail in the clouds.
B — Rain at the surface is a reliable indication of no hail aloft.
C — Hailstones may be encountered in clear air several miles from a thunderstorm.

52. Turbulence that is encountered above 15,000 feet AGL not associated with cumuliform cloudiness, including thunderstorms, should be reported as

A — severe turbulence.
B — clear air turbulence.
C — convective turbulence.

53. From which of the following can the observed temperature, wind, and temperature/dewpoint spread be determined at a specified altitude?

A — Stability Charts.
B — Winds Aloft Forecasts.
C — Constant Pressure Analysis Charts.

54. What values are used for Winds Aloft Forecasts?

A — True direction and MPH.
B — True direction and knots.
C — Magnetic direction and knots.

55. Which weather chart depicts conditions forecast to exist at a specific time in the future?

A — Freezing Level Chart.
B — Weather Depiction Chart.
C — 12-hour Significant Weather Prognostic Chart.

56. The Aviation Weather Center (AWC) prepares FA's for the contiguous U.S.

A — twice each day.
B — three times each day.
C — every 6 hours unless significant changes in weather require it more often.

57. Which conditions are favorable for the formation of a surface based temperature inversion?

A — Clear, cool nights with calm or light wind.
B — Area of unstable air rapidly transferring heat from the surface.
C — Broad areas of cumulus clouds with smooth, level bases at the same altitude.

58. Which type of jetstream can be expected to cause the greater turbulence?

A — A straight jetstream associated with a low-pressure trough.
B — A curving jetstream associated with a deep low-pressure trough.
C — A jetstream occurring during the summer at the lower latitudes.

59. (Refer to Figure 5 above.) The vertical line from point D to point G is represented on the airspeed indicator by the maximum speed limit of the

A — green arc.
B — yellow arc.
C — white arc.

60. Baggage weighing 90 pounds is placed in a normal category airplane's baggage compartment which is placarded at 100 pounds. If this airplane is subjected to a positive load factor of 3.5 Gs, the total load of the baggage would be

A — 315 pounds and would be excessive.
B — 315 pounds and would not be excessive.
C — 350 pounds and would not be excessive.

61. (Refer to Figure 20 on page 278.) Using instrument group 3, if the aircraft makes a 180° turn to the left and continues straight ahead, it will intercept which radial?

A — 135 radial.
B — 270 radial.
C — 360 radial.

62. Which is not a type of hypoxia?

A— Histotoxic.
B— Hypoxic.
C— Hypertoxic.

63. As hyperventilation progresses a pilot can experience

A— decreased breathing rate and depth.
B— heightened awareness and feeling of well-being.
C— symptoms of suffocation and drowsiness.

64. For internal cooling, reciprocating aircraft engines are especially dependent on

A— a properly functioning cowl flap augmenter.
B— the circulation of lubricating oil.
C— the proper freon/compressor output ratio.

65. What will occur if no leaning is made with the mixture control as the flight altitude increases?

A— The volume of air entering the carburetor decreases and the amount of fuel decreases.
B— The density of air entering the carburetor decreases and the amount of fuel increases.
C— The density of air entering the carburetor decreases and the amount of fuel remains constant.

66. While maintaining a constant angle of bank and altitude in a coordinated turn, an increase in airspeed will

A— decrease the rate of turn resulting in a decreased load factor.
B— decrease the rate of turn resulting in no change in load factor.
C— increase the rate of turn resulting in no change in load factor.

67. A fixed-pitch propeller is designed for best efficiency only at a given combination of

A— altitude and RPM.
B— airspeed and RPM.
C— airspeed and altitude.

68. Which of the following are considered aircraft class ratings?

A— Transport, normal, utility, and acrobatic.
B— Airplane, rotorcraft, glider, and lighter-than-air.
C— Single-engine land, multiengine land, single-engine sea, and multiengine sea.

69. No person may operate a large civil aircraft of U.S.-registry which is subject to a lease, unless the lessee has mailed a copy of the lease to the FAA Aircraft Registration Branch, Oklahoma City, OK, within how many hours of its execution?

A— 24.
B— 48.
C— 72.

70. Who is primarily responsible for maintaining an aircraft in an airworthy condition?

A— The lead mechanic responsible for that aircraft.
B— Pilot in command or operator.
C— Owner or operator of the aircraft.

71. For an airport without an approved instrument approach procedure to be listed as an alternate airport on an IFR flight plan, the forecasted weather conditions at the time of arrival must have at least a

A— ceiling of 2,000 feet and visibility 3 SM.
B— ceiling and visibility that allows for a descent, approach, and landing under basic VFR.
C— ceiling of 1,000 feet and visibility 3 NM.

72. Pilots who change their permanent mailing address and fail to notify the FAA Airmen Certification Branch of this change, are entitled to exercise the privileges of their pilot certificate for a period of

A— 30 days.
B— 60 days.
C— 90 days.

73. In the contiguous U.S., excluding the airspace at and below 2,500 feet AGL, an operable coded transponder equipped with Mode C capability is required in all airspace above

A— 10,000 feet MSL.
B— 12,500 feet MSL.
C— 14,500 feet MSL.

74. If weather conditions are such that it is required to designate an alternate airport on your IFR flight plan, you should plan to carry enough fuel to arrive at the first airport of intended landing, fly from that airport to the alternate airport, and fly thereafter for

A— 30 minutes at slow cruising speed.
B— 45 minutes at normal cruising speed.
C— 1 hour at normal cruising speed.

75. Airplane A is overtaking airplane B. Which airplane has the right-of-way?

A — Airplane A; the pilot should alter course to the right to pass.
B — Airplane B; the pilot should expect to be passed on the right.
C — Airplane B; the pilot should expect to be passed on the left.

76. NTSB Part 830 requires an immediate notification as a result of which incident?

A — Engine failure for any reason during flight.
B — Damage to the landing gear as a result of a hard landing.
C — Any required flight crewmember being unable to perform flight duties because of illness.

77. Approved flotation gear, readily available to each occupant, is required on each airplane if it is being flown for hire over water,

A — in amphibious aircraft beyond 50 NM from shore.
B — beyond power-off gliding distance from shore.
C — more than 50 statute miles from shore.

78. A new maintenance record being used for an aircraft engine rebuilt by the manufacturer must include previous

A — operating hours of the engine.
B — annual inspections performed on the engine.
C — changes as required by Airworthiness Directives.

79. No person may operate an aircraft in simulated instrument flight conditions unless the

A — other control seat is occupied by at least an appropriately rated commercial pilot.
B — pilot has filed an IFR flight plan and received an IFR clearance.
C — other control seat is occupied by a safety pilot, who holds at least a private pilot certificate and is appropriately rated.

80. A person with a Commercial Pilot certificate may act as pilot in command of an aircraft for compensation or hire, if that person

A — is qualified in accordance with 14 CFR part 61 and with the applicable parts that apply to the operation.
B — is qualified in accordance with 14 CFR part 61 and has passed a pilot competency check given by an authorized check pilot.
C — holds appropriate category, class ratings, and meets the recent flight experience requirements of 14 CFR part 61.

81. To act as pilot in command of an airplane that is equipped with retractable landing gear, flaps, and controllable pitch propeller, a person is required to

A — hold a multiengine airplane class rating.
B — make at least six takeoffs and landings in such an airplane within the preceding 6 months.
C — receive and log ground and flight training in such an airplane, and obtain a logbook endorsement certifying proficiency.

82. To act as pilot in command of a tailwheel airplane, without prior experience, a pilot must

A — log ground and flight training from an authorized instructor.
B — pass a competency check and receive an endorsement from an authorized instructor.
C — receive and log flight training from an authorized instructor.

83. If an ATC transponder installed in an aircraft has not been tested, inspected, and found to comply with regulations within a specified period, what is the limitation on its use?

A — Its use is not permitted.
B — It may be used when in Class G airspace.
C — It may be used for VFR flight only.

84. Which is the correct symbol for the stalling speed or the minimum steady flight speed in a specified configuration?

A — V_S.
B — V_{S1}.
C — V_{S0}.

85. When weather information indicates that abnormally high barometric pressure exists, or will be above ___ inches of mercury, flight operations will not be authorized contrary to the requirements published in NOTAMs.

A — 31.00
B — 32.00
C — 30.50

86. One of the main functions of flaps during the approach and landing is to

A — decrease the angle of descent without increasing the airspeed.
B — provide the same amount of lift at a slower airspeed.
C — decrease lift, thus enabling a steeper-than-normal approach to be made.

87. (Refer to Figure 52 on page 243.) (Refer to point 8.) The floor of the Class E airspace over the town of Auburn is

A — 1,200 feet MSL.
B — 700 feet AGL.
C — 1,200 feet AGL.

88. With regard to the technique required for a crosswind correction on takeoff, a pilot should use

A — aileron pressure into the wind and initiate the lift-off at a normal airspeed in both tailwheel- and nosewheel-type airplanes.
B — right rudder pressure, aileron pressure into the wind, and higher than normal lift-off airspeed in both tricycle- and conventional-gear airplanes.
C — rudder as required to maintain directional control, aileron pressure into the wind, and higher than normal lift-off airspeed in both conventional- and nosewheel-type airplanes.

89. Which is true regarding the development of convective circulation?

A — Cool air must sink to force the warm air upward.
B — Warm air is less dense and rises on its own accord.
C — Warmer air covers a larger surface area than the cool air; therefore, the warmer air is less dense and rises.

90. What feature is normally associated with the cumulus stage of a thunderstorm?

A — Roll cloud.
B — Continuous updraft.
C — Beginning of rain at the surface.

91. Select the true statement pertaining to the life cycle of a thunderstorm.

A — Updrafts continue to develop throughout the dissipating stage of a thunderstorm.
B — The beginning of rain at the Earth's surface indicates the mature stage of the thunderstorm.
C — The beginning of rain at the Earth's surface indicates the dissipating stage of the thunderstorm.

92. If severe turbulence is encountered during flight, the pilot should reduce the airspeed to

A — minimum control speed.
B — design-maneuvering speed.
C — maximum structural cruising speed.

93. (Refer to Figure 51 on page 75.) The pilot generally calls ground control after landing when the aircraft is completely clear of the runway. This is when the aircraft

A — passes the red symbol shown at the top of the figure.
B — is on the dashed-line side of the middle symbol.
C — is past the solid-line side of the middle symbol.

94. An aircraft 60 miles from a VOR station has a CDI indication of one-fifth deflection, this represents a course centerline deviation of approximately

A — 6 miles.
B — 2 miles.
C — 1 mile.

95. Which data must be recorded in the aircraft logbook or other record by a pilot making a VOR operational check for IFR operations?

A — VOR name or identification, place of operational check, amount of bearing error, and date of check.
B — Date of check, place of operational check, bearing error, and signature.
C — VOR name or identification, amount of bearing error, date of check, and signature.

96. Which procedure should you follow to avoid wake turbulence if a large jet crosses your course from left to right approximately 1 mile ahead and at your altitude?

A — Make sure you are slightly above the path of the jet.
B — Slow your airspeed to V_A and maintain altitude and course.
C — Make sure you are slightly below the path of the jet and perpendicular to the course.

97. Which is true regarding a cold front occlusion? The air ahead of the warm front

A — is colder than the air behind the overtaking cold front.
B — is warmer than the air behind the overtaking cold front.
C — has the same temperature as the air behind the overtaking cold front.

98. Weather Advisory Broadcasts, including Severe Weather Forecast Alerts (AWWs), Convective SIGMETs, and SIGMETs, are provided by

A — ARTCCs on all frequencies, except emergency, when any part of the area described is within 150 miles of the airspace under their jurisdiction.
B — FSSs on 122.2 MHz and adjacent VORs, when any part of the area described is within 200 miles of the airspace under their jurisdiction.
C — selected VOR navigational aids.

99. During an approach, the most important and most easily recognized means of being alerted to possible wind shear is monitoring the

A — amount of trim required to relieve control pressures.
B — heading changes necessary to remain on the runway centerline.
C — power and vertical velocity required to remain on the proper glidepath.

100. GIVEN:

Pressure altitude. 5,000 ft
True air temperature . . . . +30°C

From the conditions given, the approximate density altitude is

A — 7,800 feet.
B — 7,200 feet.
C — 9,000 feet.

Page Intentionally Left Blank

PRACTICE TEST LIST OF ANSWERS

The listing below gives the correct answers for your FAA commercial pilot practice knowledge test and the page number in this book on which you will find each question with the complete Gleim answer explanation.

Q. #	Answer	Page	Q. #	Answer	Page	Q. #	Answer	Page	Q. #	Answer	Page
1.	A	281	26.	B	241	51.	C	209	76.	C	127
2.	C	153	27.	B	144	52.	B	211	77.	B	120
3.	A	264	28.	A	173	53.	C	225	78.	C	125
4.	B	169	29.	C	27	54.	B	231	79.	C	112
5.	C	149	30.	C	239	55.	C	229	80.	A	108
6.	C	161	31.	A	55	56.	B	226	81.	C	103
7.	B	165	32.	A	176	57.	A	203	82.	C	103
8.	A	253	33.	C	31	58.	B	199	83.	A	124
9.	A	255	34.	A	36	59.	A	51	84.	B	99
10.	B	256	35.	C	288	60.	B	42	85.	A	114
11.	A	259	36.	B	115	61.	A	279	86.	B	26
12.	C	262	37.	C	204	62.	C	181	87.	B	240
13.	A	167	38.	C	54	63.	C	183	88.	C	286
14.	A	257	39.	C	201	64.	B	57	89.	A	206
15.	A	258	40.	B	82	65.	C	53	90.	B	207
16.	B	260	41.	A	198	66.	B	38	91.	B	208
17.	C	270	42.	B	50	67.	B	58	92.	B	288
18.	C	273	43.	A	287	68.	C	101	93.	C	74
19.	B	274	44.	C	202	69.	A	110	94.	B	276
20.	C	159	45.	A	34	70.	C	123	95.	B	116
21.	B	170	46.	C	32	71.	B	116	96.	A	84
22.	B	174	47.	B	30	72.	A	107	97.	B	197
23.	C	223	48.	C	29	73.	A	121	98.	A	221
24.	B	242	49.	B	37	74.	B	115	99.	C	213
25.	B	34	50.	B	54	75.	B	113	100.	A	142

APPENDIX B
INTERPOLATION

The following is a tutorial based on information that has appeared in the FAA's *Pilot's Handbook of Aeronautical Knowledge*. Interpolation may be required in several questions found in this book.

A. To interpolate means to compute intermediate values between a series of given values.

   1. In many instances when performance is critical, an accurate determination of the performance values is the only acceptable means to enhance safe flight.
   2. Guessing to determine these values should be avoided.

B. Interpolation is simple to perform if the method is understood. The following are examples of how to interpolate, or accurately determine the intermediate values, between a series of given values.

C. The numbers in column A range from 10 to 30, and the numbers in column B range from 50 to 100. Determine the intermediate numerical value in column B that would correspond with an intermediate value of 20 placed in column A.

A	B
10	50
20	X = Unknown
30	100

   1. It can be visualized that 20 is halfway between 10 and 30; therefore, the corresponding value of the unknown number in column B would be halfway between 50 and 100, or 75.

D. Many interpolation problems are more difficult to visualize than the preceding example; therefore, a systematic method must be used to determine the required intermediate value. The following describes one method that can be used.

   1. The numbers in column A range from 10 to 30 with intermediate values of 15, 20, and 25. Determine the intermediate numerical value in column B that would correspond with 15 in column A.

A	B
10	50
15	
20	
25	
30	100

   2. First, in column A, determine the relationship of 15 to the range between 10 and 30 as follows:

$$\frac{15 - 10}{30 - 10} = \frac{5}{20} \text{ or } 1/4$$

      a. It should be noted that 15 is 1/4 of the range between 10 and 30.

3. Now determine 1/4 of the range of column B between 50 and 100 as follows:

$$100 - 50 = 50$$
$$1/4 \text{ of } 50 = 12.5$$

   a. The answer 12.5 represents the number of units, but to arrive at the correct value, 12.5 must be added to the lower number in column B as follows:

$$50 + 12.5 = 62.5$$

4. The interpolation has been completed and 62.5 is the actual value which is 1/4 of the range of column B.

E. Another method of interpolation is shown below:

1. Using the same numbers as in the previous example, a proportion problem based on the relationship of the number can be set up.

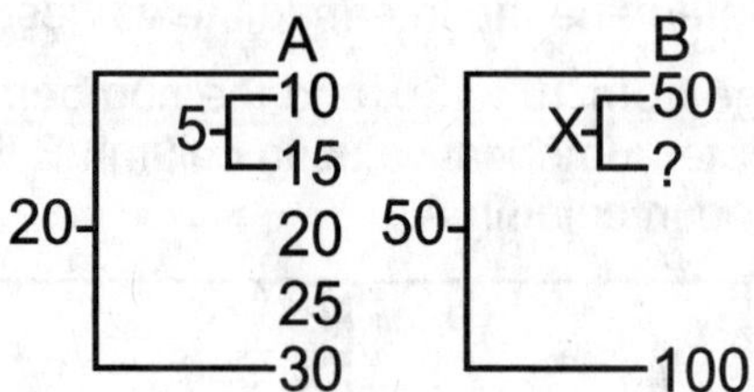

Proportion: $\frac{5}{20} = \frac{X}{50}$

$$20X = 250$$
$$X = 12.5$$

   a. The answer, 12.5, must be added to 50 to arrive at the actual value of 62.5.

F. The following example illustrates the use of interpolation applied to a problem dealing with one aspect of airplane performance:

Temperature (°F)	Takeoff Distance (ft.)
70	1,173
80	1,356

1. If a distance of 1,173 feet is required for takeoff when the temperature is 70°F and 1,356 feet is required at 80°F, what distance is required when the temperature is 75°F? The solution to the problem can be determined as follows:

10 [5 [70°, 75°], 80°]   183 [X [1,173, ?], 1,356]

$$\frac{5}{10} = \frac{X}{183}$$
$$10X = 915$$
$$X = 91.5$$

   a. The answer, 91.5, must be added to 1,173 to arrive at the actual value of 1,264.5 ft.

FAA LISTING OF LEARNING STATEMENT CODES

Reprinted below and on the following pages are all of the FAA's learning statement codes for pilots. These are the codes that will appear on your Airman Computer Test Report. See the example on page 13. Your test report will list the learning statement code of each question answered incorrectly. The statements are designed to represent the knowledge test topic areas in clear verbal terms and encourage applicants to study the entire area of identified weakness instead of merely studying a specific question area. You should discuss your test results with your CFI.

When you receive your Airman Computer Test Report, you can trace the learning statement codes listed on it to these pages to find out which topics you had difficulty with. To determine the knowledge area in which a particular question was incorrectly answered, compare the learning statement code(s) on your Airman Computer Test Report to the listing that follows. The total number of test items missed may differ from the number of learning statement codes shown on your test report because you may have missed more than one question in a certain knowledge area.

Additionally, you should trace the learning statement codes on your Airman Computer Test Report to our cross-reference listing of questions beginning on page 309. Determine which Gleim subunits you need to review.

The FAA will periodically revise the existing learning codes and add new ones. As Gleim learns about any changes, we will update our materials.

PLT001 Calculate a course intercept
PLT002 Calculate aircraft performance - airspeed
PLT003 Calculate aircraft performance - center of gravity
PLT004 Calculate aircraft performance - climb / descent / maneuvering
PLT005 Calculate aircraft performance - density altitude
PLT006 Calculate aircraft performance - glide
PLT007 Calculate aircraft performance - IAS / EPR
PLT008 Calculate aircraft performance - landing
PLT009 Calculate aircraft performance - turbine temperatures (MGT, EGT, ITT, T4, etc) / torque / horsepower
PLT010 Calculate aircraft performance - STAB TRIM
PLT011 Calculate aircraft performance - takeoff
PLT012 Calculate aircraft performance - time/speed/distance/course/fuel/wind
PLT013 Calculate crosswind / headwind components
PLT014 Calculate distance / bearing from/to a station
PLT015 Calculate flight performance / planning - range
PLT016 Calculate fuel - dump time / weight / volume / quantity / consumption
PLT017 Calculate L/D ratio
PLT018 Calculate load factor / stall speed / velocity / angle of attack
PLT019 Calculate pressure altitude
PLT020 Calculate turbulent air penetration
PLT021 Calculate weight and balance
PLT022 Define Aeronautical Decision Making (ADM)
PLT023 Define altitude - absolute / true / indicated / density / pressure
PLT024 Define atmospheric adiabatic process
PLT025 Define Bernoulli's principle
PLT026 Define ceiling
PLT027 Define coning
PLT028 Define crewmember
PLT029 Define critical phase of flight
PLT030 Define false lift
PLT031 Define isobars / associated winds
PLT032 Define MACH speed regimes
PLT033 Define MEA / MOCA / MRA
PLT034 Define stopway / clearway
PLT035 Define Vne / Vno
PLT036 Interpret a MACH meter reading
PLT037 Interpret a radar weather report
PLT038 Interpret aircraft Power Schedule Chart
PLT039 Interpret airport landing indicator
PLT040 Interpret airspace classes - charts / diagrams
PLT041 Interpret altimeter - readings / settings
PLT042 Interpret Constant Pressure charts / Isotachs Chart
PLT043 Interpret Analysis Heights / Temperature Chart
PLT044 Interpret ATC communications / instructions / terminology
PLT045 Interpret Descent Performance Chart
PLT046 Interpret drag ratio from charts
PLT047 Interpret/Program Flight Director/FMS/ Automation - modes / operation / indications / errors
PLT048 Interpret Hovering Ceiling Chart
PLT049 Interpret ILS - charts / RMI / CDI / indications
PLT050 Interpret information on a Brake Energy Limit Chart
PLT051 Interpret information on a Convective Outlook
PLT052 Interpret information on a Departure Procedure Chart
PLT053 Interpret information on a Flight Plan
PLT054 Interpret information on a Glider Performance Graph
PLT055 Interpret information on a High Altitude Chart
PLT056 Interpret information on a Horizontal Situation Indicator (HSI)
PLT057 Interpret information on a Hot Air Balloon Performance Graph
PLT058 Interpret information on a Low Altitude Chart
PLT059 Interpret information on a METAR / SPECI report
PLT060 Interpret information on a Performance Curve Chart
PLT061 Interpret information on a PIREP
PLT062 Interpret information on a Pseudo-Adiabatic Chart
PLT063 Interpret information on a Radar Summary Chart
PLT064 Interpret information on a Sectional Chart
PLT065 Interpret information on a Service Ceiling Engine Inoperative Chart

PLT066 Interpret information on a Convective Outlook Chart
PLT067 Interpret information on a SIGMET
PLT068 Interpret information on a Significant Weather Prognostic Chart
PLT069 Interpret information on a Slush/Standing Water Takeoff Chart
PLT070 Interpret information on a Stability Chart
PLT071 Interpret information on a Surface Analysis Chart
PLT072 Interpret information on a Terminal Aerodrome Forecast (TAF)
PLT073 Interpret information on a Tower Enroute Control (TEC)
PLT074 Interpret information on a Velocity/Load Factor Chart
PLT075 Interpret information on a Weather Depiction Chart
PLT076 Interpret information on a Winds and Temperatures Aloft Forecast (FB)
PLT077 Interpret information on an Airport Diagram
PLT078 Interpret information in an Airport Facility Directory (AFD)
PLT079 Interpret information on an Airways Chart
PLT080 Interpret information on an Arrival Chart
PLT081 Interpret information on an Aviation Area Forecast (FA)
PLT082 Interpret information on an IFR Alternate Airport Minimums Chart
PLT083 Interpret information on an Instrument Approach Procedures (IAP)
PLT084 Interpret information on an Observed Winds Aloft Chart
PLT085 Interpret information on Takeoff Obstacle / Field / Climb Limit Charts
PLT086 Interpret readings on a Turn and Slip Indicator
PLT087 Interpret readings on an Aircraft Course and DME Indicator
PLT088 Interpret speed indicator readings
PLT089 Interpret Takeoff Speeds Chart
PLT090 Interpret VOR - charts / indications / CDI / ADF / NAV
PLT091 Interpret VOR / ADF / NDB / CDI / RMI - illustrations / indications / procedures
PLT092 Interpret weight and balance - diagram
PLT093 Recall administration of medical oxygen
PLT094 Recall aerodynamics - airfoil design / pressure distribution / effects of altitude
PLT095 Recall aerodynamics - longitudinal axis / lateral axis
PLT096 Recall aeromedical factors - effects of altitude
PLT097 Recall aeromedical factors - effects of carbon monoxide poisoning
PLT098 Recall aeromedical factors - fitness for flight
PLT099 Recall aeromedical factors - scanning procedures
PLT100 Recall aeronautical charts - IFR En Route Low Altitude
PLT101 Recall aeronautical charts - pilotage
PLT102 Recall aeronautical charts - terminal procedures
PLT103 Recall Aeronautical Decision Making (ADM) - hazardous attitudes
PLT104 Recall Aeronautical Decision Making (ADM) - human factors / CRM
PLT105 Recall airborne radar / thunderstorm detection equipment - use / limitations
PLT106 Recall aircraft air-cycle machine
PLT107 Recall aircraft alternator / generator system
PLT108 Recall aircraft anti-icing / deicing - methods / fluids
PLT109 Recall aircraft batteries - capacity / charging / types / storage / rating / precautions
PLT110 Recall aircraft brake system
PLT111 Recall aircraft circuitry - series / parallel
PLT112 Recall aircraft controls - proper use / techniques
PLT113 Recall aircraft design - categories / limitation factors
PLT114 Recall aircraft design - construction / function
PLT115 Recall aircraft engine - detonation/backfiring/ after firing, cause/characteristics
PLT116 Recall aircraft general knowledge / publications / AIM / navigational aids
PLT117 Recall aircraft heated windshields
PLT118 Recall aircraft instruments - gyroscopic
PLT119 Recall aircraft lighting - anti-collision / landing / navigation
PLT120 Recall aircraft limitations - turbulent air penetration
PLT121 Recall aircraft loading - computations
PLT122 Recall aircraft operations - checklist usage
PLT123 Recall aircraft performance - airspeed
PLT124 Recall aircraft performance - atmospheric effects
PLT125 Recall aircraft performance - climb / descent
PLT126 Recall aircraft performance - cold weather operations
PLT127 Recall aircraft performance - density altitude
PLT128 Recall aircraft performance - effects of icing
PLT129 Recall aircraft performance - effects of runway slope / slope landing
PLT130 Recall aircraft performance - fuel
PLT131 Recall aircraft performance - ground effect
PLT132 Recall aircraft performance - instrument markings / airspeed / definitions / indications
PLT133 Recall aircraft performance - normal climb / descent rates
PLT134 Recall aircraft performance - takeoff
PLT135 Recall aircraft pressurization - system / operation
PLT136 Recall aircraft systems - anti-icing / deicing
PLT137 Recall aircraft systems - environmental control
PLT138 Recall aircraft landing gear/tires - types / characteristics
PLT139 Recall aircraft warning systems - stall / fire / retractable gear / terrain awareness
PLT140 Recall airport operations - LAHSO
PLT141 Recall airport operations - markings / signs / lighting
PLT142 Recall airport operations - noise avoidance routes
PLT143 Recall airport operations - rescue / fire fighting vehicles and types of agents
PLT144 Recall airport operations - runway conditions
PLT145 Recall airport operations - runway lighting
PLT146 Recall airport operations - traffic pattern procedures / communication procedures
PLT147 Recall airport operations - visual glideslope indicators
PLT148 Recall airport operations lighting - MALS / ALSF / RCLS / TDZL
PLT149 Recall airport preflight / taxi operations - procedures
PLT150 Recall airport traffic patterns - entry procedures
PLT151 Recall airship - buoyancy
PLT152 Recall airship - flight characteristics / controllability
PLT153 Recall airship - flight operations
PLT154 Recall airship - ground weigh-off / static / trim condition
PLT155 Recall airship - maintaining pressure
PLT156 Recall airship - maximum headway / flight at equilibrium
PLT157 Recall airship - pressure height / dampers / position
PLT158 Recall airship - pressure height / manometers
PLT159 Recall airship - pressure height / super heat / valving gas

PLT160 Recall airship - stability / control / positive superheat
PLT161 Recall airspace classes - limits / requirements / restrictions / airspeeds / equipment
PLT162 Recall airspace requirements - operations
PLT163 Recall airspace requirements - visibility / cloud clearance
PLT164 Recall airspeed - effects during a turn
PLT165 Recall altimeter - effect of temperature changes
PLT166 Recall altimeter - settings / setting procedures
PLT167 Recall altimeters - characteristics / accuracy
PLT168 Recall angle of attack - characteristics / forces / principles
PLT169 Recall antitorque system - components / functions
PLT170 Recall approach / landing / taxiing techniques
PLT171 Recall ATC - reporting
PLT172 Recall ATC - system / services
PLT173 Recall atmospheric conditions - measurements / pressure / stability
PLT174 Recall autopilot / yaw damper - components / operating principles / characteristics / failure modes
PLT175 Recall autorotation
PLT176 Recall balance tab - purpose / operation
PLT177 Recall balloon - flight operations
PLT178 Recall balloon - flight operations / gas
PLT179 Recall balloon - ground weigh-off / static equilibrium / load
PLT180 Recall balloon gas/hot air - lift / false lift / characteristics
PLT181 Recall balloon - hot air / physics
PLT182 Recall balloon - inspecting the fabric
PLT183 Recall balloon flight operations - ascent / descent
PLT184 Recall balloon flight operations - launch / landing
PLT185 Recall basic instrument flying - fundamental skills
PLT186 Recall basic instrument flying - pitch instruments
PLT187 Recall basic instrument flying - turn coordinator / turn and slip indicator
PLT188 Recall cabin atmosphere control
PLT189 Recall carburetor - effects of carburetor heat / heat control
PLT190 Recall carburetor ice - factors affecting / causing
PLT191 Recall carburetors - types / components / operating principles / characteristics
PLT192 Recall clouds - types / formation / resulting weather
PLT193 Recall cockpit voice recorder (CVR) - operating principles / characteristics / testing
PLT194 Recall collision avoidance - scanning techniques
PLT195 Recall collision avoidance - TCAS
PLT196 Recall communications - ATIS broadcasts
PLT197 Recall Coriolis effect
PLT198 Recall course / heading - effects of wind
PLT199 Recall cyclic control pressure - characteristics
PLT200 Recall dead reckoning - calculations / charts
PLT201 Recall departure procedures - ODP / SID
PLT202 Recall DME - characteristics / accuracy / indications / Arc
PLT203 Recall Earth's atmosphere - layers / characteristics / solar energy
PLT204 Recall effective communication - basic elements
PLT205 Recall effects of alcohol on the body
PLT206 Recall effects of temperature - density altitude / icing
PLT207 Recall electrical system - components / operating principles / characteristics / static bonding and shielding
PLT208 Recall emergency conditions / procedures
PLT209 Recall engine pressure ratio - EPR
PLT210 Recall engine shutdown - normal / abnormal / emergency / precautions
PLT211 Recall evaluation testing characteristics
PLT212 Recall fire extinguishing systems - components / operating principles / characteristics
PLT213 Recall flight characteristics - longitudinal stability / instability
PLT214 Recall flight characteristics - structural / wing design
PLT215 Recall flight instruments - magnetic compass
PLT216 Recall flight instruments - total energy compensators
PLT217 Recall flight maneuvers - quick stop
PLT218 Recall flight operations - common student errors
PLT219 Recall flight operations - maneuvers
PLT220 Recall flight operations - night and high altitude operations
PLT221 Recall flight operations - takeoff / landing maneuvers
PLT222 Recall flight operations - takeoff procedures
PLT223 Recall flight operations multiengine - engine inoperative procedures
PLT224 Recall flight plan - IFR
PLT225 Recall flight plan - requirements
PLT226 Recall fog - types / formation / resulting weather
PLT227 Recall FOI techniques - integrated flight instruction
PLT228 Recall FOI techniques - lesson plans
PLT229 Recall FOI techniques - professionalism
PLT230 Recall FOI techniques - responsibilities
PLT231 Recall FOI techniques / human behavior - anxiety / fear / stress
PLT232 Recall FOI techniques / human behavior - dangerous tendencies
PLT233 Recall FOI techniques / human behavior - defense mechanisms
PLT234 Recall forces acting on aircraft - 3 axis intersect
PLT235 Recall forces acting on aircraft - aerodynamics
PLT236 Recall forces acting on aircraft - airfoil / center of pressure / mean camber line
PLT237 Recall forces acting on aircraft - airspeed / air density / lift / drag
PLT238 Recall forces acting on aircraft - aspect ratio
PLT239 Recall forces acting on aircraft - buoyancy / drag / gravity / thrust
PLT240 Recall forces acting on aircraft - CG / flight characteristics
PLT241 Recall forces acting on aircraft - drag / gravity / thrust / lift
PLT242 Recall forces acting on aircraft - lift / drag / thrust / weight / stall / limitations
PLT243 Recall forces acting on aircraft - propeller / torque
PLT244 Recall forces acting on aircraft - stability / controllability
PLT245 Recall forces acting on aircraft - stalls / spins
PLT246 Recall forces acting on aircraft - steady state climb / flight
PLT247 Recall forces acting on aircraft - thrust / drag / weight / lift
PLT248 Recall forces acting on aircraft - turns
PLT249 Recall fuel - air mixture
PLT250 Recall fuel - types / characteristics / contamination / fueling / defueling / precautions
PLT251 Recall fuel characteristics / contaminants / additives
PLT252 Recall fuel dump system - components / methods
PLT253 Recall fuel system - components / operating principles / characteristics / leaks
PLT254 Recall fuel tank - components / operating principles / characteristics

PLT255 Recall fueling procedures - safety / grounding / calculating volume
PLT256 Recall glider performance - effect of loading
PLT257 Recall glider performance - speed / distance / ballast / lift / drag
PLT258 Recall ground reference maneuvers - ground track diagram
PLT259 Recall ground resonance - conditions to occur
PLT260 Recall gyroplane - aerodynamics / rotor systems
PLT261 Recall hail - characteristics / hazards
PLT262 Recall helicopter hazards - dynamic rollover / Low G / LTE
PLT263 Recall hazardous weather - fog / icing / turbulence / visibility restriction
PLT264 Recall helicopter approach - settling with power
PLT265 Recall helicopter takeoff / landing - ground resonance action required
PLT266 Recall high lift devices - characteristics / functions
PLT267 Recall hot air balloon - weigh-off procedure
PLT268 Recall hovering - aircraft performance / tendencies
PLT269 Recall human behavior - defense mechanism
PLT270 Recall human behavior - social / self fulfillment / physical
PLT271 Recall human factors (ADM) - judgment
PLT272 Recall human factors - stress management
PLT273 Recall hydraulic systems - components / operating principles / characteristics
PLT274 Recall icing - formation / characteristics
PLT275 Recall ILS - indications / HSI
PLT276 Recall ILS - indications / OBS / CDI
PLT277 Recall ILS - marker beacon / indicator lights / codes
PLT278 Recall indicating systems - airspeed / angle of attack / attitude / heading / manifold pressure / synchro / EGT
PLT279 Recall Inertial/Doppler Navigation System principles / regulations / requirements / limitations
PLT280 Recall inflight illusions - causes / sources
PLT281 Recall information in an Airport Facility Directory
PLT282 Recall information in the certificate holder's manual
PLT283 Recall information on a Constant Pressure Analysis Chart
PLT284 Recall information on a Forecast Winds and Temperatures Aloft (FD)
PLT285 Recall information on a Height Velocity Diagram
PLT286 Recall information on a Significant Weather Prognostic Chart
PLT287 Recall information on a Surface Analysis Chart
PLT288 Recall information on a Terminal Aerodrome Forecast (TAF)
PLT289 Recall information on a Weather Depiction Chart
PLT290 Recall information on AIRMETS / SIGMETS
PLT291 Recall information on an Aviation Area Forecast (FA)
PLT292 Recall information on an Instrument Approach Procedures (IAP)
PLT293 Recall information on an Instrument Departure Procedure Chart
PLT294 Recall information on Inflight Aviation Weather Advisories
PLT295 Recall instructor techniques - obstacles / planning / activities / outcome
PLT296 Recall instrument procedures - holding / circling
PLT297 Recall instrument procedures - unusual attitude / unusual attitude recovery
PLT298 Recall instrument procedures - VFR on top
PLT300 Recall instrument/navigation system checks/inspections - limits / tuning / identifying / logging
PLT301 Recall inversion layer - characteristics
PLT302 Recall jet stream - types / characteristics
PLT303 Recall L/D ratio
PLT304 Recall launch procedures
PLT305 Recall leading edge devices - types / effect / purpose / operation
PLT306 Recall learning process - levels of learning / transfer of learning / incidental learning
PLT307 Recall learning process - memory / fact / recall
PLT308 Recall learning process - laws of learning elements
PLT309 Recall load factor - angle of bank
PLT310 Recall load factor - characteristics
PLT311 Recall load factor - effect of airspeed
PLT312 Recall load factor - maneuvering / stall speed
PLT313 Recall loading – limitations / terminology
PLT314 Recall longitudinal axis - aerodynamics / center of gravity / direction of motion
PLT315 Recall Machmeter - principles / functions
PLT316 Recall meteorology - severe weather watch (WW)
PLT317 Recall microburst - characteristics / hazards
PLT318 Recall minimum fuel advisory
PLT319 Recall navigation – celestial / navigation chart / characteristics
PLT320 Recall navigation - true north / magnetic north
PLT321 Recall navigation - types of landing systems
PLT322 Recall navigation - VOR / NAV system
PLT323 Recall NOTAMS - classes / information / distribution
PLT324 Recall oil system - types / components / functions / oil specifications
PLT325 Recall operations manual - transportation of prisoner
PLT326 Recall oxygen system - components / operating principles / characteristics
PLT327 Recall oxygen system - install / inspect / repair / service / precautions / leaks
PLT328 Recall performance planning - aircraft loading
PLT329 Recall physiological factors - cabin pressure
PLT330 Recall physiological factors - cause / effects of hypoxia
PLT331 Recall physiological factors - effects of scuba diving / smoking
PLT332 Recall physiological factors - hyperventilation
PLT333 Recall physiological factors - night vision
PLT334 Recall physiological factors - spatial disorientation
PLT335 Recall pilotage - calculations
PLT336 Recall pitch control - collective / cyclic
PLT337 Recall pitot-static system - components / operating principles / characteristics
PLT338 Recall pneumatic system - operation
PLT340 Recall positive exchange of flight controls
PLT341 Recall power setting - characteristics
PLT342 Recall powerplant - controlling engine temperature
PLT343 Recall powerplant - operating principles / operational characteristics / inspecting
PLT344 Recall precipitation - types / characteristics
PLT345 Recall pressure altitude
PLT346 Recall primary / secondary flight controls - types / purpose / functionality / operation
PLT347 Recall principles of flight - critical engine
PLT348 Recall principles of flight - turns
PLT349 Recall procedures for confined areas
PLT350 Recall propeller operations - constant / variable speed
PLT351 Recall propeller system - types / components / operating principles / characteristics
PLT352 Recall purpose / operation of a stabilizer
PLT353 Recall Radar Summary Chart
PLT354 Recall radio - GPS / RNAV / RAIM

PLT355 Recall radio - HSI
PLT356 Recall radio - ILS / compass locator
PLT357 Recall radio - ILS / LDA
PLT358 Recall radio - LOC / ILS
PLT359 Deleted
PLT360 Recall radio - Microwave Landing System
PLT361 Recall radio - SDF / ILS
PLT362 Recall radio - VHF / Direction Finding
PLT363 Recall radio - VOR / VOT
PLT364 Recall radio system - license requirements / frequencies
PLT365 Recall reciprocating engine - components / operating principles / characteristics
PLT366 Recall regulations - accident / incident reporting and preserving wreckage
PLT367 Recall regulations - additional equipment/operating requirements large transport aircraft
PLT368 Recall regulations - admission to flight deck
PLT369 Recall regulations - aerobatic flight requirements
PLT370 Recall regulations - Air Traffic Control authorization / clearances
PLT371 Recall regulations - Aircraft Category / Class
PLT372 Recall regulations - aircraft inspection / records / expiration
PLT373 Recall regulations - aircraft operating limitations
PLT374 Recall regulations - aircraft owner / operator responsibilities
PLT375 Recall regulations - aircraft return to service
PLT376 Recall regulations - airspace special use / TFRS
PLT377 Recall regulations - airworthiness certificates / requirements / responsibilities
PLT378 Recall regulations - Airworthiness Directives
PLT379 Recall regulations - alternate airport requirements
PLT380 Recall regulations - alternate airport weather minima
PLT381 Recall regulations - altimeter settings
PLT382 Recall regulations - approach minima
PLT383 Recall regulations - basic flight rules
PLT384 Recall regulations - briefing of passengers
PLT385 Recall regulations - cargo in passenger compartment
PLT386 Recall regulations - certificate issuance / renewal
PLT387 Recall regulations - change of address
PLT388 Recall regulations - cockpit voice / flight data recorder(s)
PLT389 Recall regulations - commercial operation requirements / conditions / OpSpecs
PLT390 Recall regulations - communications enroute
PLT391 Recall regulations - communications failure
PLT392 Recall regulations - compliance with local regulations
PLT393 Recall regulations - controlled / restricted airspace - requirements
PLT394 Recall regulations - declaration of an emergency
PLT395 Recall regulations - definitions
PLT396 Recall regulations - departure alternate airport
PLT397 Recall regulations - destination airport visibility
PLT398 Recall regulations - dispatch
PLT399 Recall regulations - display / inspection of licenses and certificates
PLT400 Recall regulations - documents to be carried on aircraft during flight
PLT401 Recall regulations - dropping / aerial application / towing restrictions
PLT402 Recall regulations - ELT requirements
PLT403 Recall regulations - emergency deviation from regulations
PLT404 Recall regulations - emergency equipment
PLT405 Recall regulations - equipment / instrument / certificate requirements
PLT406 Recall regulations - equipment failure
PLT407 Recall regulations - experience / training requirements
PLT408 Recall regulations - fire extinguisher requirements
PLT409 Recall regulations - flight / duty time
PLT410 Recall regulations - flight engineer qualifications / privileges
PLT411 Recall regulations - flight instructor limitations / qualifications
PLT412 Recall regulations - flight release
PLT413 Recall regulations - fuel requirements
PLT414 Recall regulations - general right-of-way rules
PLT415 Recall regulations - IFR flying
PLT416 Recall regulations - immediate notification
PLT417 Recall regulations - individual flotation devices
PLT418 Recall regulations - instructor demonstrations / authorizations
PLT419 Recall regulations - instructor requirements / responsibilities
PLT420 Recall regulations - instrument approach procedures
PLT421 Recall regulations - instrument flight rules
PLT422 Recall regulations - intermediate airport authorizations
PLT423 Recall regulations - knowledge and skill test checks
PLT424 Recall regulations - limits on autopilot usage
PLT425 Recall regulations - maintenance reports / records / entries
PLT426 Recall regulations - maintenance requirements
PLT427 Recall regulations - medical certificate requirements / validity
PLT428 Recall regulations - minimum equipment list
PLT429 Recall regulations - minimum flight / navigation instruments
PLT430 Recall regulations - minimum safe / flight altitude
PLT431 Recall regulations - operating near other aircraft
PLT432 Recall regulations - operational control functions
PLT433 Recall regulations - operational flight plan requirements
PLT434 Recall regulations - operational procedures for a controlled airport
PLT435 Recall regulations - operational procedures for an uncontrolled airport
PLT436 Recall regulations - operations manual
PLT437 Recall regulations - overwater operations
PLT438 Recall regulations - oxygen requirements
PLT439 Recall regulations - persons authorized to perform maintenance
PLT440 Recall regulations - Pilot / Crew duties and responsibilities
PLT441 Recall regulations - pilot briefing
PLT442 Recall regulations - pilot currency requirements
PLT443 Recall regulations - pilot qualifications / privileges / responsibilities / crew complement
PLT444 Recall regulations - pilot-in-command authority / responsibility
PLT445 Recall regulations - preflight requirements
PLT446 Recall regulations - preventative maintenance
PLT447 Recall regulations - privileges / limitations of medical certificates
PLT448 Recall regulations - privileges / limitations of pilot certificates
PLT449 Recall regulations - proficiency check requirements
PLT450 Recall regulations - qualifications / duty time
PLT451 Recall regulations - ratings issued / experience requirements / limitations
PLT452 Recall regulations - re-dispatch
PLT453 Recall regulations - records retention for domestic / flag air carriers
PLT454 Recall regulations - required aircraft / equipment inspections

PLT455 Recall regulations - requirements of a flight plan release
PLT456 Recall regulations - runway requirements
PLT457 Recall regulations - student pilot endorsements / other endorsements
PLT458 Recall regulations - submission / revision of Policy and Procedure Manuals
PLT459 Recall regulations - takeoff procedures / minimums
PLT460 Recall regulations - training programs
PLT461 Recall regulations - use of aircraft lights
PLT462 Recall regulations - use of microphone / megaphone / interphone / public address system
PLT463 Recall regulations - alcohol or drugs
PLT464 Recall regulations - use of safety belts / harnesses (crew member)
PLT465 Recall regulations - use of seats / safety belts / harnesses (passenger)
PLT466 Recall regulations - V speeds
PLT467 Recall regulations - visual flight rules and limitations
PLT468 Recall regulations - Visual Meteorological Conditions (VMC)
PLT469 Recall regulations - weather radar
PLT470 Recall rotor system - types / components / operating principles / characteristics
PLT471 Recall rotorcraft transmission - components / operating principles / characteristics
PLT472 Recall rotorcraft vibration - characteristics / sources
PLT473 Recall secondary flight controls - types / purpose / functionality
PLT474 Recall soaring - normal procedures
PLT475 Recall squall lines - formation / characteristics / resulting weather
PLT476 Recall stabilizer - purpose / operation
PLT477 Recall stalls - characteristics / factors / recovery / precautions
PLT478 Recall starter / ignition system - types / components / operating principles / characteristics
PLT479 Recall starter system - starting procedures
PLT480 Recall static/dynamic stability/instability - characteristics
PLT481 Recall student evaluation - learning process
PLT482 Recall student evaluation - written tests / oral quiz / critiques
PLT483 Recall supercharger - characteristics / operation
PLT484 Recall symbols - chart / navigation
PLT485 Recall taxiing / crosswind / techniques
PLT486 Recall taxiing / takeoff - techniques / procedures
PLT487 Recall teaching methods - demonstration / performance
PLT488 Recall teaching methods - group / guided discussion / lecture
PLT489 Recall teaching methods - known to unknown
PLT490 Recall teaching methods - motivation / student feelings of insecurity
PLT491 Recall teaching methods - organizing material / course of training
PLT492 Recall temperature - effects on weather formations
PLT493 Recall the dynamics of frost / ice / snow formation on an aircraft
PLT494 Recall thermals - types / characteristics / formation / locating / maneuvering / corrective actions
PLT495 Recall thunderstorms - types / characteristics / formation / hazards / precipitation static
PLT496 Recall towrope - strength / safety links / positioning
PLT497 Recall transponder - codes / operations / usage
PLT498 Recall Transportation Security Regulations
PLT499 Recall turbine engines - components / operational characteristics / associated instruments
PLT500 Recall turboprop engines - components / operational characteristics
PLT501 Recall turbulence - types / characteristics / reporting / corrective actions
PLT502 Recall universal signals - hand / light / visual
PLT503 Recall use of narcotics / drugs / intoxicating liquor
PLT504 Recall use of training aids - types / function / purpose
PLT505 Recall use of training aids - usefulness / simplicity / compatibility
PLT506 Recall V speeds - maneuvering / flap extended / gear extended / V1, V2, r, ne, mo, mc, mg, etc.
PLT507 Recall VOR - indications / VOR / VOT / CDI
PLT508 Recall VOR/altimeter/transponder checks - identification / tuning / identifying / logging
PLT509 Recall wake turbulence - characteristics / avoidance techniques
PLT510 Recall weather - causes / formation
PLT511 Recall weather associated with frontal activity / air masses
PLT512 Recall weather conditions - temperature / moisture / dewpoint
PLT513 Recall weather information - TWEB broadcasts / FAA Avcams
PLT514 Recall weather reporting systems - briefings / forecasts / reports / AWOS / ASOS
PLT515 Recall weather services - EFAS / TIBS / TPC / WFO / AFSS / HIWAS
PLT516 Recall winds - types / characteristics
PLT517 Recall winds associated with high / low-pressure systems
PLT518 Recall windshear - characteristics / hazards / power management
PLT519 Recall wing spoilers - purpose / operation
PLT520 Calculate density altitude
PLT521 Recall helicopter takeoff / landing – slope operations
PLT522 Recall helicopter – Pinnacle / Ridgeline operations
PLT523 Recall vortex generators – purpose / effects / aerodynamics
PLT524 Interpret / Program information on an avionics display
PLT525 Interpret table – oxygen / fuel / oil / accumulator / fire extinguisher
PLT526 Recall near midair collision report
PLT527 Recall BASIC VFR – weather minimums

CROSS-REFERENCES TO THE FAA LEARNING STATEMENT CODES

Pages 309 through 315 contain a listing of all of the questions from our commercial pilot knowledge test bank. Non-airplane questions are excluded. The questions are in FAA learning statement code (LSC) sequence. To the right of each LSC, we present our study unit/question number and our answer. For example, look below and note that PLT001 is cross-referenced to 10-26, which represents our Study Unit 10, question 26; the correct answer is B.

Pages 303 through 308 contain a complete listing of all the FAA learning statement codes associated with all of the commercial pilot questions presented in this book. Use this list to identify the specific topic associated with each learning statement code.

The first line of each of our answer explanations in Study Units 1 through 11 contains

1. The correct answer.
2. A reference for the answer explanation, e.g., *AFH Chap 1*. If this reference is not useful, use the following chart to identify the learning statement code to determine the specific reference appropriate for the question.

FAA Learning Code	Gleim SU/ Q. No.	Gleim Answer	FAA Learning Code	Gleim SU/ Q. No.	Gleim Answer	FAA Learning Code	Gleim SU/ Q. No.	Gleim Answer
PLT001	10–26	B	PLT011	5–12	A	PLT012	9–29	A
PLT001	10–27	C	PLT011	5–13	C	PLT012	9–30	B
PLT001	10–30	B	PLT011	5–14	B	PLT012	9–31	A
PLT001	10–32	A	PLT012	5–15	B	PLT012	9–32	B
PLT001	10–33	A	PLT012	5–16	A	PLT012	9–33	A
PLT002	1–20	C	PLT012	5–17	C	PLT012	9–34	B
PLT002	1–21	A	PLT012	5–18	C	PLT012	9–35	A
PLT002	1–70	C	PLT012	5–19	B	PLT012	9–44	A
PLT004	5–20	A	PLT012	5–29	C	PLT012	9–45	B
PLT004	5–21	C	PLT012	5–30	B	PLT012	9–46	A
PLT004	5–22	C	PLT012	5–31	A	PLT012	9–48	C
PLT004	5–23	C	PLT012	5–32	C	PLT012	9–50	C
PLT004	5–24	C	PLT012	5–33	B	PLT012	9–51	B
PLT004	9–58	B	PLT012	5–37	B	PLT012	9–52	A
PLT004	9–59	B	PLT012	5–38	B	PLT012	9–53	B
PLT004	9–61	A	PLT012	5–39	C	PLT012	9–54	C
PLT004	9–62	C	PLT012	5–40	B	PLT012	9–55	C
PLT005	5–7	B	PLT012	9–20	A	PLT012	9–56	A
PLT005	5–8	A	PLT012	9–21	B	PLT012	9–57	B
PLT005	5–9	B	PLT012	9–22	C	PLT012	9–60	C
PLT006	1–39	B	PLT012	9–23	C	PLT012	9–63	C
PLT006	1–44	C	PLT012	9–24	B	PLT013	5–42	A
PLT008	5–46	B	PLT012	9–25	A	PLT013	5–43	A
PLT008	5–47	B	PLT012	9–26	A	PLT013	5–44	A
PLT008	5–48	A	PLT012	9–27	A	PLT013	5–45	C
PLT008	5–49	A	PLT012	9–28	A	PLT014	9–36	A

FAA Learning Code	Gleim SU/ Q. No.	Gleim Answer
PLT014	9–37	C
PLT014	9–38	B
PLT014	9–39	C
PLT014	9–40	C
PLT014	9–41	A
PLT014	9–42	A
PLT014	9–43	A
PLT014	9–47	A
PLT014	9–49	B
PLT014	10–3	C
PLT014	10–4	B
PLT014	10–5	C
PLT014	10–6	A
PLT014	10–7	B
PLT014	10–8	C
PLT014	10–9	C
PLT014	10–10	C
PLT014	10–11	B
PLT014	10–12	B
PLT014	10–13	B
PLT014	10–14	C
PLT014	10–15	C
PLT015	5–27	C
PLT015	5–28	B
PLT015	5–34	B
PLT015	5–35	C
PLT015	5–41	A
PLT017	1–45	C
PLT018	1–17	C
PLT018	1–69	C
PLT018	1–71	C
PLT018	1–77	A
PLT018	1–78	A
PLT021	5–50	A
PLT021	5–51	C
PLT021	5–52	B
PLT021	5–53	B
PLT021	5–54	B
PLT021	5–55	B
PLT021	5–59	B
PLT021	5–60	A
PLT021	5–61	C

FAA Learning Code	Gleim SU/ Q. No.	Gleim Answer
PLT022	6–25	A
PLT022	6–27	C
PLT022	6–28	A
PLT022	6–46	A
PLT032	1–83	C
PLT032	1–84	C
PLT035	2–2	B
PLT035	2–3	B
PLT037	8–14	C
PLT040	9–8	B
PLT040	9–10	B
PLT040	9–15	A
PLT040	9–16	B
PLT040	9–17	C
PLT041	4–69	B
PLT044	3–61	C
PLT044	3–63	A
PLT046	1–43	B
PLT056	10–31	A
PLT056	10–34	C
PLT059	8–7	B
PLT059	8–8	B
PLT059	8–9	C
PLT059	8–10	B
PLT059	8–11	A
PLT059	8–12	B
PLT059	8–13	B
PLT061	8–43	A
PLT061	8–44	A
PLT064	9–11	B
PLT064	9–12	B
PLT064	9–13	B
PLT064	9–14	B
PLT068	8–41	B
PLT070	8–49	C
PLT072	8–23	B
PLT072	8–25	C
PLT072	8–26	B
PLT074	2–4	B
PLT074	2–5	A
PLT074	2–7	C
PLT075	8–45	B

FAA Learning Code	Gleim SU/ Q. No.	Gleim Answer
PLT079	3–17	B
PLT083	9–19	B
PLT085	5–10	C
PLT085	5–11	B
PLT085	5–25	C
PLT085	5–26	B
PLT088	2–8	C
PLT090	10–21	A
PLT091	10–1	A
PLT091	10–2	B
PLT091	10–28	B
PLT091	10–29	A
PLT092	5–56	A
PLT092	5–57	A
PLT092	5–58	A
PLT094	1–6	C
PLT096	6–8	B
PLT099	6–23	C
PLT101	9–1	C
PLT101	9–2	C
PLT101	9–3	C
PLT103	6–29	C
PLT103	6–30	B
PLT103	6–31	C
PLT103	6–32	A
PLT103	6–33	A
PLT103	6–34	A
PLT103	6–35	A
PLT103	6–38	A
PLT103	6–39	C
PLT103	6–40	C
PLT103	6–41	C
PLT103	6–42	C
PLT104	6–36	B
PLT105	7–68	A
PLT113	4–105	C
PLT113	4–107	C
PLT113	4–108	B
PLT115	2–27	C
PLT115	2–28	C
PLT115	2–29	A
PLT118	2–11	A

FAA Learning Code	Gleim SU/ Q. No.	Gleim Answer	FAA Learning Code	Gleim SU/ Q. No.	Gleim Answer	FAA Learning Code	Gleim SU/ Q. No.	Gleim Answer
PLT119	3–51	A	PLT141	3–41	B	PLT189	2–24	C
PLT119	11–10	A	PLT141	3–42	A	PLT189	2–25	C
PLT120	1–13	B	PLT141	3–43	B	PLT192	7–28	C
PLT121	5–62	A	PLT141	3–46	B	PLT192	7–29	B
PLT121	5–63	B	PLT141	3–47	A	PLT192	7–30	B
PLT121	5–64	A	PLT141	3–48	C	PLT192	7–31	C
PLT121	5–65	A	PLT141	3–49	B	PLT192	7–32	B
PLT123	5–36	B	PLT146	3–20	A	PLT192	7–51	C
PLT125	1–29	C	PLT161	3–2	B	PLT192	7–59	B
PLT125	1–30	C	PLT161	3–9	A	PLT192	7–62	C
PLT126	11–11	A	PLT161	3–11	B	PLT194	3–50	C
PLT126	11–13	A	PLT161	3–13	B	PLT194	3–52	B
PLT127	5–2	B	PLT161	3–18	C	PLT194	6–21	C
PLT127	5–4	A	PLT161	4–101	A	PLT194	6–22	A
PLT129	3–66	A	PLT161	9–18	C	PLT197	7–3	A
PLT131	1–51	A	PLT162	3–1	B	PLT197	7–4	A
PLT131	1–52	A	PLT162	3–5	B	PLT197	7–13	A
PLT131	3–25	A	PLT162	3–7	A	PLT197	7–14	A
PLT131	3–44	A	PLT162	3–19	B	PLT197	7–15	B
PLT131	3–45	B	PLT163	3–14	A	PLT203	7–22	B
PLT132	1–82	C	PLT163	3–15	C	PLT205	6–9	C
PLT132	2–10	C	PLT163	4–72	B	PLT205	6–10	C
PLT136	11–12	C	PLT164	1–58	C	PLT205	6–11	C
PLT140	3–62	B	PLT166	5–3	B	PLT206	2–23	A
PLT140	3–64	A	PLT168	1–8	A	PLT208	11–9	C
PLT140	3–65	A	PLT168	1–9	C	PLT208	11–22	B
PLT140	3–67	B	PLT168	1–10	B	PLT208	11–23	B
PLT140	3–68	A	PLT 168	1–41	C	PLT213	1–56	B
PLT140	3–69	B	PLT170	4–83	A	PLT214	1–5	B
PLT141	3–26	B	PLT170	11–5	B	PLT215	2–1	B
PLT141	3–27	A	PLT171	4–85	B	PLT219	11–1	C
PLT141	3–28	A	PLT173	7–9	C	PLT220	11–19	C
PLT141	3–29	C	PLT173	7–43	B	PLT220	11–20	C
PLT141	3–30	B	PLT173	7–44	A	PLT220	11–21	B
PLT141	3–31	B	PLT173	7–45	A	PLT221	11–6	A
PLT141	3–32	B	PLT173	7–46	B	PLT222	11–8	A
PLT141	3–35	A	PLT173	7–47	C	PLT224	10–24	A
PLT141	3–36	C	PLT173	7–48	C	PLT226	7–35	C
PLT141	3–37	B	PLT173	7–52	B	PLT226	7–37	B
PLT141	3–38	A	PLT173	7–58	A	PLT226	7–39	C
PLT141	3–39	B	PLT173	7–88	A	PLT226	7–41	A
PLT141	3–40	A	PLT187	2–12	C	PLT226	7–42	C

FAA Learning Code	Gleim SU/ Q. No.	Gleim Answer
PLT235	1–31	B
PLT235	1–42	A
PLT235	1–50	B
PLT236	1–38	C
PLT236	1–46	B
PLT237	1–33	C
PLT237	1–35	C
PLT237	1–37	C
PLT237	1–49	C
PLT237	5–1	A
PLT240	1–22	A
PLT240	1–24	B
PLT242	1–4	C
PLT242	1–16	C
PLT242	1–19	C
PLT242	1–25	B
PLT242	1–64	A
PLT242	1–85	C
PLT243	2–47	B
PLT244	1–53	B
PLT244	1–57	B
PLT245	1–14	A
PLT245	1–15	A
PLT245	1–23	C
PLT246	1–32	B
PLT246	1–47	A
PLT247	1–26	A
PLT247	1–27	C
PLT248	1–28	A
PLT248	1–60	A
PLT249	2–19	B
PLT249	2–20	B
PLT253	2–13	C
PLT253	2–14	A
PLT253	2–16	A
PLT253	2–18	C
PLT261	7–74	C
PLT261	7–75	B
PLT263	7–18	A
PLT263	7–36	C
PLT263	7–38	C
PLT263	7–81	B

FAA Learning Code	Gleim SU/ Q. No.	Gleim Answer
PLT263	7–82	C
PLT263	7–83	B
PLT263	7–85	A
PLT263	7–86	A
PLT263	7–87	B
PLT263	11–7	A
PLT266	1–48	A
PLT271	6–26	C
PLT271	6–37	B
PLT271	6–45	A
PLT271	6–47	B
PLT272	6–43	C
PLT272	6–44	B
PLT276	10–16	B
PLT276	10–18	B
PLT276	10–20	B
PLT278	2–9	A
PLT280	6–24	A
PLT283	8–20	A
PLT283	8–21	C
PLT283	8–22	B
PLT284	8–48	B
PLT286	8–39	C
PLT286	8–40	B
PLT286	8–42	C
PLT287	7–5	C
PLT287	7–8	A
PLT287	8–15	B
PLT287	8–16	A
PLT287	8–17	A
PLT287	8–18	B
PLT287	8–19	A
PLT288	8–24	C
PLT288	8–27	A
PLT289	8–46	C
PLT290	8–35	A
PLT290	8–36	C
PLT291	8–28	B
PLT291	8–30	B
PLT291	8–31	C
PLT294	8–32	A
PLT294	8–33	A

FAA Learning Code	Gleim SU/ Q. No.	Gleim Answer
PLT294	8–34	C
PLT300	4–78	C
PLT300	4–79	A
PLT301	7–40	A
PLT301	7–92	B
PLT301	7–93	C
PLT301	7–94	A
PLT301	7–95	A
PLT302	7–16	B
PLT302	7–17	A
PLT302	7–21	B
PLT303	1–34	B
PLT303	1–40	A
PLT305	1–2	B
PLT309	1–68	A
PLT309	1–72	B
PLT309	1–73	B
PLT309	1–75	B
PLT310	1–66	A
PLT310	1–67	A
PLT310	1–74	A
PLT310	1–80	B
PLT310	1–81	A
PLT311	1–76	C
PLT312	1–18	A
PLT312	2–6	A
PLT312	11–15	C
PLT313	1–79	B
PLT322	10–22	C
PLT322	10–23	C
PLT322	10–25	A
PLT323	11–18	A
PLT330	6–1	C
PLT330	6–2	A
PLT332	6–13	A
PLT332	6–14	C
PLT332	6–15	B
PLT332	6–16	C
PLT333	11–17	B
PLT334	6–17	B
PLT334	6–18	A
PLT334	6–19	B

FAA Learning Code	Gleim SU/ Q. No.	Gleim Answer
PLT334	6–20	C
PLT342	2–35	B
PLT342	2–36	B
PLT342	2–37	A
PLT343	2–15	C
PLT343	2–22	C
PLT344	7–34	A
PLT344	7–76	B
PLT344	7–77	C
PLT348	1–59	B
PLT348	1–61	C
PLT348	1–62	A
PLT348	1–63	B
PLT348	1–65	B
PLT350	2–40	B
PLT350	2–41	C
PLT350	2–42	A
PLT350	2–43	B
PLT350	2–44	A
PLT350	2–45	C
PLT350	2–46	B
PLT351	1–36	B
PLT351	2–38	A
PLT351	2–39	C
PLT353	8–47	A
PLT354	10–35	A
PLT354	10–36	B
PLT354	10–37	A
PLT354	10–38	C
PLT354	10–39	B
PLT362	3–21	A
PLT365	2–17	B
PLT365	2–21	A
PLT365	2–26	C
PLT365	2–33	A
PLT366	4–129	A
PLT366	4–130	C
PLT366	4–131	C
PLT366	4–133	C
PLT366	4–134	C
PLT369	4–103	A
PLT370	3–3	B
PLT370	3–12	A
PLT371	4–13	C
PLT371	4–15	C
PLT372	4–111	B
PLT373	4–106	A
PLT374	4–49	A
PLT374	4–109	C
PLT374	4–110	C
PLT375	4–113	B
PLT377	4–125	A
PLT378	4–120	B
PLT380	4–76	B
PLT380	4–77	B
PLT382	4–81	A
PLT386	4–20	A
PLT386	4–21	A
PLT387	4–36	A
PLT389	4–47	C
PLT389	4–48	A
PLT392	4–122	B
PLT395	4–1	A
PLT395	4–2	C
PLT395	4–3	C
PLT395	4–4	C
PLT395	4–10	B
PLT395	4–11	C
PLT395	4–12	A
PLT399	4–14	B
PLT400	4–45	B
PLT400	4–87	C
PLT400	4–89	A
PLT400	4–90	A
PLT400	8–29	B
PLT401	4–38	B
PLT401	4–46	A
PLT401	4–104	B
PLT403	4–41	C
PLT403	4–70	C
PLT405	4–93	B
PLT405	4–94	A
PLT405	4–102	A
PLT406	4–86	B
PLT407	4–25	A
PLT407	4–26	B
PLT407	4–27	B
PLT407	4–30	C
PLT409	4–28	C
PLT409	4–29	C
PLT413	4–75	B
PLT414	4–63	B
PLT414	4–64	A
PLT414	4–65	B
PLT414	4–66	C
PLT414	4–67	A
PLT414	4–68	A
PLT415	4–52	C
PLT415	4–82	A
PLT416	4–124	B
PLT416	4–126	C
PLT416	4–127	A
PLT416	4–128	C
PLT416	4–132	C
PLT417	4–95	B
PLT425	4–118	C
PLT425	4–119	B
PLT425	4–121	C
PLT426	4–112	A
PLT430	4–84	C
PLT431	4–60	C
PLT431	4–61	A
PLT431	4–62	A
PLT434	3–4	B
PLT434	3–8	B
PLT434	3–10	B
PLT434	3–16	C
PLT438	4–99	C
PLT438	4–100	C
PLT442	4–33	C
PLT442	4–34	A
PLT443	4–59	C
PLT444	4–42	B
PLT444	4–43	B
PLT444	4–44	B
PLT444	4–88	B

FAA Learning Code	Gleim SU/ Q. No.	Gleim Answer
PLT444	4–91	B
PLT444	4–92	A
PLT445	4–50	B
PLT445	4–51	B
PLT445	4–53	C
PLT445	4–54	B
PLT446	4–96	C
PLT448	4–40	A
PLT448	4–123	A
PLT449	4–31	A
PLT449	4–35	C
PLT450	4–22	C
PLT450	4–23	C
PLT450	4–24	C
PLT450	4–32	C
PLT450	4–37	B
PLT450	4–39	C
PLT454	4–114	B
PLT454	4–115	C
PLT454	4–116	A
PLT454	4–117	C
PLT461	4–97	A
PLT461	4–98	C
PLT463	4–16	C
PLT463	4–17	B
PLT463	4–18	C
PLT463	4–19	C
PLT463	6–4	B
PLT463	6–5	C
PLT463	6–6	B
PLT463	6–12	C
PLT464	4–55	B
PLT464	4–56	C
PLT465	4–57	B
PLT465	4–58	B
PLT466	4–5	B
PLT466	4–6	A
PLT466	4–7	A
PLT466	4–8	A
PLT466	4–9	A
PLT467	4–71	A
PLT467	4–73	B
PLT467	4–74	B
PLT473	1–1	B
PLT475	7–63	B
PLT475	7–65	C
PLT475	7–66	C
PLT475	8–37	C
PLT477	1–11	A
PLT478	2–30	B
PLT478	2–31	A
PLT478	2–32	C
PLT478	2–34	C
PLT480	1–54	B
PLT480	1–55	A
PLT484	9–4	C
PLT484	9–5	A
PLT484	9–6	C
PLT484	9–7	B
PLT484	9–9	C
PLT485	11–2	C
PLT485	11–3	C
PLT486	11–4	C
PLT492	7–1	A
PLT492	7–23	A
PLT492	7–24	A
PLT492	7–25	C
PLT492	7–26	B
PLT492	7–27	B
PLT492	7–33	B
PLT492	7–57	B
PLT493	1–7	B
PLT494	7–54	A
PLT495	7–60	C
PLT495	7–61	B
PLT495	7–67	B
PLT495	7–69	A
PLT495	7–70	C
PLT495	7–71	C
PLT495	7–73	A
PLT495	7–79	C
PLT495	7–80	B
PLT497	3–6	A
PLT501	7–19	B
PLT501	11–14	B
PLT502	3–22	C
PLT502	3–23	B
PLT502	3–24	C
PLT502	3–33	A
PLT502	3–34	B
PLT503	6–7	B
PLT506	1–12	A
PLT506	11–16	B
PLT507	10–17	C
PLT507	10–19	B
PLT508	4–80	B
PLT509	3–53	B
PLT509	3–54	A
PLT509	3–55	A
PLT509	3–56	B
PLT509	3–57	A
PLT509	3–58	A
PLT509	3–59	C
PLT509	3–60	B
PLT510	7–49	C
PLT510	7–56	B
PLT511	7–7	B
PLT511	7–10	B
PLT511	7–50	B
PLT511	7–53	C
PLT511	7–55	C
PLT511	7–72	C
PLT511	7–78	A
PLT512	7–2	C
PLT513	8–38	A
PLT515	8–1	C
PLT515	8–2	A
PLT515	8–3	B
PLT515	8–4	B
PLT515	8–5	A
PLT515	8–6	A
PLT516	7–6	C
PLT517	7–11	A
PLT517	7–12	B
PLT518	7–20	C
PLT518	7–64	C

FAA Learning Code	Gleim SU/ Q. No.	Gleim Answer
PLT518	7–84	B
PLT518	7–89	A
PLT518	7–90	C
PLT518	7–91	C
PLT518	7–96	B
PLT519	1–3	C
PLT520	5–5	B
PLT520	5–6	A
PLT526	4–135	C
PLT526	4–136	A
PTL330	6–3	A

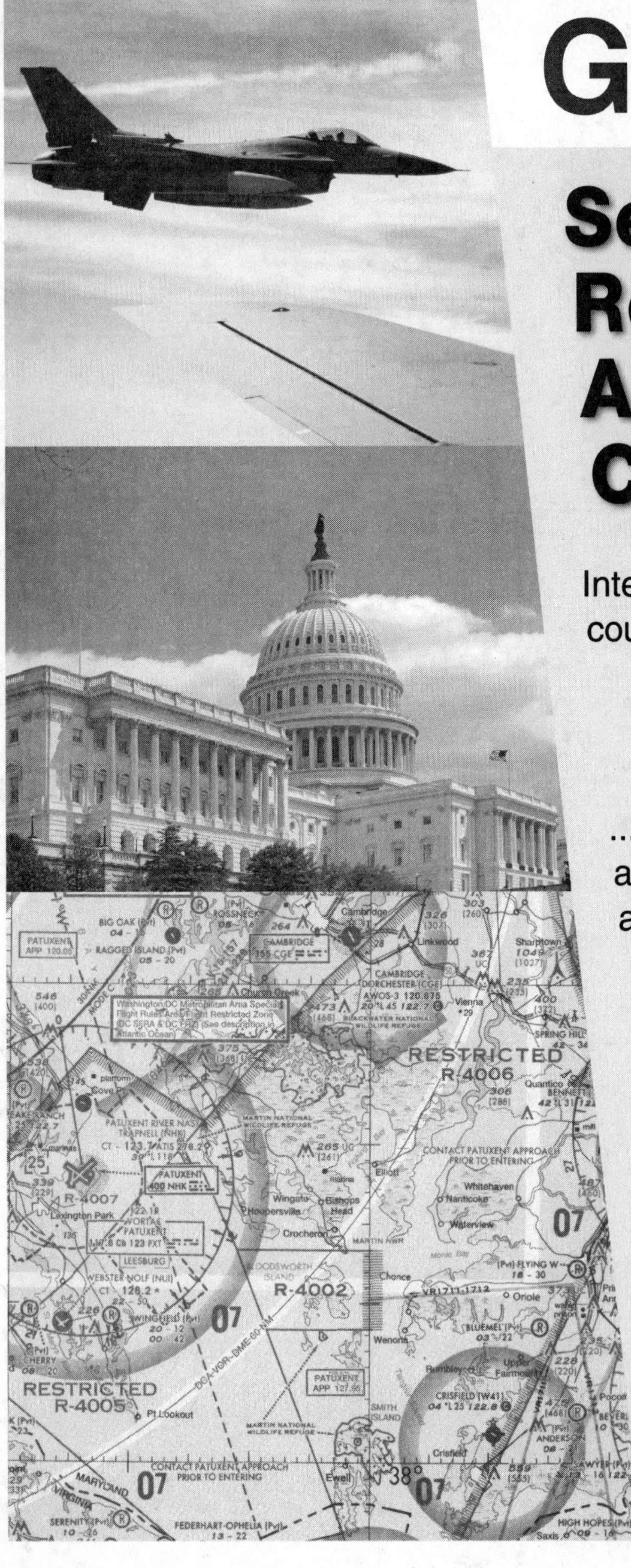

GLEIM®

Security-Related Airspace Course

Interactive ground training course designed to increase ...

- Pilots' safety
- Knowledge
- Abilities

... in regard to flying in and around the various security airspaces in the United States.

Only $29.95

For 12 months of access

gleim.com/srac
800.874.5346

INSTRUCTOR CERTIFICATION FORM
COMMERCIAL PILOT KNOWLEDGE TEST

Name: ____

I certify that I have reviewed the above individual's preparation for the FAA Commercial Pilot — Airplane knowledge test [covering the topics specified in 14 CFR 61.125(b)(1) through (16)] using the *Commercial Pilot FAA Knowledge Test* book, software, and/or online course by Irvin N. Gleim and find him/her competent to pass the pilot knowledge test.

____________________	________	____________________	____________	____________
Signed	Date	Name	CFI or CGI Number	Expiration Date N/A if CGI

GLEIM
KNOWLEDGE
TRANSFER
SYSTEMS®

ABBREVIATIONS AND ACRONYMS IN *COMMERCIAL PILOT FAA KNOWLEDGE TEST*

A/FD — *Airport/Facility Directory*
AAF — Army Airfield
AC — Advisory Circular
ACL — Aeronautical Chart Legend
ADF — automatic direction finder
AFB — Air Force Base
AFH — *Airplane Flying Handbook*
AFNA — Aerodynamics for Naval Aviators
AGL — above ground level
AIM — *Aeronautical Information Manual*
AIRMET — Airman's Meteorological Information
AME — aviation medical examiner
A&PM PH — *Airframe and Powerplant Mechanics Powerplant Handbook*
ATC — Air Traffic Control
ATCO — air tax/commercial operator
AvW — *Aviation Weather*
AWBH — *Aircraft Weight and Balance Handbook*
AWS — *Aviation Weather Services*
BHP — brake horsepower
CAT — clear air turbulence
CDI — course deviation indicator
CFI — Certificated Flight Instructor
CG — center of gravity
DUATS — Direct User Access Terminal System
ELT — emergency locator transmitter
ETE — estimated time en route
FA — area forecast
FAA — Federal Aviation Administration
FAR — Federal Aviation Regulation
FBO — Fixed-Base Operator
Fl Comp — Flight Computer
FSDO — Flight Standards District Office
FSS — Flight Service Station
GPH — gallons per hour
Hg — mercury
HSI — horizontal situation indicator
IAP — instrument approach procedure
IFH — *Instrument Flying Handbook*
IFR — instrument flight rules
ILS — instrument landing system
IR — instrument route
ISA — international standard atmosphere
L/D — Lift-to-Drag Ratio
L/D_{MAX} — Maximum Lift-to-Drag Ratio
Mb — millibar
MB — magnetic bearing
MEF — maximum elevation figure
METAR — aviation routine weather report
MH — magnetic heading
MOA — Military Operations Area
MSL — mean sea level
MTR — Military Training Routes
MVFR — marginal VFR
NAS — Naval Air Station
NDB — nondirectional radio beacon
NM — nautical mile
NOTAM — notice to airmen
NTSB — National Transportation Safety Board Regulations
OAT — outside air temperature
OBS — omnibearing selector
PHAK — *Pilot's Handbook of Aeronautical Knowledge*
PIC — pilot in command
PIREP — Pilot Weather Report
PPH — pounds per hour
RB — relative bearing
RMI — radio magnetic indicator
RNAV — area navigation
SD — Radar Weather Report
SFC — surface
SIGMET — Significant Meteorological Information
SL — sea level
SM — statute mile
ST — standard temperature
SVFR — Special VFR
TACAN — Tactical Air Navigation
TAF — terminal aerodrome forecast
TAS — true airspeed
TWEB — Transcribed Weather Broadcast
UTC — Coordinated Universal Time
V_A — maneuvering speed
V_F — design flap speed
V_{FE} — maximum flap extended speed
VFR — visual flight rules
VHF — very high frequency
VHF/DF — VHF direction finder
V_{LE} — maximum landing gear extended speed
V_{NE} — never-exceed speed
V_{NO} — maximum structural cruising speed
VOR — VHF omnidirectional range
VORTAC — Collocated VOR and TACAN
VOT — VOR test facility
VR — visual route
V_S — stalling speed or the minimum steady flight speed at which the airplane is controllable
V_{S0} — stalling speed or the minimum steady flight speed in the landing configuration
V_{S1} — stalling speed or the minimum steady flight speed obtained in a specific configuration
Z — Zulu or UTC time

INDEX OF FIGURES

INDEX

AUTHORS' RECOMMENDATIONS

The Experimental Aircraft Association, Inc., is a very successful and effective nonprofit organization that represents and serves those of us interested in flying, in general, and in sport aviation, in particular. We personally invite you to enjoy becoming a member. Visit their website at www.eaa.org.

Types of EAA Memberships:

- $40 - Individual (includes subscription to *EAA Sport Aviation* magazine)
- $50 - Family (extends all benefits to member's spouse and children under 18, except for an additional EAA magazine subscription)
- Free - Student (for those age 18 or under who have completed the EAA Young Eagles program)
- $1,295 - Lifetime

Write:	EAA Aviation Center	*Call:*	(920) 426-4800
	3000 Poberezny Rd.		(800) JOIN-EAA
	Oshkosh, WI 54902	*Email:*	membership@eaa.org

The annual EAA Oshkosh AirVenture is an unbelievable aviation spectacular with over 10,000 airplanes at one airport and virtually everything aviation-oriented you can imagine! Plan to spend at least 1 day (not everything can be seen in a day) in Oshkosh (100 miles northwest of Milwaukee). Visit the AirVenture website at www.airventure.org.

Convention dates: 2015 -- July 20 through July 26
2016 -- July 25 through July 31

The annual Sun 'n Fun EAA Fly-In is also highly recommended. It is held at the Lakeland, FL (KLAL), airport (between Orlando and Tampa). Visit the Sun 'n Fun website at www.sun-n-fun.org.

Convention dates: 2015 -- April 21 through April 26
2016 -- April 5 through April 10

AIRCRAFT OWNERS AND PILOTS ASSOCIATION

AOPA is the largest, most influential aviation association in the world, with more than 415,000 members--two thirds of all pilots in the United States. AOPA's most important contribution to the world's most accessible, safest, least expensive, friendliest, easiest-to-use general aviation environment is their lobbying on our behalf at the federal, state, and local levels. AOPA also provides legal services, advice, and other assistance to the aviation community.

We recommend that you become an AOPA member to get the most out of AOPA's resources. To join, call 1-800-USA-AOPA or visit the AOPA website at www.aopa.org.

LET'S GO FLYING!

The Aircraft Owners and Pilots Association (AOPA) hosts an informational web page on getting started in aviation. "Let's Go Flying!" contains information for those still dreaming about flying, those who are ready to begin, and those who are already making the journey.

The goal of this program is to encourage people to experience their dreams of flying through an introductory flight. Interested individuals can order a FREE copy of *Let's Go Flying: Your Invitation to Fly*, which explains how amazing it is to be a pilot. Other resources are available, such as a flight school finder, a guide on what to expect throughout training, an explanation of pilot certification options, a FREE monthly flight training newsletter, and much more. To learn more, visit www.aopa.org/letsgoflying.

GLEIM®

Reduced Vertical Separation Minimums

Training Course

800.874.5346 • gleim.com/aviation

GLEIM® - Experts in Aviation Training

SPORT	gleim.com/sport	$199.95

Deluxe Sport Pilot Kit
Includes: FAA Knowledge Test book, Flight Maneuvers and Practical Test Prep book, Syllabus book, Training Record book, Pilot Handbook, FAR/AIM book, Logbook, Gleim Online Ground School, FAA Test Prep Online, and more!

PRIVATE	gleim.com/private	$249.95

Deluxe Private Pilot Kit with Audio Review
Includes: FAA Knowledge Test book, Flight Maneuvers and Practical Test Prep book, Syllabus book, Training Record book, Pilot Handbook, FAR/AIM book, Logbook, Gleim Online Ground School, FAA Test Prep Online, Audio Review, and more!

INSTRUMENT	gleim.com/instrument	$249.95

Deluxe Instrument Pilot Kit with Audio Review
Includes: FAA Knowledge Test book, Flight Maneuvers and Practical Test Prep book, Syllabus book, Training Record book, Aviation Weather & Weather Services, Gleim Online Ground School, FAA Test Prep Online, Audio Review, and more!

COMMERCIAL	gleim.com/commercial	$174.95

Deluxe Commercial Pilot Kit
Includes: FAA Knowledge Test book, Flight Maneuvers and Practical Test Prep book, Syllabus book, Training Record book, Gleim Online Ground School, FAA Test Prep Online, and more!

INSTRUMENT/COMMERCIAL	gleim.com/IPCP	$341.95

Instrument/Commercial Pilot Kit
Includes: FAA Knowledge Test books, Flight Maneuvers and Practical Test Prep books, Syllabus books, Training Record books, Aviation Weather & Weather Services, Instrument Pilot Audio Review, Gleim Online Ground School, FAA Test Prep Online, and more!

SPORT PILOT FLIGHT INSTRUCTOR	gleim.com/sportinstructor	$174.95

Sport Pilot Flight Instructor Kit
Includes: FAA Knowledge Test books, Flight Maneuvers and Practical Test Prep books, Sport Pilot Syllabus book, Pilot Handbook, FAR/AIM book, Gleim Online Ground School, FAA Test Prep Online, and more!

FLIGHT/GROUND INSTRUCTOR	gleim.com/FIGI	$174.95

Flight/Ground Instructor + FOI Kit
Includes: FAA Knowledge Test books, Flight Instructor Flight Maneuvers and Practical Test Prep book Online, Pilot Handbook, FAR/AIM book, Gleim Online Ground School, FAA Test Prep Online, and more!

ATP	gleim.com/ATP	$189.95

Airline Transport Pilot Kit
Includes: FAA Knowledge Test book, Pilot Handbook, Aviation Weather & Weather Services, FAR/AIM book, Gleim Online Ground School, FAA Test Prep Online, and more!

FLIGHT ENGINEER	gleim.com/flightengineer	$149.95

Flight Engineer Knowledge Test
Includes: FAA Test Prep Online and Gleim Online Ground School

gleim.com • aviationteam@gleim.com • 800.874.5346 ext. 471
352.375.0772 ext. 471

Subject to change without notice. All prices before applicable shipping. 0814

If you see topics covered on your FAA knowledge test that are not contained in this book, please email us at aviation@gleim.com or mail us this form to report your experience and help us fine-tune our test preparation materials.

This form can be mailed to **Irvin N. Gleim • c/o Gleim Publications, Inc. • P.O. Box 12848 • University Station • Gainesville, Florida • 32604.** Please include your name and address so we can properly thank you for your interest.

1. ______________________________

2. ______________________________

3. ______________________________

4. ______________________________

5. ______________________________

6. ______________________________

7. ______________________________

8. ______________________________

9. ______________________________

10. ______________________________

11. ______________________________

12. ______________________________

13. ______________________________

14. ______________________________

15. ______________________________

16. ______________________________

17. ______________________________

18. ______________________________

Name: ______________________________

Address: ______________________________

City/State/Zip: ______________________________

Telephone: Home: __________ Work: __________ Fax: __________

Email: ______________________________